The Integrative Design Guide to Green Building

Redefining the Practice of Sustainability

2010

To Rachel -

My Dear Friend

Cover image:
A rendering of the Syracuse Center of Excellence designed by Toshiko Mori Architect working with Ashley McGraw Architects as the Administrative Architect and with 7group as an integrative design Consultant. Located on a severely contaminated brownfield that had previously rendered this district largely uninhabitable, the project represents a major urban revitalization in a devastated quarter of Syracuse, New York, including the creation of a public transportation hub where no such prior infrastructure existed. Opening in 2009, this building, which includes spaces that function as "laboratory" offices for testing human performance relative to various IEQ variables, serves as an example of using an integrative approach to create healthy interrelationships that sustain life." *Courtesy of Toshiko Mori Architects.*

The Integrative Design Guide to **Green Building**

Redefining the Practice of Sustainability

7group

John Boecker, Scot Horst, Tom Keiter, Andrew Lau,
Marcus Sheffer, and Brian Toevs

and Bill Reed

WILEY

John Wiley & Sons, Inc.

Published by John Wiley & Sons, Inc., Hoboken, New Jersey
Published simultaneously in Canada

Library of Congress Cataloging-in-Publication Data:

The integrative design guide to green building : redefining the practice of sustainability / by 7group (John Boecker, Scot Horst, Tom Keiter, Andrew Lau, Marcus Sheffer, and Brian Toevs) and William Reed.
    p. cm.
 ISBN 978-0-470-18110-2 (cloth)
1. Sustainable buildings--Design and construction. 2. Leadership in Energy and Environmental Design Green Building Rating System. I. Reed, William, 1953- II. 7group (Organization)
 TH880.I58 2009
 720'.47--dc22

                              2008038602

Printed in the United States of America

10 9 8 7 6 5 4 3 2 1

Contents

Chapter 6: Schematic Design_____197

Chapter 7: Design Development and Documentation_____259

Acknowledgments

Writing this book was an act of integrative design. For all who contributed their talents, knowledge, insights, and time to this process, we are grateful.

First and foremost, we needed someone to "integrate the integrators," someone to develop a narrative line and voice for all the ideas and aspects of a green design process. Shannon Murphy gave us this gift; she became a vital partner in our writing effort. As both author and translator of complex natural systems and site assessment work, she helped reframe the structure of the book and became our writing partner, not simply an editor. Shannon made our lives easier by challenging us to think as writers, not simply people conveying technical information and case studies. She deserves more thanks than we can give.

We especially thank Rick Fedrizzi of the U.S. Green Building Council for his foreword, but we also thank others who contributed their own insights directly to this book in the form of sidebars: Barbra Batshalom, Guy Sapirstein, Alex Zimmerman, James Patchett, Gerould Wilhelm, David Leventhal, Pamela Mang, Michael Ogden, Marc Rosenbaum, Max Zahniser, Elisabet Sahtouris, Christopher Brooks, Victor Canseco, Vivian Loftness, Keith Bowers, and Doug Gatlin.

We also are deeply grateful to everyone who shared their images for inclusion and for the efforts they expended in sharing them. Special thanks go to Corey Johnston for his insightful and thorough translation of the integrative design process into graphic images.

Thanks as well to our dedicated 7group staff for all of their help and long hours: Cris Argeles, Jennifer Biggs, David Blontz, Alvin Changco, Shannon Crooker, Nicole Elliott, Cam Fitzgerald, Rei Horst, Sol Lothe, Todd Reed, Sheila Sagerer, Gerren Wagner...and especially Lura Schmoyer, for her amazing skills at keeping everything organized and her constant reminders about details and deadlines.

We would also like to thank Jennifer Zurick and Christopher Magent for their engaging participation in developing some of the early materials that helped form the initial framework and outline of this book.

We offer extra thanks to our wives and children—for whom we live—with special thanks to Lisa Boecker and Ellen Reed for obliging the many weekends spent away, as well as for suffering through all of the long three-day weekends when we invaded their domestic bliss, during which their culinary delights kept us nourished throughout those twenty-hour-writing days.

We also acknowledge the work of the Whole System Integrative Process Committee whose work is also reflected in these pages: Bill Reed, John Boecker, Marcus Sheffer, Brian Toevs, Tom Keiter, Steve Bushnell, Mike Italiano, Jeff Levine, Markku Allison, Helen Kessler, Sean Culman, Kevin Settlemyre, Mitchell Swan, Gail Borthwick, Barbra Batshalom, Doug Pierce, Mike Pulaski, Muscoe Martin, Gunnar Hubbard, Alex Zimmerman, Ann Kosmal, Pam Touschner, Guy Sapirstein, Keith Winn, Kimberly Yoho, Rex Loker, Thomas Taylor, Garrick Maine, John Albrecht, Sherrie Gruder, John Montgomery, Thomas Mozina, Rick Prohov, Mandy Wong, Joel Freehling, Julie Gabrielli, John Jennings and Vuk Vujovic.

To our many clients who do not accept the status quo and are seeking a better way, we gratefully acknowledge your patience and perseverance. This book would have been a very dry and academic exercise without the stories from your projects that have enabled us to bring this subject to life. We appreciate your willingness to share your stories so that we can discover collectively a new path toward producing continually better and greener buildings.

And finally, we must thank everyone who is out in the field working every day to keep us all progressing toward a more sustainable world. We have been privileged to work with hundreds of such dedicated colleagues—far too many to name here—who share our commitment to contributing to the health of our planet. In short, this book is a reflection of all we have learned thus far on this journey with all of you, and we merely stand on the shoulders of those from whom we are learning.

Foreword

The act of building is by its very nature complex. Hundreds of linear processes must be completed in concert so that foundations can be poured, walls can rise, interiors can be fitted out, and occupancy can occur. Though practice, materials, and technology improved over time, our approach did not change much from when humans first began constructing habitats. We built where we lived, with this simple concept implied, and our structures were durable and beautiful and in harmony with their surroundings.

The Industrial Age changed all that. In the name of growth and alleged productivity, we picked places to build with little thought to that harmony; sited structures for aesthetics or economics; chose materials for their cheapness or trendiness and used them carelessly in the construction process; tacked on systems that used too much energy or too much water; threw all our leftovers into the nearest landfill; and moved people into spaces that were uncomfortable at best, unhealthy all too often; and then moved on to the next project.

But fifteen years ago, a group of leaders from every sector of the building industry came together and said: ENOUGH. We are using too many of our finite resources too fast. We are building structures as if they are as disposable as yesterday's newsprint. We are valuing cents saved over our children's health, not to mention their future. ENOUGH.

Thus was born the green building movement, and the transformation of the built environment—to one that is healthier, more sustainable, and more respectful of those who use the buildings—began. It is clear why: Buildings have a lifespan of fifty to one hundred years, throughout which they continually consume energy, water, and natural resources, thereby generating significant CO_2 emissions, the biggest contributor to climate change. In fact, buildings are responsible for 39 percent of the United States' CO_2 emissions per year. Annually, buildings account for 40 percent of primary energy use in the United States; 72 percent of U.S. electricity consumption; 13.6 percent use of our potable water per year; and 40 percent use of raw materials globally.

It is also clear *what* we need to do to build sustainably: Build so that we use less energy and less water and use fewer finite resources or figure out how to use more recycled resources. Build so that our choices deliver healthier solutions that respect the building's occupants, not compromise them. Build with an eye to future savings not first cost. Build smarter. Build so our children have a future.

What is still being formulated is *how* to do this: And this book, *The Integrative Design Guide to Green Building: Redefining the Practice of Sustainability,* is all about the how, specifically the how of integrative design. This fundamental change in the process of how we build buildings is the result of systems thinking, which—as the authors point out—has the potential to create buildings and places that (and people who) make the world a better, healthier place.

The U.S. Green Building Council's LEED® Green Building Rating System™ serves as an essential, proven tool for enabling this market transformation, and it works because it is founded on this principle of integrative design. It promotes a whole-building approach to sustainability by recognizing performance in five key areas: sustainable site development, water savings, energy efficiency, materials and resources, and indoor environmental quality, with an additional category to recognize innovation. It has become the nationally accepted benchmark, because it provides a concise framework for best practices in high-performance green building design and operations.

Equally important is the independent, third-party verification that a building meets these high-performance standards. This ensures that buildings are constructed as designed and that they perform as expected.

By every measure, green building is clearly an idea whose time is now. The USGBC tracks a host of metrics that give evidence of the rightness of the idea of sustainable design and construction, operations, and maintenance: they are, for example, visible in the number of LEED registrations and LEED Accredited Professionals; the attendance at educational courses, in person or online; the visits to our websites; and the growth in organizational membership, chapters, and volunteers.

But it is the committed, talented people behind those numbers that are making market transforma-

tion possible. The members of 7group and Bill Reed are examples writ large of the kind of leadership that is taking this idea of green building and forming it into reality by helping change minds, building practice, and design process. With this book, their individual and collective skills and experience in enhancing the design and building process are served up with thoughtful, practical guidance told through stories and examples that are at once illuminating and inspiring. It has been my great privilege to know the principals of 7group and Bill Reed individually through their many and important contributions to USGBC and to the advancement of green building practice and integrative thinking. I am grateful to have been part of this movement that continues to benefit from their work.

We understand why green buildings matter: They save energy, reduce CO_2 emissions, conserve water, improve health, increase productivity, cost less to operate and maintain, and increasingly cost no more to build than conventional structures. It is in understanding *how* to work together by utilizing the principles of integrative design to build these structures well that we will be able to deliver on our vision of green buildings for everyone within a generation.

S. Rick Fedrizzi
President, CEO, and Founding Chair
U.S. Green Building Council

Introduction: The Integrative Design Guide to Green Building—Redefining the Practice of Sustainability

This is a pragmatic book. There are many books on green design that describe the *what* of sustainability—what to do, what to use, what to design, what to buy, what *not* to buy. In this book, we talk about *how*. How to make the best decisions, how to work with others to creatively address the issues of sustainability, how to address complex issues that threaten living systems, and how to be more and more deeply purposeful in pursuing what is required of us to achieve these objectives.

How you do something is a process. This book is about redesigning the design process.

It is called the Integrative Design process (IDP). It is not our idea. This practice has emerged from the field of green and sustainable design as a natural response to the wall that we all hit when we look only at green technologies, green products, and the "objects of design." This book is based on our collective experience gained from how we've seen this process work, and its potential to create buildings, places, and people that contribute to making the world a better, healthier place.

The Integrative Design Process is how the most environmentally effective *and* cost-effective green buildings are achieved. Various rating systems such as LEED, BREEAM, and others are helpful tools, but they simply act as measures of how well we've incorporated deeper and deeper systems thinking processes through the course of design. Integrative systems design is what we do to get there—*how* we get there. Green buildings are the outcome.

In this book we define Integrative Design as a discovery process that optimizes—(i.e., makes the best use of, or creates synergy between)—the interrelationships between all the elements and entities that are directly and indirectly associated with building projects in the service of efficient and effective use of resources.

In addition to the conventional issues of building projects, this book takes the term *integration* literally and extends the identification of the systems we are integrating to a conceptually "whole" system. A whole system includes everything—human, biotic, and earth systems and the consciousness that connects them: the Whole. To achieve the health of the Whole, we must ask ourselves how the process of building can be a catalyst for a discovery process that addresses the interrelationships of all living and technical systems in the service of sustaining the health of all life. Hence, the idea of addressing interrelationships that extend well beyond our buildings and the boundaries of our construction sites is a thread that runs throughout the entire book in order to expand our scope into whole-system integrative design.

We are intentionally very explicit about the use the term "Integrative" Design instead of "Integrated"

Design. The latter term implies something that is past and completed; it implies that we're done. The word *integrative* suggests an evolving process rather than a fixed process. It implies that we're never really done. As suggested in the larger context of achieving whole-system integration, we have a long way to go before we are fully integrated.

We intend for this book to be used as a practice manual, or guide book, one with three basic divisions: The *first* provides the philosophy behind integrative design; the *second* is intended to serve as a manual for practicing professionals; and the *third* introduces deeper levels of integration.

Chapters One through Four focus on the philosophy and underpinnings of an effective IDP. These chapters address systems thinking and building and community design from a whole and living system perspective. These chapters are the foundation of this book, and as such, serve as a conceptual structure to guide the thinking that leads to a more and more deeply sustainable design process.

Chapter 5 begins the manual section of the book—the "how to do it" structure that can be used to guide the process. This begins with the Discovery Phase—the foundation of an integrative design process. It is the most important phase of a green project, and as a result, is the longest chapter. Chapters Six through Eight complete the manual and serve as a "field guide" that identifies the level of investigation required during the various stages of implementing an effective integrative design process. For the purposes of this book, we have identified thirteen explicit stages, but these are intended only as a guide that can be compressed or expanded, as necessary, to better respond to the constraints and opportunities of each project. Process outlines, practical examples, case studies, and stories are used throughout to illustrate the nature of this work.

Chapter Nine offers a view into the deeper realm of integration that we believe is required of each of us in order to truly transform our practice and our role on this planet.

You may notice that the manual section of this book provides greater detail at the beginning and then distills issues as it moves into the later stages of the integrative design process. The same is true of many of the subsections within each identified stage—more detail at the beginning than at the end. This is because the vital work of integrative design must occur at the beginning. This early work builds a proper foundation upon which all decisions are built. In addition, the further along we are in a project the more variables crop up. It is impossible to list *all* the possible flows in a single design process, but we have attempted to present a clear framework that can be applied to any situation or building type. We leave it to you, the practitioner, to use this framework to respond to the unique situation in each project.

We have delineated a process that has grown out of our experience. After several attempts to translate this experience into a list of tasks, we found describing this work through stories and examples to be more effective and meaningful. We are confident and optimistic that once you begin to implement this process, it will never play out in exactly the way that we have written it. If you keep checking back as you go, your own process will continue to evolve. And to evolve is itself a process—a valuable one, because we still have a lot to learn.

Dedicated to Gail Lindsey

SMILES . . . . wink!!!!!

1

Many Minds

People don't like change. But make the change happen fast enough and you go from one type of normal to another...

—said by novelist Terry Pratchett's character
Moist von Lipwig in *Making Money*

FROM MASTER BUILDER TO THE TWENTY-FIRST CENTURY: WHERE WE ARE AND HOW WE GOT HERE

The Master Builder

The Industrial Revolution had profound effects on human society, especially on how we build in our *places*. Only a little more than 150 years ago, local natural and human resources were the basis and the limit for what was designed and built. The resulting process was far different from contemporary practice. The architects of that time were called *Master Builders*.

Master builders were schooled through local apprenticeships, and the techniques and technologies they learned were developed from an understanding of local issues and passed down through generations. Mechanized transportation was limited, so people possessed an intimate knowledge of local materials, as well as workforce skills, economies, cultural imagery and traditions, microclimates, and soil conditions. They understood the flow of local resources and what local conditions could be limiting. The built environment was designed and constructed from a deep connection to each individual place, with the master builder conceptualizing the overall pattern and each artisan, craftsman, and journeyman then contributing layers of richness and diversity at smaller scales. What resulted were buildings and communities that truly were integrated with their environment and that lived, breathed, and grew to become timeless elements of their place.

1

▶**Figure 1-1** The peaks of the Dolomiti Lucane mountains in southern Italy (in the Basilicata region) surround and protect one of the most beautiful villages of Italy, Castelmezzano. Dating from the tenth century, the town's organic development pattern works with, rather than against, the natural formation of the mountains, and the town's buildings are oriented in alignment with the mountains to shield inhabitants from cold northeast winds and to capture solar heat from the south. *Image courtesy of John Boecker.*

◀**Figure 1-2** This view from one of the fourteen surviving thirteenth-century towers of San Gimignano, the famous Italian hill town in Tuscany, reveals the town's connection with its surrounding landscape and topography—its source for materials, food, and protection for more than 1,000 years. *Image courtesy of John Boecker.*

Understanding this process, modern architect Mario Botta recently offered this advice after designing buildings outside his native Ticino, Italy: "Build where you live." Those that have visited Ticino may recall the magical quality of the centuries-old hill towns nestled in the Swiss-Italian Alps. Built of native stone and local alpine wood, using indigenous practices and traditions handed down through generations, these towns feel organic—as if they grew out of the landscape, blurring the line between the built and natural environment, presenting a unified place. To this day, these towns remain largely self-sufficient, sustainable communities.

Many of the buildings and communities that we respect and envy today were created in this way and still thrive after centuries of vitality—so much so that many have become popular tourist destinations. Sometimes, theme parks are built to replicate these buildings and communities with the aim of capturing some hint of the life and the quality they possess. But that quality cannot be reproduced in this way, because it was generated specifically by individual master builders' intimate process of building with and within their own communities.

▲ **Figure 1-3** This picturesque Ticino hill town, located in southern Switzerland, integrates seamlessly with its Alpine terrain, the stone of its structures seemingly growing from the mountain upon which it nests. It is a distinctly Italian-style town that relies on the local hills for its farming and the adjacent river for hydroelectricity. *Image courtesy of John Boecker.*

▶ **Figure 1-4** The town of Alberobello, a UNESCO World Heritage site, contains an urban concentration of more than 1,500 Trulli dwellings, dating from the mid-fourteenth century that are still in use and were made from limestone blocks collected from surrounding fields. These indigenous structures could be quickly erected and dismantled, utilizing ancient mortarless drystone construction for their distinctive conical roofs that draw off the heat of their southern Italian climate. *Image courtesy of John Boecker.*

Figure 1-5 Matera, the "City of the Sassi" in southern Italy's Basilicata region, has been inhabited since the Stone Age and is a protected UNESCO World Heritage site consisting of nearly 3,000 cave dwellings and 150 churches carved into the rock ravine of the Torrente Gravina on which it is built, an ideal and well-protected canyon for prehistoric human habitation. *Image courtesy of John Boecker.*

Figure 1-6 The cream-colored façades of Matera, built of local tufa stone bricks, are placed in front of the many natural grottoes and carved caves to serve as entrance structures. Rainwater collection in small pools and wastewater flows were managed for 9,000 years via an ingenious system of tiny canals until overcrowding between the two world wars rendered Matera uninhabitable. Legislation in 1952 mandated restoration of the Sassi, and many of the cave dwellings and churches have been restored, transforming Matera into a breathtaking "living museum." *Image courtesy of John Boecker.*

Figure 1-7 Since structures are constructed into the rock of the ravine's steep slopes, houses were layered atop houses, so it is not unusual to encounter chimneys when walking through this ancient town, before realizing that winding roads, gardens, and other structures rest on the roofs of dwellings below. *Image courtesy of John Boecker.*

When we experience the buildings and communities that were created within the master builder process, we can see how truly integrated that process was at every level. Each person that contributed to these structures was thinking and working from a unified schema derived from a shared understanding of local patterns. This cohesive intelligence ensured that each craftsman's individual contribution would be perfectly integrated within the whole of the built environment. Not only were they working from the same place physically and culturally, but these craftsmen were also in a sense working from the same mind.

The Siena Duomo

Medieval cathedrals are familiar examples of the type of powerful coherence that characterized the built environment of the master builder. Recently we had the opportunity to visit in Italy the Duomo di Siena (cathedral of Siena), originally designed by master builders Nicola Pisano and his son Giovanni, along with pupil Arnolfo di Cambio. The Siena cathedral was largely completed between 1215 and 1263, under Pisano's guidance, with layers of work integrated into his original conception by Donatello, Michelangelo, Gian Lorenzo Bernini, and others.

The Siena Duomo occupies the highest point in Siena and seems to grow right out of the landscape, adding a physical and spiritual pinnacle to the rocky plateau. The cathedral is built primarily of local marble that the town's inhabitants gathered from nearby quarries and carted back to town. These indigenous marbles create a consistent color palette of black and white stripes with green and yellow accents. The entire complex is beautifully integrated into its place—born of the place and the people that lived there.

Figure 1-8 The awe-inspiring Siena Duomo (cathedral) appears to have grown out of the plateau upon which it sits, integrating seamlessly with its surroundings as a pinnacle that towers above the medieval town built into the hills below. *Image courtesy of John Boecker.*

Figure 1-9 The striking Romanesque marble banding of the Siena Duomo's campanile (bell tower), which was added in 1313, extends the pattern of the cathedral's exterior materials. Almost all of the marble used for the cathedral was harvested by inhabitants of the town from local quarries. *Image courtesy of John Boecker.*

Figure 1-10 Daylight streaming in from the gallery windows of the cathedral's nave highlight the signature marble stripes of the Duomo's columns. *Image courtesy of John Boecker.*

Inside the Siena Duomo, a magical vaulted space is supported by ordered rows of stone columns and piers comprised of the same horizontal black and white stripes that dominate the exterior. On a recent trip, we noticed that only a few, seemingly randomly placed columns were not striped. After looking closely for a while, we realized that these anomalous columns were far from randomly placed but were located to establish spatial hierarchies within the overall space. This architectural cipher communicated a semiotics, a natural language within the whole that revealed additional layers of meaning.

The marble floor mosaics throughout the cavernous space within the duomo remain among the world's most exquisite, each conceived and executed by a master artisan within a consistent overall pattern, each telling its own tale within the biblical stories depicted. From 1372 to 1547, these fifty-nine floor panels were executed by Siena's top artists. On our trip, we chatted with an old man we met repairing a small area of this

◀**Figure 1-11** The Duomo's mosaic floor panels depict Old Testament stories, framed by intricate patterns of local marble, composed by Siena's top artisans. *Image courtesy of John Boecker.*

▼**Figure 1-12** Meticulously executed geometric mosaic flooring patterns throughout the Duomo evoke the colors of indigenous materials used throughout Siena. *Image courtesy of John Boecker.*

marble floor. He told us that he was a descendant of the original fourteenth-century master masons, who were trained locally in a craft lovingly sustained and nurtured through generations for over seven centuries. We watched as he honed the three-inch-thick marble pieces to fit together seamlessly, with hairline joints crisper than a jigsaw puzzle.

In the 1300s, the townspeople began the construction of a transept that would make Siena's duomo the largest cathedral in Christendom. This monumental addition was intended to continue the same pattern of the structure's spatial choreography, which begins at the end of a journey through the narrow, climbing streets of the medieval town. This effort was abruptly abandoned in 1348, when over 50 percent of the town's population fell victim to the plague. What remains is a ghostlike figural void that was conceived as a roofed interior space but left virtually untouched as an exterior, "urban" room for 650 years. The space is striking in its authenticity, and acts as a permanent commemoration of the place's history.

In its totality, this spectacular cathedral complex embodies more than 350 years of continuous work, all generated from an original thirteenth-century conception that was rooted in a deep understanding of the unique interrelationships of its place, integrating landscape, materials, workforce, cultural semiotics, traditions, art forms, local climate, habitat, and urban development patterns. Nearly eight centuries later, it still leaves us marveling at the awe-inspiring result, an

accomplishment almost beyond imagining today—and on the hottest summer day, it remains the coolest space in Siena for taking a quiet respite from the sun's heat.

THE AGE OF SPECIALIZATION

With the Industrial Age came advancements that removed many of the limitations that had kept the master builder management structure in place. The evolution toward global transportation and communication meant that building materials and other resources need not be locally available and could come from anywhere. As new materials and technologies were rapidly and increasingly introduced, specialists were needed to resolve and implement the complex aspects of electricity, lighting, ergonomics, heating, cooling, ventilation, municipal waste systems, water supply, automatic climate control, smart buildings, and more; and each of these systems is now designed by different and separate professionals, and optimized in isolation.

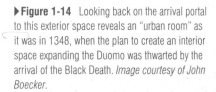

▲ **Figure 1-13** A journey though Siena's organic labyrinth of narrow medieval streets offers countless hidden and sudden views, a spatial choreography culminating at this final portal, which frames the Duomo's campanile, before arriving in the exterior space of the would-be transept nave. *Image courtesy of John Boecker.*

▶ **Figure 1-14** Looking back on the arrival portal to this exterior space reveals an "urban room" as it was in 1348, when the plan to create an interior space expanding the Duomo was thwarted by the arrival of the Black Death. *Image courtesy of John Boecker.*

Where we once had one mind—a unified intelligence—conceptualizing and integrating patterns born of the place and its people, we now involve anywhere from dozens to hundreds of disparate companies, organizations, and individuals in designing our buildings and their components. In other words, we entered what might be termed the Age of Specialization. We have fragmented the whole into myriad separate pieces.

In short order, we moved from a time of commonsense integration into a period—now more than a century and a half long—of "it's-not-my-job" specialization and "this-is-not-my-area-of-purview" disintegration. On a recent project, for example, we worked hard to convince the civil engineer that we needed him at our first predesign, goal-setting integration meeting with the owner and all members of the design team. He said, "Well, why do I need to come? You guys haven't started designing; there's nothing for me to do yet." But with some support from the owner, we were able to convince him to attend this all-day, team goal-setting session. Early on that day, after spending a couple of hours walking through site issues and discussing pre-existing site forces, conditions, flows, constraints, and opportunities, the civil engineer got up to leave, saying "OK, the rest is not my job—I'm only responsible for everything five feet from the building and beyond. You guys do whatever you want inside that…just tell me where I need to hook up your systems."

This is not to say that good work is not being done. Each specialist possesses tremendous skill for designing and optimizing the systems and components for which they alone are responsible. However, our design process is such that only pieces are optimized and not the whole. Each of these professionals is designing fully within the silo of their discipline, and the interaction between each discipline is usually kept to a minimum—limited to ensuring, for example, that the electrical engineer's supply system provides adequate power to the mechanical engineer's specified heating, ventilating, and air-conditioning (HVAC) equipment. The optimization of the building's individual systems is primarily done in isolation, based on rule-of-thumb conventions that target abstract, generalized standards. These systems are then assembled into a building.

STOP AND REFLECT: OUR CURRENT PROCESS

Siloed Optimization

We often ask our clients at the very inception of a project to reflect on today's design and construction-delivery methodology. Let's see if this sounds familiar: The project starts when the architect meets with the owner to discuss the program for the building to determine the required spaces, as well as their sizes and functions, and the relationships and proximities between them. Once this program has been documented, the architect produces a series of iterative sketches over weeks or months and presents them to the owner until they agree that everything is the right size, in the right place, and "looks good," essentially completing schematic design. These drawings are then sent to each member of the team of professionals assembled: the HVAC engineer, the electrical engineer, the plumbing engineer, the structural engineer, the civil engineer, the fire-protection consultant, the landscape architect, and others—all of whom are specialists within their disciplines, possessing tremendous acumen and skill in optimizing their systems.

The optimization of each individual system is done primarily in isolation, based on rule-of-thumb conventions and standards. Then, after each system has been designed, the drawings are sent back to the architect, who *ostensibly* coordinates everything—making sure that ducts do not run into sprinkler piping, structure, and so on. The architect then issues a final set of design documents, which results in an estimate for a building that more often than not is over budget, so we resort to "value engineering." You likely have heard the joke that value engineering is neither—since it is certainly not about value nor does it require engineering. In other words, the building is made cheaper by cutting out pieces, reducing scope, or both, often by plucking away any "green" components that appear to represent low-hanging fruit, because they were conceived as an additional layer of desired elements—in essence, eliminating things that the owner originally wanted. Once the project is back on budget, a final set of construction documents is created in the form of a large stack of drawings and a much larger stack of bound-paper specifications, which we then issue for bidding.

The Abyss Between Design and Construction Professionals

For the sake of argument, let us say that the scenario above describes a twenty-million-dollar building. How many people were involved in the building design process from the beginning of the programming effort to the day the bidding documents are put out on the street? Definitely dozens, even hundreds, if we include all of the equipment manufacturers and product representatives involved. How long did the process take? A year? Eighteen months? Two years? By doing the math, it is easy to see that what is embedded in that set of bidding documents equates to hundreds of thousands of person-hours of research, analysis, decision making, and documentation. And then what do we do? We give construction professionals (who typically are not involved in the design process) four weeks to bid on these documents, which really means two weeks or even one week, based on our conversations with contractors.

Not only are we giving contractors only a week or two to understand hundreds of thousands of hours' worth of information, but we are also asking them to put a *price* on that understanding and, further, to commit contractually to meeting that price. Then, we select the *lowest bidder,* which essentially means that we end up awarding the construction contract to the team that understands the project the least!

It gets worse. If you look around the room you are in right now, it is likely that you will see dozens of products. The chair you are sitting in, the pants you are wearing, the cup you are drinking from. Every one of these products is produced dozens if not hundreds or tens of thousands of times, built over and over again with plenty of opportunity to work out the bugs and quirks, usually accompanied by some level of quality control. However, in the case of a building—likely the most expensive product a person will buy in his or her lifetime—every single new building is entirely unique. It has never been built before. It will never be built again—even if it is a prototype that is being site adapted, the team of professionals is different, making it an absolutely unique product. Furthermore, every one of the products in the room around you was designed and constructed by the *same entity.* Our buildings, though, are designed by one set of design professionals and constructed by an entirely different set of construction professionals, with no interaction between the two of them whatsoever until construction begins. Not only does an abyss exist between these two sets of professionals, the contractual arrangement between the two actually renders them adversaries! It seems that we have created a perverse construction-delivery methodology from beginning to end.

This conventional process creates buildings that are no more than the sum of their parts—and sometimes less. The most striking innovations remain unleveraged, as any improvement that occurs is confined to its silo and secluded from the whole. The process more closely resembles assembly than integration. And because the assembly is, in a way, blind, we often face redundancies, unnecessary costs, and a great deal of wasted time and effort.

It is not surprising, then, that data from the Lawrence Berkley National Lab from a 1998 study indicates that 90 percent of U.S. buildings have either systems controls problems or nonfunctioning HVAC components upon occupancy and during the first year of operations. Further, 15 percent of our buildings are actually *missing* components that were in the construction documents and purchased by the owner in the construction contract. This is no secret to design and construction professionals. In fact, of the hundred thousand or so design and construction professionals to whom we have presented in the last ten years, when asked "When was the last time you were involved in a project that, after it was constructed and occupied, had no HVAC problems?" only one person has ever raised his hand. This person got us very excited, so we said, "Tell us about your HVAC system." He replied, "There wasn't an HVAC system. It was a cabin in the woods."

Doing Less Damage by Adding Technologies

The very system by which we certify our green buildings is illustrative of the assembly-like nature of our process. When utilizing LEED® (the U.S. Green Building Council's Leadership in Energy and Environmental Design Green Building Rating System), we whip out the LEED scorecard and begin assessing which credits are applicable and achievable. We walk the team through a credit-by-credit analysis, asking the architect, the engineers, and design team members to think about how they can make their systems and components greener by meeting the requirements of the applicable LEED credits. We ask them to consider how they can reduce the environmental impacts associated with their work in order to reduce automobile use, site disturbance, stormwater runoff, heat-island effects, and water and energy consumption. Each team member identifies and commits to the points that are achievable from within their discipline, and at the end of the day we add our points up to see whether we can target a silver, gold, or platinum rating.

Each project team member is then assigned LEED credit responsibilities, and each begins designing his or her system with the mission to achieve the identified LEED points assigned to them. For example, these responsibilities on a typical LEED project might generate the following activities:

The *Civil Engineer* adds the design of a retention basin to hold a greater percentage of stormwater on site and reserves several parking spaces for carpooling.

The *Landscape Architect* adds trees to the south side of the parking lot for shading, a bike rack, and more areas for vegetation, as well as native planting materials that do not require permanent irrigation; the landscape architect also changes site pavement materials to lighter colors.

The *Plumbing Engineer* specifies low-flow lavatory faucets, waterless urinals, and a high-efficiency domestic hot-water heater.

The *Mechanical Engineer* adds energy-recovery units, variable-speed fans, carbon dioxide sensors, and air-conditioning components that contain non-hydrochlorofluorocarbon (HCFC) refrigerants, and designs a ground-source heat pump system for heating and cooling.

Figure 1-15 A cabin with a fireplace in the Adirondacks is free from any HVAC problems. *Image courtesy of Todd McFeely.*

The *Electrical Engineer* adds a few more (but lower wattage) exterior cutoff luminaires in the parking lot, some photovoltaic panels, a few more energy-monitoring sensors, and also specifies individual lighting controls and high-efficiency compact fluorescent lighting fixtures throughout, tied to photocell sensors and dimming ballasts for daylight harvesting.

The *Architect* adds insulation to the walls and roof, several skylights for daylighting, a vegetated green roof, a few more windows comprised of triple-glazed systems for high performance, and specifies "greener" materials, such as drywall made from 100 percent recycled content.

The *Interior Designer* selects paints with low or no emission volatile organic compound (VOC) content, high recycled-content carpet, certified wood finishes, and rapidly renewable cork flooring.

The *Owner* commits to hiring a commissioning authority, a construction waste manager, and an indoor air quality testing agency.

Once all these technologies are added and the building is constructed, we have a successful green building that does less damage to the environment. Hundreds of these buildings are being constructed as you read this—they are doing their part by hurting the planet less. But where does that leave us? If you have a planet filled with millions and millions of buildings that do *less* damage, you still have not solved the problem. With thousands and thousands of talented design and construction professionals working with brilliant minds and genuine caring, we need to accomplish more than simply doing less damage—we need to do better than just slowing our way down our collision course.

There are many problems that arise with this unholistic, unintegrated approach, the most significant of which is the lack of a clear leverage point or an accepted and established methodology for changing the way that we build. Given the magnitude of the challenges that we

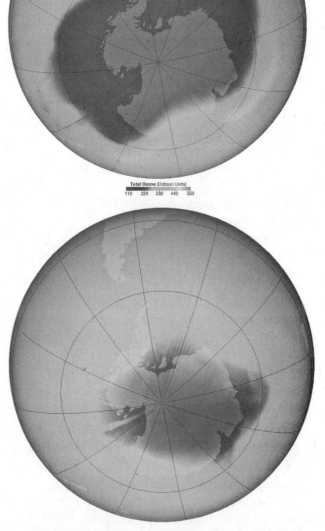

Total Ozone (Dobson Units)
110   220   330   440   550

▲▲ **Figure 1-16** The largest ozone hole over Antarctica, recorded as of September 2006. *Image courtesy of NASA.*

▲ **Figure 1-17** This image of the ozone hole in December 2007 offers hope that the Montreal Protocol on Substances that Deplete the Ozone Layer, which entered into effect in 1989, is having a positive effect. *Image courtesy of National Aeronautics and Space Administration (NASA).*

face, it will take nothing less than a massive transformation to get us out of this mess. How might that transformation occur? Where in our current design process exists the point at which we might intervene to create large-scale change? The answer, simply, is that it *does not exist* within the current process.

THE CALL BEFORE US

As our collective values have shifted toward the pursuit of sustainability, great innovations have been made.

Thousands of the best and brightest professionals are devising ways to improve the efficiency and reduce the impact of what they design. But we are still designing within a process that belongs to the Age of Specialization, and thus our solutions and approaches to sustainability are as fragmented as ever. When a technology is proposed as a solution to a green building issue, we are in effect saying that we have the answer for you. But do we? Have we even asked the right question?

These are urgent times. Depending on which reports one reads, we have only a little or almost no

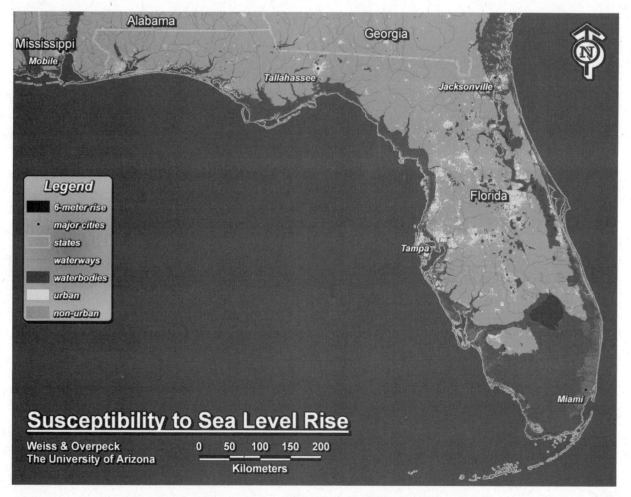

Legend
- 6-meter rise
- • major cities
- states
- waterways
- waterbodies
- urban
- non-urban

Susceptibility to Sea Level Rise

Weiss & Overpeck
The University of Arizona

0   50   100   150   200
Kilometers

Figure 1-18 Computer simulations of rising sea levels resulting from global climate change, such as this image of Florida, indicate that millions of people residing in coastal areas around the world may be displaced. *Image courtesy of Weiss and Overpeck, University of Arizona.*

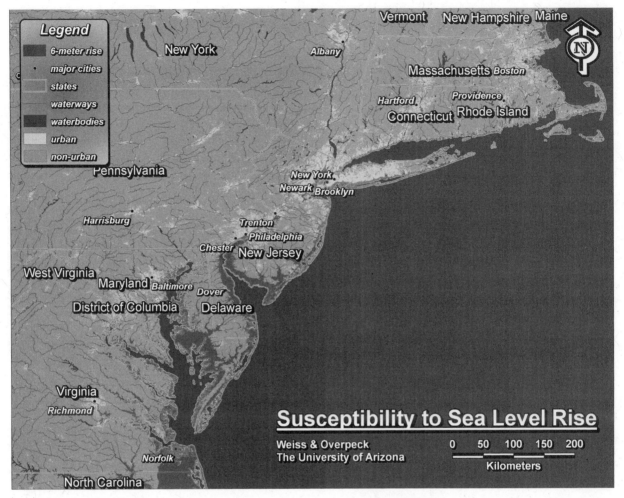

Figure 1-19 On the East Coast of the United States, rising sea levels could wipe out many major urban and residential areas. *Image courtesy of Weiss and Overpeck, University of Arizona.*

time left to change. There is a call to action before us—change the way that we build, or the Earth will change it for us. If one part of the building improves, it remains just that—an improved part. We are working brilliantly toward creating highly efficient *pieces* of buildings, but the world's most efficient HVAC system, unintegrated with the whole, is but a drop in the bucket compared to the magnitude of change that we need to create. The process by which the master build-

er produced such enduring and vital places has been lost, for the practice of development has become far too dynamic and complex for such a process to function. Even understanding the systems within a single building has become too complex for one mind, one person, to grasp completely. What is being called for is a new process of integration for the many minds devoted to each project and a new process for building the more complex systems that we inhabit.

2

Building as an Organism

English does not contain a suitable word for "system of problems." Therefore I have had to coin one. I choose to call such a system a "mess." The solution to a mess can seldom be obtained by independently solving each of the problems of which it is composed.

—Russell L. Ackoff, "Systems, Messes and Interactive Planning" from *Redesigning the Future.* New York/London: Wiley, 1974

SHIFT IN THINKING: NO PART OR SYSTEM IN ISOLATION

In the first chapter we described the shift from the "one mind" of the master builder to the many minds of the professionals and specialists that contribute their expertise to today's development projects. Yet it is not the collaboration of many minds that is the problem—it is the *process by which* they collaborate.

With these many minds, each representing an advanced discipline, we have a tremendous potential: rather than assembling our buildings from fragments that interact with one another in unplanned ways, we could be creating them as harmonious wholes whose parts support one another in mutually beneficial interrelationships. The result would be historic, tapping into the cocreative potential of our many advanced disciplines and transforming not only how we work and build but also how we live.

To do this, we need to create a shift both in process and in thinking. In fact, the two go hand in hand. Our conventional thinking treats buildings as objects, as things. Yet each building is in fact a system, with each individual part affecting the other parts and, in turn, the building as a whole. Our conventional process, however, prevents the systemic relationships between building components from being understood or even seen. On our first few projects, even when we thought we were implementing what we called integrated design, we really were not there yet.

Everyone is practicing Integrative Design . . . at least that's what they say

By Barbra Batshalom

What is this mysterious label and what does it mean? How do you know if you really are practicing integrative design or not? How does a client know who to believe when selecting a team?

With the steadily increasing demand for green building, and the proliferation of the U.S. Green Building Council's LEED Green Building Rating System, there is a heightened awareness that the design process itself determines the success and cost effectiveness of implementing green building and using rating systems. Practitioners now recognize that an integrative design process can make or break a project, but it can be difficult to achieve and depends on every member of the team participating and committing to it. The difficulty of this process is that it challenges people's ability to go outside of their comfort zone, do things differently, and refine their personal skills when encountering resistance and conflict.

When asked about green building, design professionals often respond in one of two ways. First, there are the naysayers, those who feel that green design is either a passing trend, or an expensive add-on layer superimposed onto "traditional" design. Second, there are those professing that they've been doing green design since the '70s solar craze, and that everything they do is green.

So how do you know? We suggest that to answer this question, one needs to have a set of indicators—both qualitative and quantitative criteria—that evaluate whether or not one really is working collaboratively in a team setting. The U.S. Green Building Council (USGBC) created the LEED rating system to answer the question, "what is a green building?"

Similarly, we now need to have a set of indicators that can answer the question—"how green is your process?" ...or, "how integrated is your process?"

To answer this question, it is first necessary to raise awareness about our current practice and be honest about what doesn't work in order to recognize the indicators of a "dis-integrated," or dysfunctional, process. These include:

- lack of clear and shared understanding of *project goals and basic aspirations* during conceptual and schematic design
- poor *communication* resulting in errors, omissions, and assumptions that result in over-sizing systems, redundancy, and gaps in knowledge and performance analysis
- a heightened degree of *mystery* between disciplines, particularly around specific analysis (For example, the architect doesn't understand how the mechanical engineer arrived at the current design, or what assumptions defined the system's performance analysis.)
- lack of *value* in meetings, tasks or activities—this could range from "value engineering" (which jokingly is referred to as neither) to ongoing, repetitive meetings whose outcomes are not clearly defined, and people's time is wasted.
- overlaps in roles and gaps between team members' *responsibilities* (especially in LEED projects)
- *silos*—decision making happens without collaboration (for example, the architect saying, "it's too early in design to include the mechanical engineer, interior designer, or landscape architect.")

- lack of a specific or defined *map*—the integrative design process differs in significant ways from the conventional design process to which we've become accustomed or conditioned. To succeed, the project team must intentionally map its process with clearly targeted goals and with identified decision-making paths, milestones and methodologies for analysis. Without these, the team has no idea where it will end up and will suffer added headaches and increased cost. Without a map, it's too easy to fall back into conventional practice patterns.
- *meeting structure* and flows—particularly early in the process, project teams need to engage in brainstorming, charrettes, and targeted meetings interspersed between larger group meetings. To avoid silo behavior, teams must focus on specific analyses, feedback loops and co-solving problems.

On the other hand, you know you are participating in an integrative design process when...

… you are asked for your input on a wide range of issues—including those outside of your immediate area of expertise or purview.

…a number of project team members are pushed out of their "comfort zone." (They either find this exciting and invigorating, or initially terrifying and disturbing!)

…there is a shared understanding of project goals that results from collaborative working sessions.

…the expectations of your work are clearly defined and sufficiently detailed—the results have targeted, quantified performance goals.

…other people's work depends on yours; tasks are *interdependent*—you can't just go off and hide in a corner, then push through your deliverables. Integrated systems result from an integrative process in which stakeholders co-solve problems.

…you feel that group interactions inspire creativity—working sessions are more "fun."

…you feel more respected and valued than in a traditional project, and you feel obligated to respond in kind—you sense a higher level of morale and alignment with the core values expressed by the group, resulting in an expanded degree of pride in the outcome.

…there is a focus and emphasis on process itself, including an early collaborative goal-setting session attended by all team members (no later than schematic design) to establish a shared understanding of project targets and priorities.

…the process is mapped clearly—stakeholders actually spend time planning how problems will be solved together, with decisions made in a transparent way—this defined "map" is incorporated into the main project schedule.

…innovative solutions that challenge "rules-of-thumb" are encouraged (innovation doesn't mean high-tech or risky strategies).

…decision-makers (client) and an expanded array of stakeholders are involved in a significant and valuable way.

…the project embraces issues not usually considered in the typical design process—such as the health of the watershed, the regional ecology, and the community—by engaging an ongoing process of discovery that identifies what contributes to the health of the project's context or place.

(continued)

…you feel a greater sense of ownership in the entirety (or whole), rather than in individual aspects or components.

…there is dialogue and debate surrounding design decisions, leading to a higher level of "buy-in" and consensus among the team.

However, it is important to remember that very little in life is black and white, including the design process. Most processes are neither completely collaborative nor completely dysfunctional. More likely, there are variations. One typical scenario is that a team gets off to a great start, but then the process degrades over time. At the outset, a team focused on green design will plan an initial charrette—excitement is high, enthusiasm abounds. People leave the charrette revved up and ready to charge ahead…however, ingrained habits are hard to change! Either the charrette was a one-hit wonder and didn't include a rigorous mapping process, or there wasn't enough built into the ensuing process to ensure that collaborative interaction would continue.

The first charrette isn't enough. The team's process will not be integrated unless team members continue to pay vigilant attention to it, and continue to question even their own participation and habits. A truly integrative design process will include a variety of interactions among the team—a series of larger charrette meetings with smaller focused meetings in between, all orchestrated to build on each other. Each meeting, interaction, and activity should serve to add clarity and value to the exploration, analysis, and resulting design. If not, the merits of these activities should be questioned and alternatives explored that might better serve the purpose.

The indicators of an integrative design process are reflected in both the built product and the human interaction that leads to it. Decreased costs resulting from the elimination of redundancies and streamlining systems are a solid indicator that the design team is not just piling on technology without a rigorous and carefully considered method of analysis. As a result, highly integrated building systems can't fall prey to typical value engineering methods, because components are inextricably interrelated, and they cannot be reduced by merely removing some, without significant impacts on other systems components. Clarity about both the design and the steps to be taken in the design process are another strong indicator of integrated design—the mystery surrounding who knows what and how they do what they do is lessened, thereby augmenting clarity that is visible in the final design.

Accountability is another indicator. Accountability in the form of quantifiable building performance metrics (where LEED and other rating systems play a role) gives design teams a measurable means for determining what actually has been accomplished. Such accountability in the design process requires that stakeholders are held to task for specific milestones; their input is interdependent with others and therefore critical in order to produce deliverables and meet deadlines.

The first step in assuring proficiency as an integrative designer is to pay particular attention to your own indicators—if you are reflective about your participation and the participation of others in the group, you have a much higher chance of success. In other words, look for quantifiable feedback that evaluates the collaborative nature of the process and you have a much higher chance of success.

Over the years, it has become apparent to us that virtually everyone in our current generation of design and construction professionals was trained in the process of optimizing each system in isolation, separate from other systems. Because we base our calculations on rule-of-thumb values, building systems are being optimized in relationship to an imaginary, generic building represented in the pages of the American Society of Heating, Refrigerating and Air-Conditioning Engineers (ASHRAE) tables and other design standards rather than optimized in relationship to one another and to the reality of the building being designed. The systemic relationships that make up the whole cannot be seen from the seat of any one discipline, and so the many minds participating in the process function as disparate bodies of intelligence rather than as a coherent, organized force. The result is that our buildings embody redundancy built upon redundancy—significantly oversized systems that consume more resources and energy than necessary, resulting in severe environmental impacts. These include both the impacts associated with operating the building's systems and those impacts associated with extracting materials for manufacturing and installing these systems.

So how are building components interrelated? Let's examine one rather elegant and concrete example by asking the following question: how does the selection of the paint color for interior walls impact the size of the heating, ventilating, and air-conditioning (HVAC) system? As it turns out, there is a strong relationship between the seemingly unrelated factors of paint color and reflectance, lighting, and HVAC system size. How does this work?

Every lighting designer utilizes the following equation when determining the required lighting in any given space:

$$\text{Number of light fixtures} = \frac{\text{foot-candles} \times \text{area}}{\text{lumens} \times \text{LLF} \times \text{CU}}$$

The denominator on the right side of the equation includes *light loss factor* (LLF), which is a multiplier value that estimates the degradation of the lighting system over time, a function of the selected system's lamp lumen depreciation, ballast factor, and luminaire dirt depreciation. The other variable in the denominator is the *coefficient of utilization* (CU), which is derived from a CU table similar to Figure 2-1. The way designers enter this CU chart is by selecting a *light reflectance value* (LRV) for the ceiling, wall, and floor surfaces in the space. You can see from the table that as reflectance values for these surfaces get higher (moving to the left in the top rows of the table), the corresponding CU values in the lower part of the table also get higher. If the CU gets higher, as demonstrated by the above equation, the required number of light fixtures gets lower—often the number of lighting fixtures can be reduced significantly.

On our first green school project, we discovered that the number of lighting fixtures in every classroom could be reduced by 25 percent compared to standard practice, depending on the paint color selected. How did we learn this? Late in the project's schematic design phase, we asked the architect a simple question: what is the light reflectance value of the paint color that you have selected for every classroom in the project? This question was highly unusual at the time (in 1997), and it remains highly unusual today. The architect said he had no clue. The lighting consultant said: "You might want to look at the back of the paint chip sample." The architect did, and it read: LRV 64 percent. The lighting consultant then told the architect, "If you can get that number up above 75 percent, we can reduce the number of lighting fixtures in every one of those classrooms by 25 percent."

In those days, typical 1,000-square-foot classrooms were lighted with 16 triple-lamp T12 fixtures. In the case of this early green school project, by increasing the LRV of the paint on the walls, we were able to re-

COEFFICIENTS OF UTILIZATION "SAMPLE TABLE"

Floor		effective floor cavity reflectance = .20									
Ceiling		80				70				50		
Wall		70	50	30	10	70	50	30	10	50	30	10
RC		.72	.72	.72	.72	.62	.62	.62	.62	.43	.43	.43
R	0	.66	.62	.60	.57	.56	.54	.52	.50	.37	.36	.35
	1	.60	.54	.50	.47	.51	.47	.43	.41	.33	.31	.29
	2	.54	.48	.43	.39	.46	.41	.37	.34	.29	.26	.24
	3	.49	.42	.37	.32	.42	.36	.32	.28	.25	.22	.20
	4	.45	.37	.32	.27	.39	.32	.28	.24	.23	.20	.17
	5	.41	.33	.28	.24	.35	.29	.24	.21	.20	.17	.15
	6	.38	.30	.24	.20	.33	.26	.21	.18	.18	.15	.13
	7	.35	.27	.21	.18	.30	.23	.19	.16	.16	.13	.11
	8	.33	.24	.19	.15	.28	.21	.17	.14	.15	.12	.10
	9	.30	.22	.17	.14	.26	.19	.15	.12	.13	.11	.09
	10											

Figure 2-1 Generic coefficient of utilization table. *Image courtesy of Rei Horst.*

duce the number of lighting fixtures to 12 triple-lamp T8 fixtures, a 25 percent reduction. Ten years later, we now design typical 1,000-square-foot classrooms with only 9 triple-lamp T5 fixtures, nearly cutting in half the number of fixtures per classroom but still maintaining adequate work-surface illuminance (roughly 50 foot-candles, which is the recommended illumination level for reading and other tasks performed in a typical classroom).

Reviewing our work on this early green school project, we now had 25 percent fewer light fixtures—clearly this lighting system cost less to build. Additionally, over the life of the building, we now were illuminating 25 percent fewer lights, reducing the amount of electrical energy for lighting by 25 percent in all classrooms over the life of the building and, in turn, reducing by 25 percent the environmental impacts associated with burning the fossil fuels required to create that electrical energy. As most of us know, operational costs and environmental impacts often dwarf those of initial construction, especially for lighting (see Figure 2-2).

But it gets better. What else do lights produce besides light? Heat—and a lot of it. A good rule of thumb is that for every 3 watts of energy spent to power a light, another watt of energy is required for cooling the heat generated by those lights. Let's connect that to the HVAC system.

In many climates, it is not uncommon to spend more energy cooling our commercial buildings than heating them because of internal loads, such as electrical appliances (plug loads) and the body heat of occupants, but the chief internal generator of heat frequently is lighting. Often the build-

Luminare Life Cycle Cost
Example

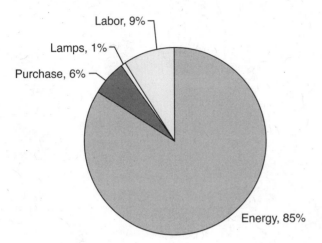

Labor, 9%
Lamps, 1%
Purchase, 6%
Energy, 85%

Figure 2-2 For most light fixtures, energy consumption is the largest component of its life cycle cost. *Image courtesy of Marcus Sheffer.*

ing's cooling system size is driven by these internal loads, and lighting is often the largest contributor to these loads. In a typical school, the lighting system can account for as much as 50 percent of the annual electrical consumption and up to 40 percent of the building's cooling loads. This internal load created by the lighting system is calculated as lighting power density (LPD), which is simply the amount of watts of connected lighting in a space divided by the square footage of that space. Mechanical engineers enter this LPD value into their block-load calculations to determine required cooling capacity and in turn to determine the size of the HVAC equipment. By reducing the number of light fixtures, and therefore LPD, mechanical engineers can significantly reduce the size and capacity of the HVAC-supply system. Further, since cooling capacity determines the size of the distribution system as well (i.e., ductwork and/or piping), the size of these components also can

be reduced (smaller ducts). This equates not only to significant savings in the first cost of construction but also to operational savings over the life of the building, since less energy is required for a smaller HVAC system.

So, let's summarize: we now have reduced first cost for lighting, first cost for HVAC-supply systems, first cost for HVAC-distribution systems, operating and energy costs for lighting, operating and energy costs for HVAC systems, environmental impacts associated with manufacturing the lighting and HVAC equipment, and the environmental impacts associated with burning the fossil fuels required to provide energy to these lighting and HVAC systems—all because of the paint color?

Well, yes. But there is a problem.

Over the past twelve years, we have asked somewhere on the order of 3,000 electrical and lighting engineers this question: "When was the last time you had a conversation with your architect to find out, before designing the lighting system, the actual light reflectance values of the surfaces in the space?" We usually are met with shrugging shoulders, or the response is "never." Then we ask: "Okay, then, since you are not using actual reflectance values when you enter the coefficient of utilization table, what reflectance values do you typically use for ceilings, walls, and floors?" In all but a few cases we hear—almost like a mantra—the same response: "80, 50, 20."

So we ask: "But what if those values actually are 90, 80, and 40 for the selected materials?"

They reply: "Well, then, we can significantly reduce the number of lighting fixtures."

Unfortunately, this almost never happens. Rather, we have found that lighting engineers rarely factor such optimal reflectance values into their calculations, so the number of lighting fixtures often ends up being far more than (often double) what it needs to be.

It gets worse.

Figure 2-3 A classroom at Clearview Elementary School in Hanover, Pennsylvania, exhibits excellent bilateral daylighting, allowing daylight to enter from both the north and the south. *Copyright © Jim Shafer.*

We then ask the HVAC engineers: "When was the last time you had a conversation with your electrical engineer to find out the actual calculated lighting power density in the spaces being cooled before sizing your cooling system?" Again, more shrugging shoulders, and nine times out of ten, we hear "never." When asked what values they use instead, these HVAC engineers typically reply that they take the LPD values out of ASHRAE tables for the associated building type, or they base these values on assumptions from past experience. It should be noted, in their defense, that part of the problem is that the lighting design typically occurs much later in the design process than the point at which load calculations are performed.

In 1997, when we were working on this early green school, the standard rule of thumb utilized by HVAC engineers to input lighting load into their equations, using LPD values right out of the ASHRAE tables, was 2 watts per square foot. We have not worked on a school in over ten years that has re-quired more than *1* watt per square foot—half the assumed LPD, hence half the heat generated. We also have seen a similar and consistent doubling of LPDs for office buildings as well (1.5 watts per square foot versus an achievable 0.75—or even 0.65—watts per square foot).

From this single example, we can see that systems as ostensibly unrelated as interior wall paint and HVAC are in fact closely related. Rather than working to deepen our understanding of these interrelationships, though, we work to optimize the individual things: the architect selects surfaces based on a preferred aesthetic, the lighting engineer uses rules of thumb to select lighting fixtures, and the HVAC engineer uses rules of thumb to size cooling equipment. In short, our current process lacks an understanding of how these systems—and many other building systems—interrelate, and, further, it lacks the communication between design professionals required to reach such an understanding.

BUILDINGS AS ORGANISMS

Quantum mechanics has established the primacy of the inseparable whole. For this reason, the basis of the new biophysics must be the insight into the fundamental interconnectedness within *the organism as well as between organisms, and that of the organism* with the environment.

—Marco Bischof, German theoretician quoted in *Science and the Akashic Field: An Integral Theory of Everything*, by Ervin Laszlo. Rochester, VT. Inner Traditions, 2004, from "Field Concepts and the Emergence of a Holistic Biophysics" (by Marco Bischof) in: Beloussov, L. V., Popp, F. A., Voeikov, V. L., and Van Wijk, R. (eds.), *Biophotonics and Coherent Systems.* Moscow University Press, Moscow 2000

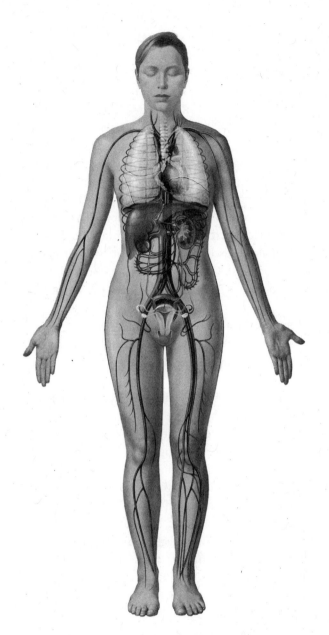

Figure 2-4 The organism of the human body is extremely elegant—each of its multitude of interrelated systems relies on the others to work as a whole with no redundancy and no waste. It also is tied to larger systems, since the waste produced by this human organism provides food for other organisms. *Nucleus Medical Illustration, Copyright ©2008 Nucleus Medical Art. All Rights Reserved; http://www.nucleusinc.com.*

One way to begin the shift toward a new process is to think of our buildings as organisms, where every system is in symbiotic relationship, such as paint color and HVAC equipment. Think for a moment about your body as an organism—an extremely elegant one at that. Your body is made up of a number of inter-related systems: immune, respiratory, digestive, and circulatory. All of these systems work in perfect concert with one another. Each of these systems impacts the others: for example, when your immune system is stressed, this impacts your circulatory system, your digestive system, and your respiratory system—and vice versa. A building's systems—the ventilation system, the electrical system, etc.—also impact one another. Perhaps we can think of a building's ventilation system functioning as its respiratory system and the electrical system as its circulatory system, and so on. A process that encourages design teams to develop an understanding of the interrelationships between a building's systems is critical for reducing construction and operating costs as well as environmental impacts.

Amory Lovins of the Rocky Mountain Institute, along with his writing partners L. Hunter Lovins and Paul Hawken, summarize the nature of these interrelationships in their book *Natural Capitalism: Creating the Next Industrial Revolution* (Boston: Little, Brown and Co., 1999) when they tell us: "Optimizing components in isolation tends to pessimize the whole system—and hence the bottom line. You can actually make a system less efficient, simply by not properly linking up those components.... If they're not designed to work with one another, they'll tend to work against one another."

Yet most of us have been conditioned and trained to design our buildings by utilizing a fragmented process that optimizes each system or subsystem in isolation, based upon conventions and rules of thumb.

Tunneling Through the Cost Barrier

So why do we continue implementing this fragmented process that we have been using for decades? The shift in thinking that is required to begin seeing our buildings as organisms is met with some very real obstacles. To return to the previous example, about the links between paint color and HVAC systems, it would seem that a relatively straightforward process adjustment—requesting that the lighting designer ask the interior designer or architect for the *actual* light reflectance values being used—could achieve the desired results. To think that this is a quick-fix solution, however, ignores the deeper issues that reinforce this fragmented process in the first place. The reason why the majority of design and development professionals do not seek out this information is not because they are stubborn or unthoughtful, but rather because they are working to meet clearly defined time and budget goals within the pressures and constraints created by a highly demanding industry. There is a disincentive for anyone to try to extend their thinking outside of, or even to

the outer limit of, their own prescribed discipline. Understandably, we begin designing right away: *Get on with it, get it done, we have to be on time and in budget.* Stopping to reconsider and question the accepted conventions that govern our design paradigms feels like a waste of time: *No, dammit, we've got work to do.*

The reason for this pressure is very real and quite valid: building a building is an extremely costly, risky, and complex endeavor. Anything that departs from the prescribed and tested is not only frowned upon but creates real uneasiness and discomfort. Further, such endeavors are perceived as adding time and cost. We in the field of green design are acutely familiar with this paradox: the number one objection or restraint to building green, coming from both our clients and from many of our fellow design professionals, is the perception of increased cost.

Our conventional process addresses cost in terms of being on time and within budget, often by *fixing* things with what we euphemistically call *value engineering*, as discussed in Chapter 1. When we want to consider sustainability, we add more considerations into the mix: energy efficiency of the envelope, new energy technologies, daylighting, solar orientation, indoor air quality (IAQ), lighting quality, equipment power density, toxicity of the built environment, materials resources, embodied energy in these materials, life cycle cost analysis, life cycle assessment of environmental impacts, habitat health, water recharge, water conservation, low-impact development design, soil health, land restoration, impacts on local economy, transportation energy, environmental impacts of infrastructure, abuse of labor practices by manufacturers, and so on.

Considering all of these issues can be overwhelming. How can we possibly address all of this and still be on time and in budget? It is easy to see that simply adding these issues to our conventional design process, as if these are technologies that we can specify or overlay on top of the design, would be a very daunting task in the face of budget and time constraints.

In other words, adding components costs money. This is obviously true. Many developers and clients are starting to come around to the realization that occupancy costs will eventually make the increased first-cost investment (or hard capital cost of construction) that a green building is assumed to require *worth it* in the *long run*. This reasoning not only lacks potency but often becomes unnecessary when an integrative, whole-systems process is used. When the building is being optimized as a whole system by a design team that focuses on the relationships between building components, single components often can be seen to perform multiple, *stacked* or *cascading* functions. This allows us to downsize or even eliminate other systems, saving not only operations costs but the ever-critical *first costs* as well.

To ensure that cascading benefits are realized, once a project team identifies some green strategy that adds cost, we encourage them to ask: What other systems will be affected by this new strategy or component? Are there any systems that can be downsized—or even eliminated—as a result of this new decision? This can almost serve as an integrative design mantra: *What other systems are impacted?* The money saved from reducing or eliminating such systems or components can then be used to pay for the additional cost of the green strategy that allowed for the reduction in the first place, hence neutralizing overall construction costs. In *Natural Capitalism,* Lovins refers to this kind of thinking as "tunneling through the cost barrier."

Lessons Learned from High-Performance Windows

As an illustration, passive solar homes—before the invention of low-emissivity glass—typically cost $5,000 more than a conventional house of the same size (2,500

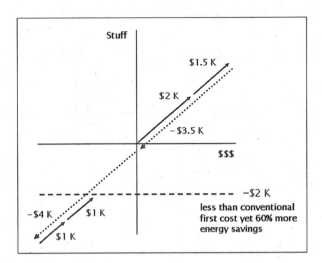

Figure 2-5 This graph depicts the cascading first-cost trade-offs for an example house that consumes 60 percent less energy than the norm: adding $2,000 for high performance windows plus another $1,500 for better insulation allows for perimeter air registers and horizontal ductwork to be eliminated for a savings of $3,500, plus another $4,000 savings by eliminating the separate heating boiler. Adding back in $1,000 for a quick recovery hot water heater to provide space heating and another $1,000 for a heat recovery ventilation system to remove moisture from spaces (which may be required due to the tightly sealed envelope) results in a total first cost savings of $2,000. *Image courtesy of Bill Reed.*

square feet). This was usually because mechanical systems had to be installed to act as backup heat sources in addition to the costs associated with larger areas of glass, increased insulation, and thermal mass.

When low-emissivity glass and high-performance windows appeared in the market, a number of cascading benefits were realized that could reduce the cost of a passive solar house to approximately $2,000 *less* than conventional construction, while at the same time reducing the yearly energy costs 50 to 70 percent by utilizing an integrative approach (see Figure 2-5).

This is because the augmented thermal properties of these windows, along with their ability to reduce solar heat gain, allow a number of reductions in other systems and elements:

■ It is possible to eliminate the usual ductwork runs to the perimeter of the house to bathe the windows with warm air. The ducts are limited to a central trunk serving all rooms from the internal walls. The well-insulated walls and windows no longer need to be warmed by a mechanically supplied heat source, and compensation for the discomfort resulting from our bodies' radiant heat loss to the cold surfaces of the glass is no longer needed, nor is it needed to reduce condensation. Money is saved.

■ Because the windows are oriented to the south and the walls and windows become more effective insulators, a boiler may no longer be needed. The house is capable of being heated with a large hot water heater. More money is saved.

■ Because the house is so tightly built, the issue of indoor air quality is a concern. The air handler in the house is replaced by an air-to-air heat exchanger with heat recovery for ventilating spaces that produce moisture, such as bathrooms and kitchens.

The approach that emerges from understanding these connections asks us to spend more money on glazing and insulation to achieve the net savings garnered from reducing ductwork and eliminating the boiler, while at the same time significant energy-consumption cost reductions and better indoor air quality also are achieved.

This works for commercial buildings as well. On an early project for Pennsylvania's Department of Environmental Protection (DEP), begun in 1999, we went to the owner and said that we would like to install triple-glazed, low-e coated, argon-filled, thermally broken windows. The owner balked, making a joke that "with all those adjectives, those windows must be very expensive." We confirmed that they were more expensive than the budgeted windows and that they would cost the owner an additional $15,000. Because this was a small building—only

about 30,000 square feet—that increase equated to roughly 50 cents per square foot on a building that in 1999 cost only $93 per square foot to build—not an insignificant inrease.

In this case, the owner was a private developer hired by the Commonwealth of Pennsylvania to design, build, manage the building, then lease it back to the DEP. He had won this contract with the state by presenting the lowest lease cost among his competitors when responding to a statewide request for proposal (RFP). This lease cost had been determined based on the construction and permanent financing he was able to procure after establishing a finite value for first construction costs. Because he was locked into the lease contract, he was also effectively locked into a first cost for construction; so, understandably, he simply could not afford to spend an extra $15,000 on windows. Even though he knew that the building would perform better in terms of energy consumption, providing a quick payback, he refused.

The owner changed his mind, though, when we explained that he could afford these windows without worrying about paybacks. Here is why: his construction budget included the installation of a perimeter heating system along the windows—a common practice for buildings in the northeast, because windows are the most vulnerable components of the building envelope in terms of heat loss. We told him that if we installed these thermally robust windows, our modeling indicated that we would be reducing heat loss to less than 100 British thermal units (Btu) per lineal foot of window, which would allow us to *eliminate* the perimeter heating system, which had a budgeted first cost of $25,000.

In this case, either the high-performance windows or the perimeter heating system were required to meet the client's performance specification, which required that when outdoor temperatures were 20°F, the interior surface temperature of the glass could be no less than 62°F. This could have been accomplished with either strategy; the high-performance windows just happened to be cheaper. Consequently, the owner was agreeable to the less-expensive option, resulting in a net savings of $10,000—but the story got better.

Due to the reduced heat gain and heat loss resulting from these more thermally robust windows, we also were able to design a smaller HVAC system, which in turn resulted in a smaller distribution system of pipes and ductwork. These reductions achieved an additional $10,000 in first-cost savings. So, by spending $15,000 on the better windows, $35,000 was saved by eliminating and reducing the size of other systems—the net $20,000 savings could then be reinvested in first costs for other systems that would return paybacks over the building's life, for example, the project's 14-kilowatt photovoltaic array on the roof.

Here we have an example of eliminating an entire redundant system (perimeter heating), significantly reducing the capacity of another system (HVAC supply and distribution), and neutralizing overall first costs—but without some understanding of how building systems are interrelated, this could not have been achieved. By analyzing the interactions between systems and eliminating redundancies between them, the project team also was able to achieve significant operational and energy cost savings over the life of the building; to eliminate the environmental impacts associated with operating these systems (again, impacts resulting from burning the fossil fuels necessary to generate this energy); and to reduce the environmental impacts associated with the extraction, manufacture, transport, and installation of materials that now were no longer necessary.

One can readily see, however, why this approach could be problematic without a fully integrated team. A construction manager reviewing the construction cost

Figure 2-6 Light shelves at south-facing windows of the Pennsylvania DEP Cambria project shade windows below from high-altitude solar radiation in the summer while allowing low-altitude winter sun to penetrate; they also bounce daylight deeper into interior spaces through the glass directly above the light shelves, reducing the need for artificial lighting. *Copyright © Jim Schafer.*

estimates during the design phase would typically look at the line-item unit cost for the high-performance windows and compare it to a database from prior similar projects. Without understanding the related impacts, the construction manager likely would eliminate the extra window costs during value engineering. Further, in early design phases, HVAC-system costs are invariably estimated in terms of dollars per square foot. Because at this stage, no equipment sizing upon which to base an accurate estimate has been done, it is unlikely that the cost estimator would be willing to reduce the HVAC-system estimate without a larger understanding of the

▲ **Figure 2-7** High-performance windows—like this triple-glazed, aluminum-clad, wood window—reduce heat loss and can eliminate the need for perimeter heating systems. *Image courtesy of Loewen. Copyright © C. P. Loewen Enterprises Ltd.*

▼ **Figure 2-8** Perimeter heating typically is supplied by air or hot water radiant systems. An example of components for a typical air system is depicted. *Image courtesy of Marcus Sheffer.*

▶ **Figure 2-9** Hot water radiant systems commonly provide perimeter heating. *Image courtesy of Marcus Sheffer.*

interrelationships between systems. In the case of the Pennsylvania DEP project, a ground-source heat pump (GSHP) system was utilized. At the time this building was constructed, GSHP systems were being installed for $19 per square foot; however, due to the capacity reductions enabled by the high-performance windows and other energy-efficiency measures (EEMs), this project's GSHP system was installed for only $12 per square foot, thereby providing a savings of $7 per square foot that offset the additional costs of the better windows and other EEMs.

PROJECT TEAMS AS ORGANISMS

All that the integrative approach requires is a process that facilitates intelligent and intentional communication between all team members, along with a willingness to reach for high-performance goals using *state-of-the-shelf* technologies. The good news here is that we now have the tools (unavailable to us 15 to 20 years ago) that allow us to examine these critical interrelationships: tools such as computer-simulated energy modeling, daylighting simulation software, and life cycle assessment (LCA) packages. These tools allow us to analyze and optimize the interactions between many systems, subsystems, and components rather than to optimize each system or component in isolation. Because of this ability to simulate the interactions between these systems, we can now begin to address more aspects of how they interrelate as a whole.

But these aspects are not *things*; they cannot simply be bought and *overlaid* onto a building design. They are aspects of a whole system of interconnected relationships. Lots of different specialists hold the knowledge about these different aspects. In our Age of Specialization, one person simply cannot address all of them. A new kind of design process is needed. To paraphrase Albert Einstein, the same design process that created the problems we face will not be able to solve them. Such a process must look at the whole, not just sets of component parts. This requires not only an understanding that every one of the building's systems impacts every other system, but it also mandates a nonlinear, holistic process where everybody integrates their work rather than designs their systems within isolated silos.

Returning to our *buildings as organisms* metaphor, we can see that the challenge is twofold. Not only does the building need to be designed to function as an organism—whereby every system and component impacts and affects all other systems—but the *design team itself* needs to be functioning as an organism. Organic systems, such as our metaphorical organisms, organize themselves through feedback processes, through communication. Our process must allow or encourage all design team members to interact on a much higher level to understand how the decisions each is making impact the decisions all others are making. In this way, high-performance teams can be built and sustained for designing high-performance buildings.

Building and Sustaining High-Performance Teams

By Guy Sapirstein, PhD

Organizations of all types have been grappling with the issue of how to build and sustain high-performance teams. This issue is particularly relevant to teams where each member has an expertise or skill set that overlaps another member's skills. As in all human interaction, there are two main dynamics that are acted out in teams: (1) issues of hierarchy, or power; and (2) issues of relatedness, or collaboration.

The issue of hierarchy is related to leadership. A leader might be appointed; that is, someone is given the authority and is designated the Leader. Another type of leader is the Emergent Leader, someone who has a unique skill set and rises to the occasion and becomes the de facto leader of the group. Identifying the emergent leader is often a difficult task a priori and requires that the situation present itself. Most work-based teams appoint a

(continued)

leader upon formation of the team rather than wait for a leader to emerge from within the team.

Relatedness and collaboration are complex dimensions of human experience. The element of initiative is implicitly included in collaboration. It is not merely a passive or submissive act of following certain rules; rather, it involves proactively seeking out how to help one another. The challenge faced by organizations and team leaders is how to bring people to the point of internalizing those concepts and integrating them into their functioning within the team.

In an attempt to integrate leadership, relatedness, and collaboration, the field of "team building" has proliferated and includes a wide variety of activities, from seminars focused on learning to use of outdoor recreational activities. These activities can be classified by using two orthogonal factors:

- *Type of teaching and learning:* didactic versus experiential
- *Focus of activity:* work versus recreation

These can be illustrated as follows (examples included in each quadrant).

	Work focused	
Lecture on team building for a specific project		Group simulation of working on a project
Didactic		**Experiential**
Teaching how to build a tree house		Rafting trip, outdoor challenge
	Recreational	

Teaching and Learning Style

When discussing styles of teaching and learning, one must first distinguish between types of knowledge or information that need to be taught or acquired. Cognitive science has identified many different kinds of knowledge, but the two that seem most appropriate to team building are *explicit* and *tacit* knowledge. *Explicit* knowledge refers to information that is easy to convey and knowledge that has already been written down and codified. Examples of explicit knowledge would be specific skills or processes such as calculating a duct or beam size in a building.

Tacit knowledge is knowledge that is not easily codified or conveyed. This type of knowledge is best imparted through interpersonal contact and experience. Michael Polanyi, who coined this term, spoke about the "we know more than we can tell" phenomenon. Most people have had the experience of trying to describe an event to someone who was not present, only to be met with a blank look indicating a lack of appreciation of the subjective experience described. We tend to mutter in response, "you had to be there." The implication is that transference of this knowledge requires a shared experience.

Given these different types of knowledge, one would expect to find different methodologies for imparting each type. *Didactic* methods optimize the amount of *explicit* knowledge that is imparted. This explicit knowledge might be *descriptive* (knowledge about things) or *procedural* (know-how, i.e., knowledge about how to do things). Didactic teaching is typically structured and scripted in form. The teacher conveys clearly articulated information about skills, rules, processes, et cetera. Didactic teaching and learning does not depend on the source of information—that source might be a person, a computer, or a book.

On the other side of the spectrum lies *experiential* teaching and learning. *Tacit* knowledge cannot easily be imparted through a book, since the source of information cannot and does not capture the multifaceted gestalt of the knowledge. The only way to acquire this type of knowledge is to have experienced it.

When helping a team become a high-performance team, it is important to ensure that team members possess not only the explicit knowledge necessary (e.g., knowledge about the integrative design process) but also tacit knowledge of the experience of being part of a high-performance team—what we know but cannot tell. The foundation of a high-performance team involves the knowledge of what it *feels like* to be a member of such a team. To be effective, this experience should capture all the stages of team development and the conflicts or struggles that a team and its members experience on the road to being a high-performance team capable of functioning effectively and innovatively.

Focus of Activity

Most team-building activities fall somewhere between *work* and *recreation* focused. While it is not clear that engaging in recreational activities as a team is sufficient to transfer needed knowledge and contribute to optimal functioning in the *work* environment, there is undoubtedly a benefit in terms of employee morale. Thus, feel-good activities should not be expected to do more than simply facilitate shared positive experiences by teams. Activities that are primarily work focused may be less fun, but they have the advantage

of disseminating knowledge that is more readily applicable to work demands and needs.

All too often, team-building activities fall into two quadrants: recreational-experiential and work-didactic. The latter is frequently associated with organizational development. The most relevant and important quadrant—work-experiential—is typically overlooked. The type of activity that would fall into this quadrant would be a simulation of a work environment. In creating that simulation, one can choose to simulate team functioning or, in other words, a view of the team at a point in time. More relevant would be simulating the process of team development; that is, creating a simulation that replicates the developmental stages of a team, allows for reflection and growth, and provides team members with the tacit knowledge of being part of a high-performance team. (Team workshops and charrettes are excellent examples of "work-experiential" activities.)

Summary

Team-building activities can be classified on two axes: *method* of teaching and learning (didactic versus experiential) and *focus* of the activity (work versus recreation scenario). The information and knowledge necessary for teams to develop into high-performing ones is primarily tacit. Such knowledge, by definition, can only be learned through doing, through personal experience. Experiential team-building exercises that are work focused and allow participants to experience all the stages of team development are most appropriate for building and sustaining high-performance teams.

Figure 2-10 The Pennsylvania DEP Cambria project is located in Ebensburg. *Image courtesy of John Boecker.*

Fostering an Interdisciplinary Process: "A Deer in the Headlights"

The Pennsylvania Department of Environmental Protection office building project just described (DEP Cambria) was 7group's second major green building project for DEP, but it represents the first time that we made a conscious decision to employ an integrative design process. This decision was based on our previous experience of working with DEP, for whom we would go on to work on a total of five projects over the years. On each of these projects, there were essentially two clients: the DEP (the building user), and the developer (the owner). The developer was responsible for designing, building, managing, and leasing each building to the Commonwealth of Pennsylvania, earning his profit from lease revenues.

It was from these projects, particularly because of the complexity of the client relationship, that we learned the importance of making sure that all of the project team members are convened in an initial session about the integrative design process as early as possible. Having touched upon this wisdom during our

first DEP project, we held an early schematic design meeting with the DEP Cambria project team members, including the project engineers, architect, contractors, developer, and DEP representatives. The schema for the design emerged as an elongated rectangle consisting of a central core and two wings (see floor plan in Figure 2-11). The plan was oriented lengthwise on an east-west axis, with the larger wing to the west and the smaller to the east. An early decision was made to couple ground-source heat pumps with underfloor supply-air-plenum distribution; to our knowledge, the building is the first in the United States to have done so.

The design architect, one of the 7group partners, had decided before this early schematic design meeting that the central HVAC equipment should be located in a penthouse on the building's roof. Given that decision, this early schematic meeting included a discussion about piping and ductwork: specifically, how best to get the piping from the ground-source heat pump well field up to the penthouse and how to distribute air ducts back down from the air-handling units into the underfloor supply-air plenums on both the first and second floors of this 30,000-square-foot building. The team engaged in a back-and-forth conversation, discussing where the piping would go, what the size of the vertical duct shafts should be, how all of this could fit into the central core, and how to avoid conflicts between these distribution components and other building elements such as elevators, structural components, sprinkler pipes, and so on. As this discussion unfolded over a period of about twenty minutes, the architect suddenly realized that this process was not, in fact, an integrative design process. Rather, this process of deciding (albeit, as a group) how best to assemble these systems amounted to little more than accelerated coordination. Further, he realized that his own decision to locate the central HVAC system components in the penthouse had been made in isolation from the seat of his own discipline, without any input from the other disciplines at the table.

The architect stopped the meeting.

Spontaneously, he looked across the table at the mechanical engineer, John Manning. "John," he asked, "if you were designing this building, where would you locate the central HVAC system components? Where's the best place for the mechanical room?"

Manning was stunned. He sat in silence; later, he said that he felt like a deer caught in headlights. The architect, noticing Manning's discomfort, asked what was wrong. John replied, "nobody's ever asked me that question before." Here we had an engineer with over twenty years' experience designing HVAC systems, yet never in his career had an architect asked him for his expert advice on where to locate the HVAC system components and the mechanical room.

It only took a couple of minutes, however, for Manning to recover. He suggested placing the eleven ground-source heat pump units in two separate mechanical spaces on the ground floor of the building (see Figure 2-11)—six units in one room (serving the

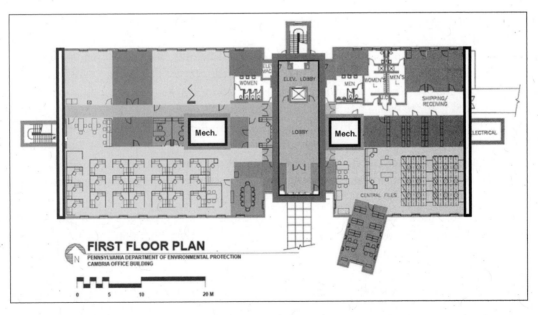

Figure 2-11 This floor plan for DEP Cambria depicts the central core, the flanking, ground-level mechanical rooms in adjacent west and east wings, and the extensions on the ends of these wings to make up for leasable space displaced by these mechanical rooms. *Image courtesy of John Boecker.*

west wing) and five in the other room (serving the east wing). He explained that he could then route supply piping from the well field directly up through the slab on grade to each of these units, thereby eliminating *all* of the piping up to the penthouse and back. Additionally, supply air could be provided directly into the first-floor air plenum with only a foot or two of ductwork in three directions. Further, only five feet of vertical ductwork would be needed to supply air to the second-floor plenum above, thereby eliminating virtually all of the ductwork that otherwise would have been needed to provide supply air from the penthouse. Further still, Manning noted that since the duct runs would be so short, less resistance to airflow would result, which meant that fan sizes could be reduced. Lastly, he explained that instead of facilities staff having to climb a ladder in the janitor's closet to get onto the roof and then go out into the snow and rain to replace filters, compressors, and so on, these activities could be performed in an easily accessible, weather-enclosed space, resulting in significantly improved ease of maintenance over the life of the building.

Manning's solution was brilliant. The rest of the design team marveled at its elegance. In fact, everyone loved the idea except for one person, the owner, who heard only that he was going to lose 400 square feet of prime lease space from the first floor of his building. Locked into a required minimum square footage of lease space, he viewed such an adjustment as impossible. But, after some discussion and calculations, we were able to report that this new idea would save him $40,000 in base construction costs.

Hearing this, the owner happily agreed to make up the lost square footage by adding an inexpensive 18 inches of length to each end of the building. Everyone was happy. The significant operational savings that would be realized from both energy savings and simplified maintenance were, as it turned out, icing on the cake. Even the sheet metal contractor, who initially balked at the idea of losing all that ductwork (asserting that such a system would never work), said by the end of the project that it was the best system he had ever installed.

So what is the lesson here? We think that there are two. The first is about the roles that we ascribe to our separate disciplines. In that meeting, the mechanical engineer was asked to think outside his normal area of purview. Instead of the architect leaning down from Parnassus, saying "it shall be thus," he instead asked the mechanical engineer to step into the architect's role. The location of the mechanical room is *always* chosen by the architect, yet who on the team is more likely to understand the best location for the central HVAC equipment than the mechanical engineer? A major shift in thinking took place by recognizing that everyone's systems interact with everyone else's; hence, *everyone's* input about how their systems and components interact with everyone else's is critical in realizing the best design. In short, everyone on the team should be invited and encouraged to extend their expertise beyond their own discipline.

The second lesson addresses the question of why the architect had put the mechanical equipment in a penthouse on the roof in the first place. When asked this question, the architect replied, "because that's what we did on the last project—it's what we've always done." If we think about how we normally go about the process of design, many such assumptions are made, and often these assumptions generate less-than-optimal results, as was the case in this instance. How many times have you heard "that's how we've always done it," or "that's how my father did it, how my grandfather did it," and so on? In order to produce a project that was much more efficient, in terms of not only operations but also initial construction cost, a willingness to question assumptions was needed. So lesson number two can be expressed simply as "question assumptions."

One commonality that we have found among all of our most successful projects is that the usual right answers were not simply assumed; rather, assumptions were questioned and new answers were discovered through an interdisciplinary process. We should not expect project team members to know everything; rather, we should expect them to question everything they know.

A Team of Colearners and the Learning Wheel

Good integration happens through a continuously dynamic, iterative process. All issues are addressed early and kept in play for as long as possible so that connections and relationships can be optimized. While a linear process approaches each problem (and system) separately, an integrative process utilizes the varied viewpoints of multiple participants to address issues from a whole-systems perspective. Through multiple iterations, greater understanding emerges, and adjustments and refinements are made—a process comparable to what the scientific community calls "progressive approximation." Exploration is encouraged, helping to ensure that the best opportunities are seen and taken advantage of.

The *Integrative Process* can be described simply as a repeating pattern of Research/Analysis and Team Workshops. The research and analysis stages involve team members analyzing systems in progressively greater detail between all-hands team meetings or workshops. Research and analysis stages also require interim integration meetings between various team members. This process is described in the "Integrative Process Overview" section of Chapter 5, and graphically depicted by the Implementation Process diagram, used throughout Chapters 5 through 8, to *map* the implementation of an *optimal* integrative design process.

The trick here is managing this process in such a way that every person is not around the table at every meeting. Each project is unique, so every project requires a project-specific roadmap (discussed later) to make sure that assignments are accomplished and issues are addressed by having the right people present at the right time. Management of this integrative process is critical if money is to be used efficiently and if the energy of team members is to be maintained.

One subtle, yet major, benefit of this process is a significantly higher level of project ownership by all team members. When the building owner, occupants, operators, builders, and designers are all active participants in the creation of the design, there is a greater level of *buy in*, since everyone has an opportunity to engage and to have their particular issues vetted by the entire team. Owners and building users are typically in a position of reacting to the architect's interpretation of their needs and desires in our conventional process. With an integrative process, though, they become an integral part of the creative process, and as a result, they embrace the solutions developed more deeply and personally (e.g., see Figure 2-12).

The intgrative process not only produces a much more successful green design—and thus lower costs over the life of the building—it also saves time, effort, and first construction costs. These savings often are a surprise to those who, groomed by a traditional process, expect a green building to be the product of adding "green stuff" to the building for which they had budgeted.

McStain Builders in Boulder, Colorado, for example, wanted to improve the environmental performance of the homes they were developing in the late 1990s. Established as the top priorities for the homes were: increasing energy efficiency, addressing materials choices, and improving indoor air quality.

Improving insulation performance and reducing air infiltration were the first strategies considered. To

Marcus,

The CUNY Law School Project was cancelled due to failure to obtain phase 2 funding in this year's legislative session. Interestingly however, the project is considered by everyone involved, including CUNY, to have been a success.

Thought you might be interested in what the Associate Dean of the Law School had to say about this project.

David R. Ortiz, P.E.
Project Manager

DMJM Harris
20 Exchange Place
New York, NY 10005
Tel: (212) 991-2141
Cell: (646) 208-6409

From: Gregory Koster [mailto:koster@mail.law.cuny.edu]
Sent: Friday, March 30, 2007 2:29 PM
To: Ortiz, David
Subject: CUNY School of Law

Dear David:

I am writing to commend you and your team for the excellent process that you established for the CUNY School of Law expansion project.

First I want to reassure you that nothing I have heard about the cancellation of this project reflects on the quality or direction of the proposals that DMJM Harris was developing. The problem is that this project has always been severely underfunded and without a commitment for the Phase II funds it is really impossible to proceed with the Phase I construction.

Second, the intensive planning process that you established for this project was a high point of all the projects that I have worked on in over twenty years at CUNY. Having all the subject matter specialists around the table from the beginning meant that we surfaced and dealt with issues like the HVAC design—and the long-term energy and personnel efficiencies—in a far more comprehensive way than I have ever seen before. I had great confidence that if we could solve the funding issues the final result of this project would have been the best overall design of any Law School building project.

Finally, it was a pleasure working with you and with each member of your team on this project. Not only did each of you inspire confidence in your specialty, but each of you was pleasant to deal with—and together we seemed to have reached an excellent group dynamic that would have helped us get through the rough patches that any project encounters.

I hope that we will have an opportunity to work together again.

Gregory Koster
Acting Associate Dean for
Administration & Finance
koster@mail.law.cuny.edu

Figure 2-12 This email expresses an owner's response to an integrative process that engages all team members from the beginning, dealing with interrelationships across disciplines. *Image courtesy of Marcus Sheffer.*

find the best technique, the builders tested three homes: one with sprayed cellulose, one with blown-in insulation, and one with fiberglass batts. The best solution, which not only increased insulation performance but also significantly reduced infiltration (from 0.5 to 0.2 air changes per hour), proved to be sprayed cellulose in the 2 × 6 wall cavities (as opposed to 2 × 4 walls).

With the building envelope so effectively sealed, the team went on to explore other strategies. Instead of a western or eastern orientation, they rotated the dominant window wall to the south and shaded it against high altitude summer solar radiation, reducing air-conditioning loads by two-thirds. An air-to-air heat exchanger was selected for installation and combined into one unit with the air handler, thus saving one motor and fan system, and thereby further reducing energy consumption. The combined effect of this heat exchanger, the insulation, and revised orientation meant that each home's entire heating demand could be satisfied with a quick-recovery, high-efficiency 50-gallon hot water heater, which replaced the boiler. Ductwork routing, in turn, was simplified, and this allowed more efficient delivery of air to each room; by eliminating 90-degree bends and extra-long runs, additional energy savings were achieved.

When all of these strategies had been decided on and integrated, the team was proud to announce that energy usage would be reduced by a significant 60 percent, with an added cost of just $7,000 per house. Much to their surprise, the production manager (who was also the owner) did not find this trade-off acceptable. Instead, he strongly suggested that the team drop all this green "silliness" (imagine a different word here).

The rest of the team felt that $7,000 in additional costs in exchange for 60 percent energy savings was well worth it—but it was not their money to spend. Rather than accepting defeat, however, the team searched for a solution. Several people around the table began to mentally scan for extraneous costs. David Johnston, the project's environmental consultant, had noticed various gable extensions and numerous projections in the design of the house's floor plan, and wondered aloud about the cost per corner for these "artful bump-outs." In response to Johnston's simple question—"how much does a corner cost?"—the team paused the meeting to calculate the costs for forming the corners in the foundation, the framing, the sheathing, and the drywall. The answer? Each of these elaborate corners had a cost of $3,500.

The Learning Wheel

By Alex Zimmerman

Describing what happens—or what should happen—at all-hands team workshops, when teams come together to share what they have accomplished since the last meeting and work to move forward with the project, is a challenge. When the process is done well, the experience seems something close to magic; when it is not done well, it seems very hard and unrewarding.

There is an experiential learning model called the Wheel of Learning (or learning wheel), described in *The Fifth Discipline Fieldbook: Strategies and Tools for Building a Learning Organization*, Peter M. Senge, Art Kleiner, Charlotte Roberts, Rick Ross, and Bryan Smith (New York: Doubleday/Currency, 1994), that helps explain the process. (See Figure 2-13.)

(continued)

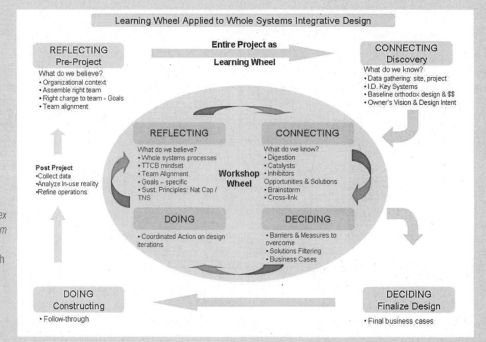

Figure 2-13 Diagram of the Learning Wheel (applied). *Courtesy of Alex Zimmerman, adapted from ideas presented in Peter M. Senge, et al.,* The Fifth Discipline Fieldbook: Strategies and Tools for Building a Learning Organization *(New York: Doubleday, 1994).*

The learning wheel relies on the observation that people learn in a cyclical fashion, moving between action and reflection, between abstract and concrete thinking. Project teams learn and make progress this way as well. This model can be used as a tool in integrative design by helping to consciously focus the team on each of the stages of the wheel before moving on to the next. The value is in taking the time to be more thoughtful and to understand what is going on before rushing to implementation. Moving slowly might actually be a way to learn faster.

The wheel consists of four stages: *reflecting*, *connecting*, *deciding,* and *doing*.

Each workshop should begin with a period of *reflection* about our own thinking and acting. We examine what we believe, take time to think about whole-system processes, get into a "tunneling through the cost barrier" mind-set, reflect on goals and team alignment around them, and reaffirm our commitment to sustainability principles.

The next stage is to make *connections* to create ideas and possibilities for action. We begin by looking at what we have done since the last meeting. We can then digest those actions and look for what Anita Burke calls catalysts and inhibitors to further actions in her work as a sustainability consultant. We brainstorm opportunities and solutions and look for synergies between them. This is a process of expansion and opening up.

The first two stages are crucial for developing shared insight and meaning.

From here we move on to *making decisions*, to winnowing the creative possibilities. We are filtering so that we are left with practical solutions that will overcome the barriers. Here we begin to capture the business case for our decisions.

The final stage is to settle on the coordinated *action that must be taken*. This is the next step's stage—who will do what by when.

Being explicit with the team about the learning wheel demystifies it and helps people to understand where they are in the cycle and why a given activity is taking place when it does. As you work with the wheel, you will also notice that different individuals will naturally be drawn to the different stages of the cycle.

This diversity is a good thing. Everyone has a different personality and different skills to contribute to a team in addition to his or her professional qualifications. We all recognize those who are impatient with process and the required discussion, who just want the action to begin. We also recognize those who keep introducing new ideas. This model acknowledges both of these styles and legitimizes places and times for people to contribute where they can do their best work.

The whole cycle is repeated at each of the all-hands sessions. The wheel also describes larger cycles within the project and, at a high enough level, describes the whole integrated-systems-process cycle.

The incremental cost savings gained by eliminating just two corners ended up neutralizing the cost of the performance enhancements for the envelope and mechanical system—the net first cost was now zero, which was quite a surprise for the project's hesitant owner. The team had engaged a colearning process that not only resulted in an incredibly efficient design but also unified the team in devising a final solution good enough to overcome even a flat-out refusal from the owner.

This colearning process is the foundation for systemic change and whole-systems solutions. Without the majority of design and building team members aligned around what needs to change and why, projects typically fall back into old patterns, resulting in designs that amount to little more than the same old thing with some improvements in efficiency. Taking time for reflection and reinvestigation in meetings will allow new ideas to emerge. Alex Zimmerman's sidebar on "The Learning Wheel" explains the simple elegance of this process.

The Composite Master Builder

This process of systems thinking can be applied to any situation. As we have seen, none of us can hold the whole alone, so we need to embrace a *Composite Master Builder* approach that consists of many people working to grow an understanding of the many subsystems within the whole system in order to create a collaborative intelligence.

Figure 2-14 illustrates conceptually how integrative design teams can function as a composite master builder. The approach depicted in the diagram differs radically from conceiving the project team as functioning within the traditional hierarchy of our normal, pyramidal organizational charts, where each team member is housed in a box reporting to another team member in another box above. Rather, the composite master builder consists of a much wider array of contributing stakeholders organized in three primary groups but

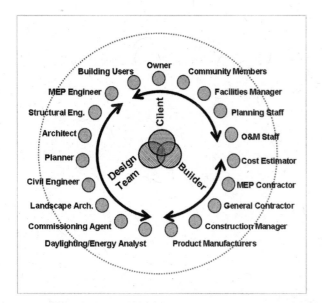

Figure 2-14 Composite Master Builder. *Image courtesy of Bill Reed and 7group; adapted from graphic by Bill Reed.*

contributing and operating in a more egalitarian circular pattern. These three primary groups are the client, the design team, and the builder, with each group comprised of multiple individual stakeholders. The Venn diagram in the center illustrates how these three groups overlap and intersect throughout a process of collaboration. As a result, the *many* minds can begin to become synthesized into a collective *one* mind.

An integrative process mandates much more collaboration and coordination. It encourages rigorous questioning. It challenges typical assumptions and rules of thumb from the very beginning of the project. Interrelating building and site systems must be addressed early and questioned before schematic design starts or, at the least, while it proceeds. Integrating the many systems involved in a building project requires that the expertise of each team member responsible for each system be brought together for the purpose of augmenting the efficiency and effectiveness of each system and team member in relation to one another: a team functioning as an organism to design a functioning organism.

Shifting from the *components* mind-set to the *organism* mind-set—and from a linear process to an integrative one—allows possibilities to increase exponentially. Suddenly the creativity that each team member has been applying to optimizing a single component is unleashed and focused on optimizing a system of relationships. True transformation can occur.

The process of transforming our buildings, our sites, our industries, and our conventions will move us from the Age of Specialization and toward the dawning Age of Integration, allowing us to meet the challenges we face. This new age asks us to devote ourselves to understanding the interrelationships extant in the complex systems we inhabit. Developing this understanding is essential if we hope to achieve sustainability on any level, local or global.

chapter

3
Reframing Sustainability

An object seen in isolation from the whole is not the real thing.

—Masanobu Fukuoka, Japanese farmer who developed a revolutionary method of sustainable agriculture, from *The One-Straw Revolution: An Introduction to Natural Farming,* Emmaus, Pennsylvania: Rodale Press, 1978

A good solution solves more than one problem, and it does not make new problems. I am talking about health as opposed to almost any cure, coherence of pattern as opposed to almost any solution produced piecemeal or in isolation.

—Wendell Berry, from "Solving for Pattern," in *The Gift of Good Land,* p. 141, North Point Press, 1981

WHAT IS SUSTAINABILITY?

Postindustrial society has created, through its products and practices, an amalgamated set of environmental challenges that we now must face together. Since a host of these problems can be traced to many of the products that we use, much of the current green movement focuses on replacing harmful or wasteful products with *green* alternative products, such as nontoxic paint or energy-efficient compact fluorescent light bulbs. New technologies are being developed and used not only to create these products, but also to measure the effects of their use and the need for developing them. This approach allows us to reduce environmental impacts in ways never before imagined; however, if we are to have any chance of creating a fundamental shift in the way that we inhabit the planet, improving our products is only part of the story.

In Chapter 2, we talked about the need to develop a "living" understanding of the interrelationships between our increasingly complex building systems and components. It is within this perspective of a building as an organism that the term *sustainability* most accurately conveys its intended meaning. Sustainability is not a deliverable. Sustainability is not a thing. Sustainability is not simply about efficient technologies and techniques. Sustainability literally is about *sustaining life*—a practice by which living things such as forests, neighborhoods, people, businesses, watersheds, mushrooms, microbes, and polar bears contribute to the interrelationships that ensure the viability of each over the long haul. Jonathon Porritt (former director of Friends of the Earth and Chairman of the UK Sustainable Development Commission) offers a straightforward (and widely quoted) way to understand this term and its intended usage within such a larger perspective: "If something is sustainable, it means we can go on doing it indefinitely. If it isn't, we can't."

There is no shortage of examples of human practices that lack this indefinite viability—they can be seen all over the world. A particularly illustrative example can be found in the massive, man-made island projects of Dubai. To maximize a certain aesthetic beauty (and the lineal footage of waterfront property), these islands have been designed in the shape of palm fronds from an aerial view and, in another case, in a map-of-the-world layout.

Unfortunately, the creation of such artificial and arbitrary landforms creates a significant liability for the islands' inhabitants and environs. First, construction of the islands themselves severely disrupted marine ecosystems, potentially threatening the only current local food source to these islands. With good intentions, it was mandated that only natural materials could be used for their foundation and structure (i.e., no concrete or steel). This led to dredging sand from the ocean floor, but there was not enough—they actually ran out of sand! As a result, distant dredging occurred

Figure 3-1 The Dubai Palms and World projects consist of artificially built islands in the Persian Gulf constructed for high-end commercial and residential development. In this image, we see (from the bottom left) Palm Jebel Ali, Palm Jumeirah, the World (configured to depict a world map when viewed from the sky), and Palm Deira, which is in the early stages. Although environmental concerns mandated that no concrete be used for these monumental engineering projects, dredging of the sand needed for the underlying structure of the islands depleted the local sea bed, so sand from the northern Persian Gulf had to be imported. *Image courtesy of NASA.*

throughout the Persian Gulf to supply the quantity of sand needed, further disrupting living systems patterns long into the future. Second, the sole source of potable water comes in the form of energy-intensive desalination plants that further threaten marine life by increasing salt concentrations offshore. With few viable local resources, the islands import almost everything (even the sand). And, while it is tempting to view these islands as the new standard-bearer for unsustainable development, the fact is that they are simply the extreme end product of the thinking and development practices being perfected all over the world.

There is a growing awareness that the common thread linking all of our environmental concerns is the enduring viability of the human species. The current trajectory of green or sustainable design, though, tends to define sustainability as an end point—if 30 percent energy savings is good and 50 percent is better, then 100 percent is sustainable. This quantitative logic is also often applied to materials selection, water conservation, and waste treatment. Yet, when we build, we are not only using materials and other resources; we also are replacing the natural environment with the built environment. More often than not, this entails the destruction of the natural system of vegetation that keeps the soil healthy, allows rainfall to soak into the water table and become potable, and provides habitat for other species—in short, the infrastructure that sustains life.

Anyone can witness this paving over of the natural system by driving through Every City, U.S.A., to see the asphalt, concrete, strip malls, and fast-food jungles that currently make up much of *our* habitat. James Howard Kunstler refers to this homogenized American landscape as "crudscape." Our current practice is one that systematically replaces a self-sustaining system with one that requires constant investment, maintenance, and replacement. Simply making this practice more resource-efficient does not address the root of the problem.

Bill Rees, developer of the ecological footprint concept, made this point during his 2007 lecture during the Seattle American Institute of Architects Committee on Architecture for Education conference: "Regrettably, most approaches to sustainability today—hybrid cars, green buildings, smart growth, the new urbanism, green consumerism, recycling— assume that sustainability resides in greater material and economic efficiency. When absolute reductions are required, growing more efficiently merely makes society more efficiently unsustainable."

Andrew Rudin expands this idea in his Web-based book *Efficology*, which is a term he coined to mean "the

Figure 3-2 Vast areas of urban sprawl have homogenized America by transforming the unique character of each place into the ubiquitous "crudscape" of junk-food jungles. *Image courtesy of Travis Church.*

study of efficiency" (www.efficology.com). An energy-management consultant who has been surveying building energy use since 1974, Rudin has collected writings from hundreds of authors for the stated purpose of helping readers to deepen their understanding of the role that efficiency plays in their lives. He expresses a belief that working to improve a system in terms of its efficiency alone can actually have many *negative* outcomes, suggesting that improved efficiency may increase personal stress and increase the rate at which we abuse natural systems. Further, he points out that improved energy efficiency does not necessarily decrease the rate at which we *use* energy. Reminding us of Bunuel's Law, Rudin states that "overdoing things is harmful in all cases, even when it comes to efficiency."

Bill McDonough, too, has offered a metaphor for working on environmental issues by only improving efficiency. He describes it as driving a car south at 70 miles per hour when your destination lies to the north. You cannot reach your destination by simply slowing down. Further, if there is a cliff ahead of you, can you avoid going off the edge by merely slowing down? As we increase our efficiency and engage in "doing less damage," we are slowing down the speed of the car—but we will still drive off the cliff; it merely takes us a bit longer.

Slowing down the environmental damage inherently created by a flawed design process will not get us where we need to go. Instead, we need a process for developing the understanding needed to change our course and turn around. The fact of the matter is that addressing energy savings, water conservation, or waste treatment simply is not enough. We might build nothing but LEED Platinum buildings with net-zero energy or water use for the next one hundred years and still succeed at destroying the system, or web of relationships, that sustains life on the planet. Building in this way cannot be done indefinitely; therefore, it is not sustainable. Trying to pack green strategies into an already overburdened process, in some ways, is like loading up the car with excess luggage as we continue to head toward the cliff.

This is not to say that efficiency is not important—it is, and vitally so. Yet it is insufficient. To be truly beneficial, improving efficiency must be done within the context of a fundamentally different process.

THE TRAJECTORY OF SUSTAINABILITY PRACTICE

Confucius advised that if we hoped to repair what was wrong in the world, we had best start with the "rectification of the names." The corruption of society begins with the failure to call things by their proper names, he maintained, and its renovation begins with the reattachment of words to real things and precise concepts. So what about this much-abused pair of names, sustainable and unsustainable?

—Michael Pollan, *New York Times Magazine*,
December 16, 2007, p. 25

When we encounter difficulty in grasping the concept of true sustainability, part of our problem lies in the homogenization or blurring of concepts. When we speak of *green* building or design, we most often are referring to some technique, product, or technology that by some definition is better for the planet than the alternative. The result is a generic, loosely used term that can describe anything from a mind-set to a light bulb. The underlying assumption is that if something is green it is universally good, when in fact the only consistent qualifier for the use of the term is that someone, somewhere, for some reason, has determined that it is less bad. Is this sustainable?

Figure 3-3 depicts sustainability as existing at the "line," or threshold point, between "below-the-line" approaches that will ultimately degrade natural systems (despite a focus on higher efficiency) and "above-the-line" approaches that can restore and regenerate them.

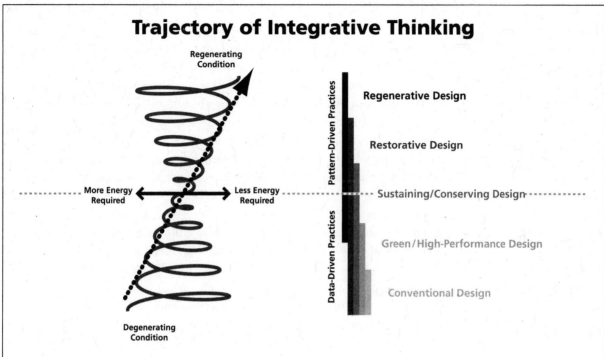

Trajectory of Integrative Thinking

Figure 3-3 Trajectory of Integrative Thinking:

DATA-DRIVEN PRACTICES (fragmented technical approaches)

Limiting the Damage

- *Green/High-Performance Design:* Design that realizes high efficiency and reduced impact in the building structure, operations, and site activities. This term can imply a more technical-efficiency approach to design and may limit an embrace of the larger natural system benefits.

Neutral

- *Sustainable/Conserving Design:* Reaching a point of being able to sustain the health of the planet's organisms and systems—including human systems—over time.

PATTERN-DRIVEN PRACTICES (increasingly more whole-living-systems approaches)

Restoration

- *Restorative Design:* This approach thinks about design in terms of using the activities of design and building to restore the capability of local natural systems to a healthy state of self-organization.

Regeneration

- *Regenerative Design:* This is a design process that engages the whole of the system of which we are part. Logically, our place—community, watershed, and bioregion—is the sphere in which we can participate. By engaging all the key stakeholders and processes of the place—humans, earth systems, and the consciousness that connects them—the design process builds the capability of the people to engage in continuous and healthy relationship. There is continuous learning and feedback so that all aspects of the system are an integral part of the process of life in that place—coevolution. Tapping into the consciousness and spirit of the people engaged in a place is likely the only way to sustain sustainability.

Image courtesy of Bill Reed, Regenesis, and 7group; graphics by Corey Johnston

To create a sustainable condition, you must work to achieve goals at both levels: limiting the damage that we create (below the line) *and* healing the natural system (above the line).

Conventional design primarily concerns itself with goals related to aesthetics, comfort, and cost. While none of these conventional qualities are mutually exclusive to sustainability, an exclusive focus at this level will produce designs that are not even remotely sustainable due to habits and rules of thumb that are already deeply ingrained.

At the level of *high-performance* design, we are increasingly working to make our human systems more effective and efficient without sacrificing concerns relating to aesthetics, comfort, and cost. As stated above, this is critically important, particularly given that decades of designing without this objective in mind have left us with the behemoths of resource consumption and waste generation that make up much of our built environment. However, if we stop at this level, our built environment will only succeed at being less bad.

At the level of *restoration,* because we are speaking of living systems, it is important to make a distinction about the way that living systems work: because life evolves and is not static, we can never restore a living system to its original condition. When we speak of restoration (of a woodland, a riparian system, a wetland) we are speaking of restoring a system's *capability* to continuously self-organize and evolve. For example, on a project in Arizona, the Game and Fish Department told us they were very concerned that the proposed development would destroy the desert ecosystem. A member of a family who had been in that place for five generations had a different perspective; he observed that the ecosystem had already been destroyed. What is now a desert had one hundred years ago been a three-foot-high dry grassland prairie with running springs. After all, he said, why did my great-grandfather bring cattle to graze here in the first place? In this case, restoration required looking at the system from a long-term evolutionary perspective, so that work could focus on bringing back the *restorative capability* of the place, as opposed to creating some immediately observable "restored" condition.

Regeneration is about designing for the whole: engaging the earth systems, the biotic systems, and the people (or human systems) of each unique place in a continuous dialogue to support their coevolutionary development. To *regenerate* means *to give new life and energy to.* Sustained life and energy can only happen in a whole system. This is not an intellectual nicety—developing relationships between the living things that make up a whole system is required to achieve a truly sustainable healthy condition.

The word *development* in its true sense supports this perspective: *to develop* does not mean *to occupy.* In its many contexts from a number of dictionary sources, the word can be used to mean "to bring out the capabilities or potential of; to bring to a more advanced state; to generate or evolve; to reveal *or* deveil." *Developing* can be seen to share its etymological roots with "de-veiling." To achieve true sustainability, we need to focus on developing (de-veiling) our awareness, our capabilities, and the potential for life to coevolve in each of the places we build.

This is not a new thought or a new practice—just a forgotten one, left behind in the wake of reductionist, industrial, Age of Specialization, and monocultural thinking. The result has produced not only destroyed landscapes and systems of life but also a forgetting of how life works in each unique place.

A good illustration of an approach that integrates green technology with above-the-line thinking comes from the Willow School project in northern New Jersey.

Figure 3-4 The founders of the Willow School recognized the unique aspects of their site in New Jersey and became intent on creating a campus that integrated the school and its students with the local community and habitat. *Image courtesy of Bill Reed.*

The Technical Story of the Willow School

A new two-hundred-student, kindergarten through eighth grade private school, the Willow School includes among its three fundamental teaching objectives the teaching of environmental stewardship; consequently, the school sought to make its site a living classroom.

A core organizing principle of the project was that the design for the treatment and utilization of water function like a natural system. The resulting solution includes a constructed wetland for wastewater treatment; use of permeable paving, living roofs, bio swales, and sixty-thousand plugs of adapted-species meadow plantings to reduce stormwater runoff; use of an extended detention, stepped-pool wetland for stormwater treatment; and collection of rainwater for irrigation and toilet-water supply. The use of nature-based systems design helps demonstrate connections to the planet by recognizing the interrelationships with both the upstream water and energy sources that supply our buildings and the downstream off-site flows emitted from our buildings.

A More Compelling and Vital Story of Place™

With the help of our "Story of Place" colleagues at Regenesis Group, the Willow School approached integrative design with a mental model that embraced both below-the-line and above-the-line aspects of ecological practice—both technologies and techniques to support efficient buildings *and* a living-system approach to address community and habitat health by understanding the way life *has* evolved and *can* evolve in that place. As

Figure 3-5 The indigenous landscaping at the Willow School utilizes native planting for gardens and woodlands to restore healthy habitat, an ongoing process that is studied as part of the student's curriculum. *Image courtesy of Bill Reed.*

such, the project recognized its role as a healing link between these two conditions, as a member of a whole system with a purpose.

After a whole-systems site assessment revealed the different successions of forest ecosystems present, design concepts for the Willow School were created with the purpose of restoring the greatest and most diverse expression of the forest that had existed. The land was replanted with native plants that will help recreate the spongelike character of the soil. Temporary deer fencing was installed, as well, to allow the diverse ecosystem to reestablish. The forest, currently at an early order of expression (i.e., low level of ecological succession), will evolve to higher levels of effectiveness and ever-evolving capability to support life while it stores, filters, and gradually releases stormwater. The school campus design provides the context for an authentic educational opportunity for

self-directed, total-immersion learning for students and the community via constant monitoring of feedback from the system. It is through this learning that the possibilities for environmental stewardship can be experienced directly and profoundly.

Re-Membering Our Role in Nature

To successfully work above the line, we must move beyond doing less damage and work to create new potential for life to evolve. This requires that we develop an understanding of how nature works in each unique place and, further, that we identify a positive role for ourselves as part of nature's family in that place. One serious impediment to this is that we have internalized a model that *separates* humans from nature.

For decades, the primary guiding model for environmental advocacy has been protection or conservation oriented. The accurate perception that the human impact on natural systems was almost exclusively negative over the last two hundred years became translated into the firm belief that the best thing that we can do to help the environment is to sequester ourselves from it. Still today a large part of our environmental strategy is to *preserve* areas of *pristine wilderness* to keep them *safe* from human *impact*. This language, commonly used among those who demonstrate the highest commitment to environmental concerns, reveals a near-universal set of assumptions—primarily, that humans are *separate* from nature.

The notion that the only way to save the planet is to keep our hands off it is fundamentally unsustainable. Our current awakening to issues surrounding global climate change has brought with it the idea that we are not truly successful if we succeed at nature's expense. Parallel to this idea is the belief that if our only environmental strategy is to sacrifice our needs for the good of nature, the deficit that we are left with will eventually manifest some selfish action in the name of human survival and viability. We have not succeeded until we see ourselves *as* nature and have designed our engagement *with* nature as a symbiosis by finding the distinct positive role that we as humans bring to the association.

Prior to this modern time, we as indigenous people—people in direct association with the land that supported us—had a very different worldview. According to Gerould S. Wilhelm, there were at one time more than 260 different Native American languages spoken in North America, and not a single one of them contained a word for *nature*. This is simply because these cultures did not conceive themselves as disconnected from natural systems; nature as a separate and distinct concept did not exist. This indigenous mindset conceives humans as an integral part of natural systems, another member of nature's many symbiotic guilds—a participant in maintaining and evolving the health of the whole.

In her book *Tending the Wild: Native American Knowledge and the Management of California's Natural Resources* (Berkeley: University of California Press, 2005), M. Kat Anderson writes: "contemporary Indians often use the word *wilderness* as a negative label for land that has not been taken care of by humans for a long time, for example, where dense understory shrubbery or thickets of young trees block visibility and movement." A common sentiment among California Indians is that a hands-off approach to nature has promoted feral landscapes that are inhospitable to life. They believe that when humans are gone from an area for too long, they lose the practical knowledge of how to interact with it, and the plants and animals retreat spiritually from the earth or hide from humans. "The white man sure ruined this country," said James Rust, a Southern Miwok elder. "It's turned back to wilderness."

This unfamiliar use of the word *wilderness* beckons us to consider that perhaps the role of humans within the natural system is not unlike that of a bee pollinating a flower, an oxpecker enjoying a meal of ticks from the back of the Cape buffalo, or an animal digesting the tough outer skin of a plant's fruit so that its interior seeds may take root in the soil. We are now rediscovering the whole system of life in each unique place, rather than focusing on the fragmented parts in which we have been taught to specialize. We are being called to become indigenous once again—to become living and contributing *members* of a particular place. We are re-*membering*.

To our modern minds, this may at first seem daunting. The idea of discovering how nature works seems, to most, mysterious and complex. In reality, though, it is a natural product of human experience—developing understanding. The missing link is not so much an intellectual or moral failure on the part of humans as much as a lack of direct *experience* with the natural systems that surround us. The often-quoted statistic that the average American spends 80 to 90 percent of their time indoors

Figure 3-6 The Eastern Forest, as we all know it today, is the result of being left largely unmanaged for nearly 300 years. *Image courtesy of Bill Reed.*

Figure 3-7 This remnant section of Eastern Forest is similar to the Eastern Forest as found by the first European settlers stretching from North Carolina to Newfoundland, Canada—a forest that was understood and tended by native peoples for millennia. *Image © 2007 Jupiter Images.*

is only part of the issue here, as much of the outdoor space we have access to in our cities and communities provides only very limited means of experiencing how natural systems work. This lack of experience is actually reinforced by the traditional conservation model and mind-set that treat nature with a nonparticipatory "hands-off" approach, as if human engagement can only degrade nature's health.

A family that is a client of ours provides an illustration. The family owns many thousands of acres and runs a very high-end breeding and milking program with special types of dairy cows that they are transitioning into an organic farming operation. When discussing the role of learning how nature works at a family business meeting, we explained how native peoples in the region used fire as an integrated forest-management tool for thousands of years. One of the daughters scoffed and asked how the natives could have figured this out. The older son was quick to point out that he himself had figured this out when he was eight years old. He explained that one of the hay fields had burned in the autumn season, and for two or three years afterwards that hayfield had, by far, the richest crop yield. This understanding comes about simply by paying attention and observing.

Reciprocal Relationships Within the Larger System

Pursuing sustainability requires an understanding of and willingness to engage in *reciprocal relationships*—the process by which living things support and are supported by a larger whole. Reciprocal relationships are fundamental characteristics of the healthy living systems of organisms that form our planet's ecology. In such systems, there is no resource that is not created from waste and no waste that is not turned into a resource. Each organism's waste, through natural processes such as decomposition and fertilization, creates food for other organisms in its ecosystem, as discussed

in the previous examples. Yet our buildings, even our high-efficiency buildings, consume resources in the form of raw materials and emit waste in the form of pollution, raw sewage, and garbage. They negatively impact both upstream input flows and downstream output flows. This fundamental difference separates a sustainable system from an unsustainable one—or, to put it more bluntly, it is the difference between a system that supports itself and evolves over time and one that will eventually destroy itself.

This means that a building cannot simply be high performance and considered sustainable. Elizabet Sahtouris addresses this by expanding the buildings-as-organisms metaphor discussed in Chapter 2. To paraphrase: Imagining a high-performance building is like imagining a high-performance liver; certainly the limitations of that liver are pretty obvious outside the context of the whole body. Buildings, neighborhoods, and cities are the same. Buildings can be designed as autonomous, but they only become meaningful and beneficial when understood as part of the living fabric of their place.

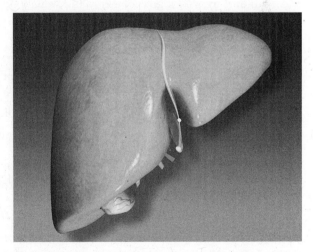

Figure 3-8 Imagining a liver outside of the context of the body's network of interrelated systems is much like conceiving a high-performance building outside the larger systems of its context. *Image courtesy of www.med-ars.it.*

Again, this insight is hardly new; but it is being rediscovered in multiple related fields after over a century of being kept alive only in the traditions and wisdom of indigenous cultures. Our purpose here is not simply to make a point but to apply this insight to the process of designing buildings that *catalyze the health* of their neighborhoods and watershed—a process that extends our understanding of a building project's context and influence beyond its site. Such understanding illuminates tangible opportunities for allowing the wisdom of natural systems to inform the design of our built environment.

THE ROLE OF THE MENTAL MODEL: FROM PRODUCTS TO A NEW MIND-SET

We in the building business are generally material oriented in our approach to design. This is understandable, because we utilize a palette of *products* to produce our buildings. However, products, as we have seen, are of limited value if viewed only as things that are added to a building to make it green. Further, the availability and performance characteristics of products are typically in a state of flux—especially in the current state of green market evolution. When we concentrate on these alone as the knowledge base for designing green buildings, we find ourselves spending more money on our projects as we engage in a continuous game of catching up to the latest level of *efficiency.*

Using green products optimally requires us to utilize *tools,* now widely available, to evaluate potential designs at the conceptual phase in terms of their performance, costs, effect on habitat and water-system health, and building massing, orientation, and zoning. Energy modeling programs, Life Cycle Assessment (LCA), and LEED are examples of such tools. But while these and other tools allow us to look at individual products within a larger context, they often are underutilized in this capacity.

On one project, we were brought on board in the middle of design development for a large office building to help the project team achieve their green objectives and LEED goals. At our first design review meeting, we asked to see the preliminary energy modeling results that would help us evaluate the current design. The HVAC engineer replied, "We don't do energy modeling until the end of design development."

We asked why, and discovered the logic behind this choice: The team viewed early energy modeling as wasteful; they believed that if they did it before the team was finished designing, they would have to model the building more than once. In their current design solution, the architecture had been designed without the HVAC engineer's input pertaining to its expected energy performance. Energy modeling—an invaluable tool for measuring the combined impact of related systems to realize new design potential—was being used merely as after-the-fact validation of building performance in order to earn LEED points.

How can we use such tools in a more meaningful and timely way? These assessment tools are discussed more fully in later chapters, but for now, let's just say that using these tools at the appropriate times in appropriate ways requires an intentional shift in our design *process.* In the above example, the energy modeling tool was simply added into the existing process as another fragment of designing systems in isolation. To utilize tools in a way that creates new possibilities, we must integrate their use into the design process from the beginning in order to inform design decisions. There is no one-size-fits-all solution, so we must approach the design process itself as a design problem. We call this *designing the design process.* This is in fact the primary focus of this book, and how to do this is explored in Chapters 5 through 8.

For now, though, we need to recognize that most of us feel we are *systems* designers by the nature of our work in delivering complex buildings—but we usually are not designing *systemically.* Instead of looking at the physical elements of the building alone, we need to understand the invisible connections between these elements (relationships and impacts that are both direct and indirect). These invisible connections and patterns may be manifest, for example, in the downstream impact of toxicants in building materials, the multiple efficiency and cost relationships between the many variables in an HVAC system and the building envelope, or impacts on social systems resulting from logging practices and other raw material extraction. This degree of analysis requires a rigorous level of enthusiastic and timely engagement from the participants and an understanding of the tools used to make these evaluations. As discussed in Chapter 1, no one person has all of this knowledge themselves; hence, the role of the team takes on great importance.

As a result, a different *mind-set*—or *mental model*—is required. This model asks us to be *open and willing* to change the way we have always done things. This change is related to a shift in mind-set from the Age of Specialization into the dawning Age of Integration—a mental model of exploring interrelationships that *contribute* to the health and wealth of each unique *place*. Such a mind-set understands *place* as the human, bi-

otic, and earth systems of a particular location and the consciousness that connects them—the *whole*.

By far, our most successful green projects have contributed to the health of their *place* because the team willingly focused on deepening their understanding of environmental issues and the invisible and critical connections within this *whole*, rather than on the addition of technology and products to the building. The team was willing to ask many questions about the potential beneficial relationships between *all* the systems in the building, site, watershed, and community. In short, assumptions were questioned. Environmental concerns were not secondary, nor were they dominant, just an integral part of the design.

Consequently, we need to shift our collective mental model from *stuff* (i.e., products and technologies) to purposeful systems thinking; it is essential to focus on the following four aspects from the top down (see Figure 3-9) if we are to address the whole:

Mental model

Process

Tools

Products and technologies

Figure 3-9 Successful integrative design requires us to shift our collective mental model from focusing on products and technologies to a mind-set of purposeful systems thinking. All four of the components in this mental-model hierarchy are necessary, but it is essential to focus on them from the top down, not bottom up. *Image courtesy of Bill Reed, Barbara Batshalom, and 7group; graphics by Nadav Malin and John Boecker.*

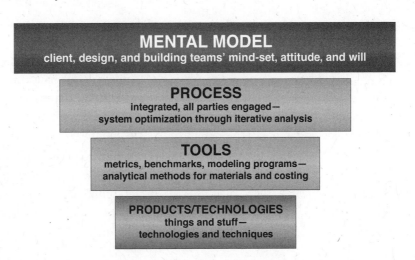

MENTAL MODEL
client, design, and building teams' mind-set, attitude, and will

PROCESS
integrated, all parties engaged—
system optimization through iterative analysis

TOOLS
metrics, benchmarks, modeling programs—
analytical methods for materials and costing

PRODUCTS/TECHNOLOGIES
things and stuff—
technologies and techniques

NESTED SUBSYSTEMS

If a problem cannot be solved, enlarge it.

—Dwight D. Eisenhower

Because our buildings are connected to larger systems through an exchange of resources and waste, the opportunity for true sustainability occurs only when we can shift our focus from individual buildings to the larger nested systems *beyond* the building—to the site, watershed, community, and larger region. In fact, we have found that as we expand our thinking to larger and larger scales of system, the possibilities for improved design expand as well. Conversely, if we were to generate design solutions within too small a system (e.g., within the building itself as opposed to within the larger context of the entire site), we would find ourselves making compromises due to limited options.

A relatively familiar example is the ground-source heat pump (GSHP). This technology integrates the building system with the larger site—specifically, the ground outside the building—to harness the heat-exchanging capacity of the Earth to the building's advantage. An oft-cited study by the U.S. Environmental Protection Agency (EPA) in 1993 claimed that "Geo-Exchange (or GSHP) systems are the most energy-efficient, environmentally clean, and cost-effective space conditioning systems available."* Yet, if we limited the scope of our thinking to the building itself and not its external environment, using a ground-source heat pump would not occur to us. The same type of leverage can be achieved by working to integrate the project with the larger nested subsystems beyond the site. (It also should be noted that looking at impacts beyond the site might lead teams not to use GSHPs in some cases, but more about this later.)

*U.S. Environmental Protection Agency (EPA), Office of Air and Radiation, "Space Conditioning: The Next Frontier," EPA 430-R-93-004 (Washington, DC: U.S. EPA, 1993).

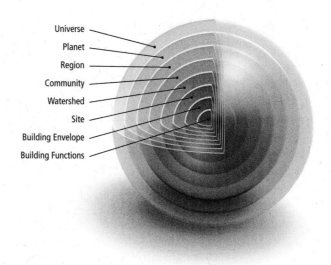

Universe
Planet
Region
Community
Watershed
Site
Building Envelope
Building Functions

Figure 3-10 Nested Systems. *Image courtesy of Bill Reed and 7group; graphics by Corey Johnston.*

The diagram in Figure 3-10 depicts a model that can help illuminate the relationship between a building and these larger systems:

- The **first system** level: optimize internal building systems, or *building functions*. For example, first reduce loads; then choose the most efficient equipment to satisfy the demand of the initial design's occupancy and load parameters.

- The **second system** level: optimize the *building envelope*. For example, with proper building orientation, daylighting, insulation, infiltration reduction, window performance, and so on, the architect can participate in reducing the size of an already efficient GSHP by another 30 percent or more (for discussion purposes).

- The **third system** level: the *site*. Use site elements to provide shade, evapotranspiration opportunities, funneling of prevailing breezes, and so on, if possible. Additional efficiency of 5 percent may be gained.

- The **fourth system** level: the *watershed*. Understanding natural water flows may not have a direct impact on energy but may have significant impacts on water issues that indirectly affect energy consumption (the significant connections between water and energy will be explored in later chapters).

- The **fifth system** level: *community*. For example, explore community-level transportation issues related to building location; these often have significant implications associated with fossil fuel consumption, and hence greenhouse gas generation and global warming. In many cases, the transportation energy used to travel to and from a commercial building exceeds the direct-energy consumption of a building by as much as eight times over the life of the building.

- The **sixth** and **seventh system** levels: *region* and *planet*. Such considerations dramatically inform choices related to a wide range of issues (which would require several more books to discuss fully).

Another restoration-oriented example of how working with the larger system can allow more highly leveraged solutions can be found on a site in a park near Baltimore, Maryland, that had a stream flowing through it. North of the stream, a large acreage of impervious surfaces in the form of buildings, parking lots, and areas of turf grass had resulted in periodic surges of runoff water during rainstorms. These flash events created flows of water that over time had ripped the streambed apart, carrying large quantities of soil and nutrients into the Chesapeake Bay. The total suspended solids (TSS) being deposited into the bay were considered to be a serious pollutant, as they were causing increased water temperatures by absorbing light and reducing plant life (and therefore oxygen content) in the water. Additionally, these solids were filling the

voids in the gravel streambeds, preventing fish from laying eggs, and smothering insect larvae.

The civil engineering firm that was hired to "fix" the TSS issue may have realized that the most leveraged solution was to address the problem upstream by reducing impervious surfaces and working to restore the spongelike quality of the land through the use of vegetation that could mitigate runoff from these rain events. But that is not generally the way things are done, and it was not the approach taken here either, primarily because the property boundary of the park defined the engineer's scope of work; even if the engineering team had been interested in pursuing this solution, they would have found it quite difficult to address issues that existed on someone else's property (as is often the case).

Without being able to address the runoff problem upstream, the engineer's solutions were limited. To solve the TSS problem, it was necessary to remove the soil from the stream. The engineer then rebuilt the stream out of concrete, as depicted in Figure 3-11. This may sound like a reasonable solution because, given the constraints, it seemed like the only option. However, when we try to stabilize nature instead of work with its patterns, we will always, *always* create more problems.

First of all, the addition of concrete required the removal of more habitat, including the gravel where fish laid eggs and insect larvae developed. Additionally, the water in the concrete stream was so shallow that it constantly overheated, creating an inhospitable breeding environment and worsening increased water temperatures downstream. The addition of concrete also required that trees be removed from the stream's edge, reducing shade and further increasing water temperatures. The groundwater could no longer be recharged by the stream, and the stream was no longer perennial due to the resultant lack of groundwater. The leaf debris that had previously served as food for the insects,

Figure 3-11 The original "concrete stream," stormwater conveyance system solution for a site in Baltimore, Maryland. *Image courtesy of Biohabitats, Inc.*

Figure 3-12 A few years later, the newly restored stream partners with nature to solve stormwater issues by understanding the larger system in ways that produce reciprocal benefits and contribute to the health of the place. *Image courtesy of Biohabitats, Inc.*

microbes, and fish now needed to be mechanically removed to keep the streamway unobstructed, and the surrounding vegetation had to be mowed (with machines driven by two-stroke internal combustion engines) and maintained to provide access for removal of the debris. Mosquitoes proliferated due to a less diverse and balanced ecosystem, and property values were reduced due to degrading habitat. Finally, in the long run, the concrete would eventually be broken apart by the natural dynamics of the traveling water, meaning that this concrete "stream" would forever be a costly maintenance and replacement burden.

Eventually, in the face of this new set of problems, a new solution was found by our colleagues at Biohabitats: Figure 3-12 depicts the same place (as Figure 3-11), only a few years later. The solution was to work as a partner with nature to address the underlying causes, rather than the symptoms, of the degradation. We are now entering a time when we recognize that nature and the health of the systems that support clean air and water cannot be addressed within the boundaries of artificial property lines. Consequently, the State of Maryland developed reasonable and sophisticated rainwater (and stormwater) management laws that require properties with impervious surfaces to retain rainwater on site for a longer period of time and to release it more slowly. This larger systems perspective allowed the park to readdress the stream and restore it to a self-organizing, complex system. Not only is the TSS issue addressed, but also the fish are back; the ecosystem is more diverse and healthy; the water table is recharging; groundwater is clean after being filtered through microbes in the plants' roots; maintenance costs are lower; and, as one can imagine, property values are higher, too—which image (Figure 3-11 or Figure 3-12) would *you* rather see? All of these benefits are in essence *free services* provided by natural systems, once engaged by a mental model that recognizes the interrelationships within the larger system.

These larger systemic relationships must be considered on each individual project. Sometimes the best solution will be counterintuitive due to the project's unique context. For example, one client—a private school in the northeast United States—expressed the desire, during the design development phase, to pursue LEED certification. The contractor was on board and had already ordered a ground-source heat pump system for the school. On the surface, it seemed like an obviously good choice, since, as we have seen, GSHPs are an extremely efficient way to heat and cool a building.

Or, rather, we should say that GSHPs are an efficient way to heat and cool a building *with* the proper subsurface geology, heat-transfer, and building-use patterns. The real efficiency for a ground-source heat pump application in the Northeast occurs in the summer months due to the limited temperature differential between indoor and average outdoor temperatures—the smaller the temperature differential, the less energy is required to achieve the desired temperature.*

One of the aspects typically addressed in energy modeling is the pattern of building occupancy. When we asked about building occupancy patterns for this project, the client told us that the school would not be open or in use during the summer months. This meant that the ground-source heat pumps would not be operating during the time of the year when they would be most effective. When we asked the client why

---

*GSHP systems are most efficient during cooling mode in the Northeast, since the temperature differential (delta-T) of around 15°F between the constant below-grade earth temperatures (approximately 55°F) and indoor thermal comfort ranges (perhaps 68°F to 72°F, or 70°F) is far closer to the 10-degree delta-T between the targeted 70°F indoor temperature and ambient summer temperatures (perhaps 80°F) than the 50-degree delta-T between the targeted 70°F indoor temperature and ambient winter temperatures (perhaps 20°F). In fact, in some climates—and particularly with a private school that does not operate in the summer—this type of cooling may be unnecessary. If this is the case, a GSHP may offer a limited benefit, based on initial cost considerations and a true reduction of global climate change impacts. For heating, natural gas can be burned on site in a boiler with greater than 90 percent efficiency. Since the production of electricity ranges from 25 to 33 percent efficient, and the GSHPs have a Coefficient of Performance (COP) of 3.3 when the whole system is evaluated, on-site energy efficiency is only slightly greater for the GSHPs (about 110 percent). If the majority of the electricity is produced from fossil fuels (primarily coal in the Northeast), CO_2 emissions will be four times greater for the GSHP system as compared to the gas boiler, despite the slightly better efficiency of the GSHPs. From an overall greenhouse gas contribution perspective in this case, the GSHPs not only cost more than a conventional system, but they contribute a greater (at best, equal) burden on the regional and planetary ecosystem. Hence, GSHP systems are not always the best investment from the standpoint of first cost, operating cost, and environmental cost.

he was using a GSHP system at all, his response was, "because it's efficient!"

With the school not operating during the months when this system would be most effective, there was no great benefit in spending the extra money for the well system necessary to transfer the heat load. It turned out that installing a very efficient gas boiler to take care of the heating needs would be more efficient from an energy perspective and would lower (or at least equal) the contribution of greenhouse gas emissions generated by the region's coal-fired power plants (see footnote, p. 57). The lesson here is that it is important to consider the whole *before* designing individual systems. The purchase of a GSHP before analyzing connections with larger systems provides just one simple example of why this kind of analysis (and mind-set) is important.

The key, once again, is that we work to optimize the *whole system*, within a larger context. All relationships should be identified for optimal results—do not value-engineer individual components, since there are a number of nested relationships within the larger whole system that impact the selection of systems in a development project. Using the above example of the school again, a design team may assume that a ground-source heat pump is one of the best choices (in terms of efficiency) for the provision of occupant comfort in the school. While this may appear to be true when comparing equipment efficiencies at the building system level, a number of larger-scale issues need to be integrated to properly optimize the system choice and size. A decision tree that addresses nested subsystems, as described above, is used to lead the design team through larger system scales. These potentially can yield more intelligent decisions in relation to environmental concerns—decisions can be made that have much more positive environmental influence than if left within the traditional boundaries of discipline-focused building design.

SOLVING FOR PATTERN

It is the nature of any organic pattern to be contained within a larger one. And so a good solution in one pattern preserves the integrity of the pattern that contains it.

—From "Solving for Pattern," in *The Gift of Good Land*, p. 144, Wendell Berry, North Point Press, 1981

Developing *mutually beneficial* relationships between humans and nature (i.e., the whole) allows us to benefit from the *free services* provided by natural systems. This means using fewer materials and technologies in constructing our buildings, which in turn means that there is less to go wrong, less work involved, less cost, and better performance—all of which are products of the same design mentality. All reflect what farmer-poet Wendell Berry calls *solving for pattern*—finding solutions that are "good in all respects," solutions that improve not just the part that seems to be the problem but all parts of the system that contains it—all components of all subsystems. As Village Homes developer Michael Corbett put it, "You know you are on the right track when your solution for one problem accidentally solves several others. You decide to minimize automobile use to conserve fossil fuels, for example, and realize that this will reduce noise, conserve land by minimizing streets and parking, multiply opportunities for social contact, beautify the neighborhood, and make it safer for children." Corbett was solving for pattern. As Christopher Alexander teaches in his famous design text, *A Pattern Language*: "When you build a thing, you cannot merely build that thing in isolation, but must also repair the world around it, and within it, so that the large world at that one place becomes more coherent, and more whole; and the thing which you make takes its place in the web of nature, as you make it."

Further, when we look for the natural patterns that have shaped a place over time, new possibilities for responsible development are revealed. This was the

◀ **Figure 3-13** The ghost of an alluvial fan (comprised of multiple stream channels formed over millennia) is barely visible beneath the grid of farm fields adjacent to the Teton River on this project site in Idaho. *Image courtesy of Tim Murphy and Bill Reed.*

▼ **Figure 3-14:** Soils map of the land depicted in Figure 3-13, demonstrating that streams were present on the site before farmers diverted them. *Image courtesy of Tim Murphy and Bill Reed.*

case on a recent project in Idaho. The aerial photo in Figure 3-13 depicts approximately 3,500 acres of current farmland along the eastern edge of the Big Hole Mountains (just west of the Grand Tetons) that was being considered for development. Looked at closely, this photo reveals that farming was superimposed on top of an alluvial fan between the stream in the mountain valley (top center of the photograph) and the river. When viewed from the air, the ghost of a delta-like pattern remains barely detectable, revealing the underlying pattern of alluvium deposition formed by the stream "firehosing" from the base of the mountains across the plain over the course of millennia. The remnant of one remaining stream (to the right in the photograph) can be seen running out of the valley in the center of the mountain range.

Originally, this mountain watercourse and alluvial fan supported beaver, otter, native cutthroat trout, salmon, turkeys, grouse, and mega-fauna such as deer, elk, and moose. These animals were all responsible for carrying nutrients back upstream into

the mountains to feed the forest and diversify the terrestrial and riparian ecosystem. The abandoned stream courses can be seen in the aerial photo as depressions—spreading out in a radial pattern from the point at which the mountain stream meets the plain—again, barely visible at first glance from the air and nearly impossible to discern from the ground without soils mapping. (The soils mapping of the same place, as seen in Figure 3-14, reveals the pattern more clearly.) Before farming took place here, these radiating streams served as corridors for wildlife moving back and forth between the mountains and the river. When farmers settled the land, they diverted this perennial stream along the highest possible course (in elevation) to irrigate fields and gridded over a highly productive and robust prairie ecosystem. This action severely simplified and destabilized the ecosystem that once was there. The farming pattern did not *preserve the integrity of the pattern* that formed this land and gave it the health that allowed farming in the first place; rather, this larger healthy pattern was obliterated, leaving only a ghost.

If we simply were to use a broadly defined "green strategy," applied abstractly from a green building rating system program to this place, we likely would strive to save these farms. Using LEED, for example, we could get a point for doing so. Often this is a good idea. However, in this case, the row-crop agriculture currently being practiced has significantly downgraded this ecosystem by cutting off the stream flow and the connectivity of a diverse animal nutrient exchange process, not to mention the increase in nitrogen concentrations and other pollutants now being deposited into the river from runoff across these fertilized fields. The ecological function of this alluvial fan, and one of the core patterns of the ecosystem in this place, is that of a "living bridge" between the mountains to the west and the Teton River. By significantly reducing irrigation and row-crop farming, the patterns of the original ecosystem could be restored, thus allowing this living bridge to work as nature intended, thereby bringing health back to both the adjacent river on the east and the foothills to the west.

The options for accomplishing this include: investing a lot of grant money to support the farmers (now economically unviable) in changing their farming practices; finding a nonprofit to buy the land as conservation easements (unlikely); or encouraging respectful human development to initiate the healing process. In this case, the process of developing human habitation actually could become a means of healing this place, because the development of homes in clusters could be used to pay for the restoration of the stream and habitat corridors that originally connected the Teton River and the mountains. Further, creating carefully delineated covenants that require open and unfenced spaces in specific locations, large habitat corridors, and native species planting (perhaps also with some local and/or organic farming to support the inhabitants of the housing), would allow for the maintaining of these newly reformed habitat and stream corridors—and the water would now become available again, because large-scale farming is no longer using it for irrigation. The stream flow and the connectivity "bridge" of nutrient exchange could become regenerated, catalyzed by humans *solving for pattern* to generate health and life in a process of coevolution. This project reveals that it is possible for humans to participate in regenerating the health of an ecosystem through development. Development, in this context, can be seen as *creating new potential*—and creating new potential, in turn, can be seen as the real purpose of development.

chapter

4

Aligning Values, Purpose, and Process

Conservation is a state of harmony between [humans] and land. By land is meant all the things on, over, or in the earth. Harmony with land is like harmony with a friend; you cannot cherish his right hand and chop off his left. That is to say, you cannot love game and hate predators; you cannot conserve the waters and waste the ranges; you cannot build the forest and mine the farm. The land is one organism. . . . A land ethic, then, reflects the existence of an ecological conscience, and this in turn reflects a conviction of individual responsibility for the health of the land. Health is the capacity of the land for self-renewal. Conservation is our effort to understand and preserve this capacity.

—Aldo Leopold, *A Sand County Almanac,* New York: Oxford University Press, 1949, p. 176 and p. 236

Caminante no hay camino; se hace camino al andar. (The road is not made; we make it as we walk along.)

—Antonio Machado

INTRODUCTION TO THE DISCOVERY PHASE

As discussed, we typically jump immediately into design once the building program has been established. We find, though, that if we are to create an integrative process from the beginning, there is something more to discover before we start drawing.

With this in mind, we recently asked the following questions at the beginning of an international corporate headquarters project. Here is a paraphrased account of the discussion that occurred with the executive vice president of the company:

Why do you need this building? (Bear with us, we know this seems obvious.)

We need more space.

Why do you need more space?

To house our growing workforce.

Why do you need to house the workforce?

To achieve a higher level of effective communication and esprit de corps.

Why will they interact better if you build the design concept that's already up there on the wall?

After thirty seconds of silence, the executive vice president exclaimed that we had just saved him thirty million dollars. Obviously curious, we asked him how. He explained that having just been asked to reflect on how his workforce would interact as a result of the design concept, he suddenly realized that a full quarter of the company's staff got no benefit at all from the building. These information technology (IT) and call center department members wore headphones all day long, and communicated with each other either over the phone or electronically. They only got together face-to-face for a staff meeting once a week, and they would likely much rather avoid the commute and work from home.

After coming to this realization, the owner chose to build a building that was 25 percent smaller, which equated to a 150,000-square-foot reduction. This is not a bad way to begin a discussion about environmental building—our questions had just opened the possibility for seriously reducing the environmental impacts of this building, not to mention saving the client a huge amount of money. Here, our approach to sustainability started with building less.

It is worth noting that diminishing resource consumption is not the same as increasing efficiency. In 1865, Stanley Jevons remarked upon this distinction: "It is a confusion of ideas to suppose that the economical use of fuel is equivalent to diminished consump-

tion. The very contrary is the truth."* The mental model that governs the practice of "building our way to sustainability" by achieving higher and higher levels of efficiency, as discussed in Chapter 3, still leads to an unsustainable condition.

The role of the question is fundamental to learning. Few of us internalize anything of value until we are ready to ask a question. That is why our predilection for focusing on products and technologies is perhaps the slowest way to achieve market transformation— when a technology is proposed as a solution to a green building issue, we are in effect saying we have the answer for you. But do we? Have we made assumptions about the need? Have we asked the right questions in the first place? If our goal is to create a sustainable condition, what are the questions that we need to ask? What is the process for finding the answers? We have found that before we create design solutions, we must engage in a process for finding the right questions. We call this the *discovery* phase.

THE FOUR *E*s

The *discovery* phase is the foundation of an integrative process. Before we make any real decisions about the actual physical building being designed, it is critical to create a foundation for working together in an integrative process.

The *discovery* phase of design can be summarized with the Four *E*s:

Everybody

Engaging

Everything

Early

---

*Presentation by William E. Rees, PhD, FRSC, entitled "Sustainable Cities: An Urban Myth? Or Getting Serious about Urban Sustainability," at the American Institute of Architects Committee on Architecture for Education Fall Conference in Seattle, Washington, September 16, 2007.

In other words, every team member should be engaged in discussions and setting performance goals for every system and issue to be considered as early as possible in the project.

Rather than imposing solutions onto the team and the project, it is important to work to *discover* solutions through a process of colearning in which we ask the right questions. To successfully discover what the design must look like, we must work together to see key relationships—relationships between building systems and the work of design team members, along with relationships between the project and the larger systems it inhabits. To illuminate these relationships, we must from the outset:

■ Question assumptions.

■ Create alignment.

■ Foster an iterative process.

QUESTIONING ASSUMPTIONS

To embark on successful discovery, we must first remove presupposed answers or solutions in order to have a clear view of all possibilities. Often we think we know the answers. But do we? We assume that technologies are the answer, or we fall back into what we have done before, what is familiar—like the mechanical penthouse on the roof of the Pennsylvania DEP Cambria project described in Chapter 2. We begin designing without first checking in on the beliefs and philosophies that are *always* beneath the decisions we make, whether they are spoken or remain unspoken. We simply do not allow ourselves the time to reveal our assumptions. Sometimes these assumptions are so deeply ingrained that we do not even recognize them as assumptions.

On a project in the late 1990s, we were brought in by the board of New York State's Syracuse Zoo to help them design and build a 20,000-square-foot edu-

cational facility within the zoo complex. The executive director and board stated that they wanted to construct a LEED Platinum building (this was before the official launch of LEED); moreover, they wanted it to be "the most advanced environmental building in the United States." They were clear and firm in their commitment to environmental responsibility.

The zoo was prepared to move the program into a new structure and out of their large existing building. We felt that we could not ignore the potential for renovating this existing underutilized structure in lieu of constructing an entirely new building under the principle that building less—or not at all—is generally the most environmentally responsible choice. We proposed this idea to the executive director, and she explained that the board wanted this new "gateway" building to establish a new image for the zoo, and all fund-raising efforts had been centered on this idea. The notion of using an existing building to create that new image was a nonstarter.

Our team was concerned that ignoring this possibility was in direct conflict with the stated goal of environmental responsibility. A week later, we approached the executive director again, requesting that we be permitted to at least perform a feasibility study and cost-benefit analysis for renovating the existing building. The answer was another and firmer "no." It remained impossible for our team to reconcile this approach with the stated environmental objectives; so we raised it one more time. The response we received was, "You're the architect, we're the client—drop it."

Soon afterward, a two-day goal-setting and design charrette was convened, which was attended by all twenty-one members of the board of directors, the MEP (mechanical, electrical, plumbing) engineers, civil engineer, contractor, and several additional architects to assist in facilitating breakout sessions. The program was presented on the morning of the first day. One of the attending architects, unaware of our repeated attempts

Figure 4-1 The Syracuse Zoo in Syracuse, New York, wanted a new building that would be as environmentally responsible as possible and found that pursuing an addition-and-renovation project instead resulted in a net reduction of 10,000 square feet of new construction. *Image courtesy of Bill Reed.*

to broach the topic, noted the existing underutilized structure and asked, "So why are we building a new building?" In the open-exploration spirit of charrettes, without asking permission, we made the spur-of-the-moment decision to ask that architect to take a third of the attendees into a separate breakout group and explore the possibilities in renovating the existing building, while the other two groups examined possibilities for the design of a new structure.

The breakout groups presented their findings that afternoon. By the end of the day, all twenty-one board members realized that they could achieve their goal of creating a beautiful building by renovating and adding a second floor to a portion of the existing structure, and agreed that a new building was the wrong decision. Prior to this, they simply could not imagine that such a solution was possible.

Unfortunately, the project's contractor, who had built the original building, informed the team that adding the second floor would require underpinning the foundation, an expensive proposition. The board of directors, realizing that they did not have the budget for this, reluctantly reverted to accepting that it was not possible to add a second story to the existing

building. The team ultimately discovered a compromise position, concluding that the most viable approach would be to renovate the existing building and construct an addition of only 10,000 square feet rather than building a new 20,000-square-foot facility.

In this example, the integrative process challenged deeply held assumptions, eventually leading to a better solution (both environmentally and functionally, not to mention aesthetically and economically). Sitting down with all stakeholders to question their assumptions early in the process was the key to successfully achieving the project's purpose and goals.

CREATING ALIGNMENT

Aligning the Team

With the diversity of individuals usually present around any design charrette table, it is a given that we will have a diversity of values, opinions, expectations, and perspectives. This diversity can be either an asset or a liability, depending on how it is managed—depending on the process. Often, project success is impeded by lack of alignment around common purpose and a commonly understood process. Over time we have found that when trying to introduce a new and unfamiliar way of thinking and designing, an intentional process for helping clients and team members understand how and why the design process must be employed differently is critical.

A major university wanted to build a teaching laboratory building and achieve LEED certification. Very early during the initial LEED goal-setting charrette, which was attended by the entire design team and the owner's representatives, the owner and architect became excited about incorporating operable windows to allow natural ventilation during spring and fall shoulder seasons in order to significantly reduce energy consumption. The campus energy specialist, from the university's facilities group, championed the idea with articles describing teaching labs at other universities that had incorporated such strategies under similar climatic conditions. Later in the day, the idea was again embraced enthusiastically during the setting of performance targets—and, yet again, the team reinforced their desire to pursue this strategy during a discussion revolving around the LEED credit for controllability of thermal comfort systems.

All of a sudden, maybe because he realized that the team was really serious and committed to employing operable windows, the HVAC engineer slammed his hand on the table and exclaimed, "We are NOT using operable windows for a lab project on my watch!" His outburst was met with stunned silence. The meeting lost its energy and focus, and then devolved into a long recovery process that focused primarily on trying to convince the HVAC engineer that this approach was possible—without success. Unfortunately, after two hours of scrambling, the team's excitement about the idea deflated, and the idea was lost.

It was evident that this engineer was bringing different perspectives and expectations to the project that were not aligned with the team's goals and purpose.

In short, even though the stated objective was to produce a green building, his primary concern was that he not make himself vulnerable to a potential lawsuit. While this was a legitimate concern, we missed the opportunity to get this on the table right up front and perhaps discuss the idea of indemnification. We could have addressed this concern throughout the day had we openly solicited each team member's aspirations more directly and explicitly. Instead, by the time the engineer's concern emerged, it trumped the team's alignment around an implicitly *assumed* and different purpose. Unfortunately, this concern was too deeply rooted and hence remained unresolved, resulting in the loss of a significant opportunity.

Too late (at least for this project), we realized that we could have engaged a much more dynamic and open discussion about the real issues and potential impacts (such as short-circuiting the cooling system, maintaining thermal comfort conditions, and additional costs for automatic window controls) behind the engineer's concern about this particular strategy. Had we more explicitly addressed each team member's values, aspirations, and objectives very early on—and reached consensus (thereby alignment) around them—before getting into a more detailed exploration of technologies and strategies, we may have been able to align the team around implementing this single strategy of using operable windows to help achieve a number of their objectives. Such objectives might have included reduced energy consumption and greenhouse gas emissions, increased thermal comfort control, better ventilation, increased connection with the outdoors, and so on. Armed with such explicitly identified values and aspirations around which the team had aligned and committed, we likely would have had a much greater chance of discovering—or at least discussing—creative solutions that might have placated the engineer's concerns without busting the budget.

Figure 4-2 The Chesapeake Bay Foundation Headquarters, Annapolis, Maryland, design team resolved the dilemma between HVAC efficiency and operable windows by installing sensors and controls that shut down the mechanical system and light a sign instructing occupants to "open windows" when outside air temperature and humidity conditions are appropriate. *Image courtesy of Marcus Sheffer.*

Other teams have done so. The Chesapeake Bay Foundation headquarters in Annapolis, Maryland, used a novel technique for using operable windows to achieve the aspirations mentioned above and to reduce energy use while minimizing any short-circuiting of the cooling system. The control system they used is simple: when the outdoor temperature and humidity are within predetermined comfort ranges, an illuminated sign that reads "Open Windows" comes on, and the cooling system shuts itself down. Then, reading the sign, the occupants crank open the windows.

Aligning with the Client

Creating alignment is also critical to the client relationship. Recently, a husband and wife development team, Sandra Kahn and David Leventhal, invited us and our colleagues at Regenesis Group to work with them on the design of Playa Viva, an ecoresort on land they had recently purchased and come to love on the west coast of Mexico. The purpose of our first visit was to understand the nature of the socioecological system and patterns of how life works—and has worked—in that place. This assessment of the land and bioregion examined soil types, geological and archeological history, aspirations of the villagers, cultural relationships, habitat, hydrology, and so on; in other words, we began by looking for large-scale patterns and relationships beyond the boundaries of the property that would be impacted significantly by the project's development. When we reported our findings at the charrette, Sandra became quite upset, because we had not specifically addressed an issue she had expected to be important in a natural history assessment—a significant tree that was meaningful to her in a key area of the property. This was a major misstep from her perspective.

David took this opportunity to pause the charrette for the purpose of making sure that the whole team, including his partner, was aligned around the same process. Sandra was upset because we were using an unfamiliar design process that was not in alignment with her expectations. In other words, she had expected us to focus on certain trees and specific issues on the site, not the larger systemic interrelationships. David, however, had spent some time on the land with Tim Murphy, a systems ecologist and permaculturist; he understood that a different process was necessary to achieve the project's ambitious sustainability goals. So, during the break in the charrette, we engaged the management team in a long discussion about the process that would need to be implemented to understand the larger ecosystem well enough to achieve their stated objectives. As a result, this management team became aligned around the process we had outlined for addressing larger-scale impacts, and the charrette continued, ultimately resulting in a successful, integrative design process. A more intentional means for creating alignment during charrettes and workshops is discussed later in this chapter under the heading "The Touchstones Exercise."

Figure 4-3 The Playa Viva ecoresort in Juluchuca is being constructed along this lagoon on Mexico's west coast. *Image courtesy of David Leventhal, Playa Viva, http://www.PlayaViva.com.*

Figure 4-4 This site plan rendering for the casitas at Playa Viva resulted from examining large-scale bioregional patterns and relation-ships beyond the project property, resulting in a "tree-house structures" concept that minimally disturbs the site's natural water flows and helps restore the ecosystem of the damaged coastal sand dunes. *Design by Regenesis and Ayrie Cunliffe. Drawing by Ayrie Cunliffe. Image courtesy of David Leventhal, Playa Viva, http://www.PlayaViva.com.*

Figure 4-5 Rendering of the tree-house concept for Playa Viva's casitas. *Design by Regenesis and Ayrie Cunliffe. Drawing by Ayrie Cunliffe. Image courtesy of David Leventhal, Playa Viva, http://www.PlayaViva.com.*

FOSTERING AN ITERATIVE PROCESS

An iterative process allows communication at every level, so that each team member's design decisions can be informed by an understanding of how their work relates to the whole. It is through iterations of developing holistic understanding informed by other disciplines that we can create the Composite Master Builder approach described in Chapter 2.

The civil engineer at the Willow School in New Jersey had proposed a stormwater management system consisting of a dry well with concrete pipes and culverts, along with a septic system to meet local building codes. At the end of schematic design, two additional team members were brought into the project, one to address the restoration of soil and habitat and the other to explore alternative ways to treat human waste. For a few weeks, these two consultants did their research and analysis independently of the team.

At the next team meeting they reported their findings. The soil percolation, it turned out, could be significantly improved by restoring the spongelike character of the soil that once supported the original forest before poor agricultural practice ruined its water recharge capability. On the issue of waste treatment, our specialist suggested replacing the approved septic system with a constructed wetland system that would clean the wastewater to drinking-water quality. At this meeting, it was suggested that the civil engineering infrastructure could be substantially reduced given these insights.

However, the civil engineer was not interested in changing his design because these new ideas were unfamiliar and untested in the state. After three more meetings and review of suggested readings, the civil engineer still refused to change his original standard design; he just could not get his mind around these different concepts. Finally, in frustration, we told the engineer to try designing the site's rainwater management without using any pipes, catch basins, or curbs.

A week later he came back with an excellent solution. Fifty percent of the infrastructure had been replaced with vegetated swales and rain gardens, taking into account the new habitat that was to be planted. The only pipes needed were for areas where the swales would have disturbed tree roots on one side of the road or the other, and where water would have sheeted across the driveways in winter and turned to ice (see Figures 4-6 and 4-7).

Without the input from these other disciplines and the ultimate acceptance of these ideas by the civil engineer, we might have been left with a more costly and less environmentally effective solution. Using natural systems in place of hard construction and honoring the way water "wants" to work is almost always the best choice. The constructed treatment wetland system that was implemented will be discussed later.

Iterating across disciplines with all stakeholders and team members early in the process is key— through an interdisciplinary approach, opportunities for deeply integrating potential solutions at increasing levels of detail are made possible, and more effective solutions result. It is critical to establish this pattern of iterative investigation—one that is aligned around the team's explicit objectives—during the *discovery* phase.

INTEGRATING INTENTIONS WITH PURPOSE

The *discovery* phase is primarily about illuminating relationships—not only the relationships between building systems but also the relationships between the project and the larger whole it occupies. The fundamental question to be answered during the *discovery* phase—the question that orients and aligns all stakeholders—is this: What is the project's *purpose*?

A few years ago, the owners of the Brattleboro Co-op invited us and our colleagues from Regenesis Group to talk to them about how to achieve a LEED Gold grocery store. The owners expressed an interest

Figure 4-6 The originally conceived curb-and-gutter system at the Willow School in New Jersey consisted of a conventional system that collects, conveys, and discharges rainwater (in pipes) away from the site. *Image courtesy of Back to Nature and Jeff Charlesworth.*

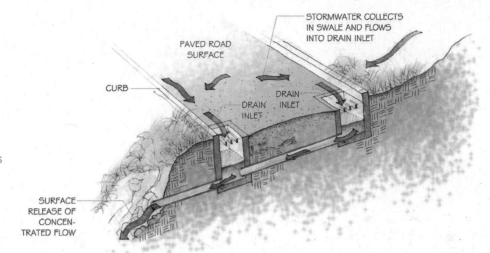

Figure 4-7 The final bioswale solution at the Willow School cleans rainwater runoff from roads via biofiltration and infiltrates this water on site—a system that contributes to the health of the place and is less expensive than one consisting of curbs, gutters, and pipes. *Image courtesy of Back to Nature and Jeff Charlesworth.*

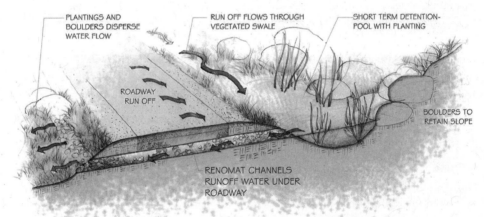

in going beyond building something that was simply more efficient and expressed curiosity about the concepts of sustainability and regeneration.

We knew from experience that it was possible to reduce the store's energy consumption by about 30 percent by applying green building practices such as augmenting thermal envelope properties, daylighting, using efficient refrigeration cases, and so on. But how could we do better? How could we do *more* rather than just "less harm"?

Asking this question led us to begin to explore the relationship between energy and food production. A quick evaluation revealed that the store's inventory included apples from New Zealand, strawberries from California, blueberries from Chile, and so forth. It became apparent that the energy associated with transporting the store's goods far exceeded the energy consumed by refrigeration and building operations. A new vision of the store's *energy footprint* began to emerge, along with the possibility of footprint reduction beyond what would have been within the scope of consideration when looking at the building's construction alone.

The team also realized, looking beyond the energy impacts associated with food transport, that the store's very ability to sustain its food supply was held in a tenuous position by the current food-delivery framework—a truckers' strike could destroy the store's viability. Equally troubling to the executive director was the threat of a corporate organic food chain coming to town with a more efficient network for delivery of the same food. As a result of this initial exploration into the deeper purpose for building the co-op, the team decided to look at the more fundamental issues of sustainability before jumping into defining a building program or assessing project goals with a LEED checklist.

This approach centered on a commitment to investing in locally produced food, which would require an examination of how to rebuild the quality of the surrounding soils and watershed. The project then became a study in understanding the local conditions in order to improve the health of the place and to sustain its inhabitants with healthy local food production. The purpose of the project shifted from simply building a grocery store to becoming a fundamental participant in the health of the place and its people.

In the end, the process of designing the grocery store included thinking more deeply into the purpose of a grocery store and what is needed to make our food supply more sustainable. The role of the physical store itself was revealed as a mere middleman in the transactions that provided food for the local popula-

tion. As a result, the program of the building could be expanded to potentially include an agricultural and soil extension service; a food canning operation for local produce; a place for hunters to dress their meat; a credit union to support local agriculture and trading; sustainable agriculture education; a day-care center; and, of course, a grocery store. This expanded program now had the potential to garner the participation of a large number of the town's inhabitants by soliciting their knowledge of the place. Not unlike the inhabitants of Siena in the building of their duomo, the inhabitants of Brattleboro, Vermont, could now participate in "building" their co-op.

The Four Key Subsystems

Each project has a distinct, purposeful contribution to make to the larger whole. To begin thinking into *purpose,* then, we must look outward and seek to understand the larger systems with which the project has interrelationships. These systems, like the building's own internal systems, cannot be optimized in isolation. Throughout the design process we need to examine iteratively and continually the relationships between smaller and larger systems. One way to do this is to see each of these systems, or subsystems, within a nested grouping of primary impacts.

The alchemists had it right—earth, wind, fire, and water are the essential elements. The sun (fire) is a bit out of our control, other than how we use its present or stored (i.e., fossil fuels) energy as a resource. However, the other elements are directly in our control and are essential to the pursuit of the sustainable conditions that serve to sustain life. Without healthy soil (earth), clean air (wind), and clean water, we will not be able to grow healthy food for all species—the essential base condition necessary to sustain life.

We have seen that *place* is not just the building and its site. Clearly, a building cannot function without

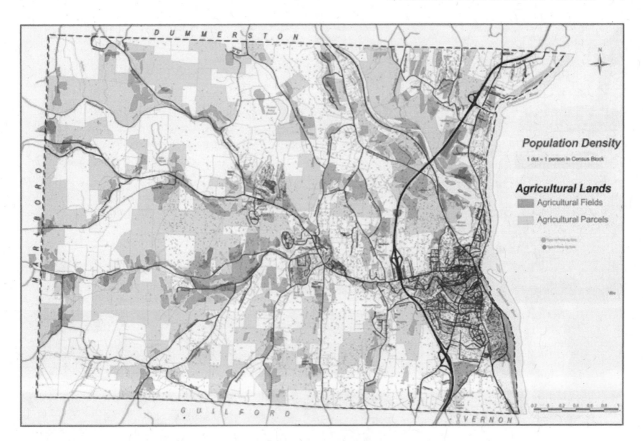

▲ **Figure 4-8** After deciding to build not just a more energy-efficient grocery store, the owners of the Brattleboro Co-op pursued a deeper purpose by exploring the relationships between energy, community, and food production, which led to their investigating the viability of selling only locally produced food. Tim Murphy of Regenesis used GIS information to create a map of the Brattleboro, Vermont, area to assist in researching local food-production capabilities. *Map courtesy of Cartographic Technologies Inc., © 2003.*

◄ **Figure 4-9** Brattleboro, Vermont, and its environs. *Image courtesy of K. Gallager.*

Figure 4-10 A desalination plant in El Paso, Texas. *Image courtesy of Texas Water Development Board.*

Figure 4-11 Construction for this desalination plant on the Taunton River near the town of Brockton, Massachusetts, started in 2006. *Image © InimaUSA.*

the contributions of water, habitat (human and other biotic), energy, and materials. Consequently, all development finds itself inherently linked and inextricably bound not only to larger nested systems but to primary subsystems within that whole, whether or not we are aware of it or intend it. For the purposes of this book, we will focus on four key subsystems:

- habitat (both human and other biotic systems)
- water
- energy
- materials

We will talk much more about each of these subsystems throughout the book, and about how looking through the lens of each can help us discover purposeful relationships between smaller and larger systems, but for now we would like to introduce the idea that all of these subsystems are deeply interrelated. We will first look concretely at the water system to see how it relates to the other systems.

In Massachusetts, at least two towns are currently building expensive, energy-intensive, and pollution-generating desalination plants in an effort to compensate for failing groundwater supply. Given the fact that Massachusetts receives an ample 40 inches of rain per year, why is this necessary?

Let's answer this question by looking at it from a systems perspective: How does the Earth get its groundwater? It catches and cleans the rain with a sponge of plants, animals, microbes, and soil. What happens if the Earth lacks a healthy sponge to catch and clean the rain? Our groundwater supply begins to disappear. In short, healthy soils generated by healthy *habitat* are required for healthy water, and hence for human survival, since without potable water the human organism cannot survive more than about three days. These two Massachusetts towns have been steadily paving and building over the local habitat for a couple of centuries now—and in the process, they have steadily destroyed their free, low-energy source of clean, fresh water.

Our failure to design in harmony with the natural system has put us in a position where we are forced to implement new and expensive technologies to produce the clean water that the Earth produces all by itself. Further, the burning of fossil fuels to generate the high levels of *energy* required to operate these desalination plants produces pollutants and other toxicants (such as concentrated brine, sulfur dioxide, and nitrous oxide, not to mention carbon dioxide that contributes to climate change) that, in turn, contribute to phenomena like acid rain, further polluting the Earth's primary source of fresh water. *Materials* systems are related as

well: instead of utilizing natural bioswales and rain gardens to capture, store, and infiltrate rain water, we build complex and materials-intensive stormwater conveyance systems to take water away—and the embodied energy to fabricate, install, and maintain them ties back to energy again.

What does this have to do with designing buildings? Well, when we build buildings, the amount of undeveloped land that allows rainwater to seep into aquifers is greatly reduced. Driveways, roofs, and parking lots cause water to run off into surface water bodies that often flood, and the threat to the groundwater supply can be serious, even with small amounts of flooding, particularly in older cities with combined stormwater and sewage systems. Furthermore, water that pools on pavement and other impermeable surfaces collects pollutants. This polluted water ends up in storm sewers, flowing directly into area lakes and streams. This affects the quality of surface water and groundwater, since some surface water soaks through lakes and streambeds to groundwater aquifers. Water runoff from impervious surfaces also tends to be far warmer than water runoff from naturally vegetated areas. The resulting thermal shock can significantly alter habitat in surface waters in proximity to areas of development.

When we have readily available tap water and use it to convey our waste, not many of us think of water's role in the larger context of sustaining habitat within the looped system of renewal that in turn sustains life. But this system represents a critical set of relationships and patterns that we usually ignore at the expense of fresh water for our future. More often than not, we ignore the ecology of water; rather, our buildings extract fresh water from aquifers and convey wastewater by means that we cannot "go on doing indefinitely," particularly since we are paving and building over the permeable surfaces (and habitat) that recharge those life-giving aquifers.

Excerpts from "The Ecology and Culture of Water"

By James M. Patchett and Gerould S. Wilhelm

All places and all living things can be defined by the way they handle water. People's relationship with water is grounded in complex interactions with local biological and mineral resources. The entire surficial environment of the earth: geology, soil, topography, flora, and fauna is mediated by water. All living things develop in an aqueous medium in their own genetically defined ways....

Although vitally important to all life systems, water remains one of the more misunderstood and mismanaged resources on earth. When we are unaware of, ignore, or are wasteful in our relationship to the interaction of water with other natural resources, water can be transformed from a vital resource into a troublesome waste product and potentially a powerful source of destruction—even as it leaves the people of the place where it fell bereft....

People of our culture have become functionally detached from an understanding of how the natural world around us works, unaware of its realities, and unmindful of its capacities. Inasmuch as we have lost touch with the importance of a sustainable cultural relationship with land and water, we have largely forsaken the human relationship with the natural environment and therefore threatened our own very well-being....

Water in the Contemporary Landscape

Embedded in the conventional doctrine of COLLECT, CONVEY, and DISCHARGE, rainwater is considered a nuisance and inculcated into the cultural psyche as "stormwater." Stormwater, as such, has become a "management" consideration in nearly every development project. Traditionally, in America, water has been viewed either as a burden, source of contagion, or as a purely utilitarian commodity. Particularly since the Clean Water Act of 1972, professionals have been trained to collect and convey surface waters as a waste product, as quickly and efficiently as the law will allow, from the site in question to areas remote from their purview, presumably to be dealt with by somebody else. They analyze, design, and construct storm drainage and detention systems that attempt to mitigate, through temporary confinement, site and regional impacts of surface water–generated storm flows.

It is rare, however, for these evaluations to consider the natural hydrologic character of the area, or the hydrologic context in which the site and surrounding natural systems formed over geologic time: time measured not by decades or lifetimes, but by thousands of years of system development. These processes were imbedded together seamlessly across the entire watershed. The floristic and faunistic elements of these systems evolved their very nature with the human cultures that depended on them and were compelled to steward their inhabitancy in perpetuity....

Much of the water falling on the ambient landscape is no longer able to infiltrate into the ground, where it once provided a constant source of groundwater seepage to sustain a stable stream hydrology, even during periods of prolonged drought. Instead of a stable watershed and associated groundwater hydrology, most systems are now dominated by erratic surface water hydrology. Waterways experience rapid fluctuations in stream-flow velocity and volume, generated almost completely in response to surface water discharges. The force of these combined stormwater flows is focused on terrestrial and aquatic ecosystems, with their inherent soils, fauna, and flora, formed with a completely different type of hydrology. The erosive and destructive power of this shift in hydrology is impressive....

Restoring a Cultural Relationship with the Land and Water

What do we mean when we say we want to restore the landscape, or restore the health of the earth? What is it that needs to be restored? How do we know when the land is healthy? Such questions can be hard to answer for a people who have become so distant and removed from the idea that their relationship with the earth is integral both to the long-term perpetuation of their culture and the renewability of the earth's living surface. One way of approaching the answers to these questions in human societies, for example, is to regard a culture healthy so long as it continues to renew itself with each new generation of individuals and families. The health of a culture is dependent upon the behavior of the individuals within it....

With an eye toward tomorrow, elders have tested the knowledge and wisdom of their forebears, made scarcely detectable modifications in response to their own experience with their people and their land, and passed it along to young ones. In this way, the health of the culture is assured, as the people, utterly respectful of the experience of the past, respond to the subtle vicissitudes of an ever changing earth, so that their culture might perpetuate itself

and replicate the full potential of human experience with each passing year....

Rates of change in human cultures and ecosystems are buffered against catastrophic collapse by an internal diversity that works to protect the whole against the development of exaggerated, untested individual behaviors or genetic malformations. Without such protections, rapid, system-wide changes can cripple the system's ability to renew itself and conserve its local knowledge of the place.

The health of an ecosystem or a culture degrades in accordance with the degree to which it destabilizes or simplifies itself, and there comes a time when there is not enough diversity within the system, with either enough memory of the past or enough potential for the future, to continue. The evolution of a system so compromised ceases.

Establishing a sustainable relationship with the living earth requires the reintroduction of a capacity for change. Water out of place is a primary agent in both cultural and ecological instability; therefore, our relationship with water is related to our ability to sustain a culture and the culture's ability to sustain the living fabric of the earth.

The Challenge to Ourselves

We believe that sustainability is an overarching principle in all of our relationships with our land and water. To support the hydrologic cycle, ecosystem stability, and other critical natural processes, it is necessary to consider local, regional, or even global issues on land use of all sizes. In contrast to a sustainable approach, much of our contemporary infrastructure and conventional planning methodologies are products of a contrived visual aesthetic with

(continued)

little understanding, relationship, or grounding in the unique realities of place.

Such methodologies represent a cultural indifference to the function of natural systems, or even the energy required to maintain this infrastructure, much less any long-term consequences. This is especially true with respect to the dynamics of water. Site planning and development, as a whole, must evaluate local natural systems and integrate their essential aspects into problem solving techniques, such that design is based on historical patterns of terrain, water, and climate....

Building a sustainable relationship with the living earth requires that our actions be grounded in environmental realities. In a culture-driven society, this requires an ethic. Since the beginning of the Holocene, and perhaps for much of the Quaternary, an important component in the shaping of the landscape has been mankind. Human beings are governed not only by random interactions within the ecosystem, but by choice. Fundamental interactions such as predation, competition, and foraging are complicated by the fact that humans can decide how to act, often with no immediate ecological parameter coming to bear on this decision, other than a human ethic.

According to Leopold [in *A Sand County Almanac*] (1966),

> All ethics so far evolved rest upon a single premise: that the individual is a member of a community of individual parts. His instincts prompt him to compete for his place in the community, but his ethics prompt him also to cooperate. The land ethic simply enlarges the boundaries of the community to include

soils, water, plants and animals, or collectively: the land. We can be ethical only in relation to something we can see, feel, understand, love and otherwise have faith in. A land ethic, then, reflects the existence of an ecological conscience, and this in turn reflects a conviction of individual responsibility for the health of the land.

The design of environments where humans and other organisms interact, where actions create reactions, where the future is built on an understanding and appreciation of the past, requires that good design and the environment be synonymous. Regardless of scale, the design of sustainable environments means facilitating human purposes in concert with natural processes.

Once we understand the realities of place, there are infinite opportunities for creative expression; true design freedom is possible only within these limits. Since every place is unique, every design will require new creativity, innovation, and technology. A new aesthetic, encompassing every aspect of infrastructure, will emerge as we become more successful at designing whole systems. This requires a design process based on the interconnection of natural systems, and an increased understanding of the relationship between an individual site, the surrounding region, and beyond. The products of such design will be both visually interesting and sustainable if they integrate basic physical and behavioral factors into the solution. (Patchett and Wilhelm 1995)

From J. M. Patchett and G. S. Wilhelm, "The Ecology and Culture of Water," Conservation Research Institute, Elmhurst, IL, Revised March, 2008, available at http://www.cdfinc.com/images/download/Ecology_and_Culture_of_Water.pdf

Figure 4-12 Historical patterns of groundwater flow paths use the natural flows of rain collection from uplands as "recharge" zones and lowlands (rivers, streams, ponds, wetlands) as "discharge" zones, resulting in continuous, clean discharge flows year-round that sustain surface and groundwater hydrology with constant water temperature and chemistry. *Image courtesy of Conservation Design Forum Inc., derived from Andrew W. Stone and Amanda J. Lindley Stone,* Wetlands and Ground Water in the United States *(Concord, N.H.: American Ground Water Trust, 1994).*

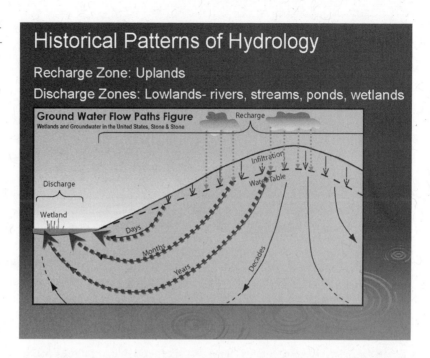

Figure 4-13 Contemporary patterns of groundwater flow paths, resulting from the doctrine of "collect, convey, and discharge," reverse those of historical hydrology: uplands become "discharge" zones, while lowland wetlands are expected to function as "recharge zones," but they cannot. This reversed hydrological pattern causes runoff containing sediments, oils, greases, salts, fertilizers, pesticides, and higher water temperatures that inundate historical systems and habitat adapted to completely different hydrological and water-quality conditions. Essentially, then, we have eliminated recharge zones due to overdevelopment and industrial agricultural practices that prohibit rainwater penetration and infiltration. The result is frequent flooding and contaminated water systems. *Image courtesy of Conservation Design Forum Inc., derived from Andrew W. Stone and Amanda J. Lindley Stone,* Wetlands and Ground Water in the United States *(Concord, N.H.: American Ground Water Trust, 1994).*

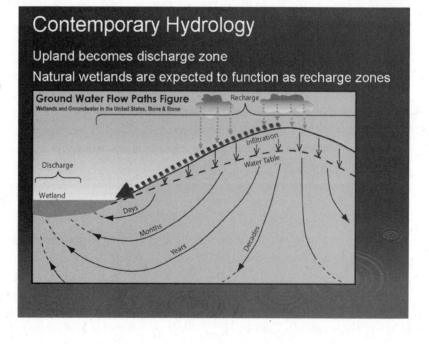

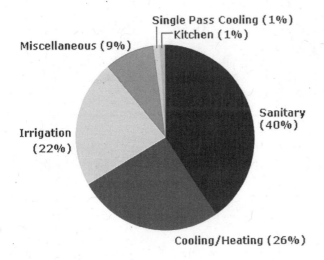

Figure 4-14 This chart illustrates the breakdown of water consumption in a typical office building. *Image courtesy of Greening EPA.*

Typically, however, water is viewed as an expendable resource, particularly in our buildings. Less than half of the domestic water use in our buildings requires drinking water, yet potable water is used for all domestic functions, including flushing away waste. Further, expensive systems are normally installed to convey rainwater away from our sites, creating problems further downstream. When project teams begin to view water differently and shift their mind-sets, they understand that our potable water supply is limited and that it is diminishing as development expands. They come to understand water as a resource, not a waste product.

Within any project site's watershed, there likely exist creeks, streams, ponds, and maybe even rivers and lakes, either above or below ground. A significant percentage of this watershed likely has been paved and covered with roofs and/or turf grass (defined by Gerould S. Wilhelm as "a drug-dependent rug, sitting atop a bed of clay, leaving the site bereft of water, and generating a daily bowel movement in New Orleans"), resulting in dirty, polluted, depleted wa-

ter with large temperature swings and high levels of heavy metals, hydrocarbons, toxins, nitrogen, phosphorous, and sediments. These sediments likely have closed fish-spawning grounds, while other riparian and/or marine habitat has been lost due to toxins resulting from eutrophication, and the health of the whole suffers dramatically—the opposite of sustaining life. Consequently, we need to ask ourselves: what is the role of our project and site in contributing to—or helping heal—these problems?

Integrating rainwater-harvesting systems into our building designs, for example, can *begin* to address these problems. Such systems collect rainwater, store it, and use it in buildings. As a result, the amount of water drawn from aquifers and municipal supplies can be reduced. For example, if we address stormwater on our site by reducing impervious surface areas, installing a green roof, and constructing a retention basin to limit stormwater runoff so that the postdevelopment rate and quantity do not exceed (or better yet, are less than) predevelopment conditions, the resulting groundwater recharge and infiltration keeps suspended solids on the site, prohibiting their conveyance into streams, bays, and oceans. At the same time, flooding and other problems associated with stormwater runoff—such as erosion, water pollution, sediment buildup, eutrophication, and expensive stormwater infrastructure costs—can be reduced as well.

This water system is only one aspect of integrative design; it is only one of the four primary subsystems mentioned above that we will address throughout this book—but again, all four are deeply interrelated. The other subsystems—habitat (both human and other biotic), energy, and materials systems—will be examined in detail during each stage of the integrative design process outlined in this book, as well as how the relationships between these systems interact within the whole.

Figure 4-15 In the DEP Southeast Regional Headquarters building in Norristown, Pennsylvania, rainwater is collected and stored in a cistern, located in the building's atrium, that is fed by exposed piping from the roof. A sediment filter and pump used to convey this harvested rainwater for flushing toilets (satisfying 100 percent of the building's toilet-flushing demand) are located in an adjacent room behind a glass partition, so that the entire system is visible to visitors as a means of providing education about rainwater harvesting (see Figure 7-11). © *Jim Shafer*.

The *four key subsystems* are associated with the fundamental principles described below.

Habitat (human, Earth, and other biotic systems)

Preserving habitat is our obligation not only to the other species with whom we share our planet but also to ourselves. Without a healthy habitat to support *us,* our capacity for basic survival is threatened. We must begin to take responsibility for developing in harmony with these other biotic systems in order to sustain life—all life. As such, we group human habitat with all other habitat systems into *one subsystem* for the purpose of engaging the following principles:

1. Partner all human activities with living systems in mutually beneficial relationships—a project should contribute to supporting the systems of life on its site and within its watershed.
2. Understand and respect local ecological and social systems.
3. Build in essential feedback mechanisms to continuously evolve these relationships.

Water

1. Make the annual water budget equal to or less than annual rainfall on site.
2. Use less water.
3. Retain all rainwater on site.
4. Manage water (rainwater or wastewater) to replicate natural flows in order to minimize water leaving the site.
5. Cascade water use to support all life (human and other biotic systems), if water will be leaving the site.
6. Recharge groundwater table (where possible).
7. Clean all water to potable standards before it leaves the site.

Energy

1. Create less demand via use of insulation, demand patterns, reduced loads, etc.
2. Use available site energies—e.g., sources and sinks—sun, wind, earth-coupling (such as ground-coupling, water-coupling, etc.), and diurnal cycles.
3. Increase the efficiency of what is left—e.g., equipment, appliances, diversity factors, parasitic losses, part-load performance, etc.
4. Minimize or neutralize carbon footprint.

Materials

1. Use less—that which is not used has no environmental impact.
2. Use materials that are abundant and renewable and that do not destroy human and/or earth systems in their extraction, manufacture, and disposal.
3. Strive to use locally sourced, recyclable, nontoxic, and/or low-embodied-energy materials. Life Cycle Assessment (LCA) tools are effective at evaluating comprehensive environmental impacts (see discussion of LCA tools in Chapters 5 and 6).

Once this type of thinking has been explored, in accordance with the fundamental principles outlined above, a project can begin to be envisioned as a contributor to, rather than a detractor from, the *whole* natural system. New questions emerge. For example, how can the project's approach to stormwater contribute to the health of the larger watershed?

If we ask this question, we might find different, creative solutions for retaining our water on site. We might consider restoring deep-rooted plant structures that reduce erosion and help generate water retention. These deeper roots add nutrients and carbon content to the soil, encourage microbial activity that filters clean water into aquifers, create animal habitat, and in turn stimulate more diverse plant growth.

By beginning to reestablish the spongelike character of the soil in this way, a rise in groundwater levels results and filtered water begins to contribute cascading benefits to the larger watershed. Eventually, more and healthier water (via underground downstream transfer) into the watershed's surface waters occurs, thus impacting a much broader scope of nested systems beyond the building and its site. Once this occurs, fish, insects, and birds that can carry nutrients upstream begin to return, further increasing the diversity of habitat on the site and beyond, throughout the watershed,…and the gyre grows.

By the way, the creative solutions for retaining water on site that generated this expansion of life are much less expensive than solving the stormwater retention issues with engineered technologies. Such strategies also consume less energy in terms of reducing the embodied energy in the components that are now unneeded, as well as reducing (in many cases) the demand for water filtration and pumping energy for water distribution. Further, fewer downstream engineering strategies are required to solve our growing water volume and sedimentation problems, again affecting a wider scope far beyond the project site with means that are cheaper. Numerous similar cost implications will be discussed later and in more detail throughout this book.

Aligning Dollars and Resources

Not everything that counts can be counted, and not everything that can be counted counts.

—sign over Albert Einstein's desk
in Princeton, New Jersey

In Chapter 2, we briefly discussed how a coherent integrative process can reduce the costs of building. Beyond that, it is worth examining the connection between costs and resources. When we expand our focus to include the larger systems outside of the building, we begin to see that natural systems are capable of providing the "free services" mentioned at the end of Chapter 3—but only if we work to sustain their generative capacity. Our economic system, however, does not fully capture the intrinsic value of the "services" and "resources" provided by natural systems.

Early on, as we began working in new ways with project teams (circa 1999), we were excited to learn of a school superintendent interested in green building. The superintendent and her school board were building a sizable high school, and they were willing to devote resources toward holding a charrette with expertise brought in to discuss integrative design principles, energy, water, materials, and indoor environmental quality (IEQ). At the time, finding successful projects was strategically important because more examples were needed to demonstrate that green building projects could be built at costs comparable to traditionally built projects.

On a typical project at this point in time, the word resource was defined strictly as the capital budget. One of the themes that continually surfaced at this particular charrette was the concept that resources included not just dollars but also the land the school was to be built on, the water that would hit the site, the energy that would be used by the building and the people getting to it, the materials in the building, and the resources needed to create those materials. Over a two-day period, we continually reviewed how the project's newly defined resources were inextricably bound to capital resources, and we explored opportunities for maximizing the potential for utilizing *all* the resources, including the "free services" available via mutually beneficial relationships with natural systems. Some of the ideas explored included alteration of building orientation to capture solar resources, optimization of bay sizing to avoid depletion of external natural resources (including energy) for materials production, change of window sizing and thermal properties, increase in envelope efficiency, and so forth. Each idea

was reviewed through a lens of tying budget resources to resources as a whole.

Unfortunately, this story does not have a happy ending. Because this charrette did not take place until after the architect had already spent a considerable amount of time producing schematic design documents, the clients found themselves in a difficult situation. Instead of pursuing opportunities to save resources as a whole, they found themselves struck by an understandable hesitancy to pay the price for altering this design. Ultimately, only a few minor changes were made on the project. It was clear to us that the few thousand dollars that were saved by not altering the schematic design were spent at the much higher cost of a vast array of other resources, including water, fossil fuels, and many thousands of additional dollars spent both on building structure and future operational costs that translate directly into further resource depletion.

Dollars and values are clearly connected. One of our colleagues, James Weiner says, "You can understand what you value by how you spend your money. Since we spend a lot of money on buildings, how we build is a reflection of our values." Further, we are discovering that dollars and resources are also connected. Mollie Beattie points to this connection when she says, "In the long term, the economy and the environment are the same thing. If it's unenvironmental, it's uneconomical. That is a rule of nature." In other words: if it's not economically sustainable, it's not sustainable.

The logical conclusion is that, through the practice of development, we need to connect our values to the vast array of noncapital resources that are at our disposal. Until the field begins to value the conservation and contribution of these "free resources" as imperative to project success—as nonnegotiable under the goal of achieving sustainability—we will continue to swim upstream in terms of both our environmental and economic challenges.

The "Touchstones" Exercise

When we first started to experiment with our projects in our consulting roles, we began each project with an exercise aimed at revealing how much the team valued each of these resources; early on, we called this our *core values* exercise. At the first workshop (or charrette) with each project team, before talking about the project design, its components, and even its program, we would simply ask the question: What are you trying to accomplish by building this project? Soon, we began to ask this question in the context of issues associated with sustainability by identifying the team's values through the lens of the following *five key environmental imperatives:*

- climate change
- potable water
- resource destruction
- habitat destruction
- pollution and toxins

As a way of exploring this, we would open a discussion about how the team thought a successful project would address each of these issues—as well as others associated with the unique specifics of the project and *place*—and how they are interrelated. In other words, we were attempting to identify primary objectives, or *touchstones,* explicitly at the outset that could help guide the team through their decision-making process, from conceptual design through occupancy. Over several iterations on several projects, we developed a rather rough technique for capturing these touchstones in this context and documenting them for the team. From there, we developed a prioritization exercise that works in the following manner.

At the initial goal-setting workshop with the entire project team, we facilitate a group brainstorming session, asking all attendees to volunteer their answers to what would constitute a successful project by asking: What are the key issues this project needs to address? These answers are recorded on flip charts. After about twenty or thirty issues are identified, everyone in the room is given a certain number of votes (for example, ten votes for each member of the architectural-engineering-site design team and twenty votes for each member of the owner's team) to allocate across any or all issues. After the votes are tabulated, the list becomes a prioritized guide for making design decisions.

Figures 4-16 and 4-17 depict examples of the results from two such value and aspiration exercises that we facilitated at two recent goal-setting workshops: one for a project pursuing LEED Platinum certification in a marginalized neighborhood of Syracuse, New York, and the other for a multiuse development of an entire block in a degraded neighborhood of Chapel Hill, North Carolina. We now call this the "touchstones" exercise (a term we learned from Sandy Wiggins), rather than a core values exercise, because it serves as an effective tool for identifying the team's goals and objectives more than it gets to the deeply held internal core values of individual and collective team members. Nonetheless, additional benefits that should not be underestimated result from the use of this exercise—for example, team alignment around explicit issues, collective and individual "buy-in" of objectives, and ownership of these issues and objectives. The results of this exercise also contribute to creating the Owner's Project Requirements, a document utilized in the commissioning process to track initial and evolving intentions from the beginning of project design all the way though construction.

It is important to note, though, that this exercise represents an entry-level process that has limits. It aligns people around basic ideas that need to be addressed in a project, but over time we began to realize that the prioritization piece of the exercise could lead team members, at times, to think that some of the identified environmental issues were less important if

TOUCHSTONES EXERCISE

King & King Architects New Office Building — Syracuse, NY

	Design Elements/Issues (Value/Aspiration)	# of votes
1.	Energy and Resource Efficiency	56
2.	Model of Restorative Approach Across Triple Bottom Line	52
3.	Achieve LEED Platinum Certification	44
4.	Establish Connections as Catalyst for Neighborhood Transition	43
5.	Beautiful Landmark	40
6.	Increased Green Space	40
7.	Better Living Conditions* for Inhabitants/Residents/Employees (*Quality of Life)	38
8.	Pedestrian Friendly	37
9.	Inclusive of Neighborhood in Design/Participation/Partnership	35
10.	Safe and Secure	32
11.	Building as Teaching Tool for Sustainability	28
12.	Inspires Responsible Growth	24
13.	Visually Aesthetic Streetscape	21
14.	Renewable Energy Generation	17
15.	Natural Systems Utilization	17
16.	Hope for the Future/Neighborhood Opportunities	10
17.	Area as Art and Cultural Destination	10
18.	Eliminate Stormwater Runoff	10
19.	Future Adaptability/Flexibility	9
20.	Improvement of Creek	9
21.	Access to Public Transportation	6
22.	Reduced Heat Islands	5
23.	Generate Improved Housing Stock	4
24.	Bike Friendly	3
25.	Reduced Automobile Use	2
26.	Appealing Tenant Space	2

Figure 4-16 Sample results from the touchstones exercise for a building renovation project in Syracuse, New York. *Image courtesy of John Boecker.*

TOUCHSTONES EXERCISE

Bluehill Green Mixed Use Project—Chapel Hill, NC

	Design Elements/Issues (Value/Aspiration)	# of votes
1.	Community Connectivity (multi-cultural/generational)	40
2.	Economic Viability/Market Desireability	27
3.	Life Cycle Assessment/Low Impact Materials	21
4.	Renewable/Solar Energy Generation and Use	19
5.	Health of Place/Biodiversity	18
6.	Reduced Ecological Footprint	18
7.	Water Conservation	17
8.	Spiritual/Historical Awareness	13
9.	Flexibility/Durability/Longevity/Legacy	12
10.	Catalyst for Changing How We Develope	11
11.	The Project Educates	11
12.	Community Participation/Involvement	9
13.	Minimize Waste—Construction and Operations	8
14.	Enhance Social Interations	7
15.	Document a Replicable Process	7
16.	On-Site Food Production	6
17.	Pedestrian Friendly	4
18.	Pride of Place	3
19.	Carbon Neutral	3
20.	Resource Exporter	2

Figure 4-17 Sample results from the touchstones exercise for a new multiuse development in Chapel Hill, North Carolina. *Image courtesy of John Boecker.*

they did not get many votes. But all issues are important; you cannot "vote on nature."

On another project this voting component momentarily trapped us. After going through the touchstones exercise on a major urban project that was pursuing not only LEED Platinum but also the Living Building Challenge, we began working collectively on conceptual design solutions. During this two-day charrette, the touchstones were frequently referred to as the team was

trying to assess conceptual design options. At one point, we were trying to decide how to deal with the project's parking needs, specifically for the high volume of cars that would be generated during special events, perhaps fifteen to twenty times per year.

A number of creative and sustainable solutions began to emerge, all in an attempt to reduce the paved area (and the associated stormwater that would be generated) and to increase the amount of open space available to native and adaptive planting areas for infiltration, educational gardens that teach about sustainable landscaping, and a constructed treatment wetland. These ideas also included things like grass-paved or open-cell pervious parking, designating parking on another part of the site, valet parking to a lot off site, and street parking to handle overflow during events. The team began to get excited about some of the potential solutions that had emerged and had begun melding into a combined array of integrated solutions, when one of the owners suddenly said, "Wait a minute!"

He said, "The number one touchstone that we as a team identified is that of being financially sustainable. Our income is heavily dependent on these events, and they are only going to be successful if people coming to them have convenient, on-site parking." He went on to assert that because this was our number one touchstone, the team must provide on-site parking in close proximity to the entrance for as many cars as possible. He then adamantly stated that none of the other, more environmentally focused solutions for parking that the team had raised would work in terms of this "number one" financial priority, and several of the other members of the owner's team agreed with him.

For the next two hours, the discussion focused on nothing but parking. It looked like things were going downhill fast. We then got to a break and asked the owner's team to convene a caucus and define for us exactly what they would and would not consider acceptable parking solutions. Some members of the owner's team advocated for other touchstones on the priority list, such as "creating a model building for going beyond green," "annual water balance," and "building serving as a teaching tool," and the caucus ultimately came to a compromise position that only slightly augmented the site's event-parking capacity. So we eventually got back on track, but we were forced into an extended divergence that should serve as a caution against placing too much emphasis on the voting results.

This experience led us to evolve the exercise again. Rather than merely prioritizing issues, we now often ask team members during the charrette to identify how any three of the identified issues are connected. Then, we ask them to select two more that have interrelationships with the first three, and then two more, and so on. In this way, project teams begin to see the interconnections more than just the fragmented issues or elements in isolation.

In thinking about this in the context of whole systems, *voting on nature* does not seem to be a very *whole* way of addressing the essential aspects required to meet a sustainable, not to mention a regenerative, condition. Applying the analogy of the whole body as a living organism, we would not vote on the function of the liver as more important than the function of the lungs…or would we?

In fact, we do this all the time in our emergency medical practices. When a person is brought into an emergency room with a bleeding and broken body, arresting loss of blood is the first priority, treating shock may be second, and setting bones third. In standard, nonemergency Western medical practices, we maintain fragmented thinking as well, often by focusing on a system or organ and treating it in isolation. Carrying this analogy to the built and natural environment, we are in an emergency situation and simple priorities can be useful in the absence of more systemic thinking about what we might do to address long-term health. However, it is time to move beyond treating only symptoms and isolated traumas.

The medical community is now working on how we promote wellness by addressing the whole of our lives—such as psychological, spiritual, *and* physical health by preventative work with diet, exercise, meditation, visualization (including some fascinating work in making changes happen quickly via "attention density" generated by group visualization), and energy flows in the body (acupuncture, chiropractic,

TOUCHSTONES EXERCISE
Phipps Conservatory

	Design Elements/Issues	# of votes
1.	Financially sustainable	85
2.	Functional efficiency that encourages team collaboration	75
3.	Building as a teaching/research tool	65
4.	Transferability to the market	56
5.	Model for beyond green	50
6.	Quantifiable results over building life cycle	39
7.	Pittsburgh's new icon of sustainable development	37
8.	Dissolve the boundaries between inside and outside	34
9.	Systems transparent to the public/visitors	31
10.	Provide a roadmap for improving future sustainable projects	31
11.	Demonstrate the connection between buildings and the environment	31
12.	Inform the development of future codes	28
13.	Influence societal behavior	27
14.	Beacon of hope related to climate change	25
15.	Create a destination venue	24
16.	Flexible/adaptable design	24
17.	Optimization of project's structure with the site	23
18.	Demonstrate achievement of the triple bottom line	22
19.	Expand project boundaries to improve health of the regional ecosystem	21
20.	Memorable spatial experience	14
21.	Encourage the question of sustainable	13
22.	Dynamic building information model	11
23.	Spark to ignite change	11
24.	Create clear linkages with adjacent park/universities/local amenities	11
25.	Engage the larger public in design and planning	11
26.	Catalyst for future innovations	9
27.	Showcase the integrative design process	8
28.	Zero construction waste	8
29.	Tangible example of the effects of human/environment interface	7
30.	Redefining building health	7
31.	Incorporate biomimicry	7
32.	The building is an embodiment of the project's ideals	7
33.	Pittsburgh's Bilbao	6

Figure 4-18 Results from the touchstones exercise for a project pursuing LEED Platinum certification and the Living Building Challenge in Pittsburgh, Pennsylvania. *Image courtesy of John Boecker.*

and ayurvedic medicine). The design of our buildings as integral to the whole system of nature and community is similarly occurring. We develop the ability to move into whole systems thinking by educating the design team and the project stakeholders about how life works in each place we design and build. The goal is to take the time to assess and understand how all the issues that relate to each subsystem are interrelated and then to resolve the interconnections in ways that serve the health of the whole.

Another powerful way to help the client and design team understand and assess these interrelated issues, while also establishing and maintaining the core purpose of a project, is to ground the significant issues to be addressed by the team in "basic principles." As such, the team's touchstones, goals, and performance targets—when explicitly identified early—are documented and referred to as the project's *basic principles*; consequently, by using such terms, the identified principles are much more likely to become internalized by team members and thereby achieved. Taking the time to understand and ground the work in such terms, these basic, unarguable principles relating to the project's place become a powerful and meaningful compass for guiding and maintaining the project's course.

For example, the following list of nine unarguable "basic principles" was generated in a workshop by the project team that worked on the development of the site adjacent to the Teton River in Idaho to guide their work (described at the end of Chapter 3):

1. Food (and healthy eating) is one of the foundations of a community.
2. Efficient transportation will minimize negative impacts on the atmosphere as well as the ecosystem of the development and community.
3. Materials should be extracted in a manner that is positive for the ecosystem and sourced in ways that are positive for the local economy (e.g., by providing jobs and creating light industry).
4. Energy should be sourced without damaging the ecosystem or atmosphere—locally or from a distance. Naturally sustained phenomena—sun, wind, and water movement—that are harnessed with minimum ancillary damage are the most sustainable energy resources.
5. Soil is the basis of a healthy ecosystem and quality of life for all species.
6. Drawing water from upstream sources and aquifers is not sustainable and ultimately creates negative impacts on ecosystem health, upstream and downstream.
7. Native vegetation has developed in this region because of diverse, self-supporting, complex, and specific habitat relationships. This matrix of life is essential for a long-term, thriving ecosystem and the health of the whole.
8. The health of this ecosystem depends on a healthy diversity of native and migratory avian, fish, and megafauna species. The ecology of this land should reestablish their ability to traverse and become an integral part of life in this place.
9. Living systems organize themselves around the flows in a system (e.g., flows of water or nutrients); if critical flows are disrupted, the system suffers and degrades.

Aligning with Values

A truly integrative process is not just about following instructions, running down a checklist, going through prescribed motions, or prioritizing issues. It requires a personal connection between and among the people involved—not just passing information back and forth but actually creating something together and collectively identifying and holding onto principles and core values—purpose. (The sidebar about Playa Viva illustrates the benefits of holding on to project principles and core values.)

Alignment for Playa Viva from the Owner's Perspective

By David Leventhal

As we started to work on the design of the Playa Viva ecoresort and community (www.PlayaViva.com) in Juluchuca, Mexico, we were unaware of the green building movement, but the concept of building green naturally aligned with our values. About three years before, we had founded a nonprofit organization (now called Rainforest2Reef.org), and we were highly dedicated to ecological and health-oriented endeavors in our lives.

In the course of engaging our design and development team in a deeply integrative Regenerative Development™ process, the consultants from Regenesis Group spoke a language that at first was strange to us, and they used unorthodox techniques. We spent a lot of time prior to our first charrette (workshop) trying to understand this language, its syntax, and terminology; we wondered what they meant by "history of place," "whole-system thinking," "living systems," et cetera. As a neophyte developer, I wasn't sure if this was new language, due to being new to the industry, or if these guys were really doing things in a new and different way.

By the time we had our first charrette, the team led us through a very rigorous process. We started the entire charrette with a day of understanding the deeper purpose and objectives of the project. They asked us big questions related to why we wanted to do this project and what we wanted to leave as a legacy. They made us think about this project from the point of view of multiple generations. We came

up with a very ambitious and clear set of objectives, for example:

- Create a living legacy.
- Be net-energy neutral or positive.
- Create community.
- Have cleaner water throughout the entire watershed.
- Create a transformative experience.
- Create a reserve to promote biodiversity.

Once we had all agreed on these and other larger driving principles, these principles became guideposts that kept us in line throughout the rest of the design process. One very contentious argument arose in the group around the issue of kitchens in the casitas (small homes). Casa Viva, our earlier project, was built around the concept of what we now call "social architecture." Social architecture is simply designing the buildings and spaces to provide a balance between private and public spaces while promoting community and communal activities. At Casa Viva, none of the main casitas (suites) have kitchens; so all hungry guests must, in general, come to a communal house to eat their meals together. Communal meals are key to the experience at Casa Viva. It is core to some of our founding values, including creating community.

However, many in the group felt that building casitas at the new Playa Viva project that didn't have kitchens made them less marketable. Who would want to buy a luxury ecovilla that had no kitchen? Plus, kitchens were necessary. Otherwise, where would you keep the food you bought, how would you cook for your family (something everyone wants to do on vacation), how would you have family meals together, where would you store your baby's milk? The discussion got contentious with the group dividing almost straight down gender lines.

One breakout workgroup had already done an energy assessment working toward our goal of being net-energy neutral. As part of the evaluation, they reported back to the larger group that adding a kitchen in each casita would double our energy consumption. At this point, the group broke into two camps, those who said the casitas had to have kitchens and those who disagreed. Just adding a refrigerator was the largest part of the energy-consumption problem. The argument became quite heated, as arguments often do, especially when the camps are divided by gender.

What got the discussion back on the right track was when the design team asked us if having kitchens fit into the goals we had all agreed upon in the first part of the charrette. Would having kitchens create com-munity? Would it make us energy neutral? Would it be a transformative experience? As a result of going back to our original principles, we were able to agree that having kitchens in the casitas did not ac-complish any of our goals.

While it may seem trivial, looking back at an argument about kitchens or no kitchens, refrigerators, or ice buckets, and so on, the process set up by the facilitators allowed us to define our own points of alignment and use those to direct us through the hard issues. We were able to address this very contentious design issue and analyze how the deci-sion fit into our overall goals. For those who want a private meal, we all agreed that room service would be good enough. In the end, the kitchen crew real-ized that we wanted people to get out of their private enclaves, come sit around the fire, cook commu-nal meals together, eat together, get to know one another, create community, have a transformative experience, and go home feeling really good about their time at Playa Viva.

An effective integrative design process challenges participants to ask deeper questions, beginning with a fundamental exploration of who we are. Who are we in relationship to each other, and who are we in relation to the project? These questions can help bring people into relationship, inviting each participant to engage, to contribute her or his expertise, and to honor the expertise of all the others. The goal is openness and clarity in inter-actions, addressing deeper issues around the basic pur-pose of the project, leading to a more robust common ground in which the team can work truly creatively.

As information is gathered, goals are articulated, and ideas begin to foment, these three lines of activity interact so that *before* talking about the project design, its components, and even its program, we ask ques-tions that bring the *whole* together:

1. What are you trying to accomplish by building this project?
2. After it is built and occupied, what will define suc-cess? What will have been achieved?
3. How will the project continue to evolve as a con-tributing member of its community and place?

In other words, how would a successful project be defined for this place not only at this time, but also for its evolution into the future?

This process encourages people to get in touch with their own personal values and to allow those values to inform their work on the project. Approached in this light, the process of developing and evaluating options and reaching decisions becomes more holistic. By incorporating core values, nonhuman stakeholders also have a place at the table and their interests are protected and articulated during dialog. Each team member becomes more engaged on a personal level—it is no longer just another building project or just a job.

How does this help in practice? At the simplest entry level, when we start going through LEED and deciding what to do and what not to do, the previously identified touchstones resulting from this process often motivate someone in the room to say something like, "well, we put 'health of occupants' high on our list, so we'd better address indoor air quality issues in terms of ventilation and carbon dioxide monitoring," which in turn affects energy, and so on. The team's values and aspirations become a framework (rather than just a checklist of issues to address) for assisting decision making not only in the first goal-setting charrette but also throughout the design and construction process, even into operations. In the end, all of this work is based on meaningful intentions and purpose—not *stuff*, not technologies.

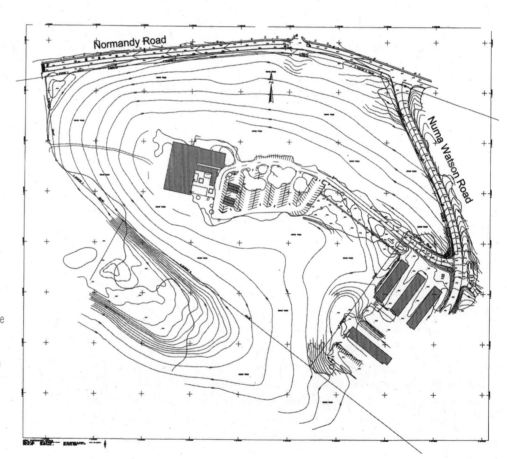

Figure 4-19 This site plan documents existing conditions at the project site prior to the design of the Chartwell School, which is located along a ridge within the former Fort Ord military base in Seaside, California. *Preliminary Landscape Plan by GLS Landscape/Architecture.*

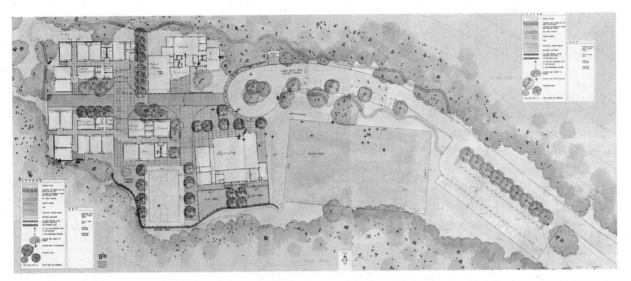

Figure 4-20 The Chartwell School site plan depicts a development footprint that uses only the areas of the site that were previously disturbed by the demolished Fort Ord Officers Club building. *Preliminary Landscape Plan by GLS Landscape/Architecture.*

Douglas Atkins, executive director of the Chartwell School, initiated a sustainable and integrative approach for achieving such an intentional purpose in the design of their new LEED Platinum school near Monterey, California. He understood that aligning the entire team around core values from the very outset—early in the *discovery* phase before initiating any building design work—was critical for the success of the project, particularly since several board members were skeptical about pursuing a green school. He describes the process as follows:

> Early on in the process our goal was not first and foremost to build green, but rather to build the best educational facility that would lead to positive education outcomes and experiences for our students. So, we began to look for the best approach to accomplish that. As we worked toward this goal, it turned out that the green building and integrative design process led us down a sort of reflective investigation of our own core values.

We saw as we engaged the criteria and the elements of green and integrative design that we were actually accomplishing the things that we had set out to do under our first priority of creating positive educational outcomes. For example, we were ensuring that we were producing an environment that was the healthiest environment for kids, so we were most sensitive to those factors that enhance educational experience, and we identified (and designed out) those factors that detracted from positive educational experiences.

Early on in this process, the teachers and faculty were led through an extensive number of charrettes and interviews by a 7group facilitator. Here, we identified our priorities and our core values; these were then merged with the LEED protocol and framework to define issues and to create a programming report that would ensure that we accomplished both ends. In this way, we made sure we weren't drifting away from what we said was most important to us from the beginning—and at the end of the day, we also benefited by having a building that earned a LEED Platinum rating.

This process resulted in the design and construction of a school driven by an explicitly documented purpose that succeeded. For example, Chartwell uses photovoltaics that produce about half of the electricity the school needs and has become a leading source of investigating the pursuit of grid-neutrality for schools. A sampling of other attributes includes copious daylighting that is provided in all educational spaces, reducing lighting demand by nearly 50 percent due to photocell controls; a rainwater harvesting system, including a sluice that not only is used by teachers to educate students about water flows but also reduces building wa-

ter use by approximately 70 percent; science gardens where students are growing organic food, composting, and learning about the food cycle, including food that is served at the school and waste that is composted back into the garden soil; natural ventilation; a web-based energy-monitoring system that is incorporated into curriculum and can be used by students to track their energy use, learn about the relationships between building performance factors and energy consumption, and compete with other classrooms for lowest energy use; salvaged materials used to build portions of the school derived from the razed Army barracks that previously existed on the former Fort Ord site; and a design that is panelized with bolted connections and special fasteners that allow for deconstructability of systems at the end of their useful life. In addition, the school cost *less*

Figure 4-21 As part of the programming effort for the Chartwell School, students were asked to make drawings depicting their vision for the new campus and school. Consistent themes emerged from the subliminal messages embedded within these drawings, revealing several insights. This example recognizes the ridgelike nature of the site and attempts to integrate the building form with the landscape. *Image courtesy of John Boecker.*

Figure 4-22 The main façade of the Chartwell School's multiuse building faces north and forms the south edge of the campus arrival court. Careful dimensioning of all components according to a 24-inch module reduced waste and cost, resulting in a 28 percent materials cost savings, which paid for the project's certified wood. *Image © Michael David Rose | Morp.*

Figure 4-23 Copious daylight fills the interior of Chartwell's multiuse room from north-facing glazing and operable windows that also provide natural ventilation. *Image © Michael David Rose | Morp.*

to build than the average cost of all elementary schools built in California in the same year, and significantly less to operate. Douglas Atkins also reports that initial post-occupancy evaluations indicate a pattern of reduced absenteeism, reduced reports of health-related issues due to IAQ issues (pending more detailed data analysis of the variables involved), and anecdotal evidence of improvements in learning and student outcomes, along with a significant increase in the enthusiasm on the part of students for engaging education.

Figure 4-24 Materials on the interior of the Chartwell School include exposed agriboard structural insulated panels (SIPs), Forest Stewardship Council (FSC) certified wood, salvaged materials from the demolished officers club, and high recycled content. Additionally, the project was designed and detailed for deconstruction and disassembly, incorporating the results from in-depth analysis of construction techniques intended to ease disassembly of building elements for reuse at the end of the building's useful life. *Image © Michael David Rose | Morp.*

Figure 4-25 The school's rainwater-collection system is integrated into the recreational space and education curriculum at the Chartwell School. *Image © Michael David Rose | Morp.*

Excerpts from "Chartwell School Programming Report, 30 September 2002"

Chartwell's mission is to provide students with specific learning difficulties (dyslexia and related symbolic language processing problems) the learning tools and personal support they need to operate effectively in "real world" situations. The single most important component of Chartwell's philosophy can be stated simply as "educating the whole child"; this means helping each student gain a sense of self. It also means transforming each student internally, so that his or her learning difficulty no longer is self-perceived as a disability.

Purpose of the Report

The Chartwell School Board of Trustees targeted the year 2004 as the school's goal for occupancy of a new permanent facility on a site that is located in Fort Ord, California. This goal recognizes that a significant opportunity exits to broaden the school's contribution to the community by expanding its enrollment capacity, providing community outreach programs, and further developing a series of research and training programs.

The purpose of this Programming Report is to identify and document the objectives that this new school must satisfy in order to be deemed successful. Accordingly, it serves as a record of the Chartwell family's best judgments about the results to be expected from the new facility. It is intended to guide the school's design team through the beginning of their design process by providing them with an initial description of program elements and priorities. It is qualitative in nature, not simply a listing of desired functions, spaces, and their required sizes. Again, this document represents the beginning of the de-

sign process, which if nothing else is a process of discovery.

Chartwell recognizes that by engaging this design process, the school's administration, faculty, staff, parents, students, and Board are participants in a dynamic, fluid process; hence, the answers that emerge from the questions posed in this report will evolve and emerge as deeper multivalent levels of investigation are pursued and integrated. These emerging answers will form the basis for an evolving diagrammatic investigation via design sketches during the design professional's schematic design process. As such, this document is intended explicitly to provide the school's design professionals with a thoughtful starting point in that process. The school understands that its contents must remain dynamic and responsive to what is learned as we proceed toward construction.

Programming Process

In June 2002, this *qualitative* programming effort commenced. What followed was a series of nine conferences aimed at investigating the school's vision for its new facility by engaging questions intended to stimulate dialogue and to generate creative problem solving—representing the beginning of an evolving process, not an end. The collective responses to these questions will likely create a tension—a fertile complexity—from which creative solutions can emerge and evolve during the design process. Indeed, one might characterize design as a process whereby one discovers simplicity from complexity. Consequently, the more fertile this programmatic soil becomes, the more robust the opportunities will grow, as solutions emerge from this program investigation.

(continued)

PROGRAMMING REPORT

TABLE OF CONTENTS

PART ONE—BACKGROUND AND PHILOSOPHY

1. PURPOSE OF THE REPORT
2. PROGRAMMING PROCESS
3. MISSION STATEMENT
4. EDUCATIONAL PHILOSOPHY AND TEACHING PRINCIPLES
5. CHARTWELL PAST AND PRESENT
6. CHARTWELL INTO THE FUTURE
7. ORGANIZATIONAL STRUCTURE
8. EXISTING SCHOOL FACILITY

PART TWO—A QUALITATIVE VISION OF THE NEW FACILITY

1. INTEGRATED DESIGN AND ENVIRONMENTAL CONCERNS
2. GOOD VALUE
3. SYMBIOSIS BETWEEN ARCHITECTURE AND EDUCATION
4. VISION FOR THE NEW CAMPUS
5. ENTRY EXPERIENCE
6. SPECIFIC PROGRAM RELATED REQUIREMENTS
7. FUNCTIONAL RELATIONSHIPS AND INTERACTIONS
8. SCHOOL COMMUNITY
9. ARCHITECTURAL CHARACTER

PART THREE—PROGRAM DATA

1. SITE INFORMATION
2. ENTITLEMENTS
3. QUANTITATIVE PROGRAM OF REQUIRED SPACES

APPENDIX

A. PROGRAM REPORT DISCUSSION POINTS AND QUESTIONS

Figure 4-26 The content of the Chartwell School's Programming Report consisted of three parts, focusing primarily on core values and vision. Only a few pages were devoted to quantitative functional program data. *Image courtesy of John Boecker, report author.*

Sample Questions

- Describe Chartwell's Mission Statement; how can this project enhance that mission?
- What do you think the school's program will look like in 5 years? 10? 20?
- What is your vision for the new campus?
- What is the most important aspect or component of Chartwell's educational philosophy?
- Can you identify specific teaching principles employed by Chartwell?
- In order to support these principles, how can the design of the building's spaces and site and their interrelationships promote these principles?
- How can provisions best be made for:
  - "decompressing" space?
  - promoting relationships to exterior spaces?
  - providing the potential for multiple ways of grouping students?
  - maximizing natural daylighting and indirect lighting strategies?
  - augmenting acoustical properties and performance?
  - augmenting indoor air quality and ventilation?
  - integrated design strategies that utilize the model of "building as organism" to eliminate redundancies and components or downsize systems in order to reduce energy and operations costs?
- What opportunities emerge by employing "nesting" strategies that promote multiple, simultaneous functions occurring within and between spaces?
- How best are spaces clustered and/or nested within the larger school organism?

- How best are spaces, functions, and buildings clustered and/or nested on and with the site to create healthy relationships?
- How can synergies occur between instructional spaces and "community" spaces?
- Could the building itself serve as a teaching tool by providing inherent learning opportunities in its design by:
  - utilizing circulation spaces as an opportunity for learning by creating a heightened sense of awareness that stimulates receptivity?
  - utilizing circulation spaces serve as galleries for student work and art?
  - providing visual and physical contact with natural systems and the environment?
- How can spaces be integrated into the site in ways that utilize exterior spaces to stimulate learning?
- Can building components instruct students about our relationship to natural phenomenon, for example, by including passive solar strategies or an integral sundial?
- Can conservation strategies such as rainwater catchment systems and photovoltaics be integrated into the design such that they provide instructional opportunities?
- How can the project contribute to the health of the place in which we are building?

These discussion points and questions represented the beginning of an evolving process, not an end.... [the intention was not to] seek correct answers; rather, it was anticipated that the collective responses to these questions would likely create a tension— a fertile complexity—from which creative solutions could emerge and evolve during the design pro-

(continued)

cess. Indeed, one might characterize design as a process whereby one discovers simplicity from complexity....

Participants within the Chartwell family were invited to engage this process as an investigation of opportunities. The were told that their input and participation would be a critical component of identifying opportunities that would give rise to designing a successful facility, one where the built environment and Chartwell's teaching principles could merge into mutually beneficial symbiosis.

The results of this investigation largely constitute the contents of this Programming Report. Responses from the nine conferences have been edited and organized herein in order to help guide the design team through the beginning of their design process, by providing them with an initial description of program elements, priorities, principles, and purpose.

Redefining Success

Projects like those just described have led us to redefine success. By looking deeply at our highest aspirations, whether building a home, a school, a grocery store, a hospital, or an office building, we see time and time again that these aspirations are in fact deeply compatible and aligned with environmental sustainability. It is this alignment that we are seeking to find when we work toward purpose. The *discovery process* is not just about discovering the relationships between building and site systems, it is also about discovering a deep and meaningful way of being ourselves in relationship with the larger system—the whole. Having seen that there are no "right" answers, we find it more helpful to think of success not as an end state but as an ongoing process. We need to examine how systems thinking and an integrative process in and of itself is not an answer but a means for accomplishing our purpose—for, without purpose, integrative design does not really integrate, and systems thinking is directionless.

chapter

5

The Discovery Phase

The loftier the building, the deeper must the foundation be laid.

—Thomas à Kempis, late Medieval German monk, mystic, writer

A great building must begin with the unmeasurable, must go through measurable means when it is being designed and in the end must be unmeasurable.

—Louis I. Kahn, architect; quoted in Green, Wilder: *Louis I. Kahn, Architect*, New York, New York, Museum of Modern Art, 1961

THIS IS NOT A COOKBOOK

A visit to any bookstore will reveal a large section of self-help books, ranging in topic from how to run, ski, hike, or climb better to how to improve your health, personal relationships, or fortune. Likewise, any magazine rack is filled with articles on how to improve yourself, your sex life, your marriage, your cooking, and so on. These articles and books are often prescriptive approaches to any given issue. For example, if you put away so much money per month in a particular investment structure, you will be wealthy enough to retire by a certain age.

This book about the design process is not intended to fit within the self-help or advice genre. It is not prescriptive. It is not intended to provide a checklist of steps that you and your design team can follow, and that will provide you with a building that does all the things you want it to do. Instead, we are trying to pro-

99

vide examples of how an integrative process can work to create better buildings. We are providing examples because we have found that there is general confusion about what tools or rating systems like LEED, among others, do for us and how we can benefit from them. Consequently, this book is focused on how to use these tools well and how to work within a larger context so that we can improve our ability to create buildings that fit within a greater whole.

Our point here is that if we were to provide a checklist for a design process that reduces environmental impacts, you—the reader—would immediately be disenchanted the first time you tried to implement this process, because it likely would not match the unique circumstances of your project. It would seem that such a process was established in a perfect world that is not attainable. Instead, we want readers to understand that this book is really about relationships. It is not only about relationships between systems; it also is about the way people interact with each other and how they can interact more effectively—and it is designed to encourage you to have your own thoughts about how to do this.

A self-help book about marriage might provide endless tips and ideas about how to engage your partner by listening better, showing concern, following through with your commitments, and so forth. As a result, you might try one or two of these ideas for a while, but you likely would find that your relationship does not change very much after implementing these strategies. Your relationship will only change when you fully understand that it *needs* to change—and when you and your partner have become fully aligned around this understanding.

Similarly, the implementation of the ideas in this book can occur only when you reach a common understanding with other design team partners about how and why you want to design and build buildings. First, you will need to internalize and understand that

your current process *needs* to change, and then you will have to align this understanding with your design team partners. Once this realignment occurs, most design teams will find that implementing the ideas in this book can assist in creating buildings that allow them to use existing tools—such as LEED—more effectively and, most importantly, to create buildings that not only function better but also have strengthened relationships and linkages with communities and natural systems.

As such, while we are attempting to provide readers with ideas about how to improve the design process, it is important to keep the main goal of understanding relationships in mind, and to understand that the process outlined in this book remains flexible. For example, on a small and less complex project, implementing the tasks discussed below for the *Discovery Phase* might be completed in a few weeks, while on a larger and more complex building project this may take many months.

With that said, it is now time to shift our discussion from establishing the foundation that supports integrative design to outlining the functional steps necessary to accomplish it. The *Implementation Outline* presented in the next four chapters introduces and describes in some detail the steps and activities that make up each stage of the integrative process. It is important to note that this process is presented as an *optimal* one that can be adjusted, applied, and tailored to fit project-specific parameters and circumstances. Accordingly, the Implementation Outline presented assumes that integrative design work starts at an optimum point—at project inception. Throughout the next four chapters, we will use the *Integrative Process* diagram (depicted in Figure 5-2 and Figure C-1) as a graphic map to identify each particular stage under discussion.

Again, it is important to note that this diagram and the stages it depicts are not to be used to dictate a linear methodology; rather, our purpose here is to identify an idealized structure and set of activities that will need to be adjusted and tailored to the parameters of each unique project and team. In other words, we suggest using the outlines presented for each stage to help guide your progress through the process, and not as a cookbook with fixed recipes.

The integrative process begins with the discovery phase, as introduced in the last chapter. To begin exploring this phase, let's first look at what a typical scenario for the beginning stages of a project might look like when a more conventional design process is used; see if this scenario sounds familiar.

HERE'S WHERE WE ARE

A major corporation wants to build a new headquarters office building and achieve LEED Silver certification. The owner hires the entire architecture and engineering team, and then decides to hire a LEED consultant who can help guide the project team through the LEED certification process.

A program document, developed by the owner and the architect, is sent to the LEED consultant so that he or she can identify the scope of services needed to help the project team better understand and document the credits that the architect has selected from the LEED checklist. The LEED consultant submits a proposal, which is accepted by the owner, and a team meeting is scheduled immediately, since land development plans need to be submitted the following month to obtain entitlement approval and secure financing.

The meeting is convened, and the project team runs through the LEED checklist to verify the architect's initial assessment. As the team reaches consensus on the LEED credits that will be pursued, the construction manager agrees, with some hesitation, that identified site strategies might be accomplished

within budget if certain other components are eliminated. The civil engineer agrees that by eliminating these components, documenting the rest can likely be accomplished within their fee structure. Various team members are assigned tasks associated with pursuing the targeted LEED credits and incorporating the required measures into the site design prior to the submittal of the land development plan drawings, with the architect and civil engineer being charged with most of the site design tasks.

Four weeks later, a set of site plan drawings is sent to the LEED consultant for review and comment to make sure that the proper components for achieving the targeted LEED credits have indeed been incorporated. Upon reviewing the documents, the LEED consultant distributes a brief report containing minor clarifications and revisions (for example, the addition of two carpooling spaces; changing the walkways from asphalt to concrete; adding more vegetated open space within the project's site boundaries) and indicates that all pursued site credits appear achievable. In short, the project team missed a few details, but otherwise they did a good job.

The architect and civil engineer incorporate the LEED consultant's recommendations into the land development drawings, submit them, and receive preliminary municipal approval. With this approval in hand, the owner is able to secure financing and schedule a second team meeting, a design charrette, with the team, saying, "We're now ready to design the building!"

STOP AND REFLECT

Sounds pretty good, right? In fairly short order, the owner has obtained approvals and financing. The architect and the civil engineer have met their contractual obligations for this phase of the work, and the project is on track for achieving its targeted LEED goals.

What's Working?

The expected results have been achieved on time and within budget. A highly efficient process was implemented—one based on an accepted and conventionalized set of values that target and are characterized by the following:

- Speed of completing this phase
- Ease of identifying cost parameters
- Ease of code approvals
- Ease of securing financing
- Clarity and simplicity of defining scope and design tasks
- Ease of setting fees to meet client expectations
- Achievement of initial LEED goals

What's Not Working?

In this case, the LEED checklist was used as if it represented the full range of possibility for creating a more sustainable project. Once items had been chosen from the checklist, all work revolved around finding a way to fit these components into the design. The larger systemic relationships influencing the building were never investigated and, as a result, possibilities for sustainable engagement with the site and its larger context of nested subsystems were likely never discovered.

How does this impact results?

- As we have seen, we often proceed without questioning our assumptions, *thereby missing opportunities.*
- We also have seen that project team members operate separately, in silos, without understanding interdisciplinary linkages, thereby missing more opportunities.
- Often, project success is impeded by lack of alignment around common purpose and a commonly understood integrative process.

You may recall from Chapter 3 the story about the team for a large office building project that asked us, at the end of the schematic design phase, to help them achieve their green objectives and LEED goals. When we asked to see the preliminary energy modeling results at our first meeting with the team, the HVAC (heating, ventilating, and air conditioning) engineer replied, "We don't do energy modeling until the end of design development."

When we asked why, we discovered that the team viewed early energy modeling as wasteful. The HVAC engineer explained that "if we did it any earlier, we'd have to model the building more than once." The architecture had been designed independently, without the HVAC engineer's input pertaining to its energy performance. Energy modeling was being used as an after-the-fact assessment of building performance to earn LEED points rather than to inform design decisions. The team's common purpose was to achieve LEED points.

This left us with three questions:

- How can we structure a process that encourages the questioning of assumptions so that we are not making design decisions before we have defined and expanded the scope of exploration—that asks exploratory questions to promote iterative discovery?
- How can we structure an interdisciplinary process that explores the linkages between technologies, techniques, and subsystems in order to understand the optimal interrelationships unique to each project and place—an *inter*disciplinary process as opposed to a *multi*disciplinary approach?
- How can we structure a process that acknowledges that each stakeholder brings different perspectives and expectations to each project *and* that encourages alignment around common values, process, and purpose? (Stakeholders include all affected systems, both human and nonhuman, organic and inorganic.)

The absence of the above three critical aspects of an integrative discovery process can lead to some very dysfunctional and/or unproductive meetings and building projects. When clients, consultants, builders, community stakeholders, and occupants are not intentional in their relationships throughout the process of realizing a new project, there inevitably will be miscommunication and missteps. The ability to develop a collective and deep understanding through dialogue, rather than debate, is an almost mandatory skill for design team members if we hope to change the nature of our understanding of and care for the environment. Engaging in these aspects of the discovery process will begin to allow us to bridge the gaps between our human-to-human and human-to-environment interrelationships to avoid unintended consequences and to address long-term ramifications.

How Can We Do (and Think about) This Differently?

Our current process is self-limiting. Our scope of exploration is limited by conditioned expectations and preconceptions that are so embedded in our conventionalized process that we do not even recognize that they need to be questioned. Even when we use LEED as our guiding framework or tool, we can find ourselves limiting our thinking to the issues defined by the tool itself, and we often end up *designing to the tool.*

INTEGRATIVE PROCESS OVERVIEW

The *integrative process* is a means of doing this differently. As we have seen, it differs from the conventional, or linear, design process. Achieving the greatest effectiveness in cost and environmental performance requires that every issue and everybody be brought into the project at the earliest point.

You may recall from Chapter 2 that the integrative process, in its simplest form, can be described simply as a repeating pattern of *Research/Analysis* and *Team Workshops.* The *Implementation Outline* presented in the next four chapters defines each of these as a "stage," and outlines suggested activities for each. The activities listed in this outline for the research and analysis stages are not intended to be engaged linearly. Rather, they should be approached as an iterative reflection process. Chapter 2 introduced the Learning Wheel, a decision-making methodology that allows new ideas to emerge. This methodology constantly alternates between questioning assumptions—engaging research and analysis to formulate hypotheses—and then testing these new ideas with quantitative tools and team workshops; the process is then repeated. The general form of this repeating pattern, Research/Analysis and Team Workshops, is depicted in Figure 5-1; this simple pattern serves as the foundation for the Integrative Process diagram presented in graphic form throughout this book and can be described as follows:

- Research/Analysis: Individual team members for each discipline initially develop a rough understanding of the issues associated with the project before meeting—for example, ecological and habitat systems, water systems, energy systems, material resources, budgetary resources. This occurs so that the design process can begin with a common understanding of base issues.

- Workshop: These team members come together with all stakeholders in the first workshop (goal-setting) to compare ideas, set performance goals, and begin forming a cohesive team that will function as a consortium of codesigners. By being in relationship to each other, each team member allows the issues associated with the system for which he or she is responsible to come into relationship with all systems so that a more integrated and optimized project results.

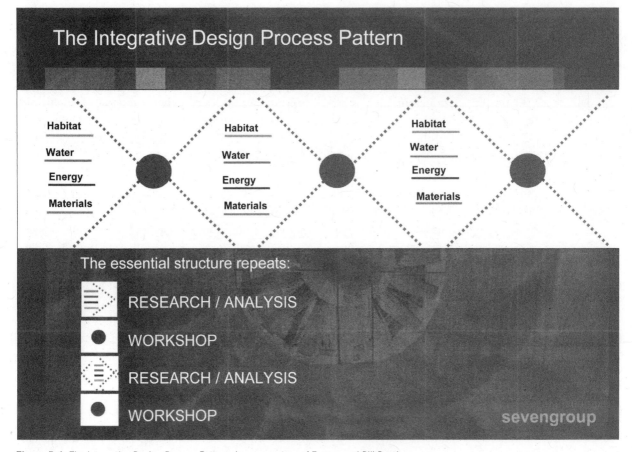

Figure 5-1 The Integrative Design Process Pattern. *Image courtesy of 7group and Bill Reed.*

- Research/Analysis: Team members go back to work on their respective issues—refining the analysis, testing alternatives, comparing notes, and generating ideas in smaller meetings.

- Workshop: The team reassembles for a deep discussion of overlapping benefits and opportunities—for example, how best to utilize the "waste" products from one system to benefit other systems. New opportunities are discovered, explored, and tested across disciplines, and new questions are raised.

- Research/Analysis: Team members separate again to design and analyze with more focus and poten-

tially with greater benefits accruing. New ideas are uncovered.

- Workshop(s): The team reassembles once again to further refine the design, to optimize systems being used (building and mechanical systems), and to integrate systems connected with the project (water, habitat, energy, materials, etc.).

This pattern continues until iterative solutions move as far as the team and client wish.

We have found that three to five charrettes or workshops are the minimum number (depending on project scale and scope) of large full-team meetings required to move integration forward in conjunction with many additional submeetings between workshops. When and how team members interact is the responsibility of the project manager or integration facilitator. Nevertheless, unless project team members meet in the interim with some level of intentional integration (and updated analysis) at least every two weeks, the momentum of exploration likely will diminish.

Throughout the remainder of the book, we will use the top diagram in Figure 5-2 (and Figure C-1) as a means of illustrating an optimal integrative process. It expands the simple pattern introduced in Figure 5-1.

Integrative Process

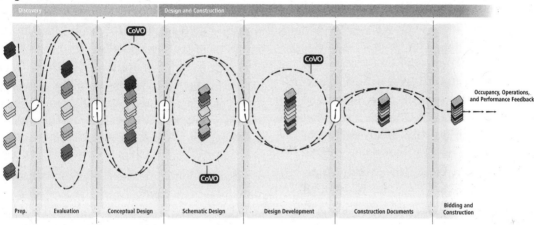

Prep.   Evaluation   Conceptual Design   Schematic Design   Design Development   Construction Documents   Bidding and Construction

Traditional Process

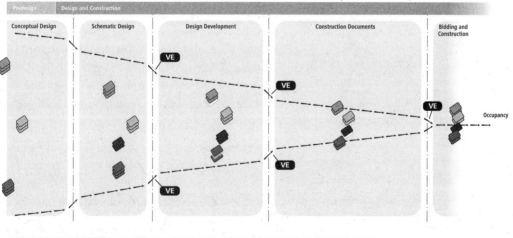

Aspects of the Key Sub-Systems	CoVO Continuous Value Optimization	Workshops and Charrettes
Scope Refinement Path	VE Value Engineering	

Figure 5-2 Integrative Process and Traditional Process (see also Figure C-1) depicting the optimal integrative process compared to the traditional process along the same time line. *Image courtesy of 7group and Bill Reed; graphics by Corey Johnston.*

This diagram graphs the *integrative process* (IP) through the design phases along the same overall time frame as the diagram of the *traditional process* (TP) below it. With all of the additional early analysis required, it is often assumed that the integrative process takes longer; but that is not necessarily true (as indicated by these diagrams, since they are plotted on the same time scale). In other words, the overall time from project inception to the delivery of bidding documents can remain the same, but the allocation of effort is redistributed. The front-end loading of analysis in the *discovery* and *schematic design* (SD) stages of the IP allows for the *construction documents* (CD) phase to be significantly reduced, as it is utilized solely for documenting earlier design decisions rather than being encumbered by continuous design changes (as it currently is, in most cases). According to the AIA's presentation on the Integrated Project Delivery Process, the Orcutt-Wislow Partnership reported the following: "We have found that when we've completed the design development phase, we're already close to 60% finished with construction documentation. [Using this process in conjunction with] the Virtual Building model, we shorten the time required in documentation, resolve design conflicts, and overall, produce better documents."

The following additional information is embedded in these diagrams:

■ The stages before schematic design (discovery) in the integrative process take nearly twice the time of the same stages in the traditional process (conceptual design) but time required in the integrative process for design development (DD) is reduced, and time in the construction documents (CD) phase can be cut by over a third or more.

■ In the traditional process, each discipline is represented by one of the "stacks of cards," each stack floating around and analyzing its system or systems in isolation. This continues though schematic design, after which cost estimates quite frequently end up over budget, and so the team engages in value engineering (VE). This is repeated one or more times through the design development and construction documents phases, as the range of decisions decreases and scope narrows, as indicated by the converging, dashed arrowhead lines in the TP diagram.

■ In the integrative process, each large lozenge represents a major, "all-hands" team integrative design workshop or charrette; a couple of these are held during the discovery phase before anybody starts designing anything. Accordingly, each discipline (represented as small "stacks of cards" in the early stages) should leave each workshop in alignment with one another, with agreed-upon performance goals and the process by which achievement of these goals will be analyzed. After each workshop or "nexus point," the scope of options becomes more focused. Accordingly, continuous value optimization is occurring (indicated by the diminished height of each successive dashed oval in the IP diagram), since the impacts of each discipline's design decisions are understood and synthesized with all other disciplines' decisions in order to understand and analyze the interactions and relationships between all systems and components. This occurs via continuous iterative analysis, as indicated by the looping dashed arrowhead lines in the IP diagram.

As discussed in Chapter 4, the foundation of this integrative design process is the discovery phase. In fact, our experience has shown us that integrative design cannot be achieved cost effectively without this discovery phase. An understanding of the invisible relationships between the basic systems and related subsystems of a project must be gained before the design of any tangible, physical relationships can begin. Every key subsystem issue (along with related budget and cost implications) needs to be brought into

Integrative Process

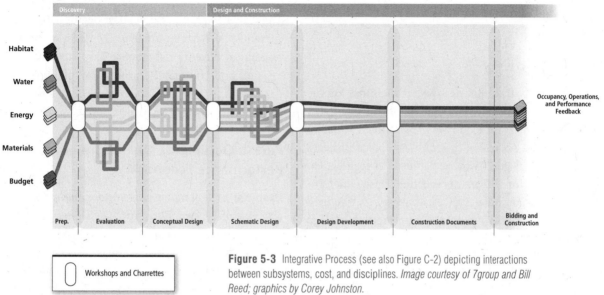

Figure 5-3 Integrative Process (see also Figure C-2) depicting interactions between subsystems, cost, and disciplines. *Image courtesy of 7group and Bill Reed; graphics by Corey Johnston.*

play—the more the better. This requires that the client, the design and construction team members, the community, and other stakeholders representing key issues and subsystems be brought into relationship with each other so that codiscovery can take place. Figure 5-3 (and Figure C-2) graphically illustrates these interactions and provides another lens through which to see the same integrative process depicted in Figure 5-2 and Figure C-1.

The design process should begin by determining, as best as possible, how to increase the beneficial interrelationships between human, biotic, technical, and earth systems (habitat, water, energy, materials). This sounds complex, but again, it is a process akin to what scientists (and structural engineers) refer to as progressive approximation, which Figure 5-3 attempts to illustrate. Understanding these interrelationships becomes the foundation for any design process aimed at saving resources, restoring the health and benefits of natural system processes, and engaging humans in discover-

ing their role in serving as effective stewards and participants in the health of any place. Over the course of the project, then, team members in the design, construction, and operations phases must actively seek to optimize these interrelationships over time—in other words, making sustainable (and best) use of resources, both technical and natural, well into the future.

THREE-PART STRUCTURE

To aid understanding of the basic structure necessary for implementing the integrative design process, we have subdivided the process into three basic parts: (A) discovery; (B) design and construction; and (C) occupancy, operations, and performance feedback. Each of these parts is then further subdivided into a series of *stages.* Following a brief description of the three basic parts, the remainder of this chapter is devoted to an integrative design *Implementation Process Outline,* which describes the tasks associated with each stage in Part A. The tasks associated with Parts B and C are described in Chapters 6 through 8.

Part A: Discovery

We repeatedly find that *discovery* is the most important aspect of integrative design, and in a sense it can be thought of as an extensive expansion of what we currently call *predesign*. It is unlikely that a project's environmental goals will be achieved cost effectively—or at all, for that matter—if this phase is not engaged with rigor and perceived as an explicitly defined phase—and as a new way of thinking about the design process.

Regardless how you may choose to implement the stages described in Part A or in what order you choose to engage this analysis, the key is that everything described in these Part A stages needs to be accomplished before "putting pencil to paper"—in other words, before beginning schematic design, this discovery work needs to be done.

Part B: Design and Construction

The *design and construction* phase begins with what we currently call *schematic design*; as such, it more closely resembles conventional practice in its structure, but it expands and enlivens the process by folding in all of the work and collective understanding of systems interactions reached in discovery.

Part C: Occupancy, Operations, and Performance Feedback

Examining the *occupancy, operations, and performance feedback* phase in any comprehensive way is beyond the scope of this book and likely requires an additional book to give it its full dimension; however, Part C must be considered while engaging parts A and B, since without feedback the relationships between building occupants and their environment do not come alive. In other words, without such postoccupancy feedback, we have no means to assess the degree to which parts A and B successfully addressed their challenges.

PART A—DISCOVERY

Stage A.1
Research and Analysis: Preparation

A.1.0 Prepare *Proposal A*

- Establish scope and fees for initial Goal-Setting Workshop

A.1.1 Fundamental Research for Workshop No. 1

- Site selection: Assess optional sites (if not already selected)
- Context: Identify base ecological conditions and perform preliminary analysis of the four key subsystems:
  - Habitat
  - Water
  - Energy
  - Materials
- Stakeholders: Identify key stakeholders—social and ecological
- Program: Develop initial functional programmatic requirements

A.1.2 Principles and Measurement

- Select rating system and performance measurement criteria

A.1.3 Cost Analysis

- Prepare integrative cost-bundling framework template

A.1.4 Schedule and Fees

- Develop a scheduling template—a *Road Map*—for assigning tasks
- Prepare Agenda for Workshop No. 1

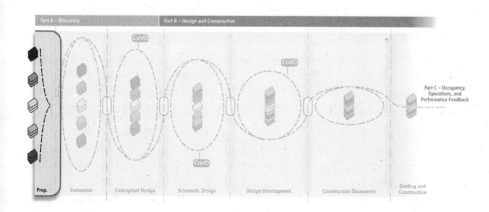

Figure 5-4 Integrative Process Stage A.1, Research and Analysis: "Preparation."*Image courtesy of 7group and Bill Reed; graphics by Corey Johnston.*

Stage A.1

Research and Analysis: Preparation

A.1.0 Prepare *Proposal A*

■ **Establish scope and fees for initial Goal-Setting Workshop**

Because the process of green design is new and the skill sets of team members vary, project design fees can have a wide range of variation. We have found that the following structure is an effective way to establish clear and fair scopes and fees:

■ *Proposal A:* Selected key consultants or team members are asked to submit a fee only for participating in the initial goal-setting workshop and preparing the background research needed for that workshop. This background research and initial goal-setting workshop can be used to set performance goals as well as to define the *integrative process road map,* a scheduling tool. With the goals and process road map established, the consultants have a much more realistic idea of the scope of work required from them for the remainder of the project.

■ *Proposal B:* With this much clearer understanding of scope and schedule, all team members can now assign more accurate fees to the tasks required for the remainder of the project. Proposal B then addresses the duration of the project and is written by each consultant based on the agreed-upon scope and schedule road map developed at the goal-setting workshop (Workshop No. 1).

This Proposal A–Proposal B approach enables a realistic fee proposal from all team members. It creates a fair process for moving forward—less guesswork and frustration for people new to the integrative design process. We have found consistently that both our clients and their design team members prefer this approach.

A.1.1 Fundamental Research for Workshop No. 1

Perform preliminary research and analysis to prepare for Workshop No. 1, the Goal-Setting Workshop (this is a component of the work defined in Proposal A). Without initial research, potential green design opportunities will not be able to be discussed with a high level of rationale (in other words, it will be a "fact-free" meeting). It helps to begin with research and analysis prior to the Goal-Setting Workshop by gathering data pertaining to the four key subsystems. This sets the stage for the initial workshop and provides a framework for continuous analysis and development throughout the entire process. Accordingly, the following should be addressed prior to the Goal-Setting Workshop:

■ **Site selection: Assess optional sites (if not already selected)**

If the site has not been selected yet, an assessment of optional sites relative to environmental impacts and benefits can be extremely beneficial. The tasks and activities listed under *Context* below provide a useful framework for conducting this assessment in order to inform the owner's site-selection decision. Sites often are selected without the benefit of this understanding.

■ **Context: Identify base ecological conditions and perform preliminary analysis of the four key subsystems**

This set of activities consists of researching the project's context; the Latin root of "context" means "weaving together all aspects." This is the beginning of an iterative process—a living research document that evolves with deepening understanding of what is needed to sustain the health of the systems that support life in *this place.*

There are two potential tracks to address—reduce consumption *and* restore the health of the key living systems that the project both influences and is a part of. It is necessary to engage in a preliminary analysis of flows, relationships, and economics between the project's program and the base conditions in the *context* of the following four key subsystems introduced in Chapter 4:

- Habitat (human and other biotic systems)
- Water
- Energy
- Materials

The interrelationships between these subsystems can provide a more integrated view of the whole, which is the essential foundation of the best design decisions.

■ **Habitat**
- Research outdoor air quality issues, for example, ambient particulates generated from any adjacent highways or other pollutant sources, average ambient carbon dioxide levels, etc.
- Investigate human, earth, and biotic systems to understand the patterns of place—a first step in solving for pattern. This involves spending time with the site. Tim Murphy from Regenesis describes this process as "dating" the site, much in the same way that you might use dating as a means of getting to know a potential romantic partner.

- Research both ecological systems (geohydrology, soils, local habitat, etc.) and social systems (history, settlement patterns, etc.). In other words, how have humans and other living and geological systems interacted over time to create the positive and negative aspects of this place? Ask, how might we now do it differently? How can this building project learn from the patterns of how this place has evolved over the past millennium and leverage a deeper understanding of—and therefore influence—the continuing evolution of this place toward more healthy interrelationships?
- Investigate patterns of life in this watershed and region 50, 100, 300, 500, 10,000, and 1 million years ago. This analysis is looking for patterns of social, cultural, and natural system interrelationships—including plant and animal species, soil types, geohydrology, fluvial geomorphology, agriculture, manufacturing, weather, geology, seismic activity, and so on—in order not just to identify what currently exists but also to identify what has existed before and what evolutionary trends toward greater diversity and resilience can be encouraged by our participation.

Design by Discovery—A Story of How Design Emerged from Place

By Pamela Mang

In September 2007, Regenesis Group was asked by Henry Miller Sustainable Partners and the Trust for Sustainable Development to develop a Story of Place™, to be presented at a November master-planning charrette for the Central Park project in McAllen, Texas.

McAllen is in the geographic center of the region termed the Borderplex (or Rioplex), which includes the four U.S. counties in the Rio Grande Valley and the Northern Mexico border cities from Matamoros to Ciudad Mier. The Borderplex population exceeds 2.5 million, placing it among the 25 largest metrolike areas in the United States. At the same time, it is one of the most ecologically diverse areas in the nation.

McAllen itself is a fast-growing, thriving, international retail, trade, and financial center that is consistently

(continued)

top-ranked nationally for its job and income growth and retail sales. In 2000, the City sponsored a visioning process in response to increasing concerns about how to sustain this growth without continued erosion of the natural environment, loss of cultural landscape, and overall poor quality of development. The final report noted the City's desire "to maintain a unique sense of place and identity, strengthen its physical image and character, and remain a leader in the Valley" while continuing to grow economically. Of the projects undertaken over the next few years toward this end, the Central Park project was one of the most complex and ambitious.

The project site, approximately 70 acres of city-owned land, was centrally located near the downtown, the airport, a new convention center, and a major mall that attracts annually nearly a million visitors from Mexico and the surrounding region. The purpose, according to the City's request for proposal (RFP), was to create "a destination attraction for tourists, convention attendees, regional visitors and McAllen residents."

Not surprisingly, given the project's significance, the City had collected a detailed list of the things it wanted, including "a public-private mixed use, lifestyle development with a predominance of higher end and specialty retailers, restaurants and unique venues," and as well "hotel, residences, professional office space, restaurants, boutiques and night clubs … a park and amphitheater, and a location for the potential construction of a museum and planetarium."

The master-planning team put together by the developers included internationally recognized leaders in New Urbanist, mixed-use town-center planning. Given the team's proven design talent—and a site

that was virtually a blank canvas, having been occupied for over sixty years by an old reservoir that the City planned to move—a conventional developer would have handed the team the City's list along with its financial parameters and set it loose to create. But these were not conventional developers.

Through long commitment to and experience in sustainable development, these developers had come to realize that, while green technologies and great design were necessary elements, they were never sufficient. They recognized that the most vital and viable as well as the most enduring sustainable developments grew out of a deep understanding of the place *as a living system* into which they were created. They knew that when that understanding served as the planning and design foundation, far more creative designs and far more effective green technologies emerged.

Given that perspective, the developers commissioned Regenesis to develop a Story of Place™ to be presented at the beginning of a five-day planning charrette. The purpose of the story was twofold: (1) to connect the design team (most of whom had never been to the area prior to the charrette) to the distinctive character and dynamics of McAllen, the region, the people, and the land, and (2) to serve as a unifying and inspiring context, as well as an organizing core for the creative work of the charrette.

Regenesis began the process of story development with research that included historical and contemporary documents, along with field visits to the city and several representative ecosystem sites in the region. A critical part of the process was a series of conversations with more than two dozen people from McAllen and the Rio Grande Valley. They reflected a broad range of historical, current, and future-oriented backgrounds and perspectives. Included were naturalists and environmental scientists and activists, cultural historians, City and community stakeholders in the Central Park project, political leaders, cultural and social activists and thought leaders, and people working on envisioning and articulating a desired future for McAllen.

Working from a framework that saw the site, the city, and the region as three nested wholes, each influencing and being influenced by the others, the team looked for patterns in what shaped the land and what is at the core of how it works; core patterns of how humans shaped and were shaped by the land; and core patterns of how human culture developed and how it works today. In particular, they looked for where ecological and human patterns mirrored and amplified each other through time as a way to begin to understand the core or essence that distinguishes McAllen (and the larger region) and that needed to shape and be reflected in the planning and design of Central Park.

One of the first insights was that the Rio Grande Valley was actually the Rio Grande Delta—the term *valley* was a misnomer, applied by early settlers who felt that the word valley was somehow more attractive. The significance of this is that natural forces, ecosystems, and humans relate and interact very differently in a delta than in a valley. The team worked back and forth between the working of the delta as a natural structure and system of systems and how human life unfolded and organized itself to thrive in that environment. With each iteration, they sought to discover and articulate an increasingly essential understanding. Gradually a triadic framework emerged

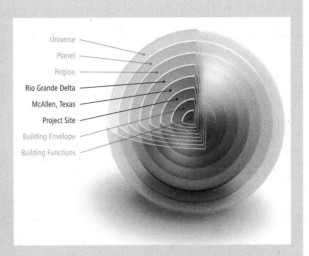

Figure 5-5 Nested systems diagram for McAllen, Texas. *Image courtesy of 7group and Bill Reed; graphics by Corey Johnston*

that depicted the core dynamics shaping the interrelationships of the place (similar to Figure 5-5). This pattern-based framework became the organizing structure for telling the story of the place.

The charrette began Monday morning with a presentation of this story to the design team, which had arrived the previous night, and about twenty local stakeholders, many of whom had participated in the research conversations. The framework was posted on the wall and used throughout the PowerPoint presentation as a way of helping people see the connections between and among the images, facts, and anecdotes presented, as well as their present and future significance for the project and the community.

A community dialogue followed the presentation, and then the design team gathered to begin its work. Given that the team was charged with presenting a substantially complete conceptual master plan, with illustrations, to the same community group on Friday

(continued)

afternoon, the pressure to immediately jump into drawing design ideas and solutions was intense. The developer, committed to creating a place-based design, slowed the team down so that Regenesis could engage them in a facilitated process to translate the story framework into design and process principles and concepts. Over the next several days of work, these became touchstones for an intense but creatively exciting design process, serving as sources of inspiration as well as means for reconciling technical and engineering issues as they came up.

The result? The City and community members greeted the conceptual master plan with excitement, pleased that the team had created a distinctive project that was an authentic reflection of their unique place. Several members of the design and development team said this process brought in a whole new level of creativity, noting that they never would have predicted the outcome based on past work and the ideas they had come in with.

As one of the developers noted, this was truly design by discovery rather than design by decision.

Perhaps equally important was the potential this process offered to the community of McAllen. A shared-story framework—one developed out of a deepening understanding of place—enables us to create our own stories within it. It is a means for keeping the *storying* process alive in how we shape our community, define our identity, and determine what we are uniquely able to contribute. By engaging McAllen with its own story, using a pattern framework, this relatively small-scale project gave the team and the community the basis for continuing the storying process, allowing them to build from the patterns they seek to embed as they continue on the wider process of recreating the physical form, image, character, and sense of place where they live.

▪ Water

- Investigate water flows, water quality, conservation methods, topography, geohydrology, soils, wetlands, adjacent bodies of water, etc.
- Research rainfall rates and perform a basic water-balance study (potential sources and waste: input and output).
- Gather the following basic data to prepare for Workshop No. 1:
  - Annual rainfall (inches per year).
  - Average monthly rainfall (inches per month).
  - Location of sewage treatment plant facilities (map and distance from site). Questions to ask include the following: Is the plant overused? Are any new plants proposed? What is the leakage rate of distribution infrastructure (estimates of infiltration of groundwater into sewage system and/or leakage of sewage into the groundwater)? What is the level of treatment quality and type of treatment? What is the carbon footprint per gallon of sewage treatment?
  - Water sources (map and description of reservoirs, aquifers, wells, lakes, rivers, etc.).
  - Groundwater depth and flow at site; determine the quality of the groundwater.
  - Average water treatment cost (per applicable unit).
  - Average potable water supply cost (per applicable unit).

The Ucross Foundation - Water Harvesting and Gray Water Management Summary for New Facilities
Natural Systems International   11-Jun-08
The following calculations outline estimates for water harvesting and gray water management for the new facilities at Ucross. The buildings can be combined into one single system (if located physically close), or can have independent systems for each of the 3 units.

1. RAINWATER HARVESTING CALCULATIONS - ROOF AREAS ONLY

Roof runoff volumes

Area

Bunkhouse	1,400	sf
Commons	1,250	sf
Existing	1,000	sf
Total Area =	3,650	sf

C =	0.9 for membrane roof	*runoff coefficient*
Collection Eff:	0.85 for membrane roof	*collection efficiency*

Runoff Volume (V = P/12 x Area x C x 7.48 x Collection Efficiency)

month	rainfall (in)	Vol Harvested (gal/month)			
		Bunkhouse	Commons	Existing	Total
Jan.	0.65	434	387	310	1,131
Feb.	0.74	494	441	353	1,288
Mar	0.79	527	471	377	1,375
Apr	0.94	628	560	448	1,636
May	1.33	888	793	634	2,315
June	1.05	701	626	501	1,828
July	2.35	1,569	1,401	1,121	**4,090**
Aug	2.17	1,449	1,293	1,035	3,777
Sept	1.52	1,015	906	725	2,646
Oct	1.11	741	662	529	1,932
Nov.	0.62	414	370	296	1,079
Dec.	0.71	474	423	339	1,236
	13.98	9,333	8,333	6,666	24,332

2. ACTIVE RAINWATER HARVESTING STRATEGY

The following strategy utilizes a subsurface cistern with irrigation pump and overflow to daylight.

Recommended Cistern Size		**3,000**	**gallons (to capture large portion of July runoff)**
Approximate Cost of Cistern	$	2.00	per gallon, installed
Approximate Cost of Cistern	$	6,000.00	installed (subsurface tank)
Approx. Cost of Irrigation pump	$	1,250.00	installed
Total Cistern Estimate =	**$**	**7,250.00**	

Total Engery Costs

Ha =   *550*PumpHP*Pump Efficiency/mass flow rate*
PumpHp =   *Ha*mass flow rate/550*eff of pump*

Irrigation Hours/Day Operation =		1 hr/d	
Pump Flow Rate, Approx =		13 gpm pump flow	1.75 lbm/sec (mass flow rate)
		754 gpd	
Design TDH (ft) for Pumping =		78 ft TDH	33.9 psi
Efficiency of pump =		0.5	
Energy Cost =	$	0.10 $/KWh	
PumpHp =		0.50 HP irrigation pump	
Energy =		0.37 kW	
		0.37 kW-hr/day	
	$	**0.04 per day**	

3. PASSIVE RAINWATER HARVESTING STRATEGY

The following strategy utilizes french drains or 'pumice wicks' to passively harvest, hold and slowly release harvested rainwater. Landscape plants are placed on both sides of the trenches.

Design Rainfall Depth =		1 inch storm
Rock void ratio =		0.4 porosity for 3/4" gravel or pumice
Wick Dimensions:		3 ft deep
		2 ft wide
Approximate Cost	$	20.00 per linear ft

Wick Sizing	Bunkhouse	Commons	Existing	Total	
Design Rainfall Total Volume =	668	596	477	1,741	gallons
Wick Volume Req'd, w/gravel	223	199	159	582	cu. Ft total volume
Total Gravel Req'd, approx =	8.3	7.4	5.9	21.5	cu. Yards gravel
Wick Length =	37	33	27	97	total linear ft
Approximate Cost =	$ 743.75	$ 664.06	$ 531.25	$ 1,939.06	approx. cost
Energy Costs =	$ -	no pumps/moving parts			

Figure 5-6 Sample of a rainfall-trending analysis. This is used to calculate the average amount of water available on a site and to a building over a number of years, which will help determine an optimally sized cistern for water storage. *Image © 2008 Natural Systems International.*

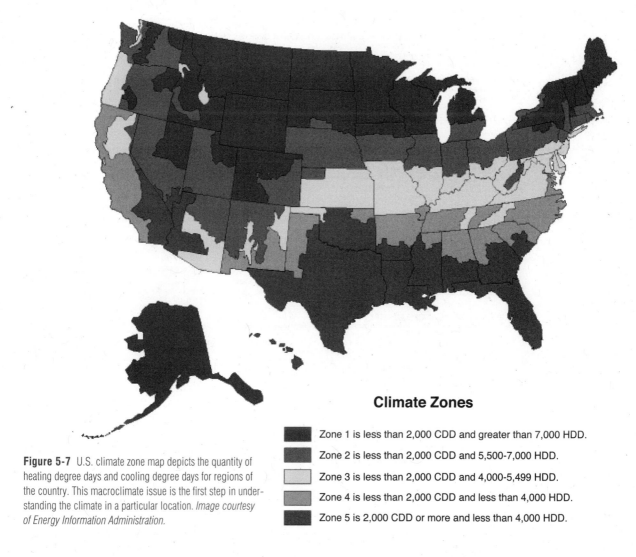

Climate Zones

Zone 1 is less than 2,000 CDD and greater than 7,000 HDD.

Zone 2 is less than 2,000 CDD and 5,500-7,000 HDD.

Zone 3 is less than 2,000 CDD and 4,000-5,499 HDD.

Zone 4 is less than 2,000 CDD and less than 4,000 HDD.

Zone 5 is 2,000 CDD or more and less than 4,000 HDD.

Figure 5-7 U.S. climate zone map depicts the quantity of heating degree days and cooling degree days for regions of the country. This macroclimate issue is the first step in understanding the climate in a particular location. *Image courtesy of Energy Information Administration.*

■ **Energy**

- Understand the climate of the place where the project is located and gather available climatic data in preparation for Workshop No. 1 such as solar and wind capacity, Heating Degree Days, Cooling Degree Days, wind rose, etc.—this should be a significant design driver for most buildings.
- Investigate energy sources, microclimates, utility providers, potential financial incentives, and any additional issues likely to affect the project's energy supply.
- Understand the building's likely distribution of energy consumption by end use.
  - Produce an extremely simple base-case (or "simple box") energy model (described below) with an assumed simple building form to inform the team about the distribution of loads by energy consumption end use in

order to identify where the leverage points are for maximizing impacts.

• Produce an energy-load-distribution chart from the above simple-box modeling output to identify where the dominant energy loads are, thereby identifying opportunities for savings that can result from integrative strategies. It is important to understand the typical heating and cooling load distribution for the projet's building type and size to understand the distribution of energy consumption by end use. The load distribution can vary considerably from project to project, depending on climate and building type. For example, in a school, the lighting typically will be a far greater contributor to overall energy consumption than in a building with high equipment and ventilation loads, such as a hospital.

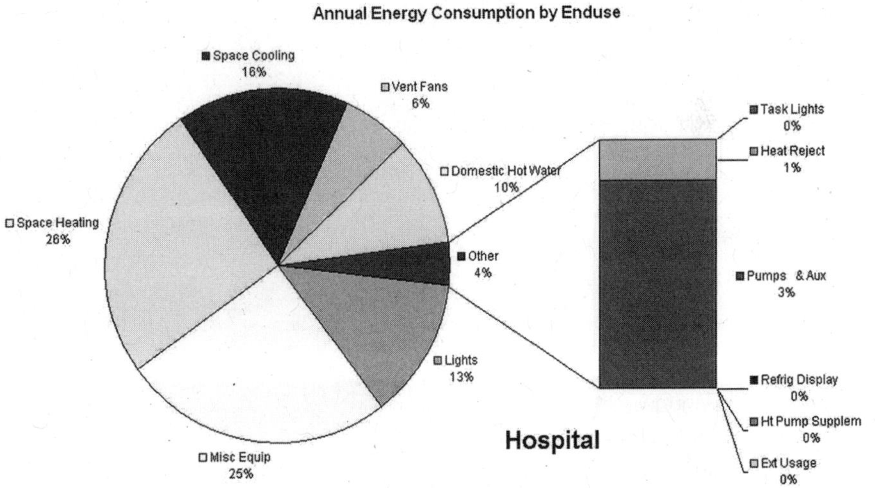

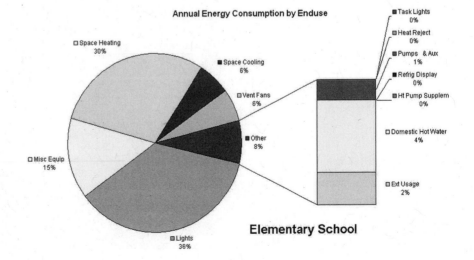

Figure 5-8 Typical energy consumption by end use for a project will vary considerably, depending on the building type, local climate, and other project-specific conditions. Hospital energy use tends to be dominated by heating and cooling loads that are driven by ventilation requirements and equipment needs. *Image courtesy of Cam Fitzgerald.*

Figure 5-9 Typical equipment loads in a school are far less than in hospitals: heating and cooling needs are driven more by the envelope, and lighting often can be the dominant energy user. *Image courtesy of Cam Fitzgerald.*

- This *simple box* (or building-massing model) energy analysis can be used to perform initial evaluation of potential overall energy strategies, such as solar orientation, insulation values, and window-performance levels. Initial modeling iterations could include the following:

1. Building-rotation evaluations demonstrating how a series of 90-degree building rotations affect energy loads.

2. Walls and roof R-value (insulation) evaluations; identify simple low, medium, and high range options.

3. Window-size variations—e.g., vary window-opening sizes by percentage to see relative impacts on energy loads; identify three appropriate options, such as 30, 50, and 70 percent window-to-wall ratios (depending on the climate).

4. Window evaluations with performance criteria for both solar heat gain coefficients and overall U-values; identify simple low, medium, and high range options for windows.

5. A matrix that shows the differences in energy use for each of the above envelope performance parameter levels (low, medium, high) as individual parameters; then put these parameters together in different combinations to see how combined options perform in aggregate relative to each other.

6. Report results in kBTU/square foot/year.

- Understand the building's heating and cooling loads based on the above analysis.

- Determine if the project is likely to be an internal- or external-load dominant building. Small commercial and most residential projects are external-load dominant—that is, exterior conditions tend to affect the building's heating and cooling loads more than internal conditions. As a result, the performance of the building's envelope tends to have a bigger impact than internal loads such as lighting. Larger commercial buildings tend to be

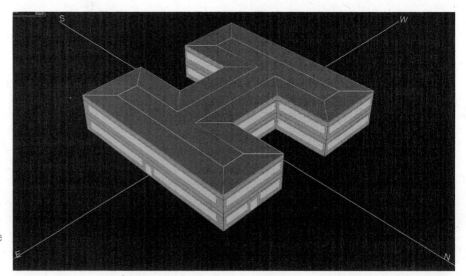

Figure 5-10 Simple box (building-massing) energy model from eQUEST software is used to understand energy distribution by end use and to evaluate early-stage energy decisions. *Image courtesy of Marcus Sheffer.*

RESIDENTIAL - EXTERIOR LOAD DOMINANT

LOAD COMPONENT	COOLING		HEATING
	SENSIBLE	LATENT	
ROOF	405	0	2,203
WALLS	2,543	0	13,023
GLASS	29,717	0	30,616
Subtotal - Shell	32,665	0	45,842
LIGHTING	5,732	0	0
EQUIPMENT	2,159	0	0
PEOPLE	1,000	800	0
VENTILATION	992	1,171	3,486
Subtotal - Internal	9,883	1,971	3,486
TOTAL:	42,548	1,971	49,328.0
SF/TON	646.9		
BTU/SF			20.6

OFFICE - INTERIOR LOAD DOMINANT

LOAD COMPONENT	COOLING		HEATING
	SENSIBLE	LATENT	
ROOF	8,500	0	46,240
WALLS	24,442	0	113,366
GLASS	216,720	0	202,560
Subtotal - Shell	249,662	0	362,166
LIGHTING	204,729	0	0
EQUIPMENT	373,325	0	0
PEOPLE	104,895	188,811	0
VENTILATION	173,442	204,768	609,452
Subtotal - Internal	856,391	393,579	609,452
TOTAL:	1,106,053	393,579	971,618.0
SF/TON	480.1		
BTU/SF			16.2

Figure 5-11 Heating and cooling HVAC load calculations comparing an office to a single-family residence. The shell components dominate the loads for a residence, while the internal loads dominate in a large office. *Image courtesy of Cam Fitzgerald.*

internal-load dominant; internal loads—such as people, equipment, and ventilation—often are far greater contributors to the overall load than the weather outside.

- Benchmark energy performance of similar buildings.
  - Research the typical energy performance for your building type and location, and prepare an *energy-performance report* of findings for presentation at Workshop No. 1. This can

be accomplished by using the Target Finder tool created by the U.S. Environmental Protection Agency (EPA): This web-based tool can be accessed from a link at www.energystar.gov/index.cfm?c=new_bldg_design.bus_target_finder (accessed January 2009).

- The EPA's Target Finder currently uses data from the 2003 Commercial Buildings Energy Consumption Survey (CBECS), a product of the U.S. Department of Energy (DOE) Energy Information Administration; this online tool provides energy data for numerous building types in different locations throughout the country; for the remainder of building types, Target Finder provides a methodology for benchmarking, using CBECS data or other sources. Employing this simple, user-friendly tool takes only a few minutes. The first step requires inputting the project's zipcode along with some brief information about the facility's characteristics, such as building type, gross floor area, operating hours, and so on. The tool can then help teams establish energy performance targets relative to similar buildings in the CBECS database. For example, by choosing a Target Rating at 50 (based on an EPA performance rating scale of 1–100, whereby 75 or higher denotes an ENERGY STAR building), the tool will display the associated energy use for an average building of similar type, size, and location; by setting the Target Rating at 90, the tool will display energy use data for a building in the 90th percentile of performance (or the top 10% of low-energy consumption), and so on. This site also allows teams to set energy performance targets by choosing an Energy Reduction Target, which is the percentage of energy consumption reduction desired relative to a benchmark building. The benchmark in Target Finder is the average energy consumption of a similar building (one with an EPA Target Rating of 50). Accordingly, choosing an Energy Reduction Target of 60% will provide energy use data for a similar building that consumes 60% less energy than this benchmark.

- Project energy performance also can be informed by the 2030 Challenge; for more information, see the Web site at www.architecture2030.org/home.html. The 2030 Challenge sets forth energy performance goals of 50 percent less energy consumption for new buildings compared to the average building as defined by the CBECS data. In 2010 the target increases to 60 percent. Then the target increases by 10 percent every five years, until we are building carbon neutral buildings by the year 2030.
- Additional potential benchmarks could include the energy used by similar facilities. The owner's existing facility could be used for comparative purposes, which may be useful to assist in the establishment of an energy performance target.
- An energy-performance report—containing all the germane information gained from the benchmark sources listed above—will serve as an effective tool at Workshop No. 1; it will provide participants with the information they will need to establish energy-performance goals (see Figure 5-12).

Materials

- Identify local building materials: sources of basic raw materials and manufacturing facilities for basic or likely materials such as concrete, stone, brick, concrete block, steel, wood, glass, etc.

- Identify alternative and indigenous building materials and building techniques used historically in the place.
- Identify local recycling infrastructure to determine capabilities for recycling construction and demolition waste.
- Evaluate alternative transportation resources and, potentially, investigate options for locating the project.
- Research potential for obtaining life cycle inventory data for the project's location and various likely materials.

Stakeholders: Identify key stakeholders—social and ecological

Identify stakeholders from key human, earth, and other biotic systems that will interact with the project. Our experience has taught us that when all identified human stakeholders work in an integrative process, the synthesis of multiple areas of expertise creates a kind of composite master builder, as discussed in Chapter 2 (See Figure 2-14). You may recall that three typical groups of stakeholders are important, hence they all should be included in the Goal-Setting Workshop, if possible: (1) all design team members; (2) the client (including the owner), and; (3) construction professionals (hopefully, the builder). Not all of the team members indicated in Figure 2-14 participate in all green projects, but each is responsible for a system or components that impact nearly all others. In addition, representatives of the ecological, social, and community context (specific to the place) are often left out of the design process. These representatives should be included, depending on the scope of the project.

- Incorporating input from all key stakeholders and members of the design team before schematic design begins is essential, particularly because 70 percent of the decisions associated with en-

Figure 5-12 Energy benchmarking report showing Target Finder results and Commercial Buildings Energy Consumption Survey (CBECS) data used to help inform team discussions (during Workshop No. 1) aimed at reaching consensus about energy-performance targets. *Image courtesy of Marcus Sheffer.*

Evaluating Building Energy Performance - Miami Trace Middle School

7group

Design Intent
To develop the buidling design to significantly reduce energy consumption and cost compared to standard practice. Frequently design decisions are made without fully assessing the impacts on future operating cost. One tool we use to establish a building performance target, evaluate building perfromance and as a reality check for the energy modeling results in US EPA's Target Finder.

Energy Star Target Finder
The US EPA's Energy Star Target Finder is a tool used to assist the design team in setting an energy performance target in terms of site energy use intensity and estimated total annual energy consumption. The database used by Target Finder is the US Department of Energy's Commercial Building Energy Consumption Survey (CBECS). By entering a few of the project's facility characteristics (i.e. location of project for local climate and weather data, building type, area, occpancy levels, and hours of operation), the CBECS data can be accessed and normalized. The normalized data is then ranked on a scale of 1-100. As the design progresses, estimated annual energy use can be compared to the normalized CBECS data to monitor the design's energy performance.

Building Characteristics

Zip Code	43160	City	Washington Court House	State		Ohio	
Space Type (see Notes below)		Gross Floor Area	Number of Occupants	Number of PCs		Operating Hours / Week	
K-12 School		92,000	622	300		60	

Utility Rates

Electricity	NA			Natural Gas	NA		

Energy Star Target Finder Results

Energy Data	50	75	90	100		
Target Finder Rating	50	75	90	100		
Site Energy Use Intensity (kBtu/Sq./yr)	73.5	58.8	44.3	27.7		
Estimated Total Annual Energy (kBtu)	6,764,050.0	5,405,912.0	4,075,473.0	2,544,147.0		
Total Annual Energy Cost ($)	$103,876	$83,019	$62,587	$39,071		
Site Energy Cost Intensity ($/Sf)	$1.13	$0.90	$0.68	$0.42	$0.00	$0.00

Notes:
The US DOE's CBECS database used in Target Finder has a limited number of building types.

Energy Star Target Finder Disclaimer:
"An incomplete energy use profile could result in a high but inaccurate rating. Total annual estimated energy use must include plug, process, and all non-regulated loads: equipment loads specified on drawings: and all fuel sources."

Energy Opportunities, Inc Disclaimer
Due to the lack of detailed information during schematic design, many assumptions and default values as described in previous sections were used for the eQuest energy analysis. The above results are not guaranteed and should be viewed in relative terms only.

Evaluating Building Energy Performance - Miami Trace Middle School

7group

US Department of Energy - Energy Information Administration
Commercial Buildings Energy Consumption Survey, 2003

CBECS data is produced by the US DOE every four years based on a survey of thousands of commercial building from all over the United States. The data is based on actual building energy consumption and cost. This data represents the average of thousands of buildings of various size, age, types of construction, location, and energy sources. It is useful to compare the modeling results to these values as a reality check and to enable realistic goal setting of project energy performance.

	Energy Intensity (kBtu/square foot)					Energy Cost ($/square foot)		
Building Type	National Average	Northeast	Middle Atlantic	Climate Zone 3	Building Type	National Average	Northeast	
All	89.8	98.5	98.3	98.5	All	$1.43	$1.65	
Education	83.1	101.6	103.1	93.5	Education	$1.22	$1.49	
Food Service	258.3	272.8	290.2	247.6	Food Service	$4.15	$4.84	
Health Care	187.7	212.2	219.0	191.4	Health Care	$2.35	$2.82	
Retail	73.9	65.0	72.3	97.1	Retail	$1.39	$1.33	
Office	92.9	101.2	98.0	95.4	Office	$1.71	$2.07	
Public Assembly	93.9	89.2	98.0	87.3	Public Assembly	$1.47	$1.27	
Public Order & Safe	115.8	132.5	NA	NA	Public Order & Safe	$1.76	$2.09	
Religious Worship	43.5	52.1	58.1	52.8	Religious Worship	$0.65	$0.68	
Warehouse	45.2	41.6	49.2	49.5	Warehouse	$0.68	$0.69	

The 2030 Challenge

The American Institue of Architects, the US Conference of Mayors, US Green Building Council and many other organizations have adopted the 2030 Challenge to eliminate fossil fuel energy use in buildings by 2030. All projects are challenged to obtain an immediate 50% reduction in energy intensity relative to the national average figures above. The reduction is scheduled to increase over time according to the following schedule:
60% in 2010
70% in 2015
80% in 2020
90% in 2025
Carbon-neutral in 2030 (using no fossil fuel GHG emitting energy to operate).
These targets may be accomplished by implementing innovative sustainable design strategies, generating on-site renewable power and/or purchasing (20% maximum) renewable energy and/or certified renewable energy credits. For more information visit - http://www.architecture2030.org

Miami Trace Middle School Target	?? kBTU/sf/year

vironmental impacts are made during the first 10 percent of the design process.

■ Select the right team members based on expertise needed to address each key subsystem; include team members who can respond to the project objectives and opportunities. Assess whether the expertise needed for each subsystem can be addressed by separate individuals or the combined knowledge of one person, based on project parameters.

■ Recognize where additional experience may be needed beyond the typical disciplines associated with the four key subsystems to achieve effective integration; consultants with such experience likely will include: an experienced energy modeler; daylighting modeler; lighting designer; landscape architect or civil engineer with an ecological systems background; building science expert; green material and specifications expert; a facilitator for team workshops; and so forth.

■ Commissioning (Cx): develop an RFP for soliciting Cx services. We have found it helpful to use a template for such an RFP that can be given to the owner before the first workshop; this template can be tailored in size, scope definition, systems to be commissioned, etc., to match the intended specifics of each particular job as it evolves. If possible, the Commissioning Authority (CxA) should be hired at this point to ensure that the CxA is available to participate in the first workshop.

■ It should be noted that additional team members may need to be added later; this will be determined by identifying any further needs at Workshop No. 1.

■ For a more advanced whole-systems approach, some additional expertise may include: a systems ecologist or systems permaculturist; geo-

hydrologist; restoration biologist; community facilitator; social historian; etc.

■ **Program: Develop initial functional programmatic requirements**

Develop an understanding of the basic areas, functions, proximities, and adjacencies of the typical building program, or "brief." This initial program document significantly informs the first pass at creating the Owner's Project Requirements (OPR) to initiate the commissioning process during *Stage A.2.*

A.1.2   Principles and Measurement

■ **Select rating system and performance measurement criteria**

The LEED program, along with other green building rating systems and assessment tools, can serve as a useful tool for establishing project targets by utilizing the benchmarks and metrics it has established, through a consensus process, for measuring performance. Other rating systems and analysis tools include: Green Guide for Healthcare (GGHC), Labs21, Living Building Challenge, CO_2 balancing, ecological footprint, life cycle assessment (LCA), Natural Step, SBTool from International Initiative for a Sustainable Built Environment (iiSBE), BREAM in the United Kingdom, CASBEE in Japan, etc.

We have found that LEED can provide a valuable framework for introducing and identifying issues to be addressed. It also can be used to look for interactions between credits and to explore strategies that contribute to earning multiple credits and achieving multiple intents, since it provides an outline of many of the issues that need to be integrated. However, LEED is *just* a tool—a tool that, if used poorly, can lead teams into a point-shopping exercise. (See the "LEED as a Tool" sidebar in *Stage A.2.*)

A.1.3 Cost Analysis

■ **Prepare integrative cost–bundling framework template**

It is a bit early to begin assigning costs to systems and components; however, it is helpful during this first stage to set up a framework of costs listed or grouped by broad function, such as foundations, envelope, mechanical systems, electrical systems, and so forth. This listing gives team members reference points for recognizing, connecting, and recording relationships between systems. In other words, it provides the framework template, in the form of a spreadsheet, for integrative *cost bundling* (see *Stage A3.3*). This document can be created with blank cells for future use; its use will be described further in subsequent stages.

A.1.4 Schedule and Fees

■ **Develop a scheduling template—a Road Map— for assigning tasks**

Develop a schedule and task spreadsheet template, or *integrative process road map* (as discussed in *Stage A.2.1* below), possibly with some assumptions about time frames and task definitions for the Discovery and Schematic Design phases that the team can begin modifying at Workshop No. 1. (An example of an Integrative Process Road Map, developed during *Stage A.3* on a recent project, is shown in Figure 5-13). This will help team members better understand:

■ The detailed scope of integrative design work (interactions and tasks) for the project.

■ The issues that will need to be addressed that may have been mentioned, but only generally or vaguely, in the RFP.

■ The specific tasks and interactions between team members, so that a *Proposal B* can be written more accurately and fairly.

■ The process of examining this detailed scheduling with the team provides a greater opportunity for team members to be aligned around the interactions required by this highly iterative process and helps them to avoid operating on more conventionalized assumptions.

■ **Prepare Agenda for Workshop No. 1**

We have found it extremely important to include input from the primary team members when developing the agenda for this first workshop. This can be accomplished by scheduling a conference call with the appropriate team leaders. The discussion during this call should center on the project team's expected outcomes so that the team's efforts can focus on and align around expectations.

A perception about the nature of agendas should be noted here: in our experience, slavish adherence to established agenda activities and time frames actually can stop valuable discussion dead in its tracks during workshops, limiting outcomes and resultant accomplishments. The most important function of an agenda is to establish and outline the purpose and objectives of the workshop. Achieving the team's objectives and alignment is the bottom-line metric for whether or not a meeting was successful, not whether or not preconceived time frames or tasks were met during the workshop. Therefore, flexibility coupled with an agenda that outlines objectives provides the best combination for success. A powerful core principle to remember when facilitating, managing, or striving to elicit successful outcomes in meetings is simply: "follow the energy in the room."

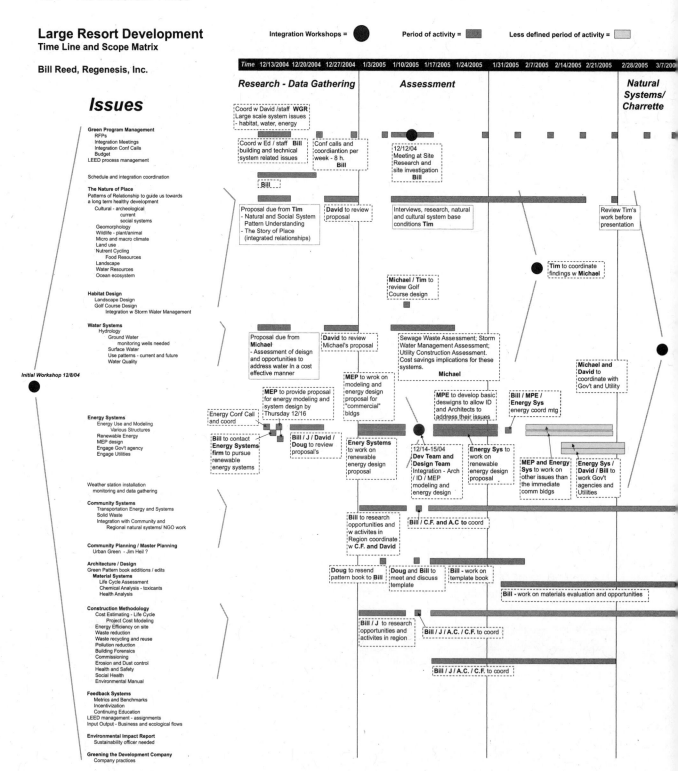

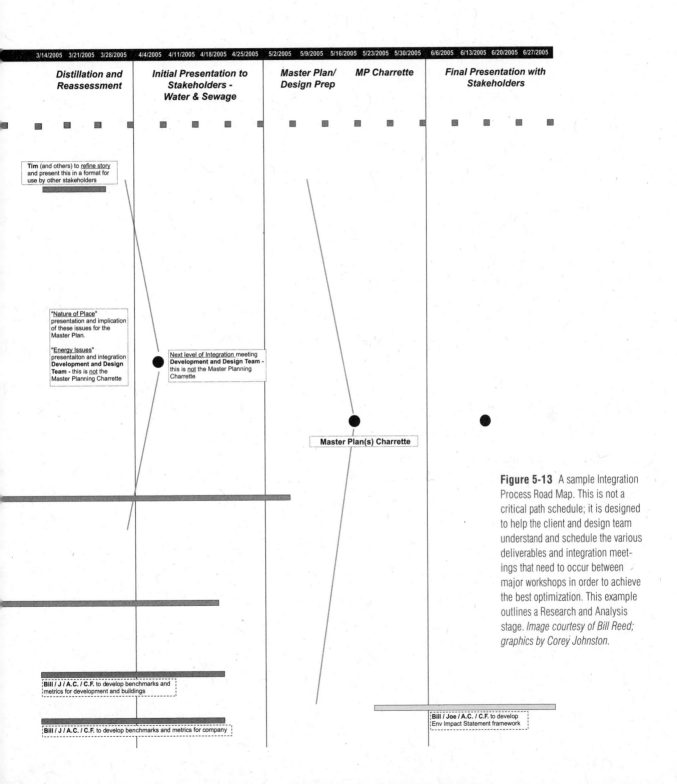

| 3/14/2005 | 3/21/2005 | 3/28/2005 | 4/4/2005 | 4/11/2005 | 4/18/2005 | 4/25/2005 | 5/2/2005 | 5/9/2005 | 5/16/2005 | 5/23/2005 | 5/30/2005 | 6/6/2005 | 6/13/2005 | 6/20/2005 | 6/27/2005 |

Distillation and Reassessment

Initial Presentation to Stakeholders - Water & Sewage

Master Plan/ Design Prep

MP Charrette

Final Presentation with Stakeholders

Tim (and others) to refine story and present this in a format for use by other stakeholders

"Nature of Place" presentation and implication of these issues for the Master Plan.

"Energy Issues" presentaiton and integration **Development and Design Team -** this is <u>not</u> the Master Planning Charrette

Next level of Integration meeting **Development and Design Team -** this is <u>not</u> the Master Planning Charrette

Master Plan(s) Charrette

Bill / J / A.C. / C.F. to develop benchmarks and metrics for development and buildings

Bill / J / A.C. / C.F. to develop benchmarks and metrics for company

Bill / Joe / A.C. / C.F. to develop Env Impact Statement framework

Figure 5-13 A sample Integration Process Road Map. This is not a critical path schedule; it is designed to help the client and design team understand and schedule the various deliverables and integration meetings that need to occur between major workshops in order to achieve the best optimization. This example outlines a Research and Analysis stage. *Image courtesy of Bill Reed; graphics by Corey Johnston.*

Stage A.2

Workshop No. 1: Alignment of Purpose and Goal-Setting

A.2.1 Workshop No. 1: Tasks and Activities

- Introduce participants to the fundamentals of the integrative design process and to systems thinking
- Elicit client's deeper intentions and purpose for the project
- Engage Touchstones exercise to elicit stakeholders' values and aspirations
- Clarify functional and programmatic goals
- Establish initial Principles, Metrics, Benchmarks, and Performance Targets for the four key subsystems:
  - Habitat
  - Water
  - Energy
  - Materials
- Generate potential strategies for achieving identified Performance Targets
- Determine order-of-magnitude cost impacts of proposed strategies
- Provide time for reflection and feedback from client and team members
- Develop an Integrative Process Road Map that identifies responsibilities, deliverables, and dates
- Commissioning: Initiate documentation of the Owner's Project Requirements (OPR)

A.2.2 Principles and Measurement

- Document Touchstones, Principles, Metrics, Benchmarks, and Performance Targets from Workshop No. 1

A.2.3 Cost Analysis

- Document order-of-magnitude cost impacts of proposed strategies to reflect input from Workshop No. 1

A.2.4 Schedule and Next Steps

- Adjust Integrative Process Road Map to reflect input from Workshop No. 1
- Distribute Workshop No. 1 report

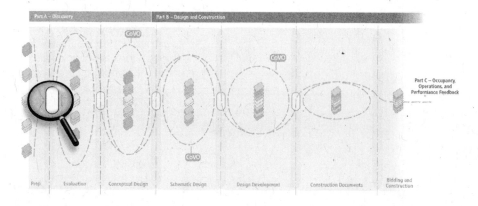

Figure 5-14 Integrative Process Stage A.2, Workshop #1: "Alignment of Purpose and Goal-Setting." *Image courtesy of 7group and Bill Reed; graphics by Corey Johnston.*

Stage A.2

Workshop No. 1: Alignment of Purpose and Goal-Setting

We recently were hired to facilitate a two-day goal-setting charrette for an ecoresort on a Caribbean island. About a week before the scheduled date of the charrette, the owner called expressing concern about the agenda we had sent her. She had two concerns: 1) time and money ("Do we really need all of these people to attend?") and 2) possible lack of alignment of goals ("There is nowhere in this agenda that talks about zero carbon, and that's our goal. I'm concerned that we are not in alignment.")

We asked, "How are you defining your carbon goals?"

She responded, "Zero carbon."

"Do you mean carbon neutrality?"

She said, "No, I mean zero carbon."

"With all due respect, that's not possible; however, we think what you are saying is that you want to neutralize your carbon footprint." Then we asked, "If that's the case, what is the scope that you want to include in calculating that footprint?"

Her reply: "Everything."

"Okay, does that include the embodied energy emissions associated with building materials—their extraction, fabrication, transportation, and construction?"

She said, "Yes, it's everything."

"Does this include transportation impacts during operations?"

She said, "Yes, it's everything." Then she elaborated, "We are planning on using vegetable oil from the island's many restaurants to fuel all of our vehicles."

We responded, "That's really good, but it doesn't completely neutralize carbon emissions, because it still involves combustion."

She replied, "Now I'm really concerned, because I don't think you get it. We want to achieve zero carbon."

At this point, it flashed through our heads that we may have reached a "go or no-go" decision point in the conversation regarding our interest in this project and our ability to develop a relationship of colearning.

So we asked, "Where is water coming from for this project?"

She replied, "We're building a desalination plant."

"Well, if that's the case, we'll need to figure out how to neutralize the emissions generated by the significant energy needed to desalinate water."

She suddenly got very quiet. After a long pause, she said, "Oh, maybe I don't understand zero carbon like I thought I did."

What happened in this conversation serves as a tiny example of why the Goal-Setting Workshop serves as a critical contributor to the integrative process—it creates alignment. Without alignment around the source and meaning of the project's goals, we may not understand the real purpose behind them, and then we might miss the larger target and its essential aspects. It also illustrates an initial example of how we need to function as colearners; in short, we needed to learn the nature of our client's goals and the purpose behind them—as did she. This discussion set the stage for much more fruitful interaction and alignment around purpose at the approaching goal-setting workshop (Workshop No. 1), thereby increasing the potential for the project's success.

On the development project in the Teton Valley, Idaho, that was introduced at the end of Chapter 3, our client became far more willing to engage the project's targeted goals—such as no pesticides, native planting, etc.—once the fundamental principles that underlie these goals were clearly explained. Then, once the client representatives gained a more complete understanding of these principles, they began to refer to them as "unarguable principles," as discussed in Chapter 4. As a result, each of the performance targets and goals (including LEED points) were viewed as far less arbitrary and far more meaningful.

In order to create such alignment, all of the project's key team members should be present at Workshop No. 1, so that team buy in and a sense of "ownership by all" develops. Accordingly, at a minimum, we have found that the following team members should participate:

- Owner
- Owner's representative with primary fiduciary responsibility
- Owner's facilities and building operations manager
- Representative building users
- Architect
- HVAC engineer
- Electrical engineer
- Plumbing engineer
- Civil engineer
- Landscape Architect
- Builder and/or Construction Manager
- Commissioning Authority

The above list of team members is intended to identify the expertise necessary at this and subsequent workshops, and it may not necessarily require that different individuals represent each of the indicated disciplines—a single individual on the team may possess adequate expertise in multiple areas. In other words, what matters is that each of these areas of expertise be represented at a level appropriate to the project.

The role of the *builder* or *constructor* deserves special mention here. It is our experience that the earlier the builder who will construct the project is involved in a meaningful way—and the more that builder's expertise is integrated into the process at the earliest possible stage—the more successful the result in all ways. This is the case not only from the standpoint of constructability and cost but also from the standpoint of the quality and elegance of the design. In some ways then, the integrative design process can be somewhat enhanced in a design-build construction delivery scenario. However, the purpose of this book is not to examine the dozens of different permutations of design-build we have seen, nor to engage in a detailed discussion of the pros and cons we have experienced in this regard; rather, suffice it to say that the earlier everybody is involved in the process, the better. Remember the four Es from Chapter 4?: Everybody, Engaging, Everything, Early.

Depending on the extent of integration, project complexity, and unique project requirements, other participants and consultants may include:

- Energy modeler (if this expertise is not possessed by the HVAC engineer)
- Daylight analyst
- Lighting designer
- Acoustical engineer
- Building forensics specialist (regarding mold, building envelope, etc.)
- Systems ecologist
- Biologist or botanist
- Permaculturist
- Habitat restoration consultant
- Productivity analyst
- Materials and LCA consultant
- Community members
- Code officials
- Municipal officials

- Traffic engineer
- Planner
- Product manufacturers

A.2.1 Workshop No. 1: Tasks and Activities (Goal-Setting Workshop)

It is important to note at this point that this book is not intended to serve as a meeting-management primer or a charrette-facilitation guide; accordingly, it will be assumed throughout that logistical issues for workshops (such as publishing agendas, arranging appropriate venues, scheduling refreshments, identifying audiovisual needs, or presenting facilitation techniques), are understood by the reader or can be researched elsewhere.* However, we have found that the following outline can be used to create an agenda for Workshop No. 1 and can be tailored to the specific parameters of each project.

■ Introduce participants to the fundamentals of the integrative design process and to systems thinking

We have found that kicking off this workshop by presenting the concept of integrative design with illustrated and concrete examples from case studies (for a total presentation time of about an hour) sets the stage for engaging teams in a systems-thinking approach. If the team already has experience with an integrative process, this presentation need not be too detailed; but it is rare that all members of a design team arrive with the same level of experience, so comprehension by all attendees should not be assumed. In some cases, the design team members might be quite familiar with an integrative approach, but project owners rarely are, so providing an educational session about this approach should not be overlooked.

■ Elicit client's deeper intentions and purpose for the project

- Leverage the client's mission (purpose) and aspirations, if possible. Spend a bit of time reflecting on how the project can help the client move toward achieving their deepest purpose and objectives. Grounding the group in the stated values and mission statement of the client's organization often allows this to happen.
- This exercise has revealed to us that profit by itself rarely is the only, or even primary, reason for building a building. Often, for example, the intentions of leaving a great legacy or helping people to achieve a higher quality of life are cited by our clients. It is important to make explicit these drivers, because they can shape a project's sustainability objectives more effectively than technical efficiency or economic examples alone.

■ Engage Touchstones exercise to elicit stakeholders' values and aspirations

- This exercise (and the evolution of our use of it) is described in detail in Chapter 4. It serves as an extremely valuable tool for gaining team alignment around performance goals and the team's ownership of the project's objectives.
- Getting alignment around the team's and stakeholder's real aspirations is essential—if this does not occur, the design process may fall back to the default mode of repeating the patterns of conventional design.

---

* Charrette facilitation resources, among others, include the following: *A Handbook for Planning and Conducting Charrettes for High Performance Projects*, National Renewable Energy Laboratory, Golden, Colorado, August 2003, http://www.eere.energy.gov/buildings/highperformance/charrette_handbook.html (accessed October 1, 2008); "Planning and Conducting Integrated Design (ID) Charrettes," Joel Ann Todd, Environmental Consultant, and Gail Lindsey, FAIA, Principal, Design Harmony (updated 5/22/08), in the *Whole Building Design Guide* (Washington, DC: National Institute of Building Sciences, 2008), http://www.wbdg.org/resources/charrettes.php (accessed October 1, 2008); "Eco-Charrettes Save Resources, Build Teams," Nathan Good (Washington, DC: American Institute of Architects, 2003), http://www.aia.org/SiteObjects/files/18-11-02.pdf; *The Charrette Handbook* [available only on the web or by taking their courses] and numerous other resources from the National Charrette Institute (NCI) at http://www.charretteinstitute.org.

■ We have found that when time allows, taking this exercise much further into an exploration of more deeply felt Core Values as a facilitated exercise can get the team more closely aligned around principles and objectives—this gives team members permission to reflect more deeply and perhaps put issues on the table that are more heartfelt and not normally addressed. The deeper the team delves into values and aspirations—and the deeper this foundation is built—the more successful the project becomes in terms of both environmental and economic performance.

■ To help make sure these values, aspirations, and environmental objectives do not get lost in the intensity of the design, construction, and operation process, it is useful to have "champions," based on their discipline, assigned to issues they particularly care about or for which their discipline is logically responsible. A manager or partner-level person, ideally, would take on the responsibility of champion for these issues, as they are ensured a powerful voice at the design table. An entry-level staff member or intern should NOT take on this role, since such staff members are rarely given a powerful enough voice.

■ Additionally, a Core Team can also be established to focus on evolving these values and aspirations. The Core Team should be composed of key team members and stakeholders who will be responsible for holding the higher aspirations of the project. This Core Team does not operate on day-to-day management issues, although some members may be in a management position; rather, the Core Team takes responsibility for holding the evolutionary capability of the project throughout its life. Its purpose is to maintain, build upon, improve, and evolve the project's aspirations for sustainable performance over time.

■ **Clarify functional and programmatic goals**

Verify and clarify the conventional functional program—space and site functions, area quantities, adjacencies, parking requirements, etc. Sometimes, this requires a separate exercise during the workshop to more clearly define the owner's program requirements and to convey a more thorough understanding of these program requirements to all team members.

■ **Establish initial Principles, Metrics, Benchmarks, and Performance Targets for the four key subsystems**

To begin this discussion we need to look at the following definitions:

Principle: a fundamental truth that is a basis for action

Metric: how we measure

Benchmark: the standard against which we measure performance

Performance Target: a measurable, quantifiable, and verifiable performance goal established by the team

Reaching initial consensus on performance goals for the four key subsystems is a primary task at this workshop, so that everyone departs in alignment and owns collectively these Principles and their related Performance Targets. The following list provides an example of one such Principle for each of the four key subsystems and a related Performance Target. Please note that there are many more principles involved, depending on how deeply the team wishes to pursue relationships with living systems; the purpose of the list below is simply to provide the reader with examples of such principles,

■ **Habitat** (human and other biotic systems)

Let's revisit from Chapter 4 the following list of fundamental principles associated with habitat:

- All human activities should partner with living systems in mutually beneficial relationships, and a project should contribute to supporting the systems of life on its site and within its watershed.
- Understand and respect local ecological and social systems.
- Build in feedback mechanisms (and pattern feedback systems), because they are essential to continuously evolving these relationships.

Here is an example of translating one of these Principles into a Performance Target:

- *Principle*: The project will support the systems of life on its site and within its watershed.
- *Performance Target* example: Select 100 percent of the plant species in the project's landscaping from options that will support the avian and terrestrial species currently or formerly present in the region.
- *To achieve this target*, the following strategies may be explored: landscape design practices such as xeriscaping, planting of indigenous species, reestablishment of ground water flows and fluvial morphology, habitat corridor connections, avoidance and/or elimination of monocultures, etc.

Water

Recall from Chapter 4 the following list of fundamental principles associated with water:

- Water budget should be equal to or less than annual rainfall on-site.
- Use less water.
- Retain all rainwater on-site.
- Manage water (rainwater or wastewater) to replicate natural flows in order to minimize water leaving the site.
- Cascade water use to support all life (human and other biotic systems), if water will be leaving the site.
- Recharge groundwater table (where possible).

- Clean all water to potable standards before it leaves the site.

Here is an example of translating one of these Principles into a Performance Target:

- *Principle:* The project will retain all rainwater on-site.
- *Performance Target* example: The project's water consumption *shall not* exceed the site's annual rainfall volume; 100% of this volume will be captured via rainwater harvesting, and 100% of wastewater generated by the building will be treated and reused on-site.
- *To achieve this target*, site water balancing analysis that calculates annual rainfall volume, annual building consumption, and annual sewage generated will need to occur; additional related issues such as water quality, wastewater treatment options, cistern options and sizing, etc., likely will need to be addressed as well.

Energy

In Chapter 4 we listed the following fundamental principles associated with energy:

- Create less demand via use of insulation, demand patterns, reduced loads, etc.
- Use available site energies—e.g., sources and sinks—sun, wind, earth coupling (such as ground coupling, water coupling, etc.), and diurnal cycles.
- Increase efficiency of what is left—e.g., equipment, appliances, diversity factors, parasitic losses, part-load performance, etc.
- Minimize or neutralize carbon footprint

Here is an example of translating one of these Principles into a Performance Target:

- *Principle*: The project will minimize its carbon footprint.
- *Performance Target* example: The project will reduce its annual energy consumption by 50

percent relative to an agreed-upon benchmark. Half of the remaining energy demand will be supplied by on-site renewable generation, and the remainder by purchasing green power.

- *To achieve this target*, overall energy performance goals and specific performance parameters and metrics related to those goals will need to be addressed and iterated via parametric energy modeling—parameters include, for example, building envelope options, lighting power density targets, square feet per ton of cooling equipment capacity, plug load power density, etc.

During the initial goal-setting workshop, it is important to discuss the overall energy performance expectations for the project. The old adage that "you can't manage what you don't measure" certainly applies to building design. Instead of establishing specific performance goals, many project teams rely on platitudes like "the project will be *energy efficient,*" without giving any meaning to that term and without quantifying any measurable target. The research and analysis prepared prior to the workshop in the preparation stage (Stage A.1), as discussed above, should be reviewed and discussed at Workshop No. 1. Data from the EPA's Target Finder, CBECS, the 2030 Challenge, and other sources should be used to establish the project's performance target.

Quite often, we have found that designers will raise the issue that much of the project's energy use is beyond their control, for example, energy consumption attributable to the building's plug loads. While this can be true to a certain extent, it is critically important for the design team to think of itself as a whole project team, one that includes the owner or representatives of the owner to adequately account for all building energy use. Energy-consuming items outside the control

Miami Trace Middle School Target	40 kBTU/sf-year

Figure 5-15 Energy efficiency can be defined by a single metric, which often is expressed in kBTU/square foot/year. The agreed-upon energy performance target discussed during Workshop No. 1 is recorded on the energy benchmarking report (see Figure 5-12). *Image courtesy of Marcus Sheffer.*

of the design team should be discussed so that the building owner can make more fully informed decisions about issues that affect project design decisions.

If we hope to produce *energy-efficient* buildings, we must define that term in the context of each specific project. Initiating the discussion in a goal-setting session is the first step.

■ Materials

Recall from Chapter 4 the following list of fundamental principles associated with materials:

- Use less—that which is not used has no environmental impact.
- Use materials that are abundant and renewable and that do not destroy human and/or earth systems in their extraction, manufacture, and disposal.
- Use locally sourced, recyclable, nontoxic, and/or low embodied energy materials.

The following is an example of translating one of these Principles into a Performance Target:

- *Principle*: The project will maximize its use of materials indigenous to its region.
- *Performance Target* example: Half (50%) of the project's materials will be harvested, extracted, recovered, and manufactured from within a one-hundred-mile radius of the project site.
- *To achieve this target,* the project team likely will need to do some product research.

Even better, the project team could use LCA tools to evaluate overall environmental impacts of materials choices relative to significant indicators such as embodied energy, human toxicity, eutrophication, ozone depletion, etc.

As discussed in *Stage A.1,* LEED can serve as a powerful tool for listing an array of project targets by utilizing the benchmarks and metrics it has established, through a consensus process, for measuring performance. Therefore, given the popularity and market transformation principles of LEED, these performance targets often are used. However, it is not difficult to shift the focus of the team onto the *intents* of each credit, since these *intent* statements serve as the basis of the metrics and benchmarks of LEED. Walking the team through the *intentions* behind the LEED checklist on a credit-by-credit basis can serve as a primary generator of the project's principles during the goal-setting workshop (Workshop No. 1). These principles can then be used to think deeply into what lies beneath the project's LEED goals, objectives, and performance targets in addition to producing an initial set of targeted LEED credits. It is useful, then, to:

- Encourage the team to look for synergies between LEED credits.
- Determine whether the LEED performance thresholds are achievable or even adequate: does the team want to target higher levels of performance relative to specific credit requirements?

■ **Generate potential strategies for achieving identified Performance Targets**

Throughout the team's discussion pertaining to Performance Targets, described above, we find it both fun and productive to also talk about what possible strategies might be considered as a means of achieving these Performance Targets. However, at this point, it usually works better to think of this discussion as a brainstorming exercise that is not limited by a commitment to any one particular strategy or definitive level of performance; rather, it is helpful if these performance targets and strategies are identified for the purpose of being tested by the research and analysis of *Stage A.3* and beyond.

LEED® as a TOOL

It is important to stress that LEED is a means, not an end. As such, it is just a tool. Tools can be used well, or they can be used badly. For example, one of our friends makes eighteenth-century furniture. Given that there was no electricity in the eighteenth century, he does this without the use of power tools. A few years ago, he bought a set of magnificent, eighteenth-century hand gouges. In his hands, these gouges are exquisite tools. In someone else's hands—someone less familiar with how to use them—those gouges are essentially useless, or perhaps a little dangerous, even.

Well, LEED is the same way. As a tool, it functions to identify in a very clear format the environmental issues that need to be addressed. Using LEED *well* as a tool means pursuing performance targets based on the *intent* of each credit and understanding that each of the "credits" represents one or more environmental issues that are deeply inter-

(continued)

related. Using LEED *poorly* means going through the credit checklist and picking individual points to pursue as though you could pick and choose the cheapest items from an *à la carte* menu, often referred to as "point shopping." The LEED program can be useful as a tool when we use it to deal with the whole, by using it to help identify all of the pieces with which we must deal—but we cannot treat the pieces as separate and separable. We must always iterate between the pieces and the whole.

In goal-setting workshops, it often is helpful to say, "If you can come up with a green strategy that begins to address at least three credits or environmental issues, you're probably on the right track." With that said, a very useful exercise at the goal-setting workshop is indeed to go through (with the entire team) the LEED checklist on a credit-by-credit basis to collectively establish, within that framework, the project's performance goals.

One way to accomplish this is to discuss each credit and determine as a team whether it is a credit that you are *definitely* going to pursue (a "YES" credit) or a credit that you definitely are *not* going to pursue (including those that are simply not applicable to the project), meaning it is a "NO" credit. Usually, a number of "MAYBE" credits also will emerge, perhaps because at this point, the team cannot yet be definitive either way about certain issues; but the team wants to leave it on the table as the process proceeds, pending additional research and analysis. In addition to this, we also find it extremely helpful to begin assigning team member responsibilities for each of the credit pursuits, as well as cost implications for each credit.

This may sound like it is in direct conflict with what was stated above about integrating costs and not

point-shopping, so bear with us a moment. One way we have found to identify these cost parameters is to assign to each credit a low-, medium-, or high-cost value, based on project-specific parameters. We start by canvassing all team members in the room to come up with an agreed-upon low-cost credit threshold by asking: "what's the amount of money that we could spend—as long as there was some benefit—without worrying too much about it?" On a five-million-dollar project, for example, this might be about $10,000. Then, to establish the high-cost-credit threshold, we ask: "What's the amount of money above which we would have to think long and hard about spending—and it must be very clear that there are significant benefits?" Everything in between, then, is a medium-cost credit.

This by no means is being done to add up all of the cost implications associated with each of the boxes you check on the scorecard—it is being done as a way of evaluating potential credits in relationship to one another in a tangible way. The purpose of identifying cost implications is to identify the range of cost savings that the team needs to neutralize via integrative design strategies. In other words, it immediately identifies where integrative design strategies are most important in terms of cost implications.

If you look at each of the LEED credits as an overlay simply superimposed on top of a conventional design, you likely will achieve some marginal environmental benefit—but at what cost? You can buy energy recovery, green roofs, daylighting components, and so on, but unless the team focuses on how these systems interrelate and can be integrated in terms of both performance and cost, the tool ends up being used badly by facilely superimposing *green* on top of convention.

Determine order-of-magnitude cost impacts of proposed strategies

Determine with the team what order-of-magnitude cost impacts might be anticipated for the identified proposed strategies. This can be accomplished by first establishing with the team what the project's dollar-value thresholds might be in terms of what constitutes "no, low, medium, and high" costs, then assign one of these four tiers of cost levels to each proposed strategy. This also can be used to reach consensus about costs associated with each identified LEED credit, but not to provide a means for "adding them up" to determine the total cost impacts; rather, the identification of these cost implications are provided in order to identify where integrative strategies are needed to neutralize first costs associated with these potential strategies, including those associated with each LEED credit. (See sidebar, "LEED as a Tool" and Figure 5-16.)

- Determine as soon as possible the project's Construction Delivery methodology—design-bid-build or design-negotiate-build, etc.—so that a contractor is on board as early as possible. It is best if the contractor or Construction Manager (CM) can be present and participate in the Goal-Setting Workshop.
- When a contractor cannot be present—as with the design-bid-build processes typically required by public procurement contracts—it is useful to have a CM and/or a cost estimator or quantity surveyor engaged to address issues of both cost and constructability.

Provide time for reflection and feedback from client and team members

We want to make sure that all key decision makers are involved in the process of establishing goals and project direction; this avoids decisions reached at the workshop from backfiring due to lack of critical support or buy-in. You may recall the story in Chapter 4 about the operable windows at a university laboratory, when the mechanical engineer essentially stopped the meeting's progress due to lack of aligned goals. Consequently, we have learned that building into the workshop intentional reflection time and feedback loops that invite participants to pause and reflect on how the meeting is progressing can help eliminate such problems. This can take the form, for example, of asking the owner's team to meet during lunch to discuss the findings of the team thus far and to report back to the group as a means of kicking off the afternoon. This has the added advantage of giving people—some of whom may feel uncomfortable sharing their thoughts in the larger group format—a voice within the comfort of a smaller group, leading to more casual conversation with their coworkers. Another form this strategy can take might be as simple as pausing—for five or ten minutes at a logical break point in conversation or at a major transition—to ask everyone to reflect on what they are experiencing through this process.

Develop an Integrative Process Road Map that identifies responsibilities, deliverables, and dates

An Integrative Process Road Map (see Figure 5-13) identifies in a detailed spreadsheet the team member responsibilities and deliverables for engaging a clearly defined and manageable integrative design process that is tied to specific tasks and dates.

- The Road Map identifies: responsibilities for action items and the champions for various environmental issues; detailed and staged deliverables (so that rational system optimization decisions can be made); and meeting schedules with purpose and expected attendees. This serves as a scheduling and process map that stipulates points of joint decision making and problem solving (not just individual assignments that are later integrated into a project).

▓ The actual scheduling process of the Road Map is best done with the entire team or with a subgroup that walks the team through the process. All members of the team are invited to comment on what is needed from the others to help them (and the project) achieve the environmental goals and performance targets. Remarkable observations sometimes occur in this process—such as "I didn't know I was responsible for an hourly simulation model," or "I didn't realize how many meetings we were going to have at the beginning of the project," or even "I don't think we're the right firm to be involved in this project."

▓ This mapping process allows for the design team to understand the scope of the work and project expectations from a very detailed perspective. As a result, there is more likely buy-in from the consultants, more accurate fees, and greater engagement in the integrative process that the project will engage to address cost and environmental effectiveness. In addition, there likely will be fewer instances of begrudging the engagement. The integrative process typically can be mapped out in detail for a three- to six-month period with reasonably frequent adjustments as the project moves forward and as inevitable changes occur. It is not the most entertaining process, but it is a very enlightening one.

For years we waved our hands in the air thinking that developers, architects, engineers, and contractors would understand the issues and process required for effective integration without the need for a detailed Road Map. "After all," some would say, "we know how to integrate; we do complex buildings all the time." The truth is that not many of us have had experience with truly integrative whole-systems thinking. Even if this was the case, a real benefit results from this mapping process if, for example,

the project manager from one of the disciplines unexpectedly leaves the project for any reason. When this happens, the first thing that might occur is that the project might be assigned to a new architect or engineer—perhaps someone unfamiliar with the integrative approach—and the pattern of work established at the charrette will not have been internalized. He or she likely will organize a process pattern for their work that they are familiar with, usually a linear one, and the opportunities for deep integration will be jeopardized.

▓ We like to use Microsoft Excel for this Road Map, since it is easy for anyone familiar with this software program to adjust schedules.

▓ It is useful to conclude the workshop with a discussion about next steps to reinforce upcoming components of the Road Map.

As discussed above, following Workshop No. 1, a Proposal B can be written with a more clearly understood and defined scope. The tasks and fees associated with this scope can now be included more accurately in various team members' proposals. These may include—but are not limited to—any from the following list, depending on project goals and parameters:

▓ Consultants may need additional fees to attend more meetings, as outlined in the Integrative Process Road Map.

▓ LEED certification project management and general consulting

▓ LEED documentation and application support

▓ Energy modeling and consulting

▓ Design-integration facilitation and planning

▓ Commissioning (with defined scope of systems to be commissioned)

▓ Daylight modeling

▓ Writing a Measurement and Verification (M&V) Plan

- Monitoring and controls system design to implement the M&V Plan
- Materials research and/or LCA
- Green and/or LEED specifications
- Cost-benefit analysis
- Drafting a Construction Waste Management Plan
- Lighting photometric plots for analyzing light pollution
- Writing a Construction Indoor Air Quality (IAQ) Management Plan
- Green housekeeping policy and plan

- Creating green and/or LEED tenant guidelines
- Providing green education components and/or marketing materials for the project

■ **Commissioning: Initiate documentation of the Owner's Project Requirements (OPR)**

It is best if the *Commissioning* process can begin at this point, so it is extremely helpful to have the Commissioning Authority (CxA) present at this goal-setting workshop to keep the team focused on the subsequent need to develop the preliminary narrative that will constitute the Owner's Project Requirements (OPR).

Owner's Project Requirements (OPR)

Commissioning activities should begin with a summary narrative describing the results from Workshop No. 1. This summary narrative will become a first pass at an Owner's Project Requirements (OPR) document. Workshop No. 1 tries to elicit the client's core purpose and objectives for the project, and the OPR should summarize the results.

The OPR should be a nontechnical narrative describing—in the owner's view—what will make the project a success. This document is needed early in the process to avoid the pitfalls of making adjustments during the latter stages of design and construction. How often are changes made late in design, or construction, simply because this is when the owner truly begins to understand the design concepts and only then begins to realize that this is what he or she—the owner—*does not want*?

In our experience, people initially react cynically to the development of the OPR as only neces-

sary to satisfy LEED paperwork requirements—but without this document, it is common for the owner's expectations to get lost in the shuffle and flurry of project design activities. Often the design team has a view of the project—one that may be driven by their own familiarity, expertise, even specialty—that can render them unable to objectively understand the owner's needs. Too often, the builder gets involved only after design is completed and is motivated primarily by maximizing profit. As a result, although the designers and builders might walk away feeling satisfied (1) because the design was really cool and just what the designers had envisioned and (2) because the contractors made a profit, the owner feels like saying: "Wait a minute. This isn't the building I wanted at all. What about *my* goals and *my* satisfaction?"

The goal of the OPR is to capture in simple terms—so that everyone can understand—what the owner

(continued)

wants. It serves as the owner's way of communicating and aligning his or her desires with the design team's conceptual thinking (i.e., what the design team is proposing in terms of program, performance issues, and general methods for achieving the project's objectives) and vice-versa. From the owner's perspective, this document communicates: "If you do these things and provide the facility described in this document, with these parts and pieces arranged accordingly, functioning like this, and performing in kind, I will be satisfied." It also evolves over time as new discoveries emerge during the design process—it tells the *story of the project*. Consequently, the development of the OPR becomes *mutually beneficial* to both the design team and the owner. It is puzzling to us, then, that we have found it a struggle on nearly every project to get this document done. It often requires of the Commissioning Authority a great deal of listening, prodding, and pulling to truly capture the core needs and desires of the owner.

The OPR is different for every project. Additionally, as mentioned above, the OPR becomes a dynamic document that changes over time as the project evolves. The OPR, then, plays an elemental role in the integrative process as design progresses. In short, one might say that this document requires continuous maintenance to record changes in thinking and to reflect decisions made that inform and influence the owner's and design team's expectations. As this happens, the OPR is adjusted to reflect these changes in thinking. As design moves into construction, more evolving decisions may be necessary. Again, each time changes occur, they should be reflected in the OPR—but from a building commissioning perspective, the exact content of the OPR is not as important as its use for the purpose of maintaining consistency between that content and the owner's current vision of the project, so that this vision matches the continuing development of the project's evolution throughout design and construction.

To overcome some of the difficulties in getting the OPR documented, we often find it helpful to provide the owner with an OPR *questionnaire* to identify the scope of what should be contained and described in the OPR—to help guide the owner's thinking about what the building needs to be and how it needs to perform. This questionnaire, then, jump starts the process of getting the owner to generate the content of the OPR document. The questions may be viewed as rhetorical, but they are intended to serve as the basis for a critical thinking exercise. Hopefully, as the questions are thought through, other more relevant questions that need to be answered will come to mind. The results of this critical thinking exercise are translated into a narrative description that describes what the owner views as a successful project—that is, the document known as the owner's project requirements (OPR). Accordingly, the questionnaire's raw questions and corresponding answers are not intended to serve as the OPR itself; rather, the questionnaire stimulates the owner's thinking and provides the owner with a clear framework for documenting his or her desires, needs, and performance goals. (See "Sample Owner's Project Requirements (OPR) Questionnaire" sidebar on the next page.)

Sample Owner's Project Requirements Questionnaire

1. **Primary Project Overview—Provide an overview of the project**

   Much of this information may be extracted from the Touchstones and/or core values exercises, along with architectural programming documentation and design meetings.

   a. Why is the project being considered?

   b. What does the owner hope to achieve by building this project?

   c. What pertinent history is there for this project (that is, the history that helps to define the present form of the project)?

   d. What is the primary purpose of this project?

   e. What is the primary intended use for this facility?

   f. What is the project schedule?

   g. Potential road blocks?

      1. Money

      2. Time

      3. Permitting or entitlements

      4. Partnering limitations

   h. What Core Values should inform the project?

   i. How will the project's specific core values be implemented to make this a high-performance building?

   j. Describe the basic building program for the project as it relates to the Core Values listed above.

   k. Is there an established level of material quality, construction cost, and anticipated operational cost? If so, what are they?

2. **Secondary Project Goals**

   a. Is the project part of a larger plan or vision?

   b. Is there future expansion anticipated beyond the primary project?

   c. Will the project be completed in phases?

   d. Will any such phases be anticipated in terms of "rough ins" required during the current phase to accommodate future needs?

   e. Will future phases pursue LEED certification and/or LEED-EBOM?

3. **Environmental and Sustainability Goals— Describe specific environmental or sustainability goals**

   a. What are the overall environmental goals for this project?

   b. What are the overall design and performance goals for this project?

   c. What are the measurable performance criteria that will determine if this project is a success or not?

4. **Energy-Efficiency Goals—Provide specific details for achieving the goals established through previous reviews (such as the LEED checklist review)**

   a. What special program and/or site parameters will influence energy use in this facility?

   b. What special landscaping features or influences on orientation will impact energy use in this facility?

   c. What special construction features will influence energy use in this facility?

   d. What are the project's energy-efficiency goals?

5. **Indoor Environmental Quality Requirements**

   a. What local building- and energy-code standards are being applied to this facility?

   b. Are there any general restrictions or limitations on this project?

   c. Will there be any provisions made for future expansions or renovations of the building's MEP systems?

(continued)

d. Will original systems be expanded to serve future tenants or expansions?

e. What are the operating systems that are being considered on this project?

6. Equipment and System Expectations

a. What are the systems in the building that will be commissioned?

b. Describe the level of quality, reliability, flexibility, and maintenance continuity expected for these systems.

c. What are the warranty requirements?

d. Are there specific efficiency targets, preferred manufacturers, or operating features that are known for these systems?

e. What are the allowable operating tolerances in the facility's systems?

f. What specific building management system controls capabilities are required?

g. What are the system's integration requirements, especially across disciplines (i.e., lighting controls integrated with HVAC controls)?

7. Building Occupancy Requirements

a. What are the user's requirements for all spaces?

b. What are the occupancy requirements for each space?

c. What is the time-occupancy schedule for each space?

d. What future occupancy requirements are currently under consideration?

e. Are occupancy-use changes in the future anticipated for the spaces created in this phase of the project?

8. Operations and Maintenance Personnel Requirements

a. What are the project documentation requirements (systems manuals)?

b. Who is (or will be) the owner's key maintenance officer?

c. What are the training requirements for the owner's personnel?

d. Are there any additional warranty requirements beyond the typical one-year-guarantees period, and if there are any such requirements, what are they?

e. What are the operational and maintenance criteria for the facility? (These criteria should reflect the owner's expectations and capabilities and realities of the facility type.)

f. What equipment and system maintainability expectations, including limitations of operating and maintenance personnel, does the owner have?

g. What is the anticipated service life of the building?

A.2.2 Principles and Measurement

■ **Document Touchstones, Principles, Metrics, Benchmarks, and Performance Targets from Workshop No. 1**

The follow-up report that documents the results from Workshop No. 1 becomes far more effective if it is a principles-based report, because it is the principles, values, and aspirations of the team that will generate the most powerful and effectively integrated solutions. Accordingly, these principles should form the basis (and even the organizational structure—perhaps around the four key subsystems) of the narrative for this report in terms of pointing the team in the appropriate direction for making discoveries and design decisions throughout the rest of the process. Additionally, this report should include an expanded and annotated LEED checklist (for LEED projects) with an additional column for detailed comments describing potential strategies, responsibilities, and the cost implications described below under *Stage A.2.3.*

A.2.3 Cost Analysis

■ **Document order-of-magnitude cost impacts of proposed strategies to reflect input from Workshop No. 1**

The order-of-magnitude cost implications that were identified in terms of "no, low, medium, and high" costs for each strategy identified in Workshop No. 1, as described above, should be documented. This documentation can identify rule-of-thumb, line-item costs associated with each strategy. Further, this documentation should not be limited to costs associated with *green* strategies alone, but it should include every strategy so that comparative conventional benchmarks that will populate the cost-bundling template, as described in *Stage A.3.3,* can be established. This sets the stage for

identifying the cost trade-offs between implementing bundled green strategies and line items of conventional strategies, so that such trade-offs can be quantified, explored, and compared in more detail during later stages.

A.2.4 Schedule and Next Steps

■ **Adjust Integrative Process Road Map to reflect input from Workshop No. 1**

This should include further input from any identified team member and/or stakeholder that may not have been present at Workshop No. 1.

■ **Distribute Workshop No. 1 report**

It is extremely important to document the results of each workshop in a report for distribution to all team members. This report should contain the following from Workshop No. 1:

- ■ Meeting agenda
- ■ Lists of attendees
- ■ Photos of activities
- ■ Results from the Touchstones (and/or Core Values) exercise
- ■ Initial OPR document or date when OPR will be written and by whom
- ■ Initial Principles, Metrics, Benchmarks, and Performance Targets (including LEED scorecard as described above)
- ■ Cost analysis (as described above), including any initial cost-bundling template input.
- ■ Integrative Process Road Map spreadsheet of schedule and tasks
- ■ Bulleted list of next steps

(Sample Goal-Setting Workshop and project charrette reports can be downloaded as pdf files from the *Resources* tab on 7groups' website at www.sevengroup.com.)

LEED for Schools Checklist: Miami Trace Middle School

Cost Implications

Yes	?	No				No	Low	Med	High
6	5	5	**Sustainable Sites**		16 Points	6	2	1	2
Y			Prereq 1	**Construction Activity Pollution Prevention**	Required	N			
Y			Prereq 2	**Environmental Site Assessment**	Required	N			
		N	Credit 1	**Site Selection**	1				
		N	Credit 2	**Development Density & Community Connectivity**	1				
		N	Credit 3	**Brownfield Redevelopment**	1				
		N	Credit 4.1	**Alternative Transportation**, Public Transportation Access	1				
		N	Credit 4.2	**Alternative Transportation**, Bicycle Use	1				
Y			Credit 4.3	**Alternative Transportation**, Low-Emitting and Fuel-Efficient Vehicles	1		L		
Y			Credit 4.4	**Alternative Transportation**, Parking Capacity	1	N			
	?		Credit 5.1	**Site Development**, Protect or Restore Habitat	1		L		
Y			Credit 5.2	**Site Development**, Maximize Open Space	1	N			
	?		Credit 6.1	**Stormwater Design**, Quantity Control	1				H
Y			Credit 6.2	**Stormwater Design**, Quality Control	1	N			
	?		Credit 7.1	**Heat Island Effect**, Non-Roof	1				H
	?		Credit 7.2	**Heat Island Effect**, Roof	1			M	
Y			Credit 8	**Light Pollution Reduction**	1	N			
	?		Credit 9	**Site Master Plan**	1	N			
Y			Credit 10	**Joint Use of Facilities**	1	N			

Yes	?	No				No	Low	Med	High
5	2		**Water Efficiency**		7 Points	6	1		
Y			Credit 1.1	**Water Efficient Landscaping**, Reduce by 50%	1	N			
Y			Credit 1.2	**Water Efficient Landscaping**, No Potable Use or No Irrigation	1	N			
	?		Credit 2	**Innovative Wastewater Technologies**	1	N			
Y			Credit 3.1	**Water Use Reduction**, 20% Reduction	1	N			
Y			Credit 3.2	**Water Use Reduction**, 30% Reduction	1	N			
Y			Credit 3.3	**Water Use Reduction**, 40% Reduction	1		L		
	?		Credit 4	**Process Water Use Reduction**	1	N			

Yes	?	No				No	Low	Med	High
13	2	2	**Energy & Atmosphere**		17 Points	12		1	2
Y			Prereq 1	**Fundamental Commissioning of the Building Energy Systems**	Required		L		
Y			Prereq 2	**Minimum Energy Performance**	Required	N			
Y			Prereq 3	**Fundamental refrigerant Management**	Required	N			
Y			Credit 1.1	**Optimize Energy Performance**, 10.5% New / 3.5% Existing	1				H
Y			Credit 1.2	**Optimize Energy Performance**, 14% New / 7% Existing	1	N			
Y			Credit 1.3	**Optimize Energy Performance**, 17.5% New /10.5% Existing	1	N			
Y			Credit 1.4	**Optimize Energy Performance**, 21% New / 14% Existing	1	N			
Y			Credit 1.5	**Optimize Energy Performance**, 24.5% New / 17.5% Existing	1	N			
Y			Credit 1.6	**Optimize Energy Performance**, 28% New / 21% Existing	1	N			
Y			Credit 1.7	**Optimize Energy Performance**, 31.5% New / 24.5% Existing	1	N			
Y			Credit 1.8	**Optimize Energy Performance**, 35% New / 28% Existing	1	N			
Y			Credit 1.9	**Optimize Energy Performance**, 38.5% New / 31.5% Existing	1	N			
Y			Credit 1.10	**Optimize Energy Performance**, 42% New / 35% Existing	1	N			
	?		Credit 2.1	**On-Site Renewable Energy**, 2.5%	1				H
		N	Credit 2.2	**On-Site Renewable Energy**, 7.5%	1				
		N	Credit 2.3	**On-Site Renewable Energy**, 12.5%	1				
Y			Credit 3	**Enhanced Commissioning**	1	N			
Y			Credit 4	**Enhanced Refrigerant Management**	1	N			
Y			Credit 5	**Measurement & Verification**	1			M	
	?		Credit 6	**Green Power**	1	N			

▶**Figure 5-16** This LEED scorecard resulting from Workshop No. 1 includes order-of-magnitude cost implications to help identify the places where the team will need to focus on integrative design strategies. Usually, this scorecard has additional columns to the right that identify potential strategies and the primary party responsible for coordinating the team's efforts relative to the issues associated with each credit's achievement. *Image courtesy of John Boecker.*

Yes	?	No				No	Low	Med	High
5	**2**	**6**	**Materials & Resources**		**13 Points**	5	1	1	
Y			Prereq 1	**Storage & Collection of Recyclables**	Required				
		N	Credit 1.1	**Building Reuse**, Maintain 75% of Existing Walls, Floors & Roof	1				
		N	Credit 1.2	**Building Reuse**, Maintain 100% of Existing Walls, Floors & Roof	1				
		N	Credit 1.3	**Building Reuse**, Maintain 50% of Interior Non-Structural Elements	1				
Y			Credit 2.1	**Construction Waste Management**, Divert 50% from Disposal	1	N			
	?		Credit 2.2	**Construction Waste Management**, Divert 75% from Disposal	1		L		
		N	Credit 3.1	**Materials Reuse**, 5%	1				
		N	Credit 3.2	**Materials Reuse**, 10%	1				
Y			Credit 4.1	**Recycled Content**, 10% (post-comsumer + 1/2 pre-consumer)	1	N			
Y			Credit 4.2	**Recycled Content**, 20% (post-comsumer + 1/2 pre-consumer)	1	N			
Y			Credit 5.1	**Regional Materials**, 10% Extracted, Processed & Manufactured Regionally	1	N			
Y			Credit 5.2	**Regional Materials**, 20% Extracted, Processed & Manufactured Regionally	1	N			
		N	Credit 6	**Rapidly Renewable Materials**	1				
	?		Credit 7	**Certified Wood**	1			M	

Yes	?	No				No	Low	Med	High
13	**5**	**2**	**Indoor Environmental Quality**		**20 Points**	14	2	1	1
Y			Prereq 1	**Minimum IAQ Performance**	Required	N			
Y			Prereq 2	**Environmental Tobacco Smoke (ETS) Control**	Required	N			
Y			Prereq 3	**Minimum Acoustical Performance**	Required	N			
Y			Credit 1	**Outdoor Air Delivery Monitoring**	1			M	
	?		Credit 2	**Increase Ventilation**	1	N			
Y			Credit 3.1	**Construction IAQ Management Plan**, During Construction	1	N			
	?		Credit 3.2	**Construction IAQ Management Plan**, Before Occupancy	1		L		
Y			Credit 4	**Low-Emitting Materials**, Adhesives & Sealants	1	N			
Y				**Low-Emitting Materials**, Paints & Coatings	1	N			
Y				**Low-Emitting Materials**, Flooring Systems OR Ceiling & Wall Systems	1	N			
Y				**Low-Emitting Materials**, Composite Wood OR Furniture & Furnishings	1	N			
		N	Credit 5	**Indoor Chemical & Pollutant Source Control**	1				
Y			Credit 6.1	**Controllability of Systems**, Lighting	1	N			
Y			Credit 6.2	**Controllability of Systems**, Thermal Comfort	1	N			
Y			Credit 7.1	**Thermal Comfort**, Design	1	N			
Y			Credit 7.2	**Thermal Comfort**, Verification	1		L		
Y			Credit 8.1	**Daylight & Views**, Daylight 75% of Classrooms	1				H
Y				**Daylight & Views**, Daylight 90% of Classrooms	1	N			
	?			**Daylight & Views**, Daylight 75% of other spaces	1	N			
	?		Credit 8.2	**Daylight & Views**, Views for 90% of Spaces	1	N			
	?		Credit 9	**Enhanced Acoustical Performance** 40dBa/ RC 32	1	N			
		N		**Enhanced Acoustical Performance** 40dBa/ RC 32	1				
Y			Credit 10	**Mold Prevention**	1	N			

Yes	?	No				No	Low	Med	High
5	**1**		**Innovation & Design Process**		**6 Points**	6			
Y			Credit 1.1	**Innovation in Design**: Exemplary Performance SSc5.2	1	N			
Y			Credit 1.2	**Innovation in Design**: Exemplary Performance WEc3	1	N			
	?		Credit 1.3	**Innovation in Design**:	1				
Y			Credit 1.4	**Innovation in Design**:	1	N			
Y			Credit 2	**LEED Accredited Professional**	1	N			
Y			Credit 3	**School As a Teaching Tool**	1	N			

Yes	?	No				No	Low	Med	High
47	**17**	**15**	**Project Totals**		**79 Points**	49	6	4	5

Certified 29-36 points **Silver** 37-43 points **Gold** 44-57 points **Platinum** 58-79 points

LEED Targeted Credits by Cost Implications

	Totals	No	Low	Med	High
Yes	47	40	3	2	2
?	17	9	3	2	3
Totals	64	49	6	4	5

Stage A.3
Research and Analysis: Evaluating Possible Strategies

A.3.0 Prepare *Proposal B*

- Develop *Proposal B*: confirm scope and fees based on Workshop No. 1 scope refinement

A.3.1 Research and Analysis Activities: First Iteration

- Explore and identify a wide range of opportunities and possible strategies before collapsing into solutions
- Expand the analysis of the four key subsystems:
  - Habitat
  - Water
  - Energy
  - Materials

A.3.2 Principles and Measurement

- Evaluate design concepts against Performance Targets from Workshop No. 1
- Commissioning: Prepare conceptual phase OPR

A.3.3 Cost Analysis

- Apply unit cost estimates to the integrative cost-bundling template

A.3.4 Schedule and Next Steps

- Update Integrative Process Road Map in preparation for Workshop No. 2
- Prepare Agenda for Workshop No. 2

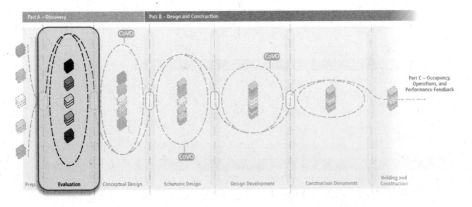

Figure 5-17 Integrative Process Stage A.3, Research and Analysis: "Evaluating Possible Strategies." *Image courtesy of 7group and Bill Reed; graphics by Corey Johnston.*

Stage A.3

Research and Analysis: Evaluating Possible Strategies

From this point forward, the process begins repeating the pattern of Research and Analysis followed by Team Workshops that was described at the beginning of this chapter. During this Research and Analysis stage, the team continues to refine initial studies, based on the understandings developed at Workshop No. 1, by testing design concepts and performance targets for feasibility. This process is highly iterative.

A.3.0 Prepare Proposal B

■ **Develop Proposal B: confirm scope and fees based on Workshop No. 1 scope refinement**

If using a two-part fee proposal, as discussed in Stage A.1, develop Proposal(s) B to define the scope of services for all team members, including any potential additional consultants needed.

■ We have found that the integrative process usually requires restructuring conventional proposals by reallocating fees per phase in order for fees to be commensurate with the effort being expended in each phase. As discussed in the Integrative Process Overview at the beginning of this chapter, much more time is required in the earlier phases compared to conventional design, particularly during the Discovery Phase. However, the construction documents (CD) phase, for example, becomes shortened and reserved solely for documentation, rather than becoming protracted and inefficient due to lack of fully informed design decisions. Consequently, the total design and documentation time frame is the same, but the allocation of effort is front-end loaded (see Figure 5-2 and Figure C-1).

■ Accordingly, teams now can be doing what the American Institute of Architects (AIA) B101™-2007 "Standard Form of Agreement between Owner and Architect" (that has replaced the former AIA B141 contract) states should be done in the CD phase—documentation.

■ We have found that shifting effort to earlier phases with deeper analysis can produce more effective solutions by making decisions during the schematic design (SD) phase that often get delayed to the CD phase in the conventional process. The resulting impacts of such conventionally delayed decisions often contribute to what might be called "design gridlock," which in turn results in significantly oversized systems, redundancies, inefficiencies, and associated increased costs. One example can be seen by revisiting the paint/lighting/HVAC story presented in Chapter 2:

■ Final lighting design typically occurs during the latter part of the CD phase (many have jokingly said that the final lighting design does not happen until addenda to the CD package are issued). One reason for this is that the lighting designer typically will not begin the lighting design until the architect provides a detailed reflected ceiling plan. Further, as you may recall from Chapter 2, lighting design typically is based on rule-of-thumb reflectance values for walls and ceilings. Almost universally, reflectances of 80-50-20 (for ceilings-walls-floor) are used by lighting designers to calculate the required number of lighting fixtures in a space, rather than the *actual* reflectances of the surfaces in the room. Lighting designers typically are forced to use such assumptions, because the architect or interior designer has not yet selected final paint colors or ceiling finishes—which sometimes does not happen until after construction contracts are awarded. Consequently, lighting capacity usually ends up being oversized, sometimes double what is required.

■ Since the final lighting design does not occur until later in the CD phase, the mechanical designer assumes code values instead of actual calculated loads for lighting. The code values—referred to as lighting power density (LPD), which are expressed in watts per square foot—are maximum allowances, so the actual value is likely to be lower—in an energy-efficient building, significantly lower. This results in HVAC systems that are significantly oversized due to a lack of coordination earlier in the design process.

The essential point here is that integrated decisions need to be made before the CD phase so that the design is already fully informed before documentation begins. In this particular case, the project team should agree on a value for lighting power density early in design—or before design begins—so that the lighting designer has a not-to-exceed target that the mechanical designer can use when calculating the building's heating and cooling loads. This will require that the lighting designer engage in the lighting system design far earlier than is the norm and coordinate with the architect or interior designer to get the reflectance values of the selected ceiling and wall surfaces *before* documentation begins.

A.3.1 Research and Analysis Activities: First Iteration

■ **Explore and identify a wide range of opportunities and possible strategies before collapsing into solutions**

This exploration involves brainstorming how loads, program elements, and systems might be downsized and possibly eliminated to achieve targeted goals. The design team should list a wide range of design ideas and opportunities in terms of interrelationships, techniques, technologies, materials, and systems to investigate.

■ We are not optimizing yet; we are just exploring possibilities that will help achieve the objectives and performance targets established in *Stage A.2*.

■ We encourage teams not to be encumbered by practicalities at this stage. This is the chance for blue-sky ideas that may not seem possible or likely and that otherwise might be left unexplored.

In other words, we are not trying to focus on solutions yet; rather, we are expanding the field of possibilities during this stage.

■ **Expand the analysis of the four key subsystems**

Expand the initial analysis of the project's context and site performed during *Stage A.1* research and analysis into more project-specific issues. This involves engaging a preliminary analysis of flows, relationships, and economics (including both construction and operations costs) between the performance targets established at the prior workshop and the project's programmed base conditions. On LEED projects, for example, this includes researching further the achievability of the LEED credits targeted at Workshop No. 1 and either verifying that they remain feasible or discovering that some of the pending "maybe" credits are achievable. More importantly, work with team members both individually and in larger groups, as necessary, to test systems associated with the four key subsystems, as described in the following examples:

■ **Habitat** (human and other biotic systems)
Perform initial analysis of potential local habitat impacts and identify potential strategies to minimize negative impacts and/or develop restorative design concepts. At this point, additional expertise may be needed or desired to engage habitat issues more fully; a list of potential systems consultants is provided in the *Stage A.5.1* discussion on habitat.

On the human side, examine potential strategies to address indoor environmental quality (IEQ) issues such as establishing daylighting criteria, initial thermal comfort parameters (including design temperatures) and potential adaptive thermal comfort strategies (see sidebar), natural or other ventilation systems, and so forth.

Adaptive Thermal Comfort

Our individual thermal comfort is determined by numerous factors. Obviously, temperature and humidity are important, but they are not the only determinants of a thermally comfortable environment; the mean radiant temperatures of surrounding surfaces, airflows, activity level, and clothing insulation also contribute to an individual's thermal comfort.

Thermal comfort is an important factor related to individual productivity; if occupants are more comfortable, they likely are more satisfied, happier, and less distracted; therefore, they can focus more on the task at hand (see "Building Investment Decision Support (BIDS): A Framework for POE" sidebar in Chapter 8). It also is a significant factor in the sizing of HVAC equipment and overall building energy use. Quite often internal thermal comfort conditions are treated as a given. For example, it is assumed in most office scenarios that temperature settings will range from, say, 72°F to 75°F year round, and humidity levels will not be allowed to exceed 55 percent RH in the summer. If these thermal comfort ranges can be extended, it is possible to reduce HVAC system size and save energy.

The chart below (Figure 5-18) demonstrates acceptable temperature settings depending on the level of clothing insulation. The warmer one dresses in the winter and the lighter one dresses in the summer can profoundly influence temperature settings. For example, our office dress code allows employees to wear shorts during the cooling season. This enables a summer temperature setting of about 80°F, which contributes to energy savings and therefore a cooling system size of approximately 1,000 square feet per ton (about 350 square feet per ton is the norm for offices in our climate). Other factors that contribute toward allowing the higher temperature settings include ceiling fans to move the air, high-performance operable windows, a well-insulated structure, and good daylighting design to minimize heat generated by light fixtures (since they can be turned off during most working hours) and to keep out the high-altitude summer sun.

A 2007 study by the Center for the Built Environment, entitled "Operable Windows and Thermal Comfort," examined how operable windows affect occupant thermal comfort; the study concluded that "our find-

Optimum and Acceptable Ranges of Operative Temperature for People During Light, Primarily Sedentary Activity (≤1.2 met) at 50% Relative Humidity and Mean Air Speed ≤0.15 m/s (30 fpm)[a]

Season	Description of Typical Clothing	I_c(clo)	Optimum Operative Temperature	Operative Temperative Range (10% Dissatisfaction Criterion)
Winter	heavy slacks, long-sleeve shirt and sweater	0.9	22°C 71°F	20-23.5°C 68-75°F
Summer	light slacks and short-sleeve shirt	0.5	24.5°C 76°F	23-26°C 73-79°F
	minimal	0.05	27°C 81°F	26-29°C 79-84°F

Figure 5-18 One of the factors that determines our individual thermal comfort is clothing. This table shows how the range of acceptable temperature settings in a space varies based on types of clothing. *Image courtesy of ASHRAE Standard 55-2004. © American Society of Heating, Refrigerating and Air-Conditioning Engineers, Inc.,* http://www.ashrae.org.

(continued)

ings reinforce the notion that the wider range of temperatures permitted under the new adaptive version of comfort standards will meet with occupant acceptance if those occupants have personal control of environmental conditions." Quite often the level of individual controllability has a profound effect on thermal comfort. Much of this may simply be psychological, in that everyone has their own personal preferences, and these may differ widely. Even the *perception* that we have some individual control can have an effect. The old joke about saving energy by installing placebo (dummy) thermostats unconnected to anything has some merit, but the effect is even greater if the controllability is real.

Factors as simple as the chair you sit in can have a relatively large impact. The trend in office seating is to use chairs that foster airflow. Instead of solid backs and seats, porous materials are used in part to encourage the flow of heat and water vapor away from our bodies. This potentially allows occupants to remain more comfortable at higher temperature settings.

The point to remember is that many small actions can combine to create a large effect. Building own-

Figure 5-19 Ceiling fans are a viable, adaptive thermal comfort strategy that increases airflow and enables temperature set points to be higher in the cooling season. The use of ceiling fans during the heating season to circulate warm air at the ceiling is a persistent energy myth. This practice does not save energy nor does it enable lower heating season temperature settings. *Image courtesy of Marcus Sheffer.*

ers should be encouraged to examine their assumptions regarding factors ostensibly unrelated to building performance, such as dress codes and furniture selection. By expanding the range of assumed thermal comfort parameters in early design, and therefore interior temperature settings during operations, project teams can potentially allow owners to downsize equipment and thereby save money and energy.

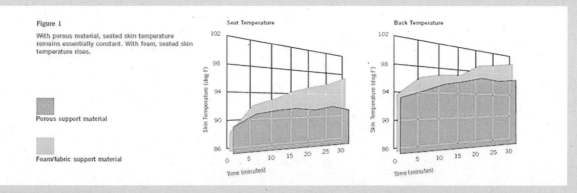

Figure 5-20 In some climates, the cost of additional air-conditioning required to counteract the insulating properties of upholstered seating can be a significant expense. A report published by the Rocky Mountain Institute estimates that an upholstered office chair, by insulating 20 to 25 percent of the body's surface, adds $140 to $290 per worker in HVAC, utility, and equipment costs (Houghten et al. 1992, from *The Attributes of Thermal Comfort,* Herman Miller, Inc., 2005). By helping to maintain neutral body temperatures, a noninsulating chair requires less cooling and no additional heating to maintain thermal comfort. *Used with permission from Herman Miller, Inc.*

Water

Investigate strategies associated with water quality and water conservation (including stormwater, soil permeability, initial quantification of annual water consumption and wastewater generation, etc.) to test the ability for achieving initial performance targets with preliminary input and output modeling. (See water balancing discussion and "The Water Balance" sidebar in *Stage A.5.1*.)

Energy

Based on the strategies and overall energy performance targets established in Workshop No. 1, the analysis in this stage begins to hone in on more specific performance goals and strategies. The strategies analyzed at this point should focus on measures that will have significant impact on the design of the building.

- The first two stages focused on establishing an overall energy performance target, typically expressed as kBTU/square foot/year. Several additional performance parameters related to the building and systems design should now be established as a subset of this overall goal. The specific parameters may vary depending on the building type and size. Examples of such parameter goals applicable to most project types include: square foot per ton of cooling, watts per square foot of lighting, watts per square foot of plug load, and thermal comfort ranges, as discussed above (see Figure 5-21).

- It is essential that these additional performance parameters be established if the project expects to achieve the overall energy performance target. Each of these specific parameters requires that individual designers address their specific systems in the context of this overall target—in relationship with numerous other systems. This helps to address one of the major limitations associated with establishing an overall energy performance target—no individual can claim stewardship of the overall performance, since it requires the cooperative participation of the entire team.

- Perform simple building-massing energy modeling options to explore "large-grain" issues, such as: site-specific solar orientation; footprint and massing relationships (e.g., two versus three floors); apertures (e.g., 20–25 percent as a starting point); load profiles; daylighting opportunities; wind profiling; potential for natural ventilation; and so forth. Whereas Stage 1 "simple-box" modeling was looking at broad-brush parameters to identify general load distributions, the preliminary modeling at this stage starts to test potential options for the issues listed above relative to the project objectives established at the goal-setting workshop. The effects of presenting such early preliminary modeling should not be underestimated; we have found that debating prescribed performance thresholds or preconceived building massing, configuration, and orientation with the team is one thing—but showing them quantified comparisons of different scenarios, accompanied with the modeling tool's graphic outputs is something quite different. This approach typically is far more convincing with regard to producing effective alternative scenarios (see Figures 5-22 through 5-25).

Materials

Develop a materials comparison using LEED criteria and/or begin initial life cycle assessment (LCA) with tools such as the ATHENA® *Impact Estimator for Buildings* to engage comparative analyses of structure and envelope systems options. A description of this tool and a detailed example of such an analysis is discussed in the "Life Cycle Assessment (LCA) Tools and Environmental Benefits" section of Chapter 6 and continued in the "Materials" section of *Stage B.2.1*.

Energy Budget	
All spaces	New construction—reduce energy cost budget by 30% compared to an ASHRAE Standard 90.1-2004 baseline building. Renovation—reduce energy cost budget by 20% compared to a pre-renovation 2003 baseline building.
Lab Spaces	< 300 kBTU/gsf/year
Office Spaces	< 40 kBTU/gsf/year
Computer Center	< 50 k BTU/gsf/year
Child Care Center	< 25 kBTU/gsf/year
Lighting Budget	
All spaces	Do not exceed the recommended light levels in the *IESNA Lighting Handbook 9th Edition*
Lab Spaces	1.00 W/gsf
Office Spaces	0.65 W/gsf
Computer Center	0.50 W/gsf
Child Care Center	0.80 W/gsf
HVAC Cooling Load	
Lab Spaces	> 250 sf/ton
Office Spaces	> 550 sf/ton
Computer Center	> 400 sf/ton
Child Care Center	> 600 sf/ton
Ventilation	
All spaces	Comply with ASHRAE Standard 62.1-2004
Lab Spaces	CO_2 levels not to exceed 500 ppm
Office Spaces	CO_2 levels not to exceed 700 ppm
Computer Center	CO_2 levels not to exceed 700 ppm
Child Care Center	CO_2 levels not to exceed 700 ppm
Glazing	
All spaces	Interior surface temperature of >62°F at outdoor temperature of 20°F
Measurement & Verification	
All building projects	Comply with the requirements of the *IPMVP Concepts and Options for Determining Energy Savings in New Construction, Volume III,* Option B or D.
Daylighting	
All Regularly Occupied Spaces	2.0% daylight factor as calculated by the International/IESNA Method
All Regularly Occupied Spaces	25–30 fc of daylight
Thermal Comfort	
All spaces	Comply with ASHRAE Standard 55-2004
Water Budget	
Office/Child Care	Do not exceed 3 gallons per person per day of potable water
Renewable Energy	
All building projects	On-site renewables
All building projects	Green power purchase which meets the Green-e requirements for 100% of electric consumption

Figure 5-21 Sample energy performance parameters from a government campus in North Carolina. Overall energy performance goals often need to be broken down into performance goals related to individual building systems, such as lighting power density (for the lighting system) or square foot per ton of cooling (for the cooling system). These values then provide coordinated guidance for the various engineers responsible for designing the lighting system, mechanical system, and so on. These parameters should be discussed at Workshop No. 2 in the context of the project's overall energy-efficiency goals. *Image courtesy of Marcus Sheffer.*

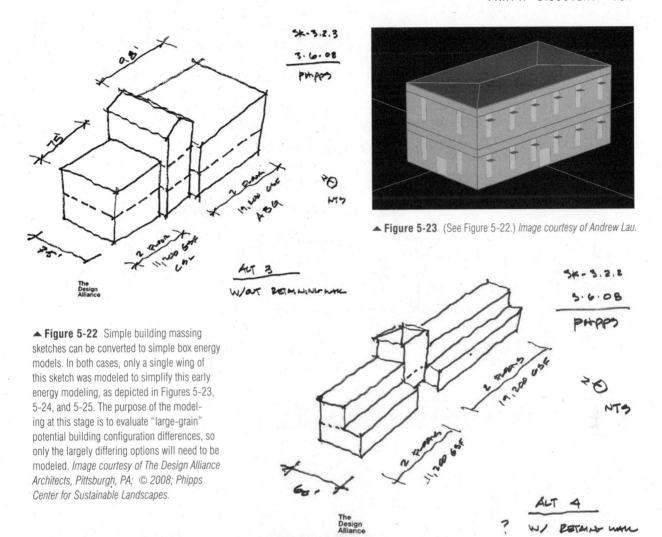

SK-3.2.3
3.6.08
PHPPS

▲ Figure 5-23 (See Figure 5-22.) *Image courtesy of Andrew Lau.*

▲ Figure 5-22 Simple building massing sketches can be converted to simple box energy models. In both cases, only a single wing of this sketch was modeled to simplify this early energy modeling, as depicted in Figures 5-23, 5-24, and 5-25. The purpose of the modeling at this stage is to evaluate "large-grain" potential building configuration differences, so only the largely differing options will need to be modeled. *Image courtesy of The Design Alliance Architects, Pittsburgh, PA; © 2008; Phipps Center for Sustainable Landscapes.*

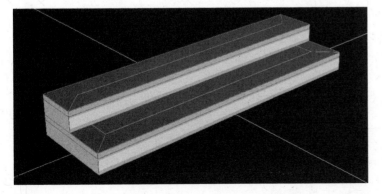

▲ Figure 5-24 (See Figure 5-22.) *Image courtesy of The Design Alliance Architects, Pittsburgh, PA; © 2008; Phipps Center for Sustainable Landscapes.*

◀ Figure 5-25 (See Figure 5-22.) *Image courtesy of Gerren Wagner.*

Life Cycle Assessment (LCA) Overview

Life cycle assessment (LCA) is a scientific methodology for holistic thinking. This holistic thinking leads us to a new decision-making model about materials. The conventional wisdom about materials is that there are "good" and "bad" materials for the environment. LCA teaches us that some materials are better than others; but, for the most part, deciding what to use is a process of determining what is most important. In other words, there is always a trade-off in terms of environmental impacts. Determining what that trade-off is becomes the responsibility of the decision maker. This is sometimes called *weighting*. In other words, what environmental impacts are most important to you? It is important to note that this question does not mean that the things we end up caring less about—or *weight* as less important—are *actually* less important. Rather, LCA provides design teams with a framework for making decisions about materials impacts. For example, if carbon dioxide emissions are deemed most important, you likely will seek materials other than concrete (due to the CO_2 emissions associated with cement production), or you might look for ways to reduce the carbon impact of your concrete via cement displacements, such as high fly ash or ground granulated blast-furnace slag (GGBFS) displacements of portland cement. If water is considered most important, then you likely will stay away from steel, as steel uses a lot of water in its processing. If land use is the most important, then you might stay away from wood. If overall environmental impact is most important, you will look for materials that already exist, so you will look for an existing building to reuse, and/or you will look to reuse salvaged materials from another building.

This decision-making model begins with the assumption that you are always making *choices* based on prioritized environmental impacts relative to another material. You are never making choices in a vacuum. Obviously, when you choose not to use a certain material, you are making that choice relative to the materials that you could have used otherwise. In other words, you are using the LCA tool to compare the impacts of a proposed design choice (of a material or assembly) relative to a benchmark case; for example, you might want to compare the overall environmental impacts of simply polishing your concrete slab instead of putting carpet on top of it. Another example might be optimizing structural components, such as engaging comparative analyses of different widths of column-bay spacing. As such, LCA tools can help designers to quantify the environmental impacts of various materials and/or assemblies in order to inform design decisions. This is described more fully in subsequent stages.

LCA is the process of looking at the building as a whole, especially related to the materials and the energy used over the life of the project. LCA leads us to a different decision-making model about materials. We are beginning to look beyond just the single attributes of any given material and to determine the overall impacts of a product's life over time across a number of environmental impact indicators. One thing becomes very clear when using LCA: all materials have an impact and determining which materials are "best" is often a subjective choice based on a trade-off of some sort (see sidebar, above).

Several major concepts come into play when using LCA and thinking from a life-cycle perspective. They include *service life, durability, delamination,* and *deconstructability*. The first of these, *service life*, refers to how long the building is being designed to last. According to J. C. Perrault, the "service life of a building is that period during which the building performs without serious breakdown, operates with reasonable economy and performs the function for which it was intended."* It is most important to establish an explicit projected service life for the building—being intentional about the service life can have a profound impact on the decisions made at this stage of design.

We ask project teams early on if they have an intended service life in mind. Heads always nod yes, with the almost constant answer being fifty to sixty years. However, we have found that this issue usually has not been well thought out, if thought about at all, in quantifiable terms. When pressing the question further, the owner is not always comfortable with the idea that the building will have to be rebuilt in fifty to sixty years, especially in institutional settings. When this conversation does not occur, a vague discussion about durable materials usually ensues, and the concepts related to durability become a proxy for service life itself. (More about service life later.)

Durability, however, functions within the context of *service life*. Any building system will last only as long as the entire combination of components of the system last. For example, a window will last as long as the weakest component of the window, which is likely to be a rubber seal. The glass might last centuries, as might cladding on a wood win-

dow frame; but all of the glass and the cladding become useless as parts of the window once the seal breaks. The same thinking applies to the rest of the building. If the design team has in mind an intended service life that can be incorporated into the project's future planning in any way, the outcome is significant. One of the most powerful and positive examples we have seen of project teams using this thinking was when an institution decided (prior to hiring their architect) that their building would be designed and built to last three hundred years. This decision altered almost every subsequent decision throughout design.

Delamination is "not using what you don't need" by eliminating layers of materials, for example, using polished concrete flooring in lieu of adding another layer of flooring material such as vinyl composition tile (VCT), rubber flooring tiles, ceramic tile, or carpet.

Deconstructability is designing for ease of disassembly after the building's useful life in order to provide feed stock of materials for future buildings, as mentioned in reference to the Chartwell School at the end of Chapter 4.

During this stage, such possibilities should be investigated and explored relative to the Principles and Performance Targets established at Workshop No. 1.

A.3.2 Principles and Measurement

■ **Evaluate design concepts against Performance Targets from Workshop No. 1**

These evaluations will require the level of analysis described above for the four key subsystems to assess in more detail the Performance Targets established by the team during Workshop No. 1 and to verify that they are capable of being achieved or exceeded by the expanded set of possible strategies being explored during this stage.

---

*"Service Life of the Building Envelope," an article published as part of the technical documentation produced for Building Science Insight '84, "Performance of Materials in Use," a series of seminars presented in major cities across Canada in 1984. Available from the National Research Council Canada website at http://irc.nrc-cnrc.gc.ca/pubs/bsi/84-1_e.html.

An architect with whom we were working recently described how the identified principles of reducing resource consumption and recycling led to an expanded set of possible strategies explored by his team on a Las Vegas casino project pursuing LEED certification. Instead of simply providing recycling infrastructure for the occupant waste streams and increasing the recycled content of the building's materials, the team proposed thinking of the entire city of casinos as a resource for future reconstruction. This seemed obvious to him, after he realized that the average life spans of casinos range from ten to fifteen years; therefore, a much larger impact could potentially be achieved by designing the casino to be *deconstructable,* thereby providing a resource pool of its materials at the end of its short useful life. The resulting strategy was based more on the team's targeted principles pertaining to resource consumption than trying to meet the LEED prerequisite for recycling occupant waste or the recycled content credit—a remarkable leap that unfortunately was considered too radical by the casino owner . . . at least for now.

- ### *Commissioning*: Prepare conceptual phase OPR

  - Using the outline provided in the OPR questionnaire discussed in the "Owner's Project Requirements (OPR)" sidebar and the "Sample Owner's Project Requirements (OPR) Questionnaire" sidebar in *Stage A.2.1,* the design team and the owner begin the process of extracting the owner's conceptual project requirements from the responses to this questionnaire and developing the first iteration of the OPR. Usually by this stage, it becomes evident that "the owner" represents more than one person, so the questionnaire may need to be distributed to a number of key people on the owner's team. If each of these people representing the var-

ied interests of "the owner" can be identified early on and resourced, the outline for the OPR can be derived from this questionnaire. The responses and results can then be collated and filtered to produce the conceptual phase OPR—a more complete and comprehensive representation of the objectives and requirements from the full owner's team that ultimately will drive the project.

  - Based on the owner's responses to the OPR questionnaire, the Commissioning Authority (CxA) may need to provide guidance to the owner in order for the owner and project team to complete the conceptual phase OPR document. Remember, that this document will evolve over time as design decisions are made; hence, as the process progresses from conceptual design to completion, similar updating exercises are recommended.

  - The CxA's input can be extremely valuable in assisting the cost-estimating tasks described in the cost analysis *Stage A3.3* (below) by helping identify various optional components that should be incorporated into the integrative cost-bundling template. For example, how complicated or simple can or should the building's control system be? In other words, what are the appropriate options to consider?

A.3.3 Cost Analysis

- ### Apply unit cost estimates to the integrative cost-bundling template

We now can begin inputting data into the cost-bundling framework, or spreadsheet template created during *Stage A.1,* and expanding it based on the strategies identified at Workshop No. 1. Strategies further explored and identified during this research and analysis stage may also be added. This template can be used to accurately portray both initial cost and life cycle cost considerations, as follows:

- Use line-item unit cost estimates as a starting point for understanding the first-cost impacts of the alternative systems components (and systems groupings) that are being tested, modeled, and considered. We do this to create a "project palette" of line-item costs for these alternatives that allows the team to see the whole set of potential project systems (and associated components) costs, so that the team can assemble, or bundle, interrelated system "groupings" or "combinations" of systems and components. In other words, we draw from this list items that are related to each other with regard to how they interact in terms of their costs. It should be noted that the line-item costs for each listed component do not need to be finely honed at this stage; it is the relative difference between the costs of each alternative "grouping" or "combination" that is being explored.
- Consider a net-present-value analysis of life cycle costs to include:
  - First cost of systems options
  - Operations, maintenance, and replacement costs
  - Productivity and environmental cost impacts, when possible

In other words, expand the list (or "palette") in the template to include life cycle cost impacts related to each systems option. Even before the project is defined with any level of specificity, it is useful to develop a cost estimating framework that lists the elements of a generic project of a similar type to use for comparisons and benchmarking purposes. Again, by establishing this list in functional groupings, the team has a tool it can use to systematically understand the impacts of one subsystem on another in subsequent phases.

- When considering a given strategy that appears to cost more as a set of line items, analyze what other systems can be downsized or eliminated to offset these first costs. As we have seen, every system is connected in multiple ways to other systems in a project and so are their costs in terms of trade-offs. Accordingly, teams should be encouraged to avoid locking into a "line-item" mentality that does not take into account the impacts that one system's cost may have on the cost of other systems or components—hence the term *cost bundling*.

A.3.4 Schedule and Next Steps

- **Update Integration Process Road Map in preparation for Workshop No. 2**

  Adjust and refine the Road Map with the project team, as necessary, and clarify next steps. At this point, the schedule of tasks, team conference calls, meetings, and analysis processes will almost always need to be altered to accommodate the interim meeting dates, times, and deliverables that occur between major workshops and charrettes.

- **Prepare Agenda for Workshop No. 2**

  The importance of developing the agenda with a stated purpose and objectives for Workshop No. 2 cannot be understated. This task is similar in nature to the discussion in *Stage A.1.4* about creating the agenda for the first workshop, but it may be even more important at this stage. Again, this can be accomplished by scheduling a conference call or two with the appropriate key team members. In addition to clarifying expected outcomes, this call also creates an opportunity for project team members to assess the status of the research and analysis that is expected to be completed in preparation for Workshop No. 2.

Stage A.4

Workshop No. 2: Conceptual Design Exploration

A.4.1 Workshop No. 2: Activities

- Assess the findings from Stage A.3 (Research and Analysis) of the four key subsystems:
  - Habitat
  - Water
  - Energy
  - Materials
- Generate conceptual site and building design concepts from:
  - Touchstones and Principles
  - Site forces
  - Community and watershed living-system patterns
  - Functional program
  - Breakout group working sessions
- Confirm alignment with Touchstones, Principles, Metrics, Benchmarks, and Performance Targets
- Review integrative cost-bundling studies in progress
- Review and adjust the Process Road Map
- Provide time for reflection and feedback from client and team members
- Commissioning: Review Owner's Project Requirements (OPR)

A.4.2 Principles and Measurement

- Document adjustments to Performance Targets to reflect input from Workshop No. 2
- Commissioning: Adjust OPR to reflect input from Workshop No. 2

A.4.3 Cost Analysis

- Update any required integrative cost-bundling templates to reflect input from Workshop No. 2

A.4.4 Schedule and Next Steps

- Update Integrative Process Road Map to reflect input from Workshop No. 2
- Distribute Workshop No. 2 Report

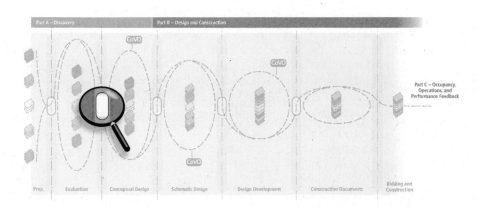

Figure 5-26 Integrative Proces Stage A.4, Workshop #2: "Conceptual Design Exploration." *Image courtesy of 7group and Bill Reed; graphics by Corey Johnston.*

Stage A.4

Workshop No. 2: Conceptual Design Exploration

This workshop, or charrette, initiates the transition from research and alignment of objectives to the actual design process. It is best when this charrette can focus on generating conceptual design ideas; but if a project enters the integrative process late, this charrette also can focus on reviewing conceptual design ideas that already have been developed and exploring alternatives.

The project's key team members who attended Workshop No. 1 should be present at Workshop No. 2 so that team buy-in and a sense of "ownership by all" continues to develop.

It should be noted that the Implementation Outline above can be used as a template for creating a Workshop No. 2 agenda and tailored to the specific parameters of each project. However, the agenda for this session needs to remain fluid and flexible during the workshop, allowing for it to change in response to the "energy in the room" (as always), the degree of progress made during

each activity, the potential exploration of new discoveries, and so forth. It also should be noted that this workshop can occur as an all-day event on a single day, or it can be structured to last as long as three or four days, depending on project complexity and the team's goals.

If the *builder* has not been involved up until now, this is an important stage at which the builder's participation becomes highly valuable. In particular, the creative experience and additional perspective on design ideas that builders can offer, not to mention their thoughts on how design impacts constructability and cost, are often overlooked. In other words, the builder is best viewed as another co-designer.

A.4.1 Workshop No. 2 Activities

- **Assess the findings from Stage 3 (Research and Analysis) of the four key subsystems**

  Review with the entire team the results of the *Stage A.3* analysis of flows, relationships between the project program and the base conditions, and impacts on economics (budget and operations costs).

Figure 5-27 The workshop kicks off by reviewing with the entire team the research and analysis results from the prior stage to inform conceptual design explorations across all four key subsystems. *Image courtesy of Marcus Sheffer.*

■ **Habitat** (human and other biotic systems)

Review *Stage A.3* analysis of potential site-specific local habitat impacts and strategies, along with IEQ approaches applicable to the project, including any associated quantified results, to inform the day's conceptual design iterations.

■ **Water**

Review *Stage A.3* findings and potential strategies applicable to the project associated with achieving initial performance targets for water quality and water conservation (including stormwater, soil permeability, quantification of annual water consumption and wastewater generation, etc.).

■ **Energy**

Review the proposed performance parameters related to HVAC system sizing, lighting power density, renewable contribution, daylighting, thermal comfort, and so on. Discuss and adjust the specific parameters that will be used to guide the initial design effort. Encourage the project team to be somewhat aggressive in their targets at this point, since these values will be revisited and adjusted as necessary.

Review results from *Stage A.3* energy modeling of options (and parameter combinations) derived from the simple building massing explorations to inform the day's conceptual design iterations. Discuss and identify potential load reduction strategies to be explored in *Stage A.5* (Research and Analysis) parametric modeling runs. Also, identify energy impacts associated with transportation issues for further analysis in *Stage A.5.*

■ **Materials**

Review materials in light of the material-selection principles and the comparative analyses conducted in *Stage A.3,* such as initial LCA results, to identify initial impacts of structure and envelope systems options.

■ **Generate conceptual site design solutions and building design concepts**

This workshop serves as a design charrette intended to generate initial conceptual design ideas that can be explored further and tested by research and analysis in *Stage 5*. Conceptual site and building design concepts result from engaging the following activities during this workshop:

■ **Touchstones and Principles**

We find it important to briefly review with the entire team the Touchstones and Principles identified at Workshop No. 1 to ensure team alignment around performance goals and the project's objectives while exploring conceptual design ideas throughout the day.

■ **Site forces**

The conceptual design effort at this charrette often begins with a group *site forces exercise*, which involves diagramming on a site-plan overlay those flows entering the site and those leaving the site. These site-specific flows can be thought of as "site forces," and they include solar orientation, prevailing winds, pedestrian and/or vehicular circulation, public transportation access, utilities access, topography, stormwater flows, views, noise sources, neighborhood connections, etc. (see Figures 5-28 and 5-30).

■ **Community and watershed living-system patterns**

A more holistic way of addressing context is to have a team member (e.g., systems ecologist, permaculturist, biologist, or other consultant) present to the team an assessment of site and neighborhood interrelationships, similar to what Pamela Mang describes in the "Design by Discovery—A Story of How Design Emerged from Place" sidebar above in *Stage A.1*.

By understating the patterns of living systems and how they worked in the past (see "Solving for

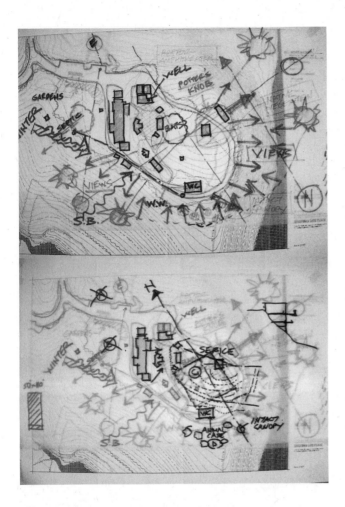

Figure 5-28 The project team for Penn State's Shaver's Creek Environmental Center reached several conclusions during the site forces exercise, including:

- Existing native vegetation and intact tree canopy to the west and south should be preserved.
- View opportunities toward the lake to the west should be exploited.
- Exterior connections to the raptor amphitheater, meadow, and bat-habitat area should be made.

Four different locations on the site were identified as primary potential candidates for the new building, as indicated in the lower sketch with the letters *A*, *B*, *C*, and *D*. During this exercise, the team reached consensus that site C would be best, with the building located approximately in the square zone depicted. The building could then best support habitat and advantageously integrate with existing slopes. *Images courtesy of John Boecker.*

Pattern" in Chapter 3), we can look to create—or rediscover—potentially healthier and mutually beneficial future relationships between the site's habitat and cultural aspects, building occupants, visiting users, the community, and the watershed. For example, we discovered on one project that some of the desert terrain areas of the Baja peninsula in California were four hundred years ago a scrub oak forest. By knowing what once was, we may be able to discover ways to recover and restore, to some degree, the prior condition.

Functional program

We often find that the above site forces exercise and/or living systems pattern explorations—along with discoveries made during breakout group work sessions during the charrette (discussed below)—inform and generate adjustments to aspects of the project's *functional program*. For instance, similar occupancy schedules for several programmed spaces may suggest groupings of functions into adjacent or consolidated mechanical zones to improve the efficiency of both distribution components and operations. As a result, a group exercise that focuses on any potential adjustments to the functional program can be extremely useful during the charrette. Also, the building program often remains somewhat nebulous, even at this point, so this exercise can serve to help clarify the functional "unknowns" or to refine the entire program. We have even experienced a project where the primary objective on the first day of a three-day charrette was to define the functional program collectively; this benefited all project team members in terms of reaching a deeper understanding of the project's purpose. Consequently, using a separate exercise to clarify and define more precisely the owner's programmatic requirements in this workshop can be very effective, since team members need to have a thorough understanding of program requirements.

Breakout group working sessions

Generally we find it quite effective to follow the above discussions with breakout group design sessions. The focus of these breakout group working sessions may vary depending on a number of factors, such as the degree to which the project design has already been developed (which, optimally, would be minimal), the complexity of the project, the project scope, site constraints, the number of workshop participants, the expertise represented by these participants, and so on. Accordingly, we have found two basic breakout group strategies to be effective, depending on the above factors. The *first* basic strategy utilizes these breakout groups to explore everything as an integrated whole. The *second* basic strategy begins by organizing the breakout groups as focused sessions on each of the key subsystems before exploring all of them collectively as a whole. In short, we have found it important to remain flexible in this regard and to discuss with the design team the approach most appropriate to the project's parameters.

The first basic strategy often consists of two rounds of breakout group working sessions; the first round asks each group to come up with a consolidated, overall design concept—a rough site plan and building idea—without trying to resolve individual program components or details. Armed with tracing paper, markers, colored pencils, and the project's Touchstones, Principles, and Performance Targets—now informed by the *site forces exercise* and the *functional program review*—each small group strives to discover a set of overall, cogent design concepts. Examples of issues to consider in this first round include the following:

- Site connections to the neighborhood
- Contextual remedies
- Functional and program components (in large chunks, not at the scale of individual spaces)
- Strategies aimed at achieving sustainability targets and LEED pursuits

Figure 5-29 The style, format, and goals of breakout groups can vary widely, but each breakout group should have cross-disciplinary representation. *Images courtesy of Marcus Sheffer* (left) *and Sandy Wiggins* (right).

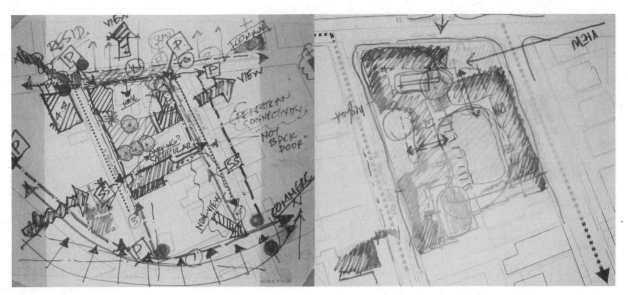

Figure 5-30 After exploring the larger community context and site forces (as depicted in the sketch on the *left*), one group focused on massing, orientation, green space, vehicular access, and parking in order to produce the sketch on the *right* during the first round of breakout work sessions for an urban project in Chapel Hill, North Carolina. *Images courtesy of Marcus Sheffer.*

- Parking, transportation, and service locations and solutions
- Image and character

The outcome of this first breakout group work session should be a single consolidated sketch from each small group for presentation to the large group. This site plan sketch should clearly depict the overarching design idea (or *parti*) and identify all key strategies, proposed site solutions, and chunks of program elements.

After representatives from each breakout group have presented the ideas that emerged from their working sessions, it is best to solicit from the large group their thoughts or reflections. Once all work from the breakout groups has been presented, we like to engage what we refer to as the "green hat, red hat" exercise.* We ask the entire group, based on what they have seen,

what concepts or ideas emerged that they absolutely "want to keep" and these are recorded on a flip chart. Then, it is time to take off the "green hat" and put on the "red hat." We ask what has emerged that the team absolutely wants to avoid, and these items are recorded as well. This identifies emerging priorities for future engagement in the discovery process.

Next, we like to ask the team how the "want-to-keep" concepts can best work together to create more whole solutions. The large group then evaluates how to reconcile any conflicts (by harmonizing, not compromising) and works to identify opportunities for integrating strategies. The resulting ideas are recorded for future iteration and refinement. Most often, this group discussion is followed by a second round of breakout group conceptual design sessions, time permitting, that takes into account the larger group feedback to develop a second iteration of ideas.

*We owe thanks to Sandy Wiggins for giving us this metaphor as a name for this exercise.

Figure 5-31 This sketch was produced by one of four breakout groups in the first round of exploring possibilities for the addition of an educational facility to the Phipps Conservatory on an extremely complex and degraded site in Pittsburgh, Pennsylvania. They focused on:

- Maximizing reuse of an existing building (box at *lower right*) or, at least, keeping or salvaging its components
- Optimizing solar orientation on east-west axis
- Creating a restored landscape zone as a linear east-west connector along a major slope that cuts through the site
- Stepped green roofs that could integrate with slopes, landscaping, and constructed wetlands
- A central piazza linked with gardens to serve as an "outdoor room" and perhaps as a future conservatory.

Image courtesy of Marcus Sheffer.

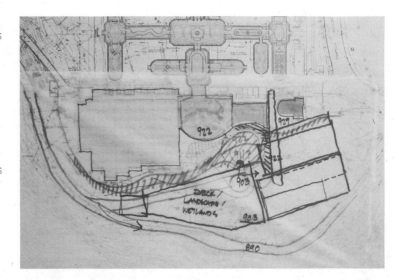

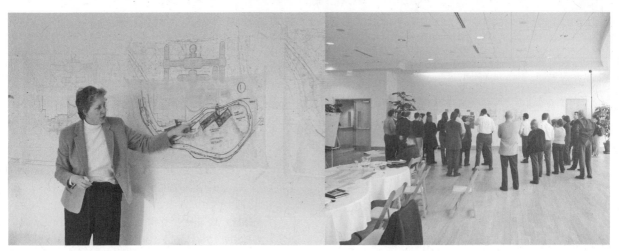

Figure 5-32 Two other breakout groups present their schemes for the Phipps Conservatory project to the larger, full team. *Images courtesy of Marcus Sheffer.*

Alternatively, the *second* basic strategy for breakout group work asks each group during the first round to focus on exploring solutions for each one of the four key subsystems. During presentations to the large group, the team's discussion centers around integrating these subsystem solutions and strategies. One group, for example, could focus on energy-related issues, while another group focuses on water and site interactions, while yet another group focuses on building design and/or indoor environmental quality issues, and so on. This is particularly appropriate for more complex projects. A second iteration of breakout group design sessions that focuses on conceptual design idea-generation can follow, as described above.

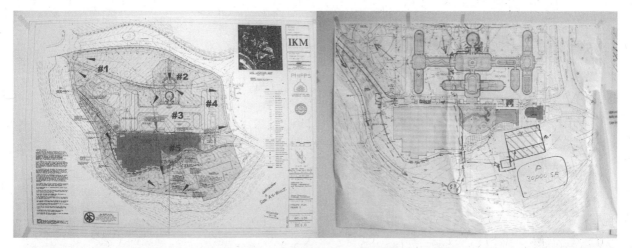

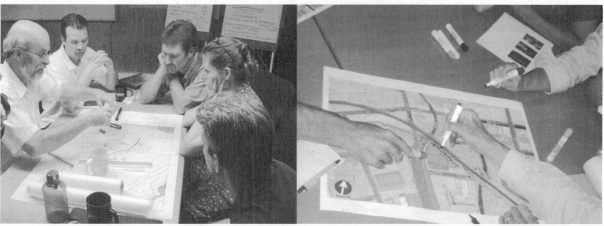

▲▲ **Figure 5-33** Four primary and distinct rainwater-collection zones were identified during research and analysis conducted prior to Workshop No. 2 for the Phipps project. The water-focused breakout group produced the sketch (on the *right*) to explore living on no more water than the site's annual rainfall by looking at storm and sanitary flows in ways that could accomplish the following integrative strategies: The 38 inches of annual rainfall likely exceeds demand, so this abundance of water could be combined with other systems to address habitat, storm water, watershed, cooling (energy), water quality, sewage conveyance, materials, and beauty by separating combined sewers, creating a constructed wetlands (the hatched box depicts the approximate size needed), designing restorative appropriate native habitat for cleaning water that flows downhill to an adjacent lake and to the Monongahela River, incorporating educational water features, and perhaps passing water through the ground for passive cooling—all with minimal pipes, no curbs, and no catch basins. *Image courtesy of Marcus Sheffer.*

▲ **Figure 5-34** Breakout groups encourage hands-on participation by all team members. The image on the *right* depicts many hands working to explore the linkages between a planned building rehabilitation project and its neighborhood on a degraded urban site in Syracuse, New York. Images courtesy of Tom Keiter *(left)* and Marcus Sheffer *(right)*.

The results from this charrette usually take the form of conceptual sketches, but these results can vary considerably depending on project complexities. We have seen such charrette results range from rough master plans or site plans with building-location options to rather developed building footprint and floor plan solutions with associated building sections.

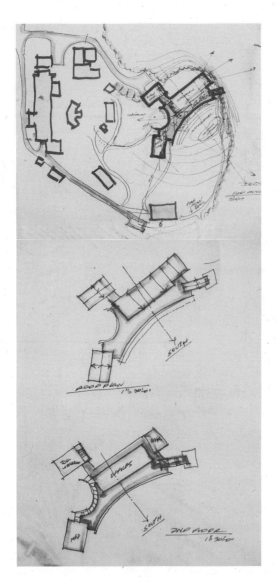

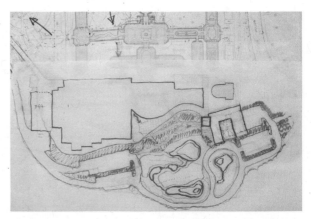

Figure 5-36 A proposed concept resulting from the two-day Workshop No. 2 for Phipps Conservatory. *Image courtesy of Marcus Sheffer.*

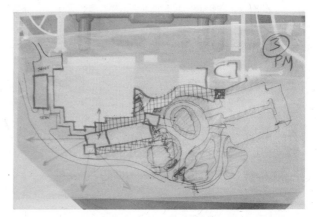

Figure 5-37 Near the end of the Phipps two-day workshop, a new idea emerged for further exploration and testing in the next research and analysis stage. *Image courtesy of Marcus Sheffer.*

▲ **Figure 5-35** The scheme produced for the Shaver's Creek project at the conclusion of a one-day conceptual design charrette. *Images courtesy of John Boecker.*

▶ **Figure 5-38** This sketch from a three-day charrette (attended by over eighty design team and community members) depicts a conceptual master plan that unifies into a single scheme the design work from six different breakout groups exploring ideas for a centralized town services facility on a degraded site in Southampton, New York. *Image courtesy of Sandy Wiggins.*

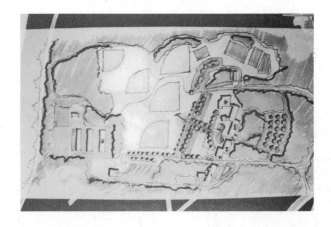

■ **Confirm alignment with Touchstones, Principles, Metrics, Benchmarks, and Performance Targets**

■ The group evaluates the potential solutions and results developed during the workshop in terms of alignment with identified Principles and Performance Targets initially established at Workshop No. 1 and adjusts these if necessary.

■ The group reviews the status of the project relative to the Benchmarks, Metrics, and goals of its green building assessment tool; for example, reevaluate strategies and proposed conceptual design solutions relative to the project's LEED goals and the targeted credit requirements.

■ At times, we have found that the conceptual design exercises during Workshop No. 2 result in discoveries or synergies that may bring back to the table a strategy rejected at the prior workshop—or one that was not considered previously. Such strategies may have impacts on the achievement of Performance Targets. For example, LEED points that may have been previously assessed as questionable or unachievable may now be considered viable or, vice versa, obviated.

■ **Review integrative cost-bundling studies in progress**

■ Refine with team, as necessary.

■ As discussed above, new discoveries of further interrelationships and associated cost tradeoffs that may have occurred during the workshop will require adjustments to the line items, components, and/or bundles of any cost-bundling templates.

By now, you may have noticed a pattern emerging of continuous iteration, whether we are discussing design strategies, performance targets, cost analysis, or next steps. This is intentional; there is a strong role for reflection, iteration, rediscovery, or discovering anew at each step throughout these early stages. (See Chapter 2, "The Learning Wheel.") As a result, many of the tasks indicated for each stage revisit the same task from the prior or earlier stages, so to avoid repetitive language, our descriptions of such tasks will start to become more and more brief. This may at times require you to go back and reference tasks from earlier stages.

■ **Review and adjust the Process Road Map**

■ Refine with team, as necessary, and identify next steps.

■ As discussed above, new discoveries of further interrelationships that may have been made during the workshop will require adjustments in turn to be made to the components of the Integrative Process Road Map, including tasks, schedule changes, anticipated meetings, and so on.

■ **Provide time for reflection and feedback from client and team members**

This idea is discussed in *Stage A.2.1,* and it bears repeating: we want to ensure that all key decision makers are involved in the process of establishing goals and project direction to avoid decisions reached at the workshop from backfiring due to lack of critical support or buy-in. Again, this buy-in process can be as simple as pausing—for five or ten minutes at a logical break point in conversation or at a major transition (or asking the owner's team to caucus during lunch)—to ask everyone to reflect on what they are experiencing and learning through this process.

■ **Commissioning: Review Owner's Project Requirements (OPR)**

A presentation of the OPR document by the design team and/or owner to the entire team can help reinforce alignment around the project goals and set the stage for developing the Basis of Design (BOD) document in the next step of the Commissioning process (see Stage *A.5.2* below for a description of this BOD).

A.4.2 Principles and Measurement

■ **Document adjustments to Performance Targets to reflect input from Workshop No. 2**

The follow-up workshop report should reflect updates to Performance Targets that may have resulted from any discoveries or explorations that occurred during Workshop No. 2, such as updating and annotating the LEED checklist.

■ **Commissioning: Adjust OPR to reflect input from Workshop No. 2**

The OPR may need to be updated by the project team to maintain consistency with the results of Workshop No. 2.

A.4.3 Cost Analysis

■ **Update any required integrated cost-bundling templates to reflect input from Workshop No. 2**

As discussed above under *Stage A.4.1,* new discoveries of further interrelationships and associated cost trade-offs that may have occurred in Workshop No. 2 will require adjustments to the components of any cost-bundling templates.

A.4.4 Schedule and Next Steps

■ **Update Integrative Process Road Map to reflect input from Workshop No. 2**

Adjust and refine with team, as necessary, and clarify next steps. This should include further input from any identified team members and/or stakeholders who may not have been present at Workshop No. 2. Again, the schedule of tasks, team conference calls, meetings, and analysis processes will almost always need to be altered to accommodate the interim meeting dates, times, and deliverables that occur between major workshops and charrettes.

■ **Distribute Workshop No. 2 Report**

As with all workshops, results should be documented in a report that is provided to all team members. This report should contain the following for Workshop No. 2:

■ Meeting agenda
■ Lists of attendees
■ Photos of activities
■ Site forces exercise sketch
■ Images of all conceptual sketches
■ Meeting notes recording additional findings, results, reflections, "what to keep," etc.
■ Touchstones, Principles, Metrics, Benchmarks, Performance Targets—including updated LEED checklist, if applicable
■ Updated integrative cost-bundling template
■ Process Road Map spreadsheet of schedule and tasks
■ Next steps

(Sample Design Charrette reports can be downloaded as pdf files from the *Resources* tab on 7group's website at www.sevengroup.com.)

Stage A.5
Research and Analysis: Testing Conceptual Design Ideas

A.5.1 Research and Analysis Activities: Explorations within individual disciplines and smaller related groups

- Test Conceptual Design schemes from Workshop No. 2 within the realities of the program and guiding principles relative to the four key subsystems:
  - Habitat
  - Water
  - Energy
  - Materials
- Coalesce findings and bring analysis to a reasonable conclusion before beginning the Schematic Design phase

A.5.2 Principles and Measurement

- Confirm and solidify Metrics, Benchmarks, and Performance Targets
- Commissioning: Develop Basis of Design (BOD)

A.5.3 Cost Analysis

- Put a price tag on every strategy and subsystem, then aggregate them into integrated cost bundles

A.5.4 Schedule and Next Steps

- Update Integrative Process Road Map in preparation for Workshop No. 3
- Prepare Agenda for Workshop No. 3

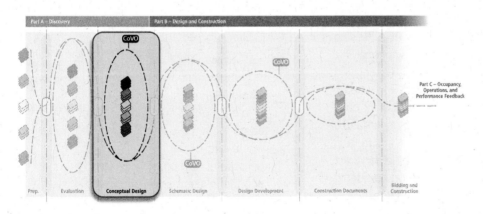

Figure 5-39 Integrative Process Stage A.5, Research and Analysis: "Testing Conceptual Design Ideas." *Image courtesy of 7group and Bill Reed; graphics by Corey Johnston.*

Stage A.5

Research and Analysis: Testing Conceptual Design Ideas

This is a critical point in the process. This stage is the bridge between discovery and schematic design. We need to be reasonably sure that we have addressed the essential form-giving issues of the key subsystems *before* giving form to the building. These should be analyzed to a level to which we can confidently commit so that they can be coalesced into a limited number of schematic design schemes.

A.5.1 Research and Analysis Activities: Explorations within individual disciplines and smaller related groups

■ **Test Conceptual Design schemes from Workshop No. 2 within the realities of the program and guiding principles relative to the four key subsystems**

Engage more detailed analysis of the four key subsystems to test the feasibility of the ideas and Conceptual Design schemes generated at Workshop No. 2 in terms of meeting programmatic requirements, budget, Principles, and Performance Targets. This work generally proceeds within each discipline and includes small cross-disciplinary group sessions and interim meetings with team members designing related systems. These sessions are informed by using various tools for such analysis. The array of analysis, tools and potential subjects is legion, and describing all of them is beyond the scope of this book. Instead, examples of the types of analysis and tools for each subsystem that can be used to help understand the interrelationships between systems are provided in the outline below. Our attempt here is to demonstrate through these examples the level of effort and depth needed at this stage in the integrative process:

■ **Habitat** (biotic systems other than human)
  • Look for opportunities to cascade water uses to support living systems. In other words, look for multiple ways to use a unit of water to support life before it leaves the site, through some of the following or other methods:
    ◦ Irrigation
    ◦ Habitat for constructed wetlands
    ◦ Vegetated roof(s)
    ◦ Groundwater recharge
    ◦ On-site pond to serve as a rainwater harvesting cistern
    ◦ Rain gardens and bioswales to both treat and infiltrate stormwater
  • Investigate planting materials appropriate to the microclimates that may result from the design of the building itself.
  • Look at opportunities for restoring plant habitat in conjunction with integrating stormwater management opportunities.
    ◦ *Example*: Reduce turf grass to reduce stormwater runoff and stormwater conveyance infrastructure.
    ◦ *Example*: As you may recall from the Willow School discussion in Chapters 3 and 4, this project looked at the characteristics of the soil and plant and animal life that had existed on the site before poor farming practices had depleted the soil; it then restored native species along with deer fencing to allow the plants to become established, which in turn recharged groundwater by allowing minimal water to leave the site.
  • **Tools** (examples)
    In late October 2004, Gerould (Gerry) Wilhelm came from Chicago to visit the properties where two of us live in Pennsylvania for the purpose of helping us understand how best to engage in site restoration. Over the course of about four hours, he was able to use his training as a botanist to inventory the plant species present on one of these properties in order to discover historical patterns and assess levels

of biodiversity that might inform restoration efforts. He did this by using the *Floristic Quality Assessment* (see sidebar) method that he began developing in the 1970s. By examining approximately eight acres (half of which was woodland), he created an inventory of the extant plant species for the purpose of determining a mean C *value* for the thirty-acre property as a whole. Then, C values were assigned to each plant species on a scale of one to ten as follows, based on the following criteria:

C *value of 0:* less than 5 percent confidence that the plant came from a *native remnant*

C *value of 5:* 95 percent confidence that the plant came from a remnant but does not attest to the quality of the remnant

C *value of 10:* 95 percent confidence that the plant came from a high quality remnant

From his inventory exercise, Jerry was able to tell us virtually everything that had happened to that property over the past three hundred years on a square meter basis. He also reported the following:

> ... you will note that the C value of your property as a whole is 3.8—even competent *de novo* restoration efforts do not yield C values much higher than 3.5 at any price, and [they] usually achieve much lower quality systems; further, woodland restorations from scratch are virtually impossible. The integrity of your property, therefore, is essentially irreplaceable and priceless.... Consider the potential your site contains when a nonlocal botanist can record 85 native species during the dormant season! I know that there is much to do here and that some of it seems perhaps discouraging. Do not let your heart be troubled, however, you are the custodian of a great little remnant of what once was Pennsylvania.

Such information provides invaluable insights into any given site and can thereby help guide design decisions, as can be seen in the example below about a site in Princeton, New Jersey (see Figure 5-40). In the case above, the information Jerry provided also created for us a stronger sense of responsibility for the health of the land; discovering that we were "the custodian of a great little remnant of what once was Pennsylvania" on property that "is essentially irreplaceable and priceless" gave us a whole new love for and connection to the place; as a result, our efforts became driven by a much deeper relationship with the land and concern for its health.

- Floristic Quality Assessment (see sidebar): This tool, as described above, can provide valuable initial site assessments, but also can be used to track changes on the same site over time to garner periodic feedback. The earlier in the process this kind of assessment can be engaged, the greater the chance that it can inform design decisions.

- Observation of living systems: This is about looking at the patterns and relationships between the aspects of life in any given place. These patterns can be seen through historical accounts and analysis of scientific data *along with* the knowledge necessary to support and confirm pattern understanding—data, or facts alone, do not reveal patterns.

- Inventories: Through a consolidated inventory of soil, plant species, animal habitat, microclimates, and evolutionary interaction of people in the project's place over time, we can learn the patterns of how life has evolved there, along with when and how it has devolved. This can help us discover the means by which we can contribute to the health of the place.

- The following represents a menu of potential systems consultants who can provide the

Coefficients of Conservatism and Floristic Quality Assessment*

Excerpted from source at www.fhsu.edu/biology/ranpers/ert/fqa_cc.htm

Floristic Quality Assessment

Floristic quality assessment is a standardized tool for natural area assessment developed by Floyd Swink and Gerould Wilhelm (1994). The method replaces very subjective measures of quality, such as "high" or "low," with a still somewhat subjective, but more dispassionate and quantitative index. This "Floristic Quality Index" allows comparison of the floristic quality among many sites and tracking changes at the same site over time. The method assigns a Coefficient of Conservatism to each native plant species based on that species tolerance for disturbance and fidelity to a particular pre-[European] settlement plant community type. The aggregate conservatism of all the plants inhabiting a site determine its floristic quality. Refer to Swink and Wilhelm (1994) for a thorough discussion of the methodology used to calculate a Floristic Quality Index.

Coefficient of Conservatism, C Value

The concept of species conservatism is the foundation of floristic quality assessment. Each native species is assigned a coefficient of conservatism (C) following the methods described by Swink and Wilhelm (1994) and Wilhelm and Masters (1995). Coefficients of conservatism range from 0 to 10 and represent an estimated probability that a plant is likely to occur in a landscape relatively unaltered from what is believed to be a pre-settlement condition. For example, a C of 0, is given to plants such as *Acer negundo,*

box elder, that have demonstrated little fidelity to any remnant natural community, i.e. may be found almost anywhere. Similarly, a C of 10 is applied to plants like *Potentilla fructicosa* (shrubby cinquefoil) that are almost always restricted to a pre-settlement remnant near Chicago, i.e., a high-quality natural area. Introduced plants were not part of the pre-settlement flora, so no C value is applied to these.

While C values are assigned based on collective extensive experience with the flora throughout an area the assignments are still somewhat subjective. The conceptual difference between a value of 0 and a value of 1, or between 9 and 10, is slight, while the difference between a value of 0 and a value of 3 is more distinct. Concerns over any particular C value are usually compensated within the floristic quality assessment method since it requires the average C value of all the individual species that occur at a site.

*References

Swink, F., and G. Wilhelm. 1994. *Plants of the Chicago Region*, 4th ed. Indianapolis, Ind.: Indiana Academy of Science.

Wilhelm, G. S., and L. A. Masters. 1995. *Floristic Quality Assessment in the Chicago Region and Application Computer Programs*. Lisle, Ill.: Morton Arboretum.

Herman, K. D., L. A. Masters, M. R. Penskar, A. A. Reznicek, G. S. Wilhelm, and W. W. Brodowicz. 1996. *Floristic Quality Assessment with Wetland Categories and Computer Application Programs for the State of Michigan*. Lansing, MI.: Michigan Department of Natural Resources, Wildlife Division, Natural Heritage Program.

Bowman's Hill Wildflower Preserve

Bowman's Hill Wildflower Preserve's Plant Stewardship Index

Description

Old Fields

Site Summary

This list contains 29 plants, of which 52% are native to NJ

Plant Stewardship Index	Total Mean C	Native Mean C	Floristic Quality Index
3.73	0.96	1.80	6.97

Description

Lewis School Woodland

Site Summary

This list contains 43 plants, of which 70% are native to NJ

Plant Stewardship Index	Total Mean C	Native Mean C	Floristic Quality Index
18.12	3.31	4.30	23.55

Figure 5-40 Indices such as coefficients of conservatism (C values) can be used to evaluate and track over time the health of a place, based on a qualitative inventory and assessment of all plant species inhabiting a site. *Image courtesy of Gerould Wilhelm.*

tools, assessments, and inventories that may be needed, depending on project specifics:

- Restoration scientists
- Fluvial morphologists (river and stream expertise)
- Geomorphologists (large scale geography)
- Soil and geotechnical consultants
- Wetlands specialists
- Water quality analysts
- Permaculturalists
- Systems permaculturalists (large scale ecological systems)
- Habitat biologists (animal and plant)
- Hydrologists (surface and groundwater)
- Social anthropologists
- Archeologists
- Historians

For many sites, it is important to conduct an ecological site assessment to determine and better understand the land and its inhabitants. On a project for the Lewis School near Princeton, we were working with an owner who was exploring the construction of a new school facility on property that was a combination of field and woodland. Site assessments were conducted by the landscape architects and a consulting botanist. The botanist used a Plant Stewardship Index tool (available through Bowman's Hill Wildflower Preserve), which is based on the same C-value (Coefficient of Conservatism) method described above. The results are presented in Figure 5-40. Partial results of the analyses conducted by the landscape architect are presented in Figures 5-41 through 5-44. To the untrained eye, the site appears to be a bucolic rural scene of farm fields interspersed with woodlands, areas that one might tend to avoid disturbing. Closer inspection via the ecological site assessment revealed that the site suffered from severe and chronic loss of water and soil, hence intense loss of biodiversity. Nonnative species dominated the fields, a significant amount of soil loss was occurring even in vegetated areas, much of the woodlands were overgrown with invasive species, and most rainwater was lost as runoff that contained high levels of nitrogen concentrations. With this knowledge in hand, the project team was better able to understand the place and move forward toward developing solutions that could mutually benefit all the inhabitants of the land.

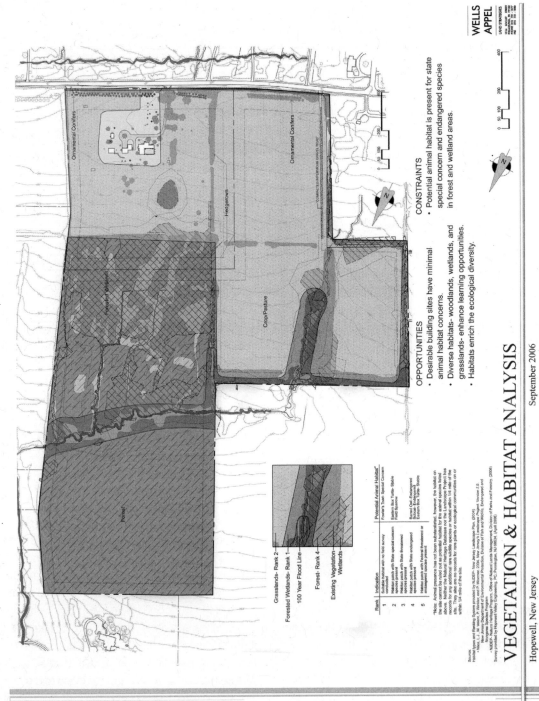

Figure 5-41 Site assessment analyses conducted early in the Discovery phase pertaining to vegetation and habitat corridors can be used to identify the opportunities and constraints of existing conditions (See also Figures 5-42, 5-43, and 5-44). *Image courtesy of Wells Appel Landscape Architecture and Planning.*

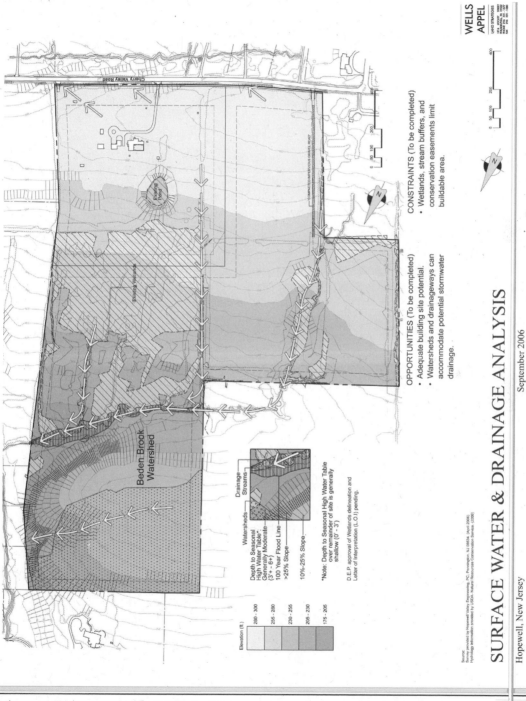

WELLS APPEL

SURFACE WATER & DRAINAGE ANALYSIS

Hopewell, New Jersey

September 2006

Figure 5-42 Site assessment analyses aimed at discovering historical and predevelopment surface water and drainage patterns early in the Discovery phase can reveal opportunities and constraints present in existing conditions. For example, road alignments and building placement should honor the force and flow of water. *Image courtesy of Wells Appel Landscape Architecture and Planning.*

THE LEWIS SCHOOL

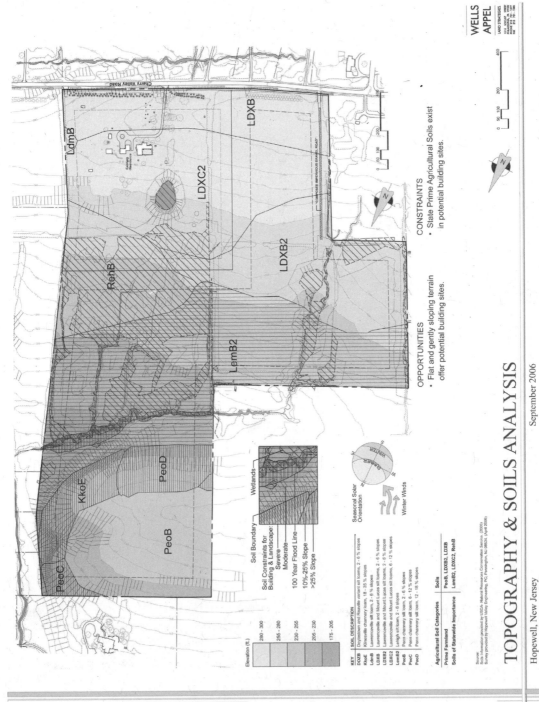

THE LEWIS SCHOOL

TOPOGRAPHY & SOILS ANALYSIS

Hopewell, New Jersey   September 2006

Figure 5-43 Topography and soils analyses prepared before Workshops No. 1 and 2 can help confirm the potential for more robust habitat in the future and help the team direct design components into areas that have the least potential for being ecologically productive. Our ultimate wealth resides in soil, and water can quickly carry it away if drainage patterns are not designed to slow and minimize runoff. *Image courtesy of Wells Appel Landscape Architecture and Planning.*

THE LEWIS SCHOOL

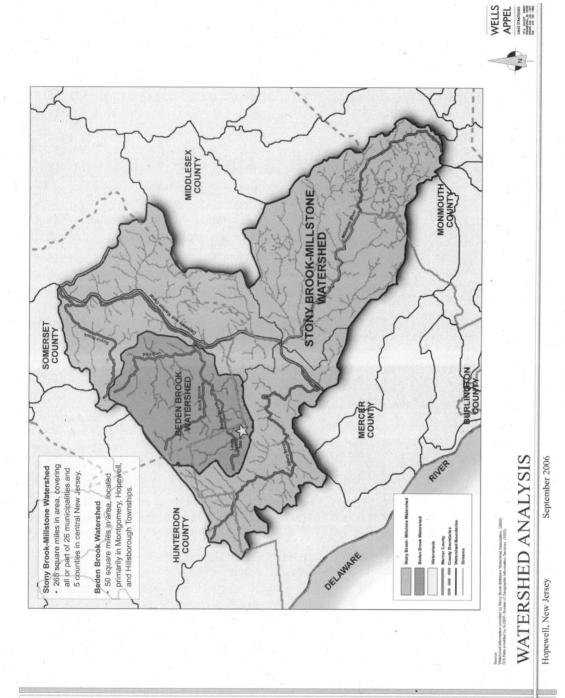

WATERSHED ANALYSIS

Hopewell, New Jersey   September 2006

Stony Brook-Millstone Watershed
- 265 square miles in area, covering all or part of 26 municipalities and 5 counties in central New Jersey.

Beden Brook Watershed
- 50 square miles in area, located primarily in Montgomery, Hopewell, and Hillsborough Townships.

Source:
Watershed information provided by Stony Brook-Millstone Watershed Association. (2006)
GIS Data provided by NJDEP- Bureau of Geographic Information Services. (1995)

Figure 5-44 Research and analysis that aims at understanding the watershed can be used during Workshops No. 1 and 2 to help understand the context of water flow. The team can then begin to understand how the site is impacted by upstream events and how it can influence downstream life. Designing to create greater health in water courses and on the surfaces that feed these water courses should be integral to any building and site design. The largest manageable watershed should be considered as the *smallest* context for any project. *Image courtesy of Wells Appel Landscape Architecture and Planning.*

- **Habitat** (human)
  - Since human habitat issues include those that impact health, safety, performance, and quality of life, examples of issues to be tested and examined in more detail include: indoor air quality, ventilation, thermal comfort, lighting, acoustics, odor, vistas and views, etc.
  - Investigate daylighting strategies (see discussion under "Tools" below).
  - Begin to discuss and consider the use of adaptive thermal comfort strategies to provide greater comfort while decreasing energy use (see "Adaptive Thermal Comfort" sidebar in *Stage A.3.1*).
  - Identify beneficial interrelationships between the project and the community; for example, transforming infrastructure disruptions into other restorative community activities underway can help the project become a catalyst to reinforce objectives (e.g., the Brattleboro Co-op example discussed in Chapter 4).
  - Identify potential source control issues associated with toxicants in materials over their entire life cycle.

The practice of evaluating toxicants in materials and buildings deserves some elaboration, particularly with regard to the interrelationships between materials and other subsystems. Our typical process for thinking about green materials is to look for their negative attributes, such as toxicants, and attempt to find alternatives that do not have those attributes. This can be a good place to start. For example, we know we can positively affect human health by using materials that do not emit volatile organic compounds (VOCs) inside the building. But what about the off-gassing or emissions that occur outside the building, or during a given material's manufacturing process, or from its disposal?

Another tendency is to focus less on materials and more on impacts associated with a building's energy use, since the total ratio of energy used over a building's life is so much greater than the energy used to make the materials for the building. But focusing on energy tells us only one—albeit important—part of a larger story. For example, many of the toxic releases that remain in our world, sometimes over indeterminate time frames, come from the extraction, production, use, and disposal of our materials.

The point here is that when we look only at the energy impacts of materials as they relate to a specific building and only relative to that building's life, materials seem not to matter too much, since the overall impacts of operating that building as an ongoing polluter over its life span (emissions associated with energy consumption and transportation, for example) seem to dwarf the impacts associated with the energy used to produce and use its materials. But when viewed more holistically, materials can have significant ongoing impacts on human health, other biotic habitat, and water quality through the *toxic releases* (and emissions) that may occur during their full life cycle, from extraction to disposal. These toxic emissions can happen both internally (affecting building occupants) and externally (affecting the larger community and ecological system).

LCA tools can be used to measure and assess these toxicant impacts over the entire life of a material. It should be noted that many of these impacts remain very difficult to measure, in particular, land use impacts and certain human health impacts; these need to be dealt with more specifically and separately from LCA, and they often require a more subjective approach to assessing impacts and value. In any case, though, it can be quite informative to consider the flow of a material over its entire life when assessing its impacts due to toxicants, beginning with the extraction of its raw materials components to its final disposal—the entire cycle, coming from nature and returning to it. We can break down this flow into stages; they often are delineated in the following way:

- Cradle to gate: includes material extraction to manufacturing
- Construction: what happens on the job site
- Use: the maintenance and replacement of a material
- End of life: the impact of land filling or recycling

Each of these stages includes both extractions from the environment and flows into the environment, most of which are measurable. LCA tools can be used to quantify these flows as they relate to a given material's toxicant impacts. Design decisions about materials options, then, can be informed by a more holistic approach that considers and compares larger impacts over longer time frames (more on LCA later).

- **Tools** (examples)

  Investigate daylighting strategies: The use of naturally lighted spaces is a particularly valuable strategy not only for achieving energy savings (and for earning LEED points across more than one credit) but daylighting also can contribute to occupant wellbeing and productivity when used carefully. Consequently, teams are encouraged to improve their ability to apply daylighting strategies in their early thinking about building design solutions. Physical models are an accurate way to evaluate the effects of daylighting as well, and they can be a cost-effective method of analysis. However, software programs are increasingly used to simulate and analyze daylighting effects. These simulation tools will be examined in detail in *Stage B.2.1.*

The LEED program currently allows verification of daylighting performance with a simplified calculation method, referred to as the *glazing factor.* This calculation takes into account window area, room floor area, window geometry, window height, and the *visible light transmittance* (or Tvis) of glazing. However, as an approximation, the calculation excludes factors such as orientation, room cavity ratios, visible access to the sky dome, latitude designation, and interior room reflectance. This limited methodology only really assesses, a bit crudely, the *quantity* of daylight. Good daylighting, though, requires addressing both its quantity and *quality*. It is possible to earn the LEED credit for daylighting, using the simplified glazing factor calculation, by designing spaces with very poor daylighting. Good daylighting design is not simply installing windows in a space. Good daylighting design is integrated into the essential fabric of the building's design—it is in the design's DNA. To be most effective, daylighting cannot be an afterthought related to the building's design, it must be one of the primary design drivers from the beginning.

Unlike artificial lighting, sunlight is highly variable and difficult to control. For most commercial spaces, the best daylighting designs bring in visible light while excluding its direct beams from entering the space, as these can cause glare and unwanted solar heat gains. *Bilateral daylighting*—bringing daylight into a space from more than one direction, optimally from the north and south—typically provides the highest quality daylighting conditions. Our visual acuity is a complex combination of light quality and quantity. When daylighting provides very high levels of light *quality,* the *quantity* of light (measured in foot-candles) can often be reduced.

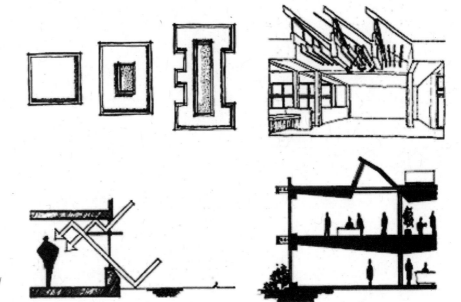

Figure 5-45 Good daylighting design begins with simple massing sketches and aperture studies. For example, these drawings from the *Whole Building Design Guide* show various building configurations, potential sections, and details regarding roof monitors and light shelves. *Image courtesy of* Whole Building Design Guide; © 2006 National Institute of Building Sciences.

Many architects understand daylighting design; but for the majority, we have found that it can be helpful to remind them of what characterizes *good* daylighting design. Initial design considerations—such as orientation, building massing, interior space configuration, and light reflectance values, window sizing and placement, shading, and so on—should be discussed and evaluated during conceptual design. Consequently, we have found it extremely helpful to convene at this point an interim meeting that focuses on daylighting with the project architect and other team members to review some design tips, so that daylighting is not something applied to the design after the fact. (A document outlining daylighting design tips can be downloaded as a pdf file from the *Resources* tab on 7group's website at www.sevengroup.com.)

- Daylighting simulation tools: Several daylighting software-analysis programs that can help

teams develop high quality daylighting are listed in *Stage B.2.1.*

- ATHENA® *Impact Estimator for Buildings:* This LCA tool can be used to assess toxicant impacts and is described in the "LCA Tools and Environmental Benefits" section at the beginning of Chapter 6.

■ **Water**

The primary activity at this stage is conducting water balancing analysis. *Water balancing* consists of understanding all water input *to* the site and building and all water output *from* the building and site. The fundamental goal is to live within the site's annual rainfall budget by keeping, treating, recharging, and maintaining all water flow from the building and site on the site. Additionally, as much water as possible should be cascaded and used to benefit all technical and living systems multiple times. As Gerry Wilhelm tells us, an adage to remember here is "let rain stay where it falls."

The Water Balance

By Michael Ogden, PE

The *water balance*—an accounting of sources and uses of water—is an essential tool in developing a sustainable project. The basic idea behind the water balance is intuitively easy to understand; stated in its simplest form, it is merely a question of how much water goes into a building, and how it is used. Typically, design professionals do not spend a lot of time thinking about the consequences their designs have on water use. Architects are trained to locate various water-consuming appliances within a building and then leave it to the engineers to design both the system that supplies the water and a wastewater collection system to remove wastewater. In this simplistic view, the design (or development) process should consist of nothing more complicated than two pipes: one for clean water and one for dirty water. The landscape architect may slightly complicate the process.

Global warming, the price of oil, droughts, and water pollution have combined to encourage design professionals to take another, more holistic view of the water balance, and ask questions related to the consequences of our designs, whether they be single family dwellings or new cities. It has become clear to many design professionals that a new building or development can have major impacts on water supply, so that questions about the sources of water must be answered first. Typically, until recently, only western states demanded an assured supply prior to issuance of building permits. But when we read that the Georgia legislature has considered moving the state line a mile north to gain access to the Tennessee River (and this is a state that normally receives 52 inches of rainwater/year), it is evident that the planning and design process needs to look beyond the expectation that the water will always be there.

Water has been priced as if it is free; only the costs of pumping, filtering, disinfecting, and the amortization of capital equipment and labor are part of the water bill. Rivers and streams are used as conveyances for our "used" water and decision makers hope that the downstream users do not object too much. As a consequence, water in most communities is relatively inexpensive, and not much thought is given to the availability of supply or the consequences of its use. As a more sophisticated approach, the water balance begins to recognize the essential value of water: in the western United States, there is no development without water. An argument can be made that in the future, periods of extended drought will make this a similar consideration in the eastern United States as well.

Recognition of the reality of a dwindling water supply requires more sophisticated tools and methods to deal with ensuring reasonable supplies. The most important change that must occur is in the master planning process itself. The planner, architect, civil engineer, landscape architect, HVAC engineer, electrical engineer, and owner/developer all must participate in a charrette process that clearly acknowledges the role of water in the development process. The water balance is the potential tool capable of dealing with a limited resource whose availability may be highly variable, subject to unpredictable future conditions. Once it is acknowledged that water

(continued)

is essential to the development process, it becomes logical to incorporate design solutions that minimize consumptive uses of water, reduce water diversions, save energy, reduce downstream impacts of storm water and wastewater, reduce groundwater depletion, and improve potable water supplies and water security.

The following list represents those elements in a water balance that constitute sources and supplies of water and the associated informational requirements.

- *Sources.* Not much will happen without a water supply. These need to be identified immediately in any design process.
  1. Municipal or water district supply. (This generally relies on a water catchment basin, e.g., New York, Los Angeles, which in turn depends on rainfall.)
  2. Rainfall on the building or property. (Western water law complicates the harvest rules.)
  3. Groundwater flows. Velocity, direction, quantity, and quality are factors.
  4. Reclaimed water. Wastewater can be treated to a level suitable for reuse as irrigation water or as a supply for toilets and urinals.
  5. Sea water. Desalinization plants provide an option for coastal regions, but are energy intensive.

- *Uses.* Each type of building will have a different water demand. Understanding the building type and its water use is the essential first step. For example, offices use about 8–13 gallons per person per day, while residences may use 45–150 gallons per person per day. Big homes use more water than small homes; large residential lots use

more water than small lots. Apartment dwellers use less water than suburbanites. Uses in buildings and large scale developments will include some or all of the following:
  1. Washing: showers, baths, laundry
  2. Culinary and drinking
  3. Flushing of toilets and urinals
  4. Cooling (chillers) and heating (steam heat, saunas)
  5. Irrigation
  6. Swimming pools, spas, architectural uses
  7. Industrial and/or food processing water

Water demand will change seasonally and daily; building occupancy, landscape demand, and cooling requirements will affect use on a daily basis as well as seasonally (e.g., ski resort in Aspen, spa in Arizona).

The type of landscape will greatly dictate water usage. Lawns are probably the most water intensive feature in the landscape. Native landscaping, or landscapes designed for local climate conditions, are usually the most frugal.

The following list is typical of the kind of information that is essential for developing the water balance. One or all of these types of buildings or structures may be included in the project. All need to be listed.

1. Number of residences with average population and roof area, type of building (single family, condo, apartment, etc.) and number of bedrooms.
2. Total area of office buildings and area of roof. Include number of parking spaces and surface area.

3. Total area of retail buildings plus roof area. Also include number of parking spaces and surface area.

4. Restaurants, cafeterias, coffee shops, and so forth. List total seating and number of meals per day.

5. Hotels and resorts. List number of rooms, class (budget, four star, etc.), restaurants, bar, spa, roof area, parking, and maximum seasonal occupancy rates.

6. List other building types such as warehouses, laboratories, industrial, or food processing facilities. Indicate roof and parking areas.

7. Landscaped area, ideally by type (percentage of high, medium, and low water use). (If not known, make some assumptions appropriate to the site and climate.)

8. Total paved area; topography, existing vegetation, and surfaces.

Once the sources and uses are identified—building types, landscapes, etc.—it is possible to address some design goals that will affect the water balance:

- *Precision.* How important is the daily or monthly demand? An office will have a different daily demand than a home. Is a monthly estimate adequate? What about rainfall? Generating daily rainfall amounts using the National Oceanic and Atmospheric Administration (NOAA) historical data will generate precipitation numbers that can be used to develop an estimate for the potential harvesting of rainwater, determine run-off, and define on-site storage requirements. Using statistical forecasting techniques and the latest climate change predictions, long-range water balance calculations can be developed.

- *Integrated "green design."* Green design principles include reuse of reclaimed water and/or harvest of rainwater for irrigation, toilet supply, and cooling; storm water can be viewed as a major asset or a major problem. The potable supply, rainfall, and reclaimed water can be utilized as both heat sources and heat sinks. Working with the HVAC engineers, designers can make projects more energy efficient by using the heat capacity of water.

- *Project phasing.* Each phase of development can be modeled to determine the water balance as the project grows.

- *Flexibility.* The water balance is easily and quickly edited to reflect changes in vision or scope.

Once all of the relevant information has been accumulated, the model can be assembled in such a way that it will produce information from inception of the project to twenty or more years in the future. The schematic diagram in Figure 5-46 shows the annual demand resulting from calculations for a typical office building in Albuquerque, New Mexico, based on an annual rainfall of 8.8 inches.

This model represents a very simple water balance, but it is illustrative of the possible outcome, which will vary from year to year. Complexity multiplies as various building types are added. Regional water balances require sophisticated computer systems, but for most developments and small communities, the water balance can be completed on a desktop personal computer.

(continued)

Figure 5-46 Water inputs and outputs that demonstrate how water can be used in multiple and cascading relationships should be diagrammed for every project so that the team can understand and help participate in exploring design improvements that support these opportunities. This schematic water balance diagram was prepared for a mixed-use development of approximately 150 homes, in the arid west. It illustrates the quantity of flow through a development incorporating residential dwellings, a school, civic and commercial buildings, and landscape. Captured rainwater and treated effluent meet the landscape water demand. This reduces the potable water required for the development by 6.14 acre-feet per year (AFY), or by approximately 2 million gallons, (6.14 x 43,560 cubic feet x 7.48 gallons/cubic foot). The diagram also shows that no captured rainwater or recycled effluent is being used for flushing urinals and water closets in the commercial and civic buildings. However, the commercial and civic buildings are dual-plumbed to make this possible in the future. 15.8 acre-feet per year (5.15 million gallons) is returned to the aquifer through a "land application system." This offsets the long-term demand on the aquifer, creating a more sustainable water profile for the development. *Image © 2008 Natural Systems International.*

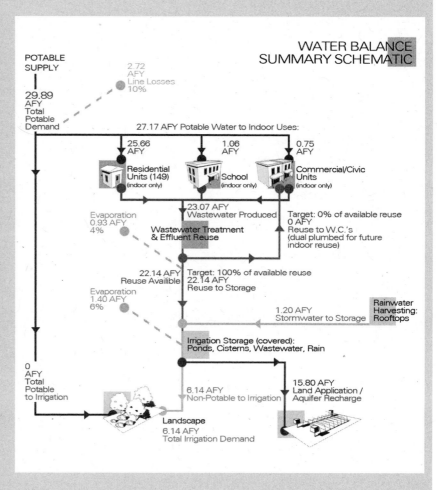

- **Tools** (example)

  Analysis depends on the scope of the hydrological cycle under consideration at this stage: for example, using rainwater harvesting cisterns versus using the cascading benefits of the natural hydrological cycle, that is, using treated wastewater from constructed wetlands to irrigate vegetation and to recharge groundwater, which uses the ground for water storage. Spreadsheets can be developed for this type of analysis (see Figure 5-47). Water balance diagrams also can be used to investigate and visually portray systems explorations (see Figure 5-46).

DEP Norristown Office Building: Monthly Stormwater Harvesting Predictions

New Hard Roof Area - Total	23,629	sq. ft.
Green Roof Area - Total	850	sq. ft.
Hard Roof Run-off	95	percent
Green Roof Run-off	50	percent
Annual Toilet Demand	250,000	gal. (See WEc2)
Daily Toilet Demand	1,000	gal. (See WEc2)
Daily Hose Bibb demand	50	gal. Atrium planting hose bibb at 5 gpm x 10 minutes/day = 50 gal/day
Annual Work days	250	
Cistern Usable Storage Capacity	4,250	gal. 5,500 gal. nominal capacity x 85% actual: sized to accommodate 4-day demand of 1,050 gal/day x 4 = 4,200 gal.

Hard Roof Default Run-off Coeff.	95.00%
Stormwater Reused	41.47%
Adjusted Hard Roof Run-off Coeff.	53.53%

Month		Average Rain Inches	Rain cu ft	Rain gal.	Green Roof stormwater gal/month	Hard Roof stormwater gal/month	Total Roof stormwater gal/month	Average Work Days per month	Daily Toilet Demand gal/day	Daily Hose Bibb Demand gal/day	Monthly Toilet Demand gal/month	Monthly Hose Bibb Demand gal/month	Total Greywater Demand gal/month	% Stormwater Recovered
Jan	Hard Roof	3.3	6,498	48,605		46,175	47,049	20.83	1,000	50	20,833	1,042	21,875	46.49
	Green Roof		234	1,748	874									
Feb	Hard Roof	3	5,907	44,186		41,977	42,772	20.83	1,000	50	20,833	1,042	21,875	51.14
	Green Roof		213	1,590	795									
Mar	Hard Roof	3.5	6,892	51,551		48,973	49,900	20.83	1,000	50	20,833	1,042	21,875	43.84
	Green Roof		248	1,854	927									
Apr	Hard Roof	3.7	7,286	54,496		51,772	52,752	20.83	1,000	50	20,833	1,042	21,875	41.47
	Green Roof		262	1,960	980									
May	Hard Roof	4.2	8,270	61,661		58,768	59,880	20.83	1,000	50	20,833	1,042	21,875	36.53
	Green Roof		298	2,225	1,113									
Jun	Hard Roof	3.6	7,089	53,023		50,372	51,326	20.83	1,000	50	20,833	1,042	21,875	42.62
	Green Roof		255	1,907	954									
Jul	Hard Roof	4.5	8,861	66,279		62,965	64,158	20.83	1,000	50	20,833	1,042	21,875	34.10
	Green Roof		319	2,384	1,192									
Aug	Hard Roof	4.1	8,073	60,388		57,368	58,455	20.83	1,000	50	20,833	1,042	21,875	37.42
	Green Roof		290	2,172	1,086									
Sept	Hard Roof	4.1	8,073	60,388		57,368	58,455	20.83	1,000	50	20,833	1,042	21,875	37.42
	Green Roof		290	2,172	1,086									
Oct	Hard Roof	3	5,907	44,186		41,977	42,772	20.83	1,000	50	20,833	1,042	21,875	51.14
	Green Roof		213	1,590	795									
Nov	Hard Roof	3.8	7,483	55,969		53,171	54,177	20.83	1,000	50	20,833	1,042	21,875	40.38
	Green Roof		269	2,013	1,007									
Dec	Hard Roof	3.6	7,089	53,023		50,372	51,326	20.83	1,000	50	20,833	1,042	21,875	42.62
	Green Roof		255	1,907	954									
Annual Totals		44.4	90,572	677,481	11,762	621,258	633,021	250			250,000	12,500	262,500	41.47
Annual totals adjusted for runoff coefficient					5,881	590,195	596,077							

L. Robert Kimball Associates

Figure 5-47 Rainwater harvesting calculations that predict supply capacity (based upon catchment areas, their runoff coefficients, and local weather data for average monthly rainfall) can be compared to demand calculations for annual toilet flushing. In this case, calculations indicate that the system's annual collection capacity equates to 596,077 gallons. Using the rule of thumb that 50 percent of the average rainfall can be used as an estimate of the low end of expected rainfall in a drought year, the system is capable of capturing 298,039 (596,077 × 0.5) gallons annually. When the hose bib's annual demand of 12,500 gallons is subtracted from this rainwater harvesting capacity, 285,539 gallons remain available for toilet flushing, which exceeds the total annual toilet flushing demand of 250,000 gallons by 14 percent. *Image courtesy of 7group.*

▪ Energy

The analysis at this stage is highly dependent on the level of conceptual design reached at Workshop No. 2, but the following assumes that a general building footprint and configuration has been initially established for a first round of conceptual testing; if not, the following level of analysis likely will need to be deferred to *Stage B.2*.

- Based on the initial research into building energy distribution and loads, performance goals, parameters, targets, early building massing models, and the potential strategies discussed in the workshops, more specific modeling runs can be undertaken to evaluate the effectiveness of individual strategies and combinations of strategies.

- The first step is to determine an appropriate baseline for comparison. The purpose of energy modeling during design is to enable the design team to make relative comparisons, not absolute predictions. Relative comparisons can be accurate without being absolutely correct in terms of actual quantities of usage. With so many variables, it is virtually impossible to accurately predict the future and match actual energy usage during occupancy. As long as the modeling results are within reason, the percentage differential between options (relative comparisons) should be enough to drive decisions at this stage. Entering modeling results into the Environmental Protection Agency's (EPA's) Target Finder (www.energystar.gov/index.cfm?c=new_bldg_design.bus_target_finder) can help teams determine if the model is yielding reasonable results. In addition to the benchmarking capabilities discussed in *Stage A.1.1*, Target Finder also allows users to compare their modeled energy consumption (Design Energy) to the target by entering an estimate from their modeling results into the tool. Target Finder will display the corresponding EPA Target Rating or Energy Reduction Target—the percentage of energy consumption reduction relative to a similar benchmark building. (See discussion of Target Finder in the "Energy" section of *Stage A.1.1*.)

- Produce conceptual parametric modeling runs of design options and individual energy-efficiency measures (EEMs) to inform schematic design options (e.g., different thermal envelope parameters, reduction in lighting power density, daylighting, and other load reduction strategies, etc.). Specific EEMs to be evaluated can vary considerably, depending on the type of project.

- At this point, modeling should focus almost entirely on load-reduction strategies before analyzing different mechanical systems options; in other words, the adage here should be *Reduce, Reduce, Reduce* the building's energy demand, instead of searching for simply more efficient mechanical equipment.

- Parametric modeling begins by analyzing individual strategies in isolation. This first pass should be used to assist in the prioritization of EEMs. Both energy-savings and load-reduction impacts should be considered in the analysis of each EEM. The EEMs are then run in combination to evaluate the optimal synergy between cost, savings, and load reduction. All of these iterations are run using the baseline model for comparison.

- It is important that load-reduction strategies are evaluated before using the model to evaluate HVAC system options. One of the goals in this round of modeling is to begin to evaluate the potential for downsizing the HVAC system. If HVAC system options are evaluated based on the baseline model's loads and parameters, then the full effect of HVAC-system-size and -cost reductions will not be accurately evaluated; hence, HVAC system options should be evaluated *after* all loads have been reduced as much as possible in the model via the most promising combina-

tion of EEMs. If the potential HVAC systems are known, then these systems should be modeled assuming the reduced loads. Depending on the software used for energy modeling, this may require the performance of HVAC load and system calculations in a separate piece of software.

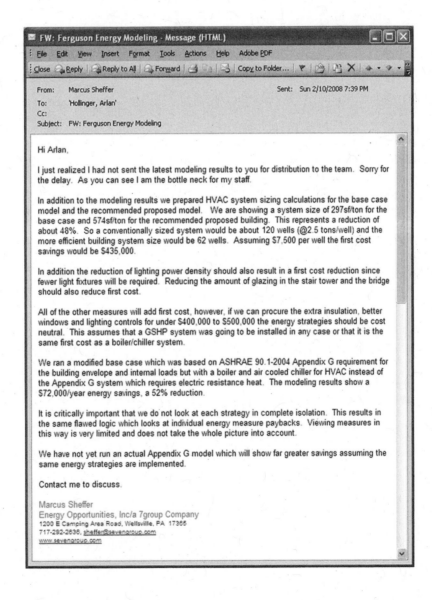

▶ **Figure 5-48** Sample e-mail correspondence summarizing initial parametric energy modeling results and HVAC system sizing impacts, including potential first-cost reductions. *Image courtesy of Marcus Sheffer.*

Ferguson Elementary
eQuest v3.6 Modeling Results Summary
Building Energy Enduse Summary for Individual Energy Efficiency Measures (EEMs)

Individual EEM Design Runs	Base Building ASHRAE 90.1-2004 Appendix G w/ modified HVAC	EEM-1 R20 Roof	EEM-2 R30 Roof	EEM-3 Triple Pane Windows	EEM-4 Reduced Lighting LPD=0.75 W/sqft	EEM-5 LPD=0.75 w/ Daylight On/Off Controls	EEM-6 Increased Wall Insulation to overall Rt=18.5	EEM-7 Slab on Grade Edge Insulation	EEM 8 Elim Bridge & South Stair Glazing
Estimated Operating Costs									
Electric	$70,611	$70,472	$69,838	$72,361	$61,214	$58,646	$70,959	$71,583	$68,914
Gas	$68,210	$67,155	$65,771	$65,850	$71,150	$71,620	$63,631	$46,499	$65,424
Total	$138,821	$137,627	$135,609	$128,211	$132,364	$130,266	$134,590	$118,082	$134,338
Cost/SqFt	$1.56	$1.55	$1.52	$1.44	$1.49	$1.46	$1.51	$1.33	$1.51
Consumption									
Site (kBtu / SqFt / Yr)	91.4	90.6	89.1	80.9	90.6	90.2	87.5	71.2	87.8
Building Electric Use (kWh)									
Total	726,722	730,864	725,871	754,987	634,267	610,662	734,861	730,443	701,324
Building Gas Use (Therms)									
Total	56,587	55,704	54,547	46,290	59,033	59,424	52,772	38,497	54,265
EEM Economics									
EEM Savings	NA	$1,194	$3,212	$10,610	$6,457	$8,555	$4,231	$20,739	$4,483

EEM Descriptions

| EEM 1 - ASHRAE Baseline but with R20 roof insulation |
| EEM 2 - ASHRAE Baseline but with R30 roof insulation |
| EEM 3 - ASHRAE Baseline but with Triple pane windows, Pella Designer Series LowE IG w/ argon w/ 3rd LowE pane, U=0.16, SHGC=0.37, Vt=0.61 |
| EEM 4 - ASHRAE Baseline but with reduced lighting power density (LPD) to 0.75 W/sqft |
| EEM 5 - ASHRAE Baseline but with reduced lighting power density (LPD) to 0.75 W/sqft and Daylighting On/Off controls for 1/3 of lights in perimeter spaces |
| EEM-6 - ASHRAE Baseline but with Wall insulation increased such that the overall wall R=18.5 |
| EEM-7 - ASHRAE Baseline but with R10 24" vertical and horizontal edge insulation added to slab on grade |
| EEM-8 - ASHRAE Baseline but eliminating all of the bridge windows and 75% of the windows in the South Stairwell. |

Figure 5-49 These sample parametric energy modeling runs analyzed individual energy-efficiency measures (EEMs) to evaluate energy savings relative to a baseline (see also Figure 5-50).
Image courtesy of Shelia Sagerer.

Ferguson Elementary
eQuest v3.6 Modeling Results Summary

Building Energy Enduse Summary for Energy Efficiency Measure (EEM) Combinations

Combined EEM Design Runs	Base Building ASHRAE 90.1-2004 Appendix G w/ modified HVAC	EEM Combo 1 EEM 2, 3, 5, 6, 7, 8 w/ modified HVAC	EEM Combo 2 EEM 2, 3, 5, 6, 7, 8 w/ groundsource heatpumps & Heat recovery on ded OA
Estimated Operating Costs			
Electric	$70,611	$55,864	$64,652
Gas	$68,210	$27,188	$1,280
Total	$138,821	$83,052	$65,932
Cost/SqFt	$1.56	$0.93	$0.74
Building Energy Use (MBtus)			
Site (kBtu / SqFt / Yr)	91.4	46.5	26.7
Building Electric Use (kWh)			
Total	726,722	555,385	671,554
Building Gas Use (Therms)			
Total	56,587	22,409	836
EEM Economics			
EEM Savings	NA	$55,769	$72,889

EEM Descriptions

Baseline building uses ASHRAE design as described on "Baseline Input Summary" tables.

EEM Combo 1 - ASHRAE building with chiller & boiler HVAC system, applying EEMs 2, 3, 5, 6, 7, & 8: R30 Roof, Pella Designer Series Triple Pane Windows U=0.16, SHGC=0.37, VLt=0.61, LPD reduced to 0.75 W/sqft, Daylight On/Off Controls for 1/3 of lights in perimeter spaces, wall insulation to overall Rt=18.5, R10 24" vertical and horizontal edge insulation, and eliminating all windows in bridge connector and 75% of windows in South Stairwell

EEM Combo 2 - ASHRAE Baseline but with GSHPs and heat recovery on dedicated OA units and applying EEMs 2, 3, 5, 6, 7, & 8: R30 Roof, Pella Designer Series Triple Pane Windows U=0.16, SHGC=0.37, VLt=0.61, LPD reduced to 0.75 W/sqft, Daylight On/Off Controls for 1/3 of lights in perimeter spaces, wall insulation to overall Rt=18.5, R10 24" vertical and horizontal edge insulation, and eliminating all windows in bridge connector and 75% of windows in South Stairwell

Figure 5-50 This sample summary of energy modeling runs shows the cumulative effect that various combinations of individual EEMs have on energy savings. The EEM Combo 2 modeling run includes a different HVAC system (in this case, ground-source heat pumps) applied to EEM Combo 1 so that the effect of the HVAC system can be isolated and compared under similar load conditions. *Image courtesy of Shelia Sagerer.*

Evaluating Building Energy Performance
for
Ferguson Elementary

Design Intent

The design intent is to make Ferguson Elementary into a "high performance building". Being early in the design development process, it would be useful to know how energy efficient the current design is. The US Environmental Protection Agency has developed a tool called Energy Star Target Finder that can be used during all stages of the design process to quickly evaluate a design's energy performance.

Energy Star Target Finder

The US EPA's Energy Star Target Finder is a tool used to assist the design team in setting an energy performance target in terms of site energy use intensity and estimated total annual energy consumption. The database used by Target Finder is the US Department of Energy's Commercial Building Energy Consumption Survey (CBECS). By entering a few of the project's facility characteristics (i.e. location of project for local climate and weather data, building type, area, occupancy levels, and hours of operation), the CBECS data can be accessed and normalized. The normalized data is then ranked on a scale of 1-100. As the design progresses, estimated annual energy use can be compared to the normalized CBECS data to monitor the design's energy performance.

Energy Opportunities, Inc has entered the energy modeling results in Target Finder and compared those results to expected energy performance at three levels of energy efficiency. The results are listed below.

Building Characteristics		
Zip Code	City	State

Facility Characteristics				
Space Type (see Notes below)	Gross Floor Area	Number of Occupants	Number of PCs	Operating Hours / Week
K-12 School	89,021	1,017	80	35
Totals	89,021 SqFt	1017	80	35

Utility Rates		
Electricity	virtual rate per KWh	$0.096 / kWh
Natural Gas	virtual rate per therm	$1.416 / CCF

Energy Star Target Finder Results					
Energy Data	50%	75% (Energy Star)	90%	EEM Combo w/ Boiler/Chiller	EEM Combo w/ GSHPs & Heat
Target Finder Rating	50	75	90	86	90
Site Energy Use Intensity (kBtu/Sq./yr)	44.7	35.8	26.7	29.3	26.7
Estimated Total Annual Site Energy (kBtu)	3,975,966.3	3,183,490.2	2,380,302.2	2,612,562.6	2,374,949.1
Total Annual Energy Cost ($)	$108,824	$87,133	$66,099	$71,507	$65,951
Average cost per kWh	$0.096 /kWh	$0.096 /kWh	$0.096 /kWh	$0.096 /kWh	$0.096 /kWh

Pollution Emissions					
CO_2 Emission (tons/year)	620	496	375	415	375
CO2 Emission Reduction (%)	0%	20%	40%	33%	40%

Figure 5-51 EPA Target Finder reports can be used as a reality check on the energy modeling results by comparing data from actual building energy consumption for similar building types to the team's modeling results. *Image courtesy of Shelia Sagerer.*

Energy Modeling Requirements

By Marc Rosenbaum, Energysmiths, Meriden, New Hampshire
Edited by Marcus Sheffer

Energy modeling is a critical item for two reasons—one is to guide good choices in envelope and systems during design phases, and the other is because it is required by LEED in most instances and by some jurisdictions.

Inputs

The owner and the architect need to understand completely the inputs as well as the outputs.

The report needs a comprehensible listing of all the inputs:

- envelope data (U-value and thermal mass inputs);
- areas of floor, wall, roof, and glazing, etc., by zone and orientation;
- U-value, Tvis, and SHGC for glazing;
- internal gains such as people and equipment;
- lighting loads and schedules;
- weather data such as Insolation (the measure of solar radiation energy received on a given surface area), Heating Degree Days, Cooling Degree Days, Wind Rose charts;
- seasonal design temperatures
- indoor conditions—occupied and unoccupied temperature set points;
- utility rates
- ventilation quantities and schedules;
- ventilation equipment recovery efficiency;
- infiltration assumptions;
- distribution equipment types and efficiencies, including fans and pumps; economizer settings, etc.

- HVAC equipment type, efficiencies, and details regarding settings.

The owner and design team should review the inputs before modeling is begun so that they can sign off on them. Advanced mechanical systems may not be easy to model in some software; use appropriate software, and make clear your assumptions if you are tweaking the software beyond its normal application.

Outputs

Outputs (or modeling results) should include the following:

- monthly and annual energy consumption for the following end uses:
- space heating
- space cooling
- fans and pumps
- domestic hot water (DHW)
- interior lighting
- exterior lighting
- equipment, including plug loads
- other ancillary or miscellaneous loads (such as for elevators)
- heating and cooling loads by building assembly type—how much is due to walls, roofs, windows, infiltration, ventilation air, lighting, people, etc. This guides us to look for the areas where we can make the biggest savings. We need this information for the baseline building (e.g., one that just meets ASHRAE 90.1,or code, or whatever is the base) and for the proposed building.

(continued)

Process

Once the inputs are agreed upon, run the base building model. Then, review the outputs to see how they compare with experience and data from actual buildings of similar occupancy (such as energy use data in Target Finder). We want to convince ourselves first that the model of the building is realistic, and then we want to be able to design parametric runs to look at variations.

Parametrics

Run the proposed building and examine areas that need more study. Vary inputs and review the results. Commonly modeled variations include envelope and glazing upgrades, equipment types and efficiencies, lighting levels and controls, and daylighting strategies.

Report

It is critical that this material be presented in a form that the design team and the owner can understand. This should include a narrative that can be understood by the project team that includes all the information listed above. Include the building area totals as a check on the area takeoffs used for the model. Produce a spreadsheet, or whatever works best, to show the energy consumption comparisons and EEM-related cost impacts in a way that is understandable. This should include breakdowns of the total energy use and cost by energy end uses as described above.

- **Tools** (examples)

  Several available energy modeling software programs can simulate whole-building energy consumption. Perhaps the simplest of these tools is Energy-10, a personal-computer-based program that enables architects to quickly identify cost-effective, energy-saving measures for commercial and residential buildings under 10,000 sq. ft. (www.nrel.gov/buildings/energy10). Larger and more complex buildings require more sophisticated programs. The most widely used of these are the following:

  - eQUEST: This building-energy-use analysis program is available at no charge at www.doe2.com.
  - VisualDOE: This energy-simulation program is available at www.archenergy.com/products/visualdoe.
  - HAP: Developed and owned by Carrier, this hourly analysis program is available at www.carrier-commercial.com/software.
  - TRACE™: This chiller plant analysis software, developed and owned by Trane, is available at www.trane.com/commercial/software.
  - EnergyPlus: This energy-simulation software from the U.S. Department of Energy merges the popular features and capabilities of the Department of Defense's BLAST and DOE-2. Graphic interfaces are under development. Available at no charge at www.energyplus.gov.
  - TRaNsient SYstems Simulation, or TRNSYS: The modular structure of this tool allows for custom configuration—available at http://sel.me.wisc.edu/trnsys/.

Materials

- *Materials Matrix:* Teams often find it useful to construct a spreadsheet matrix listing materials against the environmental criteria being considered so that materials options can be compared in a simple format. These criteria include all those that LEED addresses and more: recycled content, certified wood content, material off-gassing, distance from manufacturing and extraction, rapidly renewable content, embodied energy, waste generation, environmental stance of manufacturer, ease of disassembly, toxicants generated by manufacturing, carcinogen and endocrine disrupter content, and so forth.

- *Life Cycle Assessment (LCA):* As previously discussed, LCA tools provide a more accurate and more detailed analysis of materials impacts. These tools compare various material options in terms of their applicability to the project and their impacts over the building's service life across a range of LCA environmental impact indicators, based on quantified environmental inputs and extractions.

- *Service Life Planning.* Establish the planned service life of the building, as discussed in *Stage A.3.1:* Most impacts of buildings occur over time while the building is in operation. Energy and water use are good examples of this. The impacts accrue as energy and water are used. With materials, on the other hand, the impacts mostly occur before and during the initial stage of the building's life (extraction, manufacturing, and installation) and at the end of its useful life (disposal). This means that early assessment of a building's materials needs in terms of the building's service life is a key consideration when seeking large opportunities for reducing overall materials impacts—the longer they last, the smaller the impacts associated with their disposal and/or replacement.

A recent study by the Athena Institute shed some light on materials used in buildings by attempting to determine why buildings are torn down. The Institute obtained a database of buildings that had been demolished in a single year. Owners of these buildings were contacted and asked what the structural and envelope materials of their building were and why it was torn down. A most interesting finding was that many of the structures with the shortest service life (often less than twenty years)—namely mini-malls, strip malls, fast-food buildings, etc.—were made from the most durable materials, that is, concrete, steel, or brick. Following demolition, most of these materials typically end up in landfills. Some of them can be recycled, but this requires a significant amount of energy, and often, high-quality materials like portland cement are reduced to subbase materials.

So one might ask, if not these materials, what materials should be used for buildings with short service lives? Well, perhaps these materials in the right combination might work quite well, so long as they can be disassembled and reused more easily.

We used this thinking on a project for the U.S. Postal Service. We were told in early meetings how big the building needed to be. It seemed quite large, based on the size of the local community, so we asked "why so big?" As it turns out, this agency plans the location and size of their facilities based on projected growth patterns. In this case, projected data indicated a fast-growing area, so the building was programmed to accommodate ten years of growth. In the words of the project manager: "basically, the employees will have a ballroom to work in for the first decade."

Further discussion led to the following solution: The building was designed to utilize *structural insulated panels* (SIPs). We focused on connections for these SIPs not only for disassembly but also for ease of adding a phased expansion. As a result, the design was developed to build an initial building for five years of projected growth with plans for easily constructing an addition that could accommodate the next five years (whenever it was deemed necessary) without demolishing any of the existing building components. Piers were poured for the addition, so that site disruption would be minimized during the expansion. All structural and shell components were designed around a 24-inch module to reduce waste. Everything was designed for ease of disassembly, so that all components could be reused. In other words, all waste was designed out of both the initial project and the phased expansion. Additionally, the SIPs contributed significantly to the building's energy performance.

- **Tools** (example)
  - ATHENA® *Impact Estimator for Buildings*: This LCA tool, as mentioned above, is described in the "LCA Tools" section of Chapter 6. It can be used to analyze and compare various service life options against more than a dozen environmental impact indicators. One of the primary environmental impact indicators that LCA tools can analyze is carbon emissions, so such tools can assist in quantifying the carbon footprint of a project.

Carbon Footprinting

Carbon footprinting is a methodology for determining how much carbon dioxide is being created by the activities of a person or an organization. It is becoming more popular as awareness of climate change grows.

The process begins with an inventory of all relevant CO_2-generating activity. Calculator tools exist to assist in quantifying the carbon dioxide created per activity by assigning emissions factors to individual activities. Current calculators draw on many different data sources for calculating these factors, and the calculation methodologies used by these data sources range from the precise to the unknown, so outcomes from these tools can vary significantly. Also, these calculators can produce a wide range of results depending on how the scope of the inventory was determined, how "energy" is defined, and a number of other technical factors.

For this reason it is important to establish your purpose for undertaking a carbon inventory. If you want to know which areas of your activity are creating the most carbon dioxide for the purpose of focusing on ways to reduce the associated emissions, then it is always a useful exercise to compare strategies—regardless of how precisely the calculations are determined. If, on the other hand, you want to use this information to broadcast your good deeds, or engage in voluntary or regulatory carbon markets, then precision is much more important.

To better understand inventory scope issues, let's look at an example of a typical office building. The typical scope might begin with the following:

- On-site combustion energy use by the building
- Electricity use based on utility fuel type, i.e., combustion of coal vs. natural gas or hyroelectricity, etc.
- Employee business transportation (car, train, and air miles)
- Employee commuting transportation

Now let's say that this inventory is for an organization's new building project. Should this inventory include the extraction and manufacture of the building's materials? Should it include the transportation for getting those materials to the job site? Should it include the impacts related to the project's design and/or job-site meetings? Should it include the construction activity? And if so, should that include the transportation of the workers to the site? Should the contractor's equipment be included or should these impacts be attributed to the contractor? In other words, the scope questions abound, and their answers are not universally accepted, so if you engage carbon footprinting in order to claim that you are carbon neutral, then we must all accept that there is a great deal of uncertainty in the term "neutral."

It is always best to begin by using accepted standards for this work. Standards can be very helpful in establishing accepted practices and rules so claims of re-

duction and neutrality have real meaning. The relevant International Organization for Standardization (ISO) standards for defining this work are listed below.

Since most carbon footprinting is undertaken in order to achieve—and thereby claim—carbon neutrality, the carbon issue gets even more complicated. The most real and effective way to head toward neutrality is by implementing strategies that by various means reduce carbon impact. Most often, though, carbon offsets are purchased to reduce carbon footprints. At their best, these offsets can create markets that alter the flow of dollars into programs and projects that benefit the environment, e.g., funding carbon-reduction programs that in some cases could not exist without these dollars. At their worst, carbon offsets are nothing but dollars spent with little or no benefit to the environment. At present, the evolution of carbon footprinting requires significant research to ensure that what is being claimed as an offset is really an offset.

Example standards:

- To assist with service life planning, see ISO 15686
- To assist with carbon footprinting, see ISO 14064, 14065
- To understand LCA, see ISO 14024

Coalesce findings and bring analysis to a reasonable conclusion before beginning the Schematic Design phase

The analysis described above for *Stage A.5* may seem like an awful lot of analyses—because it is. It clearly adds more time and effort during the Discovery Phase, *but* it allows for informed decisions earlier in the process, so that later stages are not

hamstrung or paralyzed by too many variables. *Schematic Design* (SD) can now become more focused on refinement, rather than regressing to questioning fundamental issues. In short, as stated above in *Stage A.3*, the Construction Documents phase can be reserved solely for documentation, hence becoming much more efficient and taking less time. In the end, the total design time frame can remain the same, but the effort is much more front-end loaded.

By spending this upfront time to coalesce the major issues and form-givers before schematic design begins, the team has the opportunity to use the subsequent SD phase for focused design reconciliation, rather than trying to process too many new ideas at once. In other words, the range of alternatives to be explored in SD has already been significantly limited, because systemic analysis has identified and resolved many of the potential form-giving design inputs that otherwise could—and often do—overload the iterative SD exploration.

It should be noted that we have had teams reflect to us at this stage that they feel a bit confused or that this process feels awkward, since they have engaged all this analysis without yet committing to the building form, to which we respond, "Well, then, that's a good sign…you're probably on the right track."

A.5.2 Principles and Measurement

■ Confirm and solidify Metrics, Benchmarks, and Performance Targets

The testing and analyses in this stage related to the four key subsystems solidifies performance targets by tightening the initially targeted goal ranges. These targets now can be inserted into the initial Basis of Design (BOD), as described in the commissioning task discussion below. This testing and analysis also serves to define more clearly the parameters and performance targets to be pursued during schematic design iterations.

For LEED projects, the status of each pursued credit should be updated and verified in this and all stages. By engaging the systemic analyses described thus far, projects often can achieve LEED Gold and Platinum certification without much difficulty or cost, since established performance targets that address the four key subsystems also inherently address the environmental issues on which the LEED credit categories and criteria are based. However, LEED targets and benchmarks may not always be appropriate for a project's goals or for gaining a deeper understanding of what underlies these benchmarks. In some cases, project teams will need to dive into the details embedded within the benchmarks defined by LEED in order to completely understand the impacts associated with certain credits.

The current energy benchmark in LEED references ASHRAE 90.1-2007, Appendix G. Based on the building type, size, number of stories, and fuel sources, one selects an HVAC system for the baseline building. Appendix G also dictates baseline parameters for the building envelope, lighting systems, and so forth. In some cases, these baseline assumptions may not make sense if the objective is to gauge energy savings more accurately. If the baseline used for comparison is not reflective of what would have been built in the absence of LEED or an integrative design process, then the project team should discuss the components of an appropriate baseline to use for comparison, in addition to the benchmark required for calculating LEED points.

For example, if one is designing a school and the local school district mandates load-bearing masonry construction (and would not even consider steel frame), then the baseline wall construction for modeling should be masonry, instead of the steel-frame wall stipulated by Appendix G. Similarly, if Appendix G indicates electric resistance heat as the benchmark system for the school, and this system would never even be considered as an option, then an alternative baseline should be discussed that more closely matches what likely would have been constructed conventionally. Often, then, we find ourselves running modeling comparisons of the design case against two different baseline cases, one for LEED purposes and another using a benchmark defined by "what we would have done anyway."

For the purpose of establishing such a benchmark and creating a more accurate baseline, we often have engaged the project team in a discussion of what is common practice in the area. In this way, we are trying to identify a more typical building scenario in cases where Appendix G provides a less than appropriate baseline for comparison.

■ **Commissioning: Develop Basis of Design (BOD)**

At this point, the project team develops an initial Basis of Design document, based on results of Workshop No. 2 and subsequent findings. This document translates the Owner's Project Requirements narrative into a technical description of performance goals and metrics on a system-by-system basis, including all mechanical, electrical, and plumbing (MEP) and architectural systems.

The BOD is intended to provide a technical narrative explanation of the design parameters and quantified performance objectives established for the project. Creation of the BOD, in its first iteration, should precede schematic design. Ideally, future phases and design iterations will both be informed by and inform updates to the BOD with information in a feedback loop. As each phase of the design develops, the BOD will need to be updated in order to continuously reflect any new decisions and/or changes in the design (see "Sample Basis of Design Outline" sidebar).

This portion of the commissioning activity needs to be owned by the project team, not by the Commissioning Authority (CxA). The Commissioning Authority's role really is to help the design team and owner understand what needs to be incorporated into these documents and why. We have found that this often is misunderstood by project teams unfamiliar with Commissioning. As a result, we need to remind these teams repeatedly that it is critical for design team members to understand that their participation in creating and updating these OPR and BOD documents is fundamental to the success of any commissioning endeavor and ultimately to the success of the project. The CxA alone cannot and should not produce them.

A.5.3 Cost Analysis

■ **Put a price tag on every strategy and subsystem, then aggregate them into integrated cost bundles**

It bears repeating that when a potential strategy identified by the team costs more, the team should ask where other strategies (or systems and systems components) can be reduced to neutralize the project's overall first cost and simultaneously reduce environmental impacts; this is cost bundling. A separate "bundle" of cost impacts should be created for each strategy that may be difficult to resolve with consensus, and it should include all cost impacts across all systems affected by implementing that strategy.

In actual practice, we have found that certain of these strategies that emerge are often essential to making critical path design decisions, while others can wait—e.g., establishing structural bay spacing (that reduces environmental LCA impacts) is far more critical at this stage than selecting water closets and urinals (that reduce water consumption). Of course, the water-consumption issue impacts hydrological systems options and targets at this stage. We know that we can get a wide variety of different low-flow and/or dual-flush toilets across a wide range of costs, so this decision can remain flexible, but we must pin down bay spacing as soon as possible.

Sample Basis of Design Outline

The following sample BOD outline, when tailored to the specifics of a project, provides a framework for documenting the technical design parameters and quantified performance objectives.

1. Primary design assumptions
   a. Space use based on OPR
   b. Redundancy level
   c. Diversity issues
   d. Climatic conditions
   e. Space zoning
   f. Occupancy types and schedules
   g. Special requirements for indoor environmental conditions

2. Standards
   a. General building codes, guidelines, regulations
   b. LEED related additional requirements (i.e., energy-use reduction, water-use reduction, etc.)

   c. Industry-related requirements (i.e., hospital, information technology (IT), manufacturing standards)

3. Narrative descriptions and performance requirements (chronological descriptions of the main systems as they evolve over the phases of project design and construction)
   a. Architectural systems
   b. HVAC systems
   c. Building automation systems
   d. Lighting systems
   e. Water systems
   f. Power systems (normal/emergency, special metering)
   g. Communications systems
   h. Information technology systems
   i. Security and life-safety systems

A.5.4 Schedule and Next Steps

■ **Update Process Road Map in preparation for Workshop No. 3**

As with every stage, adjust and refine the Road Map with the project team, as necessary, to address evolving issues and to clarify next steps. Similar to the prior Research and Analysis stage, the schedule of tasks, team conference calls, meetings, and analysis processes will almost always need to be altered in order to accommodate the interim meeting dates, times, and deliverables that occur between major workshops.

■ **Prepare Agenda for Workshop No. 3**

Again, the importance of developing the agenda for Workshop No. 3 cannot be understated, particularly since the team is now armed with a significant volume of data and information resulting from an extensive amount of analysis. Organizing the presentation and conveying this analysis to team members can be challenging, but the task of choreographing how best to impart these results to the team is critical, since this consolidated information, as presented and discussed at Workshop No. 3, provides the foundation for proceeding into the further exploration of the Schematic Design phase. The next chapter will discuss this in detail.

chapter

6

Schematic Design

The habit of calling a finished product a Design is convenient but wrong. Design is what you do, not what you've done.

—L. Bruce Archer, engineering designer, design theorist and academic, Professor of Design Research at London's Royal College of Art

Designing is not a profession but an attitude. . . thinking in relationships. The designer must see the periphery as well as the core, the immediate and the ultimate. . . He must anchor his special job in the complex whole.

—László Moholy-Nagy, photographer, graphic designer, and cofounder of the Bauhaus, from László Moholy-Nagy, *Vision in Motion*, Chicago: Institute of Design 1947, p. 42

Design is not making beauty, beauty emerges from selection, affinities, integration, love.

—Louis Kahn, architect from Louis I. Kahn, *Writings, Lectures, Interviews*, New York: Rizzoli, 1991,"Order Is," 58–59

Design is the patterning and planning of any act toward a desired, foreseeable end . . . any attempt to separate design, to make it a thing-by-itself works counter to the fact that design is the primary underlying matrix of life.

—Victor Papanek, industrial designer, from his book *Design for the Real World*, London: Thames & Hudson, 1985

ENTERING PART B—DESIGN AND CONSTRUCTION

We are now moving into *Part B, Design and Construction*. As described in Chapter 5, this phase begins with what currently is called Schematic Design; consequently, the structure of this phase more closely resembles conventional practice. However, the activities that are engaged expand and enliven the design process by folding in all of the work and understanding of systems interactions from *Part A, Discovery*.

As a result, teams enter Schematic Design more fully informed and prepared to develop optimized and integrated design solutions.

What we have examined up to this point in the process is the production of conceptual design schemes based upon the building program, its environmental impacts, and its relationships with its larger context and place. Schematic Design typically *develops* these conceptual design ideas. As we have seen, the word "develop" in this context—and at its source—means to "reveal" or "to bring forth new potential." The opportunity at this point, then, is to discover greater potential by investigating these ideas more deeply, with more integrated and elegant solutions. This is a highly iterative process. Traditionally, though, we start solidifying these ideas right away, by translating them as quickly as possible into drawings and fixed building forms. This tends to prohibit us from further discovery, because we end up locking into finite solutions too quickly—once drawings are created, design teams often become married to them, simply by virtue of the effort involved and the fees expended.

Building Information Modeling (BIM) often is touted as the great technological answer to achieving integrative solutions. But the computer is simply a tool, a hammer of sorts. Accordingly, we need to take a moment here to warn design teams about assuming that the use of such tools results in automatic success. If team members are not engaged in solidified relationships with each other, then the technical systems and building components they are designing likely will not be either. As a result, the complex information stored in the computer ceases to be very useful.

An organization called Bioteams (www.bioteams.com) confirms this "disconnect," using data derived from numerous studies. As stated in the second page of The Bioteaming Manifesto: "The adoption of new tools without the parallel development of a new culture that supports their use and the potentialities opened by these new media scenarios is typical of all neophyte phases of technology adoption. We have yet not uncovered the full potential available to us when we operate, like nature operates, as cooperative, highly motivated teams."*

Thompson and Good's bioteaming manifesto tells us that "today's teams are a very different animal compared to those many of you grew up with…a new name is needed for today's teams," such as "Virtual Network Teams: Virtual means that the team is dependent on internet technologies more so than before. Networked means that the team is made up of dispersed and physically distant individuals who are interconnected and operate as an organic entity… thus old-fashioned command and control approaches are vastly ineffective."*

Furthermore, the authors find that:

"Statistics on IT project teams reveal some enlightening information:

Only a third of change initiatives achieve objectives…

74 percent of IT projects are unsuccessful…

Only 1 in 5 IT projects is likely to bring full satisfaction to their organizational sponsors…

These numbers reveal the quantifiable evidence that there is something deeply wrong in the way Virtual Networked Teams are operating in today's organizations."*

Contemporary design teams operate very much like a "Virtual Networked Team," as they use electronic drawings and Internet-based shared workspace sites more and more often to communicate and exchange information. Bioteams and other orga-

---

*Ken Thompson and Robin Good, "The Bioteaming Manifesto: A New Paradigm for Virtual, Networked Business Teams," November 9, 2005, http://www.bioteams.com/2005/04/06/bioteaming_a_manifesto.html (accessed October 22, 2008).

nizations, such as the National Institute of Building Standards (NIBS), are realizing that the organization and structure of such design teams (and the change-management process) need to be addressed from a sociological—not merely technological—perspective. In other words, the process of communication and the willingness to colearn across disciplines is essential for achieving success. Accordingly, for the purposes of this book, the sociological and human interrelationship issues associated with integrative design will remain our focus, not the technical tools utilized to document the results of these interactions, such as BIM and other IT solutions. Nevertheless, such tools bear mentioning, since they can be used to assist the integration process.

We are not suggesting that technologies such as BIM are not useful or important, only that they are not very effective without the interaction of the humans that use them. You may recall the Mental Model diagram from Chapter 3 (Figure 3-9), where *Tools* ranked below *Process* in the trajectory of sustainability practice; in other words, such tools are important components in the integrative design process, but alone they are insufficient. Additionally, if we move into technological documentation too quickly, we lose opportunities for further discovery and integration.

BIM: Building Information Modeling

By Max Zahniser

Strong emergence refers to instances in which attributes and behaviors of a complex system do not logically follow from the sum of the system's parts. This phenomenon is sometimes expressed in the form of a mathematical analogy: $1 + 1 = 3$. A commonly cited example of strong emergence is human consciousness, which appears to be much more than the sum of sensory organs, gray matter, and synapses. Strong emergence stands in contrast to *weak emergence*, in which the properties of a system are reducible to its individual constituent components only, and is thus easily understood; $2 = 1 + 1$. An example of weak emergence might be a brick wall emerging by stacking up several bricks.

The idea of strong emergence as presented here applies to ideas emerging from a group of professionals that no individual could have brought forth on their own. This concept often triggers skepticism and makes some scientists and philosophers uneasy, as it looks a bit like magic. A conservative scientific position might argue that if you are observing what appears to be strong emergence, then you simply have not identified all of the constituent parts of the system. I might not argue against this, but I *would* argue that the laws of physics, or even chemistry and biology, are not always perfectly analogous to systems of thought and ideas. Collective thought and creative collaboration may simply be processes that are interdependent with higher level systems than we have yet managed to fully understand scientifically. I believe that Organization Development and Industrial/Organizational Psychology, as well as some advanced neuroscience, are at their core burgeoning fields seeking to unpack some of the attributes of these higher level systems along with the work of philosophers such as Arthur Koestler, Ken Wilbur, and Mark A. Bedau. In short, we likely will not put the strong emergence debate to rest here.

(continued)

But if the goal, at least metaphorically, is to consistently yield this "magical" strong emergence in the context of building projects, then integrative design is analogous to best-practice spells or potions—and the potency of that magic elixir is strengthened when *information technology* is part of the recipe.

Design and construction professionals experienced an evolutionary, if not revolutionary, industry-wide shift in building documentation practices starting at a meaningful scale in the mid to late 1980s and extending through the 1990s by switching from hand drawings to computer-based documents and digital 3-D design. The use of computer aided drafting (CAD) tools is now a nearly universal practice among architectural and engineering (AE) firms and many builders. Over the last ten years, though, CAD tools have likely evolved to their full potential.

As CAD approached this optimization, investment of creative energy in the AE segment of the software industry shifted to developing the next evolutionary leap. That leap has landed at a set of tools that can be categorized under the term BIM (Building Information Modeling). The fundamental nature of BIM applications is completely different from CAD, aside from functioning as design and documentation tools. Most CAD applications deal strictly in geometry, color, and pattern. So CAD is really just a faster way of drawing.

BIM, however, is an entirely different way of thinking about representing a building. In fact, using a BIM tool is really a process of producing a virtual building. Whereas CAD forces one to squeeze spatial ideas into two-dimensional, representational views of a building, BIM enables designers to create the building as a building.

BIM tools can be considered simply 3-D graphical interfaces for BIM files, which are really just databases. These databases relate specific, identified objects (e.g., a wall) to attributes, like material type, connections to other objects, etc. Building Information Models, then, are 3-D virtual constructs of buildings, in which data related to each component of that building are embedded.

When drawing a building in a CAD application, one simply draws the same building from multiple views. Each time a change is made, one must determine which views are impacted, and modify each individually. Coordination across disciplines, of course, is also an important issue.

Conversely, in BIM applications, because each view of a building is exactly that, a *view* of a single database, a change made from any view modifies the virtual building itself. Thus coordination across views is not necessary. A quote used commonly in training for these tools is "a change anywhere is a change everywhere." Additionally, when using interoperable BIM tools across design disciplines (architecture, structural, mechanical, etc.), most BIM tools are capable of some level of clash detection. This means that the BIM application can determine when structure, ductwork, pipes, etc., conflict, and alerts the user. This alone can radically reduce time spent on coordination for larger projects.

Like CAD, BIM technologies crossed over from automotive and aircraft design. Also like CAD, BIM faces similar market push-back challenges related to change-management issues among its potential consumers. Despite these age-old organizational change hurdles, BIM's uptake appears to be much more rapid than CAD's was, and even LEED's, though the destinies of LEED and BIM are becoming more intertwined.

It is perhaps obvious that a software application, like any tool, in and of itself does not fundamentally shift a process or enhance its product. If you hold a hammer by its head and smack the handle against an upside down nail, it does not work very well. In fact, it makes building whatever it is you are attempting to build even harder than more primitive techniques. But holding it correctly and swinging it skillfully at a sharp, upright nail can lead to holding wood together quite effectively. This is just the nature of tools; you have to learn the skill of using them well.

Likewise, even with the most promising BIM technologies, if implementation of that technology is not well planned, its use could actually hurt the quality of output. But, much like the LEED rating system, there still is a hidden benefit, even when forced upon a project team via mandates or company policy decisions. Even in the absence of an integrative process, BIM and LEED can reveal integrating forces, albeit uncomfortable and costly ones—using LEED

likely delivers a better building than the same project would have achieved without using LEED, but perhaps not in a sustainably repeatable way without improvements in the *process*. But like LEED, BIM is forcing project team members to have conversations that may not have happened otherwise.

That said, the cost effectiveness and quality of the product (the building) will climb *enormously* by understanding both LEED and BIM as tools that require an integrative process to be used well. When woven into an integrative process, both of these tools have the potential (now often realized) of delivering an even *better* building project with cost savings, instead of cost premiums.

The photo in Figure 6-1 is a still-frame image from a video that resulted from collaboration between myself, while at the U.S. Green Building Council (USGBC), and a team at Autodesk. The aim was to envision an idealized design tool of the future. Built upon a BIM platform and intertwined with simulation engines and a digital building product marketplace, the tool would be capable of giving

Figure 6-1 Interactive multi-touch screen built by Perceptive Pixel to demonstrate the future of integrating building information modeling (BIM), building form, energy modeling, and LEED software to allow users near-real-time feedback on building performance impacts of design options (presented at the Opening Plenary of U.S. Green Building Council's annual Greenbuild, November 2007). *Image reproduced with the permission of Autodesk, Inc. ©2008. All Rights Reserved.*

(continued)

users near real-time feedback on the building performance impacts of their design changes.

It sounds and looks a bit far-fetched, and intentionally so. The interface, a 4' × 8' multitouch screen built by Perceptive Pixel, was selected to reinforce the point that this was a vision of the future—a tool that would not hit the shelves tomorrow. That said, the technologies that this application would intertwine basically exist today. As William Gibson (science-fiction author) aptly put it, "the future is already here. It's just not very evenly distributed." In fact, the primary barrier to realizing a design interface like this one comes down to the interoperability of its components, which in turn comes down to business issues and relationships among the owners of those components.

Simply stated, we are moving toward a preassembled tool kit with which project teams, when guided by integrative design principles, can *better* understand the impacts of their decisions *as they make them*. In the meantime, we can piece such a tool kit together.

In fact, BIM applications exist today that can run energy analysis at the touch of a button during design and documentation, calculate loads and size structure accordingly, do construction cost modeling in keeping with popular cost estimating compendiums, run artificial lighting and daylight modeling, run computational fluid dynamics simulations (to study airflow), and in some cases, nearly all of the above functioning interdependently—all derived from the database(s) running in the background of a BIM application.

By assembling a tool kit of BIM applications and by appropriately matching their functionality to explore interrelationships, a project team can align their process, their tools, and the building with the goals of integrative design. These BIM tool sets, then, when used across disciplines, can be seen as the design and analysis tool embodiment of systems theory— or at least as another key to illuminating the realities of systems' interdependence.

HERE'S WHERE WE ARE

We convene a team charrette, or workshop, and then we call it "integrated design." Often, though, this charrette is a team meeting convened simply to verify alignment with the project's LEED goals. Such single-meeting and single-topic scenarios are rarely capable of achieving integration. As discussed repeatedly in Chapters 4 and 5, integration requires an iterative *and* evolving process of continually deepening understanding and refining solutions.

We have found that architects want to end the schematic design phase as quickly as possible. They want to resolve and document a schematic solution that:

- meets program requirements
- establishes design character and project aesthetics
- defines building and site configuration
- complies with codes constraints
- verifies infrastructure availability
- identifies building, site, structure, and material systems
- complies with requirements of targeted LEED credits
- receives the owner's approval

Once complete, this set of schematic design documents is sent to an array of engineers (structural, mechanical, electrical, civil, etc.). Each engineer wants to start selecting their systems and documenting them as quickly as possible as well. At the same time, a land development plan that addresses zoning requirements, development footprint, parking, stormwater management, utility connections, traffic analysis, and open space areas is created and submitted to local authorities for approval. Essentially, we want to freeze the design as quickly as possible in order to maintain schedule, reduce the variables and "unknowns," obtain entitlement approvals, and get paid for this phase.

We see this happening frequently. Early in our commissioning relationship with a major hospital client, we found that there were several different architectural and engineering (A&E) teams serving the owner's numerous construction needs on a variety of projects. Each project required an orientation meeting with the team, and sometimes these occurred when projects were already well into schematic design. In one such meeting, an architect actually yelled out: "We don't have time for this Mr. Rogers exercise" and stormed out of the conference room. He later apologized and explained that he had realized that his frustration was born of the typical breakneck pace under which he and the client had been moving; with deadlines looming and expectations high, there was no time to stop and reflect: "We just had to keep moving forward—no time for reflection, only time for drawing."

STOP AND REFLECT

What's Working?

The conventional schematic design phase we currently employ can be characterized as follows:

- We work on very concrete objectives.
- We move in a generally straight-line progression toward clearly defined goals.

- We reduce variables quickly and limit unknowns.
- We perceive that we have reduced risk.
- We perceive that fast decisions keep us on schedule (time equals money).
- We receive planning approval from the local authorities.
- We confirm that we have met code compliance relative to the architectural design.
- We reconfirm that we are on track for meeting our LEED goals.
- We establish LEED-based performance targets for engineering-related issues (such as thermal comfort, ventilation rates, etc.) for the mechanical, electrical, and plumbing (MEP) engineers to verify.
- The MEP engineers begin to conceptualize appropriate systems based on the targeted LEED-performance parameters.
- The architect determines the building form and configuration and creates building plans, elevations, and sections to prepare for detailing.
- The architect identifies a potential palette of materials based on approved renderings so that detailing can begin to be explored.

We now have a clear set of documents for establishing an initial cost estimate, based upon clearly defined parameters. These documents were produced by a predictable process that enables the team to conclude this phase with a relatively small percentage of the total A&E fee expended.

What's Not Working?

The owner, design team, and zoning authorities now have locked into an image and an established building form. There is little or no turning back:

■ Site design is frozen for the most part, reinforced by submitted and approved land development and zoning documents.

■ Our focus on water issues has been narrowed to designing stormwater systems that reduce runoff and to selecting low-flow plumbing fixtures in the next phase. We have not taken into account the opportunities for the building to contribute to larger hydrologic cycles.

■ We have limited our options for affecting energy performance. By committing to footprint, massing, aperture placement, and window sizes too early, the most effective opportunities for energy savings are compromised.

■ We have unwittingly specified a significant number of materials and systems without much analysis and understanding of their impacts.

■ We think that we have done a good job addressing indoor environmental quality (IEQ) issues by targeting LEED performance criteria, but perhaps not.

We often see project teams with good intentions limiting their design explorations to the issues and metrics defined by the rating system being used (such as LEED), as discussed in Chapter 5. Because rating systems serve as tools for defining what is important in green building projects and for assessing performance, design teams tend to focus their efforts on what the rating system has chosen to measure. This focus can limit our field of vision. It encourages us to concentrate on the technical issues identified in the rating system, but not beyond—and not necessarily in ways that interlink and expose the interrelationships between the different "line-item" criteria listed in the rating system's checklist.

Further, we typically produce all of this documentation with minimal input from the builder (or construction team) or from the building's operations team, maintenance staff, and occupants. More often than not, the schematic cost estimate is over budget; this results in early "value engineering," which generally results in scope reduction or removal of system components, particularly the elimination of green features that are assumed to cost more. These green features are targeted for elimination because they are perceived as separate technologies, overlaid on top of the design solution.

In summary, lack of analysis in this early stage produces schematic solutions that lack both an understanding of systems performance and the interactions between systems—*we assume that these systems and their performance will be addressed with engineering solutions later*. We make design decisions that become fixed solutions without fully realizing how these decisions impact building performance. The resulting schematic design represents a solution based upon the function, image, and aesthetics of the *object*, but these decisions have not been informed by performance parameters or performance analysis; rather, they largely represent predetermined solutions that limit the scope of exploration. Such exploration is obviated by the demands of a shortened time frame, which in turn forces design decisions that lock us into solutions that remain unalterable in later phases ("We just have to keep moving forward—no time for reflection, only time for drawing"), thereby increasing costs, adversely impacting performance, and creating other unintended consequences.

When just 1 percent of a project's up front costs are spent . . . up to 70 percent of its life cycle costs may already be committed.

—Joseph Romm

How Can We Do (and Think about) This Differently?

Questioning Assumptions

On a project for the Sidwell Friends School, our client wanted their project to demonstrate advanced green thinking and technologies. As a result, the architect originally programmed a Living Machine® to treat wastewater—a good idea, but expensive and requiring high maintenance. The owner was completely willing to spend the extra dollars for this on-site sewage treatment technology because of the opportunity to use it as a teaching tool, one that would serve as a component of their curriculum. The team had operated on the assumption that on-site sewage treatment was more expensive than connecting to the municipal sewage system. However, we questioned this assumption by suggesting another alternative: an on-site constructed

Figure 6-2 The Sidwell Friends School installed an on-site sewage treatment constructed wetland system as the best and most cost-effective alternative. This 3-D rendering depicts the integration of the project's constructed wetlands treatment system components into the building's water supply and demand loop. *Image © Kieran Timberlake Associates.*

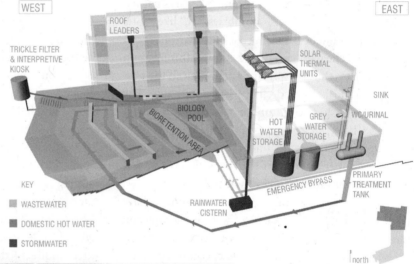

Figure 6-3 The completed constructed wetland at the Sidwell Friends School cost less than connecting to the municipal sewer system. *Image courtesy of Sidwell Friends.*

wetlands treatment system. As it turned out, the constructed wetlands not only cost less than the Living Machine (and was much less expensive to operate and maintain); it also cost less than simply connecting to the city's sewer system, because the sewage invert elevation at the road was at a higher elevation than the building, therefore requiring an expensive pumping lift station.

The Willow School team discovered the same thing; but in their case, a constructed wetlands treatment system turned out to be less expensive than a simple, conventional septic system. The original assumption was that a basic, "dumb system," like septic treatment, would be the most cost-effective—how can anything be cheaper than that? Except in this location in New Jersey, the clay soil structure required the septic tile field to be buried eight feet below grade. The excavation costs to accomplish this would have resulted in the septic system costing $30,000 more than constructed wetlands treatment. (This savings, along with further benefits of constructed wetlands systems, is discussed in more detail below).

These experiences (along with many others) have taught us that without taking the time to question the team's original assumptions, we never would have found better answers, and making decisions based on these assumptions would have cost more in terms of both money and environmental impacts

Engaging an Interdisciplinary Process

In 2002 the Neptune Township School District Board of Education decided to begin designing a new Midtown Community Elementary School. We were brought on board to begin early-stage energy modeling. The SSP Architectural Group was already engaged in early design work when we joined the team. We initially identified with the team a series of energy-efficiency measures (EEMs) specifically targeting a reduction of the building's heating and cooling loads.

Thirteen EEMs were identified; these included building orientation, reduced lighting power density, daylighting strategies (such as light shelves and photocell-sensored dimming), improved window performance, and higher levels of insulation in the walls and roof. A significant change in the early design resulting from this exercise included reorienting the building by 90 degrees to better control solar gains. This significantly reduced energy consumption at no cost. The construction manager and the design team then explored the cost of implementing the remaining measures to determine the first-cost impact associated with each EEM. This was done in parallel with analyzing each EEM in the energy model during schematic design.

As you might expect, each identified EEM strategy resulted in a first-cost increase, with the exception of the reduced lighting power density (LPD); this measure actually resulted in a reduction in the first cost of the lighting system. By reducing the LPD and by working closely with the project's lighting designer, hundreds of lighting fixtures were removed from the project without compromising the quantity of lighting throughout the building. Rather than fully direct, lay-in troffers, the lighting system was designed with pendant mounted, direct-indirect fixtures. Overall, the LPD was projected to reduce the code allowance (at the time) of 1.5 watts per square foot to just over 0.90 watts per square foot.

A parametric energy modeling run was made for each individual EEM to determine the resultant annual energy savings for implementing only that EEM relative to an ASHRAE 90.1-1999 code compliant building. The simple payback period (for each of the measures that increased first cost) ranged from about 5 to 8 years. Based upon standard EEM-evaluation techniques, several of these measures likely would have been deemed a less than worthy investment, since their payback period fell beyond acceptable time thresholds. Often, this is where such evaluations end, but this type of simplified analysis, in new construction, has severe limitations in terms of truly evaluating the full and comprehensive effect of multiple EEMs being used together.

Accordingly, we next evaluated various combinations of EEMs in order to see which combination resulted in the best optimization of energy performance and heating, ventilating, and air-conditioning (HVAC) load reductions. By also looking at the first-cost impacts associated with each combination of EEMs, the team determined that the most optimized combination of EEMs had a simple payback of 3.37 years, a significant overall reduction relative to the 5- to 8-year paybacks that resulted from looking at each EEM individually. This reduction was due to the synergies between systems, and it allowed the full set of EEMs to fall within acceptable payback time frames.

Taking the next step, we examined the effect of this optimized EEM combination on the building's HVAC loads. A set of simplified load calculations was run by the project's HVAC engineer—first for a standard school (with about 325 square feet per ton of cooling) and then with the optimized combination of EEMs applied. The combined EEMs resulted in an HVAC load reduction of 40 percent. Ground-source heat pumps (GSHPs) previously had been selected for

the HVAC system. A significant portion of the cost of this type of system is attributable to the well field. The mechanical cost estimator determined that since the 40 percent load reduction translated into needing to drill 40 percent fewer wells, a 10 percent reduction in the first cost of the overall HVAC system could result. This 10 percent cost reduction equated to an estimated first-cost savings of approximately $400,000.

The cost of implementing the combination of EEMs required to achieve this savings amounted to a total of about $125,000; hence, by spending $125,000 on energy-efficiency measures, a $400,000 first-cost savings was achieved. Consequently, the overall first cost of the project's construction was reduced by $275,000! The building cost less to build than it would have had we done nothing. At the same time, operating costs for energy were also significantly reduced due to the smaller HVAC system—and, of course, this in turn resulted in a concomitant reduction in the environmental impacts associated with burning the fossil fuels that would have been needed to produce that energy.

This $275,000 savings paid for all of our analysis, consulting time, energy modeling, *and* commissioning, leaving additional money in the owner's pocket.

Figure 6-4 The integrative process employed for analyzing energy consumption at the Neptune Township School District Midtown Community Elementary School in New Jersey showed that big savings cost less than small savings. *Image courtesy of SSP Architectural Group.*

Figure 6-5 This wall section from the Neptune Township School illustrates many of the listed energy-efficiency measures (EEMs) implemented on the project. Thirteen EEMs were analyzed via parametric energy modeling runs. *Image courtesy of SSP Architectural Group.*

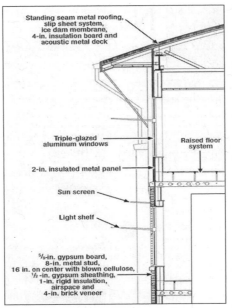

Standing seam metal roofing, slip sheet system, ice dam membrane, 4-in. insulation board and acoustic metal deck

Triple-glazed aluminum windows

Raised floor system

2-in. insulated metal panel

Sun screen

Light shelf

⅝-in. gypsum board, 8-in. metal stud, 16 in. on center with blown cellulose, ½-in. gypsum sheathing, 1-in. rigid insulation, airspace and 4-in. brick veneer

EEMs included in the project:

- solar orientation
- R27 wall w/ blown cellulose
- R30 roof insulation
- triple pane windows
- LPD = 0.92 W/sf
- solar shading
- light shelves
- daylight dimming
- ground source heat pumps
- under floor supply air
- demand controlled ventilation
- energy recovery units

Individual EEMs	First Cost	Annual Savings	Simple Payback
Reduced Lighting Power Density	-$123,887	$12,549	NA
Daylight Dimming	$90,350	$16,584	5.45
Wood Triple Pane Windows	$69,896	$9,117	7.67
R27 Wall Insulation	$46,302	$9,240	5.01
R30 Roof Insulation	$41,789	$5,186	8.06

EEMs in Combination	First Cost	Annual Savings	Simple Payback
EEMs combined	$124,450	$36,912	3.37

EEMs allowed for a 40% HVAC load and system capacity reduction

Figure 6-6 Simple paybacks were determined for both individual and combined EEM strategies for the Neptune Township school project via energy modeling runs that calculated annual energy savings relative to the associated costs for the proposed EEMs. The most efficient combination of EEMs also allowed for a 40 percent overall HVAC system load reduction. *Image courtesy of Marcus Sheffer.*

HVAC System: Ground Source Heat Pumps (GSHP)

40% reduction in GSHP capacity = $400,000 savings

Individual EEMs	First Cost	Annual Savings	Simple Payback
40% reduction in HVAC system	-$400,000	NA	NA
Implemented EEMs	$124,450	$36,912	3.37

	First Cost	Annual Savings	Simple Payback
Holistic Effect	-$275,550	$80,166	???

Figure 6-7 The 40 percent load reduction for the Neptune Township school project resulted in a 10 percent first-cost savings for the HVAC system (due to down-sizing capacity) that equated to $400,000. This reduced the building's overall first cost to $275,000 *less* than conventional construction *and* saved significantly on annual operating costs due to reduced energy consumption. *Image courtesy of Marcus Sheffer.*

Integrative Process

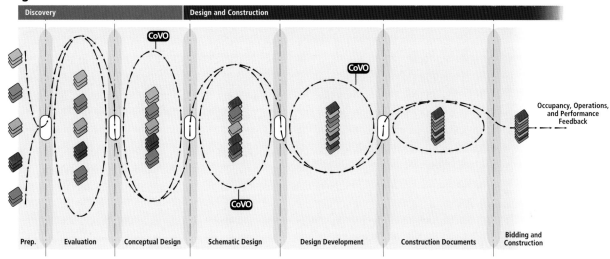

Discovery | Design and Construction

CoVO

CoVO

Occupancy, Operations, and Performance Feedback

CoVO

Prep. | Evaluation | Conceptual Design | Schematic Design | Design Development | Construction Documents | Bidding and Construction

Traditional Process

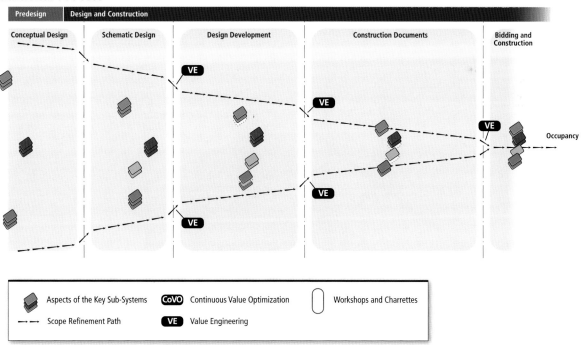

Predesign | Design and Construction

Conceptual Design | Schematic Design | Design Development | Construction Documents | Bidding and Construction

VE

VE

VE

Occupancy

VE

VE

Aspects of the Key Sub-Systems | **CoVO** Continuous Value Optimization | Workshops and Charrettes

Scope Refinement Path | **VE** Value Engineering

Figure C-1 Color version of Figure 5-2 diagramming the optimal integrative process compared to the traditional process along the same timeline. *Image courtesy of 7group and Bill Reed, graphics by Corey Johnston.*

Integrative Process

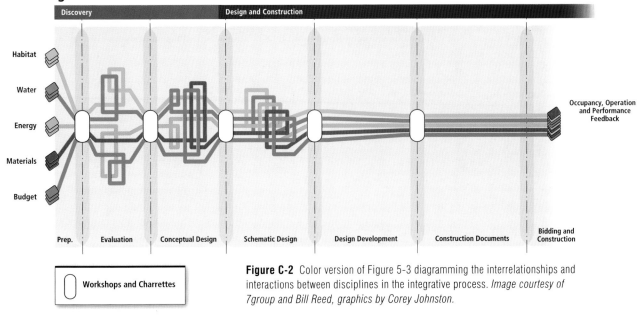

Figure C-2 Color version of Figure 5-3 diagramming the interrelationships and interactions between disciplines in the integrative process. *Image courtesy of 7group and Bill Reed, graphics by Corey Johnston.*

Figure C-3 The exterior of this building in the northeast U.S. appears to be well constructed; however, upon further inspection, the thermal envelope has failed where the exterior walls meet the roof. In this case, the attic space above the ceiling (inside the thermal envelope) has been as cold as 36°F during winter months. The infrared images depicted in Figures C-4 through C-6 reveal thermal bridging conditions, problems that are common due to lack of proper envelope detailing and/or installation during construction. The commissioning process can help project teams avoid such problems. *Image courtesy of Brian Toevs.*

Figure C-4 Infrared image taken from inside the attic of a building in Pennsylvania during the winter. This image of the building's gable end shows the failure of the thermal envelope at the roof–wall connection. The wall construction consists of concrete block, 3 rigid insulation, and brick veneer. The roof construction is corrugated metal decking with two layers of polyisocyanurate roof insulation and standing seam metal roofing. The roof overhangs the wall with soffits, and the building has no insulation between the attic and occupied spaces. *Image courtesy of Brian Toevs.*

Figure C-5 Same building as that depicted in Figure C-4 with image taken from the exterior. The ambient temperature was 6°F. As the temperature scale indicates, the areas in red are locations where the thermal envelope has failed to perform. The window is reflecting the temperature of the night sky, and it appears that the wall around the window is indicating a reflection as well. *Image courtesy of Brian Toevs.*

Figure C-6 The red areas indicate thermal envelope failure once again. The area beyond the building is the night sky. The sky always shows up as extremely cold in infrared photos. The blue band on the building is a band of glossy brick, reflecting the ambient temperature. *Image courtesy of Brian Toevs.*

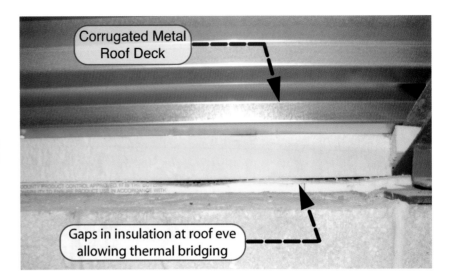

Corrugated Metal Roof Deck

Gaps in insulation at roof eve allowing thermal bridging

Figure C-7 Poor construction practices often cause thermal envelope failure; for example, the gaps depicted in this image will allow air to pass freely between the interior and exterior. Such envelope failures can be avoided by including envelope commissioning in a project's scope of commissioning services. *Image courtesy of Brian Toevs.*

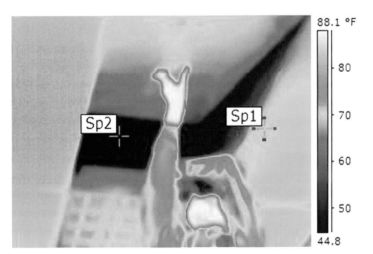

88.1 °F

80

70

60

50

44.8

Sp2

Sp1

Figure C-8 Due to the failure of the thermal envelope at the roof-wall connection, the cavity above this ceiling is just above freezing, as indicated in this infrared image. The ceiling is insulated with 2 x 4 x 6 fiberglass batt insulation located over each ceiling tile. This building is heated with ground source heat pumps that were sized for a much more thermally robust envelope. Because of this, the heating system is not able to maintain temperature above the ceiling, and the cold ceiling space then transmits negative thermal effects to occupied spaces. *Image courtesy of Brian Toevs.*

67.5 °F

66

64

62

60

59.4

Sp2

Sp1

Figure C-9 This infrared image (taken during the winter in the northeast U.S.) depicts a closet at the corner of an exterior wall. The closet's concrete block partition terminates just above the ceiling. The blue areas indicate the cold attic air (see Figure C-8) dropping down into the open cores of these block partitions. The owner has insulated the ceiling with 2 x 4 x 6 fiberglass batt insulation sections, located over each ceiling tile. Note that the suspended ceiling's metal T-grid indicates some thermal transfer from the cold attic space as well. *Image courtesy of Brian Toevs.*

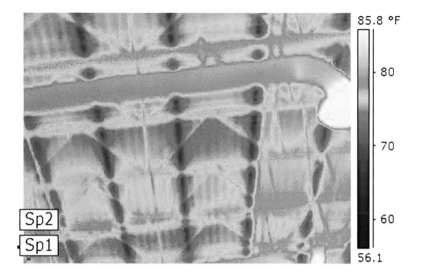

Sp2

Sp1

85.8 °F

— 80

— 70

— 60

56.1

Figure C-10 In this image, the roof of a building in the northeast United States is insulated with two layers of polyisocyanurate insulation. The blue stripes indicate areas where the roof decking is colder. It appears that these stripes are located at joints between the lower layer of roof insulation panels. The temperature difference indicates thermal bridging between the metal decking and the bottom surface of the upper layer of insulation. *Image courtesy of Brian Toevs.*

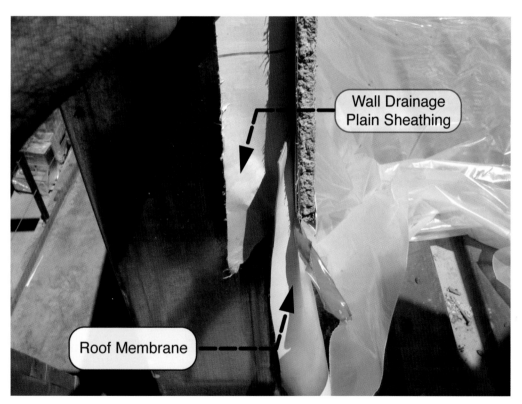

Wall Drainage
Plain Sheathing

Roof Membrane

Figure C-11 During a commissioning site visitation, the building shell installation detailing was reviewed and photographed. In this case, the roofing membrane was wrapped up the stud wall as required by the architectural specifications. Unfortunately, the installer had the wall drainage plane lapped *under* the roofing and not over. Notice that there also is no tape placed over the lap joint. Had this not been found, storm water could have drained into the building over a large atrium, saturating the fiberglass batt insulation installed in the stud wall cavity. The installers removed the wall board around the entire perimeter of this clerestory wall to properly reinstall this detail. *Image courtesy of Brian Toevs.*

Figure C-12 Chicago's City Hall was renovated with an extensive vegetated roof garden, completed in 2001, that covers more than 20,000 square feet of roof area. Effects associated with this vegetated roof decreased annual utility bills by $5,000. *Image © Conservation Design Forum, Elmhurst, IL, www.cdfine.com.*

Figure C-13 This vegetated roof on the Peggy Notebaert Nature Museum creates a beautiful landscape in Lincoln Park, Chicago. Design guidelines for green roofs can be found at www.naturemuseum.org/greenroof/planningaroof.html (accessed January 2009). *Image © Conservation Design Forum, Elmhurst, IL, www.cdfine.com.*

Figure C-14 Water passes through the roof scupper at the rear of the Peggy Notebaert Nature Museum, contributing artfully to the beauty of the project's cliff wall and educational garden. *Image © Conservation Design Forum, Elmhurst, IL, www.cdfine.com.*

◀ **Figure C-15** The Chartwell School in Seaside, California, achieved LEED® Platinum certification at a construction cost that was 11% lower than the average cost of all California schools constructed in the same year (2006) by implementing integrative design. (Architect: EHDD Architecture) *Image © Michael David Rose Photography.*

▼ **Figure C-16** The front walk leading to the Willow School's entrance in Gladstone, New Jersey, passes through native vegetation—a portion of the site's 34-acre forest—that serves as an integral component of the school's curriculum, with students participating in the project's ongoing regenerative approach. (Architect: Ford Farewell Mills and Gatsch, Architects) *Image courtesy of Mark Biedron.*

Figure C-17 The Pennsylvania Department of Environmental Protection's Cambria office building in Ebensburg, Pennsylvania, includes south-facing light shelves, rooftop solar panels, and a pair of photovoltaic trackers flanking the entrance walk. (Architect: Kulp Boecker Architects) *Image © Jim Schafer.*

▲ **Figure C-18** The Pennsylvania Department of Environmental Protection's Southeast Regional Office Building (DEP SEROB) in urban Norristown, Pennsylvania, houses more than 300 employees and incorporated Norristown's former train station, a 1931 Art Deco Historic Landmark building (on the right). This project provided both contextual remedy along Main Street and served as a stimulus for generating revitalization of this downtown district. (Architect: L. Robert Kimball & Associates) *Image © Jim Schafer.*

◀**Figure C-19** Open office spaces on the interior of the DEP SEROB project (depicted in Figure C-18) surround a four-story atrium that gathers daylight for these office spaces and contains a 5,000-gallon rainwater harvesting cistern. *Image © Jim Schafer.*

▲ **Figure C-20** The Select Medical Health Education Pavilion at the Harrisburg Area Community College in Harrisburg, Pennsylvania, utilized an integrative design process to maximize daylighting, minimize energy consumption, and achieve the owner's high performance goals. (Architect: L. Robert Kimball & Associates) *Image © Jim Schafer.*

▶ **Figure C-21** The library at the Associated Mennonite Biblical Seminary demonstrates excellent daylighting strategies. (Architect: The Troyer Group) *Image courtesy of DJ Construction.*

Figure C-22 The Lillis Business Complex at the University of Oregon creates a bridge between the older business buildings while providing daylight to lecture rooms and interior spaces via glazing with integrated photovoltaic cells embedded in the central atrium's glass. (Architect: SRG Partnership) *Image © Lara Swimmer*.

Figure C-23 Coupled with multiple daylighting strategies, integrated photovoltaic cells—clearly visible from the inside of the Lillis Business Complex—generate on-site renewable energy, allowing the Business School to sell excess power back to the utility company at a profit. *Image courtesy of Terri Meyer Boake, University of Waterloo.*

Figure C-24 The Alberici Corporate Headquarters started out as a former manufacturing facility adjacent to a three-story brick office building. After renovation, the complex was transformed into two floors of offices configured with mezzanines that provide all 300 employees with daylight and views, and it became one of the first ten Platinum LEED® certified buildings in the world. It also was one of the AIA COTE Top Ten Green Projects in 2006. The project includes a wind turbine that produces 20% of the building's annual electrical demand. The company's human resources department reported a 50% reduction in employee sick days during the first year of occupancy in the new headquarters. (Architect: Mackey Mitchell Architects) *Image courtesy of The Alberici Corporate Headquarters project, Jennifer Franko and the USGBC.*

Figure C-25 A large outdoor courtyard between the Alberici Headquarters office building and adjacent parking garage provides a relaxing space for employees to enjoy while complementing the walking trails and a boardwalk that run along the property. *Image courtesy of The Alberici Corporate Headquarters project, Jennifer Franko and the USGBC.*

▲ **Figure C-26** Located 300 feet below the eastern dam of the Diamond Valley Lake Reservoir in Hemet, California—the largest earthworks project in the U.S.—the Water + Life Museums complex is the world's first LEED® Platinum museum. It houses a significant collection of fossils and Native American artifacts that were unearthed during the reservoir's massive dig, as well as a Water Education Center that teaches visitors about water issues in Southern California and the importance of water's impact on the rest of the world. A 540-kilowatt photovoltaic array covers 50,000 square feet atop nearly the entire complex, generating nearly 70% of the project's electricity needs. (Architect: Lehrer Architects) *Image courtesy of Benny Chan/Fotoworks.*

◀ **Figure C-27** The Water + Life Museums' drought-tolerant landscaping is supported by a drip-irrigation system supplied by gray water. Plant species selections were based upon fossils discovered during the excavation, accented with rocks and boulders left over from this excavation. This landscape flourishes despite the project's harsh desert environment, where triple-digit summer temperatures are common, yet water can freeze in winter. *Image courtesy of Tom Lamb.*

Figure 6-8 This pie chart, taken from the Athena *Environmental Impact Estimator*, shows the ratio of primary energy used for operating energy as opposed to embodied energy over a sixty-year period for a sample East Coast project. If the pie chart reflected the period just following construction, the embodied impact would be the entire pie, since the operating energy accrues over time. *Image courtesy of the Athena Institute.*

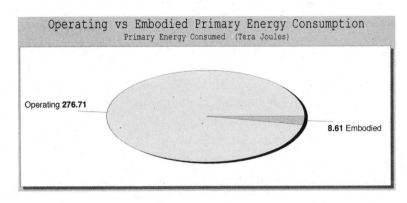

This outcome was achieved, however, only because many members of the design and construction team engaged a highly cooperative interdisciplinary effort, one that understood the building as a whole rather than as a series of component parts.

The Neptune Township example illustrates that energy modeling tools, when used to inform an interdisciplinary process and design decisions, can have a major impact on building energy use over time. Similarly, life cycle assessment (LCA) tools also can help guide a well-informed decision-making process pertaining to materials. The pie chart in Figure 6-8, taken from the ATHENA® *Impact Estimator for Buildings* LCA modeling tool (see "Life Cycle Assessment (LCA) Tools and Environmental Benefits" below), begins to show us the importance of a typical office building's energy use relative to materials in terms of global warming impacts. In this example, the office building was determined to have a sixty-year service-life expectancy; therefore, the model was set to show what the comparative carbon dioxide equivalents of energy use over that time would be, relative to those of the building's materials over sixty years.

It is interesting to note that when we build green buildings, we often add mass to the envelope as a strategy for reducing energy consumption in certain climates. These more massive materials, of course, will have a greater initial impact (e.g., embodied energy) than the materials we would use were we not focusing on reduc-

ing energy consumption. What LCA tools can help us do is find ways to reduce the impacts represented in *both* parts of the pie chart. In this case, project teams could accomplish this by exploring envelope materials options in the energy model in parallel with entering the same optional inputs into the Athena model to assess materials impacts. Accordingly, the team can then compare materials alternatives in both models, continually seeking to optimize and reduce both building energy use and materials' impacts related to global warming. (See example below illustrated by Figures 6-16 through 6-18.) This can happen only in the context of a highly integrated, interdisciplinary effort.

Creating Alignment

Chapters 4 and 5 discussed in detail the importance of creating alignment across the entire team. Although the schematic design phase is a bit late in the process for creating such alignment, sometimes we have found that a project team may need to go back and re-address alignment issues, especially if alignment was not firmly established. In any case, project teams should continually "check in" on how their decisions are maintaining alignment with their initially established values and aspirations. The following story illustrates this aspect of an integrative design process during the design of a new library for the Associated Mennonite Biblical Seminary (AMBS) in Elkhart, Indiana; it was sent to us by Eileen K. Saner, the librarian and client team leader for our work on this project:

> The initial planning for the new library of AMBS was done by the librarians, along with representatives of the faculty, students, and administration. This group produced a library building program, along with a detailed statement of the requirements of the building and the values of the institution. The new library would represent the Seminary's commitment to research and scholarship in the same way that the campus chapel represents the importance of worship and spirituality. The Library Building Committee worked with the architect to create a schematic design that was based on these requirements and values, as well as on established principles of library construction. This schematic design was used to communicate the project to donors.
>
> The design process paused for twelve months while money was raised for construction. During this time, the Librarian learned about sustainable building design. She became convinced that building a green library presented the Seminary with a unique opportunity to demonstrate a core conviction of Christian theology, creation care. "As stewards of God's earth, we are called to care for the earth and to bring rest and renewal to the land and everything that lives on it" (Article 21, "Confession of Faith in a Mennonite Perspective").
>
> After several months of research and discernment, the Seminary administration and board endorsed a resumption of the planning process with the added goal of constructing a LEED certified green building. As a theological training center for the Mennonite Church in North America, AMBS hosts students, scholars, and church leaders from around the world. A green library at AMBS has great potential for influencing many building projects, and this potential is already being realized.
>
> The advice of 7group, our green building consultant, convinced us of the value of an integrative design process. The administration decided to set aside the original schematic design for the new library and to *start over* using the integrative design process to pursue LEED certification. This decision enabled us to consider the full range of ideas that would promote sustainability in our new building, but we needed to re-align our team.
>
> We hired a project manager and selected an engineering firm with green building experience. We selected a local general contractor committed to becoming a regional leader in green building construction. We hired a conservation consulting firm committed to sustainability that could advise us on site development with attention to storm-water management and sustainable landscaping.
>
> Our green building consultant kicked off this newly aligned team endeavor by facilitating a two-day charrette with representatives from the Seminary planning committee, the architectural firm, the engineering firm, the site development consultant, and the general contractor. This charrette began with a brain-storming session aimed at identifying the core values of the group that could guide design decisions. The outcome of this charrette included a prioritized list of institutional values and an initial assessment of LEED points that could be attained for the project.
>
> The most significant physical outcome of the charrette, however, was a new and completely different footprint for the building. This new footprint incorporates two large rectangles oriented east-to-west, connected by a central service area. North-facing clerestory windows and large exterior windows bring natural light into

the building. Photosensors on the light fixtures detect the amount of daylight available and automatically provide only the level of electric lighting necessary for adequate illumination.

In addition to saving energy, this design gives daylight and views to library users seated at tables and in carrels around the perimeter. Book stacks in the interior are protected from damaging exposure to direct sunlight. The loaded book stacks prevent sound from traveling back to quiet study areas. The service desk and staff offices are centrally located, close to all collections, and also near the entrance.

For eighteen months after the initial charrette, the project team, now operating as "partners," met periodically to refine the design of the building. With owner representatives and all the professionals present at these planning sessions, decisions could be made considering the full range of possibilities, advantages and disadvantages, and potential costs. Each meeting ended with individuals taking on assignments to bring back information for the next meeting. Many options

were considered for mechanical systems, roof structure for the clerestory windows, lighting and furnishings. When fundraising lagged, we explored ways to reduce cost without compromising the sustainable features of the building. In the end, the project was fully funded and the building was constructed as designed.

The resulting new library is a dramatic and welcome change from original 1958 Seminary building with its low roof lines and dropped ceilings. The new tower draws attention to the entrance [of] ... the library and also provides a transition between the original building and the higher roof line of the added new building. The arrangement of library collections and seating is clearly visible from the entrance. The large open spaces provide flexibility that is essential as library resources and services are constantly changing.

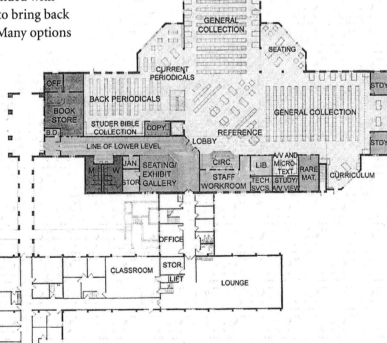

Figure 6-9 The initial floor plan of the Associated Mennonite Biblical Seminary (AMBS) project in Elkhart, Indiana, before engaging an integrative design process, was configured as a Greek cross in plan, which presented some difficulties for daylighting, energy efficiency, and other green design strategies. *Image ©2004 The Troyer Group and Associated Mennonite Biblical Seminary.*

◀ **Figure 6-10** The initial AMBS project rendering before engaging integrative design (see Figure 6-9). *Image ©2004 The Troyer Group and Associated Mennonite Biblical Seminary.*

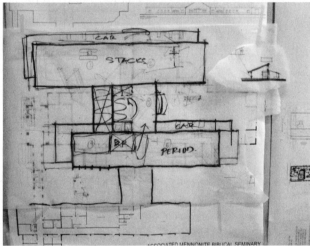

◀ **Figure 6-11** This AMBS floor plan sketch, generated in the conceptual design workshop, represents a significant departure from the original design concept. As a result of this charrette, the owner set aside the original conceptual design that had been generated to enable fundraising and pursued this new building configuration. *Image courtesy of Marcus Sheffer.*

▶ **Figure 6-12** The final floor plan of the AMBS project, reflecting the conceptual sketch generated in the conceptual design workshop, reconfigures the building as an H in plan for more effective daylighting and energy-efficiency strategies. *Image ©2004 The Troyer Group and Associated Mennonite Biblical Seminary.*

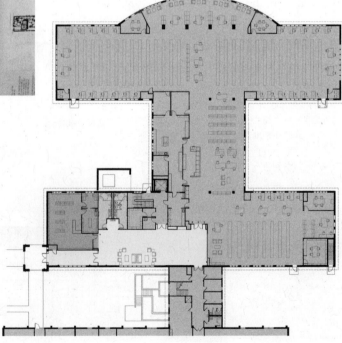

◀ **Figure 6-13** The final AMBS project rendering after engaging integrative design (see Figure 6-12). *Image ©2004 The Troyer Group and Associated Mennonite Biblical Seminary.*

▶ **Figure 6-14** The finished library at the Associated Mennonite Biblical Seminary in Elkhart, Indiana. *Image courtesy of DJ Construction.*

▶ **Figure 6-15** The finished interior of the AMBS library. *Image courtesy of DJ Construction.*

What we have learned from such projects is that it is important to keep our minds open to being continually realigned. There are multiple levels of learning—finer grains of issues and approaches—that need to be analyzed and discovered. We have found it both beneficial and necessary to pause and reflect in the fray of battle to check that we are being true to the owner's and the team's originally defined values, aspirations, and purpose, and to maintain alignment around them.

Mental Model Shift

When the minds of the entire project team can be kept open, a mental model shift occurs. This mental model shift is characterized by three simple things: the first is *allowing ourselves not to have all the answers* at this phase of design, the second is *awareness*, and the third is *observation*.

Allowing ourselves not to have all the answers too quickly is as simple as it sounds. It means being open to ideas and design options that may be coming from anyone and anywhere, even if it requires reconsidering our options. To do this, it is necessary not to overinvest time in the creation of definitive electronic drawings too early. Such an investment can become an obstacle to the good ideas that nearly always surface from an engaged interdisciplinary design team that is aligned and questioning assumptions.

Awareness is a mental state of vigilance and alertness. It is about taking everything that has been learned about the project, the people, and the place and searching for ways to integrate them.

Observation is about noticing what is actually happening with a place, with its people, and with the project. It is much more than just "looking" at something. Glenn Murcutt, an Australian architect and 2002 Pritzker Prize Laureate, has said: "We measure because we fail to observe." He speaks eloquently about observation and how he spends time in the place where he is designing a structure. He learns how wind blows through it, how water flows on and in it, how the sun impacts it, and so on. Then he designs a structure to emerge from what he has observed, so that his buildings become part of a place—instead of destroying the place.

The tools that we use to achieve this mental model shift take on different roles as we experience the shift. LEED, for example, has inspired thousands of people to think differently about their daily work. It does this by guiding project teams through a step-by-step review of a series of explicitly defined environmental issues. As we have seen, when LEED is used properly, it becomes a way to focus the conversation on how to build a better building. When it is not used properly, it becomes an end point in itself.

When LEED, and the tools we use to achieve our purpose (such as energy modeling, daylight analysis, LCA modeling), become an end point in themselves, they get in the way. This occurs when we fail to focus on the *purpose* of the tool. Without a mental model shift that embraces that purpose, tools and other methods of working result in a misalignment between goals (achieving 50 percent energy savings, achieving LEED Gold, etc.) and purpose. When this happens, tools can become a proxy for truly being involved and caring.

Life Cycle Assessment (LCA) Tools and Environmental Benefits

In the last chapter, we discussed how life cycle assessment (LCA) begins to shift our decision-making model. Once the basic structure and envelope decisions are ready to be made, LCA tools can assist in lowering the overall impact of the major elements of the building. In North America, there currently are two design-related LCA tools: One is Building for Environmental and Economic Sustainability (BEES); the other is the ATHENA® *Impact Estimator for Buildings*, along with the ATHENA® *EcoCalculator for Assemblies*, from the Athena Sustainable Materials Institute.

The BEES model was designed and is run by the National Institute of Standards and Technology

On Measuring Tools and Purpose

In an article written with Jay Hall and published in "Ultimate Home Design" Magazine, Ann Edminster, an early LEED volunteer and green practitioner, discusses the relationship between measurement tools and green buildings by asking us to think about the role of measurement in a garden:

> Imagine that your ambition is to grow the tallest sunflower in the neighborhood. It's going to be 10 feet tall! You have some seeds, a patch of soil, water, a few gardening tools, and a tape measure...but no gardening experience. What is it you need the most? Will the tape measure help you grow your coveted 10-foot sunflower?
>
> No. What you need most is the wisdom of experienced gardeners, and ideally they should be in your own community or at least share the same climatic conditions. You have a few resources to try. You start with the library and the local bookstore. That helps a bit. You take a gardening class at the local botanic garden. Better. And you talk to other local gardeners.
>
> ...Eventually you develop the confidence to begin your own gardening experiment. And your learning process continues the more you interact with others and build on their experience with your own.

The question is, what role did the measurement tool play in this process? In this particular case, the measurement device was not related to the goal at all, nor how to achieve it. The height of the sunflower and how it reached that height bear no relationship to the tape measure—the measuring tool is totally unrelated to how the goal was achieved.

Some green building rating systems are designed to function only as measurement tools—after the fact assessments. They are there to help you assess how you are doing or what you have accomplished. Other rating systems, like LEED, function more as leadership and transformational tools. In this sense, they can begin to function as guides. But guidance can have its pitfalls as well. For example, this guidance can be interpreted as "I've achieved a point, so I don't need to do anything else with that issue." No measuring tool can grow a sunflower, and no tool can design, build, or operate your building. Gardening and building are made easier and better with the use of tools, but the user always needs to know the function of these tools and fully understand their *purpose* to use them well.

(NIST). It uses both generic and product-specific life cycle inventory data. This means that the basis for the information underlying the outputs of the tool come from generic sources about things like steel and wood, as well as from specific manufacturers' products, such as Interface's carpet lines. The BEES tool mostly focuses on individual product comparisons, but it also includes some building assembly information.

The Athena *Impact Estimator for Buildings* tool uses generic data only. It is not product specific. The purpose of this Athena tool is to estimate the large impacts of different assembly groups at early phases of design so that project teams can look at alternatives and see how they might lower environmental impacts by choosing alternative assemblies. As a result, it provides a means for optimizing the large-scale materials choices of a project's core and shell components or structural systems.

By using these tools on a regular basis, we can begin to see patterns that arise in terms of the environmental impacts associated with basic material types. For example, we see significant water use related to steel, carbon dioxide emissions related to concrete, etc. These can allow us to make comparative materials decisions based upon weighting the importance of different individual materials' impacts, but it is likely that if you are designing a commercial structure, for example, you will have concrete, steel, wood, and many other materials on the project. We often find that the best opportunities for reducing impacts lie in the team's ability to optimize the collection of materials together, by looking at the collective environmental impacts of materials assemblies. This, again, helps us shift our thinking from deciding what is "good" and what is "bad" to exploring materials assemblies that collectively use what is *better*.

For example, on many projects the owner and designer have already determined from the outset that the building is going to be a certain size and that it will be made of concrete and steel with glass walls—way before schematic design starts. These predetermined assumptions are given to the structural engineer, who begins to establish sizing for bay widths, columns and beams, and floor decks and roofs, while the architect begins to consider a number of exterior wall assemblies options. All of these assemblies represent a lot of material, whose impacts can be analyzed using an LCA tool. But optimizing the size of structural bays to use the least amount of material is almost never considered. Further, looking for ways to size and configure the floor plate so that such optimal sizes of bays, columns, and beams can be achieved is another missed opportunity. Such analyses can then be followed by also analyzing the impacts of different materials options for these optimized beams. Such comprehensive holistic thinking can have a significant effect on the overall impact of the materials.

On a recent project, we used the Athena model to engage such a comprehensive analysis for optimizing

building configuration and structural components. We did this by running a number of iterations of different building shapes in order to see which structural layout would have the lowest environmental impact by using the least amount of material. The basic building was intended to be a rectangle of about 100,000 square feet. Figure 6-16 shows the modeled emissions associated with the original design, prior to optimizing sizing for bays, columns, and beams. The columns and beams, represented by the darkest bar segments (with the white square), reflect a significant opportunity to lower these emissions. Obviously, the foundation (the lightest bar segments, with the white circle)

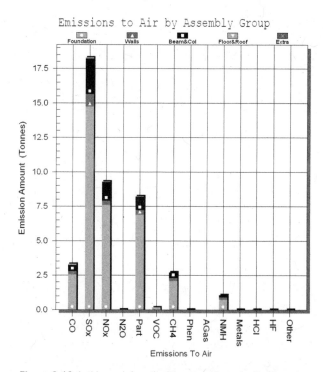

Figure 6-16 In this graph from the Athena model, we see the life cycle "emissions to air" of the base design for a recent project. It depicts which assembly groups contribute the most to various emissions types. The impacts associated with beams and columns are significant, so we used the model to evaluate optimized sizing. Foundation impacts are the largest; these are addressed later (see discussion regarding Figures 6-43 and 6-44). *Image courtesy of the Athena Institute.*

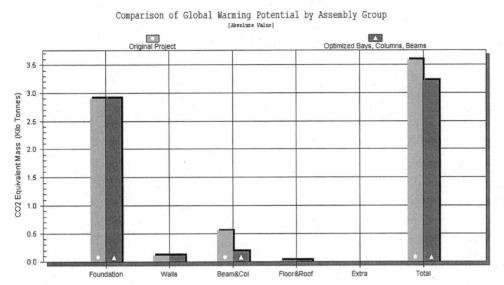

Comparison of Global Warming Potential by Assembly Group
[Absolute Value]

Original Project   Optimized Bays, Columns, Beams

CO2 Equivalent Mass (Kilo Tonnes)

Foundation   Walls   Beam&Col   Floor&Roof   Extra   Total

Figure 6-17 This Athena graph compares the global warming potential (measured in equivalent metric tons of carbon dioxide) of the original design with the reduced impacts resulting from optimized sizing of bays, columns, and beams only. Foundation impacts are addressed in a second step. (Figure 6-43 indicates a reduction in the foundation's global warming potential, resulting from fly ash displacement of portland cement in foundation concrete.) *Image courtesy of the Athena Institute.*

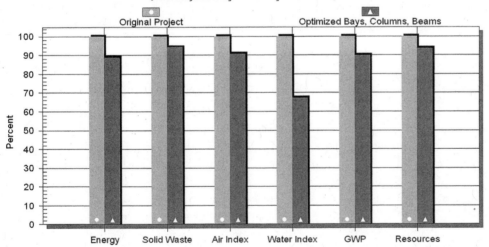

Comparison of All Measures
[With Original Project as Project Baseline]

Original Project   Optimized Bays, Columns, Beams

Percent

Energy   Solid Waste   Air Index   Water Index   GWP   Resources

Figure 6-18 The Athena life-cycle assessment model indicates sizable overall impact reductions across several indicators that resulted from a simple exercise aimed at optimizing the size of bays, columns, and beams only. This represents only one step in a series of analyses aimed at reducing overall impacts. *Image courtesy of the Athena Institute.*

represents the greatest opportunity to optimize the building shape and its structural components. We will discuss the results of this analysis later, in the "Materials" section of *Stage B.2.1*.

Figure 6-17 depicts what happened after several iterations aimed at optimized bay sizing. This graph shows the relative impacts by assembly type, compar-ing the original design to the optimized bays, columns, and beams iteration in terms of global warming po-tential. The improvement was made possible by slight-ly elongating the structure and aligning interior wall components with altered bays. Figure 6-18 compares impact reductions across a number of environmental indicators that resulted from this exercise.

Energy-Modeling Tools and Cost Benefits

Our energy modeling analysis on numerous projects over the years has shown us that *BIG* savings cost less than *small* savings. What does this mean?

As discussed in Chapter 2, the Rocky Mountain Institute refers to this concept as "tunneling through the cost barrier." Quite often, examining the full impacts of many energy-saving strategies more comprehensively across numerous systems can reduce the project's initial cost, while at the same time generating very high levels of cost benefits in terms of energy savings. This integrative concept has been discussed already with a number of examples, but it bears revisiting.

The story above about the Neptune Midtown Community Elementary School illustrates this quite well. This story demonstrates that achieving high levels of energy performance—big savings—requires that more comprehensive financial analysis be engaged in parallel with parametric energy modeling. The small savings—also known as incremental efficiency improvements—result from using financial analysis tools unrelated to the reality of the building's design as a whole—by looking at line item costs associated with energy-efficiency measures such as specifying more energy-efficient HVAC equipment.

The traditional method for analyzing a project's energy saving opportunities utilizes a "simple-payback" or perhaps a "return-on-investment" approach. This method provides a reasonable metric in certain situations where a given strategy's interactions with other building systems are minimal or where only one system is undergoing change. For example, a single energy-saving strategy for retrofitting an existing facility, such as replacing lighting fixtures, is typically analyzed in this way. However, this methodology does not provide a reasonable metric in most new construction projects or in facilities undergoing more comprehensive system retrofits or replacements. The results of such an analysis are simply incomplete.

A simple payback analysis tends to model energy-saving strategies (or energy-efficiency measures) as isolated opportunities. Such analysis typically does not examine the interactive nature of combining many individual energy-saving strategies. In a new construction project, a whole series of decisions are being made as the various building systems (envelope, lighting, HVAC, etc.) are developed. Using simple payback requires that all other variables remain fixed while an individual strategy—or fragment—is modeled in isolation.

Suppose additional roof insulation is being considered; the typical approach would be to determine the added cost for the insulation and then use an energy model to determine the resultant annual energy savings. Cost divided by annual savings equals simple payback. As one adds more insulation, energy savings incrementally decrease. This is referred to as the *law of diminishing returns*. When only one such item is examined, this law applies; but the reality of building projects is that project teams are not considering just one item in isolation. The amount of roof insulation also will affect other building systems, such as the size of the HVAC equipment or the height of the parapet, for example. Examining roof insulation as a strategy in isolation does not provide enough information— or even the right information—needed to make a fully informed decision, since such limited analysis does not examine the full financial effect.

Further, when modeling a series of energy-saving strategies individually, the energy-use reductions resulting from each measure cannot simply be added together. Just as an energy model is needed to analyze a series of interactive strategies to accurately determine energy savings, integrative cost bundling is necessary to fully analyze the associated financial implications. Many energy-saving strategies, particularly when combined with others, can have a significant effect on the size of the HVAC system, as the Neptune Elementary School example from Figures 6-4 to 6-7 demonstrates.

A downsized, smaller HVAC system costs less to purchase. The savings resulting from this smaller HVAC system can be used to pay for the energy-saving strategies that allowed for the smaller HVAC system in the first place. We often have been able to garner enough savings from such systems downsizing (or elimination) to pay the full cost of all of a project's energy-savings strategies. Consequently, significant energy savings and reduced operations costs can be achieved, while also neutralizing overall first-cost impacts.

Achieving significant energy savings and reduced first costs requires a new way of thinking about how one analyzes energy-saving measures and financial return. Simple payback for a single EEM becomes a small portion of the analysis, not the sole metric by which decisions are made. By "tunneling through the cost barrier" and treating the law of diminishing returns as a situational condition, project teams often can justify big-cost benefits in terms of energy savings with little or no additional first-cost expenditure.

Revisiting Nested Subsystems

As we proceed into schematic design, we want to continually examine each of the four key subsystems (i.e., habitat, both human and other biotic systems; water; energy; and materials) with more and more detailed analysis, but we need to remember that the essential aspect of integrative design is realizing that these subsystems *interrelate*. We must constantly seek to discover the connections between them by understanding them as nested subsystems (as discussed in Chapter 4; also, see the *holons* discussion and sidebar in *Stage B.1.1*). This requires that project teams continually attempt to link the cascading and stacked benefits of these systems in order to achieve more elegance in the solution, both in terms of cost and environmental benefits. Nature works this way too—the more closely aligned we become with the way life works (living systems) in the place we are building, the more likely the design choices we make will nest with each other in mutually supportive ways.

There are many different primary entry points into these nested subsystems. For example, the more local materials we use, the less total energy is required to construct the building and the more appropriate the building's character will be to its place, like the Siena Duomo; the more indigenous the plants are to the place, the less water will be needed for irrigation and the more appropriate these plants will be to supporting diverse life in that place, in turn creating a healthy habitat that can treat and hold water without the need for technological treatment and conveyance solutions. In schematic design, then, we are searching to more completely link these living systems.

PART B—DESIGN AND CONSTRUCTION

Stage B.1

Workshop No. 3: Schematic Design Kickoff—Bringing It All Together (without committing to building form)

B.1.1 Workshop No. 3 Activities

- Present sketch concepts, supporting data, and discoveries from *Stage A.5* Research and Analysis
- Develop site and building configuration sketch solutions by evaluating flows and exploring interrelationships between the four key subsystems:
  - Habitat
  - Water
  - Energy
  - Materials
- Assess the realistic potential for achieving Performance Targets and review commitment to Touchstones and Principles
- Identify the systems that require more extensive cost bundling analysis, including life cycle cost impacts
- Provide time for reflection and feedback from client and team members
- Commissioning: Identify where the OPR and BOD will need refinement based upon new discoveries

B.1.2 Principles and Measurement

- Document adjustments to Performance Targets to reflect input from Workshop No. 3
- Commissioning: Adjust OPR and BOD to reflect input from Workshop No. 3

B.1.3 Cost Analysis

- Update any required integrative cost bundling templates to reflect input from Workshop No. 3

B.1.4 Schedule and Next Steps

- Refine and extend forward the Integrative Process Road Map tasks and schedule into future phases to reflect input from Workshop No. 3
- Distribute Workshop No. 3 report

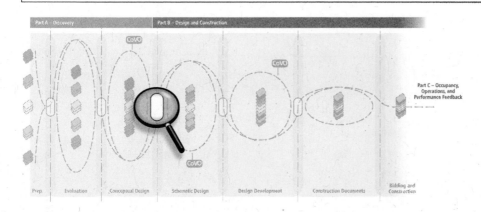

Figure 6-19 Integrative Process Stage B.1, Workshop #3: Schematic Design Kickoff. *Image courtesy of 7group and Bill Reed; graphics by Corey Johnston.*

Stage B.1

WORKSHOP No. 3: Schematic Design Kickoff—Bringing it All Together (without committing to building form)

At this point, team members have analyzed major subsystems, including options for the building's architectural form and massing, but we have yet to put these pieces together in a whole building design. Nevertheless, we still need to restrain ourselves from locking into what the building looks like too soon. If we focus too quickly on the architectural form and/or aesthetic, we tend to pessimize performance and downgrade the whole. In other words, this stage begins by ensuring that we have refined each of the major subsystems to a relatively high degree via reasonably thorough analyses before giving final form to the building.

During Workshop No. 2 (*Stage A.4*) we looked at how these systems might interact with each other conceptually. We then tested these conceptual ideas and systems performance during the Research and Analysis of *Stage A.5*; now, during Schematic Design stages, it is time to put these systems together in greater detail to see how they will support each other and, most importantly, to discover how the design evolves from integrating these various pieces. We can, then, iterate these systems in relationship and mutual support of one another, thereby allowing this process to inform the building's architectural form and solution. At the same time, we are continuing to look at these systems and their components in continually finer detail and progressive approximation with a finer grain of analysis. This Schematic Design effort is kicked off in Workshop No. 3.

Similar to Workshop No. 2, the Implementation Outline above can be used as a template for creating an agenda for Workshop No. 3; but, again, the agenda for this session needs to remain fluid and flexible during the workshop, as the team makes new discoveries. It also should be noted, again, that this workshop can occur as an all-day event on a single day, or it can be structured to last as long as three or four days, depending upon project complexity and the team's goals. Lastly, the builder's participation becomes even more valuable at this workshop and should be encouraged (if at all possible), so that the project's construction professionals can be included as codesigners.

B.1.1 Workshop No. 3 Activities

■ **Present sketch concepts, supporting data, and discoveries from Stage A.5 Research and Analysis**

This workshop can begin by presenting discoveries and analysis of the leading options for solutions regarding each of the four key subsystems, followed by exercises aimed at mapping out the relationships between them in detail—but without committing yet to what the building looks like. To begin, then, each team member presents the results of their *Stage A.5* Research and Analysis to the team in the form of sketch concepts and supporting data in order to iterate ideas and to look for synchronicity between systems.

On a recent project seeking LEED Platinum certification and pursuing the Living Building Challenge, team members brought the following documents to this workshop:

■ Refined conceptual building footprint and phasing diagram options

■ Refined program data

■ Site analysis of vehicular flows, parking options, utility connections, water flows, soils data, key habitat and restoration zones diagrams, list of potential native plant species, site-program elements, and phasing

■ Location and sizing options for infiltration and constructed wetlands resulting from analysis of demand, supply, and topography

■ Initial water balance analysis targeting net-zero-water use, including: calculations of water demand, wastewater generation, water availability from the projected roof and site areas

- Potential for renewable energy supply—optional sources and initial loads to determine requirements for achieving net-zero energy
- Building massing option sketches with alternatives for fenestration patterns and window-to-wall percentages
- Simple box energy model comparisons of the above options, along with an initial list of potential EEM options
- Rough sketches of initial daylighting strategies with optional configurations
- Initial LCA of core and shell materials options, along with associated carbon footprint calculations
- List of potential salvaged materials from the existing on-site building scheduled for demolition
- Initial draft of the BOD for Commissioning
- Cost bundling analysis for various combinations of EEMs
- Updated LEED assessment

During the presentation of each key subsystem's *Stage A.5* findings, a facilitated discussion looks at flows and interrelationships between the subsystems and their components. The whole group then assesses and identifies how the systems are interrelated and how they can mutually support one another—not only in direct relationship but in various combinations and nestings of subsystems and components—as *holons* in *holarchy,* from the Greek *holos*, meaning "whole" (see *Holons* sidebar and Figure 6-20). The workshop facilitator records these results for use in the breakout work sessions and for referencing during future stages.

- **Develop site and building configuration sketch solutions by evaluating flows and exploring interrelationships between the four key subsystems**

Now it is time to start making some decisions about the four key subsystems and their interrelationships. We often have found it effective to break into at least two small design team groups of four to five team members with expertise for each subsystem evenly distributed to each group. These small groups "roll up their sleeves" and start sketching schematic solutions that address all of the following subsystem issues in a single

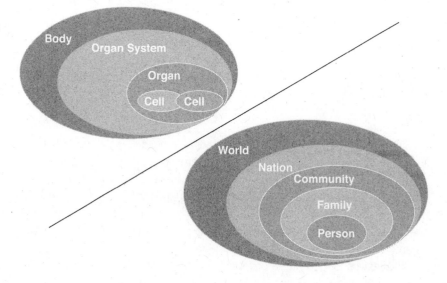

Figure 6-20 "All living systems are arranged as holarchies. That's Arthur Koestler's elegant word for the embeddedness and interdependence of natural entities, which he calls holons. Holarchy is nestedness, distinguishing it from pyramidal hierarchy (which implies superiority at the top and is the metaphor for command-and-control systems). You, as a body, are this kind of holarchy (depicted in this diagram)—cells within organs within organ systems within bodies." The key subsystems are similarly nested within larger systems. *Image and caption content courtesy of Elisabet Sahtouris, from her book* Earthdance: Living Systems in Evolution *(Ingram, NY: iUnivers. com, 2000), http://www.sahtouris.com.*

Holons*

A *holon* is a system (or phenomenon) that is a whole in itself as well as a part of a larger system. It can be conceived as systems nested within each other. Every system can be considered a holon, from a subatomic particle to the universe as a whole. On a nonphysical level, words, ideas, sounds, emotions—everything that can be identified—is simultaneously part of something *and* can be viewed as having parts of its own...

Since a holon is embedded in larger wholes, it is influenced by and influences these larger wholes. And since a holon also contains subsystems, or parts, it is similarly influenced by and influences these parts. Information flows bidirectionally between smaller and larger systems as well as by rhizomatic contagion. When this bidirectionality of information flow and understanding of role is compromised, for whatever reason, the system begins to break down: wholes no longer recognize their dependence on their subsidiary parts, and parts no longer recognize the organizing authority of the wholes. Cancer may be understood as such a breakdown in the biological realm.

A hierarchy of holons is called a *holarchy*. The holarchic model can be seen as an attempt to modify and modernize perceptions of natural hierarchy.

In the terminology of Arthur Koestler, holarchy is a hierarchy of self-regulating holons—where a holon is both a part and a whole. The term [holon] was coined in Koestler's 1967 book *The Ghost in the Machine*. The term is also used extensively by American philosopher and writer Ken Wilber.

Ken Wilber comments that the test of holon hierarchy (e.g., holarchy) is that if a type of holon is removed from existence, then all other holons of which it formed a part must necessarily cease to exist too. Thus an atom is of a lower standing in the hierarchy than a molecule, because if you removed all molecules, atoms could still exist, whereas if you removed all atoms, molecules, in a strict sense, would cease to exist. Wilber's concept is known as the doctrine of the fundamental and the significant. A hydrogen atom is more fundamental than an ant, but an ant is more significant.

The "nested" nature of holons, where one holon can be considered as part of another, is similar to the term Panarchy as used by Adaptive Management theorists Lance Gunderson and C. S. Holling.

The universe as a whole is an example of a holarchy, or holarchical system, and every other holarchy we are aware of is a part of this larger holarchy.

*References

"Living Systems, the Internet and the Human Future," Elisabet Sahtouris, PhD, talk presented May 13, 2000, at Planetwork, Global Ecology, and Information Technology, a conference held at the San Francisco Presidio. Notes developed by Carol Sanford of Interoctave, Inc., Seattle, Washington.

scheme. In other words, these breakout groups not only refine the interrelationships of components within each subsystem, but they also are challenged to explore potential synergies between subsystems—as holons. Depending on the size and complexity of the project, this can occur with one or many design team groups looking at all four key subsystems; for larger projects with many stakeholders present, several groups may be optimal.

■ **Habitat** (biotic systems other than human)

- Discuss the specific roles of habitat in relation to thermal control (wind and shading), water quality, rainwater management, connectivity to larger nested systems such as nearby streams, habitat corridors within the larger watershed, opportunities for microclimates around each side of the building to shelter and support various plants and other species, etc.

- *Example:* Let's revisit the project in Idaho near the Teton River that was discussed near the end of Chapter 3 in a bit more detail. You may recall that the developer asked us to help his team gain an understanding of the interrelationships between habitat and his development. This required a deeper way of thinking about habitat than simply preserving agricultural land or planting native species, so this issue was discussed extensively at the workshop.

The land in question was to be developed with approximately 1,000 homes on 3,200 acres of farmland. On the surface, this sounds like a bad idea from an environmental perspective. However, by looking at the larger systems of farm economics and how the farms had interrupted and eliminated the streams and habitat corridors that connected the mountains and the river, it became apparent that the farms were the original problem as discussed earlier; their presence eliminated natural water flows, fish-spawning streams, related soil replenishment, and habitat corridors for beaver, smaller animals, and megafauna. The farms were originally subsistence farms that could no longer support commodity crops in the short growing season—the farmers were bankrupt. There was no one offering to pay the farmers for their land except for the large-scale developer.

The original scheme assumed selling the land and building a home on every twenty acres; but this would have meant a continuation of the disconnection between the mountains and the stream, as we have seen. The opportunity that emerged, then, was driven by investigating the possibility of using the entire development as a means for developing new potential for this land in partnership with human habitation. The resulting scheme eliminates the farm irrigation (thus reducing water use by 75 percent—irrigation uses a tremendous amount of water), diverts rainwater to the old stream beds (still visible beneath the fields—see Figure 3-13), redistributes treated wastewater, and requires native plantings without fences to interrupt habitat flow.

As a result, it is anticipated that the human development can bring back the living connections between the mountains and the river, thereby reestablishing the diversity of life; this would not have occurred had the developer followed overly generalized checklists of average-practice environmental criteria. The larger holon of the watershed informed the design's fundamental approach. With this core principle in place, the design and development team had a basic principle to govern integrated decision-making. Again, the resulting project potentially utilizes development to improve the ecosystem, thus *bringing forth new potential*—the true definition of development.

■ **Habitat** (human)

- Identify and determine where daylighting is important (habitable spaces should be a priority in terms of available window budget) and which design strategies analyzed during *Stage A.5* need to be pursued to daylight these spaces, including: window sizing and location, room-cavity ratio, distance to glazing, orientation, bilateral capability (daylighting from two opposite sides of a given space), etc. As a reminder, these considerations need to be addressed specifically in the DNA of the schematic design and should be a basic, driving principle from the outset. They cannot be added as a superimposed layer on top of a preconceived design solution.

- Refine thermal comfort parameters and the desired level of individual control (extent and locations of operable windows, underfloor air, etc.).
- Refine ventilation parameters (natural vs. mechanical, desired volumes of outside air relative to functions, temperature settings, impacts on thermal comfort parameters, etc.).
- Determine parameters for pollutant source control issues—e.g., toxicant levels in materials, means for pollutant source isolation, housekeeping products, etc.
- Identify benefits and opportunities to pursue for the site, the building, and its occupants to support and be supported by the community—how can this project be in a more interactive and mutually beneficial relationship? In other words, how will the building occupants be inspired to understand—and better yet, care for—the water cycle, natural habitat, edible plants, fruit trees, perhaps polyphase agriculture, stream corridors that support a diversity of life, and community-gathering places?
- *Example:* Daylighting

As discussed in *Stage A.5.1*, good daylighting design is both quantitative and qualitative. There are basic strategies for introducing daylight into a space—sidelighting, toplighting, and optimally a bilateral condition, which may include a combination of strategies. Options for such strategies should be examined at the workshop. (A Daylighting Design Tips pdf file can be downloaded from the *Resources* tab on 7group's website at www.sevengroup.com.)

Sidelighting is the strategy of bringing daylight in through the vertical surfaces of a space. The rule of thumb is that effective daylight penetration equates to about one-and-a-half times the window head height; with the use of a light shelf (see Figures 6-21 and 6-22), this penetration can increase up to two-and-a-half times the window height. An initial starting point for adequate daylighting in schematic design is to target approximately 15 percent as a glazing-to-floor area ratio for spaces on the south and about 20 percent for those on the north, if sidelighting is being used from a single orientation.

Toplighting includes several strategies for bringing in daylight through the roof. The most effective means of toplighting is through the use of clerestories or roof monitors (see Figures 6-23 and 6-24). The use of skylights requires a special balance between lighting needs and the reduction of solar heat gain. An initial design starting point in schematic design is to target approximately 7 to 10 percent as a glazing-to-floor area ratio for toplighting. Clerestories can represent either a sidelighting or toplighting strategy, and they can be used individually or in a series of sawtooths. Clerestories function best if they face either north or south; if facing south, baffles or diffuse glazing might be needed to eliminate direct solar gain and glare.

Figure 6-21 Interior light shelves reflect daylight that enters through the upper section of window glass deeper into the space. This portion of glass above the light shelf is selected for its daylighting properties and has a higher visible light transmittance than the vision glazing below. *Image courtesy of Todd Reed.*

Figure 6-22 Exterior light shelves shade the lower vision glass from high-altitude direct solar penetration in the summer, while bouncing daylight through the upper daylighting glass deeper into the space. *Image courtesy of Todd Reed.*

Figure 6-23 These clerestory windows at the AMBS project provide effective toplight daylighting for producing even illumination within the library space. *Image courtesy of Marcus Sheffer.*

Figure 6-24 The north-facing clerestory windows at the DEP Cambria, Pennsylvania, project provide bilateral daylighting to create balanced lighting-level distributions in this open office space; punched openings on the opposite lower wall (not depicted) introduce daylight into the same space from the south. *Image ©2000 Jim Shafer.*

Roof monitors are a form of toplighting that allow daylight to enter from multiple directions. On a small scale, this strategy can be an effective alternative to skylights. At a larger scale, monitors can be used to effectively illuminate high-volume spaces, as depicted in Figure 6-25.

Bilateral daylighting consists of a combination of both sidelighting and toplighting or of sidelighting from more than one side of a space, usually from the north and south (see Figure 6-26). Bilateral daylighting provides the highest quality daylighting conditions, since it balances the lighting-level distributions in the space. This strategy also reduces the glare and high contrast ratios that can result from sidelighting alone.

▲ **Figure 6-25** These clerestory roof monitors bring copious daylight into the main map room of the DEP Cambria project from all four directions, allowing for the photocell sensor (center) to fully dim the lighting fixtures during most daylight hours. This toplighting strategy is often used to illuminate common areas such as lobbies. *Image courtesy of John Boecker.*

▼ **Figure 6-26** An example of bilateral daylighting at the Willow School. These two images depict two opposite sides of the same space: one looking north and the other looking south. *Image courtesy of Todd Reed.*

■ **Water**

- Evaluate integrative solutions for water conservation, water quality, and water balance strategies. Again, the goal here is to use water for multiple purposes as it moves through the building and the site—a cascading of uses, as described in the example below.

- Identify the natural and technical systems and components that can address these issues (it is more than just reducing plumbing fixture flow-and-flush rates).

- *Example:* You may recall from Chapter 4 that the civil engineer for the Willow School was very frustrated. We kept telling him at the workshop that his design was too technical, relying on technologies and built infrastructure to solve the problem; instead, we were trying to work with the topography and let the water flow to areas of habitat where it could serve the purpose of supporting new life. In frustration, we finally gave him a straightforward strategy: "Keep it simple: no curbs, no catch basins, no culverts." He came back a week later with an apology and an excellent design. He said he pretty much tried what we asked him to do, but he was not entirely successful:

  > I had to add a few culverts. I tried to use as many vegetated swales as possible, but then I came to this large tree and realized I'd be cutting the roots with the swale, so I sent the water to the other side of the road with a pipe. Then there was the curve in the driveway, and the water sheeting over it in the winter might freeze and create a driving hazard, so I had to pipe it under the road as well.

  We were very impressed; he fully got the idea and used technical solutions only where it was needed, not as a rule. The rainwater design

Figure 6-27 This rain garden captures and infiltrates the rainwater runoff from the adjacent paved surfaces via slotted gutters. *Image ©2008. Conservation Design Forum, Elmhurst, IL, http://www.cdfine.com.*

worked beautifully, habitat was encouraged and fed, and the site infrastructure costs were reduced by 50 percent.

■ **Energy**

- Review the results of the initial energy modeling parametric runs from *Stage A.5.1.* Discuss the modeling inputs to be sure that the project team is in alignment with them.

- Narrow the range of possibilities related to general building massing, orientation, and rough percentage of glazing openings.

- Establish thermal envelope initial parameters and identify additional options for parametric modeling.

- Identify potential additional systems that need to be modeled, such as ground-source heat pumps, solar thermal, etc.

- Identify a list of energy-efficiency measures (EEMs) or energy-conservation measures (ECMs) to investigate, model, and determine initial cost implications for further cost-bundling analyses.

- Discuss operations:
  - Decide on comfort ranges and adaptive thermal comfort parameters.
  - Assess level of automation vs. active participation in operations.
  - Evaluate the level of sophistication of maintenance and operations staff in relation to the desired complexity of controls systems. An overly complex building management system (BMS) is useless if staff cannot operate or understand it. (How many times have you seen control systems components disabled during the first year of occupancy?)
  - Begin to identify actual occupancy schedules—these can have a huge impact on modeled-energy consumption. Discuss options for occupancy periods and equipment schedules, and examine daily and/or seasonal fluctuations in occupancy where applicable (e.g., schools, resorts, alternative work shifts, after-hour activities, shared occupancies, etc.)
- Establish criteria for determining Service Life of mechanical systems (see Figure 6-28).
- Revisit all energy-related performance parameters to ensure that the project design is in alignment with the options to be analyzed in the next stage.
- Discuss potential local incentives, rebates, grants, and other funding sources related to energy efficiency.
- *Example*: An architectural firm hired us to coach their green design and construction process for a large call-center project in Florida. At the first workshop, we were surprised to find that the design team was already committed to a build-

Figure 6-28 This ASHRAE Table identifying the Service Life of various types of mechanical equipment can assist teams in Life Cycle Cost Analysis evaluations. *Image courtesy of ASHRAE Standard 55-2004. © American Society of Heating, Refrigerating and Air-Conditioning Engineers, Inc., http://www.ashrae.org.*

Table 3   Estimates of Service Lives of Various System Components[a]

Equipment Item	Median Years	Equipment Item	Median Years	Equipment Item	Median Years
Air conditioners		Air terminals		Air-cooled condensers	20
Window unit	10	Diffusers, grilles, and registers	27	Evaporative condensers	20
Residential single or split package	15	Induction and fan-coil units	20	Insulation	
Commercial through-the-wall	15	VAV and double-duct boxes	20	Molded	20
Water-cooled package	15	Air washers	17	Blanket	24
Heat pumps		Ductwork	30	Pumps	
Residential air-to-air	15[b]	Dampers	20	Base-mounted	20
Commercial air-to-air	15	Fans		Pipe-mounted	10
Commercial water-to-air	19	Centrifugal	25	Sump and well	10
Roof-top air conditioners		Axial	20	Condensate	15
Single-zone	15	Propeller	15	Reciprocating engines	20
Multizone	15	Ventilating roof-mounted	20	Steam turbines	30
Boilers, hot water (steam)		Coils		Electric motors	18
Steel water-tube	24 (30)	DX, water, or steam	20	Motor starters	17
Steel fire-tube	25 (25)	Electric	15	Electric transformers	30
Cast iron	35 (30)	Heat Exchangers		Controls	
Electric	15	Shell-and-tube	24	Pneumatic	20
Burners	21	Reciprocating compressors	20	Electric	16
Furnaces		Package chillers		Electronic	15
Gas- or oil-fired	18	Reciprocating	20	Valve actuators	
Unit heaters		Centrifugal	23	Hydraulic	15
Gas or electric	13	Absorption	23	Pneumatic	20
Hot water or steam	20	Cooling towers		Self-contained	10
Radiant heaters		Galvanized metal	20		
Electric	10	Wood	20		
Hot water or steam	25	Ceramic	34		

Source: Data obtained from a survey of the United States by ASHRAE Technical Committee TC 1.8 (Akalin 1978).
[a]See Lovvorn and Hiller (1985) and Easton Consultants (1986) for further information.
[b]Data updated by TC 1.8 in 1986.

Figure 6-29 Breakout groups are an effective means of getting into a significantly greater level of detail with a smaller group at a team workshop. In this case, the breakout group is discussing potential energy strategies. *Image courtesy of Marcus Sheffer.*

ing form that included a 300-foot long, 20-foot high wall of glass that looked onto some adjacent woods—a form that was meant to provide views that could support the well-being of the building's occupants. Unfortunately, the wall of glass faced east. In Florida, this is not a good approach in terms of energy and daylighting due to the cooling demand resulting from this solar orientation. We suggested that the design should be reconsidered if the team was really interested in meeting their goals for energy efficiency (and achieving their desired LEED Gold certification). Apparently, we mentioned the need to reconsider the building orientation five times during the workshop, because they told us this the next day: "We are very disappointed in your performance...perhaps you aren't the best firm for the job, since you're questioning the architect's design." We apologized for giving offense, and the project moved forward as originally designed.

At the beginning of design development, the energy modeler presented his near-final analysis, indicating barely two LEED points for energy (a 14 percent energy cost reduction). We got a call from the same project manager telling us how disappointed they were with our ability to give them an energy-efficient building. We thought they were joking. It became clear that throughout the design process, the team was not able to connect the idea that the building form had that big an effect on energy; despite our attempting, admittedly obliquely, to help them understand that all the other techniques being employed could not make up for their desire to have an unobstructed east-facing view with clear glazing that had a high solar heat gain coefficient (SHGC). We made this point again, but a bit more clearly—now supported by energy modeling results. After further discussion, they finally understood, and to their credit, they addressed the problem with a variety of techniques that still allowed the view—among them, using a higher-performing window wall, shading elements, and trees.

■ Materials

- Establish structural system materials options and parameters based upon *Stage A.5* analysis, such as steel vs. concrete, structural bay sizing, etc.
- Establish building Service Life criteria for architectural and structural systems.
- Prioritize environmental indicators for informing LCA-based materials decisions and selections, such as human toxicant limits and prohibitions, embodied-energy targets, carbon footprint budget, etc.
- *Example*: At this workshop, when breakout groups focus on materials, they are presented with some unique challenges. Determining the level of thinking that team members bring to this session requires education as well as good listening skills on the part of the group leader or facilitator. The team may not be completely on board with the objectives of the charrette, or they may be overly enthusiastic about materials-specific issues. The goal should be to ensure that everyone understands and discusses viable options for structure and envelope decisions and is fully aware of the implications.

For example, on a recent project, we saw from early energy models that a steel-stud exterior wall with six inches of insulation and a thermal break had the same energy performance as an insulated concrete form (ICF) wall. However, from viewing our infrared photos of actual construction sites, we have seen that the steel-stud option is associated with a higher incidence of human error during con-

struction, opening the possibility for the creation of numerous small holes, gaps, and thermal bridges that can add up to a significant difference in overall performance. This cannot be accounted for in any of the models, so it is all the more important that the builder be engaged in this discussion.

Also, if the group can have such a discussion, then the team can examine a variety of envelope options by analyzing Athena models in parallel with energy models to see what the comparative environmental impacts of these options may be from an LCA perspective. If the LCA modeler cannot perform the work at the workshop, the team can review a variety of options as a group and then analyze modeled results at a follow-up interim meeting (see "Interim Meetings" in *Stage B.2*). If LCA-based modeled options can be reviewed at the workshop, the team can look together for ways to lower overall impacts by comparing proposed options for assembly types.

In the case of the above-referenced project, we began by modeling a steel-stud exterior wall with brick cladding and comparing that to ICFs. The ICF option had an overall greater LCA impact, but it eliminated the possible construction flaws due to the monolithic nature of this envelope system. The team then sought ways to lower the overall impact of the exterior wall assembly by viewing other cladding options. The breakout group took the ideas back to the larger team, and it was determined at the workshop that several other options should be modeled from an LCA standpoint and reviewed at an interim team meeting focused on integrating envelope issues (more about this in *Stage B.2.1*).

■ **Assess the realistic potential for achieving Performance Targets and review commitment to Touchstones and Principles**

  ■ Similar to Workshop No. 2, a representative from each breakout group presents the ideas that emerged from their working session to solicit from the *large* group their thoughts or reflections. Once all breakout groups present, the large group once again can engage a *green hat, red hat* exercise and record "what to keep" and "what to avoid." This can occur for as many rounds as time allows, depending upon the duration of this workshop. For single-day workshops, at least two rounds of such presentations are preferable, so that breakout groups are able to incorporate emerging priorities and integrative ideas from the first round into their second round of explorations.

  ■ The resulting outcome from this workshop usually takes the form of site and building sketches; but, of course, these results can vary considerably depending upon project complexities. The targeted goal should be to have the team hone in on a limited number of overall design solutions that integrate all four subsystems.

  ■ The group evaluates potential solutions developed by the breakout groups in terms of alignment with the project's initial targeted performance objectives and principles.

  ■ The group reviews the status of the project relative to its green building assessment tool goals; for example, evaluating strategies relative to the project's LEED goals and the requirements of pursued credits.

  ■ Evaluate the potential for achieving the targeted levels of performance—the group should focus on realistic yet aggressive-as-possible objectives, since the scheme is gradually getting more real.

  ■ *Ask*: Are the metrics and benchmarks still appropriate? If not, adjust them.

■ **Identify the systems that require more extensive cost bundling analysis, including life cycle cost impacts**

  ■ Identify major sets of systems and components that need to be analyzed as related bundles of costs and refine with team, as necessary.

  ■ For example, let's return to the Willow School's creation of a constructed waste–treatment wetland that initially was considered to be too costly. The treatment wetland in this case consisted of a primary treatment tank and a leeching field—just like a septic system. However, a wetland and sand filter are installed between the tank and the field to add a much higher level of treatment. Of course, everyone thought that these so-called extra components would add cost—except that in this location in New Jersey, where an eight-foot layer of relatively impermeable clay typically needs to be excavated to install the leech lines for a conventional septic drainage field. With a wetland filtering the septic tank effluent before it goes into the field (called a dosing field, in this case), there are no solids going into the field; therefore, the lines could be placed at only 14 inches below grade—saving significant excavation costs and also eliminating the need for a reserve leeching field, since the field that is tied to the constructed wetland will never have to be abandoned due to oversaturation of solids. As discussed previously, a bundled cost estimate demonstrated that when the entire system design was considered, the constructed wetland treatment actually cost $30,000 *less* than the septic system.

  Further, we discovered that at eight feet below grade, effluent from typical septic systems leeches directly into the water table through fractured sandstone, since there is no aerated soil layer to effectively treat the waste with microbes. So for less money, the school got a better system that doesn't clog, doesn't pollute the water table, doesn't add any burden to the municipal treatment system, consumes less water, produces water than can be recycled back into the building, promotes habitat and biodiversity, and serves as an effective teaching tool for their students and the community—and at a lower cost.

■ Provide time for reflection and feedback from client and team members

Once again, ask everyone to reflect on what they are experiencing and learning at the workshop during logical break points or at major transitions, such as during lunch or coffee breaks—especially the owner's team—and set aside time for them to convey their reflections back to the group.

■ Commissioning: Identify where the OPR and BOD will need refinement based upon new discoveries

As analyses and solutions become more refined, the Owner's Project Requirements (OPR) and the Basis of Design (BOD) need to be updated to reflect them. The team should review an outline of the BOD, agree on updates, and add to the BOD any revisions in outline form. Consequently, the Commissioning Authority reminds everyone at the workshop to update the components of the OPR and BOD that relate to their systems.

As design elements are identified and refined through this evolution and various iterations, there may be a need to expand the number of individuals serving as team members; there is good reason to believe that the process will be enhanced by such fresh eyes and ears. The Commissioning Authority, then, might look for opportunities from these newer team members to inject new thoughts into a process that otherwise may be subject to a tendency for seeking "sameness," even in new things.

B.1.2 Principles and Measurement

■ Document adjustments to Performance Targets to reflect input from Workshop No. 3

As Performance Targets are revised, based upon discussions and discoveries during the Workshop and throughout the process, adjustments to these Performance Targets need to be documented and distributed to the project team in the workshop report. If the project is pursuing LEED certification, this report should include a revised LEED scorecard that documents updates and revisions to the status of each credit being pursued, along with the current strategies under consideration for meeting targeted credit requirements.

■ Commissioning: Adjust OPR and BOD to reflect input from Workshop No. 3

The design team, with owner input, makes any revisions to the OPR and publishes this revised document to the project team. As noted above, the OPR is a dynamic document that evolves as a reflection of the current status of the design.

The design team also needs to update the BOD, based upon both the OPR revisions described above and the discoveries and decisions reached at Workshop No. 3, and then distribute this revised document. Like the OPR, the BOD is a dynamic document that continuously evolves. It also needs to describe the *story of why* decisions have been made at various points in the process and what generated these decisions in order to inform work on future phases and to capture the evolutionary nature of how these technical thresholds and performance targets were determined, then met. In other words, the BOD answers: how does the building have to work as a whole to achieve these performance targets?

The important point here is that the sooner these key documents are developed, the more effectively they can evolve with the project. As explained in Chapter 5, they cannot and should not be static, in as much as the process of integrative design and construction is not static. However, even when the OPR and BOD are not created at the very beginning, they still can add value. An example of this comes from our experience on a recent project:

Following some successful LEED project commissioning efforts for a major hospital organization, we were invited to commission their data backup facility, which was already under construction, but not pursuing LEED certification. At our initial interview, we encountered the information technology (IT) manager, who was serving as the "owner" for the project. It did not take long for us to affirm what we had heard from other members of the design team, that this fellow was an IT wizard. He expressed an absolute need for guaranteed perfection, but his appreciation for building design and construction was limited. He welcomed and easily consumed his initial assignment for completing the OPR questionnaire for the "infrastructure," or building elements, of the project. He completed it within a day of distribution, leaving other team members simply to fall in behind his responses, since he had answered all of the questions about all of the systems for *all* the owner's team members.

At the second meeting, we watched and listened as he continued to answer questions for everybody else on the team. He possessed a fair command of the project's electrical necessities, but when it came to the HVAC elements, it was clear that he lacked thorough knowledge of these systems, and was reflecting what he had been told by trusted IT consultants. We finally were able to slow him down a bit with questions rooted in recent ASHRAE studies pertaining to the full set of loads, energy requirements, and efficiencies—impacts on HVAC systems related to IT systems. This gave the HVAC design team members a chance to join the discussion and add valuable input that was missing from the OPR questionnaire responses associated with specific HVAC system needs, which in turn impacted the content of the BOD significantly.

With that accomplished, we then asked him privately if he had given much thought to what his needs were for data storage systems, particularly in the case of a power outage. He said he would get back to us, as he had to think about an answer. He had just learned the need for including other team members before responding, so a few days later, we were invited to participate in a conference call with his IT consultants and in-house IT staff who previously had not been involved in any of the team effort. While on the call, he pointedly asked what steps we would be taking to commission his data-collection system, and he asked us to describe for his IT team the commissioning process as it related to the IT system. After a quick primer (likening commissioning to a "shakedown cruise," using the nautical parlance—where commissioning originated), we started to get some feedback from the rest of the participants but related only to elements of the building's "infrastructure," nothing about the IT system.

So, at that point, we realized that we needed to focus the discussion back onto the IT system requirements, so we asked: "How would you test your IT system's ability to serve as the active data storage center in the case of a power outage without a real "lights-out" event to test it?" (This system served three major hospitals and a hundred satellite facilities.) The phone lines went silent; the owner said that he would get back to us. Within the hour, we received his call. "Thanks so much," he started. "Up until this point I could not get my IT staff to buy into this concept of integrative design and commissioning for our facility." Instead, he said: "We were all looking at the IT stuff as something that we would handle simply by setting standards for others to follow. When you hit us with the question about how will we test our system, it became quite clear to everyone that we need to apply commissioning to *all* our systems—IT systems included, not just the building's 'infrastructure' systems."

It should be noted that one of the virtues of the OPR and the BOD is that these documents can be initiated at any time in the process of design, construction, or occupancy, since the information gathered for these documents is always valuable—whenever it is obtained. But the earlier the OPR and BOD are addressed, the more valuable they can become for a project.

If started early, these documents have the added value of maintaining a historic record of the team's decisions and *why* they were made by documenting them in a dynamic series of updates. This dynamic nature also serves an evolutionary function; these documents can and should be tailored in such a way that initially they simply identify the project's initial vision, but they then can be expanded in complexity and detail as subsequent visions and analyses develop. Again, these documents provide the entire team with a valuable record of not only *what* but *why*. In effect, these documents become the evolving story of the project that can inform all participants, regardless of whether they were on the team from day one or joined the team during operations.

B.1.3 Cost Analysis

■ **Update any required integrative cost bundling templates to reflect input from Workshop No. 3**

At this point, project teams probably will have this analyses pared down to only one or two, perhaps

three, cost bundling templates or only one to three groupings of components. These are then refined as information is obtained in subsequent stages.

B.1.4 Schedule and Next Steps

■ **Refine and extend forward the Integrative Process Road Map tasks and schedule into future phases to reflect input from Workshop No. 3**

Review next steps, adjust overall schedule, and set target dates for the tasks and meetings needed to accommodate the necessary communication and studies in subsequent *Part B* phases.

■ **Distribute Workshop No. 3 report**

As indicated for prior workshops, it is important to document the results of each workshop and to distribute a report containing the following for Workshop No. 3:

- ■ Meeting agenda
- ■ Lists of attendees
- ■ Photos of activities
- ■ Images of all sketches of proposed solutions
- ■ Meeting notes recording additional findings, results, reflections, etc.
- ■ Updated Metrics and Performance Targets, include updated LEED checklist (if applicable)
- ■ Updated integrative cost-bundling template
- ■ Process Road Map spreadsheet of schedule and tasks
- ■ Updated OPR and BOD
- ■ Next Steps

Stage B.2

Research and Analysis: Schematic Design—Bringing It All Together (and now committing to building form)

B.2.1 Research and Analysis Activities: Schematic Design

- Engage a more informed schematic design process and develop building form solutions from conceptual sketches produced in Workshop No. 3.
- Iterate, iterate, iterate, with meetings, conference calls, etc., to integrate the four key subsystems with building form
  - Habitat
  - Water
  - Energy
  - Materials

B.2.2 Principles and Measurement

- Test building performance in detail and evaluate results against Performance Targets
- Commissioning: Adjust the OPR and BOD to reflect proposed schematic design

B.2.3 Cost Analysis

- Refine integrated cost bundling numbers to ensure that proposed schemes, systems combinations, and cost scenarios can be evaluated with increasing accuracy

B.2.4 Schedule and Next Steps

- Adjust and prepare Integrative Process Road Map for team review to include tasks and schedule impacts that have emerged from schematic design discoveries
- Prepare Agenda for Workshop No. 4

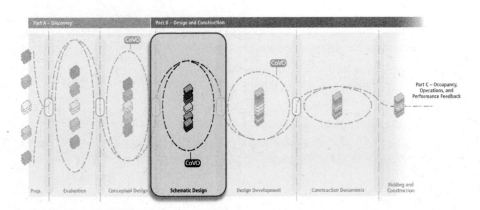

Figure 6-30 Integrative Proces Stage B.2, Research and Analysis: Schematic Design. *Image courtesy of 7group and Bill Reed; graphics by Corey Johnston.*

Stage B.2

Research and Analysis: Schematic Design—Bringing It All Together (and now committing to building form)

Schematic design now begins in earnest. This Research and Analysis period is focused on iterating and refining the results of all previous work and developing a project solution or solutions that address multiple issues with minimal materials, systems, and expense. Also, this process focuses on using the opportunity of building to restore and contribute to the health of local living systems—in other words, elegant design.

Interim Meetings

Although the process outline being presented here does not explicitly identify schematic workshops or meetings other than the Schematic Design Kickoff (Stage B.1), successful systems integration mandates a series of interim subteam meetings during schematic design to focus on incorporating integrative discoveries that impact multiple team members and their disciplines. In reality, then, this Research and Analysis stage consists of a number of such smaller team meetings, the subject of which may vary considerably for each project, depending upon the targeted performance goals. These smaller interim meetings likely begin within each discipline by analyzing the integration of elements within each key subsystem, but then the subject matter quickly expands to enfold interrelationships with the other key subsystems in progressive and subsequent meetings across disciplines.

The purpose of this book is not to prescribe what these meetings need to address, how many might be needed, or when such meetings need to happen; it would be impossible to anticipate all the variables that may crop up in your projects. Consequently, only a few examples of such meetings are being identified in the outline below to avoid presenting a prescriptive methodology.

B.2.1 Research and Analysis Activities: Schematic Design

■ **Engage a more informed schematic design process and develop building form solutions from conceptual sketches produced in Workshop No. 3**

The architect can now dive headlong into developing design solutions, building form, and aesthetic iterations; the design palette has now been enriched with a wider range of possibilities and potentialities than in a conventional process. These possibilities are far less accessible and concretized—if simply not available—without engaging the Discovery process described in the prior stages. Further, an expanded framework has already been established in the integrative process that provides a clear initial starting point for form development, instead of beginning in isolation with a blank piece of paper; generating schematic solutions is now informed by a wider scope—with a larger sandbox, it is more fun to play. Design decisions are not being driven merely by building form and aesthetic considerations; rather, performance analyses and systems interactions help drive design decisions. As a result, a much more comprehensive aesthetic is being addressed. The resulting beauty and elegance far exceeds mere visual aesthetics in its richness and honesty, because the project's aesthetic is informed by both rational analysis and the model provided by nature.

■ **Iterate, iterate, iterate, with meetings, conference calls, etc., to integrate the four key subsystems with building form**

The success of integrating the key systems (habitat, water, energy, materials) depends upon how detailed and how much exploratory work and understanding of the environmental issues was previously accomplished—and, most importantly, how these systems are working in relationship with one another.

Ask questions, answer questions, ask questions, answer questions: Environmentally effective design solutions require very quick cycles of iteration between the key systems in the project to explore their interrelationships. In Schematic Design, we are exploring how these systems are brought together as a *whole* design and how they nest together in more effective relationships; this is an enriched iteration process, since more issues are in play. These issues are addressed at interim meetings, as discussed above, within each discipline and across disciplines. These sessions are informed by using various tools for such analysis, but the array of available tools is wide; therefore, for the purpose of simplicity, we again (as in *Stage A.5)* provide only a few examples of such tools in the outline below where particularly appropriate.

It is worth mentioning that as integrative solutions are developed, the dividing lines between the four key subsystems should begin to blur. Consequently, you may notice that the examples described below may not fall so clearly within only one of the key subsystems; rather, these examples of solutions intentionally address multiple subsystems simultaneously.

- **Habitat** (biotic systems other than human)
  Explore strategies and components that promote habitat and biodiversity in ways that also can be synthesized with other systems, such as rainwater, wastewater, energy, etc.
  - *Examples:*
    - Habitat doubling as treatment for human waste in a constructed wetland.
    - Installing a vegetated green roof or constructed wetlands on the roof to reduce heat island effects, provide cooling mass, reduce peak-cooling capacity via reduced intake-air temperature at air-handling units, retain storm water, and reduce noise.

    - Utilizing stormwater infrastructure to promote habitat, such as bioswales, rain gardens, open cell pervious paving, etc. Better yet, reduce impervious surfaces and/or install meadows or planted areas with higher infiltration rates to reduce stormwater runoff quantities and infiltrate rainwater from groundwater recharge.
    - Designing earth berms and other vegetation to reduce wind exposure, impact solar exposures, reduce building envelope thermal losses and gains, address force-protection issues, etc.

- **Habitat** (human)
  Explore interrelationships between indoor environmental systems and components that impact human health, performance, productivity, and quality of life.
  - Test various daylighting strategies by engaging preliminary daylighting analysis and modeling in parallel with energy modeling, as discussed in the "Energy" section below.
  - Daylight analysis can be very simple or very complicated, depending upon the project's complexity and performance goals. It should be used to guide design decisions—make them proactive, not reactive. There are two basic parts to daylighting analysis: one is direct solar analysis, and the other is the actual measurement of lighting levels. Both aspects of the analysis require a basic understanding of site-related solar geometry and climate data.
  - Examine the direct solar access on the site and the building. This could include the use of inexpensive tools and/or refined computer programs. Simple solar access tools can be used to determine the extent to which surrounding objects will cast a shadow, depending on factors such as the time of year (see Figure 6-31).

Figure 6-31 A simple solar access tool can be used to determine shading obstructions. The image on the *left* is the Solar PathFinder tool. The photograph is used to create the sky-vault chart on the *right*, which shows the shading pattern at various times of the day and months of the year. *Image © Solar Pathfinder.*

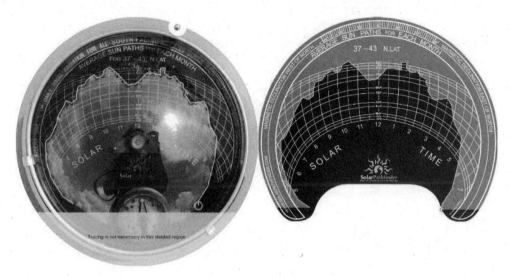

These tools are used to help determine placement on the site, not necessarily the actual effect upon the building. From a daylighting perspective, a project team can use this tool to identify when and where on the site there is shading and conversely, access to daylight.

Many tools that the architect currently uses can provide the information for the next step in this direct solar access analysis (see list of daylighting simulation tools below). SketchUp and other three-dimensional (3-D) modeling software packages can replicate the solar geometry of the project's location and examine building-shading effects. More refined programs, such as ECOTECT, provide a more comprehensive and in-depth analysis. These tools are used to examine exterior shading and the potential effects of direct solar penetration (see Figures 6-32 and 6-33).

- Model individual spaces or combinations of spaces to quantify daylighting performance. An efficient method is to create as few models as possible by using a single model for many different analyses; a single model can represent many spaces of similar size and geom-

etries. To save time at this stage, small details and nonpermanent elements should not be included in the models.

Generally, daylight performance is measured at the equinox and solstices under clear and overcast sky conditions. The data from the analysis on these dates can then be extrapolated to the remainder of the year. The analysis should be geared to determine the best strategies for the project site's typical sky conditions, either clear or overcast.

Daylight can be measured several ways. A simple measure is the use of daylight factor—that is, the ratio of exterior lighting levels to interior lighting levels. A daylight factor of 2 percent is considered good performance; daylight factor expresses the ratio of outside illuminance to indoor illuminance (with the lights off) as a percentage, so 30 foot-candles (fc) of interior illuminace equates to a daylight factor of 2% on a cloudy day when sky dome illuminance might equal 1,500 fc. However, using daylight factors alone will not provide an accurate assessment of daylight quality

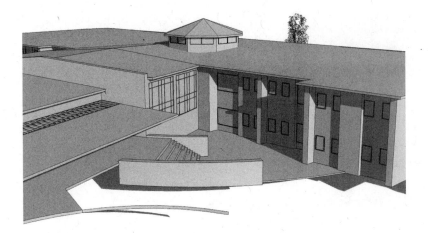

◀ **Figure 6-32** SketchUp models can be used to evaluate shading effects. Several pieces of software allow movies to be created that quickly show shading effects over any given set of hours or days throughout the year in 3-D imagery. *Image courtesy of Todd Reed.*

▶ **Figure 6-33** This sun path diagram model from ECOTECT can be used to evaluate solar position and its effect on building design. *Image courtesy of Todd Reed. Image produced using ECOTECT; ©2008. http://www.autodesk.com.*

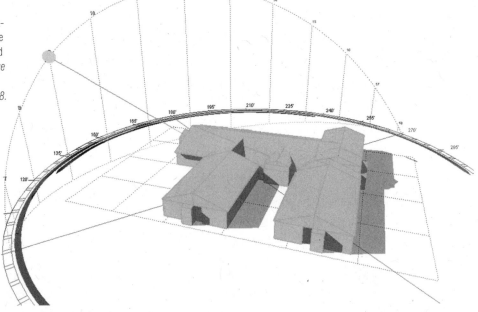

with regard to uniformity and contrast ratio. As we have seen, good daylighting addresses both the quantity and quality of light. When examining issues such as glare and contrast, actual foot-candle measurements, relative values, and distribution provide a more accurate picture (see Figures 6-34 and 6-36).

- Another metric to examine is daylight autonomy factor (DAF). The DAF quantifies the percentage of time during the year when a space will have sufficient lighting levels from daylight to allow for the electrical lighting system to be turned off. Analyzing the daylight levels with this metric begins the process of integrating

Figure 6-34 Foot-candle measurements plotted in a classroom at desk height provide the quantitative analysis necessary for evaluating daylighting design performance. *Image courtesy of Todd Reed. Image created using AGi32 software.*

daylight analysis with the energy model, and it provides a more comprehensive picture of overall building performance. A relatively simple tool to use for analyzing daylight autonomy factor is SPOT (see Figure 6-35).

The key criteria for assessing whether a space is well daylighted, though, are: even distribution of light (see Figure 6-36), minimal glare, and low contrast ratio. Balancing all three of these

elements is crucial to providing quality daylighting design. These are the qualitative aspects of daylighting design that should be analyzed beyond simple quantities of daylight penetration.

An additional benefit of daylight modeling simulations is their potential for generating 3-D models that can visually illustrate a space. Many daylighting software tools, such as AGI32, can produce photo-realistic

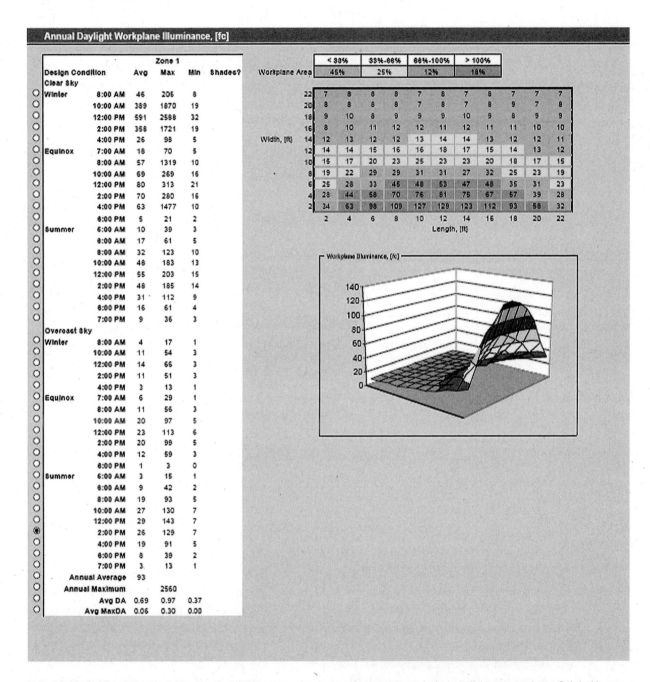

Figure 6-35 SPOT modeling results showing workplane illuminance levels; the software program calculates daylight autonomy factor (DA). In this case, the DA is 0.69, which means that daylighting will provide the targeted illuminance levels with the lights turned off for 69 percent of the time over an entire year during daylight hours. *Image courtesy of Todd Reed.*

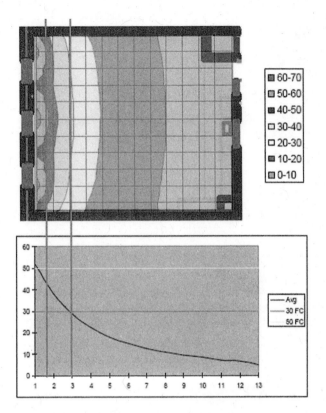

Legend:
- 60-70
- 50-60
- 40-50
- 30-40
- 20-30
- 10-20
- 0-10

Figure 6-36 The uniformity of daylighting plotted in plan and in section can help designers evaluate the evenness of daylighting distribution in a space. As with electrical lighting system design, this is an important design consideration, since good daylighting design minimizes contrast ratios in a space. *Image courtesy of Todd Reed.*

images. While this level of detail is not required for analyzing daylighting performance, it can help owners and designers envision the results more clearly; but even more simple daylight modeling visual illustrations can give the team a good feel for the space and help them to identify potential problems. During schematic design for a major university's School of Music building, the visual illustrations generated by our daylight modeling revealed that direct beams of sunlight from clerestory windows fell

directly on the director's podium in the primary orchestral and choir rehearsal space, which would have blinded the director from seeing the choir and the orchestra. The original clerestory configuration was revised to avoid this problem. Muscoe Martin relates a similar story from the design of the Cusano Environmental Education Center for which the rendered lighting analysis showed that interpretive display cases would have had their contents obscured by veiling reflections from the daylighting. The architect (Susan Maxman Partners) then designed these display cases with sloped fronts to fix the problem.

- During this stage, the architect should be working closely with the daylight modeler and using the output of the daylighting analysis to inform the project's design. This will typically require several iterative modeling runs and interim meetings during the schematic design phase.
- Daylighting simulation tools:
  Several daylighting software-analysis programs can help address these factors, thereby allowing teams to develop more sophisticated design strategies and higher quality daylighting. Some currently available programs include:
  - Radiance: Developed by the Lawrence Berkeley National Laboratory for UNIX-based computers, this program is available at no charge at http://radsite.lbl.gov/radiance/HOME.html.
  - Lumen Designer: This software developed by Lighting Technologies Inc. is a successor to Lumen Micro. It is available at http://www.lighting-technologies.com.
  - AGI32: Developed by Lighting Analysts Inc., this lighting design software can be used for calculations and modeling. It is available at http://www.agi32.com.

Figure 6-37 Three-dimensional daylight modeling simulations also can be useful for giving building users a sense of what the space will look like under varying daylit conditions. In this case, the model depicts the same space as Figure 6-23, but from a slightly different viewpoint (and with no electrical lighting turned on) to see the effects of the book stacks on daylight levels for the AMBS library project. *Image courtesy of Robert Thomas. Image created by AGI32 software.*

- ECOTECT: Daylighting module included as a part of building-analysis software offered by Autodesk. Available at http://ecotect.com.
- IES-VE: This daylighting module, a component of a Revit-based suite of analysis tools, is closest to BIM. Developed by Integrated Environmental Solutions Inc., this module is available at http://www.iesve.com.
- DAYSIM: This tool calculates Daylight Autonomy Ratio, and its output can be used by other software simulations modeling the same space. This is useful, since the first step in daylighting analysis is to build a 3D model; this model can be built in one piece of software and then used by another for analy-

sis, or sometimes the model is built within the analysis software itself. More information and a free download available at http://irc.nrc-cnrc.gc.ca/ie/lighting/daylight/daysim_e.html.

- SPOT: Sensor Placement + Optimization Tool focused on calculation of DAR and daylight-sensor placement. From Architectural Energy Corporation at http://www.archenergy.com/SPOT.

Output from such daylighting programs can provide designers with luminance and illuminance values, lighting level plots and contours, visual comfort levels, photo-quality images, and video solar-shading diagrams with animations. Design teams familiar with thesefundamental factors, as well as the effects of glazing characteristics, will be able to effectively evaluate alternative daylighting parameters and components and their impacts on other systems. We often have used these tools to help optimize the configuration and dimensions of window openings, shading devices, overhangs, etc.

- Thermal comfort analysis
  - Determine final comfort settings and parameters.
  - Determine the level of individual control (operable windows, underfloor air, etc.) provided to the occupants.
  - Begin to examine the effects of issues related to the interaction of HVAC system components. For example, if humidification will be required to meet performance requirements and economizer cooling is being considered, then the desire for free cooling should be weighed against the need for humidification.
  - Thermal analysis modeling can be particularly helpful in complex building design and airflow scenarios. Software such as TRNSYS can be used to evaluate indoor conditions based on HVAC system design and building envelope performance.
  - Specific envelope configurations and window-wall sections can be evaluated with software such as WINDOW and THERM 5.2 to determine heat-transfer effects. This analysis can be used to identify thermal bridging in the building's structural and envelope systems, which can help identify potential issues related to condensation, moisture problems, cold surfaces (a component of thermal comfort referred to as mean radiant temperature), and heat loss. The software is available as a free download at http://windows.lbl.gov/software/default.htm.

- Ventilation analysis
  - Determine the location(s) of outside air intakes and coordinate with roof material selection, if applicable. Quite often, the outside air intakes for a building are located on the roof. A white or green vegetated roof can have an ambient temperature that is 60°F to 80°F lower when the sun is shining during the cooling season, potentially resulting in considerable additional energy savings.
  - Consider whether *computational fluid dynamics* (CFD) is needed for the project. If necessary, CFD software can be used to model airflows, heat transfer, and thermal comfort. It is particularly useful in large volume spaces such as an atrium, complex envelope assemblies (such as a double-envelope scenarios), and for analyzing airflows for ventilation systems. If the project is considering the use of displacement ventilation (underfloor air distribution, for example) or natural ventilation strategies, the use of CFD can test and compare various strategies (see Figure 6-38). The CFD studies will need to be closely coordinated with energy-modeling efforts and often are performed by the same firm.
  - One of the more commonly used CFD software packages is produced by Fluent and is available at http://www.fluent.com.

- Pollutant source control
  - Identify operational pollutant sources that need to be addressed with regard to their location within the building's floor plan or layout and with regard to isolating potential air transfer from these spaces to adjoining spaces; analyze architectural and HVAC system impacts resulting from the elimination of such cross-contamination. Explore potentially

Figure 6-38 Floor geometry model for Syracuse Center of Excellence Headquarters Building, Syracuse, New York. The Syracuse Center of Excellence is a mix of laboratory, office, and classroom spaces that used computational fluid dynamics (CFD) to test the temperatures, airflows, and radiant temperatures for a scheme with underfloor air and a double-skin corridor. This snapshot image from Airpack software models the layout of Level 3; the corridor at the bottom of the image faces south and is located adjacent to the proposed double-skin façade. Such modeling determined that the proposed scheme provides acceptable classroom conditions for both winter and summer comfort. The corridor rises toward 85°F during the summer. During the winter, the corridor is near 64°F near the floor. *Image and caption content courtesy of Arup.*

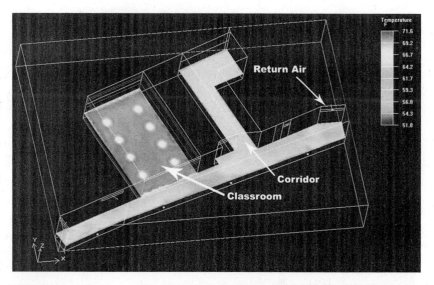

Figure 6-39 Renderings of the proposed Syracuse Center of Excellence project, which is pursuing LEED Platinum certification, depict south-facing glazed walls (image on the *right*) for this cold climate along with extensive green roofs. *Images courtesy of Toshiko Mori Architect.*

reducing both exhaust duct runs and fan capacity by grouping or stacking such spaces.
- Identify any air-filtration requirement impacts on HVAC system components.
- Acoustics
  - Identify impacts on building envelope, architectural configuration, HVAC system com-

ponents, materials selection, etc., related to acoustical properties and performance targets.
- It should be noted that LEED for Schools now requires achievement of acoustical performance as both a prerequisite and as an optional credit.

Integrating Acoustics into Building Design 101

By Christopher Brooks, senior consultant with Acoustic Dimensions

Every aspect of a building affects its acoustics, and thus (if considered in the design) acoustics affects every building system. Even if not considered in the design, there will be acoustic consequences (desirable or undesirable) from nearly every building system.

If the clients and designers would prefer the acoustic aspects of their building to have intentional results, acoustics must be considered throughout design and construction. This is obviously crucial when acoustics is a primary focus of the program, such as worship and performance spaces, but it is also important where the acoustic program is more utilitarian (just one of many competing interests) such as in schools, offices, and residential buildings.

Acoustics and buildings relate in several ways:

- The scale and form of a room fundamentally determine its acoustic character.
- Materials affect how sound behaves within a space and the transmission of sound between spaces.
- Mechanical and electrical systems create noise. Designing for low noise requires serious consideration of budget and building configuration.
- Electro-acoustics systems require locations for their components and a room that is acoustically friendly.

Scale and Form

For a building with a program centered on acoustics, scale and form are fundamental. The mere scale of a room affects how many people a room can hold and who can perform there. A string quartet cannot perform in the Houston Astrodome; nor can the Marine Band perform in my living room. For a less extreme example, a classroom that is too large will result in poor speech intelligibility.

The form of a major concert hall is essential to its primary function, and the design of such a form is still an art. The twentieth century saw numerous mediocre-to-awful concert halls based on a flawed conception of their geometry. The first successful modern concert hall—the acoustically superb Meyerson in Dallas—resulted from a radical insight into the geometry required for such a room.

For any room where sound isolation is important (concert halls, worship spaces, auditoriums, conference rooms, private offices, audio-editing suites, etc.), location must be considered carefully. The most cost-effective way to isolate a room from the noisy outside world, adjacent rooms, or from noise equipment is by location.

For rooms where acoustics is less critical to the program, the form of a room can still create problems (an inadvertent echo from a curved rear wall), or opportunities (a speech-supporting shape above a conference room table).

Acoustic program, scale, form, and location are issues best decided in the earliest stages of design.

Materials

Materials affect sound by absorbing or by acting as a more-or-less effective barrier to sound. Products can also be intentionally shaped to scatter sound. None of these attributes is positive or negative in

(continued)

itself. Materials must be carefully chosen for both their properties and location, then integrated with other design requirements.

The term "acoustical" is often used to denote materials that absorb sound (and sometimes to denote some other property related to sound); the implication being that "acoustical" materials are always good for acoustics. This is false. Materials are good for acoustics if they are appropriately chosen and located to serve the acoustic function of a room.

The best solution is often to choose materials that can integrate several desired functions. For instance, a hard surface for walking on catwalks can usefully reflect sound in the stage below. Acoustic tile is not appropriate everywhere, but where it is appropriate, it is cost effective, reflects light, hides unsightly structure, and controls excessive reverberation. Great, if that is what the acoustic program calls for.

The acoustic performance of a material also depends on where it is located and how it is installed. Material choice cannot be separated from the more fundamental issues of acoustic program, form and function, and construction.

Mechanical and Electrical Systems

Mechanical and electrical systems generally affect acoustics negatively, by making noise. A great deal of money and effort is spent to ascertain the appropriate levels of noise from these systems and then to design and build them to meet these noise criteria. This can be a challenge since some desiderata for mechanical design conflict directly with acoustic

requirements. For instance, turbulence helps mix air (good for comfort), but turbulence creates noise (bad for acoustics).

Yet, there are some opportunities for integration; for instance, surfaces with an acoustic function such as acoustic "clouds" can be used to help distribute air, or "white" noise from air-distribution can contribute to speech privacy. In performance and worship spaces, supplying air from below audience (or congregation) seating, and returning it high, may be more expensive, but this approach can be quieter, more energy efficient, and removes contaminants from the air. Underfloor air distribution systems provide extremely quiet acoustic environments for office and educational spaces as well.

Mechanical and acoustic requirements can be reconciled—with difficulty. The earlier this challenge is addressed, the more likely a successful outcome.

Electro-acoustics systems (or AV)

Electro-acoustics systems require locations for their components—including sometimes highly visible loudspeakers—and a room that suits them acoustically. In addition, many audiovisual (AV) components are cooled by fans that create noise that has to be controlled to suit other aspects of the acoustic program.

Audiovisual (or electro-acoustic) systems have, unfortunately, contributed to the idea that acoustics is just another item of equipment that one tacks on after the design is finished. This isn't even true for spaces where AV is the primary acoustic function of a room!—much less in a room where AV is one of many acoustic functions, such as a multipurpose auditorium.

Integrating Acoustics

Acoustics is one aspect of a building's program. Its level of importance in that program may be incidental, or it may be the building's *raison d'être*. Even when its importance to the overall program is low, however, acoustic problems can be disruptive, sometimes significantly.

With the exception of AV drawings, there are no separate "acoustics drawings." Good design requires that acoustics be thoughtfully integrated into every stage and every aspect of a building's development from programming through final commissioning.

Figure 6-40 This illustration is from an EASE (Electro-Acoustic Simulator for Engineers) acoustic model of a synagogue. Acoustic requirements for Jewish worship activities drove the geometry of the room's height to provide support and blend for chanted prayer; wall articulation for acoustic clarity; slanted walls to avoid echoes and boominess. The model was developed to investigate these acoustic properties quantitatively. *Image courtesy of Chris Brooks.*

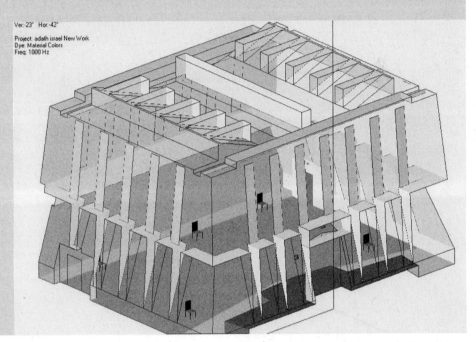

Ver: 23" Hor: 42"

Project: adath israel New Work
Dye: Material Colors
Freq: 1000 Hz

■ Water

Explore water input and output flows to and from each system and component so that they are understood and can be integrated in such a way that each element of the system serves more than one function or purpose in the project's water balance schema.

- *Examples*
  - Reducing water demand via low-flow fixtures usually is the first step; often, simply installing dual-flush toilets, waterless urinals, 0.5 gallons per minute (gpm) lavatory faucets, automatic faucet controls, and 1.5 gpm shower heads can reduce potable consumption by 40 to 50 percent, and lead to cost savings.
  - Use cooling system condensate water, gray water, and/or captured rainwater for flushing toilets, irrigation, and/or groundwater recharge.
  - Explore treatment of wastewater from toilets in constructed wetlands on-site to create

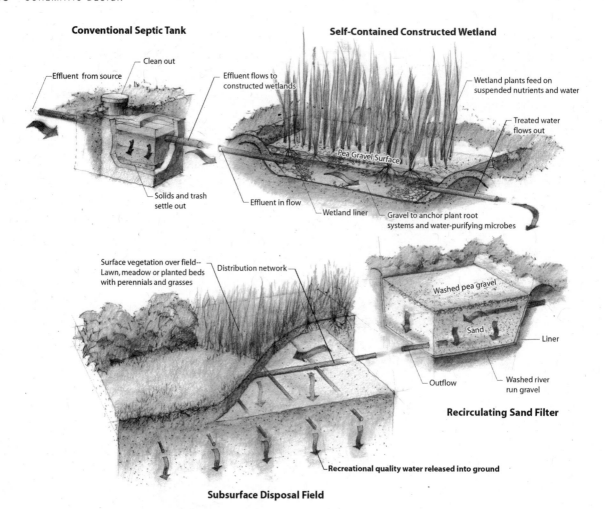

Figure 6-41 Constructed wetlands can cost-effectively integrate wastewater treatment, habitat, and water quality in ways that strongly contribute to water balance. This diagram depicts the components of a typical waste treatment constructed wetland. *Image courtesy of Jeff Charlesworth and Back to Nature, Oldwick, NJ.*

habitat, to recharge groundwater, or to be recirculated back into the building. It should be noted that in many cases where the larger hydrological loop is being considered, the use of ultra low-flow toilets and urinals is not necessary—or even desired—due to the need for effluent to feed the wetlands.

- Verify the quantity of captured rainwater, gray water, and/or condensate in order to balance this supply quantity with the wastewater demand of the constructed wetlands, habitat, and/or groundwater recharge; again, counter-intuitively, low-flow fixtures may not always be the best solution.

- Consider using composting toilets to avoid water use and wastewater generation altogether, with the added benefit of generating high-quality soil to augment habitat on site.

Energy

Explore and analyze interactions between all systems that impact energy performance and energy consumption via iterative parametric modeling and parallel life cycle cost analysis to inform design decisions.

- Lock into general building massing, orientation, and percentage glazing openings during this stage (Schematic Design).
- The energy model should evolve as the project's design evolves. Update the model and complete modeling runs for any additional energy-efficiency measures (individual parameters) identified during Workshop No. 3.
- Perform initial and subsequent iterations of combination parametric modeling runs to optimize system size reduction strategies by exploring various combinations of EEMs to discover which combination best balances energy performance with first-costs and operational-cost impacts
- Based upon HVAC system options initially identified in Workshop No. 3, perform additional modeling runs to inform life cycle cost analyses as a mechanism for selecting an HVAC system. Once the building loads have been reduced to be as low as possible, the next step is to use the model to assist in the selection of an HVAC system. It is important to perform this step *after* the load-reduction strategies have been modeled and agreed upon. Performing the life cycle cost analysis (LCCA) before load reduction will result in overstated values for energy use, since loads have not been optimally reduced. If this LCCA precedes serious explorations and evaluations of load reduction, then the potentially overstated energy use may produce a completely different conclusion than if the HVAC

comparison is based upon much more efficient envelope and lighting design.

On a recent project, the design engineers performed a LCCA based upon the building's projected energy use, using performance data from a previous elementary school design (that was built conventionally) that they then extrapolated and applied to a much larger high school. Their LCCA concluded that the best HVAC system for the project was a four-pipe variable air volume (VAV) system with a water-cooled chiller and gas boiler. Instead of using this projection, we suggested running the energy model with an efficient envelope and a reduced lighting load. When our "reduced-consumption" modeling results were used in the LCCA, the conclusion changed, with ground-source heat pumps turning out to be the best choice. The conclusion that the project was going to have reduced heating and cooling loads beyond the norm changed the results of the LCCA and, in turn, the HVAC system selection (see Figure 6-42).

- Complete comprehensive life cycle cost analysis, informed by the energy-modeling runs identified above, in order to select the most cost-effective HVAC system, based upon optimized load reductions.
- Initial HVAC load calculations should be performed along with energy-modeling runs to take optimum advantage of system downsizing. Many mechanical engineers are reluctant to perform load calculations at this phase until the building's floor plan and elevations have "settled down" and are not likely to change significantly. The reason given is that they do not have the budget for performing the load calculations multiple times. Full scale load calculations, however, do not have to be performed

Figure 6-42 Sample Energy Modeling for HVAC Selection: This set of energy modeling results compares four distinct HVAC systems for a recent project; these modeling runs were used as part of a life cycle costing analysis for selecting the HVAC system with the lowest life cycle cost. Descriptions of the four modeled systems are as follows:

HVAC-1: Ground-Source Heat Pumps (GSHP), 16 EER, 3.8 COP, ground-loop heat exchanger is provided by 320 vertical wells, individual ground-source heat pump units with ventilation provided by dedicated OA (outside air) GSHP units with heat recovery and CO_2 sensors, large spaces served by ground-source heat pump heat-recovery units.

HVAC-2: Conventional Water-Source Heat Pumps (CWSP), 14 EER, 5 COP, natural gas boiler @ 88% AFUE (annual fuel utilization efficiency), cooling tower @ 50 gpm/horse power, individual water-source heat pump units with ventilation provided by dedicated OA GSHP units with heat-recovery and CO_2 sensors, large spaces served by water-source heat pump heat-recovery units.

HVAC-3: Fan-Powered VAV, 2 water-cooled chillers 6 COP, 2 natural gas boilers @ 88% AFUE, cooling tower @ 50gpm/hp, VAV with VAV boxes, reheat and CO_2 sensors; large spaces served by heat-recovery units with hot water and chilled water coils.

HVAC-4: Fan Coil Units, 2 water-cooled chillers 6 COP, 2 natural gas boilers @ 88% AFUE, cooling tower @ 50gpm/hp, individual fan coil units with ventilation provided by dedicated OA units with hot water and chilled water coils, heat recovery and CO_2 sensors, large spaces served by heat-recovery units with hot water and chilled water coils.

Model Assumptions for all four systems are as follows:

Building envelope: 13' 0" floor-to-floor

height with Gymnasium and Auditorium as 2-story spaces, Mass Walls—4" face brick, 3" polyisocyanurate insulation, 8" block (overall U-value = 0.041, R-24); Steel Stud Walls (at glass walls only)—steel siding, air space, 3" polyisocyanurate insulation, 5/8" gypsum wallboard (overall U-value = 0.042, R-24); Roof—3" polyisocyanurate overall U-value = 0.037, R-27; glass—clear, double-pane, low-e, Vision "Solarscreen" VRE 1-46, overall U-value = 0.30, SHGC = 0.28, Visible Transmittance = 43%. The loads associated with the indoor pool are not accounted for in these models.

Internal loads: Lighting—0.85 W/sq. ft.; Plug—0.7 W/sq. ft., based upon ASHRAE densities and common sense.

Utilities: Electric—PECO GS single meter rate (assumed no summer session and thus no ratchet applies); Gas—PECO GC rate (gas-fired domestic water heaters and boilers for all but GSHP systems).

Schedule: A single schedule was used for this model based upon a 9-month school year with no summer classes.

Defaults: Standard eQuest defaults were used whenever possible, including, but not limited to, domestic hot water usage and percentage of floor area for each type of space. Any inaccuracies introduced by using defaults will be consistent for all systems and as such will not affect the system comparison.

Image courtesy of Cam Fitzgerald.

Upper Dublin High School
eQuest v3.60b Modeling Results Summary
Building Energy Enduse Summary for HVAC System Alternatives

Individual EEM Design Runs	HVAC-1 GSHP	HVAC-2 WSHP	HVAC-3 4-Pipe FP VAV	HVAC-4 4-Pipe FCU
Estimated Operating Costs				
Electric	$323,790	$347,456	$354,808	$325,906
Gas	$32,309	$36,244	$52,578	$41,664
Total	**$356,099**	**$383,700**	**$407,386**	**$367,570**
Cost/SqFt	**$1.00**	**$1.08**	**$1.14**	**$1.03**
Consumption				
Site (kBtu / SqFt / Yr)	32.0	34.3	38.4	34.7
Source (kBtu / SqFt / Yr)	82.5	87.8	93.4	86.9
Building Electric Use (kWh)				
Lights	881,635	881,635	881,635	881,635
Task Lights	447,638	447,638	447,638	447,638
Misc. Equip.	370,597	370,597	370,597	370,597
Space Heat	21,313	14,705	0	0
Space Cool	380,269	499,057	355,965	378,261
Heat Rejection	0	0	2,850	2,140
Pumps & Aux.	183,715	219,114	239,768	260,483
Ventilation Fans	270,754	270,751	479,861	292,957
Refrig Display	0	0	0	0
Ht Pump Supplement	0	0	0	0
Domestic Hot Water	0	0	0	0
Exterior Usage	86,613	86,613	86,613	86,613
Total	**2,642,534**	**2,790,110**	**2,864,927**	**2,720,324**
Building Gas Use (Therms)				
Cooking	6,956	6,956	6,956	6,956
Space Heat	0	3,031	15,606	7,214
Domestic Hot Water	16,546	16,546	16,546	16,546
Total	**23,502**	**26,533**	**39,108**	**30,716**

at this phase. For many projects—schools, hospitals, office buildings, etc.—a wing or pod of the building can be used as representative, or in some cases (like a school), an entire wing can be estimated based on the loads from one room if it is a dominant repetitive component.

- When a major project goal is to reduce HVAC system sizing, the mechanical engineer should be prepared to examine a variety of options and their effect on the building's loads.
- Consider the impacts on mechanical, electrical, and plumbing layout and design relative to enabling the submetering of systems as part of the postoccupancy *measurement and verification* (M&V) effort. Agree to the general M&V approach so that the MEP systems layout (and controls) can be informed by the data collection needs identified during prior stages.
- *Example*

The holy grail of building performance simulation is the proverbial set of simulation buttons that integrally link to three-dimensional design software. Push the energy button, and the software spits out the energy-use impact of a recent design change. Push the daylighting button, and the light-level grid appears on the drawing. As design tools evolve, we are getting closer all the time to this ideal, but the current reality (for nearly all projects) is that we are not quite there yet. As a result, it usually is necessary to run multiple simulation tools in parallel.

For example, when examining daylighting strategies, it is often necessary to run energy simulations to evaluate the full impact of a variety of design decisions. For a recent project we examined several design options for providing effective daylighting in a second floor space. The options included a variety of roof config-

urations—flat roof with skylights, sloped roof with clerestories, flat roof with a sawtooth, and so forth. These different room configurations were analyzed concurrently for both daylight performance (in daylighting simulations) and for impacts on energy use (in energy-modeling software). Solving for one issue alone will not enable the project team to produce optimal solutions. As BIM tools evolve, concurrent analysis in a single tool will become more commonplace and will expedite this process significantly.

Materials

Explore and analyze options for structural and envelope systems, along with the interrelationships between these components and other subsystems to inform design decisions.

- Based upon the parameters defined in Workshop No. 3, perform LCA analysis of structural and envelope systems using the tools described in *Stages A.3.1* and *A.5.1* to inform design decisions.
- Review comparisons of assembly options to lower environmental burdens based on project goals.
- Review inputs for structural live-load requirements.
- Review all opportunities to optimize sizing for bay-spacing, columns and beams, floor, and roof decks.
- Consider all structural innovations that reduce material needs.
- Based on the LCA modeling runs in prior stages, review the largest impacts by building assembly, and seek opportunities for reducing impacts for these assemblies. An example might include reducing portland cement use in concrete (to reduce CO_2 emissions), which

requires the involvement of the structural engineer.

- *Examples*

Revisiting the LCA exercise discussed in "Life Cycle Assessment (LCA) Tools and Environmental Benefits" at the beginning of this chapter, you may recall that we began the process of using LCA for this project by inputting the basic structural and envelope components into the ATHENA® *Impact Estimator for Buildings* model. This allowed us to see comparisons of the emissions and global warming impacts associated with each of the project's various structural and envelope assembly groups. This, in turn, helped us set priorities on where to focus our efforts. First, we optimized bay-spacing, columns, and beams (see Figures 6-17 and 6-18). The initial analysis, though, clearly indicated that the emissions and global warming impacts of the structural and envelope components were dominated by the foundation (see Figures 6-16 and 6-17).

This realization led us to review options for reducing the impacts associated with this foundation. We regularly seek ways to lower the amount of portland cement used in concrete to reduce CO_2 emissions. Efforts include seeking technical input from cement manufacturers, working closely with the structural engineer, and making sure that any issues that may impact project schedules are addressed as soon as the general contractor is on board.

In this case, displacing 35 percent of the portland cement in the foundation concrete reduced the associated CO_2 emissions by approximately 6,000 tons—more than the total CO_2 impacts from all of the other structural and envelope assembly groups combined. In conjunction with the optimized bays-columns-beams, the global warming potential (measured in generated CO_2 equivalent mass) for the project's structure and envelope was reduced by a little over 25 percent (compare Figure 6-43 to Figure 6-17).

We also worked in conjunction with the energy modeler to identify a collection of other strategies. A steel-stud wall with brick cladding had been chosen for the original design. Instead of spending dollars on brick, it was decided to invest that money in insulated concrete form walls (which also improved energy performance) and change the cladding to wood. The amount of portland cement also was reduced in the ICF walls.

Figure 6-44 shows the Athena output that resulted from analyzing the combination of these strategies employed to lower the impacts of the project's building materials; it depicts the overall embodied effects of the three design options: The baseline project includes the original steel-stud walls, typical concrete mix, brick cladding, and nonoptimized bay sizing. The next lowest bar represents optimized bays, columns, and beams. The third and lowest bar depicts reduced portland cement in the foundation and walls, ICF walls, and changing the cladding to wood.

B.2.2 Principles and Measurement

■ Test building performance in detail and evaluate results against Performance Targets

- ▩ Based upon all of the analyses described above, adjust and fully document impacts of all design decisions in detail relative to the resultant schematic design's conformance with previously es-

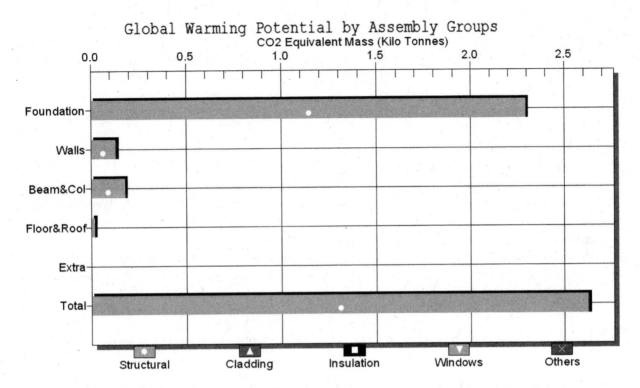

Figure 6-43 This Athena model graph indicates the relative global warming impacts of the sample project's various assemblies, providing guidance on where to focus priorities—in this case, the dominant impacts are associated with the foundation. By displacing 35 percent of the foundation concrete's portland cement, the results in this graph indicate a 6,000 equivalent metric ton reduction in CO_2 emissions when compared to the originally specified foundation concrete graphed in Figure 6-17; this reduction equates to more than the total impacts of all other structural and shell assemblies combined. *Image courtesy of the Athena Institute.*

tablished Performance Targets, and update if necessary.

- For projects pursuing LEED certification, revisit compliance with previously established LEED goals and performance thresholds relative to all pursued LEED credits. This process involves continuously refining targeted performance goals in further detail, informed by the above analyses. You can use the LEED targets to assist the refinement of these goals by looking for interactions between credits.

One difficulty that we and others have encountered on LEED projects is that focusing

solely on performance targets can lead to performance optimization in silos. Further, and more fundamentally, the tasks and responsibilities assigned to team members at workshops simply do not get done in many instances. Accordingly, it is critical to convene interim team meetings and subteam meetings to assess the status of the necessary research and analysis that was identified in the full team workshops; otherwise, it is quite easy for teams to fall back into a conventional mode of design and documentation in isolation. Also, these interim meetings are used to identify and pursue systems interactions that are being discovered as design options are explored.

- At the conclusion of this stage, the project team should fully evaluate the schematic design against all Performance Targets and the project's previously established Purpose, values, and aspirations.

- **Commissioning: Adjust the OPR and BOD to reflect proposed schematic design**

The design team and owner ensure that the OPR and BOD have been updated with input from all team members to reflect the current schematic design solutions. All such updates should be incorporated into the OPR and BOD in preparation for review by the entire team at Workshop No. 4.

To reiterate, the responsibility for creating and generating these OPR and BOD documents must fall on the owner and design team, respectively. The Commissioning Authority uses these guiding documents to compare the schematic design's consistency with the project team's intentions, as defined in the OPR and BOD.

B.2.3 Cost Analysis

- **Refine integrated cost bundling numbers to ensure that proposed schemes, systems combinations, and cost scenarios can be evaluated with increasing accuracy**

It is best to build a Uniformat cost-estimating model (or spreadsheet of unit costs) for each identifiable

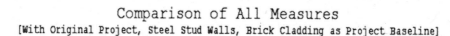
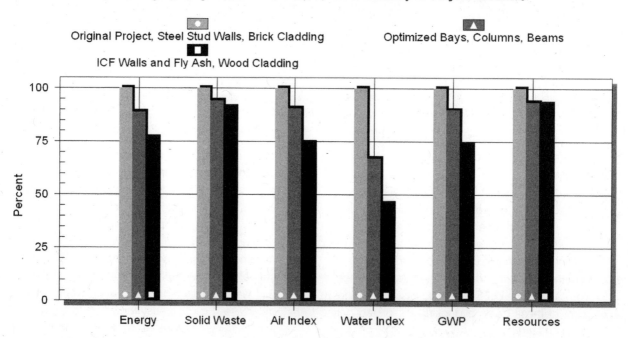

Figure 6-44 We used the ATHENA model to analyze the impacts of various measures aimed at lowering our overall impact over a number of indicators. This output indicates impact reductions relative to the original design baseline. *Image courtesy of the Athena Institute.*

grouping of system elements and components in the project. Having this list of elements helps to easily evaluate and group the materials and subsystems of the project that need to be bundled to understand the true first cost of integrative decisions and operating costs.

To illustrate cost bundling, let's look at how early-stage cost estimating traditionally occurs for HVAC systems. Schematic (and often design development) HVAC system estimates are nearly always based on a database of cost per square foot. Since the HVAC design typically has not yet begun in earnest, the HVAC cost estimator has little detail upon which to base the estimate, so there is no alternative. Usually, the HVAC system type has been broadly identified by the end of Schematic Design—there may be an outline specification, but there are few known details; hence, a cost per square foot value is used. This cost per square foot value typically is based on past experience with similar systems for similar building types, along with a few other factors that might be taken into account, such as recent bid results from similar projects.

The major problem with this approach on an integrated project's schematic design is that we often are trying to significantly reduce the size of the HVAC system by reducing the building's loads. Often, system-size reductions of 40 to 50 percent are possible compared to standard practice (as the Neptune Midtown Community School example at the beginning of this chapter illustrates). Since the data used to estimate HVAC system costs are based on conventionally sized projects, the cost of the HVAC system tends to be overestimated at this stage for energy-efficient projects. However, in an early-stage cost estimate, it is very likely that architectural enhancements and energy-efficiency measures that are necessary to reduce the HVAC loads will have been identified—usually as cost increases. These include potential load-reduction strategies like extra insulation, triple-pane windows, daylighting design, and so on.

So, the early-stage cost estimate often includes pricing for all of these "extra" items, but none of the first-cost savings due to systems integration and system down-sizing have been captured. The project appears overbudget. Consequently, many of the energy-saving, green features are abandoned in the name of value engineering. With an integrative process, performance requirements have been established, and the development of the design is significantly more advanced at this stage. Since the cost estimator knows more—particularly in terms of cost savings associated with downsized HVAC components, in this case—a more accurate holistic accounting of the true overall cost of the project can be developed.

The various cost reductions resulting from downsized HVAC components can now be bundled with corresponding combinations of estimated costs (and/or savings) associated with the EEMs that allowed for this downsizing to occur—EEMs such as better-performing windows, more insulation, energy recovery, daylighting components (photocell sensors, dimming ballasts, clerestories, etc.), underfloor air system, associated reduction in ductwork, lighting power density reductions, elimination of perimeter heating systems, and so on. When the cost impacts of these EEMs are bundled in combinations that match the various EEM combinations run in the energy model—and bundled with the various cost savings associated with downsized HVAC equipment—the project team can compare the cost bundles of various combinations of strategies against one another and against the original estimate. In this way, the project's overall first costs often can be neutralized, while operating cost associated with energy consumption are significantly reduced.

For example, an early-stage cost estimate for one of our Pennsylvania DEP projects included an estimate for an underfloor air (UFA) system. Since this was the first time that that particular estimator had priced an underfloor system, we expected his natural tendency might be to cover himself with a value that was on the high side, which he did. But he also included the full cost of installing ductwork in the project. Often, UFA systems will displace 80 to 90 percent of a project's ductwork, so the estimator's price included the full cost of both. To the credit of the design team, in this case, these kinds of discrepancies were identified and the cost estimate adjusted. Cost estimating on a line-item basis will often yield the wrong answer, just as designing building systems in isolation will produce redundancies and not an optimal solution.

B.2.4 Schedule and Next Steps

■ **Adjust and prepare Integrative Process Road Map for team review to include tasks and schedule impacts that have emerged from schematic design discoveries**

Adjust and refine this Road Map with the team, as necessary, and clarify next steps. Similar to the prior Research and Analysis stages, the schedule of tasks, team conference calls, meetings, and analysis processes will almost always need to be altered to accommodate the interim meeting dates, times, and deliverables that occur between major workshops and charrettes.

■ **Prepare Agenda for Workshop No. 4**

The primary difference between the agenda for Workshop No. 4 and all prior workshops is that the scope of possible design solutions has been considerably narrowed to a single architectural solution, with possible variants—it is not subject to wholesale or major reconfigurations. The difference here from conventional practice is that all MEP and other systems have been evaluated in parallel with architectural solutions, rather than waiting for the architecture to be locked in before any of the engineers begin their design work. Consequently, agenda items for Workshop No. 4 can be far more focused on presenting holistic solutions based upon interactions between systems, quantified performance analyses, and cost implications. As a result, activities at the workshop can focus on collectively finalizing major design decisions and verifying their conformance with Performance Targets prior to moving into the next stage, Design Development, where the focus becomes *optimizing* these interactions. The next chapter discusses this in detail.

chapter

7

Design Development and Documentation

It is one of our most exciting discoveries that local discovery leads to a complex of further discoveries. Corollary to this we find that we no sooner get a problem solved than we are overwhelmed with a multiplicity of additional problems in a most beautiful payoff of heretofore unknown, previously unrecognized, and as-yet unsolved problems.

—R. Buckminster Fuller, from *Synergetics: Explorations in the Geometry of Thinking,* written in collaboration with E. J. Applewhite, New York: Macmillan, 1975. Text available at: http://www.rwgrayprojects.com/synergetics/ toc/status.html © 1997 by the Estate of R. Buckminster Fuller (accessed 15 December 2008)

The only progress that knowledge allows is in enabling us to describe more and more in detail the world we see and its evolution.

—Albert Schweitzer, quoted by Gunnar Jahn in his presentation speech awarding Schweitzer the 1952 Nobel Peace Prize, from *Civilization and Ethics* (3rd ed., translated by C. T. Campion, revised by Mrs. Charles E. B. Russell. London: A. & C. Black, 1946), pp. 240–242

Activities during the Design Development phase are meant to do just as the name of this phase indicates: develop an already-conceived design. At this point in our process, we have produced substantially more than just an established building form, since *all* of the building's systems have been addressed to a schematic level and analyzed to discover interactions between them. The mechanical, electrical, structural, civil engineering, water, habitat, landscape, and materials systems have been progressing in unison to a reasonably resolved state.

Using the metaphor of a landscape painting, at this point in our process the structural composition of the painting is set on the artist's canvas, the scope of the scene to be depicted is defined and drawn, the color palette is understood, and the relationships between the objects and terrain are established. Developing the painting is now about the nuances, shadings, and details of expression. The way we typically design a building with our conventional process would be akin to starting with a blank canvas and working at a high level of detail from one corner of the frame to the other. With this approach, we likely will find ourselves without enough room to depict the intended scene, or with an imbalanced composition, once we reach the lower corner of the canvas.

For a building project implementing integrative design, the engineering and land-related systems—and their relationship to the building design—should be understood and agreed upon at the end of Schematic Design. Midlevel calculations should have been performed to substantiate these general conclusions, so there is no need to rethink fundamental decisions about building form, structure, envelope, mechanical, electrical, plumbing, and landscape systems during Design Development. All the systems in the project, then, have been brought to a similar level of committed design and performance with an understanding of their interrelationships *before* Design Development begins—things are no longer being added or taken away. The purpose of Design Development is to *optimize* this design—that is, "*to make the best or most effective use of*" the systems already agreed upon.

Of course, there are always exceptions, and a great idea may appear in the course of the development process that could motivate the team to reconsider some major issue—but in general, this is the time to fine-tune the design solution with more detailed performance calculations.

Documenting the developed design during Construction Documents (CD), then, follows as the last phase before final project pricing. The CD phase is not entirely a mechanistic process of putting lines on paper or into computer-aided design (CAD) files, but the focus should be documenting decisions that were made during Design Development at an even higher level of detail. Fine-tuning and adjustments will need to be addressed as surprises and opportunities are found, but any decisions being made should occur only at a very, very fine level of detail during the CD phase.

HERE'S WHERE WE ARE

There appears to be a commonly understood break between the Schematic Design and Design Development phases in the conventional design process; in practice, however, we have seen fewer and fewer clear divisions between these phases. Generally speaking, though, we typically have accomplished the following at the end of conventional Schematic Design:

- The building is designed architecturally, that is, the building form—what it looks like—is firmly established, and we have a visual representation of it documented in plans, elevations, and sections.
- Land development plans have been approved—all impervious surfaces are defined and configured, vegetated open space is defined, stormwater infrastructure is defined and configured, parking areas have been determined and documented.
- Water and wastewater service utility locations are identified.
- Rainwater harvesting may have been identified as a possibility.

- An outline description or narrative describes mechanical, electrical, and plumbing (MEP) systems, perhaps with an option or two.

- Electrical service size as well as size and location of basic building service components, such as transformer and main utility service lines have been estimated.

- The structural grid is established and the type of structural system has been determined (steel, concrete, load-bearing masonry, etc.).

- A significant percentage of materials for the building's structure and envelope have been selected, as indicated on the elevations.

- The architect has completed and conveyed visual deliverables to the owner in order to conclude this phase and to submit invoices for design fees.

- Code analysis has been completed for determining building occupants, egress requirements, and plumbing fixture counts.

- Legal issues pertaining to site and environmental impact requirements are documented.

- Targeted LEED certification level is established, based on identified credits that can be achieved most easily.

Leaving Schematic Design and entering conventional Design Development (DD), we send the schematic drawings off to all team members and have them design their systems. This work includes the following:

- The architect draws building sections, dimensioned floor plans, detailed elevations, and detailed wall sections.

- The civil engineer finalizes all documentation to conclude permitting.

- The landscape architect (if one is on the team) lays out planting plans for DD pricing.

- The HVAC (heating, ventilating, and air-conditioning) engineer performs block-load and peak-demand calculations to size central supply components and major equipment; these are entered into a schedule—e.g., boilers, air handlers, chillers.

- Single-line drawings of distribution systems are created for ductwork and piping.

- Energy modeling begins after load calculations have been completed near the end of DD or later.

- Cost estimates are established, based on unit costs, such as dollars per square foot for the HVAC system.

- Value engineering brings the project back into budget by reducing scope and/or quality.

- Each team member tries to determine which of the LEED "question mark" credits are the least expensive to convert to "yes" credits on a credit-by-credit basis.

In the conventional process, the conclusion of Design Development often occurs at an undefined point, blending and blurring into the CD phase. During the CD phase, all team members document their systems and final cost estimating occurs, as follows:

- All design team members make final decisions about the systems within their disciplines and document them for bidding.

- Specifications for each system and its components are developed and finalized during this phase by specification (or spec) writers.

- Near the conclusion of the CD phase, final cost estimating takes place, usually followed by one more round of value engineering, again bringing the project back into budget by reducing scope and/or quality.

STOP AND REFLECT

What's Working?

Issues identified during Schematic Design are explored and pursued in more detail during current Design Development activities, as described above. Analyses for each individual system may inform some of the large-scale decisions previously made, often resulting in reconsideration of these issues to improve performance and/or achieve budget objectives. The Construction Documents phase then documents these decisions. This process includes the following benefits:

- A clearly understood convention for acceptable deliverables and compensation (fees) is used by all team members for DD and CD.

- Design and documentation tasks are clearly defined, and everyone knows what they need to do by investigating and defining their systems components in more detail and then documenting them.

- Budgetary issues are addressed through cost estimating, and the means for meeting cost constraints is generally agreed upon through accepted value engineering practices.

- Clearer definitions of systems and components are developed and documented.

- Each team member evaluates and documents potential achievement of LEED credits being pursued on a credit-by-credit basis to ensure achievement of targeted LEED certification level, then submits this documentation at the end of the CD phase.

What's Not Working?

Major design decisions continue to be made in isolation for each system during Design Development and Construction Documents (a continuation of the same conventional linear process implemented for Schematic Design) that protract the duration of design decision-making. Such decision making extends into the DD and CD phases, thereby eliminating the team's ability to explore detailed analysis aimed at optimization.

For example, as previously discussed, engineers usually wait to begin designing their systems until the architectural design is solidified, for fear that it will change. Generally, this is because the engineers have only enough fee to size and document their systems once; there is not enough time or fee to investigate alternative design possibilities and iterations. Consequently, their analysis surrounding major design decisions is initiated in late Design Development, only after the architectural design has been completed. This is a linear, rather than holistic, approach that leaves barely enough time to size and document systems and their components, let alone optimize them. We have often heard engineers say, "How can I size my systems before you guys are done with the building design?" The architects say, "How can you possibly run an energy model, if I haven't finished designing the building yet?"

As a result, energy modeling generally occurs only after the architectural design is finalized and, worse, after all engineering load calculations have been completed. The HVAC engineer, therefore, spends little or no time focusing on load reductions, because there are no measurable means to do so—and little time left in this phase, since so much of it is spent waiting for final architectural design solutions and performing load calculations for equipment sizing. Accordingly, energy modeling often is relegated to an after-the-fact assessment of performance, so it cannot be used to inform design decisions. Further, when load reductions *are* addressed, they largely are limited solely to those that can be achieved within the purview of the HVAC engineer (higher efficiency equipment), as we have seen. The HVAC engineer does not analyze options for all other components that can impact loads, such as augmenting the thermal properties of the building envelope, because

HVAC design does not begin until the architectural design is complete—this is a fragmented process and a circular dead end in terms of energy performance.

Additionally, previously allotted mechanical space in this near-final architectural solution often is discovered to be inadequate—or is not provided at all until late in the DD phase. This results in compromises elsewhere and more delays, further limiting analysis time and any potential efficiencies associated with HVAC distribution systems.

Team members are incentivized to complete design as quickly as possible to meet contractual obligations and receive payment, often by using off-the-shelf solutions, instead of exploring interrelationships and potential for optimization. In brief, the primary consequences of our nonintegrative conventional process during Design Development and Construction Documents include the following:

- Land development plan approvals lock the team into stormwater solutions before design has been analyzed and completed.

- Landscape and building solutions are viewed as separate from each other, thereby missing significant opportunities for promoting habitat and biodiversity in mutually beneficial ways that can contribute to the health of the place.

- A lack of systems analysis and coordination during Schematic Design limits the opportunities to further analyze and optimize systems interactions in DD.

- The design of major systems does not begin until late in this phase: Often, the selection of HVAC equipment is not even done during DD, and is put off until the CD phase, thereby limiting the ability to explore optimization and the accuracy of cost estimates or cost bundling.

- Project-specific specifications for these equipment selections (and virtually all other building systems) usually have not begun until the CD phase, which further limits accurate cost estimating during DD.

- Value engineering eliminates components and green technologies, since these are seen as isolated or superimposed technologies or products that have not been designed as interdependent and interrelated, nor optimized into a holistic solution.

- LEED credits are pursued in isolation, often by adding technologies within the bounds of conventional practice or by adding less conventional products that easily become low-hanging fruit for elimination during value engineering at the beginning and end of DD.

In short, we have not even finished making design decisions about many systems by the end of DD, let alone invested time in optimizing these systems. As a result, major design decisions are left for the Construction Documents phase, a phase during which we should be documenting, not designing—this leaves little or no time for optimization, so it rarely happens.

How Can We Do (and Think about) This Differently?

Design Development is about looking in detail at systems interrelationships and fine-tuning systems components via iterative and more progressively detailed analysis. Integrative design assures that *major design decisions* already have been made by the end of Schematic Design, so that such analysis can occur. Design Development is about optimizing these decisions—first, by verifying that the team's agreed-upon range of Performance Targets has been met, then by fine-tuning component selections, so that these components and systems can be properly sized, configured, and optimized to meet more specific and detailed Performance Targets.

In the integrative design process, Design Development can accomplish this in less time than the conventional process, as indicated in the Integrative Design Process diagram discussed at the beginning of Chapter 5 (see Figure 5-2 or C-1). This is because we already have explored and analyzed interrelationships between the four key subsystems (habitat, water, energy, and materials) and many of their components in order to ensure that the range of Performance Targets established early on can be achieved and often exceeded. So, for example, at the beginning of DD in an integrative design process, we have already:

- integrated wastewater and stormwater systems with promoting habitat.

- analyzed water balancing strategies.

- tested and integrated into the project's DNA daylighting concepts via schematic daylighting simulation models.

- completed load reduction analyses via parametric energy modeling in conjunction with orientation, building envelope, lighting, and HVAC systems options.

- analyzed these HVAC systems options for meeting the established range of reduced loads and performance targets, and selected the most appropriate HVAC system type (ground-source heat pump [GSHP], boiler, chiller, etc.), or at worst, limited this selection to no more than one or two systems with variants.

- analyzed major materials systems options (at least for structure and envelope systems) over a wide range of environmental impact indicators via life cycle assessment (LCA).

- performed cost bundling analyses for systems combinations (rather than line items only) to evaluate cost scenarios with increasing accuracy.

Since this analysis already has been completed, we can make more informed and optimized final design decisions during DD. The team can focus on ever-increasing levels of detailed analysis and cost-estimating to make these final smaller-scale design decisions, which might include, for example: the layout of efficient distribution systems, final sizing of all system components, completion of draft specifications, and cost analyses for all major systems and components that accurately assess bundled cost impacts.

As a result, at the end of Design Development, the design is completed. We sometimes like to say that concluding "DD" means *Design is Done*. This means that the team needs to recognize the DD phase as having a defined duration with an explicit end point. The Construction Documents phase, then, can consist of *documenting*, as intended by its very name. It can proceed by documenting the design, not by designing while documenting. Therefore, significantly less time is required for this phase as well, which makes up for the additional time required during the Discovery phase, again as indicated in the Integrative Design Process diagram discussed in Chapter 5 (see Figure 5-2 or C-1).

Further, we have seen that when the CD phase is characterized by "documenting the design," not by "designing while documenting," fewer errors and omissions generally result, primarily due to the inherent coordination of all systems. The conventional process typically depends on an eleventh-hour attempt to achieve such coordination between systems via a *quality control* review of the 90-percent-complete CD sets of documents submitted by all disciplines. By contrast, coordination between systems is *built into* the design throughout the integrative process. As a result, this inherent coordination can significantly reduce change orders. The U.S. Navy reports that a deeply integrated green process, along with design-build delivery (ensuring participation of the builder during design), has consistently allowed them to reduce change orders by 90 percent on their LEED Gold projects. Since the Navy typically holds 6 to 10 percent contingency for change orders on their projects, this translates to LEED Gold buildings coming in at 1 to 2 percent less than conventional construction cost.

The point is that integrative design is really nothing but good systems design. Good systems design requires that the people representing each system need to be in close and continuous relationship to discover synergies between systems, as we have tried to drive home throughout this book. Therefore, good integrative design really constitutes high levels of Total Quality Management.

In summary, we have found that if design teams have not done the necessary systems thinking, integration, and analyses described in Chapters 5 and 6 during the Discovery and Schematic Design phases, there are few interventions—if any—that can be made during the DD and CD phases to improve systems optimization and improve quality control cost-effectively and in a timely manner—hence the conventional adage "pick any two: good, fast, or cheap."

Mental Model Shift

If the mental model for Schematic Design is allowing oneself not to have the answers too quickly, Design Development is about selecting and finalizing the best answers.

Such a mental model shift mandates thinking of DD as a *discrete* phase, not just an initial part of the Construction Documents phase, as mentioned above.

To reiterate, the end of this phase should constitute the conclusion of making design decisions; again, at the end of this stage, DD stands for "Design is Done," but during this stage, it stands for *Designing in Detail.*

As we have seen, this mental model focuses on thoroughly vetting design ideas with increasingly higher levels of detail, requiring a continuous process of design iterations and communication between all team members from the outset. A quote from *The Toyota Way—14 Management Principles* captures this model succinctly:

> The key to the Toyota Way and what makes Toyota stand out is not any of the individual elements....But what is important is having all the elements together as a system. It must be practiced every day in a very consistent manner—not in spurts.

Continually focusing design activities on the interactions between *all* systems, beginning from the earliest stages in the design process, allows for a progressively higher level of detailed analysis of *all* systems in Design Development, thereby reducing the time and fee required to complete this phase and, in turn, reducing the time required to complete Construction Documents. Conversely, the CD phase in the conventional process often proceeds in spurts, frequently taking two steps forward, then one backward. One of our partners describes this by remembering the wry advice he was given by the CD production manager at his first architectural firm: "Never draw more in the morning than you can erase in the afternoon."

Stage B.3
Workshop No. 4: Design Development Kickoff—It Is Brought Together; Does It Work?

B.3.1 Workshop No. 4 Activities

- Present schematic design solutions from *Stage B.2* Research and Analysis and verify that the ranges of Performance Targets are being met for the four key subsystems:

  - Habitat
  - Water
  - Energy
  - Materials

- Verify that schematic design solution meets building program requirements and environmental performance objectives
- Commit to building form, configuration, and systems interrelationships that will be analyzed in further detail for optimization during *Stage B.4* Research and Analysis
- Identify the systems components variants that will require more detailed cost bundling analysis
- Identify Measurement and Verification (M&V) methods and opportunities for providing continuous performance feedback
- Commissioning: Identify where the OPR and BOD require updating

B.3.2 Principles and Measurement

- Document adjustments to Performance Targets that reflect schematic design solution
- Commissioning: Adjust OPR and BOD to reflect schematic design solution

B.3.3 Cost Analysis

- Expand any integrative cost bundling templates to reflect input from Workshop No. 4

B.3.4 Schedule and Next Steps

- Refine and extend forward the Integrative Process Road Map tasks and schedule through Design Development
- Distribute Workshop No. 4 Report

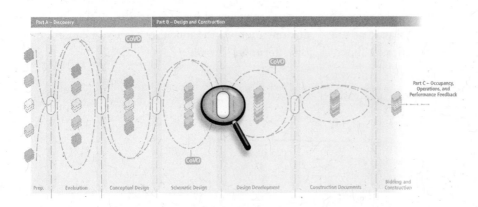

Figure 7-1 Integrative Process Stage B.3, Workshop #4: Design Development Kick-Off. *Image courtesy of 7group and Bill Reed; graphics by Corey Johnston.*

Stage B.3

WORKSHOP No. 4: Design Development Kickoff—It Is Brought Together; Does It Work?

At this point, Schematic Design documents have been submitted to the owner as a single architectural solution, with possible variants. The team now has an understanding of the interrelationships between the four key subsystems and the project's potential for achieving the Performance Targets within the ranges defined during Discovery and analyzed during Schematic Design. The pieces have been brought together into a building form to which the team now needs to commit collectively by validating that the schematic solution falls within these ranges for all Performance Targets, before engaging more detailed optimization analysis in *Stage B.4,* Design Development.

In essence, Workshop No. 4 functions both as a Schematic Design sign-off and as an organizational meeting for outlining Design Development activities. The benefit of breakout groups at this point likely is limited; rather, the team as a whole needs to verify that all the threads have been brought together. Then the team needs to identify any gaps in the schematic analyses that will need to be addressed, by engaging more refined analysis, in order to reach higher levels of performance within these ranges of Performance Targets.

B.3.1 Workshop No. 4 Activities

■ **Present schematic design solutions from *Stage B.2* Research and Analysis and verify that the ranges of Performance Targets are being met for the four key subsystems**

This workshop can begin by presenting the team's final schematic design solution (with optional variants) that resulted from *Stage B.2* Research and Analysis, in the form of drawings and supporting quantified data regarding systems performance. The purpose of this workshop is to validate col-

lectively as a team that all the systems have been brought together in supportive relationship with one another during Schematic Design. The focus here is to ensure that the four key subsystems are working together as a whole: Does it all work? Are these systems reinforcing one another? Are we meeting all of our Performance Targets? Further, can we find even more overlap between systems? Can we push Performance Targets to a higher level? As we will see, asking these and other questions leads to more highly integrated solutions that augment performance, sometimes via counterintuitive discoveries.

■ **Habitat** (biotic systems other than human)

- Verify the relationship of the proposed systems and building form with objectives aimed at the health of biotic systems relative to Performance Targets, and identify any potential gaps for further detailed analysis. Ask, for example:
  - Have the landscaped areas, green roofs, bioswales, and other infiltration strategies been sized collectively to neutralize runoff quantity, to meet the water quality targets, and to meet biodiversity goals?
  - Is there adequate rainwater retention capability between all strategies and components (cisterns, xeriscaping, irrigation system efficiencies, planting densities, etc.) to accommodate irrigation requirements based on varying rainfall patterns?
  - Are there adequate constructed wetland areas to accommodate waste demand flows and contributions to stormwater management and groundwater recharge?
  - What are the quantified results, according to the energy modeling results, of the landscaping scheme's impact on thermal comfort, e.g. the impact of shading of south-facing glazing?

- Do we have adequate habitat corridors and vegetated areas to accommodate the proposed habitat needs of specific species, both flora and fauna?

■ **Habitat** (human)

- Verify the relationship of the proposed systems and building form with human health and performance objectives relative to Performance Targets, and identify any potential gaps for further detailed analysis. Ask, for example:
  - Have targeted daylighting performance objectives been met in terms of providing adequate footcandles and glare reductions over varying times of the year and solar exposures (as modeled by daylighting software) in conjunction with meeting modeled energy targets via parallel energy modeling? Additional levels of details to consider might include the precise placement and dimensions of exterior shading devices, visible light transmission of the glazing, and internal glare controls.
  - Does thermal comfort analysis indicate that targeted thermal comfort ranges and individual thermal comfort goals have been met while achieving energy Performance Targets, perhaps via nonmechanical means, such as natural ventilation strategies? Discuss the design implications of the chosen strategies.
  - Have targeted ventilation capacities for all occupancy functions, ventilation effectiveness, and air filtration criteria been met without negatively impacting overall energy performance, such as needing to increase fan size and capacity? If not, how can this be addressed?
  - Do the targeted levels of indoor air quality appear achievable relative to proposed materials choices and pollutant source control strategies?

- Have acoustical performance criteria been met in terms of sound transmission class and background noise relative to proposed materials selection, daylighting strategies, window orientation away from noise sources, and locations of HVAC equipment noise sources?

- *Example*: In 2002, during the Design Development kickoff stage for our third Pennsylvania (PA) Department of Environmental Protection (DEP) project (a 20,000 square foot rural field-office building), the owner-developer called us with a concern: He said, "I need help: I just realized that one of my staff underestimated the project's construction cost when we submitted our lease numbers to the state. Is there anything at all we can do to reduce the project cost, since I'm contractually obligated to meet these numbers?" This was the second DEP project that we had worked on with this developer, so he was familiar with the trade-offs between thermal envelope, HVAC system sizing, perimeter heating, and energy savings that we had learned on the prior project with him (DEP Cambria). Nevertheless, he suggested (among other things) that one option might be to replace the triple-glazed windows with double glazing for the north-facing clerestories that ran the entire length of the building. He told us that this could save around $7,000—relative to the project's size, this was not a small savings, around $0.35 per square foot. We replied that we did not think we could do this because of those trade-offs. But he pushed us to at least run this option through our energy modeling analysis.

We did so reluctantly. The modeling results told us that this change would result in a surprisingly low energy cost increase of less than $150 per year. We were shocked, and at first we could not figure it out: "Why is the impact so low?!"

Then it dawned on us: Of course! The double-glazed windows have a higher visible light transmittance (Tvis). As a result, since all of the lighting in the spaces daylighted by these clerestories was controlled with photocell sensors and dimming ballasts, the lights now would be completely dimmed far more often, consuming less energy for lighting and producing less heat that would need to be cooled by the HVAC system. The energy increase for heating and cooling due to the heat gain and heat loss through less insulating windows was almost completely offset by the energy reductions associated with the lights being on far less often.

▶**Figure 7-2** Using double-glazed windows for the north-facing clerestories *(upper right)* instead of triple-glazed windows for our third Pennsylvania DEP project (the DEP California field office) resulted from counterintuitive energy modeling results. *Image courtesy of John Boecker.*

▼**Figure 7-3** Solar shading devices on the south-facing windows of the DEP California project are part of an integrative approach that reduced the HVAC system's cooling capacity by 50 percent and annual energy costs by over 40 percent. *Images courtesy of John Boecker.*

Consequently, the simple payback for the triple glazing turned out to be nearly fifty years. Also, since these clerestories were located an adequate distance from occupants in the center of the building, any impacts relative to perimeter thermal comfort were obviated. In short, the triple glazing could not be justified. We called the developer and told him the good news.

What we learned from this is that not all solutions are applicable to all projects. Every project is unique. What works well for one project, might not be the best answer for another—question assumptions. Sometimes, analysis produces counterintuitive results.

Water

- Verify the relationship of the proposed systems and building form with water conservation and quality objectives relative to Performance Targets, and identify any potential gaps for further detailed analysis. Ask, for example:
  - Have all the water-related systems in the building and on the site been analyzed and quantified in terms of potable water consumption and quantified cascading benefits—not simply the water efficiency impacts of toilet room fixtures, but all systems related to water flows, such as cooling tower water makeup, equipment washing, process water use, habitat irrigation, groundwater recharge, waste treatment, gray water, rainwater catchment, and so on?
  - Does the quantity and availability of treated wastewater, rainwater, and/or process water, such as cooling coil condensate, meet the quantified demand for use in toilets and other potential nonpotable uses, such as irrigation?
- *Example*: During a recent Goal-Setting Workshop for the Miami Trace Middle School project

in central Ohio, the project team was reviewing the pursuit of LEED-NC Sustainable Sites Credit 5.1, which required (for this previously developed site) that 50 percent of the site area, exclusive of the building footprint, be restored with native and adaptive vegetation. Based on pricing estimated by the landscape architect for specifying native planting, the team believed that this would be too costly, since the required restored area equated to twenty-one acres. So the credit was left as a low-priority question mark.

This issue came up again later, during a stormwater management discussion with the civil engineer and the team. During this discussion, it was mentioned that a new elementary school had just been completed on a somewhat smaller site, directly adjacent to the planned middle school. Since the ground sloped minimally toward the road, a huge stormwater detention basin had been installed in front of the elementary school. This basin was a visual eyesore that the community did not like. The landscape architect then spoke up: "What if we create a rain garden planted with native plants in front of the new school that could serve as stormwater retention?" His idea linked native planting with stormwater management, groundwater recharge, habitat health, aesthetics, and an educational function since this new wetland could provide middle school students an opportunity on site for studying botany and biology. Everyone agreed that this was a great suggestion. Breakout groups worked to develop this idea, including connecting this rain garden to another one in the courtyard that was emerging in several design schemes.

As it turned out, further analysis later revealed that this solution, when cost bundled, garnered

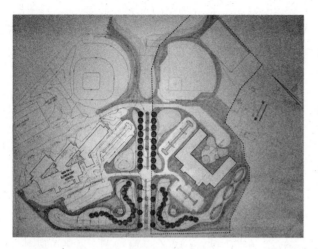

Figure 7-4 This sketch presented by the landscape architect at a Miami Trace Middle School team workshop depicts large wetland and rain garden areas that collect and infiltrate rainwater, thereby eliminating a much more costly system of stormwater detention and conveyance for the new middle school (located to the right of the road). The concept was generated at an earlier team workshop (see Figure 7-5). *Image courtesy of Marcus Sheffer.*

enough savings from eliminating most of the stormwater conveyance system to pay for this rain garden and all of the required native planting for the rest of the site. Not only that, but enough money was left over to renovate the detention basin on the elementary school site into a rain garden as well, thereby eliminating the eyesore on the adjacent site left over from the previous project. It also should be noted that the facilities manager calculated an annual maintenance savings of several thousand dollars due to the elimination of mowing what otherwise would have been turf grass.

Energy

- Verify the relationship of the proposed systems and building form with energy efficiency and renewable energy objectives relative to Performance Targets, and identify any potential gaps for further detailed analysis. Ask, for example:

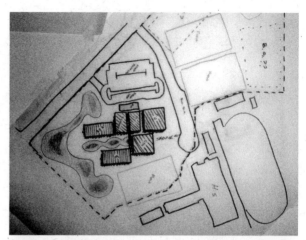

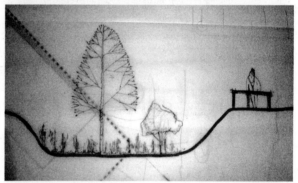

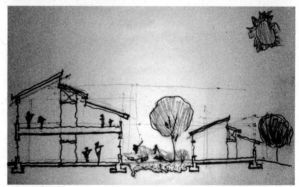

Figure 7-5 Sketches from an early design workshop breakout group depict the first ideas for the rain gardens concept at Miami Trace Middle School that later developed into the solution depicted in Figure 7-4. *Images courtesy of Marcus Sheffer.*

- Which combination of energy-efficiency measures (EEMs) from parametric energy modeling runs appears to result in the most efficient building in terms of both energy consumption and cost? Have all the related systems been analyzed and designed to contribute? Such systems would include building orientation, thermal envelope, shading devices, daylighting strategies, percentage of glazing openings, thermal comfort parameters, ventilation approaches, water conveyance strategies, HVAC system type, renewable energy generation, etc.
- Have all possible load reduction parameters that might be used to augment energy performance been analyzed in the parametric modeling effort? Often, for example, exterior aspects of the building are not considered, such as tree shading and nearby shading from other buildings, prevailing winds, etc.
- Has thermal comfort been analyzed from the perspective of its impact on energy performance via strategies like operable windows and other hybrid cooling techniques such as ceiling fans, controlled natural ventilation, whole building ventilation, and so on?
- Now that we have optimized the larger-load impacts on the HVAC system, we need to optimize the design details. What are the potential options that could be evaluated by the energy model during the DD phase to optimize HVAC system performance?
- *Example*: A new office building in the intermountain western U.S. debated using a direct-indirect evaporative cooling system instead of vapor compressive air-conditioning. However, there was a problem: for a week or two in the summer, the humidity was calculated to be too high to bring the indoor sensible temperature down enough to fall within comfort range. The energy savings offered by the evaporative cooling were significant but needed to be augmented through the use of ceiling fans and operable windows. The client had a very important role to play in the decision. They could decide on business as usual, or they could consider the benefits of operating a building that would require more engaged occupants for two weeks out of the year. Occupants would have to be taught that a thermostat is not the only control mechanism, and that opening windows and using ceiling fans could provide a comfortable environment. In this case, the building owner (and his assessment of occupant participation) became the deciding factor for an efficient building—not just the engineers and architect.

Materials

- Verify the relationship of the proposed systems and building form with material choices relative to Performance Targets, and identify any potential gaps for further detailed analysis. Ask, for example:
  - Do the results of the LCA indicate that the environmental impact targets (prioritized in *Stage B.1*) have been met for the building's structural and envelope systems—metrics such as embodied-energy targets, carbon footprint budget, human toxicant limits, etc.?
  - Are the proposed materials for structural and envelope systems likely to support as many environmental objectives as possible, considering factors such as intended service life, manufacturers' social responsibility, community safety, habitat health and stability, long-term living system viability, local and atmospheric toxicant burden due to leeching and disposal, etc.?

- Are the proposed materials for structural and envelope systems able to be disassembled easily and redistributed or reused when the building reaches the end of its Service Life?
- Are the proposed materials consistent with the Service Life criteria established in *Stage B.1*?
- Are proposed materials able to be reabsorbed into the local ecosystem when disposed?
- Once these questions have been explored, the team should continue by:
  - Beginning a focused discussion on finish materials.
  - Seeking opportunities to use structure as finish.
  - Framing the research and analysis structure for investigating finnish materials during Design Development.
  - Choosing appropriate LCA model for finishes. (In North America BEES is the most appropriate.)

- *Example:* One of the general principles in building near the ocean is that one should not build on a coastal sand dune, due to its ecosystem and the protection it offers the estuary system and land behind it. We and our colleagues at Regenesis were confronted with just this compromising situation at the Playa Viva project, the ecoresort project in Juluchuca, Mexico, that was discussed in Chapter 4. We had originally assumed that we would be building on the land inland from the estuary systems, but due to the low elevation of this land, the client wanted to locate some casitas (small houses) on the coastal dune. We refused and offered to leave the project because of the ethical compromise this represented for us. The client, David Leventhal, challenged us to live up to our belief that most situations can be reconciled (harmonized) and not simply compromised (conceded). Af-

Figure 7-6 These images show tests used to evaluate the ability of transplanted palms (technically a grass) to reestablish themselves such that they are able to hold the living matrix of sand and soil together (they did) and the process of structural testing to use them as "living columns" for casitas at Playa Viva, an ecoresort in Juluchuca, Mexico. *Images by David Leventhal, Playa Viva, http://www. PlayaViva.com.*

ter a two-hour meeting, we agreed that the only way to effectively "build" on a sand dune would be to avoid concrete and rigid surfaces and to use only plants to help hold and restore the already damaged dune system. We spent a few weeks researching the possibility of using the abandoned palm trees from the palm plantation that was on the site, and we found that mature trees are easily transplanted. By transplanting these mature palms, we could use them to form a matrix of "living columns" to support the casita platforms with their roots knitting together and stabilizing the dune. In addition, it turned out that the casitas could be built entirely from these palm trees as well—beams, flooring, palapas (palm-leaf thatching). Eventually, however, another local wood was substituted for the beams due to the short structural life span (service life) of the palm wood. The structure was local, living, easily repaired or rebuilt in the event of future storm events, and it helped stabilize the dunes to support habitat health.

■ **Verify that schematic design solution meets building program requirements and environmental performance objectives**

- ■ As discussed above, the group evaluates the schematic design solution in terms of alignment with the project's Performance Targets and also with its initially established purpose, values, aspirations, and principles. This is the final opportunity for ensuring alignment with these guiding principles and for making any significant changes.

- ■ The group reviews the status of the project relative to its green building assessment tool goals. If pursuing LEED, verify the status of all targeted credits.

■ **Commit to building form, configuration, and systems interrelationships that will be analyzed in**

further detail for optimization during *Stage B.4* **Research and Analysis**

- ■ The team collectively commits to the building form resulting from Schematic Design efforts, including any potential variants that may need to be addressed during the more detailed analysis of *Stage B.4*—another reinforcement that the design is fully "owned" by all team members.

- ■ Evaluate the quantified data from the Schematic Design effort, and identify where potential augmentation might be possible via deeper interrelationships or adjustments. Outline procedures for the detailed analysis to be engaged for optimizing and verifying performance during *Stage B.4* Research and Analysis.

■ **Identify the systems components variants that will require more detailed cost bundling analysis**

Identify any variants, changes in components, or systems design adjustments that emerge during Workshop No. 4 and may have cascading cost impacts; consequently, any such impacts should be discussed, so that additional cost bundling analysis can be conducted during *Stage B.4.*

■ **Identify Measurement and Verification (M&V) methods and opportunities for providing continuous performance feedback**

The team needs to discuss the methodology that will be employed to provide performance feedback to establish the parameters for creating a draft Measurement and Verification (M&V) plan during *Stage B.4* by asking:

- ■ How will the energy (and water) consumption savings be predicted?

- ■ What will be the extent of the built-in monitoring and/or submetering?

- ■ What end uses or systems are intended to be measured and how?

- ▥ Which of these systems can be configured, zoned, and circuited to enable the use of portable data loggers or clamp-on meters?
- ▥ Are the systems and end uses simple enough that submetering will not be necessary?
- ▥ Who will collect the required data, calibrate the calculations used to make predictions, compare measured versus projected performance, and reconcile the difference?
- ▥ Will additional expertise beyond the capabilities of the building facilities managers be required to implement the M&V Plan?

▥ Commissioning: Identify where the OPR and BOD require updating

The ways in which any adjustments to the Schematic Design solution and/or Performance Targets may affect the evolving Owner's Project Requirements (OPR) and Basis of Design (BOD) need to be identified during the workshop, so that these documents can be updated accordingly. The Commissioning Authority can facilitate this discussion.

B.3.2   Principles and Measurement

▥ Document adjustments to Performance Targets that reflect schematic design solution

Any performance adjustments resulting from Workshop No. 4, as described above, need to be documented and distributed to the project team to ensure that all team members understand their responsibilities for engaging, coordinating, and integrating the identified detailed analysis required during *Stage B.4.* For projects pursuing LEED certification, a revised LEED scorecard also should be distributed to the project team that documents updates and revisions to the status of each credit being pursued.

▥ Commissioning: Adjust OPR and BOD to reflect schematic design solution

- ▥ Again, it is the design team's responsibility, with owner input, to make any revisions to the OPR and BOD that reflect any adjustments resulting from Workshop No. 4, as described above. At this point, however, such revisions become fewer and fewer, so that maintenance of these documents may become a task of merely reflecting decisions made by the team. Such documentation is still critical to avoid having to reconstruct it later in the process. Remember, these documents are intended to convey to the construction professionals the story of *why* systems have been designed the way they have been.

- ▥ It is important to note that the OPR and BOD also serve as tools for helping the owner's nontechnical representatives understand what they are getting, so that they are not surprised when they walk in the building. As the OPR and BOD henceforth evolve during the DD and CD phases, though, there also can be impacts of an increasingly technical nature, particularly with regard to more detailed specific parameters and team members' responsibilities. While at this stage, the impacts tend to be more subtle than pronounced, the subtleties beg an even more intentional update of these documents. These updated documents need to be distributed to the entire team, and each team member should be asked to provide their approval, indicating that they understand and agree with the provisions within them. Their approval of the technical aspects of these documents is important, since the OPR and BOD really provide the only vehicle for nontechnical stakeholders to understand the building systems.

- ▥ At this point, the Commissioning Authority is beginning to frame the thinking that will create a Commissioning Plan, which is informed and guided by the OPR and the BOD. Again, the Commissioning process is aimed at assuring that the final outcome represents a building design that is based on the owner's requirements.

B.3.3 Cost Analysis

■ **Expand any integrative cost bundling templates to reflect input from Workshop No. 4**

Additional cost bundling analysis identified during Workshop No. 4 activities, as described above, likely will be required only where cascading cost impacts are not obvious or simply combined with already-established bundles. Also, as a Construction Phase Commissioning Plan begins to take shape, cost considerations for contractor involvement in commissioning during construction must be estimated and realistically revealed. This is not to say that significant additional cost is expected, but it should now become a real consideration—and quantified if applicable. This is discussed further in *Stage B.5.3* below.

B.3.4 Schedule and Next Steps

■ **Refine and extend forward the Integrative Process Road Map tasks and schedule through Design Development**

Adjust overall schedule and set target dates for tasks associated with integrating the more detailed analysis to be engaged during *Stage B.4*—identify meetings that will be required to accommodate the necessary communication between team members as all systems are fine-tuned.

Although this constant reminder about updating the Road Map may appear to be redundant, we have seen repeatedly that without the rigor of such process mapping, team members at this point often return to their silos and to the conditioned and familiar pattern of "optimizing components in isolation"; when this happens, performance becomes compromised. The challenge we face, then, is to maintain deeper levels of interaction between team members so this siloing tendency can be avoided. Additionally, this Road Map encourages more sharing of the development sketches and analysis being generated, so that the impacts of all decisions on all systems are known to all.

In other words, it is at this point that we see many design teams collapse in their effort to achieve deep integration and revert back to "getting the job done." This is the point in the process when good intentions and the results from earlier stages can be jeopardized unless there is a coordinated effort to continue integrating and confirming "true performance." The client is a critical driver at this stage—i.e., the client can become the cheerleader inspiring the team to strive for deeper achievement.

■ **Distribute Workshop No. 4 Report**

Once again, it is important to document the results of each workshop and therefore distribute a report containing the following for Workshop No. 4:

■ Meeting notes recording the assessment of all Performance Targets, additional findings, results, reflections, etc.

■ Updated Metrics and Performance Targets—include updated LEED checklist, if applicable

■ Updated integrative cost bundling template for any new and more detailed analysis identified

■ Process Road Map spreadsheet of schedule and tasks

■ Updated OPR and BOD for team approval

■ Next Steps

Stage B.4
Research and Analysis: Design Development—Optimization

B.4.1 Research and Analysis Activities: Design Development

- Engage detailed analysis of systems interrelationships with continuous iterations between disciplines
- Validate achievement of Performance Targets for specific components of the four key subsystems
  - Habitat
  - Water
  - Energy
  - Materials
- Obtain input and feedback from builder on all systems

B.4.2 Principles and Measurement

- Document in detail and validate building performance results against Performance Targets
- Prepare draft Measurement and Verification (M&V) Plan
- Commissioning
  - Invite the Commissioning Authority to review design progress and identify opportunities for further optimization and potential conflicts
  - Identify the preliminary list of systems to be commissioned
  - Prepare preliminary Commissioning Plan

B.4.3 Cost Analysis

- Utilize integrated cost bundling templates to optimize value and performance (true value engineering) to conclude cost analysis for all major systems

B.4.4 Schedule and Next Steps

- Extend forward the Integrative Process Road Map tasks and schedule through the Documentation phase and begin integrating with the builder if this has not yet occurred
- Prepare Agenda for Workshop No. 5

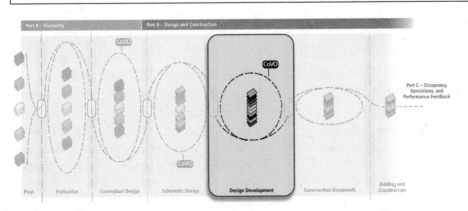

Figure 7-7 Integrative Process Stage B.4, Research and Analysis: Design Development. *Image courtesy of 7group and Bill Reed; graphics by Corey Johnston.*

Stage B.4

Research and Analysis: Design Development (Optimization)

As described at the beginning of this chapter, Design Development is about *optimization.* Accordingly, during this stage, team members are fine-tuning the details of their systems, components, and system interrelationships via iterative and more progressively detailed analysis. The conclusion of Design Development constitutes the conclusion of making design decisions. It bears repeating, then, that activities during DD focus on "Designing in Detail," except for at the finest level, which remains for Construction Documents; therefore, "Design is Done" at the end of this stage. What is meant by "Done" here is that the design of all systems that support the Performance Targets for all four key subsystems is complete. All that is left for the CD phase, then, is ultrafine detail: "Do the screw heads line up?"

Interim Meetings

Again, just like *Stage B.2* (Schematic Design), the process outline presented here does not explicitly identify specific Design Development (DD) team meetings other than the Design Development Kickoff *(Stage B.1)*. Successful systems integration, though, mandates a series of interim subteam meetings during DD, so that the impacts of all decisions on all systems are known to all team members as detailed analysis proceeds. Consequently, since the intention of this book is not to prescribe a cookbook approach to what these meetings need to address (nor could we if we tried, since each project is different), only a few examples of such meetings are mentioned below.

B.4.1 Research and Analysis Activities: Design Development

■ **Engage detailed analysis of systems interrelationships with continuous iterations between disciplines**

The analysis here should address *in detail* the project-specific questions about systems interrelationships that were asked during Workshop No. 4 pertaining to the four key subsystems. Interim meetings between team members are essential to accomplish this.

■ **Validate achievement of Performance Targets for specific components of the four key subsystems**

If solutions for integrating the four key subsystems are not completed in detail during this Stage, and their Performance Targets are not verified by detailed analysis, then it likely will be too late to realize integrative solutions—the design will not be "Done." Accordingly, this detailed analysis should address questions similar to the examples referenced above in the text for *Stage B.3.1.* Such questions are highly project specific, so presenting a comprehensive list of the types of analysis to be engaged during this stage would be impossible (and well beyond the scope of this book), since the nature of such analysis varies as widely as design parameters differ from project to project. The examples presented below, then, are intended to illustrate what *level* of detail should be addressed in the systems integration analysis during DD.

■ **Habitat** (biotic systems other than human)
  • *Example:*
    The landscape architect for a recent project in the Northeast created a landscaping plan during DD to illustrate the planting scheme for a constructed treatment wetland and presented it to our team. This plan depicted groupings of different plant species that he had selected and arranged in a pattern of separate but interlinked zones. The plan was beautiful, but it did not work very well. By "work," we mean that although the selected plants and groupings may have looked pretty, they were not in close and symbiotic relationship with each other. We had experienced this problem on a previous project,

Figure 7-8 A constructed wetland that had been planned in monocultural zones; this wetland required a much longer period of time (three years) to establish a rich and healthy diversity of plant life than similar wetlands that mix various species together and become profuse within a year. *Image courtesy of Bill Reed.*

where it took almost three years for the plants to self-organize into a thriving ecology and to revive the operative microbes (see Figure 7-8). We discovered that if the plants are seeded by utilizing a broadcast method, mixing the various species together, the wetland becomes a profuse and healthy system within a year. As E.O. Wilson says, "Better amok than regimented."

■ **Habitat** (human)

● *Examples:*

For most projects, daylight glazing on the western façade presents the problem of direct solar gain due to low sun angles for much of the year. These low sun angles present potential glare problems due to direct sunlight penetration. In addition, excess heat gain occurs during the cooling season, which increases energy use and affects the sizing of the cooling system, since the building's peak loads typically occur on a hot day during the afternoon—an even worse condition than the east-facing glass façade discussed in *Stage B.1.1*, because by mid-to-late afternoon the building has had all day to heat up.

The media center space for a recent project was located on the building's western façade; a large storefront glazing system was planned for this façade in the original design. The best solution, in most cases, is to significantly minimize west-facing glazing, since the low sun angles cannot be eliminated. In this case, the designers were not willing to reduce the glazing but were very interested in minimizing the problem to the greatest extent possible. Initial daylighting analysis demonstrated considerable hours of direct solar penetration, especially during the cooling season (see Figure 7-9). Subsequent analysis with daylighting modeling during DD examined both interior and exterior light shelves and adjustments to the glazing's solar heat gain coefficient (SHGC). As a result, the direct solar gain was minimized, reducing

▲▲ **Figure 7-9** Initial daylighting analysis depicting direct solar penetration through a project's west-facing storefront glazing system. *Image courtesy of Todd Reed. Image created by AGi32.*

▲ **Figure 7-10** Design Development analysis included both interior and exterior light shelves and adjustments to the glazing system's solar heat gain coefficient, significantly reducing direct solar penetration relative to the initial analysis depicted in Figure 7-9. *Image courtesy of Todd Reed. Image created by AGi32.*

glare issues and heat gain (see Figure 7-10). We typically use daylighting simulation tools (such as those described in *Stage B.2.1*) to optimize the configuration of such light shelves and shading devices by running various options through the model, then iteratively adjusting their geometry and dimensions.

On another recent project, a hospital wanted to provide patients with daylight and views to the outdoor gardens. Views to such gardens and the outdoors have been shown to increase psychological comfort, promote health, contribute to productivity gains, and decrease recovery time in health care facilities* (see related discussions in Chapter 8 regarding post-occupancy evaluations). The design team created gardens in this case that were comprised of native plantings to promote habitat, which in turn helped establish deeper root zones that allowed for increased rainwater absorption by the soil. But these plantings also helped with energy performance, by providing increased shading that reduced solar heat gain through glazing. We modeled the effect of these plantings using energy simulation tools during DD in a collaborative effort that helped select planting species and sizes, based on their effect at varying ages of maturity.

■ **Water**

• *Example:*

This example describes another lesson learned: On our fifth project for the Pennsylvania DEP, a 110,000-square-foot office building in urban Norristown, Pennsylvania, the rainwater harvesting system was designed to store

---

* Many case study examples are detailed in Robin Guenther and Gail Vittori's book *Sustainable Healthcare Architecture*, New Jersey: John Wiley & Sons, 2008.

captured rainwater from the roof in a 5,000-gallon cistern that was located in the building's central 4-story atrium, as depicted in Figure 4-15. Calculations used for sizing the cistern's capacity (which in earlier stages informed the cistern's location and associated structural implications) were based on the monthly stormwater harvesting predictions spreadsheet depicted in Figure 5-47 and as described in the "Water" section of *Stage A.5.1*. During Design Development, this cistern was equipped with an overflow pipe for cases when storm events might exceed cistern capacity. Conversely, to address drought conditions, a float valve was placed in the cistern as a control device to fill the tank from the municipal water supply in the absence of rain, since this cistern was sized to provide 100 percent of the water required for flushing all of the toilets in the building. This float valve was strategically placed to trigger adding potable water to the tank only when water levels sunk to less than a third of the tank's capacity. This strategy meant that the cistern was able to receive nearly its full capacity with rainwater from the majority of storm events, but potable water would be used to fill the tank to only one-third of its capacity when significant time had elapsed without precipitation—so if a storm event immediately followed such filling, two-thirds of the cistern's volume would still be available for capturing the rainwater.

However, once the building was occupied an excessively high volume of water consumption appeared on the first month's extremely high water bill. After a brief investigation, it was discovered that the float valve had malfunctioned and was continuously triggering refill mode. All of that excess water was simply draining through the overflow pipe. The lesson we learned (the hard way) here was that such devices should be configured to alarm the building's control system when the valve remains open for longer periods than required to fill the tank. Such details—and components for all systems that impact performance—should be incorporated into the specifications and BOD document during this stage as a component to be commissioned. The Commissioning Authority should then verify their inclusion in the

Figure 7-11 Harvested rainwater stored in the cistern at DEP's Norristown, Pennsylvania facility satisfies 100 percent of the building's annual toilet-flushing demand. The system's sediment filter and pumps are housed in an adjacent room behind a glass partition as a means of educating visitors about the system. *Image ©2004 Jim Schafer.*

DD and CD drawings and specifications when reviewing these documents.

Energy

- *Example:*

  Now that the specific HVAC system has been selected and downsized, the system components and sequence of operations will need to be optimized. The energy model should be updated and used to guide remaining design decisions pertaining to more detailed issues such as the use of premium-efficiency motors, variable frequency drives for pumps and fan motors, specific equipment efficiency, heat recovery, economizers, waste heat recovery, and so on, that should be evaluated, depending on the selected HVAC system. In addition, issues related to the HVAC sequence of operations should be analyzed, such as optimal start-stop, unoccupied temperature settings, boiler/chiller water temperature reset controls, demand-controlled ventilation, water/air economizer operation, and so on.

▲ **Figure 7-12** The rainwater-harvesting cistern of the DEP Norristown project is located in the building's atrium and also supplies water to a hose bib for watering atrium plants. *Image ©2004 Jim Schafer.*

▶ **Figure 7-13** The DEP Norristown building filled in a vacant urban lot along Main Street and incorporated into its programmed space the renovation of the town's previously abandoned 1931 Art Deco commuter train station, a registered Historic Landmark building (seen here on the right). *Image ©2004 Jim Schafer.*

This detailed analysis during DD is critical for questioning assumptions at this level of detail. For example, it often is assumed that ventilation air heat recovery (VAHR) systems will save energy, since generally, these VAHR systems can reduce the installed capacity (and first cost) of heating and cooling equipment by reducing the load associated with having to heat and cool this outside air to maintain thermal comfort ranges—especially for buildings requiring large amounts of outside air for ventilation, like schools. In very hot and very cold weather, VAHR can reduce HVAC energy usage significantly.

However, our recent experience with several green building projects indicates that there are times when VAHR systems may not save energy. In fact, there are two reasons why a VAHR system might *increase* annual energy usage. One is the substantial fan power required to move the air through the heat-recovery heat exchanger. The other is that, at times, ventilation air alone *could* be used to cool the building via the "free cooling" of an air-side economizer (ASE) when outside air temperatures are appropriate—but VAHR systems will often continue to operate in heat-recovery mode, with their associated fans running needlessly, under these same circumstances. Because of this, ASE operation can substantially reduce or eliminate the cooling load on the HVAC system, and in turn significantly reduce cooling-energy use. This is particularly true for green buildings that are well insulated and have low balance temperatures, since in many climates such buildings need space cooling most of the time—even during reasonably cold outdoor air conditions (see Figure 7-14).

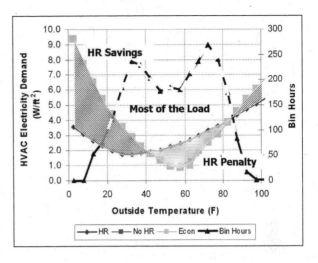

Figure 7-14 The graph illustrates that heat-recovery (HR) systems will save energy (HR savings) at temperatures below 40°F and above 85°F. In this example, the HR system actually uses more energy than it saves (HR penalty) between these temperatures; since most of the heating and cooling load in the climate analyzed occurs between 40°F and 85°F, the HR penalty outweighs the HR savings on an annual basis. *Image courtesy of Andy Lau.*

Consequently, energy modeling results during DD often show that VAHR alone is not the best option with regard to energy use. Rather, we have found that if a VAHR system is installed in a building to reduce the installed system capacities, the system also should have the option of bypassing the VAHR system and using an ASE when outside air conditions are advantageous.

Materials
- *Example:*

  The Pennsylvania DEP Cambria facility discussed in prior chapters is a rural office building located in a wooded area of an industrial park; it was designed to function as a district office for the mining division of Pennsylvania's Department of Environmental Protection. The proposed cladding material was originally intended to be steel siding, due to its recycled content, and because its look would have fit with other buildings in the industrial park.

We proposed another idea, though, after giving a lot of thought to the notion that a green building might change in appearance over time, and that such changes might reflect the building's climate, context, and varying solar exposures. We questioned what this might look like and concluded that wood siding without a finish would be perfect for the conditions present. It would darken on the north side of the building and bleach out on the south side of the building where the sun would hit it regularly. Additionally, wood siding, while seemingly unsuitable for a state office building, blended very well with the indigenous context. Many of the century-old barns in the area had been built (mostly by German and Swiss immigrants who settled the land) with local hemlock siding that had not been painted or finished in any way, and had held up well for well over one hundred years. So we proposed rough-sawn, unfinished, locally harvested hemlock wood siding—just like those barns—for much of the building's exterior.

Naturally, this was not an easy idea to sell to the client, as it did not fit many people's concept of what a commercial office structure should look like. The state facilities people immediately came up with many reasons to reject a material that their own ancestors had considered a primary cladding material. Objections abounded, including "we can't afford wood siding," "it will rot," "bugs will infest it," "it won't look right," and "we'll have to hire a full-time person to maintain it."

We were able to demonstrate through our LCA model, though, that this locally harvested hemlock was environmentally preferable to any of the alternatives being considered. What finally convinced the state that this was a direction worth pursuing was a quick cost comparison. The local hemlock (indigenous to central Pennsylvania) was a fraction of the price of steel siding. Therefore, we could show that even in the unlikely case that rotting became an issue, its reduced cost would allow for 60 percent of it to be replaced over a fifty-year period, including installation and accounting for inflation. In fact, the wood was about one-quarter the cost of steel for this project, and its life cycle impacts were far lower as well.

Figure 7-15 Unpainted, locally harvested hemlock siding at the DEP Cambria, Pennsylvania, building significantly reduced costs and environmental impacts; its board and batten installation allows it to dry while on the building, thereby reducing the embodied energy and emissions associated with typical kiln drying. *Image ©2001 Jim Schafer.*

Figure 7-16 The Clearview Elementary School in Hanover, Pennsylvania, also incorporated local indigenous hemlock siding; in addition to its environmental benefits, it reflects the local, agricultural, and rural architectural context of century-old wood barns in nearby surrounding areas. *Image ©2003 Jim Schafer.*

Additionally, as we sought other ways to lower the impact of each material, we learned during Design Development when developing wall section details that one of the significant environmental impacts associated with manufacturing wood is the drying process. This can be done naturally over a very long period of time, or it can be accomplished quickly by using heat in a kiln. Wood is dried in a kiln to help it reach ambient humidity and thereby stabilize its movement. In this case, we realized that we need not concern ourselves so much about movement if we detailed a board and batten system of fastening. The board is fastened on one side and left to float on the other side where it is held down by another batten. This means the wood can move and not crack as the humidity changes. As a result, we were able to use wood that had been recently harvested and milled locally without drying it in a kiln. For nearly ten years now, it has dried naturally on the wall of the building without any need for painting, finishing, or maintenance—and without any problems.

■ **Obtain input and feedback from Builder on all systems**

The builder's role at this point can be critical. Of course, the earlier the builder is present and engaged, the better the outcome of project, as discussed in Chapter 5. This is due to aligning the design *and* construction team around purpose, problem solving, constructability issues, and certainly cost ramifications, that is, refining the cost estimate. If possible, the builder (or, if the builder has not yet been selected, someone with similar expertise) should be in attendance at most meetings during this phase to comment and provide

Wood and Life Cycle Impacts

Wood is almost always preferred in LCA. This is because it soaks up carbon dioxide (and creates oxygen) while it is being produced, takes very little energy to extract, requires very little energy to mill and make usable, requires very little maintenance (under most circumstances), and can often be re-used at the end of a building's useful life. What LCA does not show us about the use of wood, though, are the impacts on land use. This is extremely difficult to measure, and therefore it needs to be dealt with in other ways. For our purposes on the Pennsylvania DEP Cambria project, we chose to look locally and sought pricing for hemlock from local wood mills. The mill we ended up using was close to the site and harvested its logs from local farmers' wood lots. These lots had been managed by farmers for a couple of hundred years as the area was settled. Where they still exist, they usually are about two acres in size. Managed and selective harvesting from these lots provided building material, logs for use on the farm, and fire wood for cooking and heating in the winter while maintaining the health of the wooded land. These lots have fallen out of use in this regard over the last few decades, and currently they provide little to the farmers, except for the value of the logs.

The land use issues associated with using the wood from these logs as a building material should be investigated. For example, in the eastern forest, wood lots are harvested in a very specific way because of the high-quality hardwood species in them. The greatest value logs are veneer logs. These are from large trees with few imperfections, so that they can be rotary sliced into veneer materials and sold at a high cost. Therefore, these hardwood trees are always left to grow as large as possible. As such, many of the local loggers suggest selectively harvesting a wood lot every fifteen to twenty years. This allows the larger trees to be cut for high-quality use, while the middle size trees are left to grow larger within that time. The result is a healthy biodiverse breeding ground for building materials that provides a diverse, albeit relatively small, area for flora, fauna, and habitat.

input into the detailed design solutions under consideration.

B.4.2 Principles and Measurement

■ **Document in detail and validate building performance results against Performance Targets**

- ■ Provide detailed calculations to justify and "prove" the achievement of Performance Targets for all desired environmental performance thresholds across the four key subsystems. Again, if specific Performance Targets are not verified during DD, it probably will be too late, and it probably will not happen. As Ronald Reagan once stated, "Specificity is the soul of credibility."

- ■ For projects pursuing LEED certification, verify compliance with all previously established LEED goals and performance thresholds relative to all pursued LEED credits. This process involves refining targeted performance goals and continuously looking for more synergies between credits. As discussed in *Stage B.2,* interim meetings should be convened, as applicable, to address such cross-disciplinary LEED issues as stormwater management and landscaping, energy performance, daylighting, etc.

■ **Prepare draft Measurement And Verification (M&V) Plan**

Consultation, primarily with the building owner and MEP design engineers, should occur to discuss the project's specific M&V strategies. This meeting will determine the basic approach, the scope of necessary data gathering, and the parties responsible for performing the individual tasks outlined in the M&V plan. The outcome should clarify in more detail the responses to the M&V questions asked during Workshop No. 4, as outlined in *Stage B.3.1.* The basic outline of the M&V plan needs to include the following:

■ How savings are going to be predicted for both water and energy by end use.

■ The specific methodologies for collecting data in the facility post-occupancy, to verify the accuracy of input assumptions used in the predictive calculations. In most cases, these calculations will be those produced by the energy model, with additional spreadsheet calculations of water use.

■ How data collection will be used to modify and adjust the predictive calculations. In many cases, the energy model is calibrated to the building's actual performance by adjusting predictive modeling inputs to actual operating data obtained by the submetering of individual energy end uses, along with additional data gathered with portable meters, staff interviews regarding operations and occupancy, weather files, etc.

■ The adjusted predictive calculations (i.e., the adjusted or calibrated energy-modeling results) are then reconciled with the actual utility bills received during the time frame identified for the M&V effort.

■ Based on the calibrated and reconciled version of the model, a new base case is developed by removing all of the energy-saving strategies and creating a code-compliant version of the model or another agreed-upon base case. The difference between the calibrated model and the revised base case represents the actual savings, as compared to the predictive savings generated during the modeling effort in design.

■ Finally, the plan should include recommendations based on the findings of the M&V effort for areas of potential additional savings. Identify specific energy-efficiency and water-saving measures with calculated savings and costs where applicable. These recommendations should be a part of the development of an action plan in case the predicted savings do not match the actual savings—likely due to the wide array of issues that might not have been predictable during design.

■ **Commissioning**

■ **Invite the Commissioning Authority to review design progress and identify opportunities for further optimization and potential conflicts**

• Up to this point, the responsibility for ensuring that the OPR and BOD are updated at each phase of the project has remained with the design team, as facilitated by the Commissioning Authority. Now that Design Development iterations and associated detailed analysis are being captured and documented, the Commissioning Authority can begin to perform meaningful reviews of this documentation.

• The focus of these reviews is first and foremost to check for consistency between the OPR, BOD, and current DD documentation to identify conflicts that might exist in terms of purpose, Performance Targets, and systems functions.

- The Commissioning Authority also can serve a valuable function during these reviews by exposing the team to places where even deeper integration opportunities might exist to augment optimization, since the Commissioning Authority offers a uniquely objective and holistic viewpoint across systems and disciplines.
- This review should take the form of written comments authored and distributed by the Commissioning Authority to all team members. Each team member considers the comments relative to their documentation and responds to the Commissioning Authority's comments in order to document any impacts.
- This review also should remain sensitive to the progressive nature of the documents. Regardless, comments need to be taken seriously by the design team, respecting the fact that the Commissioning Authority's perspective is intentionally different than that of the designers.
- DD documents should be back-checked by the Commissioning Authority to ensure that revisions and/or responses to all comments have been provided by the appropriate team member, so that these documents can be forwarded to the owner for approval.
- The Commissioning design review, at this stage, should not be reduced to just checking drawings, since the Commissioning Authority is now becoming more focused toward final outcomes, functional testing, and maintenance. As has been stated, designers involved in this process must open themselves and their work to this perspective before their efforts take shape in the field.

A very simple example is found in how HVAC equipment is often scheduled: The designer's first priority is to document the capacity of equipment. Schedules that list equipment with a singular reference applied to multiple units of identical capacity may be easy for the engineer to create, but will not present the entire picture. Equipment must eventually be identified for control programming, for accurate installation, for facility staff access, and for maintenance documentation; so DD documentation of equipment should include clear identifiers for each piece of equipment that will link it to its complete application through installation and operations. For example, equipment schedules that list only 10 unit types, each of which might be applied 5 times, let's say, for a total of 50 units, each intended for a different location in the building do not serve the owner's interest. The implications of such equipment schedules is discussed further in *Stage B.6.2*. Designers accustomed to traditional design and documentation methods typically are resistive to comments of this type in a Commissioning review. But integrative design requires a spirit of cooperation that goes beyond what is the easiest way for one team member to accomplish their task in isolation from the whole.

- It should be noted that in situations where a project is one of multiple projects for a single owner (maybe a hospital or university), the Commissioning Authority may be the only team member with a technical background common to these multiple projects. The Commissioning Authority, then, can serve as the common thread linking together all of the owner's more technical requirements, thereby bringing consistency to the various design teams that may be working on these multiple projects, each of whom brings their own (and usually different) perspectives to this process.

■ **Identify the preliminary list of systems to be commissioned**

- The list of systems to be commissioned likely will start from a generic list, including items such as HVAC systems, lighting systems, plumbing systems, renewable energy systems, controls, and building envelope tailored to project-specific parameters. (See Figure 7-25.)

- The list can become more comprehensive and expanded to include systems such as emergency power, fire suppression, fire alarm, security, key card access, computer data collection, soap dispensing, etc.

- Optimally, specific HVAC system types have been selected at this stage; but, in some cases, such selections may not be able to be finalized at the beginning of DD, depending on project complexity. For instance, reaching final decisions about system types (centralized chiller/boiler plant versus distributed HVAC, ground-source heat pumps versus closed loop or other water-source heat pumps and boilers, etc.) may need another round of analysis and parametric energy modeling runs in the earliest stages of DD to compare the performance of these system types options in more detail—and may include a comparative analysis of emissions generated by the project's available energy sources.

- While specific systems types may not be finalized yet, the range of systems alternatives should be limited to only a few candidates or variants by the end of Schematic Design, so that this detailed optimization analysis can finalize system-type selection very early in this stage at the latest.

- Besides commissioning of primary HVAC systems, building-envelope commissioning is next in importance, if not equally important. In

short, we have found through experience that even if an HVAC system's components are functioning perfectly in accordance with testing and sequence of operations criteria, the HVAC system may fail completely if the building envelope does not perform.

As an illustrative example, several years ago we commissioned a multistory, 100,000-square-foot office building that achieved LEED Gold certification. We were under contract to provide building energy systems commissioning but not building envelope commissioning. Near the end of construction in 2003, we received an admission from the HVAC control technician that he could not achieve enough static pressure to pressurize the building. Imagine the implications of this puzzling piece of news.

This building included a four-story open atrium, served by a complex overhead underfloor air-delivery HVAC system. For us, this admission was not only frustrating, but it also started us on a long journey of discovery that began in construction and continued into the second year of occupancy, which in turn led us back to Design Development envelope detailing. To be fair to the design team, the detailing component of this story is not so much related to this particular building, but it has led us to look for similar problems on almost every subsequent building we have commissioned.

The building was designed with both underfloor air-delivery (the dominant system) and overhead VAV air–delivery arrangements, supplied from the same air-handling unit with the same temperature air to both delivery arrangements. With this type of combined system, coupled with the fact that all four floors intercommunicate through a central open atrium, there

Figure 7-17 Care must be taken during construction to maintain the integrity of the minimally pressurized plenum of underfloor supply-air distribution systems, but performance gains prove the effort worthwhile. An in-depth study on underfloor air systems published in 2002 that identified over 300 case studies reported performance gains for thermal comfort, indoor air quality, energy savings, productivity, churn cost, and overall first-cost savings for underfloor systems. (Loftness, Brahme, Mondazzi [from Carnegie Mellon's Center for Building Performance and Diagnostics], Vineyard, & McDonald [from Oak Ridge National Laboratory], "Energy Savings Potential of Flexible and Adaptive HVAC Distribution Systems for Office Buildings.") *Image courtesy of John Boecker.*

was no way to isolate an individual floor and address the pressurization issues incrementally. When we began addressing the building's lack of ability to maintain pressure, we initially were confronted with too many issues at once to be able to effectively isolate any one issue and deal with it on an individual level. It seemed like we were chasing a moving target, running around in circles, adjusting system-pressure set points, air-delivery temperatures, night-setback temperatures, then performing smoke tests and checking the trending data in a vain effort to discover the source of the problem. We checked the roof curbs around the smoke-evacuation fans for leaks. We verified positive closure of the dampers in the smoke-evacuation fans above the atrium. We verified that the smoke-evacuation fans were actually off. We double-checked the functional performance

of the air-delivery systems. In the summer, we were seeing some spaces overheating, while others were comfortable. In the winter, we saw areas that could not get warm, while others were overheating. We discovered that we had underfloor air-pressurization problems, along with the original building-pressurization problem. In addition, we found that the return-air temperatures were only a few degrees warmer than the supply-air temperatures. We checked and rechecked everything we could think of from an HVAC perspective, but we kept coming up with very little—nothing, in fact, that we could identify as the cause of the overarching problem.

Slowly, we began to understand the sources of the underfloor pressurization issues and focus on them, hoping that this would help. We actively addressed these by sealing the floor

Figure 7-18 Floor diffusers for underfloor air distribution (such as these manufactured by Krantz) serve as metering devices that afford occupants individual thermal-comfort control. *Image ©2001 Jim Schafer.*

plenums (where the contractor, in a few instances, had left large holes in various zones) and making modifications to the ductwork serving the underfloor supply-air system. We began getting somewhat better results, and comfort seemed to be improving, but inconsistently. Further, we still had the original building-pressurization problem. The owner, justifiably, remained unsatisfied.

It was not until the second winter, well over a year into occupancy, that we began to understand the primary cause of the building-pressurization issue. During a site visit on a particularly cold winter day, we noticed ice inside the building below a window. This was in an enclosed office, one of the spaces in which maintaining temperature had been particularly difficult. Further investigation led to discovering significant air infiltration under and around almost every window. We removed the wood trim from around the first window and saw daylight between the window frame and the adjacent steel stud. This initiated a campaign of removing the wood trim from around every window in the entire building. We discovered that the contractor had installed the windows with the standard gap between the window frame and the rough window framing, and as detailed in the CDs, had filled this gap with foam backer rods in some locations—but not well, and without sealant caulking. In many other locations, no backer rod was installed at all. The exterior trim had been installed with a bead of caulking, but there was no proper seal of the air gap to prevent infiltration and exfiltration. The space between the rough opening and the window frames simply had been covered with wood trim—the only air barrier in the entire installation was the intermittent foam backer rod, and this, of course, was not working. (See Figures 7-19 and 7-20.)

The solution was to remove all the foam backer rods at all windows throughout the building and fill the gaps with minimal-expanding-spray polyurethane foam. After the spray foam was installed, we experienced—not surprisingly—a miraculous turn of events. All of a sudden we were able to pressurize the building, and

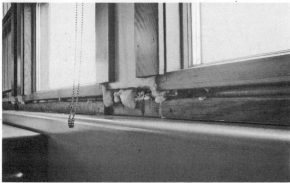

Figure 7-19 This image shows the gap between the window frame and the adjacent rough-opening framing that was discovered during Commissioning as having been left unsealed. The gap size works well, though, when proper sealing of this opening is installed. A gap too small cannot be properly sealed and will be a significant source of infiltration. *Image courtesy Brian Toevs.*

Figure 7-20 Spray foam works better in filling the gap than preformed foam backer rods, because the gap can be filled continuously with no separations. *Image courtesy Brian Toevs.*

the formerly uncontrollable spaces were now maintaining temperature.

The lesson learned from this experience was that HVAC problems are not always the result of HVAC systems in isolation. From this expe-

rience, we learned how significantly envelope detailing and installation impacts proper operation of the building as a whole. We began to recognize more deeply the interrelationships of the building's component parts and how buildings truly function like organisms—if any major component is not functioning well, the ripple effect can be felt in ways that are almost unimaginable. We also now make it a policy to pursue building envelope commissioning on nearly every project. This envelope commissioning is best begun during Design Development document reviews.

A year or so later, we were performing building commissioning services for a school in central Pennsylvania. The school achieved LEED silver certification, but the project team chose not pursue the enhanced commissioning credit, so unfortunately, design reviews were not part of the scope of work.

Armed with the lessons we had learned about building-envelope performance, we made regular site visitations throughout construction, to review the building-shell components, as well as other typically commissioned systems—we were particularly interested in the building-shell construction, having just come off the previous project with all its building-shell problems. We made it a point to pay close attention to the windows; but in this case, with brick and block cavity-wall construction, the opening details were well done and generated little concern.

As the walls and roof went up, and the building was closing in, we started looking at the roof-wall connections. The building's construction consisted of structural steel framing, concrete block and brick veneer with 3 inches of rigid insulation between the brick and block, and a pitched roof with a 4 in 12 slope that created roof overhangs with soffits. The roof construction consisted of corrugated steel decking on structural steel beams with rigid insulation on top of the decking, covered by standing-seam metal roofing.

The issue that emerged with this building also was a building envelope problem, but this time it was related to the air and thermal barrier at the juncture between wall and roofing systems. This story can be told either as a design-focused story or as a construction-focused story; but in this case, the root of many of the issues that led to construction shortcomings can be found in the design detailing. Details depicting where the corrugated roof decking rests on the top of exterior walls called for gaps at the corrugations to be filled with batt insulation or mineral wool, sometimes referred to as "rotten cotton." This rather standard detail became the focus of a threefold set of problems: The first and most obvious issue resulted from the contractor not installing any insulation in many of the corrugations, which is not uncommon. The second problem presented itself where the insulation *was* installed, but it acted more as an air *filter* than an air *barrier*. The third, and worst, issue was that the decking was acoustical; as a result, the sound absorbing perforations along the length of its corrugations allowed not only sound but also air to pass through the decking into and from the uninsulated soffit, with no air barrier between this soffit and the interior space. We identified these issues during construction, bringing them to the attention of the owner, the architect, and the contractor. But the problems were not properly addressed during construction, as evidenced by

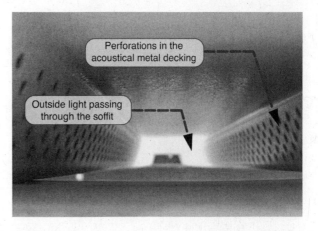

Figure 7-21 This image is taken from inside the gymnasium, up at the roof deck. The image shows the acoustical metal roof decking resting on the exterior masonry wall. The roof decking passes over the wall and a soffit encapsulates the exterior edge of the decking. The image is taken in the middle of the day, and the light shining on the decking is daylight passing through the perforated soffit. This was finished construction, and clearly the flute in the roof-decking corrugation was not filled. (See Figures C-4 through C-7). *Image courtesy Brian Toevs.*

Figure 7-21 and the infrared images depicted in Figures C-4 through C-7—images that we took last winter, nearly three years after construction was completed.

This example illustrates how teams not properly aligned around the more detailed analysis required for high-performance buildings can, with the best intentions, allow themselves to revert to standard practice in Design Development, documentation, and construction. We have come to realize that implementing standard building construction techniques and conventional design practices—"doing it how we've always done it"—will fail more often than not when pursuing the enhanced needs and aspirations of higher-performing buildings. High-performance buildings mandate high-performance design, a process driven by an integrated team aligned around Purpose.

Figures C-3 through C-11 depict images of typical building envelope issues that we have documented on commissioning projects.

■ Prepare preliminary Commissioning Plan

- While the Commissioning Plan is an evolving document, similar to the OPR and BOD in this regard, it is one component of Commissioning (Cx) that needs less attention at this phase. Nevertheless, the importance of a Cx plan cannot be overstated, so preparing a draft of this plan should begin during DD.
- The preliminary draft Commissioning Plan should include an overview of the Cx process in accordance with the contractually agreed-upon scope of services. It serves as a guide for implementing the requirements of the Cx process; this process is detailed in the project's commissioning-related specifications.
- The plan should include the current OPR and BOD, along with their previous iterations, at least in their main outline formats to reinforce that the thrust of the commissioning effort is to serve as a tool for achieving the owner's requirements throughout design and construction.
- Likely, the preliminary Cx Plan will begin as a relatively short (15-page) document. It becomes the outline for the final Commissioning Report. Eventually, as appendices are added, it could evolve into multiple, large-volume, three-ring binders. While this final version of the Cx Plan can take many forms, we have found that keeping the original fifteen-page document format (with multiple indexed appendices) remains the most manageable, since the original fifteen or so pages can remain relatively unchanged or be modified easily, serving as an outline of sorts for appending the plan as additional sections are developed.

- The activities and responsibilities defined in the Cx Plan will need to be developed in close coordination with the project specifications, particularly the spec sections related to Commissioning. These specifications are discussed in the next two stages.

B.4.3   Cost Analysis

■ Utilize integrated cost-bundling templates to optimize value and performance (true value engineering) to conclude cost analysis for all major systems

When faced with apparent cost overages, the big temptation at this point in the design process is to have the builder huddle with the building team and value-engineer the project. It cannot be stressed enough how important it is that this *not* be allowed to occur. An integrated team approach, one that includes all key owner, design, and building team members, is necessary to review pricing and determine optimal ways of cutting costs. This is the purpose of the cost bundling template. It is used to analyze cost more holistically to achieve *true* value—or true value engineering. Team members are there to assure that "value" is maintained via integrated and engineered solutions. Often, great solutions come out of this process. If nothing else, the truths of the design solutions result from this intense scrutiny.

Recently, a university laboratory-classroom project that had theoretically been designed with an integrative approach from the very beginning faced a cost challenge. The president of a very large architecture firm personally attended the integration workshops to encourage the design team—in particular the mechanical engineer—to look aggressively at "right sizing" the mechanical equipment, because he

▶ **Figure 7-22** Table of Contents from a sample Commissioning Plan. *Courtesy of Brian Toevs.*

Commissioning Plan—Construction Phase
Table of Contents

(continued)

knew cost would be a pressure point on this tightly budgeted project. Throughout the project the engineers had firmly stated they had been very rigorous in their energy analysis and that the system, as designed, was the best they could do. We thought otherwise but did not have the opportunity to do a peer review. At the value-engineering session, it became apparent that the mechanical system was the deal breaker on the project, and the project would not be given the go-ahead for construction; the engineers acknowledged that they might be able to pare down the chiller and heat-recovery sizes. After more rigorous and detailed analysis that looked at systems impacts more comprehensively, they came back with a 50 percent reduction in the mechanical system cost—allowing the project to be built.

This story is not unique; subsequently, we experienced almost exactly the same scenario on a $285 million hospital project pursuing LEED Silver level certification, but without utilizing a very rigorous integrative process. We were asked to join the team after the conclusion of schematic design. Again, we were not convinced that systems had been "right-sized" based on our first round of energy modeling analysis during DD. We repeatedly stated our case, but again the design engineers held steadfast to their position that the HVAC systems had been "optimized." Fortunately the project team included an excellent Commissioning Authority who reviewed the design documents and determined independently that HVAC system components were *significantly* oversized. It was clear that systems had been sized based on rules of thumb, without taking into account the interrelationships of the numerous energy-efficiency measures (EEMs) being employed for other systems. The very high cost estimates for the associated HVAC system almost killed the project. The Owner mandated that the HVAC systems be redesigned and resized, taking into account all of the EEMs, and after an additional two months devoted to this effort, an HVAC system was documented that met the budget and resulted in a 20% annual energy savings.

B.4.4 Schedule and Next Steps

■ **Extend forward the Integrative Process Road Map tasks and schedule through the Documentation phase and begin integrating with the builder if this has not yet occurred**

The tasks and schedule in the Integration Process Road Map need to be extended through the documentation phase, and this road map should now begin integrating with the builder, if this has not yet occurred.

At this point, the process of moving into Construction Documentation can be made smoother by beginning to develop the specifications, so that they are more than legalese—they are instructive to the contractors and trades. Specifications are critically important documents for clearly defining and holding the unique aspects of a green building. Initiating the writing of specifications as a team in an integrated process, particularly where issues cross disciplines, helps ensure that the design team is aligned around what needs to be communicated to construction professionals. This is best accomplished by involving the builder in this process, if possible. This full team involvement contrasts dramatically from the conventional approach of relegating wholesale the spec-writing to a detached spec-writer decoupled from the team and is an important step in helping ease the frustration that sometimes accompanies the introduction of unfamiliar ideas, techniques, and technologies.

A detailed description of the specific content required in these specifications is beyond the scope of this book; further, there are numerous resources currently available in the marketplace devoted to this subject, so we need not repeat those efforts here. However, the purpose and general structure of specifications will be explored further in the next two stages.

■ **Prepare Agenda for Workshop No. 5**

This next workshop is the point at which all issues are finalized. It is the last efficient point for resolving and addressing with the entire team any outstanding issues with regard to achieving high environmental Performance Targets. All key stakeholders should attend.

Stage B.5

Workshop No. 5: Construction Documents Kickoff—Performance Verification and Quality Control

B.5.1 Workshop No. 5 Activities

- Verify achievement of all Performance Targets
- Present and verify the integrated performance of the project as an interrelated whole
- Identify where Specifications will need to be altered to effectively document project performance and integrate the four key subsystems (habitat, water, energy, and materials)
- Verify final cost bundling analysis and cost impacts related to all major systems and components
- Commissioning: Review Commissioning Plan for alignment with BOD and schedule Commissioning review at mid-construction-documents phase

B.5.2 Principles and Measurement

- Document final Performance Targets
- Review draft Measurement and Verification (M&V) Plan
- Commissioning: Update OPR, BOD, and Commissioning Plan to reflect input from Workshop No. 5

B.5.3 Cost Analysis

- Document integrated cost implications of final design decisions

B.5.4 Schedule and Next Steps

- Plan quality control review process of Construction Documents
- Distribute Workshop No. 5 Report

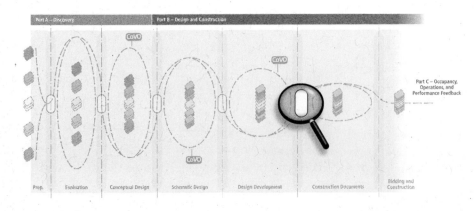

Figure 7-23 Integrative Process Stage B.5, Workshop #5: Construction Documents Kick-Off. *Image courtesy of 7 group and Bill Reed; graphics by Corey Johnston.*

Stage B.5

Workshop No. 5: Construction Documents Kickoff—Performance Verification and Quality Control

The design is done. The four key subsystems are no longer separate. They are now part of a whole. To proceed confidently with the documentation phase, it will be worthwhile to have a final review of project intentions. Did we miss anything during the intensity of the DD stage? Are there any last opportunities to integrate systems that may have slipped through the process? In preparing for this workshop, make sure the data to support the actual achievement of expected performance results is available. All generalizations and guesswork should now be put to rest with concrete performance calculations.

The principal objective in this workshop is to design the documentation process in ways that can best integrate and communicate the details of the project, so that the systems can be effectively priced and constructed. In addition to clear, communicative drawings, designing a process for developing meaningful, thorough, and understandable specifications is a key aspect of this phase; this process needs to be addressed by the entire team at the workshop.

B.5.1 Workshop No. 5 Activities

■ **Verify achievement of all Performance Targets**

Documentation of all performance criteria related to design Performance Targets should be complete or very near completion. Documentation protocols and/or templates for documenting the design Performance Targets related to construction issues should also be established; these relate to issues over which the builder has final control, such as materials procurement, construction and demolition waste, construction indoor air quality measures, building-envelope integrity, air infiltration, and so on.

If the documentation of design Performance Targets is not complete, develop a plan for doing so.

For LEED projects, the status of achieving the requirements for all targeted credits should be finalized, and responsibilities for producing required documentation for all design credits should be discussed and clarified.

■ **Present and verify the integrated performance of the project as an interrelated whole**

All disciplines should have coordinated and integrated the systems for which they are responsible in a way that accounts for overlapping benefits. There will be performance results that are dependent on the performance of other systems. Are the boundaries and overlaps as they relate to documentation responsibilities specifically understood and addressed?

■ **Identify where Specifications will need to be altered to effectively document project performance and integrate the four key subsystems (habitat, water, energy, and materials)**

It is necessary for the design team, and also the building team (if possible), to come to an agreement on the design of the specification structure and philosophy. There are a few different philosophies about specification structure and purpose. We have found that these range across three primary areas of focus: *first*, that specs serve primarily a legal function; *second*, that the specs are manuals that stipulate project systems for the purpose of pricing and purchasing products and their installation; and *third*, that specs are instruction books with a subtext that explains the rationale for systems, so that these systems are more likely to be installed and perform correctly.

In conventional construction, where many systems are purchased and installed in a conventional manner, there is not great need for a set of detailed instructions—these systems generally are those with which tradespeople have had years of experience. A relatively straightforward legal and performance specification approach is adequate to achieve a satisfactory result.

However, new technologies, products, construction techniques, and commissioned installation methods that benefit from a more integrated systems approach may require the specifications to be more explicit about why and how the expected results are to be achieved. This is especially true with issues relating to the achievement of high performance for the components of the four key subsystems and to the commissioning process.

This is not to say that legal issues should not to be addressed; they need to be included, but perhaps in a different location or with sections structured so as not to confuse the new information that needs to be conveyed to the trades in the field with legal boilerplate. Often, specifications suffer from an overabundance of legalistic terms and technical references that in the reality of work in the field are never consulted, unless the project goes into litigation—not a very smart way to achieve an expected result.

Victor Canseco, a builder-construction manager with whom we have worked repeatedly over the years, issues what he calls "Bidding Guides" to each trade during bidding. These guides include a project description, scope of work, insurance rider, bid form, instructions to bidders, a job-information sheet that consolidates legal requirements and boilerplate issues into a brief document, and significantly streamlined germane specifications that he calls "primary specification sections." He strips away everything but the essential information required for both pricing and construction, removing the layers of legalese and references to arcane standards; in other words, he issues this "essentialized" spec to each potential subcontractor. This streamlined version of the specifications addresses in clear, simple terms—using language understood by tradespeople in the field, not just attorneys and estimators back in the office—what the performance standards and criteria need to be for providing and executing each product and system. He reports that when he began doing this fifteen years ago, he started getting tighter bid results and better performance in the field. He also claims that he has yet to be sued. Victor once demonstrated this approach for a relatively small project by holding up the project's spec book; it was several inches thick. He then held up a second stack of the specification pages from the project's Bidding Guides that he had issued, containing what he had determined was the essential information required to price and construct the project in the field; this stack was less than one inch thick.

Such approaches, along with the structure and philosophy of the specifications, should be discussed and a plan of action agreed upon at this workshop.

■ **Verify final cost bundling analysis and cost impacts related to all major systems and components**

This is the time that cost bundling can be very important with regard to preparing for final estimating. The overly simplistic approach to value engineering again needs to be resisted; that is to say, avoid the temptation to reduce the quality of a product or remove a product or system from the project on a line-item cost basis. The impact on and performance of the whole project needs to be analyzed when attempting to understand whether a product or systems should be removed. Providing bidding alternates is a common practice, but caution should be exercised to avoid eliminating key system elements that will degrade the whole. Consequently, strategies for bidding alternates should be discussed, so that any and all alternates can be identified at this workshop.

It is useful at this workshop to set up a few cost-focused engineering meetings with the estimator and builder (if possible) that include key client team members, the architect, engineers, and systems designers. Isolated meetings with only the builder and architect or owner—without the expertise and input of other team members to constitute a composite master builder—often do significant damage to the performance, and ultimately the cost benefit, of projects.

■ **Commissioning: Review Commissioning Plan for alignment with BOD and schedule Commissioning review at mid-construction-documents phase**

Specific dates for review of construction documents midway through their production need to be discussed and coordinated with all team members, with allowances threaded into the schedule for the Commissioning Authority's review time, along with the team's time frame for responding to these comments. Appropriate deadlines should be defined at this workshop.

As indicated above, specifications will inform the contractors of their process responsibilities related to Commissioning. With the BOD evolving and with possible updates relative to cost estimating, this is the stage where any realistically foreseeable cost impact for commissioning should be revealed and discussed, as mentioned in *Stage B.3.3*. The Commissioning Authority will know the extent of primary systems to be commissioned, based on their involvement during design, along with where Commissioning specifications will begin to address quantifiable expectations relative to the contractor's involvement in the process. Construction estimators will need to see where real cost impacts on contractors might appear, such as keeping current construction checklists, involvement in the functional testing, and furnishing devices for these tests. What needs to be understood by the team is that the "cost of commissioning" should not be freely incorporated, based solely on someone's "pitch" or on the number of pages in a specification or drawing set. Estimators of such costs need to understand that they must discern the difference between where the commissioning process is really adding work and where it is simply verifying work as a standard element—though an element not always delivered—of the traditional design and construction process.

B.5.2 Principles and Measurement

■ **Document final Performance Targets**

As with all prior workshops, any performance adjustments resulting from Workshop No. 5, as described above, need to be distributed to the project team in order to ensure that all team members understand their responsibilities for documenting their systems accordingly during *Stage B.6*. At this point in the process, all performance criteria should be finalized, pending only very minor adjustments, if necessary.

For projects pursuing LEED certification, a revised LEED scorecard should be distributed to the project team that documents the status of all pursued credits. Decisions pertaining to all design-phase credits should be finalized. Responsibilities for incorporating LEED requirements into the CDs should be clearly defined and assigned to all appropriate team members. Also, the various components of documentation required for submission to the U.S. Green Building Council (USGBC) for all design credits should be assigned to appropriate team members as well, so that this documentation can be completed in parallel with the completion of Construction Documents.

■ **Review draft Measurement and Verification (M&V) Plan**

The draft M&V plan should be reviewed with the entire team to verify that it includes all appropriate components for providing the desired feedback after construction and revised as necessary. Responsibilities for each affected team member should be identified for all components of the plan (as described in *Stage B.4.2*) regarding the components that will need to be incorporated into the Construction Documents drawings and specifications, such as controls systems metering and/or submetering devices for identified end uses, data loggers, etc.

- ■ **Commissioning: Update OPR, BOD, and Commissioning Plan to reflect input from Workshop No. 5**

The final Performance Targets determined by the team at Workshop No. 5 should be fully integrated into the OPR and BOD documents. Performance Targets constitute a critical component of the Commissioning process; the Commissioning Authority will incorporate them into the checklists and performance tests that will be created for all related systems during *Stage B.6*.

B.5.3 Cost Analysis

- ■ **Document integrated cost implications of final design decisions**

Typically, in the midst of the pressure to produce final bidding documents, there often is a temptation to pull elements out of the project to achieve lower costs. Evidence that the team has analyzed integrated cost bundles, in the form of cost bun-

dling spreadsheets, can avoid this problem. The cost bundles can demonstrate that the elimination of some line items may be very expensive if pursued outside of the context of the whole project cost and in light of operations cost returns.

For example, removing exterior shading devices will have implications for daylighting design, glare control, window selection, and HVAC system sizing. All components are connected; some of these connections have potentially greater cost implications than others.

B.5.4 Schedule and Next Steps

- ■ **Plan quality control review process of Construction Documents**

Specify the dates, specific disciplines to be addressed, and review methods to coordinate the check sets and final set of CDs. This now includes incorporation of the Commissioning Authority's Design reviews and team responses.

- ■ **Distribute Workshop No. 5 report**

This report should primarily be focused on process due dates, interim check-set deliverables, team member responsibilities, and coordination meetings necessary to achieve a final set of coherent and integrated drawings and specifications documents.

Stage B.6
Construction Documents—No More Designing

B.6.1 Documentation Activities

- Complete Bidding Documents with thorough Specifications that communicate both performance requirements and project intentions for integrating the four key subsystems

- Commissioning: Update Commissioning Plan and insert Commissioning requirements into Specifications

B.6.2 Principles and Measurement

- Finalize performance calculations to validate final design and document results

- Produce final Measurement and Verification (M&V) Plan to build performance measurement and feedback mechanisms into project

- Commissioning: Perform detailed review of Drawings and Specifications to ensure consistency with OPR and BOD

B.6.3 Cost Analysis

- Review unique cost implications with builder and finalize cost estimate

B.6.4 Schedule and Next Steps

- Schedule quality control reviews of Construction Documents

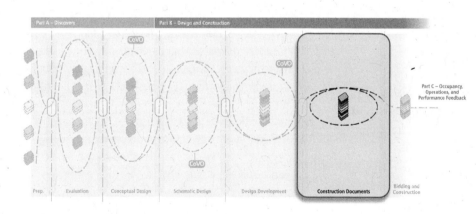

Figure 7-24 Integrative Process Stage B.6, Construction Documents. *Image courtesy of 7 group and Bill Reed; graphics by Corey Johnston.*

Stage B.6

Construction Documents—No More Designing

In the best of worlds, this stage is a disciplined process of drawing and specification documentation. *Disciplined* means that there are check points along the way that will verify the systemic integration and coordination of systems through the Construction Documents. We need to state—somewhat facetiously—that this is more than the typical process of checking to ensure that beams do not conflict with sprinkler pipes or ductwork that, in turn, do not conflict with light fixtures, etc. To achieve a deep optimization of systems, almost every decision and interrelationship needs to be understood and reconfirmed. It is necessary to make sure that the people doing the technical documentation understand why and how decisions have been made, so that they can "think into" the issues and resolve any remaining discrepancies with the same level of creativity and understanding that informed the design team's integration of the four key subsystems. This is where the Building Information Modeling (BIM) tools discussed at the beginning of Chapter 6 will be very useful.

B.6.1 Documentation Activities

- **Complete Bidding Documents with thorough Specifications that communicate both performance requirements and project intentions for integrating the four key subsystems**

  We have found that currently the level of green building knowledge and experience differs in every region and that the level of understanding of such projects on the part of various builders and subcontractors varies in each city and place. The drawings and, in particular, the specifications should be produced and written in a way that conveys the information in a clear and comprehensible manner; how that information ultimately is conveyed may need to be tai-

lored to the knowledge base of the contracting pool in a given place.

Recently, in a city where the economic climate was very healthy, few subcontractors were interested in working on green projects, because they had all the work they needed and more. When approached with a specification that mentioned green and LEED, their almost automatic reaction was to add 20 percent to their bids in order to deal with the "hassle factor" of unusual requirements. In this case, for a public project that precluded design-phase builder involvement, we pulled all references to *green* out of the specification and used what we named a *bait-and-teach* approach. Once the apparent low and responsible bidder was told they had received the award for their portion of the work on the project, we invited them to discuss some possible options—such as alternate materials or Construction and Demolition waste management protocols. We found the subcontractors were much more willing to learn and experience something new when they believed that they had already been awarded the work. This context made them more open to understanding the purpose of the new ideas, and to seeing that these options were not that alien to their normal practices. This practice only lasted a year or two, until there was more interest in environmental work and green buildings in that area. We mention this to make the point that it is necessary to know the local skill sets and competition that exist in the project's place. In other locations, by the way, we have seen strong interest in green buildings where builders have begun to use their experience on such projects as a market differentiator.

- **Commissioning: Update Commissioning Plan and insert Commissioning requirements into Specifications**

  - The systems to be commissioned are gathered from the effort to date and posted in commissioning specifications, as well as in the draft ver-

HVAC System	Electrical System
Water Source Heat Pumps	Power Distribution System—Switchboards
Hydronic Piping Systems	Variable Speed Drives
HVAC Pumps	Engine Generators
Various Unit Heaters	Transfer Switches
HVAC Chemical Treatment System	Lighting Control Systems
Air Handling Units	Installation of Individual Motor Control
Radiant Heating and Cooling Units	Equipment Systems Power
Building Maintenance and Control System (DCC)—Including an intentional sequence of operation	Fire Alarm and Interface Items with HVAC (i.e.: smoke evacuation, smoke dampers, et cetera)
Ductwork	**Other**
Fire/Smoke Dampers	Building Insulation Installation
Centrifugal Fans	Building Roof Installation Methods
Testing, Adjusting, & Balancing	Doors & Windows Installation Methods
Building/Space Pressurization	Water Infiltration/Shell Drainage Plain
Fire Pumps and Controllers	Shell Flashing Details

Figure 7-25 List of systems to be commissioned from a sample project.

sion of a Commissioning Plan. Systems that are most commonly considered appear in Figure 7-25. Any renewable energy systems should be included as well.

▦ Once the systems to be commissioned are established, a list of the equipment in each of these systems is developed. The result of this effort is the creation of a tracking form in the Commissioning Plan.

▦ From the tracking form, individual construction checklists for each piece of equipment to be commissioned are created in the Commission-

ing Plan as well. Development of construction checklists begins as specific equipment is identified. As part of this process, it is necessary first to identify on these checklists the equipment and associated parameters as they are defined in the Basis of Design document. This carries the earmarks of the BOD into the field and provides a comparative standard for evaluating potential alternatives and substitutions. Accordingly, space is dedicated on these checklists for documenting what is submitted by contractors through the construction submittal process, again providing a chance to reflect on the details of the BOD for comparative purposes when evaluating specific equipment submissions. Finally, space is allotted for recording what is actually installed. Again, contractors may look upon this as wasteful and time-consuming paperwork, but this paperwork draws people into focusing on details that are very important to the integrity of the team's efforts—a process aimed at satisfying the goals of the OPR through the defined performance parameters of the BOD that are then translated into the field.

- Development of a Functional Performance Tests (FPT) tracking form in the Commissioning Plan follows, based on the systems listed above. This serves as a guide for creating functional performance tests of all commissioned systems and equipment. It outlines a methodology for gathering the related information from submittals and design documents that will enable the Commissioning Authority to develop testing protocols and performance parameters to verify that the intended sequences of operations are functional.

- Commissioning specifications (developed in parallel with the Commission Plan) typically impact several sections of the administrative divisions of a project's specifications, including such sections as Project Management and Coordination, Submittal Procedures, Quality Requirements, Closeout Procedures, Operations and Maintenance, Data and Demonstration, and Training—all are touched by the commissioning process. More pointedly, a dedicated General Commissioning Requirements specification section is often nested in Division 1 with other specifications joined to the traditional 15000 (Mechanical Systems) and 16000 (Electrical Systems) Divisions that will spell out trade responsibilities related to installation commissioning. It also provides examples of related documentation tools, such as construc-

tion checklists and functional performance test tracking forms (more about these in Chapter 8).

B.6.2 Principles and Measurement

- **Finalize performance calculations to validate final design and document results**

This is self-explanatory—all final calculations verifying achievement of Performance Targets should be cross-checked with final documentation of all related systems.

- **Produce final Measurement and Verification (M&V) Plan to build performance measurement and feedback mechanisms into project**

The final M&V plan should be prepared as outlined in *Stage B.4.2*. The submetering needs identified in the plan should be incorporated into the final construction documents. If the submetering will be tied to the building's energy management system, then coordination with the building controls system components will be necessary. The post-occupancy implementation of the plan should be discussed so that any contractual arrangements necessary to implement the M&V plan post-occupancy can be agreed upon and executed.

- **Commissioning: Perform detailed review of Drawings and Specifications to ensure consistency with OPR and BOD**

Perspective is very important at this stage. The Commissioning Authority is more than a drawing checker. Redlining obvious incompleteness and noncompliance with the BOD does little to build relationships with the design team, so the Commissioning Authority can be most helpful by also adopting the perspective of the eventual facility manager. As such, the Commissioning Authority can help the team gain early insight into how the documented design conveys both installation instruction and end-user accessibility. A good example of these two perspectives can be illustrated in the review of equipment schedules for major HVAC systems. So what is in the name assigned to a piece of equipment?

For example, an *air handler* is scheduled for a designated area of service. It follows that the area of service defines the area of load for that air handler, and thereby its capacity. Typically, an air handler will *support* numerous local-zone fan coils, VAV units, or heat pumps on one side, and it may *be supported by* various pumps and heat exchangers on the other—an entire system of components, with the air handler in the center of a very specific set of localized circumstances. In the scheduling of this air handling unit, though, engineers are chiefly concerned with capacities and ease of documentation, so they frequently schedule major equipment based on capacity, and then assign the same unit number (e.g., AHU-1, or air handling unit 1) to all similar units serving various other spaces or zones in multiple locations throughout the building. The same name, AHU-1, is used in both the equipment schedule and on the mechanical plans for each of these locations, for example, in seven different places. Although all seven of these units may be identical, the individual location-specific issues associated with each can differ considerably in the field.

The Commissioning Authority, then, might think about who is affected by naming all of these units AHU-1 once they find their way into the field. Delivering and storing each air handler upon arrival involves trade contractors, haulers, factory workers, and product reps. Setting and installing the air handler into its correct place at the center of each location-specific system then involves the HVAC contractor, the electrician, perhaps the plumber, the fire alarm installer, the controls provider, the test and balance technician, various building code inspectors, and the Commissioning Authority, all of whom likely will need to coordinate their issues about AHU-1, but which one are we talking about when they all have the same name?

Once each air handler is started and commissioned, it becomes the responsibility of the owner and his facilities team. How do we introduce each of these air handlers to the maintenance technician? Do we show him on the equipment schedule that this is AHU-1 and walk away? What is the number one concern that the maintenance technician has about each air handler? He wants to know what area, or areas, of the building each specific unit serves. And what about all of the equipment supported by AHU-1?

For each piece of HVAC equipment (e.g., a series of heat pumps, each called HP-2) we can assign the same litany of localized connections and conditions that we have identified for AHU-1. Then we might also have a similar set of players all trying to coordinate installation and connections to HP-2—again, which HP-2 are we talking about? And for each of these pieces of equipment, the maintenance technician will have the same chief concern he had about AHU-1.

So much depends on the designers' scheduled equipment identification, from delivery through installation and into operations. Unless the engineer begins with some geographic orientation for naming equipment in the schedules, the installation process will be confusing at best and will not meet the owner's end-use needs or performance targets. When asked to consider such location-specific naming in a Commissioning design review log, designers will often object, making reference to how room numbers are not complete or are subject to change, so there is no point in doing it that way—but there are other ways to schedule a piece of equipment so that it is tied to a specific location in the building. Resolving this issue early in the process is just one more example of where OPR and BOD must converge to inform design documentation, not only for achieving end results but also for affecting the required steps leading to those end results in the field.

B.6.3 Cost Analysis

■ **Review unique cost implications with builder and finalize cost estimate**

This may seem like a late date to be determining the cost of the building, but the reality is that you will not know for sure what the costs are even now. Estimating is a process of progressive confirmation, and this is the case no matter what design process you are using. However, project-specific unique components are particularly germane to green projects, so this serves simply as a reminder

to ensure that they are discussed and understood in the final estimate.

B.6.4 Schedule and Next Steps

■ **Schedule quality control reviews of construction documents**

Depending on the complexity of the project, quality control reviews may include peer review of the CD package, or these may have been addressed via BIM tools. Ultimately, quality control is about getting the team to take the time to collectively walk through the construction documents conceptually with a focus on the intended performance of the project, so that the team is in alignment with the final documents that will guide construction and operations, which is the subject of the next chapter.

8

Construction, Operations, and Feedback

Perfection is achieved not when there is nothing more to add, but when there is nothing left to take away.

—Antoine de Saint-Exupéry, aviator, writer, and philosopher; translated from the French, "Il semble que la perfection soit atteinte non quand il n'y a plus rien à ajouter, mais quand il n'y a plus rien à retrancher." From Antoine de Saint-Exupéry, *Terre des Hommes (Land of Men),* Paris: Gallimard Education, 1998, original copyright 1939 (Translated into English as *Wind, Sand, and Stars* in 1939)

However beautiful the strategy, you should occasionally look at the results.

—Winston Churchill

At this point in the process we have completed a final set of construction documents that now is ready for bidding. Generally speaking, this documentation takes the form of a large stack of drawings and a much larger stack of bound paper and/or electronic specifications that are issued to contractors for final pricing. As you may recall from Chapter 1, our conventional process faces an abyss that exists between design and construction professionals. We expect construction professionals during bidding to understand the hundreds of thousands of person-hours of research, analysis, decision making, and documentation that are embedded into these bidding documents in a matter of a mere week or two. This "understanding" is reached by multiple separate contractors and subcontractors reviewing fragmented and incomplete sets of bidding documents in isolation from one other.

These bidding contractors and construction professionals often understand quite well *how* to build what is documented, and they generally understand the basic concepts behind the design of the systems they are pricing. But in a conventional process no communication is provided to them about *why* these systems were designed the way they were. They likely do not even know what decisions were made and what options were discarded, much less what intentions drove these choices. Hence, bidding contractors may be seeing what needs to be done through the lens of "how we've always done it." This perception can potentially be magnified when an integrative process is implemented. The design team's intentions and discoveries are likely to lead to less conventional solutions and interrelationships when all systems have been analyzed through the lens of a larger whole, as opposed to conventionally optimized systems in isolation—and another layer of misunderstanding is likely to emerge.

Further, the conventional bidding process is conducted by breaking the whole of the design (which was assembled in fragments to begin with) into fragmented pieces again, with each system being priced in isolation by separate construction professionals. Each prime contractor or subcontractor typically gets only a small piece of the bidding documents—the sections that pertain only to his or her area of purview. These sections are sometimes not even full systems by themselves. Like the design professionals, these construction professionals possess tremendous acumen in understanding the systems within their purview; but also, like the designers, these contractors find themselves stuck within silos that have them looking at their components in isolation. In many cases, they are contractually obligated to do so.

Worse yet, the construction professionals conventionally have had little or no input into the design and decision-making process. The abyss is widened and deepened, since no interaction whatsoever occurs between design and construction professionals until bidding and construction begin. And then, as mentioned in Chapter 1, this very complex and unique product (a building) that never has been built before (nor will be again) is constructed with no opportunity for working out the bugs until it is being constructed or is completed. Finally, it gets worse yet again: this process is implemented by construction and design professionals that more or less are obligated to function as adversaries, due to a contractually reinforced misalignment of purpose.

In short, this "perverse construction delivery methodology" leaves innovations unleveraged, because any improvements that occur are confined to their silos and secluded from the whole. Consequently, our buildings are fraught with redundancies, unnecessary costs, and a great deal of wasted time and effort, not to mention a whole set of malfunctioning components. Revisited in this context, it is not surprising that 90 percent[*] of the buildings in the United States experience either controls problems or nonfunctioning heating, ventilating, and air-conditioning (HVAC) components—or both—upon occupancy and during the first year of operations. This number may in fact be higher—perhaps even 100 percent. Remember the cabin in the woods from Figure 1-15?

THE EVOLVING COMMISSIONING PROCESS

We believe that these malfunctions are the result of a fragmented design and construction process exacerbated by an utter lack of any quality control (QC) mechanism. The integrative design and commissioning process provides a means for beginning to fill this quality control gap and for bridging the disconnect

---

[*]Based on data from the Lawrence Berkley National Laboratory in a survey of 60 newly constructed buildings in 1998. Remarkably, 15% of these buildings were *missing* equipment that had been specified and documented in the construction documents.

between design and construction professionals, as we have discussed in prior chapters. High-quality commissioning, then, is a critical component of the integrative design process.

One of our partners recently quipped: "Every project in America has a Commissioning Plan, and here it is: We know it's not going to work once occupied, so we're going to fix it during the warranty period, and then we're going to pay additional fees in service calls or service contracts to fix problems that didn't get solved during that warranty period." This observation invites the question: how can we construct an *intentional* commissioning plan aimed at overcoming this condition? Owners have begun asking this question. They have recognized the current condition as untenable and unacceptable. Many want to engage such an intentional commissioning plan, but they are still trying to figure out exactly what is the best form or process for implementing that plan. One thing is for sure: the process of commissioning is still evolving, and what we believe to be correct today may or may not be the best process tomorrow—commissioning itself is evolving.

What we see today is that commissioning is not construction, and it is not design—but it *influences* both. The Commissioning Authority (CxA) is an odd term, because the CxA has no actual contractual authority to change the design at any time in the project or to direct construction activities. With these apparent drawbacks, the CxA must rely on other skill sets to accomplish the work of ensuring design compliance and systems performance during construction. Besides technical expertise, some of the most important skills required of a good CxA are the ability to communicate, collaborate, mediate, remain objective, and most of all, remain calm. This becomes especially important in the midst of what remains—in the minds of many—essentially a traditional construction process with an extra player. The CxA often is perceived as

either just another inspector—another cop—or conversely, and even worse, as a troubleshooting tool for helping contractors complete their final closeout.

So what is construction phase commissioning, really? Well in short, it is quality control, right? But how is that implemented? What is the process? Currently, most presentations and seminars aimed at teaching the commissioning process identify three phases: design, construction, and acceptance. From our traditional process, all of us can identify the design phase as quite discrete, and we certainly recognize the duration of the construction phase; the design phase ends with the completion of Construction Documents, and the construction phase generally ends at "substantial completion," named such because this milestone generates substantial payment and the commencement of the warranty period. But where in the traditional process do we find an identifiable acceptance phase? Where in this process does the functional performance of the building's systems get verified? The simple answer is nowhere. This phase is new. As we have identified above, most of the time, the "acceptance phase," currently, consists of fixing problems through the warranty period to some nebulous point beyond: Engineers often tell us that they commission every project—it just occurs over the first five years of occupancy, and they have no documentation to show for it, other than invoices for their services.

Where in this process might "functional completion" occur? Perhaps an equivalent in the traditional process might be the completion of an engineer's punch list? Providing inspection certifications and operations and maintenance (O&M) documentation? Issuing an occupancy permit? The problem here is that each of these events is a static representation of a dynamic, almost organic, living project. When are components even tested for functional performance, let alone deemed functionally complete? For building conditioning systems, "testing, adjusting, and balancing" occurs, but even testing, adjusting, and balancing (TAB) reports represent isolated static conditions prior to the actual use of a fully functioning facility. So, again, we conclude that the traditional 12-month warranty period of the conventional construction delivery methodology serves, more often than not, as a less than ad hoc acceptance phase. During this period, functional performance is tested by means of addressing complaints and premature failure. This may correct system deficiencies, but it does not provide any feedback for improving the overall design process nor does it test systems performance—and it comes nowhere close to measuring the resources lost to well-intended equipment installation that perhaps never gains the full benefit of efficient operation. In the traditional construction delivery process, then, not only is there no defined acceptance period but what constitutes acceptance and functional completion goes undefined as well.

An *intentional* commissioning process establishes a discrete acceptance phase and defines criteria for functional completion. Performing successful functional tests in accordance with the Commissioning Plan's clearly defined protocols and quantified compliance constitutes functional completion. The commissioning plan generally identifies that undefined gray area between *substantial completion* and *occupancy* as where the acceptance phase for such functional testing wants to reside. However, although the acceptance phase truly is an extension of construction, it also seems to want to occur during early occupancy, when system use actually begins and loads on these systems are real. Facilities such as hospitals and public safety institutions may not lend themselves to testing during occupancy, but these are exceptions to the majority of building types that do indeed lend themselves to early occupancy testing and tune-ups. Buildings like schools, offices, university facilities, and other non-critical buildings can benefit from a slightly delayed

functional testing period. Every project suffers from completion anxiety; often, a delayed functional testing period will allow the trades to properly complete last-minute items that can become critical to delivering a successful project.

Defining what *successful* means is, in fact, part of the Commissioning process. If success means bridging the communication gap between design and construction professionals and also bridging the gap between abstract design intentions and actual building performance, then our experience with the commissioning process gives us cause for optimism about the future. If the purpose of commissioning is to build both better relationships and better buildings, we see signs that these early commissioning efforts hold great promise for the building industry. Perhaps the most important bridge that commissioning will provide, as it evolves, is the bridge from our current fragmented process to a future in which commissioning will no longer be necessary.

LEARNING FROM FEEDBACK

Such a future will depend on how our process evolves, which in turn is dependent on continuously inputting feedback from the results of our integrative process into that process for the purpose of evolving it further. According to Wikipedia, "Feedback is a process whereby some proportion of the output signal of a system is passed (fed back) to the input. This is often used to control the dynamic behavior of the system." (http://en.wikipedia.org/wiki/Feedback, accessed June 2008) Within the design and construction industry, there is a definitive lack of feedback. As we have seen, much of the feedback that currently is received comes in the form of major problems during the facility's initial warranty period, requiring designers and contractors to revisit and troubleshoot in search of a solution. This feedback is almost always negative—complaints about this or that system not working properly; therefore, designers and contractors usually are reluctant to share any lessons learned for fear of scaring away future clients. Positive feedback tends to be strictly anecdotal, such as the owner telling the architect that they like this or that aspect of the building.

To create better buildings that achieve a far greater level of performance, the building industry needs to create additional avenues of feedback in order to learn and evolve. Too often, designers and contractors keep doing the same thing over and over, not necessarily because it really works well, but because they have not received any negative feedback in the form of too many complaints (or lawsuits). Building owners, designers, and contractors should be investing time to create opportunities for receiving feedback in the interest of learning how to improve the performance of future projects.

In its simplest form, this feedback can consist of activities ranging from simple follow-through to gathering performance data, such as energy use and cost. Feedback also could include more sophisticated data gathering, such as post-occupancy evaluations (POE) or complex analysis of multiple systems, such as full Measurement and Verification (M&V) studies, both of which have already been introduced, but will be discussed in detail later in this chapter. Whatever form it takes, the purpose of generating feedback is to learn from what works and what does not work, so that we can do a better job next time.

Post-occupancy evaluation is an important practice that addresses how buildings and their occupants perform in relation to each other and to their larger context. Beyond the relatively simple measurement and verification of energy performance—based on quantifiable indicators such as utility bills, energy metering, and so on—POE addresses issues that quantify and assess the quality of life and health of a building, its place, and its occupants and, in the future, will address the health of the living systems of the site and region that are impacted by our structures and operation.

FEEDBACK LOOPS

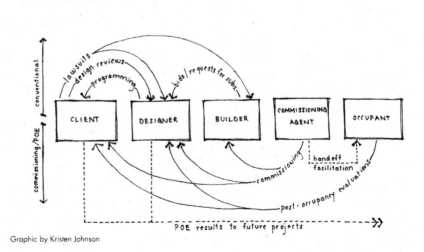

Figure 8-1 Feedback loops from commissioning and post-occupancy evaluations (POEs) reach far beyond those of the standard design and construction process. The information and insights from this feedback can improve the current project and inform future projects. *This graph by Kristen Johnson originally appeared in "Post-Occupancy Evaluations Learning from Experience with Green Buildings,"* Environmental Building News, *September 2003.*

Graphic by Kristen Johnson

Post-occupancy evaluations can be a one-time event. However, these evaluations are most effective when implemented as a continuous process of feedback. In terms of practicality, there are systems whose performance can be measured continuously with relative ease, by looking at factors such as energy consumption and maintenance costs. Other, less quantifiable metrics—such as employee productivity, wellness, psychological health, and the health of other natural systems—beyond the building's physical systems are assessed periodically.

To close the loop on design, POE is necessary. This loop consists of gathering feedback to inform both the current project's performance and the evolution of the design process. Measured outputs from the building's systems are passed back as input for the purpose of making adjustments and improving their performance; via such feedback mechanisms, we can understand the effectiveness of our design decisions—we can then improve how and what we think about, allowing us to address more systematically and intentionally future design endeavors. Like with any organism, feedback from a building's systems (including its occupants) serves a vital function in terms of sustaining an organic and healthy whole system.

HERE'S WHERE WE ARE

We have completed the construction documents. Again, we now have large stacks of drawings and specifications (or huge electronic files) that are issued for bidding. These documents are distributed to all potential prime bidders and subcontractors, who are given four weeks or so (which in reality means one or two weeks) to put a price on the work defined by these documents.

Not long after bidding documents hit the street, a Pre-Bid Conference is convened to review bidding procedures, clarify alternates, point out special conditions, and identify unique aspects of the project with prospective bidders.

Somewhere in the middle of this pricing effort, a series of clarification questions are submitted to the architecture and engineering (A/E) team. Often, responses to these questions and requests for clarifications are accompanied by addenda to the bidding documents. More often, *addenda* are published that alter the bidding documents to incorporate additional documentation that was not completed by the out-to-bid deadline.

Submitting contractors consolidate the bid numbers that they have gathered from various trades and submit their final bid to the owner. The owner's project team evaluates these bids, and the owner awards contracts to the lowest "qualified" bidders. Not long afterward, a Pre-Construction Conference is convened with the successful bidder(s) for the purpose of reinforcing the project's unique aspects and explaining administrative procedures, communication channels, and the chain of command.

Within a few weeks, the builder mobilizes and construction begins under a command-and-control hierarchy using a conventional process and techniques that everyone understands. This process has evolved in a way that allows construction to proceed with a minimum amount of communication required—to make things easier. It allows for everyone to proceed doing what they do best without being told what to do—it encourages independent action. And everyone is comfortable with this, since procedures generally rest on collective understanding of common practices, conventions, and assumptions. Each trade has specific and, in general, clearly defined tasks within their contract.

Design team members most often are contractually obligated to *observe* construction but only to evaluate conformance with the Construction Documents (CDs), since these documents define what the owner has purchased by accepting construction bids. Frequently, A/E firms utilize their Construction Administration department's staff to monitor these construction activities. The level of involvement in construction activities that this staff engages generally includes attending biweekly job-site conferences, reviewing shop drawings and submittals, responding to *requests for information* (RFIs), approving payment applications, and processing change orders.

Change orders are used to resolve conflicts, errors, and omissions. Many of these conflicts directly result from the rush to complete construction documents. Others result from a lack of coordination between design consultants and between systems. Still more arise in the field due to unanticipated conflicts between components and trades, along with other unforeseen conditions. Change orders are generally paid from the project's budgeted contingency, which usually amounts to 5 to 10 percent of the contractually defined construction cost.

Tradespeople and subcontractors attend biweekly job conferences to assess and report project status to the owner. Other than these meetings, interactions between these contractors and trades occur only when conflicts between systems and responsibilities arise.

The Commissioning Authority is brought to the site to confirm that building energy systems equipment and components (such as HVAC and electrical systems) are installed and functioning in accordance with the Owner's Project Requirements (OPR), the design team's Basis of Design (BOD), and project specifications.

Construction proceeds until *Substantial Completion.* At this point, substantial payment is made to all contractors and subcontractors, and everybody leaves, except for a few people involved with addressing punch-list items. Soon afterward, construction re-tainage is released, and all contractors and A/E team members are paid their final fees.

Occupancy follows in short order, warranty periods begin, and the building is turned over to the owner's facilities staff; this staff enters operations mode with a sophisticated set of controls. When these controls, equipment, or systems malfunction during the standard twelve-month warranty period, contractors are called back to the site to fix lingering problems.

Final LEED documentation is gathered and submitted to the U.S. Green Building Council (USGBC), LEED certification is awarded, and the process ends here.

STOP AND REFLECT

What's Working?

Of course, the process described above is a generalized one, consisting of almost infinite variants, but its essential aspects are familiar, right? Familiarity makes it work; utilizing this conventional process, projects are delivered within reasonably consistent cost and time expectations. The final results fit generally accepted performance criteria. There are few surprises, and while everyone expects there to be problems, we do not have to reinvent the wheel for each project. We are comfortable with this way of bidding and building. Once we learn the conventions, the complex processes of realizing a building are almost automatic, so expectations are easily met.

The bidding process works very efficiently for the most part. The quality specified is generally achieved with the lowest practicable price. Market-driven competitive pricing generally keeps costs within fairly predictable ranges. The feedback of the marketplace ensures that artificially low prices and low-quality construction are not repeated too often.

Well executed construction documents and specifications define responsibilities of all parties, so there is little question of expected deliverables.

Workplace safety is generally well managed. Occupational Safety and Health Agency (OSHA) regulations and insurance practices are effective.

Life-safety codes and ADA (Americans with Disabilities Act) compliance are enforced through inspections by public agencies, generally providing high levels of protection and accessibility to the public.

Unfortunately, though, this list of "what's working" is short. We struggled to come up with additional positive aspects.

What's Not Working?

Given the short time frame of the bidding process and the lack of builder involvement in the design process, further fragmentation of an already unintegrated whole system occurs. Specification sections are distributed to the subcontractors and vendors as independent pieces. Each system or component is priced in isolation. Problems occur when a subcontractor assumes the system they are pricing is connected to other systems in a conventional way. The implications and resulting consequences of building systems that may have been downsized or eliminated through earlier system's integration and optimization processes have likely not been communicated to the subcontractors. We have found that final prices, more often than not, are based on the premises, "Well, we thought you must have meant this" and "we've never seen anyone build it this way before," so "why would we bid it that way? Here's the way we've priced it." Or more specifically, regarding HVAC systems, for example, "We didn't think you were really going to use that sequence, so we didn't bother to program it into the HVAC control system."

Additionally, since so many design changes occur during the conventional construction documents phase, effective integration of these changes rarely occurs, inevitably leading to addenda during bidding and change orders, often costly, during construction. Further, although the "final pricing" of the bidding process establishes a bottom-line number, it is not unusual to see an additional 10 to 20 percent added in the form of such addenda and change orders, depending on the quality of the bidding documents.

The typical construction process is rigorously hierarchal. Its efficiency is based on collective conventions that allow relatively fast command-and-control decisions to be made via a vertically organized hierarchy of decision making. Without the benefit of easy feedback mechanisms to inform and adjust these decisions, it is difficult for the bidding and construction process to respond to new techniques and more integrated system relationships.

The subcontracting trades often get in each other's way. Previously installed systems may need to be partially undone and redone to accommodate systems installed improperly or in the wrong sequence. When the "it's not my job" issue is raised, change order negotiations begin for time extensions and extra cost. Sometimes, these changes and construction revisions impact other systems in unanticipated and surprising ways, unknown or unforeseeable to unintegrated construction teams that did not participate in the analysis of systems interrelationships and cost bundling, potentially resulting in long-range significant cost impacts that extend well beyond construction.

For example, the following story illustrates how problems during construction, such as improper installation, can have major cost impacts well into occupancy (unless discovered by the Commissioning Authority). We were involved in the renovation of a one-hundred-year-old, nine-story office building in downtown Baltimore, Maryland, one of our early projects. Our role in the project was fundamental building commissioning to satisfy LEED requirements. The building was being completely gutted, and all the mechanical and electrical systems were being replaced. The mechanical system being installed was a primary and secondary water-loop heating system with three 1-million Btu boilers. The piping system in the mechanical room consisted of 6-inch and 8-inch welded steel. During one of our midconstruction commissioning site visitations, we were on-site specifically to verify installation by tracing this piping system. At this point in construction, most of the piping system had been installed, but the large welded steel piping was only tack welded in place and the system was not yet filled with water. One of our goals for the day was to trace the piping for the primary and secondary loops in the mechanical room. We followed each fitting, valve, and connection as it was installed, comparing what we saw to what was on the construction drawings.

This type of system has two piping loops. The primary loop includes pumps, piping, and boilers. The purpose of the primary loop is to continuously circulate plus or minus 180°F heating water through the boilers and to maintain a source of heating water in case the building needs heat. The secondary loop includes piping and pumps as well; it circulates water through all the heating devices in the building. The primary and secondary loops operate independently of each other, while sharing a common body of heating water. There are two piping connections between the primary and secondary loops. The secondary-loop *return* piping has an open connection to the primary-loop return piping. The primary-loop *supply* piping is connected to the secondary loop with a control valve (on the suction side of the pumps). If the secondary loop needs more heating water, then the control valve will open between the two loops, allowing some of the 180°F heating water from the primary loop to mix with the return water from the secondary loop. One reason for using this type of heating system is to save energy by adjusting or resetting the heating water

temperature to match the heating load, depending on outdoor air temperatures.

The two piping connections that join the primary and secondary loops are the most critical connections in the system. The return connection from the secondary loop must be downstream of the supply connection from the primary loop. If these connections are reversed, then return water from the secondary loop will always mix with the primary loop's 180°F water, cooling it substantially before it is fed into the secondary supply piping. If this occurs, the building's heating system will not be capable of achieving anywhere near its full heating capacity. The result, of course, is that demand for heating cannot be met in heating mode, and the building will remain cold. In some cases, this mistake has been the cause of entire building sections experiencing chronic pipe-freezing problems for years, until the mistake is discovered—that is, if it ever *is* discovered.

In this case, as can be seen in Figure 8-2, the two piping connections were only one fitting apart. Having the return connection on the opposite side of one fitting—an easy mistake to commit—was all it took for the system to be piped incorrectly. This mistake likely would not have been discovered during start-up since the building was completed in May, months prior to the need for heating. It was estimated that the cost of fixing it post-occupancy—were it to be discovered at all—would have exceeded $50,000 (more than the CxA's fee) by the time the system was drained, the welded connection cut, the pipe relocated, the water loops recharged, the start-up procedures redone, and the system rebalanced. This estimate did not include the incalculable cost of having to shut down the entire building during this period and the associated lost lease revenue. It is quite likely, though, that this mistake would have remained undetected for many years, in which case the cost implications are staggering in terms of the years of building operations fraught with

This pipe was originally connected to this tee incorrectly.

Figure 8-2 Commissioning field observations found this piping mistake early in construction, revealing that the return piping of the building's secondary heating loop was tied into the primary boiler loop in the wrong location. At the time, the piping was only tack welded in place, and the system was not yet filled with water. Had this incorrect piping arrangement not been found, the building would have had far less than adequate heating capacity. *Image courtesy of Brian Toevs.*

inflated energy consumption, freeze-ups, repairs, reduced productivity due to lack of thermal comfort, potential lost lease revenue from low occupancy rates, and so on.

The site observation that enabled avoiding this fate was a planned activity. Such visits should be built into every commissioning project. It is this type of site observation that is intended to help both the engineer and the contractor provide the owner a better product. Catching mistakes like this early, when the piping is unfinished and the system is dry, means that they are relatively inexpensive to fix. Finding such mistakes after systems are complete and operational is much more expensive, and failing to discover such mistakes until ten or fifteen years of operations have passed results in unimaginable and unnecessary high costs and environmental impacts.

On another project, a green condominium development in Massachusetts had four air handlers. They all "worked" at substantial completion. In other words, they all turned on. That was the level of functional test-

ing that was done for this system. Unfortunately, for the first year of occupancy, many of the apartments were uncomfortable and energy bills were quite high. Finally, the owner decided to commission the project. A not-too-subtle problem was found. A motor for one of the air handlers had been installed with reverse polarity, causing it to run backward. This was a problem that could have been addressed if proper *Testing and Balancing* of the ductwork truly had been implemented and commissioned. The Commissioning process is designed to avoid just such issues.

These stories illustrate the lack of real quality control in our current construction process, especially at the end of a project when sophisticated equipment and controls are installed. These are just two examples from dozens and dozens of similar cases we have encountered while commissioning projects over the past several years. Many projects suffer delays for various and often unpredictable reasons, thereby putting tremendous pressure on subcontractors by forcing them to complete their installations as quickly as possible in order to get to the next job, where in all likelihood, they will be late getting started again. How assured are we that a well-integrated installation is being achieved under this scenario?

Frustration with this lack of quality control occurs on even the smallest projects. In a small house with radiant floor heating, a pump motor burned out. The HVAC and plumbing contractor who installed the system had disappeared—on to the next job, late. There were no operating instructions provided for this heating unit. A new HVAC firm was brought in. The motor burned out two more times, frustrating everybody. Finally the owner put her ear to the pipes to locate an irritating noise that had been present the whole time. Assuming that a lack of noise meant something positive, she opened a valve slightly with a one-eighth-inch turn, and the noise went away. After testing over a few days, no more burning out of the pump occurred, and heat delivery has been effective ever since. No one has any idea why it is working, but they now know the proper setting for that valve.

The point is that our current construction practices have no real mechanism for quality control. Perhaps the only quality control measure, when commissioning is not implemented in any rigorous way, is the conventional process of testing, adjusting, and balancing (TAB). Have you ever read a TAB report? If you have, please accept our sympathy; they can be soporific. Nevertheless, TAB represents a critical component of achieving functional completion. However, we have asked over two thousand engineers at our training and educational workshops the following question: What percentage of the content in a typical TAB report would you say is *nonfiction*? The highest answer we have ever heard is 50 percent. Usually, responses range from 0 to 10 percent.

One of the components of a TAB effort includes testing airflow in ducts. Such tests are conducted by inserting measurement probes every six inches around the perimeter of a duct (in cross-section) and averaging their airflow readings. Once the probes are removed, what is left in the duct? Holes. These are then plugged. So we then ask our engineers: How often after reading airflow test results in a TAB report have you found holes in the subject duct? One of our partners reports that, before we began commissioning, he never found them. So, we ask rhetorically, since the tests were not done, where did the airflow results indicated in the TAB report come from? Hmmm. And perhaps this is understandable on one level: Who pays the TAB subcontractor? The HVAC contractor. Does the TAB professional have any real incentive for finding problems?

The point here is that without commissioning, TAB theoretically represents the only component of quality control in conventional construction. But, in reality, these efforts are not particularly effective in achieving proper functional completion. This is not to say that all TAB reports are worthless (there are many conscientious TAB professionals), but evidence indicates a clear tendency in this direction.

We were in the functional testing phase of Commissioning an addition and renovation project for a Career and Technology Educational Center in Ohio. We had been asking for the TAB report for weeks and needed it to begin our work. After many delays and promises, the TAB report was finally delivered. Due to delays, time limitations, and scheduling, we were beginning the functional testing at the same time that the engineer was reviewing the TAB report. The first unit scheduled for functional testing was a small make-up air handler with very little ductwork, serving an existing machine shop classroom. We verified that all the devices on the unit operated properly before we began the first functional test. The first test was to turn the unit on and verify the airflow indicated in the balancing report. The balancer was not available for the testing that day, so we needed to check the report without his presence. With the unit operating, we could not get an acceptable reading on the airflow. This did not make any sense, given that the unit was exposed in the classroom—there were only four diffusers on a short duct run, and the outside air intake was directly above the unit. We double-checked all the dampers and actuators, and we could find no obstructions in any components, all of which had been installed per the design. After a half day of testing, verification, and searching, we could not determine why there was no airflow. We could not verify the balancing report. The functional testing for this unit had failed almost before it began.

In discussing the issue with the school's maintenance staff, we came to realize that this unit was using an existing roof opening and hood. The previous purpose of this opening was for exhaust, and the maintenance staff recalled that this hood had a back-draft damper in the opening. We returned to the space with the contractor, who removed the hood from the opening in the roof, and we found the back-draft damper still in place and closed (see Figure 8-3). After the back-draft damper was removed, the rest of the functional test was completed without issue.

The TAB report indicated that all tested components of this unit were performing within acceptable ranges, including correct motor amperage and *airflow*. The question is: Was the back-draft damper open during balancing and somehow closed after balancing was complete? Or was balancing ever really performed on this unit?

Later that day, after this unit was functionally complete, we began verifying proper operation of new variable air volume (VAV) boxes serving tech labs from a large existing air-handling unit. There were around fifty VAV boxes with hot water reheat coils on this system. The first VAV box we checked would not deliver warm air. We checked the operation of the control valve and verified that the balancing valve was opened. Still no heat. We traced the piping back to the main and found the branch isolation valves closed. We opened them. With the isolation valves opened, the VAV box operated correctly. The second VAV box had the same issue—closed isolation valves.

Again, the TAB report indicated that both of these VAV boxes were delivering designed water flow to the heating coils. And again, the question is: Were the valves open when the testing occurred and then somehow closed afterward? Or was the balancing ever actually performed?

At this point, we had completed a full day of functional testing and had a success rate of zero. Our confidence in the balancing report was gone. The next morning, we called for a commissioning team meeting and reviewed this report in detail to be sure the work had actually been performed. Because of the issues with the TAB report, functional testing was postponed and did not resume for three months.

Figure 8-3 *Top image:* Functional testing of a new makeup-air unit tied to this existing hood and roof opening for outside air intake resulted in no airflow, but we could not understand why. Everything else we tested and checked on the system worked fine, but from below we could not see up into this roof opening. We wanted to uncover the mystery, so we removed the hood without knowing what we would find.
Bottom image: After removing the hood from the roof opening, we found an existing back-draft damper that was closed, prohibiting air intake, but the testing, adjusting, and balancing (TAB) report indicated that airflow for this unit met the design exactly. *Images courtesy of Brian Toevs.*

An abbreviated summary of other aspects of our conventional construction process and operations that we would classify as "what's not working" include:

■ Product substitutions frequently occur, and as a result performance may suffer. For example, a chiller substitution was made to a seemingly identical chiller from another manufacturer. After the installation was complete, we realized that the substitute chiller would not operate at variable water-flow rates as designed. The chiller pumps were taken off automatic and placed in manual mode, thus negating any potential pump- and/or chiller-energy savings.

■ We rarely count the environmental impacts associated with the construction process beyond implementing Construction Waste Management Plans and Construction Indoor Air Quality Management Plans. A thoughtful builder of a project on Cape Cod in Massachusetts initiated a discussion about this issue. He assessed how far his subcontractors on the project had to drive to work. Since Cape Cod does not have the density to support a variety of trades, tradespeople typically must drive to the cape from the north. He calculated an average round trip of three-and-a-half hours. As a result, he rented some apartments for the duration of the project, and many of the subcontractors stayed overnight when they had consecutive days on the job—saving money, time, fuel cost, and a little over two metric tons of CO_2 emissions per week.

■ Workplace safety during construction is limited in scope; indoor air quality (IAQ) and toxicant issues remain unaddressed in terms of their impacts on construction workers.

■ Construction usually remains uncompleted: Have you ever seen a totally completed punch list? Rarely, in our experience. Everyone eventually gives up, often due to frustration and the pressures of the next job. It is frequently impossible to get subcontractors and trades back on the site, even when retaining a portion of final payment. Everyone just seems to fade away, a very dissatisfying conclusion to a grueling process—no acceptance phase and no functional completion.

■ Operations staffs usually inherit a building that they do not understand; they had little or nothing to do with its design or controls. When controls systems critical to building systems operations are not understood, performance suffers. Sometimes this lack of understanding results in sophisticated controls systems being simply overridden and placed into manual mode—often with systems left running 24/7.

■ The only feedback we receive generally consists of complaints about "what's *not* working." These complaints usually are not measured or quantified, so we rarely can assess the source. We rarely even address the complaint. We have no intentional feedback mechanisms built into the process to assess whether or not what we intended in the design actually is performing as expected after construction, or how what was built impacts the performance of building occupants. How often do architects go back to survey occupant satisfaction of the buildings they have designed? Rarely. There is little incentive to do so, and clients are just beginning to think that it may be valuable to elicit these observations.

In conclusion, current practice produces a product that more often than not does not perform well. In most cases, we do not fully quantify performance expectations, nor do we create metrics and feedback mechanisms to assess performance. Energy efficiency is defined as meeting or barely exceeding code requirements, building operators do not understand the intention of the designers, unresolved problems in the building linger for years, and so on; in short, a myriad of issues can be used to exemplify the problems with current practice. If we expect our buildings to perform at a higher level, we must consciously establish aggressive performance goals with an integrated team, design and construct the project with these goals in mind, and check back on the actual results.

How Can We Do (and Think About) This Differently?

Essentially, construction is a mysterious process: We saw in Chapter 1 that every building is an entirely unique product that has never been built before and will never be built again. Each building is entirely unique every time—we really do not know how it is going to go together until we actually build it. Furthermore, we have a different team every time. Imagine if the team responsible for building the project was a football team. Each building project would be like playing a game every Sunday with a different set of teammates, using a different set of plays, on a different field, in front of a different crowd, with none of your games being played on your home field.

Consequently, we need to dispel the mystery. We can make this a less mysterious process by getting builders involved early. Again, they need to become part of the colearning design team—and then we need to extend this shared knowledge and colearning a level deeper, to the subcontractors and tradespeople.

Building information modeling (BIM) may be a tool that can help us make this a less mysterious process—an opportunity to build the building electronically before it is built physically, as discussed at the beginning of Chapter 6.

Another significant problem that needs to be addressed is the nearly ubiquitous policy of using low bids as a credible basis for selecting construction professionals. It is not hard to understand the perversity inherent in this practice and the disincentives that arise from it. One of our clients made it a policy several years ago to select bidders only from the middle of the bell curve—from the middle range of submitted prices. Even when all bidders are prequalified and theoretically "responsible," there are substantive reasons why bids are high or low; more often than not, this is due to something being missed or to varying degrees

of "pencil sharpening." In other words, even responsible bidders can make mistakes. Our clients tell us that when they award their bids to the lowest responsible contractor, invariably something gets missed—and what is missing often remains unseen, sometimes until deep into construction.

Perhaps the most important aspect of this stage about which we must ask "how can we do this differently" is simply this: We have no quality control process to link intentions with outcomes in construction, as we have seen in our above discussions on commissioning. We need to engage such a quality control process because of the huge gap that exists between an abstract *representation* of a building—drawings of plans, sections, elevations, and specifications—and the *reality* of actual construction. This gap results from the wide range and array of possible interpretations between the building *represented* in the construction documents and the *actual* building. Drawings and specs are really just symbols; they are an attempt at representing reality, but not reality themselves. This interpretive gap is exacerbated by the gap in communication—the abyss we have described—that currently exists between design and construction professionals.

Before litigation issues (in our opinion) trumped common sense, we used to have a clerk-of-the-works on-site who served as a link between the design team and the builder in terms of helping bridge the interpretation and communication gap. Since that role no longer exists, these gaps are now somewhat bridged by the Commissioning Authority (CxA). As we have seen, the role of the CxA essentially is one of quality control, which is achieved by bridging both the interpretation and communication gaps as a key member of the composite master builder team.

In our Age of Specialization and complex contemporary building systems, we have moved beyond the capabilities of a single master builder's mind to hold the whole, so we are suggesting our idealized model of a composite master builder (from Chapter 2) as a means for addressing the downward spiral of fragmented expertise (architecture, mechanical engineering, electrical engineering, etc.) no longer versed in the knowledge of other disciplines. Adding to this, each profession is competing for work in an arena that requires lower margins and less profit across the board. Quite literally, the building design profession has become more like a commodity and less like the practice of providing professional services. Design professionals no longer can compete in today's marketplace and continue to provide the full range of services as in the past.

So where do these professionals currently cut to stay competitive? They know that their design services can suffer only so much reduction in scope before the product delivered becomes incomplete or laden with liabilities. So there are only a few ways to reduce costs and stay competitive. One is to recycle as much of the design as possible. This means reusing details and schedules, running the risk of producing final construction documents that include details and schedules that may not be entirely applicable to project specifics or that are incomplete, incorrect, or mismatched.

Another way design professionals have reduced scope is by cutting construction administration services. This means few or no site observations. As the design industry has evolved over the past several decades, the limited site observation and field work by design professionals has contributed significantly to widening of the abyss between design and construction professionals. Young design professionals coming into the industry today with no field experience have little opportunity to obtain it. Designers of today tend to know the components in their designs as lines on paper or in computer-aided design (CAD) programs or as pictures in a product catalog—*representations* of a built reality, but not the thing itself. Further, we have found that many designers have no desire to gain experience on the job site—"It's not my job."

Design firms also have reduced cost by having only a small pool of professionally trained architects or engineers, supported by a large pool of CAD operators working under them. These CAD operators are educated in operating computer-aided design tools but have little or no real engineering or architectural education—and no field experience. The engineer or architect is often spread too thin, overseeing too many projects, unable to properly check the work of these CAD operators. (Again, BIM might be a tool that could help address this in the future.)

So how *can* we think about and do this differently?

Throwing money at these problems will not fix them. The design industry of today can be likened to an automobile manufacturer that is currently tooled up to produce large sport-utility vehicles (SUVs). The manufacturer cannot convert the plant overnight into a facility that manufactures smaller, more energy-efficient cars, as evidenced by the recent economic crisis in the American automobile industry. This requires first the *will* to do so and a clearly defined *purpose*—followed by retooling, changing manufacturing equipment, changing out the entire stock of parts and components, and so on, to pursue that purpose. Like the car manufacturer, design firms need to retool *their* process and equipment—their *people*—by actively pursuing the mental model shift that we have discussed throughout this book. This too cannot be done overnight. It requires openness to change and evolving our process.

For example, we often have encountered owners who say, "Aren't I already paying my engineer to perform the activities associated with the commissioning process?" The answer is *no*. If an owner is paying standard market fees for engineering and architectural design services, this owner is getting the Commissioning-Plan-of-every-project-in-America: "We know it won't work, so we'll pay to fix it later." Even if the owner chooses to pay more to design professionals, hoping to receive enhanced services in this regard, it is likely that the owner will not receive the best value for the dollars spent, given today's fragmented practices. We cannot retool overnight—shifting mental models and reversing our Age of Specialization is a process of evolution, a shift to a mental model that understands all design and construction team members *functioning as an organism to build a functioning organism.*

As we have seen, a building project consists of a series of components and systems combined to create a larger system within yet larger nested systems, and connections between those components and systems offer the best opportunities for integration. The creation of feedback mechanisms is essential in a process aimed at integrating these systems for the purpose of creating optimally performing buildings or to produce any truly functional system. The first step requires owners, designers, and contractors to align and commit to producing an integrated building project that performs to expectations, but then make an additional commitment to enabling feedback that can further our knowledge about how we can integrate better and improve performance.

Observations from a Builder and Construction Manager

By Victor Canseco, Sandpebble Builders

A municipal client's request for information, on what it would take to design and construct its new village hall as a green building, led me to a seminar given by two 7group partners. It would completely change the direction of what was at that point my 33-year career in construction.

Together with 150 or so other people in the industry, I learned that the thousands of buildings we had been collectively responsible for producing had, by many accounts, major flaws resulting in grave effects on both their inhabitants and the world around us.

To say the least, it was quite sobering to learn that in the process of creating indoor environments, which rank among the most unhealthy of all places that people spend their time, we had, among other things, consumed unconscionable quantities of our environmental capital while becoming the prime contributor to global climate change and the enormous quantities of trash in our landfills.

The good news was that the solution did not require years of new research and technology or premium project costs but, rather, simply to change the mind-set of those involved in planning and constructing new buildings.

The task at hand was and continues to be to convert the current methods of designing and constructing buildings into an integrative process involving the owner and design team members, as well as the facilities and construction personnel. (A mind-set change was required.)

This was in sharp contrast to the traditional approach in which architects complete the schematic phase on their own without much outside input except for programming information.

Their initial architectural design is then "reacted to" by the rest of the stakeholders. The engineers design their systems around the schematic plan, and the input of the owner and facilities and construction personnel is generally limited to minor adjustments to it. (Mind-set change!)

General contractors then would bid on the work and when the bids came in over budget, the "value engineering" process would be used to delete items from the scope of work according to some set of priorities that reduced the ability of the building to perform its function in a way that best met the needs of the stakeholders. (Ironically, "value engineering" on a construction project actually decreases the value of the finished product!) (Mind-set change!)

In the integrative process, the proactive participation by all the stakeholders from the outset results in a design that is driven by consensus. The building then performs its function much more effectively, its systems are more efficient and the environmental costs can be vastly reduced. The economic benefits of the first two are enormous; those of the last item are way beyond economic and are of course immeasurable. (Mind-set change!)

In addition, when using this process, there are significantly fewer design-driven change orders during the construction phase because all the issues are worked through during the design phase and not reacted to during the construction part of the project. Change orders are the main cause of projects exceeding their budgets, and the majority of all change orders are caused by design changes.

Public awareness about the "green tsunami" occurring around the world has no doubt helped increase the ranks of design professionals who have bought into this new approach. Even so, it will be a while before the integrative design approach is the norm as opposed to the exception.

In the process of redefining the way in which buildings are designed, construction trade personnel have been left behind. Although "project" managers are more and more apt to be at the table during the design phases, the need for "construction" managers is often not fulfilled until the "construction phase" is closer at hand. (Mind-set change!)

In addition, early participation by a general contractor precludes the competitive bidding process once the plans are complete, and therefore it is not an option unless a "cost-plus" arrangement is opted for. Ironically, this is not generally regarded to be in the best interests of the owner. (Mind-set change!)

Changing the mind-set of the field tradespeople that carry out the intent and requirements of high-performance design during the construction phase has been and will continue to be a far more difficult task until the time when green building has become more of the norm. There are several reasons for this:

- The construction documents for a project represent the distillation of ideas, calculations, input, failures, and energies of a group of people during many months if not years of planning.
- Although the purpose of these documents is to convey the intent of the design team to those charged with the task of transforming paper into bricks, at best they are usually only 80 to 90 percent successful. The goals of a green project, as they differ from a traditional one, are difficult to articulate in these documents.

(continued)

■ Traditionally, specifications have consisted of very lengthy descriptions of materials and performance requirements for the project. They are usually very formal, and on larger private and all public projects they provide reading for few others than estimators and lawyers. They are of little use to a job superintendent trying to explain the principles and requirements of green building to the work crews. This has become a major stumbling block in getting green buildings built in the spirit in which they were designed.

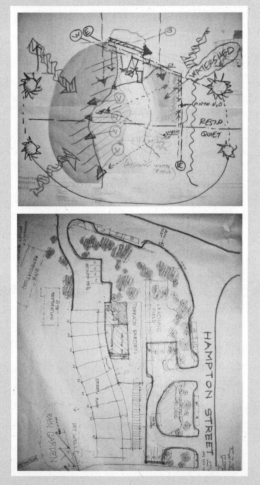

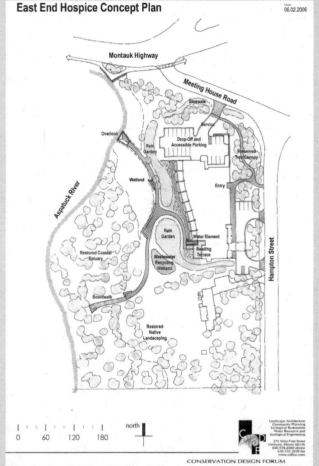

Figure 8-4 The East End Hospice is one of several projects on Long Island in New York resulting from the efforts Victor Canseco, owner of Sandpebble Builders. Located adjacent to a sensitive estuary, the project focused on the restoration of this estuary. The design integrates both visually and physically with the renewal and regeneration of life as an appropriate theme. These three sketches from team workshops depict the development of the scheme, from the site-forces exercise on *top left,* to the conceptual plan produced at the team's conceptual design workshop at *bottom left,* to the schematic site plan on the *right. Two left images courtesy of John Boecker. Right image ©2008 Conservation Design Forum, Inc.*

■ Trade contractors spend but a few days or weeks in formulating a bid for their part of the work, and a successful general contractor must spend the same time accumulating bids to insure that nothing is left out. Estimators performing takeoffs are not concerned with the intent of the documents but, rather, that nothing that might result in a non-profitable bid is mistakenly left off their estimate.

■ After but a few weeks of bidding, a successful contractor dispatches its field people to the job to begin. From the very first day on the job, they begin the work shown on the plans and perhaps one sheet of "must do's" excerpted from the specifications by the estimator back in the office where the spec book usually remains.

Green buildings struggle to get built by a large team of field personnel who have not participated in the conception and design of the building. Their valuable input and ideas, the result of years and years of experience, are not part of the plan. With no such "buy in," they have little interest and the value of their input is totally overlooked. (A typical $10 million project will involve the efforts of no fewer than two hundred construction people. Assuming an average of ten years experience per person, the result is 2,000 years of experience totally omitted from the design and planning process. (Mind-set change!)

It is not difficult to understand why it has been so difficult to get a green project done. Introducing construction personnel to a project twelve months or so after its conception, not to mention with nothing more than traditional plans and partial specifications to describe the work, cannot help but leave them completely in the dark.

What we have found to be of significant value in mitigating this problem has been the evolution of a booklet containing a distillation and conversion of the specifications and other construction information into "plain language" with an emphasis on the hows and whys of a sustainable project.

This begins to convey how the design was developed to meet the goals of the stakeholders and why certain systems appear different than in a traditionally designed project. The next step will be to convert some of this information into a short video that can be viewed by all trade personnel before beginning work on the first day on the job.

Without question, the overwhelming benefits and environmental demands of sustainability in current and future design, construction and renovation of the built environment will drive its ultimate acceptance as the norm. With the environmental and other clocks ticking, however, time is of the essence, and the sooner the construction people are engaged in this interactive process the faster the transformation—the mind-set change—will occur.

Mental Model Shift

The overarching shift required is this: we no longer can function in fragmented silos and expect to perform as an organic whole—as a composite master builder. We need to move from a command-and-control model to a structure that understands design and construction as a continuum of relationship-building. Mechanisms for openly sharing and incorporating the opinions, experience, and creativity of all participants—both design and construction professionals—are required.

The design and construction industry needs to become more vertically integrated to bridge both the interpretation and communication gaps that currently exist between design and construction professionals. Designing and building processes need to be structured so that neither designers nor builders are either subservient or in full control at any stage—rather, they must be equal partners, fully integrated as one team.

We understand that there are institutional and attitudinal barriers that separate designers and builders; however, there is tremendous opportunity for both designers and builders who can offer greater value to both their clients and the planet by working as an integrated whole for the purpose of achieving both cost-effective and highly environmentally effective projects.

Our (potentially naïve) advice is this: Ignore the lawyers. Architects and engineers no longer *actively* participate in the Construction Administration process primarily due to liability avoidance. Consequently, they have methodically abdicated responsibility and extracted themselves from this process; even their contracts limit their involvement to a single verb: observe. Their attorneys' advice is: "Do not discuss means and methods." Not long ago, we used to accept responsibility for problems and resolve them together as a team. We need to shift our mental model toward doing so again . . . because creating a sustainable planet is not just one profession's job, but everyone's. If we can do this, we may find that more risk means greater reward—and that the risk of *not* doing it may in fact be greater.

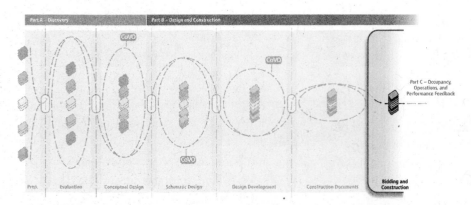

▶ **Figure 8-5** Integrative Process Stage B.7, Bidding and Construction. *Image courtesy of 7group and Bill Reed; graphics by Corey Johnston.*

Stage B.7
Bidding and Construction—Aligning with the Builder: Becoming a Team

B.7.1   Bidding and Construction Activities

- Explain unique aspects of project and the integration of all systems at the Pre-Bid and Pre-Construction conferences

- Review with builder's team (all trades and subcontractors) their roles and responsibilities prior to commencing construction regarding:
  - Subcontractors' roles in supporting the integration of their work into the whole
  - Each subcontractor's role in supporting the documentation necessary to demonstrate achievement of Performance Targets

- Review builder submittals through the unique filters of environmental performance

- Commissioning: Coordinate with builder's team installation of all systems regarding achievement of Performance Targets
  - Perform site observations
  - Incorporate Commissioning schedule into construction schedule
  - Review submittals
  - Develop construction checklists and functional tests
  - Witness start-up
  - Perform functional tests
  - Verify training of building operations team
  - Prepare final Commissioning report
  - Produce systems manuals

B.7.2   Principles and Measurement

- Manage the collection of documents that verify achievement of Performance Targets

- Commissioning: Document prefunctional and functional testing results and prepare Commissioning (Cx) reports and Recommissioning Plan

B.7.3   Cost Analysis

- Coordinate with builder to ensure that subcontracts are awarded based on performance requirements, not just price

B.7.4   Schedule and Next Steps

- Ensure systematic communication between design and building teams

Stage B.7

Bidding and Construction—Aligning with the Builder: Becoming a Team

The *Implementation Process Outline* for these last two stages is not intended to provide a comprehensive or detailed outline of the myriad activities and variables associated with construction and occupancy. Rather, our intended purpose here is to provide a general overview of the aspects associated with integrative design that affect team members as they engage construction and occupancy activities.

B.7.1 Bidding and Construction Activities

- ■ **Explain unique aspects of project and the integration of all systems at the Pre-Bid and Pre-Construction conferences**

  We actually need to entirely rethink Pre-Bid conferences (common to design-bid-build construction delivery) and their purpose, because under our current process the wrong people attend, since currently attendees primarily consist of estimators that have no involvement with the building whatsoever; further, the competition is in the room, so people are reluctant to ask questions or raise issues. We have found that this problem can largely be obviated with a negotiated contract and certain design-build scenarios.

  The right people need to be at the Pre-Construction conference as well. The trade supervisors who will actually be on the job need to attend. In addition to the typical logistical issues and contractual obligations, a detailed review of the OPR and BOD should be a primary focus of this meeting, so that everyone on the team understands the "why" of their work—generally, they already understand the "how" and "what" of their systems.

  Address non-building-related sustainability issues at both of these meetings. The reason for this is that most builders are concentrating on the building form, its components, and general site issues; but the project's interrelationships and its relationship with living systems also need to be understood. Some of the issues that could be raised as significant might include a project's more detailed landscape-habitat design, site stormwater systems, natural waste systems, operational and embodied-emissions targets, indoor air quality concerns, recycling programs, education programs, and so on.

- ■ **Review with builder's team (all trades and subcontractors) their roles and responsibilities prior to commencing construction regarding:**

  - ■ **Subcontractors' roles in supporting the integration of their work into the whole**

    Builders and tradespeople need to understand that their components are part of a larger whole, and this likely requires them to be made aware of the components in the project that will require products and installation processes that fall outside of conventionalized norms. Accordingly, we have found it useful to convene meetings with tradespeople—those who actually will be on-site doing the work—at several points in the construction process. These multiple meetings need to be scheduled contemporaneously with the specific work being performed at various stages of construction; examples include:

    - An early meeting with all tradespeople associated with shell construction to discuss issues like water penetration, air infiltration, and the importance of maintaining the integrity of the building envelope, since the HVAC and other systems are highly dependent on building envelope performance, and these other related systems were designed and sized accordingly.
    - An early midstage meeting between the general contractor (GC), mechanical contractor, and electrical contractor, along with special-

ized flooring tradespeople—when, for example, an underfloor air-supply system is being installed—to ensure that each installer understands the need to keep the underfloor plenum not only clean but sealed to maintain pressure (sealing holes for electrical and/or duct penetrations through this plenum, etc.). These individuals likely will be different from those involved in shell construction.

- A midstage meeting between the general, mechanical, and electrical contractors, along with specialized controls tradespeople, in order for everyone to understand the intention and components of the building's control systems so that when controls codes are written they match the intent of the OPR and the sequence of operations in the BOD. Otherwise a "canned" program likely will get installed. Also, the controls systems' impacts on other trades need to be understood, including issues such as: the mechanical installer properly placing dampers, the GC properly locating access panels to provide accessibility to actuators and dampers, coordinating the electrical installer's electrical connections (such as low versus line voltage, transformer locations, etc.), and so forth.

- Even if the design team has been diligent in developing a relationship with the builder and the trade supervisors, there is still the matter of integrating the people actually constructing and installing their respective systems. This gap is where many slips "between cup and lip" occur. A few decades ago, an institutional client insisted that we meet with each trade before they were allowed to begin their work on the site. We reviewed the related specification section(s) with the entire field crew of each trade. The comments received were the clas-

sic ones: "My grandfather didn't do it that way, my father didn't do it that way, and I'm sure not going to do it that way." Or: "Is that really what we're supposed to do? We didn't price it that way." The end result was reconsideration by the subs about what and how they were building, and the nature of the work they were being paid to deliver. After some grumbling and some beer and pretzels—it was a Friday afternoon—a common ground and partnership emerged between the design team and the guys and gals in the field.

■ **Each subcontractor's role in supporting the documentation necessary to demonstrate achievement of Performance Targets**

Again, the "why" of Performance Targets is as important—if not more important—than the actual documentation of what will be needed to verify performance, so that each of the trades can understand the purpose behind this documentation and why it is needed. This includes their role in documenting the requirements of the Cx process (such as providing completed construction checklists)—and for LEED projects, the submittals related to their work associated with credits being pursued (such as volatile organic compound [VOC] content of adhesives, solar reflectance index [SRI] of roofing and paving materials, recycled content of materials, photos of construction IAQ measures implemented in the field, etc.).

■ **Review builder submittals through the unique filters of environmental performance**

For example, we normally select materials and products on the basis of cost, quality, availability, and aesthetics. Now we are adding a few more selection criteria related to environmental impacts and human health, such as recycled content, embodied energy, toxicants, VOC content, and so on. Accordingly, since specifications now include language that addresses these additional criteria and characteristics, the submittal review process must verify compliance with these unconventional specification requirements.

■ **Commissioning: Coordinate with builder's team installation of all systems regarding achievement of Performance Targets**

After all the time and effort expended establishing and verifying Performance Targets during design, if Commissioning is not implemented in the field, these targets likely will not be met: Commissioning is where the rubber meets the road.

Today's traditional buildings have built-in redundancies and "safety factors" to overcome the inadequacies of typical construction methods—for example, to account for the impacts on the HVAC system that result from how a commercial building's envelope is constructed; additional heating and cooling are provided, often unknowingly, to compensate for a leaky building shell. While most commercial buildings are not constructed well, and the systems installed within them often do not operate correctly or at all, these buildings limp along, and most people are none the wiser.

When it comes to integrated higher-performing buildings, Commissioning becomes of the utmost importance, since interrelated systems must be installed properly (and function correctly) to achieve the project's established Performance Targets. Using the prior example, the building shell must perform as designed (with no air infiltration in many climates) for the HVAC system to function properly, because most of the previously needed HVAC safety factors and redundancies likely were removed from the calculations that determined the system's capacity. We have seen a number of green buildings achieve nowhere near their intended potential—and in some cases fail (as previously described in several examples)—because high-performance designs were constructed with standard and substandard building practices and techniques. Commissioning is a means for verifying the quality of installation required to achieve the performance targets.

Additionally, high-performance buildings often utilize new technologies and techniques unfamiliar to builders. This requires contractors to be purchasing, installing, and coordinating systems that are new and different from standard same-old-same-old construction practices. And later, the owner's O&M staff must continue to maintain systems and equipment with which they are often equally unfamiliar.

This is where Commissioning becomes indispensable. Along with the standard gaps between design and construction, these new design ideas create potentially more and wider gaps between construction and operations—holes that need to be filled, sometimes quite literally. The commissioning process provides the vehicle for ensuring that these holes receive the attention they deserve. Commissioning does not bring a whole bunch of new experts to the table of a project; rather, the commissioning process is intended to help the experts, already gathered around the table, be more effective at managing the process of designing, constructing, and operating a high-performance building—and understanding its integrative nature, again for the purpose of achieving the project's performance targets.

Once again, Commissioning attempts to infuse a currently nonexistent quality control methodology into the process of designing and constructing buildings. When visiting a manufacturing facility, it is usually easy to identify the quality control practices being enforced; they are established to help reduce errors and improve the quality of whatever product is being manufactured. One can usually find the quality control office and recognize the relatively static QC procedures in place to ensure that each identical product meets the same quality standards (the product's performance targets). For a building design and construction process, as we have seen, every project is unique, having a different set of intentions, designers, contractors, site issues, spaces, equipment, materials, construction parameters, and so on—the circumstances surrounding the making of this product are always changing, as are the performance targets. So, the QC process and procedures must be adapted to each project. Commissioning has become the current best method for bringing such dynamic QC practices to this industry.

Such Commissioning practices are derived from a general set of procedures that must be tailored to the specific issues of each project and at the same time engage a litany of variants related to the construction process. Consequently, we have attempted in the outline below to identify only the most important areas where commissioning commonly engages this construction process for most projects. However, since every project is different, every project's needs related to the commissioning process will vary; hence, how to apply the outline below will differ for each project.

■ **Perform site observations**

Performing site observations during the construction phase affords the CxA a great opportunity to share a better understanding of the "why" of the project's components with tradespeople and those in the field who have pretty good command of the "how" and "what." These visits also serve to help bridge the gap inherent in the aforementioned adversarial relationship between contractors and designers. A starting place might include sharing and discussing the OPR and BOD with the contractors, especially since those documents ideally have been employed—in an inte-

grative process—for developing the construction documents and commissioning plan.

The initial Commissioning meeting is the place to start this essential communication process. Candor can be a valuable tool for introducing and clarifying the CxA's role—letting the contractors know that the CxA is not the police. Setting aside preconceived notions and replacing them with an open forum for people to share understanding is the only way to overcome traditional tendencies and adversities. Remember, the contractor is responsible for installing what the owner purchased in the construction contract, which is based on what the designers designed, documented, and approved for installation. It is the CxA's responsibility to ensure that the owner's project requirements are not lost in the transition between paper design and physical installation.

As mentioned previously, one unique perspective the CxA brings is seeing installation through the lens of operations and maintenance. As such, the CxA will be looking closely at accessibility, potential problems generated by substitutions, and misunderstandings of design intent. These site observations are not inspections; they do not come from a perspective of codes or construction administration. They are intended to focus attention on the functional performance of the design and, ultimately, the operation of the facility. Thus, it does not serve the project well to be *policing* a project; rather, the CxA is *collaborating* with the installers as systems come together.

■ **Incorporate Commissioning schedule into construction schedule**

The process of incorporating key commissioning points into the construction schedule is one that requires evolution. Beginning with a list of generic commissioning milestones (a pdf file of sample

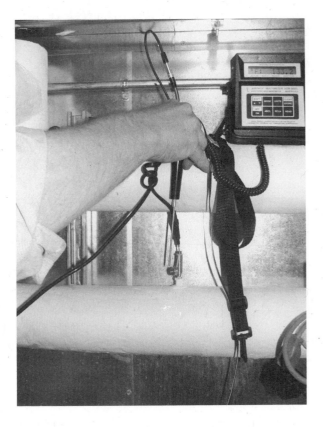

◀ **Figure 8-6** Commissioning of this pressure-temperature (PT) port, installed in a custom air handler built by a manufacturer and delivered to the project site, revealed that the PT port was inaccessible due to the pipe above being too close, obstructing access to the temperature probe. *Image courtesy of Brian Toevs.*

▼ **Figure 8-7** We cut the insulation and found that the PT port from Figure 8-6 was installed with unions. The contractor was able to loosen the unions and roll the fitting over to provide temperature probe access for future testing. *Image courtesy of Brian Toevs.*

Cx milestones can be downloaded from the *Resources* tab on 7group's website at www.sevengroup.com), the contractor can begin to merge commissioning activities into the evolving construction schedule to ensure that the two processes inform and support one another. An obvious connecting point would be the submittal review of commissioned systems that takes place in parallel with the designers' review of submittals (see below); this should be scheduled with a beginning date and an agreed-upon set duration. Less obvious, but ultimately more important to success, are planned and well-timed executions of specific tasks. Witnessing wall mock-ups might take place at any point in the duration of that event, while witnessing the installation of the first window

can only take place on the day it is installed. As the Commissioning Authority is not a daily visitor to the site, there is a need for timely and intentional communication, usually initiated by the contractors. Without these efforts to maintain the merger, these two schedules will grow apart, driven by the forces of traditional construction administration and tendencies to avoid job-site "inspections."

■ **Review Submittals**

The Commissioning Submittal review should run parallel with the design team's review of contractors' submittals, but the commissioning review should come from a much different perspective. While the designers' reviews focus on meeting the capacity and performance criteria of the specification, the commissioning review is more focused on the features that make the equipment meet the unique applications of the project. Not a substitution for the designer's effort, but an enhancement, Cx reviews from this perspective pertain to end-use viability and can improve the traditional review process in a number of ways. In the case of substituted items, the subtle differences in the application of options for single components will often play out differently when viewed in the context of *systems* applications.

For example, one manufacturer's chiller may operate with entering condenser water temperature at 55°F, while a seemingly equal chiller of the same capacity from another manufacturer requires 65°F. These two pieces of equipment cannot easily be accepted as equal within the focused, integrative design process that we advocate here for achieving performance targets. Even equipment of exactly equal capacity and performance features can have subtle differences of utility connection points, footprint, and dedicated access that may not honor the operation and maintenance needs of the project. Since the CxA is more directly engaged with the field circumstances of all the building's systems, the resulting familiarity with physical project particulars provides a valuable perspective.

◼ Develop construction checklists and functional tests

The submittal review process has provided the opportunity for the CxA to become even more familiar with the project's design objectives and equipment particulars, and it delivers valuable information for creating practical construction checklists and functional tests. While the checklists and tests are based on generic variations, even these variations are dynamic, evolving constantly from both individual experience and association with others in the commissioning field. In keeping with all that has been said, these tests must recognize the unique features of each proj-

ect. This can be achieved through close attention to the project-specific particulars of approved documentation and submittals. This is the time in the process, then, to publish the draft version of project-specific checklists and functional tests documents. This draft should be reviewed by the contractors to assist their understanding of systems and testing procedures and to allow them to raise any issues from their perspective.

Construction Checklists (also known as Prefunctional Checklists or System Verification Checklists) are checklists that focus on the component level of systems. These checklists are intended to track components from submittal, to installation, and through start-up—all of which are construction-related activities, thus the name Construction Checklists. These typically are developed by the CxA and completed by the appropriate contractor. (A sample construction checklist can be downloaded from the *Resources* tab on 7group's website at www.sevengroup.com.)

As important as it is to assure that equipment is finally accepted, based on conformance with the OPR and BOD, it is even more important to be sure that the equipment is installed correctly and can properly and completely satisfy the conditions for which it was intended. Starting at the component level, we need to verify that the individual parts are not only received undamaged but installed appropriately and started-up properly. Using the design documents, submittals, and product-specific installation manuals for the selected equipment or component, checklists are created that will help guide the installer toward making the equipment system ready and improving the efficiency of installation and start-up. While it has to be assumed that the contractor has every intention and ability to do a good job, the object here is to ensure a *better* job. The repeatability promoted by the checklist is a proven method for achieving enhanced performance.

Tracking Form for Construction Checklists									
Date Developed	Received Submittal	Bldg. Section	Bldg. Floor	Symbol	Schedule Title	Schedule	Drawing	Service	Location
9/28/2007	X	A	First	EF-1A	Exhaust Fan	M602	M101	IDF A140	IDF A140
10/2/2007	X	A	First	FPV-7A	Fan Powered VAV Box	M603	M101	Music Classroom A124	
10/2/2007	X	A	First	FPV-8A	Fan Powered VAV Box	M603	M101	Computer Lab A136	
10/2/2007	X	A	First	FPV-9A	Fan Powered VAV Box	M603	M101	Classroom A135	
9/28/2007	X	A	First	CH-1A	Hot Water Cabinet Heater	M604	M101	Vestibule A119	Vestibule A119
10/2/2007	X	B	First	VAV-5B	Variable Air Volume Box	M602	M102	Corridor B102	
9/28/2007	X	A	Second	EF-2A	Exhaust Fan	M602	M108	IDF A210	IDF A210
9/28/2007	X	A	Second	EF-6A	Exhaust Fan	M602	M108	Kiln Exhaust	Ceramic A209C
10/1/2007	X	A	Second	HRU-5	Heat Recovery Unit	M601	M403	Auditoriam	Mechanical Room A208
9/28/2007	X	A	Second	UH-1A	Hot Water Unit Heater	M602	M403	Mechanical Room A208	Mechanical Room A208
9/28/2007	X	A	Second	UH-2A	Hot Water Unit Heater	M602	M403	Mechanical Room A208	Mechanical Room A208
10/1/2007	X	B	First	CH-5B	Hot Water Cabinet Heater	M604	M102	Vestibule B118	Vestibule B118
10/1/2007	X	B	First	CH-6B	Hot Water Cabinet Heater	M604	M102	Vestibule B124	Vestibule B124
9/28/2007	X	B	First	EF-1B	Exhaust Fan	M602	M102	Womens Toilet Rm.B109	Womens Toilet Rm.B109
9/28/2007	X	B	First	EF-2B	Exhaust Fan	M602	M102	Mens Toilet Rm B119	Mens Toilet Rm B119
10/2/2007	X	B	First	FPV-7B	Fan Powered VAV Box	M603	M102	Corridor B134 & G103	
10/1/2007	X	B	First	HRU-7	Heat Recovery Unit	M601	M402	Cafeteria & Kitchen	Mechanical Room B130
9/28/2007	X	B	First	UH-1B	Hot Water Unit Heater	M602	M102	Equipment B126A	Equipment B126A
9/28/2007	X	B	First	UH-2B	Hot Water Unit Heater	M602	M102	Equipment B126B	Equipment B126B
9/28/2007	X	B	First	UH-3B	Hot Water Unit Heater	M602	M102	Equipment B129A	Equipment B129A
10/2/2007	X	B	First	VAV-4B	Variable Air Volume Box	M602	M102	Coach B121	
10/1/2007	X	B	Second	AHU-1	Air Handling Unit	M601	M404	Technical Education	Mechanical Room B202
10/1/2007	X	B	Second	AHU-2	Air Handling Unit	M601	M404	Stage	Mechanical Room B202
10/1/2007	X	A	Second	AHU-3	Air Handling Unit	M601	M403	Administration	Mechanical Room A208
10/1/2007	X	B	Second	AHU-4	Air Handling Unit	M601	M404	Auxiliary Gymnasium	Mechanical Room B202
10/1/2007	X	B	Second	HRU-6	Heat Recovery Unit	M601	M404	Media Center	Mechanical Room B202
10/1/2007	X	B	Second	HRU-8	Heat Recovery Unit	M601	M404	Locker Rooms	Mechanical Room B202
10/1/2007	X	B	Second	HRU-9	Heat Recovery Unit	M601	M404	Main Gym	Mechanical Room B202
9/28/2007	X	B	Second	UH-4B	Hot Water Unit Heater	M602	M404	Mechanical Room B201	Mechanical Room B201
9/28/2007	X	B	Second	UH-5B	Hot Water Unit Heater	M602	M404	Mechanical Room B202	Mechanical Room B202
10/1/2007	X	D	First	B-1	Boiler	M601	M401		Mechanical Room D107
10/1/2007	X	D	First	B-2	Boiler	M601	M401		Mechanical Room D107
10/1/2007	X	D	First	B-3	Boiler	M601	M401		Mechanical Room D107
10/1/2007	X	D	First	CHL-1	Air Cooled Chiller	M601	M401		Mechanical Room D107
10/1/2007	X	D	First	CHL-2	Air Cooled Chiller	M601	M401		Mechanical Room D107
10/1/2007	X	D	First	P-1	Pump	M601	M401		Mechanical Room D107
10/1/2007	X	D	First	P-2	Pump	M601	M401		Mechanical Room D107
10/1/2007	X	D	First	P-7	Pump	M601	M401		Mechanical Room D107
9/28/2007	X	D	First	UH-1D	Hot Water Unit Heater	M602	M401	Mechanical Room D107	Mechanical Room D107
9/28/2007	X	D	First	UH-2D	Hot Water Unit Heater	M602	M401	Mechanical Room D107	Mechanical Room D107
9/28/2007	X	D	First	UH-3D	Hot Water Unit Heater	M602	M401	Mechanical Room D107	Mechanical Room D107
9/28/2007	X	D	First	UH-4D	Hot Water Unit Heater	M602	M401	Pump Rm D107C	Pump Rm D107C
9/28/2007	X	D	First	UH-5D	Hot Water Unit Heater	M602	M401	Generator D107B	Generator D107B
9/28/2007	X	D	First	UH-6D	Hot Water Unit Heater	M602	M104	Receiving D112	Receiving D112
10/2/2007	X	D	First	VAV-1D	Variable Air Volume Box	M602	M104	Serving D108	
10/1/2007	X	E	First	CH-6E	Hot Water Cabinet Heater	M604	M105	Vestibule E131	Vestibule E131
10/1/2007	X	E	First	CH-7E	Hot Water Cabinet Heater	M604	M105	Stair E2-1	Stair E2-1
9/28/2007	X	E	First	EF-1E	Exhaust Fan	M602	M105	IDF E121	IDF E121
9/28/2007	X	E	First	EF-3E	Exhaust Fan	M602	M105	Electrical E120	Electrical E120
10/3/2007	X	E	First	FPV-1E	Fan Powered VAV Box	M603	M105	Classroom E101	
10/3/2007	X	E	First	FPV-2E	Fan Powered VAV Box	M603	M105	Classroom E102	
10/3/2007	X	E	First	FPV-3E	Fan Powered VAV Box	M603	M105	Classroom E104	
10/2/2007	X	E	First	VAV-2E	Variable Air Volume Box	M602	M105	IPC E119	
10/2/2007	X	E	First	VAV-3E	Variable Air Volume Box	M602	M105	Science Prep E111A	
10/2/2007	X	E	First	VAV-4E	Variable Air Volume Box	M602	M105	Small Group E123	
10/2/2007	X	E	First	VAV-5E	Variable Air Volume Box	M602	M105	Small Group E124	
9/28/2007	X	E	Second	EF-2E	Exhaust Fan	M602	M112	IDF E221	IDF E221
9/28/2007	X	E	Second	EF-4E	Exhaust Fan	M602	M112	Electrical E220	Electrical E220
10/3/2007	X	E	Second	FPV-15E	Fan Powered VAV Box	M603	M112	Classroom E201	
10/4/2007	X	E	Second	FPV-27E	Fan Powered VAV Box	M603	M112	Student Project E222	
10/4/2007	X	E	Second	FPV-28E	Fan Powered VAV Box	M603	M112	Corridor E225	
10/4/2007	X	E	Second	FPV-29E	Fan Powered VAV Box	M603	M112	Corridor E228	
10/2/2007	X	E	Second	VAV-6E	Variable Air Volume Box	M602	M112	Science Prep E204A	
10/2/2007	X	E	Second	VAV-7E	Variable Air Volume Box	M602	M112	IPC E219	
10/2/2007	X	E	Second	VAV-8E	Variable Air Volume Box	M602	M112	Science Prep E211A	
10/2/2007	X	E	Second	VAV-9E	Variable Air Volume Box	M602	M112	Small Group E223	
10/2/2007	X	E	Second	VAV-10E	Variable Air Volume Box	M602	M112	Small Group E224	
10/1/2007	X	E	Pent-House	HRU-1	Heat Recovery Unit	M601	M405	Classroom Wing North	Mechanical Room E301
9/28/2007	X	E	Pent-House	UH-1E	Hot Water Unit Heater	M602	M405	Mechanical Room E301	Mechanical Room E301
10/1/2007	X	F	First	CH-1F	Hot Water Cabinet Heater	M604	M106	Corridor F130B	Corridor F130B
10/1/2007	X	F	First	CH-2F	Hot Water Cabinet Heater	M604	M106	Stair F1-1	Stair F1-1
10/1/2007	X	F	First	CH-3F	Hot Water Cabinet Heater	M604	M106	Vestibule F129	Vestibule F129
10/1/2007	X	F	First	CH-4F	Hot Water Cabinet Heater	M604	M106	Corridor F125	Corridor F125
10/1/2007	X	F	First	CH-5F	Hot Water Cabinet Heater	M604	M106	Corridor F130B	Corridor F130B
9/28/2007	X	F	First	EF-1F	Exhaust Fan	M602	M106	IDF F121	IDF F121
9/28/2007	X	F	First	EF-3F	Exhaust Fan	M602	M106	Electrical F120	Electrical F120
10/4/2007	X	F	First	FPV-1F	Fan Powered VAV Box	M603	M106	Classroom F101	
10/4/2007	X	F	First	FPV-2F	Fan Powered VAV Box	M603	M106	Classroom F102	
10/4/2007	X	F	First	FPV-3F	Fan Powered VAV Box	M603	M106	Classroom F104	

Middle School Construction Checklists

1a		1b		2a		2b		2c		2d		2e		2f		2g		2h		3a		3b		3c		3d			
Checklists issued for Contractor completion																													
in	out	in	out	in	out	in	out	in	out	in	out	in	out	in	out	in	out	in	out	in	out	in	out	in	out	in	out	Issued	Returned
						x	x					x	x	x	x	x	x	x	x			x	x	x	x	x	x	April-08	
												x	x	x	x			x	x			x	x			x	x	April-08	
												x	x	x				x	x			x	x			x	x	April-08	
												x	x	x				x	x			x	x			x	x	April-08	
									x	x	x	x	x	x	x	x	x	x			x	x	x	x	x	x	April-08	
								x	x			x	x	x	x			x	x			x	x			x	x	April-08	
						x	x					x	x	x	x	x	x	x	x			x	x	x	x	x	x	April-08	
						x	x					x	x	x	x	x	x	x	x			x	x	x	x	x	x	April-08	
																		x	x			x	x			x	x	April-08	
										x	x	x	x	x	x	x	x	x	x			x	x	x	x	x	x	April-08	
										x	x	x	x	x	x	x	x	x	x			x	x	x	x	x	x	April-08	
										x	x	x	x	x	x	x	x	x	x			x	x	x	x	x	x	April-08	
						x	x					x	x	x	x	x	x	x	x			x	x	x	x	x	x	April-08	
						x	x					x	x	x	x	x	x	x	x			x	x	x	x	x	x	April-08	
												x	x	x				x	x			x	x			x	x	April-08	
																		x	x			x	x			x	x	April-08	
										x	x	x	x	x	x	x	x	x	x			x	x	x	x	x	x	April-08	
										x	x	x	x	x	x	x	x	x	x			x	x	x	x	x	x	April-08	
								x	x			x	x	x	x			x	x			x	x			x	x	April-08	
																		x	x			x	x			x	x	April-08	
																		x	x			x	x			x	x	April-08	
																		x	x			x	x			x	x	April-08	
																		x	x			x	x			x	x	April-08	
																		x	x			x	x			x	x	April-08	
																		x	x			x	x			x	x	April-08	
																		x	x			x	x			x	x	April-08	
										x	x	x	x	x	x	x	x	x	x			x	x	x	x	x	x	April-08	
										x	x	x	x	x	x	x	x	x	x			x	x	x	x	x	x	April-08	
												x	x	x	x	x	x	x	x			x	x	x	x	x	x	April-08	
												x	x	x	x	x	x	x	x			x	x	x	x	x	x	April-08	
										x	x	x	x	x	x			x	x			x	x			x	x	April-08	
										x	x	x	x	x	x			x	x			x	x			x	x	April-08	
										x	x	x	x	x	x			x	x			x	x	x	x	x	x	April-08	
										x	x	x	x	x				x	x			x	x			x	x	April-08	
										x	x	x	x	x	x	x	x	x	x			x	x	x	x	x	x	April-08	
										x	x	x	x	x	x	x	x	x	x			x	x	x	x	x	x	April-08	
										x	x	x	x	x	x	x	x	x	x			x	x	x	x	x	x	April-08	
										x	x	x	x	x	x	x	x	x	x			x	x	x	x	x	x	April-08	
								x	x			x	x	x	x			x	x			x	x			x	x	April-08	
										x	x	x	x	x	x	x	x	x	x			x	x	x	x	x	x	April-08	
										x	x	x	x	x	x	x	x	x	x			x	x	x	x	x	x	April-08	
						x	x					x	x	x	x	x	x	x	x			x	x	x	x	x	x	April-08	
						x	x					x	x	x	x	x	x	x	x			x	x	x	x	x	x	April-08	
												x	x	x	x			x	x			x	x			x	x	April-08	
												x	x	x	x			x	x			x	x			x	x	April-08	
												x	x	x	x			x	x			x	x			x	x	April-08	
								x	x			x	x	x	x			x	x			x	x			x	x	April-08	
								x	x			x	x	x	x			x	x			x	x			x	x	April-08	
								x	x			x	x	x	x			x	x			x	x			x	x	April-08	
								x	x			x	x	x	x			x	x			x	x			x	x	April-08	
						x	x					x	x	x	x	x	x	x	x			x	x	x	x	x	x	April-08	
						x	x					x	x	x	x	x	x	x	x			x	x	x	x	x	x	April-08	
												x	x	x	x			x	x			x	x			x	x	April-08	
												x	x	x	x			x	x			x	x			x	x	April-08	
												x	x	x	x			x	x			x	x			x	x	April-08	
								x	x			x	x	x	x			x	x			x	x			x	x	April-08	
								x	x			x	x	x	x			x	x			x	x			x	x	April-08	
								x	x			x	x	x	x			x	x			x	x			x	x	April-08	
								x	x			x	x	x	x			x	x			x	x			x	x	April-08	
						x	x					x	x	x	x	x	x	x	x			x	x	x	x	x	x	April-08	
						x	x					x	x	x	x	x	x	x	x			x	x	x	x	x	x	April-08	
												x	x	x	x			x	x			x	x			x	x	April-08	
												x	x	x	x			x	x			x	x			x	x	April-08	
												x	x	x	x			x	x			x	x			x	x	April-08	
								x	x			x	x	x	x			x	x			x	x			x	x	April-08	
								x	x			x	x	x	x			x	x			x	x			x	x	April-08	
								x	x			x	x	x	x			x	x			x	x			x	x	April-08	
								x	x			x	x	x	x			x	x			x	x			x	x	April-08	
								x	x			x	x	x	x			x	x			x	x			x	x	April-08	
																		x	x			x	x			x	x	April-08	
										x	x	x	x	x	x	x	x	x	x			x	x	x	x	x	x	April-08	
										x	x	x	x	x	x	x	x	x	x			x	x	x	x	x	x	April-08	
										x	x	x	x	x	x	x	x	x	x			x	x	x	x	x	x	April-08	
										x	x	x	x	x	x	x	x	x	x			x	x	x	x	x	x	April-08	
										x	x	x	x	x	x	x	x	x	x			x	x	x	x	x	x	April-08	
										x	x	x	x	x	x	x	x	x	x			x	x	x	x	x	x	April-08	
						x	x					x	x	x	x	x	x	x	x			x	x	x	x	x	x	April-08	
						x	x					x	x	x	x	x	x	x	x			x	x	x	x	x	x	April-08	
												x	x	x	x			x	x			x	x			x	x	April-08	
												x	x	x	x			x	x			x	x			x	x	April-08	
												x	x	x	x			x	x			x	x			x	x	April-08	

Figure 8-8 Sample Tracking Form for Construction Checklists. *Image courtesy of Brian Toevs.*

Tracking Form for Functional Tests

Note: MC=Mechanical Contractor; CC=Controls Contractor, EC=Electrical Contractor, MR=Manufacture Rep., SM= Sheet Metal Contractor, O=Owner, CX=Commissioning Agent

Date Developed	Building Area	Building Floor	Equip. Tag	Equipment Description	Room Name
11/8/2007	Roof	Helipad		Snow Melting System	Helipad
11/8/2007	A	Level 1		Hot Water System	Mechanical Room
11/8/2007	A	Level 1		Glycol Hot Water System	Mechanical Room
11/5/2007	A	Level 1		Chilled Water System	Mechanical Room
11/5/2007	B	Level 1	AHU-1	Air Handling Unit	Mechanical Room
11/5/2007	B	Level 1	AHU-2	Air Handling Unit	Mechanical Room
11/5/2007	B	Level 1	AHU-3	Air Handling Unit	Mechanical Room
11/5/2007	B	Level 1	AHU-4	Air Handling Unit	Mechanical Room
11/5/2007	C	Level 1	AHU-6	Air Handling Unit	Mechanical Room 2
	C	Level 1	AHU-7	Air Handling Unit	Mechanical Room 2
11/6/2007		Level 2		VAV Assoc AHU-1	
11/62007		Level 3		VAV Assoc AHU-2	
11/6/2007		Level 3		VAV Assoc AHU-3	
11/6/2007		Level 3		VAV Assoc AHU-4	
11/62007		Level 1		VAV Assoc AHU-6	
11/8/2007				Exhaust CV AHU-2 & 3	
1/17/2008		Level 2	FC-B-2	Fan Coil Unit	Stair B
1/17/2008		Level 3	FC-B-3	Fan Coil Unit	Stair B
1/17/2008		Elev. Lobby.	FC-4-C	Fan Coil Unit	L4003
1/17/2008		Level 5	FC-5-A	Fan Coil Unit	Bed Tower link
1/17/2008		Elev.	FC-5-B	Fan Coil Unit	L5002
1/17/2008		Elect. Rm.	FC-E2	Fan Coil Unit	L1001
11/8/2007	A	Level 1	UH-1-1	Unit Heaters	Mechanical Room
11/8/2007	A	Level 1	UH-1-5	Unit Heaters	Water
11/8/2007	A	Level 1	UH-1-6	Unit Heaters	Med Gas
11/8/2007	E	Level 2	CUH-1	Cabinet Unit Heaters	Vestibule
11/8/2007	C	Level 2	CUH-3	Cabinet Unit Heaters	Vestibule
111/8/2007		Level 5	UH-5-2	Unit Heaters	Level 5
11/8/2007			UH-1-7	Unit Heaters	Chiller Addition
		Level 2	DH-1	Air curtain/ Door heater	Ambulance vestibule
11/8/2007		Level 1	EF-1	Exh Fans General CV	Central Sterile
11/8/2007		Level 1	EF-5	Exh Fans General CV	Toilet Exhaust
11/8/2007		Level 1	Ef-6	Exh Fans General CV	General Exhaust
11/8/2007		Level 7	EF-2	Exh Fans Variable Volume	Emergency Room
11/8/2007		Level 7	EF-3	Exh Fans Variable Volume	West ISO Rooms
11/8/2007		Level 7	EF-4	Exh Fans Variable Volume	East ISO Rooms
8/15/2007	A	Level 1	EM. GEN	Emergency Generator	Generator Room
8/16/2007	A	Level 1	UPS	Uninterruptible Power Supply	Electrical Room
11/13/2007	A	Level 1		PLC Auto-Transfer System	Electrical Room

Figure 8-9 Sample Tracking Form for Functional Tests. *Image courtesy of Brian Toevs.*

Critical Care Hospital Facility

Room Number	Anticipated Duration in Days		Date Functionally Tested	Status
Helipad	0.500			
L1001	0.500		5/20/2008	Complete
L1001	0.500		5/20/2008	Incomplete
	1.000	2.5		
L1001	1.000		6/18/2008	Incomplete
L1001	1.000		6/17/2008	Incomplete
L1001	1.000		6/17/2008 / 6/18/2008	Incomplete
L1001	1.000		5/22/2008 / 6/18/2008	Incomplete
L1020	1.000		5/29/2008 / 6/19/2008	Incomplete
L1020	1.000			
	3.000		5/27 - 5/28/2008	
	2.000			
	2.000			
	2.000		5/23/2008	Complete
	2.000		5/28 - 6/ /2008	Complete
	4.0	21.0		
	0.125		5/6/2008	Complete
	0.125		5/6/2008	Complete
	0.125		Future	
	0.125		6/19/2008	Complete
	0.125		Future	
	0.125	0.8	5/21/2008	
L1001	0.125		5/5/2008	Complete
L1006	0.125		5/5/2008	Complete
L1007	0.125		5/5/2008	Complete
L2001	0.125		6/19/2008	Complete
L2178	0.125		6/19/2008	Complete
L 5001	0.125		5/5/2008	Complete
	0.125			
L2110	0.125	1.000	5/21/2008	
L1152	0.250			
L1201	0.250			
L1201	0.250			
L2002,3,4	0.500			
L2094,95	0.500			
L2082,83,84	0.500	2.250		
L1003	1.000			
L1002	0.500			
L1002	0.500	2.000		
	29.5	29.5		

The contractors are given the blank checklists and are expected to complete them as the course of construction progresses. These checklists are intended to help contractors establish a disciplined approach to the repetitive tasks of supervising their own crews during the installation process—a task that sometimes suffers from a loss of focus. For example, while the installation of each of one hundred identical fan coil units will require the same basic repetitive steps, each installation will also require adaptation to the unique physical circumstances of one hundred different locations. In reality each unit's installation never happened before and will never again, exactly. Nevertheless, checking these individual units can become totally repetitious. It is precisely in this repetition that contractors can benefit from the value of performing the checkout in exactly the same way every time, therefore assuring that each and every component gets the same attention as all the others.

Functional tests are testing protocols used to verify that systems and their components operate in unison and as designed. (A sample functional test can be downloaded from the *Resources* tab on 7group's website at www.sevengroup.com.) Functional tests should be developed as early as possible in the project. If comprehensive sequences of operations are developed during the design stage, then the functional tests can be started when equipment is installed and ready. However, finalization of the functional tests cannot occur until after all submittals are approved and operations and maintenance documentation is available for the specific equipment of the project.

The construction checklists and functional tests developed for any project will become fairly sizable in volume, and this documentation needs to be tracked. If good tracking tools are not utilized, much of this documentation will likely be lost, or simply not referenced, during the course of construction. There has been many a project where this set of documents has been created, only to find itself left dormant in the contractor's trailer until the end of the project, at which point it gets collected and organized as an empty, literally useless set of forms.

We have developed a Tracking Form for Construction Checklists (see Figure 8-8) and a Tracking Form for Functional Tests (see Figure 8-9) to help guard against this. We have found additional value in the construction checklist tracking form; while seemingly obvious, it was only after the development of this form that we realized its value in identifying many of the specific submittals we need to review related to commissioning.

Witness start-up

Often, equipment start-up is far more important to functional operation than the credit it is given in the traditional construction process. Start-up is usually left as an exercise between a visiting factory technician and a less interested mechanic, usually without the attendance of any of the owner's maintenance personnel. In most cases the owner's personnel, who will assume responsibility for operating the equipment and systems, only come to know the equipment's operative features through its failure, after everyone is gone. Start-up offers invaluable training opportunities for facilities staff, providing a level of familiarity that cannot be duplicated.

Start-up should also ensure that equipment is being positioned optimally within its *system,* and therefore should include start-up settings and adjustments that prepare the equipment for its linkage—and responses to its linkage—with other system components. Failure to recognize these linkages, or an incorrect sequence of linkages, often results in failed or incomplete start-up and failed functional tests. Just as the integrative process results in a unique facility (never built before and never built again), each component piece has a unique place in the system. It is that basic. And yet the mundane, repetitive, detailed nature of the task becomes the enemy of this basic understanding (many in the field find start-up just plain boring) and needs to be overcome by recognizing the importance of these start-up procedures relative to achieving the building's performance targets.

While the master builder of antiquity had the benefit of tools—albeit arduous and challenging by current standards—with which he was intimately familiar (and to which he was physically linked) due to use over long periods of time, today's contractor is challenged by the ostensible benefit of ever-changing technology. It can be quite difficult for the contractor to develop any sense of personal involvement through the use of these technologies. Checklists and witnessed start-ups are important tools that promote the ownership, involvement, and, we daresay, pride of effort that we consistently see improves outcomes and performance. Much can be gained in this regard by reminding contractors of the purpose behind these efforts—again, achieving the building's performance targets.

Perform functional tests

Once substantial completion has occurred and the acceptance phase of construction begins, it is time for functional testing. The functional testing is where the commissioning authority takes control of the process and oversees the execution of the tests. Experience has taught us that functional testing can only serve its purpose after systems are installed and started, control points are checked and verified, balancing reports are approved, and engineer's punch lists are completed. Testing requires close documentation by the commissioning team. This documentation not only affirms that the correct installation of

systems meets the engineer's original sequence of operations, but it also provides a record for the future that will allow the facilities staff to return the system to its original, optimal operating condition in the future—a guide for future operations.

Functional testing provides an opportunity to discover and correct any mistakes resulting from improper or incomplete installation that in the conventional process are left for facilities and maintenance staff to discover much later over the course of operations. Accordingly, one clear value of functional testing is that it allows maintenance staff to focus on the random problems associated with normal equipment operation. Another significant value is gained when maintenance staff witnesses and participates in the process of functional testing—the value of this opportunity cannot be overstated. These tests are events that typically occur only once to this level of detail. There is a great deal of time spent unpacking a sequence of operations for the first time, waiting to see what happens, and deciding if the actual results are consistent with the expected results. So, if these opportunities for training are missed, it is unlikely that they can or will be duplicated.

Verify training of building operations team

Now that the building is operational, one of the final construction tasks is to provide training for the operations and maintenance staff charged with taking care of the building. As with the construction checklists, since the contractors are responsible for the installation of all components and equipment, contractors also should be responsible for providing all necessary training. These installing contractors are more familiar than anyone at this point with the nuances and idiosyncrasies of each unique installation. The training required will have been considered and identified long before the end of construction, in the form of a training matrix (see Figure 8-10). Evolving OPR and BOD considerations, as well as possible changes in personnel, might well require a current update at this point. This training matrix is derived from the OPR and the specifications, along with the start-up and troubleshooting guides provided with the installed equipment. This matrix can be useful in matching systems with the appropriate key people who will participate in the live training. It also can be used to schedule and sequence training events in progressive ways. It makes sense that if multiple components of systems will require training, these training sessions should be organized in an escalating fashion. In other words, plan training to be sequential, starting with individual components, and then progressing to overall systems. Of all the training vehicles available, the functional testing referenced above may be one of the best methods for familiarizing facilities staff with the basic operating nature of the systems, although formalized training is still necessary. With so many technologies available, recording and documenting training can take many forms; but at minimum, these events should be organized with a training agenda, a record of attendance, and a video recording of the training as it takes place, which can be used for future reference.

▦ Prepare final Commissioning report

As each phase of the project is completed, commissioning activities for that phase should be concurrently completed and cumulatively summarized in a report. All phase-related documentation should be collected and placed in appendices that support the work of that particular phase. For example, there should be a design phase report, a construction phase report, an acceptance phase report, and so on. The final Commissioning report should simply be an organized collection of all previous documentation and phase reports.

Establishing early on the protocol for the Commissioning process with construction managers

EARLY PHASE TRAINING MATRIX

The following table summarizes the current training requirements listed in the specification. This is initiated by the Commissioning Authority for review and completion by the owner, through the various contractors and the Construction Manager, as applies.

Specification Section	System	Duration
131100.1.12.B	Swimming Pool	32 Hrs. 2 sessions – 1st for 16 hrs. on pool systems, 2nd for 16 hrs anytime up to 1 year after acceptance.
142400.3.5.A	Hydraulic elevators	
144200.3.5.A	Vertical Platform lift	
212200.3.9	Clean Agent Fire Suppression System	
230513.13.3.5.	Variable Frequency Drives	
230924.3.9	Direct Digital Temperature Controls	24 hrs
232500.1.6.D	HVAC Water Treatment	2 hrs
235233.14.3.2.A	High Efficiency Condensing Boilers	2 days minimum on 2 separate visits
236400.3.2	Packaged Water Chillers	2 days minimum on 2 separate visits
237413.3.3	Packaged Natatorium Dehumidification Unit	8 hrs minimum over 2 visits
260944.3.3	Digital Network Lighting Controls	
263213.4.5	Emergency / Standby Power Systems	8 hrs per 5 people
265100.3.6	Interior Lighting	2 hrs
265561.2.12	Auditorium Theatrical Lighting System	2 sessions – 1st for 4 hr minimum. 2nd w/in 60 days of owner acceptance for 2 hr minimum
275124.1.7.A & 3.5.C	Intercom & Master Clock	
275124.01.2.5.A	Auditorium Sound Reinforcement System	Each system 2 sessions @ 2 Hrs. ea. & 1 @ 1 Hr within 60 days of owner acceptance.
275124.02.2.5.A	Band/Choral Rooms Sound Reinforcement System	
275124.03.2.5.A	Cafeteria Sound Reinforcement System	
275124.04.2.5.A	Gymnasium Sound Reinforcement System	
275124.05.2.5.A	Natatorium Sound Reinforcement System	
275132.3.2.A	RF Broadband Video Distribution System	2 Hrs.
275132.01.3.2.B	Media Management Subsystem	16 Hrs. Hands on & * Hrs. technical.
283100.1.5.A	Fire Alarm Network & Detection System	4 Hrs.

Figure 8-10 Sample Early Phase Training Matrix. *Image courtesy of Brian Toevs.*

and contractors during this stage will save confusion, time, and lost momentum. Commissioning is a parallel process that will, from time to time, impose serious questions that are important to the implementation of the OPR through the BOD during construction. Again, the more clear the OPR and the BOD (including their ongoing, documented maintenance during design), the smoother will be the entire commissioning process during this stage and the easier will be the task of tracking established milestones—and successfully achieving performance targets.

▦ Produce systems manuals

The *systems manuals,* or *recommissioning manuals,* do not typically contain any new or different information than that produced by the contractors, designers, or CxA. The systems manuals can take many forms, but they are consistently a collection of existing documentation reorganized into sections that mimic the systems found in a project. We have come to view systems manuals as more than just troubleshooting guides, but as documents to be utilized when the systems in a building are operating normally. During normal operation, systems need standard scheduled

Lessons from the Systems Manuals For Automobiles

During any building's normal operation, its systems will require standard scheduled maintenance to perform well and to avoid the need for premature replacement. This set of operations issues mimics that of car ownership, whereby standard scheduled maintenance, instituted by the Japanese automakers in the late 1970s, has resulted in more than tripling the average useful life of a new automobile in the intervening thirty years.

Additionally, a building's systems manuals define the parameters for maintaining performance levels. You may recall from Chapter 2 the story about systems interrelationships that describes how the selection of the paint color (with high light reflectance values) for interior walls on our first green school project helped reduce the size of the building's HVAC system. This story was revisited in Chapter 5 (*Stage A.3*) to emphasize that such interrelationships need to be analyzed as early as possible so that more effective integrated solutions and decisions can be made during the schematic design (SD) phase. These early decisions can significantly affect operations decisions throughout the building's life. So what happens 10 or 20 years after occupancy when someone wants to paint the walls a darker color? Doing so could now potentially render the cooling capacity of the HVAC system inadequate, right?

The answer lies in the systems manual.

When you buy a $20,000 automobile, what do you get as the owner of that fairly complex product to operate it? A pretty good owner's manual, right? It tells you everything you need to know about how to operate that vehicle and maintain it to ensure performance. But when you buy a $20-million building (three orders of magnitude more expensive), what do you as the owner get to operate that *very* complex product? Often when we ask this question in workshops, the response we hear is "nothing"—or "a key." As the owner, though, you often receive what's *called* an owner's manual, but what is this really? Generally, it consists of a stack of three-ring binders stuffed with cut sheets of equipment and components—if you are lucky, the correct model numbers for the installed equipment are circled. But this "manual" tells you nothing about how to operate or maintain your building. That would be like getting an owner's manual for your car consisting of cut sheets for things like the compressor (for the air conditioning system) under the hood, with no information at all about how to set temperatures or what button to press to cool the cabin.

In the case of the paint color for repainting interior walls, the systems manual will stipulate the light reflectance values required in certain spaces to maintain adequate lighting system performance and in turn to ensure adequate cooling system performance—not unlike the owner's manual for a car mandating that 10w-40 synthetic motor oil is required to maintain engine performance.

maintenance (such as filter changes, lubrication, occasional checks, and so on) to ensure that operation is remaining consistent with the original intent over long-term operations.

B.7.2 Principles and Measurement

■ **Manage the collection of documents that verify achievement of Performance Targets**

The Cx report serves this purpose quite well for most systems. Projects pursuing LEED will need to collect documentation from the builder and subcontractors required to verify achievement of the LEED credits being pursued. Since this generally falls outside the standard of care for the scope of services in design and construction contracts, it is likely that additional fees will need to be allocated, or the owner will need to devote staff time for managing this process.

Examples of LEED documentation required from contractors include materials cost, construction waste management reports, photographs depicting construction indoor air quality measures, recycled content information from manufacturers, and so on. Since this documentation may be unfamiliar to many construction professionals, it often gets overlooked or deferred to the end, at which point reconstructing this documentation can become quite onerous—"OK, we will get to that later." Consequently, we have found that it can be vitally important to require that submittals documenting environmental performance and LEED credits not be divorced from the standard submittal process; rather, specifications should require this documentation on an ongoing basis, accompanying normal product submittals. We also have found it effective to require that regular periodic progress reports be submitted with monthly certificates and applications for payment, tying payment approvals to periodic submission of documentation such as construction waste management logs and status reports on the

implementation of construction IAQ management plans, and so forth.

■ **Commissioning: Document prefunctional and functional testing results and prepare Commissioning reports and Recommissioning Plan**

As stated above, commissioning is not design, and it is not construction. There is no need to duplicate design or construction documentation in the commissioning report. As such, the final commissioning report should be limited to reporting the specific activities related to the commissioning process (see Figure 8-11). Similar to training, the reports generated during a project related to commissioning ideally should be progressive in nature. Also included in the final report should be an executive summary of the successes and failures of the commissioning activities throughout the entire project. The executive summary should be short, only three to five pages in length, and specific, highlighting only those important points that drove the project's commissioning successes and/or failures.

The recommissioning, or systems, manuals should include abbreviated versions of the design documents, commissioning documentation, and operations and maintenance information. If significant problems arise with systems (or components within systems), the systems manuals provide only the initial step in diagnosing the problem. As problems arise, it makes sense to progress from the systems manuals, to the full set of design (or as-built) drawings and specs, along with O&M documentation, to outside assistance—as necessary—to diagnose and solve the problem.

B.7.3 Cost Analysis

■ **Coordinate with builder to ensure that subcontracts are awarded based on performance requirements, not just price**

SAMPLE   *Contents*

Final Commissioning Report
  Executive Summary
  The Commissioning Plan
  LEED Score Card

  Appendix A.   Design Intent and Basis of Design
    Design Intent Report
    Basis of Design Comments

  Appendix B.   Design Review Comments
    50% CD Review
    90% CD Review

  Appendix C.   Submittal review Comments
    Submittal review comments

  Appendix D.   Field Observation Reports
    Field Observation Issues Log

  Appendix E.   Construction Check Lists
    Completed Construction Checklists

  Appendix F.   Functional Performance Test and Results
    Completed Functional Tests
    Blank Functional Tests

  Appendix G. Issues Report
    Issues Report Log

  Appendix H. Training
    Training Plan

  Appendix H.   Warranty

  Appendix J.   Photographs

7group 183 West Main Street Kutztown, PA 19530 1.610.683.0890 www.sevengroup.com

---

Figure 8-11 Sample Commissioning Report Table of Contents. *Image courtesy of Brian Toevs.*

As a component of the *construction partnering* process described throughout this chapter, we have found it important that the activities described (above) in *Stage B.7.1* be implemented in two stages: The *first* step includes a review of performance criteria and unique aspects of the project with the builder, *prior* to subcontractor selection. As a result, award of subcontracts is not based merely on low-est price; rather, it is also based on subcontractors' thorough understanding of the project's Performance Targets. The *second* step is implementing all of the post-award activities described above.

On an early LEED project, a carpentry subcontractor in the process of submitting a bid for a major University project asked us to clarify the impacts LEED had on materials selection and documentation requirements in order to better understand how to construct their bid. We have experienced this kind of inquiry from numerous subcontractors, so we now recommend that construction teams take the time to understand these implications as part of positioning or differentiating themselves in a competitive marketplace that is demanding green buildings more and more.

B.7.4 Schedule and Next Steps

■ **Ensure systematic communication between design and building teams**

We have found it quite effective to require in the specifications that various topics related to Performance Targets be included as regular agenda items at all job conferences for the purpose of updating status, coordinating trades, and sequencing appropriately. This often requires interim meetings and/or communication between various team members; not at all unlike the traditional construction process, but environmental performance issues and system interrelationships are now thrown into the mix with equal priority. Throughout this process, the incorporation of feedback mechanisms should remain part of all discussions to ensure that building and occupants have the capability to measure and assess operational performance. *Stage C.1* outlines such considerations and aspects of performance measurement and feedback.

PART C—OCCUPANCY, OPERATIONS, AND PERFORMANCE FEEDBACK

Stage C.1
Occupancy: Feedback from All Systems

C.1.1   Operations Activities

- Establish operations team consisting of key stakeholders responsible for continuously monitoring, maintaining, and improving environmental performance
- Establish and implement standard operating procedures (SOPs) that provide continuous feedback regarding performance of the four key subsystems:
  - Habitat
  - Water
  - Energy
  - Materials
- Commissioning: Conduct periodic Recommissioning in accordance with Recommissioning Manual

C.1.2   Principles and Measurement

- Document key indicators that serve as proxies for the health of the larger ecosystem
- Document occupant surveys and reconcile results with building systems performance
- Implement Measurement and Verification (M&V) plan continuously over the life of the building
- Insert results of periodic Recommissioning into Recommissioning Manual

C.1.3   Cost Analysis

- Track economic performance of the four key subsystems

C.1.4   Schedule and Next Steps

- Implement all of the above forever

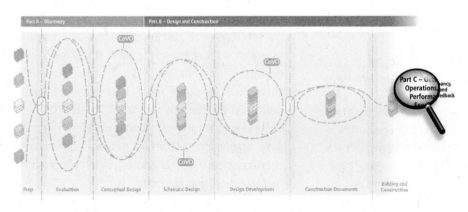

Figure 8-12 Integrative Process Stage C.1, Occupancy. *Image courtesy of 7group and Bill Reed; graphics by Corey Johnston.*

Stage C.1

Occupancy: Feedback from All Systems

The Call for Performance Feedback

We are now moving into Part C—Occupancy, Operations, and Performance Feedback. At this point, construction has been completed and the operations phase begins. Our intent here is not to describe, in any comprehensive way, how to operate a building, since the procedures and impacts associated with building operations are far beyond the scope of this book. Rather, our purpose here is to explore what needs to be measured and how. Accordingly, we focus our discussion in this last stage on how to go about engaging performance measurement and creating performance feedback mechanisms. Such measurement and feedback is critical for informing the operations of the facility, so that we can assess the degree to which established Performance Targets have been met.

Such feedback also helps designers, builders, and owners better understand the implications that their process and decisions might have on future project outcomes, so long as this feedback can be identified and documented. In other words, performance feedback can help us understand the results of our integrative process, so that we can continually evolve our process toward better and more effective integration.

We have found that convening a project team meeting post-occupancy can be extremely useful in this regard. The purpose of this meeting is to generate a discussion with all team members about lessons learned. An effective framework for this discussion includes exploring: What worked? What did not work? How could we do and think about this differently? This will enable the further development and ongoing evolution of the mental model shift required to become more integrated, based on outcomes in the form of measured performance data.

Generally speaking, the level of measuring energy performance in our buildings currently consists of simply paying utility bills and monitoring annual increases in cost—are this year's bills higher than last year's? The next step, less often undertaken, is analyzing utility billing data to determine what underlies those costs: did my usage by fuel source go up, and/or did my rate structure change? Were weather conditions (HDD and CDD) different? However, we *should* be comparing that utility data to our targeted energy performance benchmark and verifying energy savings by implementing a measurement and verification (M&V) plan, as addressed in more detail below.

But what other performance indicators can and should be measured?

An emerging field of study, Post-Occupancy Evaluation (POE), measures factors that can influence human performance. These factors might include measuring levels of indoor air quality, daylighting, acoustics, thermal comfort levels, and so on.

Some studies now go beyond measuring just the factors that *influence* human performance by attempting to measure human performance itself. These studies measure things like productivity—currently with metrics such as absenteeism, turnover rates, and reduced error rates, among others. Much of this current work in the United States is being done by Carnegie Mellon's Center for Building Performance and Diagnostics (see *BIDS* sidebar), Syracuse University, Judith Heerwagen, and others. However, even though much work on such studies has been launched, there currently exists a dearth of conclusive data in this regard. Environmental psychologist Heerwagen, who focuses on these issues, concludes that "more time and creativity has gone into designing natural habitats for zoo animals than in creating comfortable office spaces for humans."

But the early returns from such studies are quite positive—several have documented statistically significant increases in productivity in simple terms. One example, from Joseph J. Romm's and William D. Browning's *Greening the Building and the Bottom Line: Increasing Productivity through Energy-Efficient Design* (Snowmass,

Building Investment Decision Support (BIDS): A Framework for Post-Occupancy Evaluation (POE)

Vivian Loftness of Carnegie Mellon University says sustainability is, in truth, all about health. Energy and material extraction and use, as well as atmospheric, water, and land pollution are as significantly health-related issues as they are environmental conservation issues. The following has been excerpted from papers and reports that she and her colleagues have published.*

The work of the faculty, researchers, and graduate students of the Center for Building Performance and Diagnostics at Carnegie Mellon and the Advanced Building Systems Integration Consortium, link the quality of buildings to productivity, health, and life cycle sustainability. As part of this research, a new Building Investment Decision Support tool—BIDS™—has been developed (see http://cbpd.arc.cmu.edu/ebids). This cost-benefit decision support tool presents the results and life cycle data from over 150 field case studies, laboratory studies, simulation studies, and other research efforts. The substantial environmental cost-benefits of a range of advanced and innovative building systems—such as delivering privacy and interaction, ergonomics, lighting control, thermal control, network flexibility, and access to the natural environment—can now be quantified by professionals. This tool illustrates the amazing return on investments possible, through a range of cost-benefits—from the "immediate dollars" of energy efficiency, waste management, and churn, to the "long term dollars" of improved indoor environmental quality, productivity, and health. Environmental design principles and life-cycle decision-making are critical to our professional commitment to improving quality of life.

The Center for Building Performance and Diagnostics uses the following principles and guidelines as a framework for Post-Occupancy Evaluation in support of what they are calling high performance buildings and productive organizations:

1. **Move beyond broad definitions of sustainability to justify high performance materials and assemblies.**
   Environmental designers often argue for broad sustainability objectives without further detail.... However, investors and clients will need to understand the specific quality differences of sustainable design alternatives—component by component—if they are to move beyond least-first-cost decision-making.

2. **To justify high performance building components and systems, understand the Cost of Ownership.**
   In order to promote investment in sustainable, high quality buildings, it will be critical to prove to the client that the real cost of doing business is realized over time, not in first construction costs. Careful bookkeeping will reveal that "cheap" buildings and infrastructures, and "cheap" building delivery processes, result in major costs over time.

3. **Facilities Management Cost Savings**
   Maintenance and Repair; Energy, Water, and Other Utilities; Cost of Discomfort; Employee Retention and Training; Failure Costs: High performance buildings have the potential to generate significant operational cost savings, ranging from energy and other utility efficiencies, to fa-

cility management effectiveness, to the potential for reducing failure costs and measurable lost work time due to system failures. 25–50% energy savings, for example, can be achieved in most existing buildings and…new construction.…At present, energy use is typically 1–2% of current plant value, and facility management / maintenance and repair costs are typically 2–4% of current plant value, indicating the importance of pinpointing the costs of discomfort and failure due to inadequate investments.

4. Individual Productivity Cost Savings

Speed and Accuracy; Effectiveness; Creativity; Motivation; Absenteeism: Since a majority of the cost of doing business is for salaries (as much as 60%), any innovation that will clearly increase productivity even by a small percentage will quickly pay back investments in quality products and systems. Adrian Leaman, in England, estimates the potential impact for buildings on overall productivity as +12.5% (improved performance) and –17% (hampered performance), for an overall 30% change in worker performance between the best and worst buildings.

5. Attraction/Retention or Turnover Cost Savings

Time and Cost to Attract; Quality Attracted; Training Costs; Retention Rates: Another aspect of the productivity cost-benefit equation is the ability to attract and keep the best workers, the time needed for training, and the commitment of those workers to their work, including unpaid overtime. Average turnover rates for private professional positions are 20.3% with 6.8% rates for government positions. A 2000 study by Jac Fitz-Enz identified four costs associated with employee turnover: termination, vacancy, replacement, and productivity loss.

Total cost of turnover for one position
 Termination $ 1,000
 Replacement $ 9,000
 Productivity $15,875 (3 months baseline salary and benefits)
Total $25,875—with 20.3% turnover rate [this equates to] $5,300 per employee per year

6. Health Cost Savings

Workman's Compensation; Medical Insurance Costs; Health Litigation Costs; Environmental Evaluation & Remediation; Lost Work Time: After salary, the second major annual cost of an employee is benefits, including medical and insurance costs, as well as workman's compensation. Measured reductions in these costs would justify investment in better quality environments.

The most easily identified health cost–savings linked to the quality of buildings are within workman's compensation, especially as related to muscular skeletal disorders (MSD). In the State of Washington, workers compensation claims for muscular skeletal disorders average over 43,000 per year with an average 1.84 workdays lost per employee. Given average claim rates of 3.6% per workforce and median MSD cost of $470, the average MSD cost per employee per year is $17, which can be substantially offset (over 80%) through ergonomic furniture and employee training. The annual cost of muscular skeletal disorders may be only "the tip of the building-related iceberg," since the annual workman's compensation costs per employee exceeds over $500 per year according to Bureau of Labor Statistics data.

(continued)

7. Spatial Renewability: Organizational Churn Cost Savings

Labor and material costs for reconfiguring workstations and workgroups; HVAC/Lighting/Networking System Modification Costs; Occupant Down-Time: There are significant cost-benefits to investing in renewable, quality building systems to reduce the cost of "churn." The International Facility Management Association (IFMA) reports a mean churn rate of 41% for all types of facilities…the average cost per move was $809,

while the median cost per move was $479. These significant annual expenses are incurred to support the cost of: reconfiguring working groups and individual space; accommodating changes in functions, densities, and work hours; and accommodating rapid changes in technologies on the desktop.

8. Access to the Natural Environment: Daylight and Natural Ventilation

Effective daylighting can yield 10–60% reductions in annual lighting energy consumption,

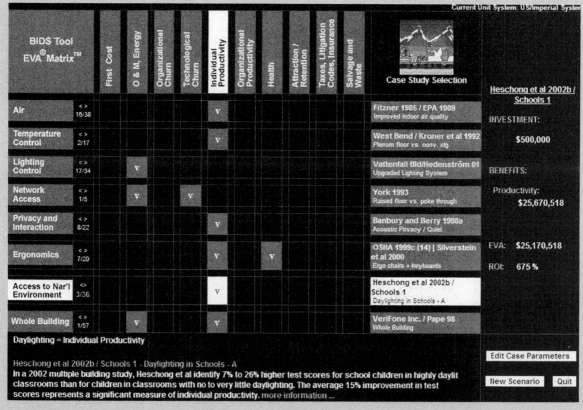

Figure 8-13 This screen capture (from the online BIDS tool) depicts a matrix that can be used to access POE results from the case studies in the database and illustrates that remarkable returns on investment are possible over a range of strategies for green buildings. *Image courtesy of Vivian Loftness, FAIA, University Professor of Architecture at the Center for Building Performances & Diagnostics.*

Figure 8-14 This graph summarizes the relative returns on investment (ROIs) associated with various attributes of green buildings as derived from 276 studies. Even the lowest ROI, which resulted from looking at impacts at the whole building level for 191 projects, indicates extremely attractive financial performance at 19 percent. *Image courtesy of Vivian Loftness, FAIA, University Professor of Architecture at the Center for Building Performances & Diagnostics.*

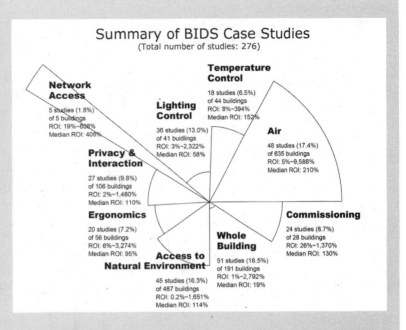

Summary of BIDS Case Studies
(Total number of studies: 276)

Network Access
5 studies (1.8%)
of 5 buildings
ROI: 19%~808%
Median ROI: 408%

Temperature Control
18 studies (6.5%)
of 44 buildings
ROI: 8%~394%
Median ROI: 152%

Lighting Control
36 studies (13.0%)
of 41 buidlings
ROI: 3%~2,322%
Median ROI: 58%

Air
48 studies (17.4%)
of 635 buildings
ROI: 5%~9,588%
Median ROI: 210%

Privacy & Interaction
27 studies (9.8%)
of 106 buildings
ROI: 2%~1,460%
Median ROI: 110%

Commissioning
24 studies (8.7%)
of 28 buildings
ROI: 26%~1,370%
Median ROI: 130%

Ergonomics
20 studies (7.2%)
of 56 buildings
ROI: 6%~3,274%
Median ROI: 95%

Whole Building
51 studies (18.5%)
of 191 buildings
ROI: 1%~2,792%
Median ROI: 19%

Access to Natural Environment
45 studies (16.3%)
of 487 buildings
ROI: 0.2%~1,651%
Median ROI: 114%

with average energy savings for introducing daylight dimming technologies in existing buildings at over 30%. Emerging mixed-mode HVAC systems that interactively support natural ventilation and air conditioning are demonstrating 40–75% reductions in annual HVAC energy consumption for cooling. Moreover, design for access to the natural environment, including daylighting and natural ventilation strategies, has shown measurable gains for productivity and health in the workplace.

9. High Performance Equipment

The first trade-off in a value engineering exercise is typically to reduce the quality of the equipment and appliances that have been specified. Even short-term energy savings do not seem to be enough to drive decision-makers. For example, the introduction of California, and then national, standards for equipment and appliance efficiency has had a major impact on national energy use, reducing overall energy consumption for heating, cooling and refrigeration by 25%, 40% and 75% respectively.

High Performance Lighting Pays!

Replace outdated office lighting with quality electric lighting systems featuring high-performance lamps, ballasts, fixtures, and advanced controls for 27–87% lighting energy savings, 0.7–26 % productivity gains, and 27% headache reduction, with ROIs over 236%.

10. Shading, Cool Roofs and Cool Communities

Where once shading through massing, orientation, external and internal shading devices was integral with the aesthetics of place, the shading of buildings and communities today is a lost art. Again, first-least-cost decision-making will not support the dynamic and elegantly crafted solutions for shading that are invaluable to sustainable environments. Consequently, we must

(continued)

build the life-cycle proofs to support shading, landscaping and cool roof technologies.

Cool Roofs Pay!

Replace conventional dark roofs with cool roofing for 2–79% cooling energy savings and 14–79% peak cooling demand reduction.

11. Innovative Systems Integration

There are a growing number of LEED® Silver, Gold and Platinum projects that have demonstrated measurable energy benefits, as well as reduced absenteeism, quicker attraction rates, better health statistics, and more. The difficulty lies in determining which elements of the building contributed most significantly to those gains—one systems integration innovation, the use of underfloor air to ensure task air for each individual, has demonstrated life cycle benefits.

Task Air Pays!

Underfloor Air Systems:

Implement underfloor air systems to ensure 5–34% annual HVAC energy savings and 67–90% annual churn costs savings, for an ROI of at least 115%.

*Much of the content of this sidebar is taken from Vivian Loftness, Volker Hartkopf, Beran Gurtekin, Ying Hua, Ming Qu, Megan Snyder, Yun Gu, and Xiaodi Yang, Carnegie Mellon University Center for Building Performance and Diagnostics, "Building Investment Decision Support (BIDS™), 2005.

Colo.: Rocky Mountain Institute, 1994; http://www.rmi.org/images/PDFs/BuildingsLand/D94-27_GBBL.pdf), indicates that productivity gains can be as high as 16 percent.

Clearly, writing and implementing M&V plans and POE studies requires additional effort well outside the standard for scope and fees. How can we encourage and incentivize such invaluable studies? Why would an owner pay for these? In short, what is their value? It is important to answer this question to ensure that such studies are funded and implemented.

First, engaging such studies requires that the relationship between design teams and owners be extended well into occupancy. This sustained relationship can do nothing but serve both parties well, as the results can be applied in multiple ways. Owners, for example, can alter operations and/or future design pursuits for the benefit of their employees and their bottom line. Designers can apply the implications of these results to their future work. And, in many cases, the sustained relationship between owners and de-

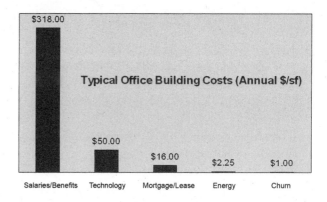

Figure 8-15 This data from U.S. office buildings reveals that an increase in employee productivity of less than 1 percent would pay an owner's entire energy bill (by comparing annual employee salaries and benefits costs to annual energy costs). Productivity increases of 5 percent would pay for an owner's entire mortgage or lease costs. Productivity gains in green buildings have been shown to be as high as 16 percent. *Graph courtesy of Marcus Sheffer, who adapted this bar chart from Environmental Building News, which was derived from data provided by Carnegie Mellon Center for Building Performance and Diagnostics extracted from the Rocky Mountain Institute's documentation based on data from Building Owners and Managers Association (BOMA) International.*

signers can inform their future work together, further fusing their relationship.

Owners who build only a single building will need to understand the value of performance feedback if they are to be willing to pay for it—or to pursue other funding sources to support the effort involved. Hence, implementing such studies that produce measurable, quantified results as a means for providing statistical evidence linking the relationship between building performance and human productivity can serve as strong motivation. Their purpose for conducting such studies can then be understood as a means for improving not just building performance, but also productivity and their bottom line (see Figure 8-15).

Potential mechanisms for encouraging the implementation of feedback mechanisms include the use of performance contracting and performance-based fees. Both mechanisms tie a portion of the designers' and builders' fees to the ultimate performance of the project.

Performance contracting taps into the savings generated by the project, relative to an agreed-upon benchmark, as a means for paying a portion of the design and construction fees. For example, energy savings confirmed through M&V efforts produce a revenue stream that can be used to pay these fees.

Performance-based fees allow the owner to retain a portion of the design and construction fees until performance is measured and verified: If the building performs well (again, relative to an agreed-upon benchmark), designers and builders get paid additional fees on a sliding scale: the better the building performs, the more fees are earned; if the building performs poorly, less fees are paid.

This certainly sounds like a reasonable approach, right? Well, these performance-based contracting and fee structures are currently unusual, due to the complexities associated with the range of variables involved in determining the benchmarks against which to measure performance. Is this because such an approach is too naïve in the context of current practice, or because we simply do not yet understand the complexity of how to incorporate all of the variables fairly and accurately enough to assess performance? In either case, perhaps a more clearly defined and understood integrative process could enable such fee structures by more clearly defining performance parameters, and, with more data, by more clearly predicting outcomes.

The performance data currently generated by the building industry is severely lacking. This directly reflects the nearly complete absence of research and development (R&D) investment with regard to building performance, relative to the average percentage of annual revenue that most industries devote to R&D. The average U.S. industry invests 3 percent of its annual sales in R&D, while industries that produce more complex products spend far more, as illustrated in Figure 8-16. The U.S. design and construction industry spends a paltry 0.4 percent; yet, as we have seen, a building is perhaps the most complex and expensive product that any human will buy in their lifetime.

Our call is clear. We in the building industry must devote more time, energy, and resources to measuring, understanding, and improving building performance. Such performance studies of our buildings are essential if we hope to link more effective integration to better performance. However, the value derived from these studies extends well beyond the project being analyzed. Given the value to the industry as a whole—or, dare we say, to humanity or living systems—single projects perhaps should not be expected to bear the cost burden alone. We argue that large-scale institutional funding is needed to support industry-wide R&D efforts pertaining to building performance and human productivity. Participants could include universities, U.S. Department of Energy labs (such as National Renewable Energy Laboratory, NREL), utilities, foundations, design and construction professionals, building owners, developers, insurance companies, product manufacturers, and others. The drivers behind the creation of such funding, such as global climate change and rapidly increasing energy costs, are

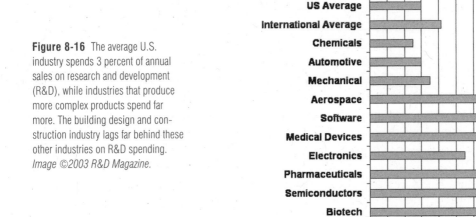

R&D Spending by Industry Average

US Design/Construction Industry
US Average
International Average
Chemicals
Automotive
Mechanical
Aerospace
Software
Medical Devices
Electronics
Pharmaceuticals
Semiconductors
Biotech

0 1 2 3 4 5 6 7 8 9 10 11 12 13 14 15
% of Annual Sales

Source: R&D Magazine, 2003 Annual R&D Funding Forecast

Figure 8-16 The average U.S. industry spends 3 percent of annual sales on research and development (R&D), while industries that produce more complex products spend far more. The building design and construction industry lags far behind these other industries on R&D spending. *Image ©2003 R&D Magazine.*

becoming increasingly recognized—the more serious we are about addressing climate change and energy costs, the greater the need for building-industry R&D. Such research does not pertain solely to what happens within the building, although that would be a good start; as we have seen, it must expand the gathering of feedback to address larger and larger nested systems.

C.1.1   Operations Activities

■ **Establish Operations team consisting of key stakeholders responsible for continuously monitoring, maintaining, and improving environmental performance**

The Operations team generally is led by the building owner; if the owner does not take the lead in coordinating and implementing this effort, it likely will not happen. The specific key team members responsible for performing the required monitoring tasks vary, but usually this effort is lead by the owner's facilities managers in conjunction with other germane participants, such as the company responsible for providing and/ or installing the building's controls systems.

To hold the project's aspirations and vision, the operations team must also consist of other key stakeholders beyond facility operators. Key participants in this effort may include: the project architect, engineers, builder, energy modeler, commissioning authority, POE researchers, and other specialized consultants relative to building-specific functions.

Continuous systems training for new staff and refresher courses for all staff should be conducted pertaining to all systems. One of the best ways we have found to reproduce training activities after the project is complete and the owner has taken occupancy is to be sure that all training has been videotaped, as mentioned above. With today's video recording technology, it is easy to document every training event and produce a DVD that can be easily duplicated and viewed as many times as necessary by anyone needing initial training or a refresher.

■ **Establish and implement standard operating procedures (SOPs) that provide continuous feedback regarding performance of the four key subsystems**

It is not the intent of this book to provide a comprehensive list of all potential feedback sources and indicators; rather, the examples provided for each of the four key subsystems below are intended to identify the range and scope of the most useful opportunities for receiving feedback that are common to most projects. For each of these indicators, it is important to identify and document the mechanism by which feedback will be received over the life of the project, including the data that needs to be collected, the means for gathering this data, how the data will be analyzed (including the metrics and benchmarks that will used), and how the resultant information will be communicated. Once procedures are established for collecting and reporting feedback, they need to be incorporated into the project's standard operational practices.

■ **Habitat** (biotic systems other than human)
  • Gather measurements of key indicators of the ecosystem; examples include the following:
    • macro-invertebrate inventories, dissolved oxygen, nitrogen, pH levels, and turbidity in surface water
    • soil organic matter, chemical composition, and infiltration testing
    • ongoing Floristic Quality Assessment and C values over time, as discussed in *Stage A.5.1*
    • continuously updated assessments of biodiversity (see *Key Considerations...* sidebar)

Key Considerations when Planning for Biodiversity during Land Development Activities

By Keith Bowers, Biohabitats, Inc., Baltimore, MD

Conserving and restoring biodiversity should be one of the primary focuses of any land development or land modification activity. Here are a few key considerations when planning for the conservation and restoration of biodiversity at a development site and for monitoring biodiversity over time.

1. Perform a comprehensive site assessment to identify the flora and fauna and their associated habitat that use the project site for part or all of their life cycle.

2. Contact the state Natural Heritage Program (along with other relevant programs) to determine if the project site supports, or has the potential to support endemic, rare, threatened, or endangered species or rare or significantly important habitat. Protect and wherever possible restore RT&E species and significantly important habitat.

3. Consider the geographic and temporal scale of the species and habitats of interest. Look beyond the project site boundaries to the surrounding ecosystems, landscapes, bioregions, and biomes. Also focus on the niches and populations of specific species and their relations to the project site. Temporal considerations should focus on species migrations, foraging, nesting, and hibernation cycles, along with natural disturbance regimes.

4. Context of the project site counts. Identify landscape patterns at a broad scale to

(continued)

determine habitat patches, connectivity, and the underlying matrix, or relationships of land uses.

5. Connectivity of habitat is key. Well-connected habitat provides species the opportunity to move throughout the landscape. Avoid habitat fragmentation and wherever possible restore habitat connectivity. Connectivity of habitat can provide refugia for species that migrate due to disturbance regimes and the effects of climate change.

6. Size of habitat matters. Large patches of similar habitat protect interior species and species with large home ranges. The core area of the patch, along with its shape, amount of edge, and proximity to other habitat patches can be key to maintaining biodiversity.

7. Consider the potential impacts that the development and operations will have on habitat and its associated biodiversity and how those impacts will be very different depending on the characteristics of the development and its associated footprint.

8. Recognize that ecosystems are going through profound abiotic and biotic changes. Look for ways that development and operations activities not only regenerate reference ecosystem processes and functions but also facilitate the creation of novel ecosystems to enhance biodiversity.

9. Biodiversity and culture go hand-in-hand. Explore how human habitat and wildlife habitat can commingle in a way that supports the evolutionary trajectory of both.

10. Apply an adaptive management strategy to biodiversity conservation and restoration. Adaptive management is a learning process that allows for the modification of long term management strategies based on the success or failure of past strategies.

Every place we inhabit is unique. Each place requires the tracking of performance indicators that are unique to that project and place. These indicators are not static; they may address certain aspects within the immediate time frame that, because life evolves, may change over time as new species emerge and new relationships form. This evolution is influenced by the improving or degrading impact of human presence as well. As the situation changes, different indicators may be more important to gauge.

On one of our projects, there was an immediate need to diversify the plant species in order to provide greater resiliency over the long term, as well as to help increase the soil absorption capability and groundwater recharge to support a nearby stream. As the situation improved, the operations plan included periodic evaluations of the quality of water within the stream and the diversity of additional water species to monitor the progress of improvements.

The plan of action needs to address the expectation of improvement, but there is no guarantee that life will proceed as we expect. Therefore, the narrative of where we hope things will go and what to look for is probably as important as any set of indicators.

- *Example*: For a large project that served as a connector to two formerly linked ecosystems, the following issues needed to be addressed and monitored:
  - Stream restoration: Channel-shape assessments, so neither degrading nor aggrading (sediment erosion or buildup) takes place; monitoring rifle pool sequences for trout habitat and water oxygenation; investigations of the floodplain to assess and stabilize locations for plant- and tree-restoration plantings.
  - Wildlife habitat: Focal species monitoring; shrubland and grassland plant-community diversity assessments; status of security islands for small species with lesser mobility; management of threatened bird species to preserves that include roosts, buffers, and large areas of emergent wetlands; upland forest management programs and trails to reduce stress from human use; thinning of forest for fire protection; annual burn protocols to restore healthy forest floor, meadow, and prairie vegetation; increase of organic matter in revegetation areas; monitoring habitat movement through corridors; taking particular care to understand and minimize levels of encroachment and understand the impact of encroachment.
- Protection of soils and water resources from impacts of erosion, invasive species, and overuse.

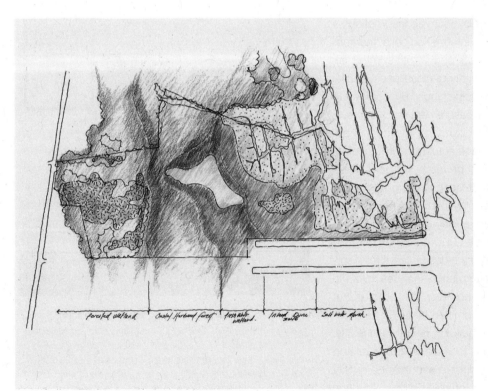

Figure 8-17 Plant-type zones are identified on a future development parcel as the land rises in elevation and distance from the Chesapeake Bay. These zones will inform the types of plants to be restored and monitored on future buildings lots within each zone as the development's plan for biodiversity—realizing a similar pattern of living system relationships that was originally on the site before it was simplified due to the previous owner's having scraped the site clean of all habitat. *Image courtesy of Torti Gallas and Partners, Tim Murphy of Regenesis.*

■ **Habitat** (human)

• Perform post-occupancy evaluation (POE) studies to measure the factors that influence human performance (indoor air quality, daylighting, acoustics, thermal comfort levels, etc.), as discussed above. Various POE methodologies evaluate the performance of occupied buildings relative to their initial performance targets. This set of tasks includes the systematic gathering of data about the building's performance; it includes measurement and analysis of both quantitative and qualitative information collected from both the building and its occupants (via occupant surveys). Information collected through measurement can consist of data from water and electric bills, measurements of indoor air quality (IAQ), daylighting and/or electric lighting levels, energy consumption by end use, and more. Information collected from surveys provides data on thermal comfort, air quality, acoustics, lighting, cleanliness, spatial layout, and office furnishings. By comparing data from both measurement and surveys, we can better understand the relationship between conceptual and actual performance, as well as identify other performance parameters that need to be addressed in design.

• *Examples:* We recently performed a POE for a facility that had achieved LEED Certification. Using tools like LEED during design can provide guidance to the design team for incorporating high performance features into the project. Ultimately, however, the proof is not in the paperwork submitted for LEED certification but in how the building performs in reality. This particular study focused on issues related to IAQ, lighting, indoor environmental quality (IEQ), and analysis of utility billing. The first

step in a POE is to devise the mechanisms to be used for gathering data. In this case, the data included air samples, temperature, humidity and CO_2 measurements, light levels, IEQ survey results, and data from utility bills.

POE studies often include a survey of the building occupants to gather feedback on their comfort and the performance of the building and its systems. The Center for the Built Environment (http://www.cbe.berkeley.edu/index.

Figure 8-18 Air sampling using a test kit can identify potential indoor air quality issues. The test kit shown here draws an air sample from an area of about 1,000 square feet, which is then sent to a lab for analysis. The IAQ parameters tested, in this case, yielded results for total volatile organic compounds, formaldehyde, and mold. *Image courtesy of Todd Reed.*

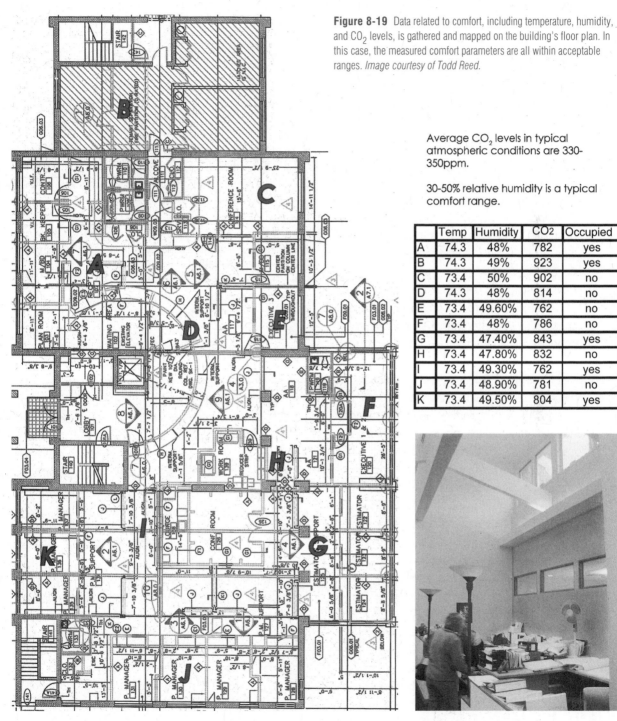

Figure 8-19 Data related to comfort, including temperature, humidity, and CO_2 levels, is gathered and mapped on the building's floor plan. In this case, the measured comfort parameters are all within acceptable ranges. *Image courtesy of Todd Reed.*

Average CO_2 levels in typical atmospheric conditions are 330-350ppm.

30-50% relative humidity is a typical comfort range.

	Temp	Humidity	CO2	Occupied
A	74.3	48%	782	yes
B	74.3	49%	923	yes
C	73.4	50%	902	no
D	74.3	48%	814	no
E	73.4	49.60%	762	no
F	73.4	48%	786	no
G	73.4	47.40%	843	yes
H	73.4	47.80%	832	no
I	73.4	49.30%	762	yes
J	73.4	48.90%	781	no
K	73.4	49.50%	804	yes

htm) offers an online survey that addresses the issues below; it can be modified to address others (see Figures 8-20 and 8-24):

- Office layout
- Office furnishings
- Thermal comfort
- Air quality
- Lighting
- Acoustic quality
- Cleanliness and maintenance

Project teams conducting this type of survey can qualify for a point in the LEED IEQ category of credits, since it serves as the primary measure of a thermally comfortable environment. According to the American Society of Heating, Refrigerating and Air-Conditioning Engineers (ASHRAE), if 80 percent of occupants express satisfaction (or better) with the thermal comfort conditions, then the space is considered thermally comfortable. When reviewing this LEED credit with project teams, we are surprised at the number of building owners that choose to pass up this opportunity because they do not want to know the results or provide occupants with a vehicle for their complaints. This evidences that we almost expect to produce uncomfortable spaces as the norm—or that we have given up trying to provide adequate flexibility in systems design to allow for greater levels of individual control. Survey data is a vital feedback mechanism that can help us produce healthier, more productive human habitat for people with varying needs, rather than a one-size fits all approach.

The POEs that measure human performance (with metrics such as absenteeism, turnover rates, productivity, error rates, etc.) differ from POEs that focus on building performance. The latter type of POE focuses on the factors that

9.2 How satisfied are you with the temperature in your workspace?

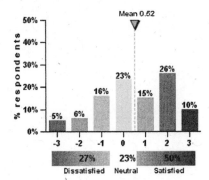

Figure 8-20 Survey questions are used as a component of a POE to determine occupant satisfaction related to building performance. Respondents expressing dissatisfaction are asked to attribute a reason for their discomfort. This information can enable adjustments to be made in the building systems to improve the satisfaction rate. *Image ©2008 Center for the Built Environment.*

influence human performance, while the former focuses on the measurement of human performance itself, as mentioned above. As a result, the first set of data can be correlated with the second, in an attempt to analyze and determine causality. Adjustments can then be made accordingly to improve performance and inform performance targets for future design efforts.

■ **Water**

The benefit to monitoring long-term water quality will certainly be useful to the building project, its occupants, and the larger living system it inhabits. In addition, this information could potentially influence changes in building codes by demonstrating the measurable benefit of alternative systems. An example of this resulted from monitoring the quality of water that exits from the constructed wetlands systems installed on a variety of projects on which we have worked. We find it ironic that this water is often significantly cleaner than the municipally supplied water our projects are typically required to use. However, the governing agencies we have established to protect our health and safety are understandably concerned about "new" technologies that are represented by a minimal number of installations. Evidence and the performance tracking of alternative systems will help move us toward better systems in the future.

- Site water use:

  The typical indicators used for water quality on or near a site help to determine impacts from improper human waste treatment, overfertilization, poor agricultural practices, erosion of soils, chemical pollution from industrial wastes, excess animal waste, improper chemical treatment of water, and so on; these indicators include the following:

  - Biochemical oxygen demand
  - Biological monitoring
  - Chemical oxygen demand
  - Coliform bacteria
  - Dissolved organic carbon
  - Fecal coliforms
  - Hypoxia (environmental)
  - Nitrate
  - Oxygen saturation
  - PH
  - Salinity
  - Total suspended solids
  - Turbidity

- Monitor building water use and cost:

  Water use and cost are similar to energy in that the data should be gathered, analyzed, and benchmarked. Water use is typically less complicated to monitor than energy use, unless there are substantial process water uses or more complicated gray water or rainwater harvesting systems. Process water is generally referred to as water use outside the typical water consumption in buildings. Typical water consumption includes water used for irrigation and water used by flush fixtures (toilets, urinals) and flow fixtures (faucets, showerheads). Process water could include water used by commercial dishwashers, cooling towers, manufacturing processes, and so on.

- Benchmark building water use against the original target and/or similar facilities:

  Unfortunately there is not yet a database of commercial building water consumption similar to that used by the Target Finder tool for energy (as discussed under the "Energy" sections of in *Stages A.1.1* and *A.5.1*). However, numerous publications related to public water supply and plumbing design refer to water-use values, typically reported as gallons per person per day. This benchmark can be calculated rather easily for many facilities.

- Benchmark building water use against the calculated prediction:

  In many cases, the calculations generated when completing the LEED documentation related to water use can serve as the calculation methodology for predicted water use, excluding process water.

- Gather data required for the M&V effort:

  Also similar to the effort for energy, data related to water use will need to be gathered as part of the M&V effort.

- *Example:* W. S. Cumby, a builder and construction management firm near Philadelphia, Pennsylvania, renovated a senior housing facility into office space that was then LEED Certified. We conducted a POE study for this project that included an analysis and benchmarking of the project's water use. Water use was benchmarked relative to the predictions of water use in the LEED submission and against typical

Water Consumption

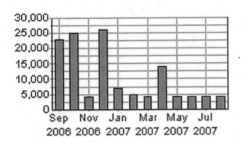

Figure 8-21 Monthly water use was graphed for 2006–2007 as part of a POE study for this project. What caused the spikes in water use during this year is currently unknown. By monitoring water use on a more regular basis, these increases in usage can be identified more quickly, so that the source of any problems can be remedied. *Image courtesy of Brad Kise.*

water-consumption values in office buildings. The predicted water use was 66,638 gallons per year. The benchmark for a comparable office building, based on typical water-use data, was 75,400 gallons per year. The first year's actual consumption was 124,000 gallons. Closer examination revealed that there were four months of anomalous consumption with much higher water use than the other eight months (see Figure 8-21). As of this writing the reasons for the excess consumption during those four months have not yet been determined, but if the eight "typical" months are more indicative of normal use, then the project could be consuming just around 60,000 gallons per year. However, the simple process of tracking the data can help to point out problems by identifying anomalies that need to be investigated and/or corrected, as in this example.

■ **Energy**
- Monitor energy use and cost:
  Facility owners typically track energy costs and sometimes energy usage. This information is rarely analyzed beyond making a comparison to the previous year when the cost significantly increases. Rarer yet is the design firm or builder who tracks the energy performance of their projects. Without gathering and analyzing this data, how does a project team know if they have designed and built an energy hog or not? If they have, what could have been done differently to minimize the problem? If not, how close are they to achieving their performance targets, and how might performance be improved? Since most owners have the data, or can easily obtain it, conducting the analysis is a relatively simple undertaking.
- Benchmark energy use against the original performance target:
  Once the energy cost and consumption data has been gathered, it should be benchmarked against the original energy target established for the project during design. Has the performance target been met? If not, then the question should be: Why not? Thus begins the pursuit of reducing the facility's energy use over time.
- Benchmark energy use against similar facilities:
  The energy cost and consumption data should also be benchmarked against similar facilities. As discussed several times, beginning back in *Stage A.1,* the U.S. Environmental Protection Agency's (EPA's) Target Finder tool can be used to compare actual utility data to data from similar facilities that has been normalized for location and building size. Other potential benchmarks could include data from similar facilities owned by the same owner (e.g., other buildings on a university campus), data from similar facilities in the same area, or Commercial Buildings Energy Consumption Survey (CBECS) data. The CBECS data is the basis for Target Finder and for the targets in the 2030 Challenge (also discussed in *Stage A.1.1*).

Comparisons to CBECS data can be used to measure performance against these targets.

- Benchmark against the energy modeling results: It is very tempting for projects to immediately compare the actual utility bills to the energy modeling results. While this is a fair comparison, it is important to understand that the energy model is a prediction of performance based on a long series of assumptions. Often the assumptions do not pan out in reality (see M&V discussion below in *Stage C.1.2*), and as a result, the values predicted by the model do not match actual energy consumption. A better comparison is to use the energy model as part of the M&V effort. During this process, the energy model is calibrated to match actual utility bills. The first step in the M&V process is to gather data required for the M&V effort, including utility billing data, submetered consumption data, information stored in the controls system's data logger (if applicable), detailed occupancy schedules, actual weather data for the year being analyzed, and so on, in accordance with the M&V plan.

- *Example:* A POE study can include simplified analysis and benchmarking of the project's energy use and cost. For the W. S. Cumby office

Evaluating Building Energy Performance - W.S. Cumby & Son

Energy Star Target Finder

The US EPA's Energy Star Target Finder is a tool used to assist the design team in setting an energy performance target and evaluating a building's actual energy performance in terms of site energy use intensity and estimated and actual total annual energy consumption. The database used by Target Finder is the US Department of Energy's Commercial Building Energy Consumption Survey (CBECS). By entering a few of the project's facility characteristics (i.e. location of project for local climate and weather data, building type, area, occpancy levels, and hours of operation), the CBECS data can be accessed and normalized. The normalized data is then ranked on a scale of 1-100. As the design progresses, estimated annual energy use can be compared to the normalized CBECS data to monitor the design's energy performance. After occupancy the actual data can be entered and compared to the database to evaluate final building energy performance.

Building Characteristics

Zip Code	19064	City	Springfield	State		Pennsylvania	
Space Type (see Notes below)		Gross Floor Area	Number of Occupants	Number of PCs		Operating Hours / Week	
Office		14,000	29	29		60	

Utility Rates

Electricity		$0.1225948/kWh		Natural Gas		NA	

Energy Star Target Finder Results

Energy Data	Actual Performance	Target Finder 75	Target Finder 90	Target Finder 100			
Target Finder Rating	88	75	90	100			
Site Energy Use Intensity (kBtu/Sq./yr)	31.8	40.8	30.6	16.4			
Estimated Total Annual Energy (kBtu)	444,553.0	571,545.0	428,225.0	230,221.0			
Total Annual Energy Cost ($)	$15,973	$20,536	$15,386	$8,272			
Site Energy Cost Intensity ($/Sf)	$1.14	$1.47	$1.10	$0.59	$0.00	$0.00	

Based on the data provided the project would qualify as an Energy Star rated building.

Notes:

The US DOE's CBECS database used in Target Finder has a limited number of building types.

Energy Star Target Finder Disclaimer:

"An incomplete energy use profile could result in a high but inaccurate rating. Total annual estimated energy use must include plug, process, and all non-regulated loads: equipment loads specified on drawings: and all fuel sources."

Figure 8-22 Actual building performance can be benchmarked within the U.S. Environmental Protection Agency's Target Finder. This particular project scored an 88 in Target Finder. Additional Target Finder scores also were entered to provide a point of reference and establish a goal for future energy improvements. *Image courtesy of Marcus Sheffer.*

Evaluating Building Energy Performance - W.S. Cumby & Son

US Department of Energy - Energy Information Administration
Commercial Buildings Energy Consumption Survey, 2003

CBECS data is produced by the US DOE every four years based on a survey of thousands of commercial building from all over the United States. The data is based on actual building energy consumption and cost. This data represents the average of thousands of buildings of various size, age, types of construction, location, and energy sources. It is useful to compare the modeling results to these values as a reality check and to enable realistic goal setting of project energy performance. In addition it is useful for making comparisons to actual building energy use to gauge building energy performance.

Energy Intensity (kBTU/square foot)					Energy Cost ($/square foot)		
Building Type	National Average	Northeast	Middle Atlantic	Climate Zone 3	Building Type	National Average	Northeast
All	89.8	98.5	98.3	98.5	All	$1.43	$1.65
Education	83.1	101.6	103.1	93.5	Education	$1.22	$1.49
Food Service	258.3	272.8	290.2	247.6	Food Service	$4.15	$4.84
Health Care	187.7	212.2	219.0	191.4	Health Care	$2.35	$2.82
Retail	73.9	65.0	72.3	97.1	Retail	$1.39	$1.33
Office	92.9	101.2	98.0	95.4	Office	$1.71	$2.07
Public Assembly	93.9	89.2	98.0	87.3	Public Assembly	$1.47	$1.27
Public Order & Saf	115.8	132.5	NA	NA	Public Order & Saf	$1.76	$2.09
Religious Worship	43.5	52.1	58.1	52.8	Religious Worship	$0.65	$0.68
Warehouse	45.2	41.6	49.2	49.5	Warehouse	$0.68	$0.69

The 2030 Challenge

The American Institue of Architects, the US Conference of Mayors, US Green Building Council and many other organizations have adopted the 2030 Challenge to eliminate fossil fuel energy use in buildings by 2030. All projects are challenged to obtain an immediate 50% reduction in energy intensity relative to the national average figures above. The reduction is scheduled to increase over time according to the following schedule:
60% in 2010   70% in 2015   80% in 2020   90% in 2025
Carbon-neutral in 2030 (using no fossil fuel GHG emitting energy to operate).
These targets may be accomplished by implementing innovative sustainable design strategies, generating on-site renewable power and/or purchasing (20% maximum) renewable energy and/or certified renewable energy credits. For more information visit - http://www.architecture2030.org

Actual Energy Performance	**31.8 kBTU/sf-year**		**2030 Challenge target**	**46.45 kBTU/sf-year**

Actual performance exceeds the 2030 Challege by 31.5%

Figure 8-23 The 2030 Challenge targets also can be used as a benchmark for comparison. Based on Commercial Buildings Energy Consumption Survey (CBECS) data, the current goal is a 50 percent reduction compared to the average building. This project exceeded the goal by 31.5 percent. *Image courtesy of Marcus Sheffer.*

facility discussed above, we benchmarked utility bills against Target Finder (Figure 8-22) and the 2030 Challenge (Figure 8-23). The project scored an 88 in Target Finder, which exceeds the 75 score required to qualify it as an Energy Star Building. The measured performance also exceeded the 2030 Challenge's current target by more than 30 percent.

■ **Materials**

We saw in Schematic Design (Chapter 6) that the operational impacts of a building's energy accrue over time but that impacts related to materials choices stay relatively static. The exception to the nonaccruing nature of materials impacts is associated with impacts resulting from their maintenance and replacement, which *do* accrue over time. Many people are surprised to hear that the maintenance of a floor—when regularly cleaned with heavy chemicals, waxed, stripped, and rewaxed, for example—can have a greater environmental impact than the total impacts associated with the extraction, production, and disposal of that flooring material.

The initial inclination is to purchase materials that are known to require low maintenance. We have found this idea to be completely subjective, however, and the concept of maintenance for one person or institution can be completely different from another.

The complexity of maintenance and replacement is compounded by the fact that the maintenance staff is rarely involved in design decisions. When they are involved, we have experienced an unfortunate tendency to select and maintain materials to fit within their current maintenance pattern. In schools, for example, we have noticed a propensity for waxing vinyl composition tile (VCT) floors during every break. This is often done on top of floors that have a finish designed to last decades without wax, generating significant impacts on indoor air quality—and needlessly consuming time, energy, and money. Instead, the team should explore ways to lower environmental impacts and cost, while establishing a maintenance and replacement schedule that ensures longevity—all the while with an eye toward the aesthetic concerns of cleanliness and beauty.

The design team should create an outline of all finish materials that indicates why they were chosen, their expected life, their anticipated replacement schedule, and the intended maintenance recommended by the manufacturer, where applicable. In a sophisticated process, the design team will be fully aware of the expected maintenance requirements for finish materials and will write a plan that addresses three key issues: alignment with service-life planning (documented in early design), maintenance and replacement, and green housekeeping. The goal of this plan should be to reduce the amount of maintenance and replacement required, then to use cleaning products and equipment that have lower environmental and IAQ impacts than more conventional options.

- Alignment with service-life planning:
  If during the Discovery phase, the project team undertook a serious effort to determine a close approximation of the building's service life, as discussed in *Stage A.3.1,* finish materials that match the expected life of the building could have been selected. If the team also sought ways to delaminate materials, finish materials that integrate with structural components could have been selected. For example, if the building is likely to change substantively or be replaced within a twenty-year time frame, the finish materials optimally would have been designed to be easily removed and chosen for their ability to be recycled or reused. If, on the other hand, the building is intended to stand for centuries, every effort will have been made to avoid adhesives, for example (as they are most likely to fail over time), and to integrate finish materials into the structure of the building—perhaps using the structural components themselves as finishes. We have found, though, that such alignment of materials selection with maintenance requirements *and* service life is almost never considered. In other words, a material that is expected to be recycled within thirty years, as opposed to a material that is expected to stay in place for two hundred years, likely will require different scheduled-maintenance procedures, and these need to be taken into consideration.

This alignment requires careful planning on a case-by-case basis with regard to the amount and type of use for any given material. If the design team did its job well, for example, there will not be carpet to maintain in extremely high-traffic areas. These areas should have been designed to be easily cleaned and maintained without requiring heavy coatings and waxes. If for some reason carpet was selected for such an area, carpet tiles that can be replaced easily (without replacing the carpet over the entire area) should have been considered.

Another example might be a wood floor that gets heavy traffic over a long service life, whose maintenance requires a regular coating, perhaps every ten years. In this case, coatings such as a modified oil rather than a static urethane should be considered so that each new coating can be applied without completely stripping the old coating and decreasing the overall life of the wood floor.

A good example of material delamination that integrates a finish material with structural components is a polished concrete floor slab. We have discussed the benefits of this option on many projects and have had great success in recent years. We have found that this integration of structure and finish can dramatically decrease maintenance requirements. It should be noted that examples such as this can benefit buildings with either a short- or long-term expected service life.

- Maintenance and replacement:
When the people responsible for maintaining a material or product in a building are aware of (or involved with) how it was designed and intended to be cared for, they can adjust accordingly. Without this information, they likely will tend to maintain each material in the same way as every other material, resulting in, for example, overmaintenance or applications of unneeded coatings and chemicals.

Likewise, the expected replacement of a material should be made known to the people maintaining the building, especially when that replacement may have an impact on the longevity of other materials. The expected life of a roof provides an excellent example. Let's say a membrane roof uses a seam sealer that is expected to last forty years. It may be obvious when that seam begins to fail, but perhaps extremely small leaks not easily seen will emerge beforehand that cause damage to interior spaces. Maintenance staff should know when to begin to look for such issues.

Typical behavior with regard to paint is a good example for illustrating replacement issues as they relate to maintenance. Institutions often repaint on a regular basis whether the need exists or not. A maintenance plan could instead encourage regular wall cleaning and touch-up rather than full paint replacement. This requires a consistent supply of original paint types and colors, of course.

- Green housekeeping:
Fortunately, green housekeeping is well known in today's building industry. In fact, once it is used and tried, most owners and maintenance professionals are overwhelmed with the improvement in indoor air quality and pleased with the performance of cleaning products that contain no toxicants and low VOCs. Green cleaning programs should be taken seriously, and the maintenance plan should provide training of staff on the types of cleaning products and equipment to be used for various materials, including instruction on how much of each cleaning product should be used. Lack of train-

ing almost always leads to overuse of cleaning products and thereby increased costs. It is our experience that there is no reason to use conventional chemicals for maintenance and housekeeping.

- *Example:* We recently worked with a school district that had tried two different types of coatings on their gymnasium floors. One type, a polyurethane, was thought to be more permanent and was beneficial in some ways due to its low VOC content. The other type, an oil-modified urethane, had a higher VOC content. The two finishes were compared relative to how they were maintained and replaced. The *polyurethane* was waxed regularly, but it still collected permanent scratches that required removal of the entire surface by sanding on a regular basis. The *modified urethane* had never been waxed or replaced, but every five to ten years a new layer was added as needed. The results were not quantified, but it was clear that the quantity of VOCs that came with regular waxing were much greater than the VOCs that came from recoating when quantified on a long-term basis. Likewise, the floors that used the modified urethane lasted longer, because they were not subjected to sanding; this sanding tended to remove nearly one-eighth of an inch every time it occurred. The energy it took to refinish the polyurethane coated floors (relative to none for the modified urethane) was never quantified either. If a comprehensive comparison were to be fully studied, though, it is obvious that the modified urethane, while initially having a higher VOC content, has a significantly lower overall impact in total VOC exposure, plus significantly lower maintenance and replacement costs and impacts over its service life.

■ **Commissioning: Conduct periodic Recommissioning in accordance with Recommissioning Manual**

The recommissioning of a building should rest squarely on the shoulders of those who will be operating and maintaining the facility. While it is possible to hire the original CxA or some other outside firm to come in and retest the systems, it makes the most sense for those intimate with the day-to-day operations of a facility to be directly involved with ensuring that the facility continues to function smoothly. Short of expensive automation, the best way to recommission a facility is to duplicate the efforts of the functional testing activities that occurred during the acceptance phase of the original commissioning process. Usually these functional tests have been written in simple, easy-to-read language describing processes and procedures, contained in the original commissioning report. At the completion of the original commissioning activities, blank functional test forms for all commissioned systems are provided to the owner, along with completed forms recording the original commissioning results, so that the blank forms can be used in the future, during recommissioning, to enable comparisons with the original results.

For example, we recently commissioned an ambulatory care medical facility. The heating system is hydronic hot water with primary and secondary pump and piping arrangements. During the functional testing of this system, we identified a subtle issue with the three-way mixing valve that provides the interface between the primary and secondary piping systems. The temperature outside was above 60°F, and the reset schedule called for a heating water temperature of 120°F when the outside air temperature is 60°F. The actual temperature, however, on the supply side of the secondary loop was 145°F. Other than this difference in water temperature, the system seemed to operate as designed. Since this water temperature was incorrect, the expected result of the functional test was not achieved. We identified the issue and moved on to the next test.

Later that day, the controls contractor stayed late in an attempt to resolve issues from the day's commissioning efforts, so we could follow up the next day and successfully complete any functional tests with remaining outstanding issues. He found that the mixing valve (actually one of two butterfly valves tied together with linkage) had been overturned (beyond 90 degrees), which had damaged the rubber seat. At full closure, the valve was bleeding water from the secondary return line. Because the return was leaking, the heating water supply also was leaking, thus causing the elevated secondary supply temperature. The butterfly valve was replaced. After the replacement valve was installed, the temperatures in the system came right into alignment and the functional test was successful.

In this instance, the discovered issue would not have caused the system to fail. However, the issue would have remained undetected by the conventional construction process; hence, the system in all likelihood would never have been in tune, and additional energy would have been wasted over the life of the facility.

C.1.2 Principles and Measurement

LEED for Existing Buildings: Operations and Maintenance (LEED-EBOM) can serve as a valuable tool for helping teams measure the performance of operations and maintenance procedures within the building and its immediate site and provide performance feedback over the life of the building (see *LEED-EBOM* sidebar).

■ **Document key indicators that serve as proxies for the health of the larger ecosystem**

Each project will have unique indicators. These will be determined by the key issues addressed at the point of the project's initial habitation, whether the

project involved new construction or repurposing of an existing building and property. An initial assessment of native plant species' tolerance for disturbance and/or fidelity to a particular presettlement plant community is important. The same goes for animal species. Monitoring of the increased viability and diversity of the guild of relationships between the plants and animals can then ensue. As the project evolves, other species that are important to track may emerge. Human aspirations and understanding will also evolve, and the goals that originally had been set for the project may change, based on unexpected and newly emergent species (life happens!). The role of continuous or periodic feedback is as essential with living systems as it is with mechanical systems.

■ **Document occupant surveys and reconcile results with building systems performance**

As we have seen, POE data enables feedback from which we can learn much. Not only can we begin to understand how buildings perform, we also can explore how the occupants respond to conditions in a space and to various construction materials and methods. By comparing POE data of actual building performance with conceptual predictions, we can begin to improve both the overall performance of buildings and our process for designing them. The goal is to gather and document the "lessons learned" from these building projects, so that we can improve the design and construction process and elevate current practice.

The final POE studies should be performed and the results documented. A report is generated that summarizes the results; it should also compare measured performance to performance targets and other national and/or regional benchmarks.

To enable feedback, the results of POE studies should be shared with the design and construction

LEED for Existing Buildings: Operations & Maintenance (LEED-EBOM)— Sustainability for Your Facilities

By Doug Gatlin VP, Market Development, US Green Building Council

The current commercial buildings market in the United States is vast and aging. Spanning over 5 million individual facilities and comprising 70 billion square feet, U.S. commercial buildings—including offices, retail facilities, schools, and public buildings—are over 30 years old on average. Many could benefit from the use of green operations and maintenance strategies addressed in the US Green Building Council's (USGBC) new rating system, LEED for Existing Buildings: Operations and Maintenance.

Launched in January of 2008, the LEED for Existing Buildings: O&M Rating System is a tool for maximizing efficient operations in existing buildings. It identifies and rewards best practices across the spectrum of building management issues, including energy and water efficiency, resource conservation, recycling, environmentally preferable purchasing, and green cleaning. LEED for Existing Buildings: O&M also serves as an outline for implementing improvements, and provides a reference to the technologies and strategies that will help you along your journey toward sustainable facilities operations.

USGBC also provides independent third-party verification of the green performance levels of the buildings that pursue LEED certification. Already prevalent in the new construction arena, LEED certification is now gaining popularity among existing buildings' operations, as owners seek to quantify the performance of their buildings across a range of key areas such as carbon emissions, sustainable site management, water conservation, and indoor envi-

ronmental quality. Over 1,000 building projects as of this writing have registered their intent to achieve LEED Existing Buildings: O&M certification, and dozens more join the ranks every week.

LEED for Existing Buildings: O&M is the result of major revisions to the LEED for Existing Buildings Rating System, first launched in 2004. The new version has a clearer focus on green operations, as opposed to construction, making it a more useful tool for implementing sustainability across the board in an organization's facilities. The other goals of the new system are streamlined reporting requirements for earning LEED certification, and increased focus on measured environmental outcomes.

Aligning LEED with issues of growing global concern, the new rating system also contains 50% greater point allocation for energy efficiency and double the numbers of points for water use reductions. In addition, greater emphasis has been added for achieving a comprehensive green cleaning program and use of performance metrics for cleaning effectiveness.

LEED Existing Buildings: O&M—A Path for Sustainable Facility Management

The journey toward sustainability begins with creating a plan for improving existing facility performance and operations practices. The collection of measures, known as credits, in the LEED for Existing Buildings: O&M rating system can be used as the basis for this plan. This can be done at the level of

(continued)

an individual building, or can be applied to dozens or even hundreds of buildings across a portfolio. Here's a suggested path to getting started:

First, explore the Green Cleaning credits listed in LEED for Existing Buildings: O&M. These include specifications for sustainable cleaning products and materials, sustainable cleaning equipment, and integrated pest management. In addition, the rating system contains an innovative system for measuring custodial effectiveness. Many of these greening improvements can be applied universally across a portfolio of buildings, through group acquisition of sustainable cleaning products and equipment, and also through selection of the green cleaning option provided through a growing number of janitorial and custodial services contracts.

Next look at opportunities to trim unnecessary waste through increased company-wide recycling initiatives. The Materials and Resources (MR) section of LEED for Existing Buildings: O&M provides guidance on increasing recycling levels, assessing the composition of the waste stream, and setting up a system for safe handling and disposal of toxic mercury-containing fluorescent lamps. The MR section also provides guidance for sustainable product purchase of office paper and supplies, durable goods such as printers and photocopy machines, and also provides specifications for sustainable facilities improvements and alterations.

Crucial to sustainability, energy and water efficiency are addressed through the establishment of minimum performance thresholds (prerequisites for USGBC certification), as well as a host of optional credits, including a focus on building commissioning, metering and sub-metering, energy and water system upgrades, energy benchmarking, and use of renewable energy. The new rating system even explores options for reducing water use through proper management of cooling towers.

All of the above measures, plus a strong set of indoor environmental quality requirements and a number of innovative strategies for sustainable site management make up the new LEED for Existing Buildings: O&M rating system. Many of the items can be implemented quickly at no cost and will garner immediate environmental benefits. Others can be implemented over time as part of a comprehensive upgrade plan. Taken together the measures help answer the question, "how green are my facilities?"

In short, the LEED for Existing Buildings: O&M Rating System provides an industry-approved framework for improving the performance, comfort, health and environmental footprint of commercial buildings. Facility managers can also apply the best practices in LEED to a large number of buildings, by implementing green O&M measures incrementally across a portfolio of buildings to yield top green building performance while moving their organizations ahead in the journey toward sustainability.

team. Of potentially greater value is sharing these results with the larger building industry. Many folks are reluctant to share this information, since it can be viewed as proprietary, or their reluctance might stem from fears about revealing their mistakes to

the world. One way to address these concerns is to aggregate the results from multiple projects into a larger data set and report them collectively. This type of research is currently being carried out by the Center for the Built Environment, New Buildings

Figure 8-24 The overall occupant survey results from a POE study. The diamonds represent the score for this particular project, while the circles represent the average results from fifteen other LEED certified projects. With the exception of acoustics, this project scored as well as or better than comparable buildings. *Image based on the results of an Occupant Indoor Environmental Quality Survey by the Center for the Built Environment, courtesy of Todd Reed.*

Institute, U.S. Green Building Council, National Renewable Energy Laboratory, and many others.

▪ Implement Measurement and Verification (M&V) plan continuously over the life of the building

The primary purpose of the M&V plan, prepared during the construction documents stage, is to verify that the predicted savings come to fruition during occupancy. Once the plan has been implemented, the final results should determine actual savings, typically for both water and energy. The final report also should identify potential areas for future savings.

The preferred methodology used in new construction projects for documenting actual energy savings is referred to as calibrated simulation. The energy model is calibrated, based on the data gathered during occupancy, and reconciled with the utility bills. A revised baseline is then established, which determines savings.

The determination of actual savings is only the end game for M&V. The real value often lies in the lessons learned, while performing the M&V, about how

facilities are actually operated relative to a prediction. It will come as no surprise to designers and builders that buildings often are operated differently than intended or expected.

We participated in an M&V effort sponsored by the National Renewable Energy Laboratory on the Pennsylvania DEP Cambria project, and the information garnered from that process was documented in a comprehensive report that can be obtained from the U.S. Department of Energy's High Performance Buildings Web site (http://www.eere.energy.gov/buildings/highperformance/), entitled "Analysis of the Design and Energy Performance of the Pennsylvania Department of Environmental Protection Cambria Office Building" (March 2005).

The report details what worked and what did not, then determined the reasons why predicted energy savings did not meet expectations. As shown in Figure 8-25, the actual savings were 40 percent better than the baseline (which was a minimally code-compliant version of the project). The *predicted* energy

	Cost		Total Site Energy		Total Source Energy	
	$/ft²·yr ($/m²·yr)	Percent Savings	kBtu/ft²·yr (MJ/m²·yr)	Percent Savings	kBtu/ft²·yr (MJ/m²·yr)	Percent Savings
Baseline	$1.80 ($19.38)	43%	57 (642)	40%	180 (1,800)	40%
As-Built	$1.02 ($10.89)		34 (386)		108 (1,226)	

Figure 8-25 The actual energy cost and usage (as-built) is compared to the revised baseline in order to show the actual energy savings resulting from the measurement and verification effort for the Pennsylvania DEP Cambria project. Metric units are shown in parentheses. Site energy is energy used on-site. Source energy includes the original energy source used to produce the electricity and represents combustion and line losses in the production of the electricity. *Image from http://www.eere.energy.gov/buildings/highperformance/.*

savings, however, were on the order of 52 percent. There were several reasons why the actual savings fell short of predictions. First and foremost, the energy model did not account for the fact that the building's plug loads (computers, printers, etc.) were in actuality not turned off during unoccupied periods. One-half of the building's measured plug load was operating 24/7, as illustrated in Figure 8-26, which was not anticipated in the original model. The other prime contributor was due to a faulty inverter on the photovoltaic system that resulted in far less solar electricity being generated than was predicted. These POE results allowed for the energy model to be calibrated with measured performance and operations, thus creating a very accurate predictor of any future savings. It was calculated that if the majority of the plug loads were turned off during unoccupied periods, the actual savings would increase to approximately 50 percent and be in far greater alignment with the overall modeled prediction.

At the conclusion of the initial M&V period, it is no longer necessary to calculate savings relative to an agreed-upon baseline; the new baseline becomes the original utility bills generated during the first year or two of occupancy. Any submeters used in this initial M&V effort now become very useful trouble-

shooting tools for identifying and pinpointing operations issues that relate to energy performance. At this point, M&V becomes a continuous monitoring effort over the life of the building.

■ **Insert results of periodic Recommissioning into Recommissioning Manual**

As stated above, one of the purposes of the commissioning documentation is to provide a vehicle for operations and maintenance staff to use when recommissioning their building in the future. In particular, functional tests are ideal when attempting to verify that a facility or system is continuing to operate as originally installed. Recommissioning, or systems, manuals, if set up correctly and used consistently, will become the living history of the facility and a diary for documenting the operational issues, repairs, changes, and updates that occur. While the systems manuals contain other documentation (such as the sequence of operations, basis of design, abbreviated O&M data with troubleshooting guides, etc.), the one place where historical and evolutionary data will consistently show up is in the collection of functional tests forms that are repeatedly filled out. As systems are upgraded and possibly changed, other sections may need updating. But it is the everyday grind that will be reflected in

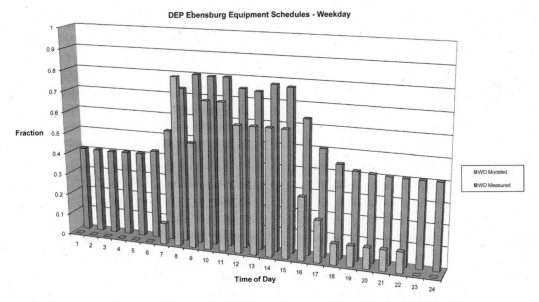

DEP Ebensburg Equipment Schedules - Weekday

Figure 8-26 This graph plots the amount of plug-load energy use during each hour of a typical workday. The solid bars represent the actual submetered consumption measured in the facility. Note that about half of this load is left running all night. This same phenomenon occurs all weekend as well. The hatched bars represent the amount of consumption predicted in the original energy model. The model assumed that the equipment would be shut down at night and over the weekends. *Image courtesy of Andrew Lau.*

the results of each future functional test. These future results become the starting point for any substantial overhauls or upgrades necessary to keep the systems in top operating condition. If performed regularly (possibly annually), these tests will help maintain performance levels—and largely mitigate most catastrophic failures.

C.1.3   Cost Analysis

■ **Track economic performance of the four key subsystems**

This is the real opportunity to demonstrate—or learn—how quality design, long-term ecological health considerations, and diligent maintenance can improve the return on investment of projects, as well as inform cost-benefit evaluations for future projects. The following list provides several examples of economic performance issues that are useful to track.

■ **Habitat** (biotic systems other than human)
- Difference in site-construction costs due to use of topography and biological systems rather than hardscape, pipes, and technological solutions for stormwater management
- Property values due to the health of the ecosystem
- Speed of environmental reviews (time to market) for zoning approvals and entitlements
- Maintenance costs for meadow grass "lawns"
- Frequency of roof replacement with living roofs

■ **Habitat** (human)
- Productivity studies due to individual control of HVAC at workstations
- Absenteeism
- Rate and cost of workmen's compensation claims

- Health of occupants due to daylighting
- Employee turnover from the implementation of many of these strategies
- See *BIDS* sidebar (at the beginning of *Stage C.1*)

■ **Water**
- Difference in site construction costs due to use of topography and biological systems rather than hardscape, pipes, and technological solutions for stormwater management
- Reduced first-cost and operating cost for natural systems waste treatment, such as constructed wetlands
- Water bills

■ **Energy**
- Energy costs for thermal comfort
- Energy costs for nonregulated, process energy loads

- Maintenance frequency related to energy savings and equipment service life
- Reduced lighting costs due to daylighting
- Energy bills
- Continued functionality of building control systems
- Operational procedures to address energy use

■ **Materials**
- Maintenance costs
- Replacement costs (related to service life)
- Cost of maintainability

C.1.4   Schedule and Next Steps

For the "completed" project: Implement all of the above, *forever.*

For the next project: Go back to *Stage A.1* and begin again!

Epilogue—
Evolving the Field

Synergy is the only word in our language that means behavior of whole systems unpredicted by the separately observed behaviors of any of the system's separate parts or any subassembly of the system's parts. There is nothing in the chemistry of a toenail that predicts the existence of a human being.

—R. Buckminster Fuller, from *Operating Manual for Spaceship Earth*, New York: E.P. Dutton & Co., 1963. Text available at: http://bfi.org/node/422 ©2005–7 by the Buckminster Fuller Institute (accessed December 2008)

The deeper we look into nature, the more we recognize that it is full of life, and the more profoundly we know that all life is a secret and that we are united with all life that is in nature. Man can no longer live for himself alone. We realize that all life is valuable, and that we are united to all this life. From this knowledge comes our spiritual relationship to the universe.

—Albert Schweitzer, from *The Spiritual Life* (1947)

The way to solve conflict between human values and technological needs is not to run away from technology. That's impossible. The way to resolve the conflict is to break down the barriers of dualistic thought that prevent a real understanding of what technology is—not an exploitation of nature, but a fusion of nature and the human spirit into a new kind of creation that transcends both.

—Robert Pirsig, from his exploration of quality in *Zen and the Art of Motorcycle Maintenance*, London: Bodley Head (1974)

A man is never the same for long. He is continually changing. He seldom remains the same even for half an hour . . . .

—George Gurdjieff, spiritual teacher, quoted by his student P. D. Ouspensky in *In Search of the Miraculous: Fragments of an Unknown Teaching*, New York: Harcourt, Brace (1949)

A TRANSFORMATIONAL PROCESS

The bottom line is that we need to change the field of development. In the bigger picture we need to change the way that human beings inhabit the planet. The good news is that our experience has taught us that the process of integration is by nature a transformational process. Recently we went back through our work history to identify those projects that were truly successful—that is, those that achieved higher-order sustainability goals on time and in budget. The number was low: maybe around 10 percent. Looking for a common denominator to the success of these projects, we were surprised at how clearly visible it was: first, we realized that we had become good friends with the clients and team members that had achieved the highest levels of success. Then we noticed that every one of these successful projects included a principal team member who was undergoing a personal process of transformation. From Alcoholics Anonymous to marriage counseling to spiritual work, some *transformational process* was occurring independently, in parts of their lives not directly connected with the project.

Reflecting on this, we realized that to be successful in this work, we have to change—transform. This change cannot be achieved superficially, by just altering our actions. That level of change never holds and is not deep enough; success comes from a more pervasive process of change. Each of us must change our *self,* our way of seeing the world, and our beliefs—our mind-set. This change is both something that we have to will ourselves to do *and* something that we must *allow* to happen. The evolution of consciousness is, after all, instrumental to the evolution of our practice and our field—and, in the bigger picture, instrumental to the evolution of life on Earth.

Folks that have had the experience of working with an integrative process on their projects consistently tell us that their understanding and values shifted during the process. More specifically, their internal world somehow aligned with their vocation, their values reconciled with how they earned their living, and they experienced something powerful. Ray Anderson (founder and former CEO of Interface Inc.), for example, explains this kind of shift in perspective as "doing well by doing good." Our partner Andy Lau refers to this by using the Buddhist concept of "right livelihood," borrowing from the Noble Eightfold Path. One of our clients described this experience as follows:

> Some esoteric chemistry took place with the team's willingness to explore new solutions without having to know the answers…My life changed—not immediately, but it was a transformative process over time…. We established performance criteria, but we didn't try to tell anyone how to achieve those goals…. It became more than a job—it became a personal passion…and this from a career bureaucrat?!?
>
> —Jim Toothaker, Pennsylvania Department of Environmental Protection

We like to think about this transformational process in the following way:

To do different things, we need to *do* things differently.

To do things differently, we need to *think* about them differently.

To think differently, we need to *become* different.

The conventional wisdom of our time teaches that if we want to work to save the environment (to do different things), the best thing that we can do is to separate humans from nature—to leave it alone (to do things differently). Throughout this book, though, we have sought to illuminate what we believe to be the most fundamental human imperative: the need for

Figure 9-1 The project team leader on the Pennsylvania Department of Environmental Protection Cambria project, Jim Toothaker, says that working on this project changed his life. *Image ©2000 Jim Schafer.*

integrating humans with nature—for understanding their interrelationships (to *think* differently). While reading the previous chapters, you may have asked the question: where do we stop integrating? We suggest that our integration work is not over until we have become a *part* of nature, until nature is not seen or thought about as something separate, until we become whole again (*become* different).

SHIFTING THE PARADIGM

Pioneering environmental scientist and systems analyst Donella Meadows explains in her article "Leverage Points: Places to Intervene in a System,"* that the fastest way to change a system (e.g., a person, a profession, a society, an ecosystem) occurs by changing your mental model—shifting the paradigm. She proposes twelve leverage points for intervening in a system

and ranks changing "the mindset or paradigm out of which the system arises" second only to "the power to *transcend* paradigms" as the most effective. She writes: "You could say paradigms are harder to change than anything else about a system, and therefore this item should be lowest on the list, not second-to-highest. But there's nothing physical or expensive or even slow about paradigm change. In a single individual it can happen in a millisecond. All it takes is a click in the mind, a falling of scales from eyes, a new way of seeing. Whole societies are another matter. They resist challenges to their paradigm harder than they resist anything else."

Over time, as we have watched people progress through different levels of capability with respect to

_____

*Donella H. Meadows, "Leverage Points: Places to Intervene in a System," ©1999 by the Sustainability Institute and available on the web at http://www.sustainabilityinstitute.org/pubs/Leverage_Points.pdf (accessed December 2008).

this way of working and looking for leverage points, we have realized that there is a difference between wanting something good to happen and having the capability to make that good thing come into being. It is not enough to simply believe that we should save the planet—we also must commit to understanding what that means in each particular place, with each particular project. The nature of this process, therefore, is inherently *developmental*. As we iterate between creating goals for integration and developing the type of thinking required to achieve that integration, our paradigm begins to shift.

Mark Biedron of the Willow School describes a moment at the conception of that project where his paradigm shifted. When he and his wife, Gretchen, started the school, paramount among their founding concepts was the idea of Core Virtues. The program's goal was to develop ethical relationships between humans through a values-based curriculum that focused on the virtues of responsibility, honesty, respect, and compassion. Also important to its founders was that the school be environmentally sustainable.

It was not long after we began working with the Willow School that the idea of humans being a part of nature clicked into place with Mark and Gretchen. As Mark describes it, he realized that if we are in fact a part of nature, how can we mentor an ethical relationship between individual humans without also mentoring an ethical relationship between humans and nature? Not fully understanding what this meant but knowing with certainty that it was important, Mark set about the process of discovering what doing that might look like. Pursuing the goal of environmental sustainability triggered a paradigm shift that ultimately led to a higher-order understanding of what it meant to be successful at achieving the project's goals for education.

When all was said and done, the Willow School ended up with not only a highly sustainable solution to the design of the campus and its buildings but also an integrated curriculum that engages students in developing an understanding of how the school itself works with nature. The school's integrated design becomes the subject matter for student exercises in various subjects. Students draw pictures of the components of the school's water-cycling system—from toilets to rooftop harvesting to wetlands—in art class. They write descriptions of these same systems in language arts class, calculate water savings in math class, study the working of the campus wetlands system for science class, and overall engage in activities aimed at establishing greater and more healthy diversity in the forest. This achievement was the direct product of Mark's and others' efforts to expand the philosophical framework, or paradigm, of what constitutes Core Virtues to include not only human relationships but also the larger systemic interrelationships between humans and nature.

We are only beginning to explore the potential for transformation. As we shift our mental model from *stopping the damage* to one where humans are an integral part of nature, we also shift our consciousness. As we begin to participate with nature, we discover that humans working with healing nature will ultimately heal and grow themselves as well. This transformation does not happen overnight, but it is rather a continuous process of healing or making whole*—*wholing*.

When we work to stop the damage, we must make a constant investment of energy to just break even—like paddling water out of a rowboat with a hole in the bottom. Partnering with nature, conversely, is hugely inspiring and actually creates energy, because we are investing our effort into a living system that is capable of its own growth and evolution. Imagine those cit-

---

*The etymology of "heal" traces its roots to the Proto-Germanic *khailaz*, meaning "to make whole," which is the source of the Old English *haelan*, meaning "make whole, sound, and well." (Source: Online Etymology Dictionary at www.etymonline.com; accessed December 2008.)

ies and municipalities that are trying to stop damage by organizing cleanup efforts to clear litter and debris from barren roadsides and medians. Now imagine investing that effort into replanting guilds of native trees and shrubs that had once grown there. When the growth begins to take hold and the flourishing ecosystem begins to attract species of native fauna, then entirely new plants grow in its understory that were seeded by the droppings of the returning bird and animal populations, do you think that passersby will be more or less inclined to toss their garbage onto the ground in these places?

Imagine that you own a piece of forested land. Imagine that you begin to devote meaningful time to understanding how this forest works, seeking to form a deeper relationship with the land. You may do some research to learn which plants in the forest tend to cluster together and how nutrients are exchanged throughout the biotic community. Maybe one day you will stumble across a portion of the forest that has been lightly grazed by fire, and maybe the following spring you will notice the riot of growth that sprouts on the charcoal-fertilized ground. Maybe you will begin to understand, as many indigenous cultures have, that there are ways that you can assist the forest in its own evolution and health. You may begin to thin invasive species of plants or to practice annual controlled burns to remove crowded understory elements while simultaneously improving the quality of the soil, helping new seedlings to flourish on the forest floor. You understand how to do this not because you have mastered or conquered nature, but because you *are* nature—your mind and muscle were shaped by the same metaprocesses that created our planet and its many forests, its deserts, its mountains and oceans and rivers. Your understanding of the forest stems from your relationship with it and evolves as the relationship grows.

It is this relationship that feeds and nourishes us, if only we work to reform it. It does not matter if you live in a rural area or an urban center, if you are looking at an already-healthy piece of land or one that has been assaulted and degraded over time, if you are working on the design of a single building or urban planning for an entire new or existing city. We *are* in relationship with nature.

Finnish-American architect Eliel Saarinen recognized this relationship when exploring urban planning principles. For decades, he looked at the development patterns of how medieval towns evolved "to explain the physical order of the urban community much in the same manner as one understands organic order in any living organism."* He looked at medieval towns and wrote in his treatise on town-building, published in 1943, that visitors to these towns "invariably terminate their visit refreshed in mind and enlivened in spirit."* Making the same case for visitors to most modern cities would be extremely difficult. Saarinen argues that this is because contemporary gridiron plans result in "three-dimensional form-disorder," as "each new building or three-dimensional element is separately and randomly placed on the preconceived pattern of a fabricated, flat, spiritless scheme."* By contrast, as we saw in Chapter 1, pre-industrial master builders worked in cooperation with natural patterns. Saarinen explains it this way:

> No preconceived design pattern was imposed upon the town, but its formation emerged indigenously from local conditions of life and from topographical circumstances. This was perfectly in accord with the laws of nature.
> ... The medieval town builder, just as life manifestations in nature, sensed intuitively the fundamental principles that govern things in all creation.*

---

*Saarinen, Eliel. *Search for Form: A Fundamental Approach to Art*, New York: Reinhold Publishing Corp, 1948, pp. x, 49, 44, 25, respectively.

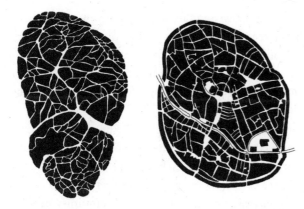

Figure 9-2 The pattern of human musculature depicted in the image on the left reflects a constructional similarity with the figure-ground plan of a medieval town on the left—both the result of organic growth formation. *Image courtesy of Jenn Biggs; derived from an idea described by Eliel Saarinen in his writings on urban planning.*

As evidence of this, Saarinen asks us to compare medieval town plans with the cell fabric of organic life. He compares a microscopic image of healthy cell tissue to the town plans of Noerdlingen (Germany), Carcassonne (France), Udine (Italy), and others. The similarity in character is remarkable—especially given that the existence of cells was unknown to the medieval town builder. In another case, he asks us to compare a cross section through the human sartorius muscle with the town plan of Malines, Belgium (see Figure 9-2). So what is it that Saarinen is trying to tell us? He is explicit:

> The three faculties of apprehension (intuition, instinct, and imagination) are the most precious gifts bestowed upon man . . . through these—and only these—man is able to penetrate the mysteries of nature. Increasing *knowledge* about these mysteries is not the essential thing . . . *increasing sensitiveness* to these mysteries by means of intuition, instinct, and imagination is the essential thing in the search. (Saarinen's italics)*

Intuition. Instinct. Imagination. These are the essential things in a transformative and developmental process, not knowledge alone. Integrating ourselves and our living patterns into the fabric of life in each unique place with *increasing sensitiveness*, is the next big step toward realizing the possibilities of integrative design—engaging the process of becoming one with all life. From the perspective of western thinking, this synergy requires a big leap. This leap can be encouraged and supported by an *intentional* developmental process, one aimed at shifting the paradigm from only collecting data, or knowledge, to understanding the mutually supportive interrelationships of the *whole* for the purpose of healing—or again, *wholing*. This requires all participants to engage in an integrative design process by intentionally exploring and discovering their relationship with each place—a paradigm shift into the right hemisphere of the brain.

A paradigm shift, as Meadows points out, is the most effective leverage point, or step toward allowing us to see new possibilities for higher-order success; but to realize that success, we must engage in a constant process of developing understanding through *both* knowledge and increasing sensitiveness. What we lost when we destroyed our indigenous cultures and dismantled the system that our master builders and medieval town planners functioned within was our understanding of place. When we build on a site using a conventional process, we take inventory of "what the place is like" by collecting data or accumulating *knowledge* about it. But there is a critical distinction between knowing the facts and figures of a place and developing an understanding of how a place works and has evolved as a whole system. Data-filled reports on soil, hydrology, habitat, and social statistics alone are not sufficient to understand *patterns* of life. In other

---

*Saarinen, Eliel. *The City: Its Growth, Its Decay, Its Future*, New York: Reinhold Publishing Corp., 1943, p. 71.

words, more than learning just the *what* of the place, we need to understand the *who* of the place.

Imagine for a moment a close friend of yours. If someone asked what your friend was like, you could respond by saying that she is five-foot five, weighs 130 pounds, has blue eyes and brown hair, and wears green a lot. This would provide some knowledge of your friend—but no understanding of her, of who she is. In order to understand *who* your friend is, you would have to explain the way she is in terms of her relationships: how she interacts with you, what types of people she has dated, what her family is like, how her career has progressed. Only after you describe these *patterns of relationships* would the asker experience deeper understanding. As a result, if the asker ever did end up meeting your friend, he or she would have some understanding of how to better engage your friend to develop their own relationship.

Similarly, each place has a unique identity that can only be understood by those who can either directly or indirectly (through stories, for example) experience the different *patterns of relationships* that make it what it is. Shifting and expanding our paradigm to finding ways that contribute to the health of natural systems is only part of the work that must be done; but it provides the motivation to develop a deeper and deeper understanding of how to develop that contributory relationship. Efforts to save the world flounder for many reasons, and the main reason is that you cannot create a positive impact on something that you are not in relationship with. To integrate ourselves with nature, we must work on our *relationship* with it, in each unique *place*.

A Story of Place™—Developing a History of "Who" This Place Is …

By David Leventhal

Early on in the design process for Playa Viva, when we brought in Regenesis, we started to work on a process of understanding the history or "Story of Place."™ for the selected site in Mexico. This was a new concept and term for our team, and we really did not understand the deep work that was involved and the value of the results to the overall design process. We started the work on the history with a set of interviews with town elders. This was done by inviting them into the home of one of the town leaders and speaking with them frankly about their hopes and aspirations for the town. We spoke of the "good old times," of what the town was like, and of how life was different back then. We also spoke of how life has changed over time, change that resulted from the construction of new highways in the 1940s and 1950s, changes due to migration patterns to "el norte," et cetera. They took us into their homes and showed us clay figurines that they had found in their backyards, artifacts from their ancestors connecting them to a noble pre-Hispanic past.

Through the interview process, we learned that the town had moved over time to where it is today as a result of flooding from the nearby Juluchuca River. We learned that the men used to work in the estuary "farming" salt, working together as a community, not as individuals competing against each other as they do today. We heard from them how they wanted to retain many of their old customs and the hardships experienced in passing these rituals along to the youngest generation. Their aspirations were to bring back good jobs to their town in order to keep their young at home and their families together.

(continued)

They remembered a time when things were more abundant, especially wildlife. This theme of the memory of the abundance of natural systems was striking to us all.

As part of the work on history of place, we also brought in an archaeologist and worked uncovering more detailed information about the pre-Hispanic history of this particular place. We found records, Aztec records of tribute showing that cotton and fabrics, cacao, and salt were all important tributes from this area. As a result, when we brought in the permaculture team to work on restoring and regenerating the land, we wanted to bring back cotton and cacao. We searched and eventually found a virgin forest nearby that had fortunately not become a victim of the massive slash-and-burn agricultural initiatives of the early 1900s that had resulted in destroying coastal forests and creating massive coconut palm plantations, such as the land upon which Playa Viva is located. As a result, we were able to bring back many native species and even found a native cacao. We have started the process of regeneration with the goal of bringing back some of the abundance of nature that once abounded in this area.

As part of the story of place, the team walked the land, and the members of the team—especially the permaculture specialists—identified that the land forms seemed, in their words, "unnatural, almost man-made." Further refinement of the topographical maps revealed some surprises. First, several small hills in the north part of the property were square in form and their contours ran in intervals that were too regular. Most importantly, the peaks of two of these mounds aligned along a north–south axis. All of this was too much of a coincidence for natural formations. The assumption was that we had an archaeological site under foot. As a result, we invited the

Instituto Nacional de Antropología e Historia (INAH, or the National Institute of Archaeology and History) to come investigate. Sure enough, these mounds were agricultural terraces inhabited by the original peoples of the town of Xuluchucan, the ancient city of Juluchuca. In our meetings with them, the town elders told of how the town had migrated about 1.5 kilometers from the ancient city that now forms the archaeological site to its current site.

The importance and amount of attention that our consultants placed on the history of the place, while frustrating to a team that was not used to this process at first, soon became a source of pride for the team and began to drive many of the team's design decisions, overall values, aspirations, and purpose for the project. What once was a strange term to us—Story of Place—is now the core to our understanding of how the location should evolve. Our understanding of the history and Story of Place had evolved. Just as you cannot grow in your relationship with another person until you fully understand who they are and where they came from, you cannot understand what a place will become, and your role as a developer in that evolution, until you know from "what" the place evolved.

We recently met with the governor of the Mexican State of Guererro (where Playa Viva is located) to see how we could work together with the governor in promoting sustainable tourism and projects similar to Playa Viva. The Governor saw sustainable tourism as part of the future of the state (tourism is one of the top three contributors to Mexico's gross domestic product [GDP] and number one in states like Guererro that do not have oil revenues). He asked us how he could help us, and we settled on the State of Guererro assisting by building the road from the main highway to Playa Viva.

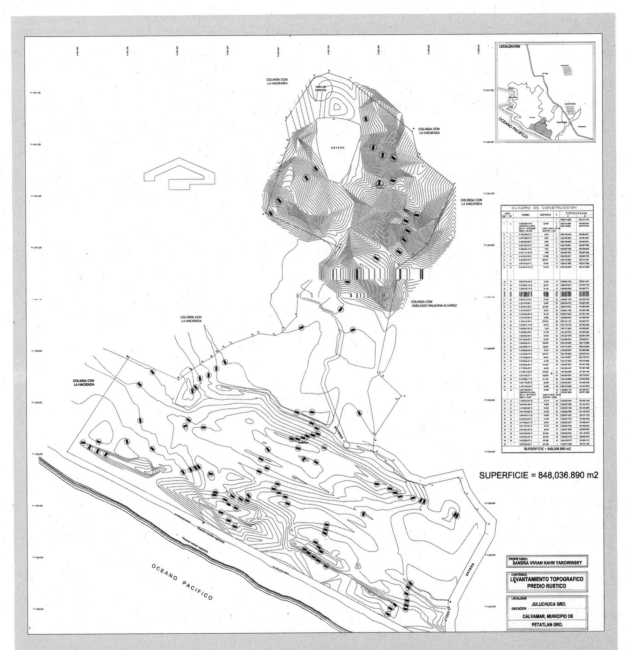

Figure 9-3 This topographic map of the Playa Viva site exhibits evidence of prior settlements in the area. Notice the evenly and closely spaced contour lines with corners indicating what could be a former terrace farming system or a pyramidlike structure. *Image courtesy of David Leventhal, Playa Viva, http://www.PlayaViva.com.*

(continued)

Figure 9-4 A predevelopment view of the Playa Viva site. *Image courtesy of David Leventhal, Playa Viva, http://www.PlayaViva.com.*

Figure 9-5 An archaeological dig at Playa Viva uncovers a large pot from the prior inhabitants of the site. *Image courtesy of David Leventhal, Playa Viva, http://www.PlayaViva.com.*

The governor, accustomed to working with more traditional developers, expected the road to be cut through the shortest path from the highway to our development. The current road into Playa Viva is actually the ancient road used by pre-Hispanics, as they traveled up and down the coasts. As mentioned, the town had moved about 1.5 kilometers further down this road from the entrance to Playa Viva and the archaeological site. We could either cut a road directly north, the shortest route to connect to the highway and bypass the town, or we could pave the existing dirt road that connected the town to Playa Viva, even though it was a longer route and would divert tourists through the town. The traditional resort developer would not want to "dirty" the entrance to their project by winding through the town; but for us this was not

only a way of maintaining our authenticity, this connection was core to our values for the project, values that evolved from the process of learning our story.

Through the process of our deep work with the team and of working with the history of this place, we began to understand the deeper meaning and connection that existed: Playa Viva represented a connection between the old city of Xuluchucan, the archaeological site, and the new town of Juluchuca. We, Playa Viva, were the cultural bridge between *what was* and *what could be* for this small town of 500 people. We helped these humble people connect to the most deeply held values of their noble past and the abundance of place. The road had to be built between Playa Viva and Juluchuca; it would not bypass the town. Our entrance had to include a museum to the archaeological site of Xuluchucan, and we had to include the townspeople's private collection of artifacts, providing them with a place to honor their past while creating a place that provides pride in their future.

The work with Regenesis on the history and Story of Place took a significant amount of time, energy, and effort, over and above what would normally be part of a development project. But the results provide us with a better understanding of where we come from and how place naturally evolves. What you read above is only part of the process covering a small part of the land, but it is integral to how working this way provided a better result even if it meant going slower and spending more resources.

In addition to the road, our permaculture team has begun restoring the old agricultural terraces of the archaeological site. The land contours formed over a thousand years ago were easy to uncover, trace, and rebuild. We have created a nursery with over forty-thousand plants and trees, mostly native, brought in from one of the few remaining virgin coastal forests, and we are slowly restoring and regenerating the land. We have cleared away many invasive species brought in by cattle, and we are working to allow the natural vegetation to take root. The permaculture team is most proud of its work resulting in restoration of the mangroves along the edge of the estuary. The work of regeneration will take a long time; but in this tropical environment, nature is extremely resilient and rapidly renews itself. We are already seeing the fruits of our labor pay off with more abundance. The abundance that the town elders spoke about so fondly is coming back to Playa Viva.

THE FIFTH SYSTEM

When a deep connectivity or relationship is clearly felt, it can be transformative. Within this context, we can revisit our four key elements or subsystems— habitat (both human and other biotic systems), water, energy, and materials—and now identify a fifth (from eastern traditions): the *system of human consciousness*. As we continually seek to rediscover our role in relationship to the systems of life, we embark on a collective shift in consciousness, a consciousness that also must be nurtured and developed. Each of us must find our own discipline for doing this developmental work, for finding the internal leverage point that will shift our consciousness to become integral with the whole.

Donella Meadows cautions us that "magical leverage points are not easily accessible, even if we know where they are and which direction to push them. There are no cheap tricks to mastery. You have to work at it, whether that means rigorously analyzing a system or rigorously casting off your own paradigms and throwing yourself into the humility of Not Knowing."

We do not know what this shift in consciousness will look like for ourelves or our culture. But we see examples of integrated consciousness in cultures, past and present. Almost every religious tradition—and even quantum mechanics—points toward a trajectory of oneness, unity, and the whole. The paradigm has shifted in the same direction within the scientific community as well. Systems theorist and scientist, Ervin Laszlo quotes Marco Bischof in *Science and the*

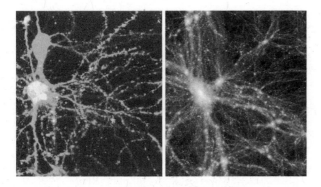

Figure 9-6 On the *left* is a stained slice of a mouse's brain showing the brain's neurons and how they connect, created by Mark Miller, a student at Brandeis University. And a strikingly similar structure is seen in the image on the *right,* of a computer-simulated universe created by the Virgo Consortium for Cosmological Supercomputer Simulations. *Image on left courtesy of Mark N. Miller, Biology Dept., Brandeis University. Image on right courtesy of Max-Planck-Institute for Astrophysics, Garching, Germany.*

Akashic Field on this point: "Quantum mechanics has established the primacy of the inseparable whole. For this reason, the basis of the new biophysics must be the insight into the fundamental interconnectedness *within* the organism as well as *between* organisms, and that of the organism *with the environment*" (Bischof's italics)."*

---

*Ervin Laszlo, *Science and the Akashic Field: An Integral Theory of Everything* (Rochester, Vt.: Inner Traditions, 2004).

Every project we work on can be an opportunity to expand our collective understanding and insights into this fundamental interconnectedness by deepening our relationships—all relationships. What then is the *deliverable* for a project? Certainly the *stuff* is important—the research reports, analysis outputs, drawings, physical buildings, and so on. But equally critical is the deepening of our understanding about how we are healing ourselves and the places we are working. In fact, it can be *through* the places we are working that we deepen our understanding of the interrelationships that make up the whole. By employing our intuition and instinct, not just our intellect, we move into a process of developing both our internal and external worlds for the purpose of becoming whole—in other words, nurturing, shifting, and expanding our consciousness. There are many approaches and methodologies we can employ for this developmental process, but the most important step is that we begin by exercising the *will and intention* to do so—by *choosing* to move beyond our current paradigm and by asking questions that will help us discover new and increasing levels of integration.

Integrating this type of consciousness-shifting developmental process into the activities associated with design and development means asking continually more penetrating questions. The question that keeps coming up, the one that we invite you to ask, is this:

Where do we stop integrating?

Index